Inside Microsoft® SQL Server™ 2005: T-SQL Programming

Itzik Ben-Gan
(Solid Quality Learning)

Dejan Sarka

Roger Wolter

PUBLISHED BY
Microsoft Press
A Division of Microsoft Corporation
One Microsoft Way
Redmond, Washington 98052-6399

ISBN-13: 978-0-7356-2197-8
ISBN-10: 0-7356-2197-7
Library of Congress Control Number 2006924463

Printed and bound in the United States of America.

1 2 3 4 5 6 7 8 9   QWT   1 0 9 8 7 6

Distributed in Canada by H.B. Fenn and Company Ltd.

A CIP catalogue record for this book is available from the British Library.

Microsoft Press books are available through booksellers and distributors worldwide. For further information about international editions, contact your local Microsoft Corporation office or contact Microsoft Press International directly at fax (425) 936-7329. Visit our Web site at www.microsoft.com/mspress. Send comments to mspinput@microsoft.com.

Acquisitions Editor: Ben Ryan
Project Editor: Kristine Haugseth
Technical Editor: Steve Kass
Indexers: Tony Ross and Lee Ross
Copy Editor: Roger LeBlanc

Body Part No. X11-97537

This Book Is Dedicated To My Grandparents

In memory of:
Lazar Fine–the noble
Tamara Ben-Gan–the saint
Abraham Ben-Gan–the strong and courageous
I miss you all so much...

And to Rita, my nana, my friend, whom I love deeply
I wish us many more years together

Contents

Foreword

Shortly after Microsoft SQL Server 7.0 shipped in the late 1990s, I quizzed a senior developer in the Microsoft IT department about the programming languages she and her team were using when working with SQL Server. "In the past we were writing code in C and Visual Basic, but now we are developing only in T-SQL." This revelation was an eye opener for me. At that time, I had been working on developing new versions of SQL Server for about three years, and it was only then that I realized that very large projects were being developed using T-SQL and that the T-SQL programming language had become the tool of the trade for many individuals. Since then, Microsoft has invested heavily in the new releases of SQL Server including significant enhancements to the T-SQL language. The number of SQL Server installations worldwide has increased by an order of magnitude, and today there are many developers, database administrators, data analysts, testers, and architects for whom T-SQL is the programming language of choice and, in many cases, the only programming tool they use.

A closer look at the T-SQL constructs reveals two kinds of statements—those that extract, insert, and manipulate data in the database and those that provide control of flow, output, variable declaration and manipulation, and other functions we find in most non-database programming languages. SELECT, INSERT, SEND, and RECEIVE are examples of the first kind and DECLARE, BEGIN, IF, ELSE, WAITFOR, and PRINT are examples of the second kind of statements in T-SQL. Itzik used the approximate line between the two classes of statements to split his T-SQL material into two books—*Inside Microsoft SQL Server 2005: T-SQL Querying* and *Inside Microsoft SQL Server 2005: T-SQL Programming*.

Neither of these books is a complete language reference, and there is no need to write one because you can download it from the Microsoft Web site at *http://www.microsoft.com/technet/prodtechnol/sql/2005/downloads/books.mspx*. Instead, Itzik used his vast T-SQL teaching experience to include the more intricate subjects in his books, together with those new to SQL Server 2005. Another advantage of having a teacher write a book is that he has addressed hundreds of questions related to the subject from his students. Itzik very skillfully uses this experience to present the material as if answering potential questions and includes many examples and tips throughout the book. My favorite tip is in the first chapter. It explains how you can use a small test table to find out if your ALTER TABLE statement against a huge table in your database will take seconds or hours. This great tip can be a real lifesaver (or career enhancer?)—but be careful and don't forget to use a non-empty test table!

My favorite example in the book is the Dynamic Pivot in Chapter 4, "Dynamic SQL." SQL Server 2005 introduced PIVOT and UNPIVOT statements, but they cannot handle rotating an unknown number of elements. This restriction has been loudly and frequently criticized by various audiences. Itzik shows how you can achieve dynamic pivoting by using a batch consisting of three(!) statements (if you don't count the variable declarations) in SQL Server 2005. If you are not using the newest version of SQL Server, you will find the pre-2005 version of the dynamic pivot batch in the book as well. It uses 10 statements, and comparison of the two versions of the pivot batch is a startling example of the increased programmability power of SQL Server 2005. Including the pre-2005 code snippets and command alternatives makes the book attractive even to programmers who are not using SQL Server 2005 yet; they can still apply the pre-2005 solutions immediately.

The T-SQL Programming book is generously laced with practical code samples you can easily use in your own work. The authors think beyond the correctness of the samples and take security, performance, and potential blocking into consideration as well. Therefore, the book contains numerous examples in which the query plans are examined and compared with alternative plans. For instance, in Chapter 9, you will find information about how to use dynamic management views (DMVs) to troubleshoot blocking scenarios. DMVs were newly introduced in SQL Server 2005 to provide information about the server state that can be used to monitor the health of a server instance, diagnose problems, and tune performance.

SQL Server is a complex product, and consequently it offers more than one way to solve almost any problem. Itzik and the coauthors thoroughly examine the multiple options and explain how you should choose among them. Sometimes one of the solutions is universally better but more often there are pros and cons, and the authors provide criteria for making the correct choice. For example, in Chapter 1, you will learn why you should use '20060212' instead of '02/12/06' or '12/02/06' in the T-SQL code to represent February 12, 2006. Chapter 2 presents a face-off between table variables and temporary tables. You will learn when to use, and even more importantly, when not to use cursors in the Chapter 3. Chapter 4 covers discrepancies between EXEC and sp_executesql. Next, in Chapter 5, you will learn when to use Common Table Expressions (CTE), which are new in SQL Server 2005, instead of creating views. Chapter 7, which covers stored procedures, explains why the names of objects should be schema-qualified. Chapter 8 clarifies when you should move the content of the inserted or deleted table inside the triggers into a temporary table for performance reasons. In Chapter 11, you will learn when to use Service Broker and when it is better to use MSMQ or BizTalk. This list is far from being exhaustive, but it gives you a taste of some of the book's many contributions.

Lubor Kollar
Group Program Manager
Microsoft SQL Server

Preface

This book and its predecessor—*Inside Microsoft SQL Server 2005: T-SQL Querying*—cover advanced T-SQL querying, query tuning, and programming in SQL Server 2005. They are designed for programmers and DBAs who need to write and optimize code in both SQL Server 2000 and 2005. For brevity, I'll refer to the books as *Inside T-SQL Programming* and *Inside T-SQL Querying*.

The books focus on practical common problems, discussing several approaches to tackle each. You will be introduced to many polished techniques that will enhance your toolbox and coding vocabulary, allowing you to provide efficient solutions in a natural manner.

The books unveil the power of set-based querying, and explain why it's usually superior to procedural programming with cursors and the like. At the same time, it teaches you how to identify the few scenarios where cursor-based solutions are superior to set-based ones.

The books also cover other much debated constructs—such as temporary tables, dynamic execution, XML and .NET integration—which hold great power, but at the same time great risk. These constructs require programmatic maturity. These books will teach you how to use them wisely, in efficient and safe ways where they are relevant.

The first book—*Inside T-SQL Querying*—focuses on set-based querying, and I recommend that you read it first. The second book—*Inside T-SQL Programming*—focuses on procedural programming and assumes you read the first book or have sufficient querying background.

Inside T-SQL Querying starts with three chapters that lay the foundation of logical and physical query processing required to gain the most from the rest of the chapters.

The first chapter covers logical query processing. It describes in detail the logical phases involved in processing queries, the unique aspects of SQL querying, and the special mindset you need to shift to in order to program in a relational, set oriented environment.

The second chapter covers physical query processing. It describes in detail the way the SQL Server engine processes queries, and compares and contrasts physical query processing with logical query processing. This chapter was written by Lubor Kollar. Lubor was a group program manager during the SQL Server 2005 development and his team was responsible for the "bottom" part of the Relational Engine—from query compilation and optimization to query execution, transactional consistency, backup/restore, and high availability. Table and Index Partitioning, Database Mirroring, Database Snapshot, Snapshot Isolation, Recursive Queries and other T-SQL query improvements, Database Tuning Advisor, and Online Index creation and maintenance were the major SQL Server 2005 features his team has been working on. Few people in the world probably know the subject of query optimization as well as Lubor does. I find it a privilege to have one of the designers of the optimizer explain it in his own words.

The third chapter covers a query tuning methodology we developed in our company (Solid Quality Learning) and have been applying in production systems. The chapter also covers working with indexes and analyzing execution plans. This chapter provides the important background knowledge required for the chapters that follow, which as a practice talk about working with indexes and analyzing execution plans. These are important aspects of querying and query tuning.

The chapters that follow delve into advanced querying and query tuning, where both logical and physical aspects of your code are intertwined. These chapters include: "Subqueries, Table Expressions, and Ranking Functions"; "Joins and Set Operations"; "Aggregating and Pivoting Data" (including a section about CLR user-defined aggregates, which was written by Dejan Sarka); "TOP and APPLY"; "Data Modification"; and "Graphs, Trees, Hierarchies, and Recursive Queries."

Appendix A covers pure logic puzzles. Here you have a chance to practice logical puzzles to improve your logic skills. SQL querying essentially deals with logic. I find it important to practice pure logic to improve your query problem-solving capabilities. I also find these puzzles fun and challenging, and you can practice them with the entire family. These puzzles are a compilation of the logic puzzles that I covered in my T-SQL column in *SQL Server Magazine*. I'd like to thank *SQL Server Magazine* for allowing me to share these puzzles with the book's readers.

The second book—*Inside T-SQL Programming*—focuses on programmatic T-SQL constructs and expands its coverage to treatment of XML and .NET integration. The topics it covers include: datatype-related problems, including XML and CLR user-defined types (UDTs); temporary tables; cursors; dynamic execution; views; user-defined functions, including CLR UDFs; stored procedures, including CLR procedures; triggers, including DDL and CLR triggers; transactions, including coverage of the new snapshot-based isolation levels; exception handling; and service broker.

The sections in the book that cover XML and .NET integration ("User-Defined Types," "User-Defined Functions," "Stored Procedures," and "Triggers") were written by Dejan Sarka. Dejan is a SQL Server expert, and he is extremely knowledgeable in the relational model. He has fascinating views about the way these new constructs can fit with the relational model when used sensibly. I found it important to have someone with a strong grasp of the relational model to cover these much debated areas of the product. All CLR code samples are provided in both C# and Visual Basic .NET.

The last chapter, covering Service Broker, was written by Roger Wolter. Roger is the program manager with the SQL Server development team in charge of Service Broker. Again, nothing like having the designer of a component explain it in his own words.

Last but not least, Steve Kass was the technical editor of the books. Steve is an extremely sharp guy. He is a SQL Server MVP, and he teaches mathematics at Drew University. He has extensive knowledge of SQL Server and logic, and his contribution to the books was invaluable.

And to you, the reader of these books, I'd like to say that for me SQL is science, logic, and art. I've been cooking up books such as these for a long time, and I've poured into these two books all my passion and many years of experience. I hope that you will find the books useful and interesting, and that you will find SQL a source of inspiration like I do. If you have any comments or corrections that you'd like to share, I'd love to hear them. You can contact me through *http://www.insidetsql.com*.

Acknowledgments

Most readers usually skip the acknowledgments section, and many authors usually make this section very short. I really don't want to judge anyone; I can only guess that authors think it might look kitsch if they exposed their emotions, or that doing so is awkward. Well, many people contributed their heart and soul to these books, and I don't care how this section might seem. I'd like them to be recognized for their contribution!

My deepest gratitude goes to all those who took part or contributed in any way to the books. Some spent countless hours directly involved in the project, and some of them had an impact on me and my work that implicitly affected the books.

To the guest authors Lubor Kollar, Dejan Sarka, and Roger Wolter: thanks for taking part in this project and adding your invaluable insight. It's been an honor and a pleasure to work with you. Lubor, your depth of knowledge and passion are a source of inspiration. Dejko, my good friend, I'm constantly learning new things from you. I find your views of the database world simply fascinating. Roger, I greatly appreciate the fact that you agreed to contribute to the books. Service Broker—your baby—brings an important dimension to SQL Server that was never there before. I'm sure that companies will find it extremely valuable, and I'm eager to see how the queuing technology will be implemented—it has such great potential.

To Steve Kass, the technical editor of the books: Steve, I have no words to describe how much I value your contribution. You're simply brilliant and amazing, and one can only hope to have half the wit and logic that you were blessed with. Remind me never to end up in a battle of wits with you. You've spent so much time on the project and provided so many insightful suggestions that I feel you've practically helped author the books. I hope that in future editions of the books you will take an official authoring role.

To David Campbell and Lubor Kollar who wrote the forewords: your work and achievements are a guiding light to many of us. SQL Server has grown up to be a mature and fascinating product—one well worth dedicating our professional careers to and to focus our passion on. Thank you both for agreeing to write the forewords. This is truly an honor! To all contributors, I'm looking forward to doing many future projects together. I, for one, have already started cooking up ideas for future editions of the books.

Many thanks to the team at Microsoft Press: Ben Ryan, Kristine Haugseth, Roger LeBlanc, and probably numerous others who took part in the making of the books. Ben, I'm sorry to have been such a pain, and for wanting to be involved in every small detail that I could. Perfection and candor are my two guidelines, though one can only strive to achieve the former. I believe that by following this path, the end result can only improve, and regardless, I believe that there's no other path. Thanks for being so attentive. Kristine, you are simply great! Devoted, professional, caring, and steering the project so elegantly. On a more personal level, I feel that

I've earned a new friend. Roger, I don't envy you for the countless hours you had to spend on editing the books. Thanks for helping to improve their quality. And I'm sure there were many others at Microsoft Press who worked long hours behind the scenes to allow the books to see the light of day.

I'd like to thank Kalen Delaney. Kalen's previous *Inside Microsoft SQL Server* books were a bible to me with regard to SQL Server internals, and I'm eager to read her new coverage of SQL Server 2005's internals in her new volumes. Kalen was also the one who initially asked me to write the T-SQL volumes now that the product has grown so large.

Many people provided extremely valuable feedback by unofficially reviewing the books. Among them members of the SQL Server development team, mentors from Solid Quality Learning, and MVPs. You didn't have to do this, and you did this voluntarily, so my gratitude goes to you from the bottom of my heart.

To the team at *SQL Server Magazine*: you're family to me. We've been working together for years and have grown and evolved together. I'm sure that I'm not the only one who believes that *SQL Server Magazine* is the world's best magazine for SQL Server professionals. These books are in great part due to what I absorbed and learned while working with you.

To my friends, partners, and colleagues at Solid Quality Learning: this company is by far the best thing that happened to me in my professional career, and in many ways in my personal life. It's simply a dream come true. With regard to the books, many of you contributed much to them through your reviews and through the work we've done together, which is naturally reflected in the books. But far beyond that, you're family, friends, and more than anyone could wish for. I still need to pinch myself to make sure this is reality and not a dream. And to Fernando: all of us share the opinion that you're the reason Solid Quality Learning came to life, and without you, it would not be. Your vision, patience, attentiveness, passion, and heart are an inspiration to us all. No words that I say or write can express the gratitude I have in my heart for you and how much I value your friendship.

I find that there are three key elements shaping a person's knowledge and ability: teachers, students, and passion. Passion is the seed that must come from within oneself, and I have great passion for SQL. I've been blessed with great teachers–Lubor Kollar and Sensei Leon Pantanowitz (Yehuda). Lubor, your passion and deep knowledge of SQL and its optimization, your seeking of new knowledge, your humility, the spark in your eyes, and your fondness for logic are all a source of inspiration to me. I'm so grateful that we came to know each other, and I cherish our friendship. Sensei Yehuda, though your world may seem to you to have nothing to do with SQL, to me, it has everything to do with it. Your advice, teaching, guidance, and friendship helped me in the SQL world in more ways than you will know. You and Sensei Higaonna are sources of great inspiration to me; you're living proof that nothing is impossible–that if we work diligently and constantly strive for perfection, we can improve and achieve great things in life. The focus on small details, never giving up, controlling excitement by thinking that "it's just another day in the office," honesty, dealing with the ugly parts of life...these are just a few examples of advice that has helped me in many ways. Writing for endless hours was extremely hard, but I attribute the fact that I managed to do it largely to you. I always thought of the experience as a long GoJu training.

To my students: I learned and continue to learn much through teaching. In fact, teaching is my true passion, and you are the main reason that I wrote these books. In the last few years, I've been traveling around the globe teaching. I spent very little time at home, sacrificing a lot to pursue my passion. My true hope is that after reading these books, we will end up meeting in class—my favorite dojo for learning and practicing SQL.

To my parents: my only regret in doing so much traveling is that it came at the expense of not spending time with you. I remember a surrealistic moment where you sat in a session I delivered about partitioned tables and indexes in SQL Server 2005 to see me after we hadn't seen each other for three months. I apologize and hope you understand that I need to pursue my passion to be fulfilled. Pa, thanks for all the help in mathematics and logic. Ma, stop yelling at father when he gives me a new puzzle over the phone in cross-Atlantic calls; he can't help it, and I can't either.

Lilach, my love and my anchor: the only thing that keeps me sane while I'm away from home is the fact that you're with me. I think that the rest I will tell you in person; we don't want to embarrass ourselves in front of the readers. ;-)

Introduction

This book is targeted at experienced T-SQL programmers and database professionals that need to write or review T-SQL code. The book covers advanced T-SQL programming, assuming that you already have a good grasp of the basic and intermediate levels of the subject matter and are ready to proceed to the next level.

Organization of This Book

This book is the second of two volumes. It covers advanced T-SQL programming. The first volume—*Inside Microsoft SQL Server 2005: T-SQL Querying*—covers advanced T-SQL querying. The second volume assumes that you read the first, or have equivalent background. For more details about the organization of the two volumes, please see the book's Preface.

System Requirements

You'll need the following hardware and software to build and run the code samples for this book:

- Microsoft Windows XP with Service Pack 2, Microsoft Windows Server 2003 with Service Pack 1, or Microsoft Windows 2000 with Service Pack 4

- Microsoft SQL Server 2005 Standard, Developer, or Enterprise Edition

- Microsoft Visual Studio 2005 Standard Edition or Microsoft Visual Studio 2005 Professional Edition

- 600-MHz Pentium or compatible processor (1-GHz Pentium recommended)

- 512 MB RAM (1 GB or more recommended)

- Video (800 by 600 or higher resolution) monitor with at least 256 colors (1024 by 768 High Color 16-bit recommended)

- CD-ROM or DVD-ROM drive

- Microsoft mouse or compatible pointing device

For more details about the system requirements and about installing SQL Server 2005, please visit the section "Preparing to Install SQL Server 2005" in SQL Server 2005 Books Online.

Installing Sample Databases

This book requires that you create and use the Northwind and pubs sample databases. The Northwind and pubs sample databases are not installed by default in SQL Server 2005. These databases can be downloaded from the Microsoft Download Center at the following address:

http://go.microsoft.com/fwlink/?LinkId=30196

Alternatively, you can download the scripts that create the Northwind and pubs databases as part of the code samples for the book. Instructions for downloading the code samples for the book will be provided shortly.

Updates

You can find the latest updates related to SQL Server at the following address:

http://www.microsoft.com/sql/

You can find resources related to the book at the following address:

http://www.insidetsql.com/

Code Samples

All the code samples discussed in this book can be downloaded from the book's companion content page at the following address:

http://www.microsoft.com/mspress/companion/0-7356-2197-7/

Or alternatively, they can be downloaded at the following address:

http://www.insidetsql.com/

Support for This Book

Every effort has been made to ensure the accuracy of this book and the companion content.

Microsoft Learning provides support for books and companion content through the Web at the following address:

http://www.microsoft.com/learning/support/books/

To search for book and CD corrections, go to:

http://www.microsoft.com/learning/support/search.asp

If you have comments, questions, or ideas regarding the book or the companion content, or if you have questions that are not answered by querying the Knowledge Base, please send them to Microsoft Press using either of the following methods:

E-mail:

mspinput@microsoft.com

Postal mail:

Microsoft Press

Attn: *Inside Microsoft SQL Server 2005: T-SQL Programming* Editor

One Microsoft Way

Redmond, WA 98052-6399

Please note that Microsoft software product support is not offered through these addresses. For support information, please visit the Microsoft Product Support Web site at:

http://support.microsoft.com

You can also contact me through the Web site I created for the book at the following address:

http://www.insidetsql.com/

Chapter 1

Datatype-Related Problems, XML, and CLR UDTs

This book explores the programmatic elements of Microsoft SQL Server 2005 with a focus on T-SQL, but it also covers other elements that have T-SQL interfaces, such as XML, .NET integration, and Service Broker. I'm assuming that you've already read my companion book to this one, *Inside Microsoft SQL Server 2005: T-SQL Querying* (Microsoft Press, 2006) or have equivalent querying and query-tuning background. For the sake of brevity, I will refer throughout this book to the T-SQL Querying volume as *Inside T-SQL Querying*.

> **More Info**   Note that you can download the source code for both *Inside T-SQL* books, send comments or corrections, and access resources related to the books at the Web site *http://www.insidetsql.com*.

Datatypes play a key role in the database. Your choices of datatypes will affect both the functionality and performance of applications interacting with your database. Schema changes related to datatypes—for example, changing a column that allows NULLs to not allow NULLs, changing an INT column to a BIGINT one, and so on—can take some time to complete and might result in the tables involved being unavailable for a while. Furthermore, some changes might cause data loss—such as shortening the length of a dynamic column, changing a NUMERIC(12, 2) column to INT, and so on. Therefore, if you're the designer involved in making datatype choices, a DBA implementing them, or a programmer interacting with the objects, studying datatypes in depth, down to the level of their internals, is time well spent. But most importantly, use extra caution when choosing datatypes because changes in a production environment can be very problematic.

Tip   You can use a simple test to check whether a certain schema change requires physical access to the data and might therefore take a while, or whether it is merely a metadata change. Turn on the STATISTICS IO option in your session, and perform the schema change against a small test table. If no I/O is reported, you know that the change didn't involve access to the base data and therefore will be fast. For example, enhancing a VARCHAR column to a larger size will involve no I/O against the base data and will be instantaneous. On the other hand, shortening a VARCHAR column will require access to the base data and might take a while to complete against a large table.

Also, in production environments with large tables, refrain from making schema changes using graphical tools such as Enterprise Manager or SQL Server Management Studio (SSMS). These tools, in many cases, use unnecessary activities to achieve the change—such as creating a new table, copying the data, dropping the original table, and renaming the new table to the original table name. As a good practice, perform schema changes using your own T-SQL code.

I urge you to take the time to study datatypes and their internals, which are covered in depth in *Inside SQL Server 2005: The Storage Engine* (Microsoft Press, 2006) by Kalen Delaney. In this chapter, I'll cover some T-SQL programming issues related to datatypes, focusing on DATETIME, character manipulations, large objects, and new functionality in Microsoft SQL Server 2005.

DATETIME Datatypes

Note   SQL Server supports two date and time–related datatypes: DATETIME and SMALL-DATETIME. Most of the discussions in this chapter are relevant to both types, but for simplicity's sake, I will typically refer to just DATETIME. When discussing aspects that are specific to one of the types, I'll refer to DATETIME and SMALLDATETIME separately.

DATETIME is one of the most frequently used datatypes and one of the most problematic ones, if not *the* most problematic. There are misconceptions regarding the storage format of DATETIME, many issues related to the different representation conventions, and many interesting querying problems related to this datatype.

Storage Format of DATETIME

One misconception that should be corrected before I cover this datatype pertains to its storage format. Internally, DATETIME doesn't remotely resemble formats used to represent DATETIME literals for input and output purposes. In particular, the familiar parts of a DATETIME–year, month, day, hour, minute, second, and millisecond–are not stored as separate values. Instead, a DATETIME value is represented internally using two four-byte integers.

A single DATETIME value requires eight bytes in all. The first four bytes represent the date, as the number of days before or after January 1, 1900. The remaining four bytes represent the time of day, measured in $3\frac{1}{3}$ -millisecond units after midnight. I'll discuss programmatic problems related to accuracy and rounding shortly. The supported range of dates for DATETIME is January 1, 1753, through December 31, 9999, and you might wonder why, because technically, the datatype could support earlier dates. This limitation is related to the shift from the Julian to Gregorian calendar. For details, see the "Why Is 1753 the Earliest Date for DATETIME?" sidebar.

Why Is 1753 the Earliest Date for DATETIME?

By Tibor Karaszi, SQL Server MVP, Solid Quality Learning

Good question. There are historical reasons for this limitation. In what we sometimes refer to as the "Western world," there have been two calendars in modern times: the Julian and Gregorian calendars. These calendars were a number of days apart (depending on which century you looked at), so when a culture that used the Julian calendar moved to the Gregorian calendar, it removed from 10 to 13 days. Great Britain made this shift in 1752. (So, in that year, September 2, 1752 was followed by September 14, 1752.)

An educated guess as to why Sybase SQL Server—the predecessor of Microsoft SQL Server—selected 1753 as the earliest date is that if you were to store a date earlier than 1753, you would also have to know which country was using which calendar and also handle this 10- to 13-day jump. So Sybase decided to not allow dates earlier than 1753. Note, too, that other countries made the shift later than 1752. Turkey, for instance, did it in 1927.

Being Swedish, I find it amusing that Sweden had the weirdest implementation. Sweden originally planned to skip every February 29, leap day, over a period of 40 years (from 1700 to 1740) so that Sweden would be in sync with the Gregorian calendar after 1740 (but meanwhile not in sync with anyone else). However, in 1704 and 1708 the leap day wasn't skipped for some reason, so in 1712 (which was a leap year), Sweden inserted yet one more extra day (imagine being born in Feb 30!) and then made the shift over a day, in 1753, in a similar manner to everyone else.

For more information, refer to "The ultimate guide to the DATETIME datatypes" published on my Web site at *http://www.karaszi.com/SQLServer/info_datetime.asp*.

SMALLDATETIME consumes four bytes in total. Two bytes represent the whole number of days after the base date January 1, 1900. The other two bytes represent the time, measured in minutes after midnight. The supported range for SMALLDATETIME is January 1, 1900, through June 6, 2079.

Datetime Manipulation

Datetime manipulation can be quite challenging. What's the correct way to express DATETIME literals? What happens when you enter a value that cannot be represented exactly—for example, '20060211 23:59:59.999'? How do you separate date and time? The following sections provide some answers to these questions.

Literals

Expressing DATETIME literals for data entry in T-SQL is tricky business. When you need to express one, you use a character string that is implicitly convertible to DATETIME. If a string appears in a context where a DATETIME is expected—for example, as the target value of a DATETIME column in an INSERT or UPDATE statement—it will be implicitly converted to DATETIME. Also, when expressions contain operands with different datatypes, normally the highest in precedence determines the datatype of all operands. Datetime has a higher precedence than a character string. So, for example, if you compare two values, one of which is a DATETIME and the other is a character string, the character string gets implicitly converted to a DATETIME.

To add to the confusion, there are various conventions for expressing DATETIME values. The value '02/12/06' means different things to different people. When this string must be converted to a DATETIME, SQL Server will convert it based on the language settings of the session. The session's language is determined by the login's default language, but it can be overridden by using the SET LANGUAGE session option. You can also control how DATETIME literals comprising digits and separators are interpreted by using the SET DATE-FORMAT option, specifying a combination of the characters d, m, and y. For example, *mdy* would mean month, day, year. By the way, SET LANGUAGE implicitly sets DATEFORMAT to match the language's convention for date formatting.

So you have tools to control the way some DATETIME literals will be interpreted, but you realize that by issuing one of the aforementioned SET options, you're changing the behavior of the whole session. What if other code that will end up running in your session is supposed to be dependent on the login's default language? This consideration is especially important with international applications.

Whenever possible, I write code that is independent of any settings or switches in the system. There are two literal DATETIME formats in SQL Server that are independent of any settings. I particularly like the one of these formats that has no separators between the date portions: '[yy]yymmdd[hh:mi[:ss][.mmm]]'. Examples of DATETIME literals in this format are '20060212', '060212', and '20060211 23:59:59.997'. The DATEFORMAT and LANGUAGE settings do not affect the interpretation of DATETIME strings in this format. If you would rather use separators between the date parts, you can use the other setting-independent format in SQL Server: 'yyyy-mm-ddThh:mi:ss[.mmm]'. An example of this format is '2006-02-12T14:23:05'. The time portion cannot be omitted when this format is used.

Another technique you can use to specify DATETIME values is to explicitly convert the character string to a DATETIME using the T-SQL function CONVERT, specifying the option style parameter in the function call. For example, if you want to use the British/French style with two digits for the year, specify style 3: CONVERT(DATETIME, '12/02/06', 3). For the full list of supported styles, please refer to Books Online, under the subject CAST and CONVERT (Transact-SQL).

At some point, you may see a date or time literal such as {d '2006-02-12'}. This is an ODBC format that can be used in some APIs. I wouldn't recommend using such literals because even though they are independent of settings, they are API dependent.

Rounding Issues

Conversions between DATETIME values and strings are not always exact. For example, if '20060923 03:23:47.001' is converted to DATETIME, it will be rounded to the nearest three-hundredth of a second, which is a millisecond earlier than the string indicates. If the same string is converted to SMALLDATETIME, it will be rounded to the nearest minute, almost 13 seconds later than the string indicates. Datetime-to-string conversions are not always exact, either. When converted to a string format that includes milliseconds, DATETIME values will be rounded to the nearest millisecond. Otherwise, time fields not in the destination format will be truncated.

With regard to DATETIME, be aware that values that cannot be represented exactly are rounded to the nearest DATETIME value that can be represented. This behavior is inconsistent with conversions between some other datatypes (for example, from DECIMAL to INT) where the value is simply truncated. (For example, 10.99 DECIMAL is converted to 10 INT). The milliseconds part of a DATETIME datatype will match the pattern [0-9][0-9][037] when displayed to millisecond precision. If, for example, you specify 994 as the milliseconds part of a DATETIME value, the actual value stored will contain 993 $\frac{1}{3}$ milliseconds, and it will appear to contain 993 milliseconds when viewed as a character string. The value 996 will be rounded to 997. The value 999 will be rounded to 000 in the next second. This can be especially tricky if you try to specify the last moment of a particular date. If you specify '20060211 23:59:59.999' SQL Server cannot exactly represent the value, and it is rounded to the nearest DATETIME value: '20060212 00:00:00.000'. That's why it's not a good idea to use a filter such as the following when looking for rows where a DATETIME column (call it *dt*) falls on a particular date:

```
WHERE dt BETWEEN '20060211 00:00:00.000' AND '20060211 23:59:59.999'
```

Rows where *dt* is equal to '20060212 00:00:00.000' will also qualify. If you are certain *dt* will always be a DATETIME column, and never a SMALLDATETIME column, you could instead use 997 as the milliseconds portion in the upper bound. Better yet, use the following predicate, which works regardless of whether *dt* is DATETIME or SMALLDATETIME, and which does not depend on the particular precision of SQL Server's DATETIME types:

```
WHERE dt >= '20060211 00:00:00.000' AND dt < '20060212 00:00:00.000'
```

Some programmers prefer to omit the time portion when using this form of predicate, in which case SQL Server will interpret the string as midnight on the specified date:

```
WHERE dt >= '20060211' AND dt < '20060212'
```

This predicate is a Search Argument (SARG), meaning that the optimizer can consider the potential of using an index seek operation. Although you can also write this predicate using a function to extract the date portion, the result is not a SARG, so for better performance, refrain from using a predicate such as the following:

```
WHERE CONVERT(VARCHAR(8), dt, 112) = '20060211'
```

DATETIME Functions

The list of DATETIME functions supported by SQL Server is short, but the functions are handy. These functions perform correct DATETIME calculations and take into account leap years (to some extent) and other calendar details. Therefore, it's advisable to use them whenever possible and avoid using your own string manipulations.

I'll describe the list of functions briefly. I'll make use of them in the "DATETIME-Related Querying Problems" section.

DATEADD allows you to add a specified number of some DATETIME unit to a given DATETIME value. For example, the expression *DATEADD(month, 1, '20060725 12:00:00.000')* adds one month to July 25, 2006, noon. Subtraction is achieved by adding a negative number of units.

> **Tip** To add or subtract a number of days, you can use the + and - operators with an integer as an alternative to using the DATEADD function. For example, *DATEADD(day, 1, dt)* is equivalent to *dt + 1*.

DATEDIFF calculates the difference in a specified date part between two DATETIME values. For example, the expression *DATEDIFF(month, '20060725', '20060825')* calculates the difference in months between July 25, 2006 and August 25, 2006.

> **Caution** The DATEDIFF function doesn't take into consideration higher levels of granularity than the specified date part; rather, it takes into consideration only lower ones. For example, when you calculate this difference in years between two very close values: *DATEDIFF(year, '20061231 23:59:59.997', '20070101 00:00:00.000')*, you get 1. DATEDIFF ignores those part of the DATETIME values that have a higher level of granularity than year (that is, it ignores the month, day, and so on).

Using DATEPART, you can extract a specified DATETIME part from a DATETIME value, and it gives an integer result. For example, the expression *DATEPART(hour, '20060118 14:39:05.370')* extracts the hour portion of the input DATETIME value. The YEAR, MONTH, and DAY functions are abbreviations of the DATEPART function that return the year, month, and day of the month, respectively. DATENAME is similar to DATEPART, but it returns the name of the date part (or the numeral if there is no name) as a character string. For example,

the expression *DATENAME(weekday, '20060118 14:39:05.370')* returns the weekday name of the input DATETIME value.

Note that some of the results that you will get from expressions involving DATETIME functions are language-dependent. For example, the expression *DATENAME(weekday, '20060118 14:39:05.370')* will return 'wednesday' if the session's language is set to us_english, and 'mercoledi' if it is set to Italian.

GETDATE gives you the server's local DATETIME value, and GETUTCDATE gives you the current Coordinated Universal Time (UTC), which is calculated from the server's local time and time zone settings. Finally, CURRENT_TIMESTAMP is the ANSI form of GETDATE. The last three functions accept no arguments.

For more details about DATETIME functions, please consult Books Online.

No Separation Between Date and Time

SQL Server, at the time of this writing, has never supported separate DATE and TIME datatypes. Support for these types is probably one of the more necessary features missing from the product. Interestingly, early beta builds of SQL Server 2005 implemented DATE and TIME types, but as CLR user-defined types, not as native datatypes. These were eventually pulled out of the product because of compatibility issues with existing datatypes and code, and because they were non-standard in important ways. There wasn't enough time left in the development schedule to implement those datatypes as native ones, or to make the required adjustments to the CLR UDTs, so unfortunately we don't have separate DATE and TIME in SQL Server 2005. We might see them in the next version of SQL Server. Of course, if you like, you can create your own DATE and TIME as CLR-based UDTs.

For now, you need to make due with the whole DATETIME package, even when you need to represent only a date or only a time. When you need to specify only dates, you omit the time portion. When converted to DATETIME, such a value will still contain a time portion, but it will represent midnight. Similarly, when a character string with only a time portion is converted to DATETIME, SQL Server will set the date part to its base date of January 1, 1900.

If you care only about the date or only about the time, specify only the part you care about and allow SQL Server to assume the defaults I mentioned earlier. This will simplify manipulation of those values. For example, suppose that you want to create a DEFAULT constraint that stores the current date in a column named *dt*. If you simply use the GETDATE function as *dt*'s default, you will need to use range filters when looking for a particular date. Instead, extract only the date portion from GETDATE for the default definition. You will get that date at midnight. A recommended expression for *dt*'s default would be: *DATEADD(d,DATEDIFF(d,0,GETDATE()),0)* or *CAST(CONVERT(CHAR(8),GETDATE(),112) AS DATETIME)*. Similar to the last expression, use styles 108 or 114 to extract only the time portion of GETDATE. The former's highest granularity is seconds, whereas the latter's is milliseconds.

Datetime-Related Querying Problems

Now that the fundamentals of DATETIME have been covered, the next section will explore querying problems related to DATETIME.

The Birthday Problem

The first DATETIME-related problem is to calculate the date of the nearest birthday based on a person's birth date and today's date. This problem demonstrates how to correctly handle leap years by using DATETIME-related functions. To be more specific, using the Employees table in the Northwind database, your query needs to return the date of each employee's nearest birthday, as of today's date, based on the stored *BirthDate* and GETDATE values. If this year's birthday date has already passed, your query should return the birthday date for next year; otherwise, it should return this year's date.

> **Note**   DATEADD and other DATETIME functions only deal with leap years to the extent that they don't ever give results like February 29, 2006. People still need to make definitions that take leap years into account. If the system's default behavior does not meet your needs, you will need to make the appropriate adjustments to your expressions. The default behavior of DATEADD when adding a certain number of years to a date that falls on February 29, is to return a date with February 29 if the target year is a leap year, and February 28 if it isn't. Most people born on February 29 in a leap year celebrate their birthday on March 1 in a non-leap year (also for many legal purposes), and that's the approach that we will apply in our solution. For example, if today's date is September 26, 2005, someone born on February 29, 1972 should get back from your query the nearest birthday date March 1, 2006. If today's date is September 26, 2007, the query should return February 29, 2008.

Before you start working on a solution, run the following code, which adds two employees to the Employees table:

```
SET NOCOUNT ON;
USE Northwind;

INSERT INTO dbo.Employees(LastName, FirstName, BirthDate)
  VALUES('Leaping', 'George', '19720229');
INSERT INTO dbo.Employees(LastName, FirstName, BirthDate)
  VALUES('Today', 'Mary', CAST(CONVERT(CHAR(8), GETDATE(), 112) AS DATETIME));
```

George Leaping was born on February 29, 1972, and Mary Today was born today. Here's the solution query:

```
WITH Args1 AS
(
  SELECT LastName, FirstName, BirthDate,
    DATEDIFF(year, BirthDate, GETDATE()) AS Diff,
    CAST(CONVERT(CHAR(8), GETDATE(), 112) AS DATETIME) AS Today
  FROM dbo.Employees
),
```

```
Args2 AS
(
  SELECT LastName, FirstName, BirthDate, Today,
    DATEADD(year, Diff, BirthDate) AS BDCur,
    DATEADD(year, Diff + 1, BirthDate) AS BDNxt
  FROM Args1
),
Args3 AS
(
  SELECT LastName, FirstName, BirthDate, Today,
    BDCur + CASE WHEN DAY(BirthDate) = 29 AND DAY(BDCur) = 28
      THEN 1 ELSE 0 END AS BDCur,
    BDNxt + CASE WHEN DAY(BirthDate) = 29 AND DAY(BDNxt) = 28
      THEN 1 ELSE 0 END AS BDNxt
  FROM Args2
)
SELECT LastName, FirstName, BirthDate,
  CASE WHEN BDCur >= Today THEN BDCur ELSE BDNxt END AS BirthDay
FROM Args3;
```

The query defining the CTE Args1 calculates for each employee the difference in years between the birth date and today's date (*Diff*), and it also calculates today's date at midnight (*Today*). If you highlight and run only the query defining the CTE Args1, you get the output shown in Table 1-1, assuming today's date is September 26, 2005.

Table 1-1   Arguments for the Birthday Calculation

LastName	FirstName	BirthDate	Diff	Today
Davolio	Nancy	1948-12-08 00:00:00.000	57	2005-09-26 00:00:00.000
Fuller	Andrew	1952-02-19 00:00:00.000	53	2005-09-26 00:00:00.000
Leverling	Janet	1963-08-30 00:00:00.000	42	2005-09-26 00:00:00.000
Peacock	Margaret	1937-09-19 00:00:00.000	68	2005-09-26 00:00:00.000
Buchanan	Steven	1955-03-04 00:00:00.000	50	2005-09-26 00:00:00.000
Suyama	Michael	1963-07-02 00:00:00.000	42	2005-09-26 00:00:00.000
King	Robert	1960-05-29 00:00:00.000	45	2005-09-26 00:00:00.000
Callahan	Laura	1958-01-09 00:00:00.000	47	2005-09-26 00:00:00.000
Dodsworth	Anne	1966-01-27 00:00:00.000	39	2005-09-26 00:00:00.000
Leaping	George	1972-02-29 00:00:00.000	33	2005-09-26 00:00:00.000
Today	Mary	2005-09-26 00:00:00.000	0	2005-09-26 00:00:00.000

To calculate the date of the nearest birthday for a given employee, you need to add *Diff* years to *Birthdate*. If the result is less than *Today*, you would need to add another year. The query defining the CTE Args2 adds to Args1 two attributes called *BDCur* and *BDNxt* which hold the birthday dates this year and next year, respectively. Note though, that if *BirthDate* falls on February 29, and the target date (*BDCur* or *BDNxt*) is not in a leap year, it will contain February 28 and not March 1. The query defining the CTE Args3 adjusts the dates in *BDCur* and *BDNxt* to March 1 if needed. The outer query returns *BDCur* as the nearest birthday if it is greater than or equal to today's date, and *BDNxt* otherwise. The output of the solution query is shown in Table 1-2, again assuming today's date is September 26, 2005.

Table 1-2 Nearest Birthday for Each Employee

LastName	FirstName	BirthDate	BirthDay
Davolio	Nancy	1948-12-08 00:00:00.000	2005-12-08 00:00:00.000
Fuller	Andrew	1952-02-19 00:00:00.000	2006-02-19 00:00:00.000
Leverling	Janet	1963-08-30 00:00:00.000	2006-08-30 00:00:00.000
Peacock	Margaret	1937-09-19 00:00:00.000	2006-09-19 00:00:00.000
Buchanan	Steven	1955-03-04 00:00:00.000	2006-03-04 00:00:00.000
Suyama	Michael	1963-07-02 00:00:00.000	2006-07-02 00:00:00.000
King	Robert	1960-05-29 00:00:00.000	2006-05-29 00:00:00.000
Callahan	Laura	1958-01-09 00:00:00.000	2006-01-09 00:00:00.000
Dodsworth	Anne	1966-01-27 00:00:00.000	2006-01-27 00:00:00.000
Leaping	George	1972-02-29 00:00:00.000	2006-03-01 00:00:00.000
Today	Mary	2005-09-26 00:00:00.000	2005-09-26 00:00:00.000

You can see that George Leaping's nearest birthday will occur next year, on March 1. Mary Today's birthday is, not surprisingly, today.

To clean up, delete the two added employees by running the following code:

```
DELETE FROM dbo.Employees WHERE EmployeeID > 9;
```

Overlaps

Many temporal querying problems require you to identify overlapping periods. Here I'll present a few such problems. In my examples, I'll use the Sessions table, which you create and populate by running the code in Listing 1-1.

Listing 1-1 Creating and populating the Sessions table

```
USE tempdb;
GO
IF OBJECT_ID('dbo.Sessions') IS NOT NULL
  DROP TABLE dbo.Sessions;
GO

CREATE TABLE dbo.Sessions
(
  keycol    INT        NOT NULL IDENTITY PRIMARY KEY,
  app       VARCHAR(10) NOT NULL,
  usr       VARCHAR(10) NOT NULL,
  starttime DATETIME   NOT NULL,
  endtime   DATETIME   NOT NULL,
  CHECK(endtime > starttime)
);
```

```
INSERT INTO dbo.Sessions(app, usr, starttime, endtime)
  VALUES('app1', 'user1', '20060212 08:30', '20060212 10:30');
INSERT INTO dbo.Sessions(app, usr, starttime, endtime)
  VALUES('app1', 'user2', '20060212 08:30', '20060212 08:45');
INSERT INTO dbo.Sessions(app, usr, starttime, endtime)
  VALUES('app1', 'user1', '20060212 09:00', '20060212 09:30');
INSERT INTO dbo.Sessions(app, usr, starttime, endtime)
  VALUES('app1', 'user2', '20060212 09:15', '20060212 10:30');
INSERT INTO dbo.Sessions(app, usr, starttime, endtime)
  VALUES('app1', 'user1', '20060212 09:15', '20060212 09:30');
INSERT INTO dbo.Sessions(app, usr, starttime, endtime)
  VALUES('app1', 'user2', '20060212 10:30', '20060212 14:30');
INSERT INTO dbo.Sessions(app, usr, starttime, endtime)
  VALUES('app1', 'user1', '20060212 10:45', '20060212 11:30');
INSERT INTO dbo.Sessions(app, usr, starttime, endtime)
  VALUES('app1', 'user2', '20060212 11:00', '20060212 12:30');
INSERT INTO dbo.Sessions(app, usr, starttime, endtime)
  VALUES('app2', 'user1', '20060212 08:30', '20060212 08:45');
INSERT INTO dbo.Sessions(app, usr, starttime, endtime)
  VALUES('app2', 'user2', '20060212 09:00', '20060212 09:30');
INSERT INTO dbo.Sessions(app, usr, starttime, endtime)
  VALUES('app2', 'user1', '20060212 11:45', '20060212 12:00');
INSERT INTO dbo.Sessions(app, usr, starttime, endtime)
  VALUES('app2', 'user2', '20060212 12:30', '20060212 14:00');
INSERT INTO dbo.Sessions(app, usr, starttime, endtime)
  VALUES('app2', 'user1', '20060212 12:45', '20060212 13:30');
INSERT INTO dbo.Sessions(app, usr, starttime, endtime)
  VALUES('app2', 'user2', '20060212 13:00', '20060212 14:00');
INSERT INTO dbo.Sessions(app, usr, starttime, endtime)
  VALUES('app2', 'user1', '20060212 14:00', '20060212 16:30');
INSERT INTO dbo.Sessions(app, usr, starttime, endtime)
  VALUES('app2', 'user2', '20060212 15:30', '20060212 17:00');

CREATE UNIQUE INDEX idx_app_usr_s_e_key
  ON dbo.Sessions(app, usr, starttime, endtime, keycol);
CREATE INDEX idx_app_s_e ON dbo.Sessions(app, starttime, endtime);
GO
```

The Sessions table tracks sessions of users in applications for billing and other purposes. A session can represent an open connection to the Internet, for example, with some Internet provider that charges by connectivity time. Each row contains a key (*keycol*), application name (*app*), user name (*usr*), start time (*starttime*), and end time (*endtime*). Listing 1-1 also creates indexes to speed the queries that I'll present in my solutions. I'll cover discuss three techniques that involve overlaps: identifying overlaps, grouping overlaps, and max overlaps.

Identifying Overlaps   To illustrate how to identify overlaps, I'll suppose that you get a request to identify, for each session, all sessions (including self) with the same application and user that overlap. That is, per each session (call it S), you need to identify all sessions that were active at any point in time that S was active. You need to join two instances of Sessions (call them *S1* and *S2*) based on application and user matches, with another logical expression that checks whether the two sessions overlap. Most programmers will probably come up with the following expression, which uses OR logic to express the idea that one session begins during the other:

```
S2.starttime BETWEEN S1.starttime AND S1.endtime
OR S1.starttime BETWEEN S2.starttime AND S2.endtime
```

Here's the full query, which produces the output shown in Table 1-3 (with dates omitted for brevity because all are the same—February 12, 2006):

```
SELECT S1.app, S1.usr,
  S1.keycol AS key1, S1.starttime AS start1, S1.endtime AS end1,
  S2.keycol AS key2, S2.starttime AS start2, S2.endtime AS end2
FROM dbo.Sessions AS S1
  JOIN dbo.Sessions AS S2
    ON S2.app = S1.app
    AND S2.usr = S1.usr
    AND (S2.starttime BETWEEN S1.starttime AND S1.endtime
         OR S1.starttime BETWEEN S2.starttime AND S2.endtime);
```

Table 1-3   Overlaps

app	usr	key1	start1	end1	key2	start2	end2
app1	user1	1	08:30	10:30	1	08:30	10:30
app1	user1	1	08:30	10:30	3	09:00	09:30
app1	user1	1	08:30	10:30	5	09:15	09:30
app1	user1	3	09:00	09:30	1	08:30	10:30
app1	user1	3	09:00	09:30	3	09:00	09:30
app1	user1	3	09:00	09:30	5	09:15	09:30
app1	user1	5	09:15	09:30	1	08:30	10:30
app1	user1	5	09:15	09:30	3	09:00	09:30
app1	user1	5	09:15	09:30	5	09:15	09:30
app1	user1	7	10:45	11:30	7	10:45	11:30
app1	user2	2	08:30	08:45	2	08:30	08:45
app1	user2	4	09:15	10:30	4	09:15	10:30
app1	user2	4	09:15	10:30	6	10:30	14:30
app1	user2	6	10:30	14:30	4	09:15	10:30
app1	user2	6	10:30	14:30	6	10:30	14:30
app1	user2	6	10:30	14:30	8	11:00	12:30
app1	user2	8	11:00	12:30	6	10:30	14:30
app1	user2	8	11:00	12:30	8	11:00	12:30
app2	user1	9	08:30	08:45	9	08:30	08:45
app2	user1	11	11:45	12:00	11	11:45	12:00
app2	user1	13	12:45	13:30	13	12:45	13:30
app2	user1	15	14:00	16:30	15	14:00	16:30
app2	user2	10	09:00	09:30	10	09:00	09:30
app2	user2	12	12:30	14:00	12	12:30	14:00

Table 1-3   Overlaps

app	usr	key1	start1	end1	key2	start2	end2
app2	user2	12	12:30	14:00	14	13:00	14:00
app2	user2	14	13:00	14:00	12	12:30	14:00
app2	user2	14	13:00	14:00	14	13:00	14:00
app2	user2	16	15:30	17:00	16	15:30	17:00

Note that you can safely use an inner join here, rather than an outer join; sessions that don't overlap with any other session will still show up, because they will get a self match. If you don't want to return self matches, add the expression *S1.keycol <> S2.keycol* to the join condition. Just remember that if you make this change, sessions that don't overlap with any other session will not show up—which may very well be desired behavior. If you do want such sessions to show up, make sure that you change the join type to an outer join.

You can perform logical transformation, converting the OR logic in the join condition to AND logic, and produce a shorter expression:

```
S2.endtime >= S1.starttime AND S2.starttime <= S1.endtime
```

If you think about it, for two sessions to overlap, one must end on or after the other starts, and start on or before the other ends. AND logic transformed from OR logic is usually more confusing and tricky than the source. It requires some getting used to. But converting to AND logic might be worthwhile because the optimizer can handle AND logic more efficiently. Here's the full solution query:

```
SELECT S1.app, S1.usr,
  S1.keycol AS key1, S1.starttime AS start1, S1.endtime AS end1,
  S2.keycol AS key2, S2.starttime AS start2, S2.endtime AS end2
FROM dbo.Sessions AS S1
  JOIN dbo.Sessions AS S2
    ON S2.app = S1.app
    AND S2.usr = S1.usr
    AND (S2.endtime >= S1.starttime
        AND S2.starttime <= S1.endtime);
```

Grouping Overlaps   Another request involving overlaps is to combine overlapping sessions with the same application and user into a single session. The next problem we'll look at requires you to collapse all overlapping sessions for each application and user into one session group, returning the application, user, start time, and end time of the session group. The purpose of such a request is to determine the amount of time a user was connected to an application, regardless of the number of simultaneous active sessions the user had. This solution to this problem would be especially helpful to service providers that allow multiple sessions at no extra charge.

You might want to tackle the problem in steps: identify starting times of session groups, identify ending times of session groups, and then match each ending time to its corresponding starting time.

To isolate starting times of session groups, you first need to come up with a logical way of identifying them. A start time S starts a group if no session (for the same *app* and *usr*) starts before S and continues until S or later. With this definition of a session group start time, if you have multiple identical start times, you will get them all. By applying DISTINCT, you will get only one occurrence of each unique start time. Here's the query that translates this logic to T-SQL, returning the output shown in Table 1-4:

```
SELECT DISTINCT app, usr, starttime AS s
FROM dbo.Sessions AS O
WHERE NOT EXISTS
  (SELECT * FROM dbo.Sessions AS I
   WHERE I.app = O.app
     AND I.usr = O.usr
     AND O.starttime > I.starttime
     AND O.starttime <= I.endtime);
```

Table 1-4   Session Group Starting Times

app	usr	s
app1	user1	08:30
app1	user1	10:45
app1	user2	08:30
app1	user2	09:15
app2	user1	08:30
app2	user1	11:45
app2	user1	12:45
app2	user1	14:00
app2	user2	09:00
app2	user2	12:30
app2	user2	15:30

To identify end times of session groups, you essentially use the inverse of the previous logic. An end time E ends a group if there is no session (for the same *app* and *usr*) that had already begun by time E but that ends after E. Here's the query returning the ending times of session groups shown in Table 1-5:

```
SELECT DISTINCT app, usr, endtime AS e
FROM dbo.Sessions AS O
WHERE NOT EXISTS
  (SELECT * FROM dbo.Sessions AS I
   WHERE I.app = O.app
     AND I.usr = O.usr
     AND O.endtime >= I.starttime
     AND O.endtime < I.endtime);
```

Table 1-5   Session Group Ending Times

app	usr	e
app1	user1	10:30
app1	user1	11:30
app1	user2	08:45
app1	user2	14:30
app2	user1	08:45
app2	user1	12:00
app2	user1	13:30
app2	user1	16:30
app2	user2	09:30
app2	user2	14:00
app2	user2	17:00

Next, you need to match a session group ending time to each session group starting time. This step is fairly simple, because for each starting time, the ending time is the nearest to it (that is, the minimum ending time that is greater than or equal to the starting time).

You can use any form of table expression that you find convenient to encapsulate the starting times and ending times queries. Here's an example using CTEs, which returns the output shown in Table 1-6:

```
WITH StartTimes AS
(
  SELECT DISTINCT app, usr, starttime AS s
  FROM dbo.Sessions AS O
  WHERE NOT EXISTS
    (SELECT * FROM dbo.Sessions AS I
    WHERE I.app = O.app
      AND I.usr = O.usr
      AND O.starttime > I.starttime
      AND O.starttime <= I.endtime)
),
EndTimes AS
(
  SELECT DISTINCT app, usr, endtime AS e
  FROM dbo.Sessions AS O
  WHERE NOT EXISTS
    (SELECT * FROM dbo.Sessions AS I
    WHERE I.app = O.app
      AND I.usr = O.usr
      AND O.endtime >= I.starttime
      AND O.endtime < I.endtime)
),
SessionGroups AS
(
  SELECT app, usr, s,
```

```
    (SELECT MIN(e)
     FROM EndTimes AS EP
     WHERE EP.app = SP.app
       AND EP.usr = SP.usr
       AND e >= s) AS e
  FROM StartTimes AS SP
)
SELECT app, usr, s, e
FROM SessionGroups;
```

Table 1-6   Session Groups

app	usr	s	e
app1	user1	08:30	10:30
app1	user1	10:45	11:30
app1	user2	08:30	08:45
app1	user2	09:15	14:30
app2	user1	08:30	08:45
app2	user1	11:45	12:00
app2	user1	12:45	13:30
app2	user1	14:00	16:30
app2	user2	09:00	09:30
app2	user2	12:30	14:00
app2	user2	15:30	17:00

In SQL Server 2000, you can use derived tables instead of CTEs. I find the solution using CTEs much clearer.

Maximum Number of Overlapping Sessions (Set-Based Solution)   This is the last problem I'll cover involving overlapping periods. The request is to return, for each application, the maximum number of concurrent sessions. Concurrent sessions are sessions that were active at the same time. Some services charge by a license called *per concurrent user*, which is based on a maximum number of concurrent connections. Note that you need to determine first whether two sessions, where one starts when the other ends, are considered to be concurrent where they overlap. For the sake of our problem, assume that these are not considered concurrent.

To tackle this problem, you might want to use an auxiliary table containing a time series with all possible timestamps in the covered period (for example, a month). For each application and point in time, you can count the number of active sessions. Then, in an outer query, you can group the data by application and return the maximum count.

Such an approach is very inefficient because there are periods in which the number of concurrent sessions doesn't change. To make things manageable, think of a start of a session as an event that increases the count of concurrent sessions, and an end of a session as decreasing the count. So, the number of concurrent sessions can only increase at the beginning of a session, and the maximum number of concurrent sessions can be identified by counting active sessions only at session start times. Because multiple sessions can start at the same time, you might want to apply DISTINCT to get only distinct start times before you do the counting. The following query returns the application names and timestamps shown in Table 1-7, which you will later use as your auxiliary table:

```
SELECT DISTINCT app, starttime AS ts
FROM dbo.Sessions;
```

Table 1-7   Timestamps

app	ts
app1	2006-02-12 08:30:00.000
app1	2006-02-12 09:00:00.000
app1	2006-02-12 09:15:00.000
app1	2006-02-12 10:30:00.000
app1	2006-02-12 10:45:00.000
app1	2006-02-12 11:00:00.000
app2	2006-02-12 08:30:00.000
app2	2006-02-12 09:00:00.000
app2	2006-02-12 11:45:00.000
app2	2006-02-12 12:30:00.000
app2	2006-02-12 12:45:00.000
app2	2006-02-12 13:00:00.000
app2	2006-02-12 14:00:00.000
app2	2006-02-12 15:30:00.000

Next, for each application and *ts* value, count the number of concurrent sessions for that application at time *ts*, using the following query, which returns the output shown in Table 1-8:

```
SELECT app,
  (SELECT COUNT(*) FROM dbo.Sessions AS C
   WHERE ts >= starttime
     AND ts < endtime) AS cnt
FROM (SELECT DISTINCT app, starttime AS ts
      FROM dbo.Sessions) AS T;
```

Table 1-8   Count of Overlaps per Application and Timestamp

app	cnt
app1	3
app1	3
app1	5
app1	1
app1	2
app1	3

Table 1-8   Count of Overlaps per Application and Timestamp

app	cnt
app2	3
app2	3
app2	3
app2	2
app2	3
app2	4
app2	2
app2	2

Remember that if one session starts exactly when another session ends, you don't consider them as concurrent. Also, you are considering a session as active at its exact start time but inactive at its exact end time (and thereafter). That's why I used the predicate *ts >= starttime AND ts < endtime* and not the predicate *ts BETWEEN starttime AND endtime*.

Finally, create a derived table out of the previous query (call it D), group the data by application, and return the maximum count for each application. Here's the final solution query, which returns the output shown in Table 1-9:

```
SELECT app, MAX(cnt) AS mx
FROM (SELECT app,
        (SELECT COUNT(*) FROM dbo.Sessions AS C
          WHERE ts >= starttime
            AND ts < endtime) AS cnt
      FROM (SELECT DISTINCT app, starttime AS ts
          FROM dbo.Sessions) AS T) AS D
GROUP BY app;
```

Table 1-9   Maximum Number of Concurrent Sessions per Application

app	mx
app1	5
app2	4

The performance of this solution will depend heavily on the existence of an index on *app, starttime, endtime*; the number of rows in the table; and the average number of overlapping sessions. In fact, this is one of the uncommon cases in which a cursor-based solution can yield better performance. I'll discuss such a solution and ways of achieving better performance in Chapter 3.

Identifying Weekday

Identifying the weekday of a given date is a much trickier problem than it might seem. Say, for example, that you were asked to return all orders from the Orders table in the Northwind database that were placed on a Tuesday. The DATEPART function using the weekday unit allows you to extract the weekday number (1 through 7) of a given DATETIME value. However, the weekday number that you will get for a given DATETIME value will vary depending on the setting of the session option DATEFIRST, which determines the first day of the week. If you set it to 1, you instruct SQL Server to consider Monday as the first day of the week, in which case you will filter orders with the weekday 2 for Tuesday. Setting DATEFIRST to 2 means that Tuesday will be considered the first day of the week, and so on.

If the DATEFIRST session option is not set explicitly, the session will set it implicitly based on your language settings. This is yet another example where you might not want to change a setting so that you avoid affecting other code in your session that depends on the current setting. Using the DATENAME to identify a certain weekday as an alternative does not solve the problem because the weekday name for a given DATETIME value can also vary based on your language settings. In short, you should look for an independent way to identify a weekday—one that is not based on settings or switches in the system.

The solution lies in logic. Think of the relationship between some value f (the DATEFIRST value) and the weekday number you will get back from the DATEPART function for a given DATETIME value d. The two values have an inverse relationship. That is, if you increase f by n, d is decreased by n. For example, if you set the DATEFIRST value to 1, meaning that Monday is the first day of the week. Given a DATETIME value that falls on a Tuesday, you will get 2 as the weekday number back from the DATEPART function. Now, increase the value of DATEFIRST by 1, setting it to 2, meaning that Tuesday is now the first day of the week. Now the weekday number that you will get back from the DATEPART function will be decreased by 1—namely, you will get 1 back. Keep in mind that the weekday numbers axis is cyclic. Cyclic nature will add a bit of complexity to the inverse relationship calculations. There's a whole branch in mathematics that deals with cyclic axes. For example, here are a few calculations based on the weekday numbers axis: $1 + 1 = 2$; $7 + 1 = 1$; $7 - 1 = 6$; $1 - 1 = 7$.

Note that you have access to the session's effective DATEFIRST value through the @@DATEFIRST value. Bearing this in mind, and the inverse relationship between the DATEFIRST setting and the weekday number you get back from the DATEPART function, here's what you can do. Add @@DATEFIRST days to the given DATETIME value, and this way, you neutralize the effect of the DATEFIRST setting. Take the date '20051004' as an example, which happens to fall on Tuesday. Check the result of the expression after setting DATEFIRST to any value you want:

```
SELECT DATEPART(weekday, CAST('20051004' AS DATETIME) + @@DATEFIRST);
```

You will always get 3, as if you set DATEFIRST to 7. If you want to "logically" set DATEFIRST to 1, simply subtract the constant 1 from the date:

```
SELECT DATEPART(weekday, CAST('20051004' AS DATETIME) + @@DATEFIRST - 1);
```

If you do this, you will always get 2 for a Tuesday regardless of the DATEFIRST setting. To generalize the formula, you can get an independent weekday number for a given DATETIME value dt, as if DATEFIRST was logically set to n, by using the following expression:

```
DATEPART(weekday, dt + @@DATEFIRST - n)
```

Now we'll deal with the original request. To get all orders placed on a Tuesday, assuming Monday as the first day of the week, use the following query:

```
USE Northwind;

SELECT OrderID, OrderDate
FROM dbo.Orders
WHERE DATEPART(weekday, OrderDate + @@DATEFIRST - 1) = 2;
```

The ability to calculate an independent weekday can come in handy when dealing with other problems that involve controlling which day of the week is considered first without changing the session's DATEFIRST setting.

Steve Kass, the technical editor of the *Inside T-SQL* books, suggests the following neat solution:

The question "which orders were placed on a Tuesday?" can be answered simply with one easy-to-generalize idea. A date is a Tuesday means that the number of days between that date and another Tuesday is divisible by 7. For this kind of problem, a reference date is a valuable and general idea. It is handy to remember that January 1, 1900 was a Monday. Bearing this in mind, to return orders that were placed on a Tuesday, filter the rows where the difference in days between a reference date which is a Tuesday and the *OrderDate* modulo 7 is equal to zero, like so:

```
SELECT OrderID, OrderDate
FROM dbo.Orders
WHERE DATEDIFF(day, '19000102', OrderDate) % 7 = 0;
```

Grouping by the Week

The problem that I will discuss in this section involves grouping data by the week. I will rely on the techniques I described earlier to calculate an independent weekday.

When you need to aggregate data based on DATETIME parts, usually the grouping elements can be easily derived from the original DATETIME value. However, when you need to group data by the week, the task is more challenging. To accomplish the task, suppose that you were asked to return the weekly count of orders. You don't need to return weeks with no orders. If you use the DATEPART function with the week part, you will get back different week numbers for dates within a week that happens to span two years.

Instead of requesting the week number within the year, you can calculate a grouping factor for each order date. The grouping factor value must be the same for all orders within the same week and different from the value generated for orders placed on other weeks. An example of a grouping factor that fits these criteria is a common day within the input order date's week—for example, the week start date or end date. Given an input order date, to return the start date of the week you simply need to subtract as many days as the input date's weekday number and add one. Similarly, to return the end date of the week, you need to add 7 and subtract the weekday number.

Now that you know how to calculate an independent weekday number, you can group orders by the week, having full control over the first day of the week without changing the setting of DATEFIRST. Here's the solution query, which returns the weekly count of orders shown in Table 1-10 (abbreviated):

```
SELECT od - wd + 1 AS week_start, od + 7 - wd AS week_end,
  COUNT(*) AS numorders
FROM (SELECT OrderID AS oid, OrderDate AS od,
        DATEPART(weekday, OrderDate + @@DATEFIRST - 1) AS wd
      FROM dbo.Orders) AS D
GROUP BY od - wd + 1, od + 7 - wd;
```

Table 1-10   Weekly Counts of Orders (abbreviated)

week_start	week_end	numorders
1996-07-01 00:00:00.000	1996-07-07 00:00:00.000	2
1996-07-08 00:00:00.000	1996-07-14 00:00:00.000	6
1996-07-15 00:00:00.000	1996-07-21 00:00:00.000	6
1996-07-22 00:00:00.000	1996-07-28 00:00:00.000	5
1996-07-29 00:00:00.000	1996-08-04 00:00:00.000	6
1996-08-05 00:00:00.000	1996-08-11 00:00:00.000	5
1996-08-12 00:00:00.000	1996-08-18 00:00:00.000	6
1996-08-19 00:00:00.000	1996-08-25 00:00:00.000	5
1996-08-26 00:00:00.000	1996-09-01 00:00:00.000	6
1996-09-02 00:00:00.000	1996-09-08 00:00:00.000	5

The derived table query simply calculates an independent weekday (*wd*) for each order date (*od*), assuming Monday as the first day of the week. The outer query then groups the data by week start (*od* − *wd* + 1) and week end (*od* + 7 − *wd*), returning the count of orders for each week.

Another approach to solve the problem is to rely on Steve's reference date idea, using the following query:

```
DECLARE @RefDay AS DATETIME;
SET @RefDay = '19000101'; -- Monday

WITH NumWksAfter1900 AS
(
  SELECT
    DATEDIFF(day, @RefDay, OrderDate) / 7 AS weeks
  FROM dbo.Orders
),
WeekRanges AS
(
  SELECT
    DATEADD(day, 7 * weeks, @RefDay)     AS week_start,
    DATEADD(day, 7 * weeks, @RefDay) + 6 AS week_end
  FROM NumWksAfter1900
)
```

```
SELECT week_start, week_end, COUNT(*) AS numorders
FROM WeekRanges
GROUP BY week_start, week_end;
```

The code initializes the variable *@RefDay* with a reference date that falls on a day that you consider as the week start day (Monday, in our case). The CTE NumWksAfter1900 calculates, for each order, the number of whole weeks that passed since the reference date (*weeks* attribute). The CTE WeekRanges calculates the week boundaries for each *weeks* value from NumWksAfter1900; *week_start* is calculated by adding *week* * 7 days to the reference date, and *week_end* is calculated as the week start date plus 6 additional days. The outer query simply groups the data by the week boundaries, and returns the count of rows for each week.

ISO Week

The ISO week is a week-numbering standard by which a week number is not broken if the week spans two years. Week 1 of year Y is the week (Monday through Sunday) containing January 4 of year Y. To implement the ISO week-numbering standard, you need to consider two special cases: when January 1 through 3 belongs to the previous year, and when December 29 through 31 belongs to the next year. One might argue that it's just as annoying to have the week number of January 1 be 53, or of December 30 to be 1 as the alternative. But it should be stressed that the ISO standard is a widely used international standard.

Run the code in Listing 1-2 to create the ISOweek function implementation, which appears in Books Online.

Listing 1-2   Creation script for the ISOweek function

```
IF OBJECT_ID (N'dbo.ISOweek', N'FN') IS NOT NULL
    DROP FUNCTION dbo.ISOweek;
GO
CREATE FUNCTION dbo.ISOweek (@DATE DATETIME)
RETURNS int
WITH EXECUTE AS CALLER
AS
BEGIN
    DECLARE @ISOweek int
    SET @ISOweek= DATEPART(wk,@DATE)+1
        -DATEPART(wk,CAST(DATEPART(yy,@DATE) as CHAR(4))+'0104')
--Special case: Jan 1-3 might belong to the previous year
    IF (@ISOweek=0)
        SET @ISOweek=dbo.ISOweek(CAST(DATEPART(yy,@DATE)-1
            AS CHAR(4))+'12'+ CAST(24+DATEPART(DAY,@DATE) AS CHAR(2)))+1
--Special case: Dec 29-31 might belong to the next year
    IF ((DATEPART(mm,@DATE)=12) AND
        ((DATEPART(dd,@DATE)-DATEPART(dw,@DATE))>= 28))
        SET @ISOweek=1
    RETURN(@ISOweek)
END;
GO
```

Note that you need to set DATEFIRST to 1 before invoking the function. To test the function, run the following code, which invokes it against dates at the beginning and end of a year and returns the output shown in Table 1-11:

```
DECLARE @DF AS INT;
SET @DF = @@DATEFIRST;
SET DATEFIRST 1;

WITH Dates AS
(
  SELECT CAST('20050101' AS DATETIME) AS dt
  UNION ALL SELECT '20050102'
  UNION ALL SELECT '20050103'
  UNION ALL SELECT '20051231'
  UNION ALL SELECT '20060101'
  UNION ALL SELECT '20060102'
)
SELECT dt, dbo.ISOweek(dt) AS wk, DATENAME(weekday, dt) AS wd
FROM Dates;

SET DATEFIRST @DF;
```

Table 1-11   ISO Weeks

dt	wk	wd
2005-01-01 00:00:00.000	53	Saturday
2005-01-02 00:00:00.000	53	Sunday
2005-01-03 00:00:00.000	1	Monday
2005-12-31 00:00:00.000	52	Saturday
2006-01-01 00:00:00.000	52	Sunday
2006-01-02 00:00:00.000	1	Monday

Working Days

Calculating the number of working days between two given dates is quite a common request. Note that both inclusive and non-inclusive counts are useful. In inclusive counts, I'm referring to taking into account the start and end dates of the range. I'll be demonstrating techniques to calculate an inclusive count. In cases for which you need to consider weekends, holidays, and other special events as nonworking days, you might want to use an auxiliary table of dates. You mark each date as working or nonworking, and when requested to calculate the number of working days, you count the rows representing working days between the two given dates. You can even optimize the solution by keeping an attribute with a cumulative count of working days as of some base date. To calculate working days, simply retrieve the cumulative values of the given input dates and subtract one from another.

However, when you want to consider only weekends as nonworking days, you don't need an auxiliary table at all. Instead, here's a solution for calculating the number of working days between @s and @e, which can be local variables or input arguments of a routine:

```
DECLARE @s AS DATETIME, @e AS DATETIME;
SET @s = '20050101';
SET @e = '20051231';

SELECT
  days/7*5 + days%7
    - CASE WHEN 6 BETWEEN wd AND wd + days%7-1 THEN 1 ELSE 0 END
    - CASE WHEN 7 BETWEEN wd AND wd + days%7-1 THEN 1 ELSE 0 END
FROM (SELECT
        DATEDIFF(day, @s, @e) + 1 AS days,
        DATEPART(weekday, @s + @@DATEFIRST - 1) AS wd
     ) AS D;
```

The solution is very fast because it involves no I/O. The derived table query calculates the number of days (*days*) between @s and @e, inclusive of both @s and @e, and the weekday number (*wd*) of the date @s assuming Monday as the first day of the week. The outer query calculates the following: the number of working days in whole weeks covered by the range (*days/7*5*) plus the number of days in the partial week, if any (*days%7*), minus 1 if the partial week contains weekday 6 and minus 1 again if the partial week contains weekday 7. For the given dates—January 1, 2005 through December 31, 2005—you get 260 working days.

Generating a Series of Dates

You might need a series of all possible dates between two input dates. Such a series could be used, for example, to populate a time dimension in Analysis Services. An auxiliary table of numbers makes the solution quite simple. Here's the code to create the Nums table:

```
SET NOCOUNT ON;
USE tempdb;
GO

IF OBJECT_ID('dbo.Nums') IS NOT NULL
  DROP TABLE dbo.Nums;
GO
CREATE TABLE dbo.Nums(n INT NOT NULL PRIMARY KEY);
DECLARE @max AS INT, @rc AS INT;
SET @max = 1000000;
SET @rc = 1;

INSERT INTO Nums VALUES(1);
WHILE @rc * 2 <= @max
BEGIN
  INSERT INTO dbo.Nums SELECT n + @rc FROM dbo.Nums;
  SET @rc = @rc * 2;
END

INSERT INTO dbo.Nums
  SELECT n + @rc FROM dbo.Nums WHERE n + @rc <= @max;
```

I described the auxiliary table of numbers and the logic behind the code that populates it in *Inside T-SQL Querying*. Note that I'll continue to refer to the Nums table throughout the book because it's a very handy auxiliary table.

Here's the code to generate the series of dates:

```
DECLARE @s AS DATETIME, @e AS DATETIME;
SET @s = '20060101';
SET @e = '20061231';

SELECT @s + n - 1 AS dt
FROM dbo.Nums
WHERE n <= DATEDIFF(day, @s, @e) + 1;
```

If you don't have a Nums table and are not allowed to create new tables, you can use one of the table-valued function implementations that I showed in *Inside T-SQL Querying*. For example, I presented the User Defined Function (UDF) shown in Listing 1-3, which accepts the desired number of rows as input and returns a sequence of numbers accordingly.

Listing 1-3   UDF returning an auxiliary table of numbers

```
CREATE FUNCTION dbo.fn_nums(@n AS BIGINT) RETURNS TABLE
AS
RETURN
  WITH
  L0   AS(SELECT 1 AS c UNION ALL SELECT 1),
  L1   AS(SELECT 1 AS c FROM L0 AS A, L0 AS B),
  L2   AS(SELECT 1 AS c FROM L1 AS A, L1 AS B),
  L3   AS(SELECT 1 AS c FROM L2 AS A, L2 AS B),
  L4   AS(SELECT 1 AS c FROM L3 AS A, L3 AS B),
  L5   AS(SELECT 1 AS c FROM L4 AS A, L4 AS B),
  Nums AS(SELECT ROW_NUMBER() OVER(ORDER BY c) AS n FROM L5)
  SELECT n FROM Nums WHERE n <= @n;
GO
```

Once the function is created, you can use it just like you use the Nums table:

```
DECLARE @s AS DATETIME, @e AS DATETIME;
SET @s = '20060101';
SET @e = '20061231';

SELECT @s + n - 1 AS dt
FROM dbo.fn_nums(DATEDIFF(day, @s, @e) + 1) AS Nums;
```

Character-Related Problems

This section demonstrates some of the aspects and challenges of working with character data. I'll cover character-related problems, including pattern matching, parsing, and case sensitivity.

Pattern Matching

SQL Server has limited support for pattern matching through the LIKE predicate and PATINDEX function. There's still no support for regular expressions in T-SQL. ANSI supports regular expressions through an operator called SIMILAR TO.

Regarding the optimization of LIKE expressions, to be able to use an index efficiently in SQL Server 2000 you had to use a constant at the beginning of the pattern—for example, *LastName LIKE N'A%'*. Note that the optimizer could decide to use an index even when the pattern started with a wildcard based on generic query selectivity estimates, but those estimates were not very accurate. SQL Server 2005 enhances the optimization of LIKE predicates by collecting statistics about substrings within string column values, resulting in more accurate selectivity estimates. The optimizer will determine whether to use an index when the pattern starts with a wildcard in a more accurate manner than in SQL Server 2000.

If you manipulate the base column by using a function instead of the LIKE predicate, the expression won't be a SARG, and an ordered index access method will not be considered. For example, the following code contains two queries that are logically equivalent—each returning the customers whose ID starts with the letter A:

```
USE Northwind;

SELECT CustomerID, CompanyName, Country
FROM dbo.Customers
WHERE LEFT(CustomerID, 1) = N'A';

SELECT CustomerID, CompanyName, Country
FROM dbo.Customers
WHERE CustomerID LIKE N'A%';
```

The first query manipulates the base column using the LEFT function, and the second query uses the LIKE predicate. Examine the execution plans generated for these queries, which are shown in Figure 1-1.

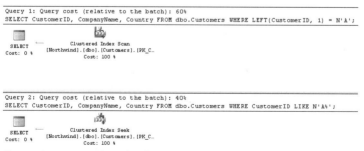

Figure 1-1   Execution plan for LIKE vs. LEFT in WHERE filter

You will see that the plan for the LIKE query uses the index efficiently, whereas the plan for the LEFT query doesn't.

As I mentioned earlier, LIKE predicates are limited to basic pattern matching. For example, they have no notion of repetitions. When you need to check for repetitions of a certain pattern, the task can be quite challenging. For example, say you have a VARCHAR column called *sn* in a table representing a serial number. You're supposed to write a CHECK constraint that allows only digits in *sn*. If the length of the serial number you're supporting is short and of a fixed length (say, 10 digits), the task is simple. Use the following CHECK constraint:

```
CHECK(sn LIKE '[0-9][0-9][0-9][0-9][0-9][0-9][0-9][0-9][0-9][0-9]')
```

However, if the length of the serial number can vary, you need a more dynamic solution that takes the actual length into consideration:

```
CHECK(sn LIKE REPLICATE('[0-9]', LEN(sn)))
```

That's all nice and well as long as the serial numbers are fairly short. However, if you need to support lengthy ones, this solution is inefficient and will slow down insertions into the table. Sometimes applying reverse logic can get you further than applying positive logic. Well, this case qualifies. Instead of using positive logic that says "all characters must be digits," use negative logic that says "no character can be a non-digit". In T-SQL, this translates to

```
CHECK(sn NOT LIKE '%[^0-9]%')
```

Some CHECK constraints involving pattern matching can be much more elaborate. For example, you're given the following IPs table:

```
CREATE TABLE dbo.IPs(ip varchar(15) NOT NULL PRIMARY KEY);
```

And you're supposed to add a CHECK constraint that validates IPs. For the sake of our exercise, a valid IP consists of four parts (octets) separated by dots, and each octet is a number in the range 0 through 255. Try to limit yourself to using pattern matching only. Bear in mind that if you attempt to convert substrings to numerics and they are not convertible, you will get a conversion error and not a CHECK constraint violation.

Here's an example for a CHECK constraint that validates IPs using exclusively pattern-matching techniques:

```
ALTER TABLE dbo.IPs ADD CONSTRAINT CHK_IP_valid CHECK
(
    -- 3 periods and no empty octets
    ip LIKE '_%._%._%._%'
  AND
    -- not 4 periods or more
    ip NOT LIKE '%.%.%.%.%'
  AND
    -- no characters other than digits and periods
    ip NOT LIKE '%[^0-9.]%'
  AND
    -- not more than 3 digits per octet
    ip NOT LIKE '%[0-9][0-9][0-9][0-9]%'
```

```
  AND
    -- NOT 300 - 999
    ip NOT LIKE '%[3-9][0-9][0-9]%'
  AND
    -- NOT 260 - 299
    ip NOT LIKE '%2[6-9][0-9]%'
  AND
    -- NOT 256 - 259
    ip NOT LIKE '%25[6-9]%'
);
```

The first two expressions verify that there are exactly three dots (at least 3, and not 4 or more) and at least one character in each octet. The third expression verifies that there are only digits and dots in the string. The rest actually verifies that the number in each octet is in the correct range. The first of those expressions verifies that four contiguous digits cannot be found—namely, there are at most 3. This means that the value is at most 999. The second expression verifies that if 3 contiguous digits are found, the first is not in the range 3 through 9, meaning that the value is at most 299. Similarly, the third expression verifies that if 3 contiguous digits are found and the first of them is 2, the second cannot be in the range 6 through 9, meaning that the value is at most 259. Finally, the last expression verifies that a three-digit value starting with 25 does not end with a value in the range 6 through 9, meaning that the value can be at most 255.

To test the CHECK constraint, run the following code, which adds valid IPs to the table, and notice that no error is generated:

```
INSERT INTO dbo.IPs VALUES('131.107.2.201');
INSERT INTO dbo.IPs VALUES('131.33.2.201');
INSERT INTO dbo.IPs VALUES('131.33.2.202');
INSERT INTO dbo.IPs VALUES('3.107.2.4');
INSERT INTO dbo.IPs VALUES('3.107.3.169');
INSERT INTO dbo.IPs VALUES('3.107.104.172');
INSERT INTO dbo.IPs VALUES('22.107.202.123');
INSERT INTO dbo.IPs VALUES('22.20.2.77');
INSERT INTO dbo.IPs VALUES('22.156.9.91');
INSERT INTO dbo.IPs VALUES('22.156.89.32');
```

Next, run the following code, which inserts invalid IPs, and notice that all inserts produce a CHECK constraint violation:

```
INSERT INTO dbo.IPs VALUES('1.1.1.256');
INSERT INTO dbo.IPs VALUES('1.1.1.1.1');
INSERT INTO dbo.IPs VALUES('1.1.1');
INSERT INTO dbo.IPs VALUES('1..1.1');
INSERT INTO dbo.IPs VALUES('.1.1.1');
INSERT INTO dbo.IPs VALUES('a.1.1.1');
```

Parsing character strings can also involve pattern matching. For example, suppose that you were asked to extract the individual octets of the IP addresses. Of course, the task would have been much simpler to begin with if you stored each IP address in four TINYINT columns, one for each octet. Or you could store IPs in a single column with a fixed-length portion dedicated to each octet—for example, BINARY(4). However, sometimes you need to cope with an existing design over which you have no control. Assume that this is such a case, and that you need to extract the individual octets out of the VARCHAR(15) IP strings stored in the IPs table.

The number of possible patterns for an IP address is limited because there are only up to 3 digits in each octet and in total only 4 octets. So there are only 81 (3^4) different patterns. You can create an auxiliary table and populate it with all possible patterns. For each pattern, you can also store the starting position and length of each octet, which you will later use in your SUBSTRING functions to extract octets. You can either manually populate such an auxiliary table, or create a virtual one with a query, and encapsulate it in a view as follows:

```
CREATE VIEW dbo.IPPatterns
AS

SELECT
  REPLICATE('_', N1.n) + '.' + REPLICATE('_', N2.n) + '.'
    + REPLICATE('_', N3.n) + '.' + REPLICATE('_', N4.n) AS pattern,
  N1.n AS l1, N2.n AS l2, N3.n AS l3, N4.n AS l4,
  1 AS s1, N1.n+2 AS s2, N1.n+N2.n+3 AS s3, N1.n+N2.n+N3.n+4 AS s4
FROM dbo.Nums AS N1, dbo.Nums AS N2, dbo.Nums AS N3, dbo.Nums AS N4
WHERE N1.n <= 3 AND N2.n <= 3 AND N3.n <= 3 AND N4.n <= 3;
GO
```

To identify IP patterns using Nums you basically cross-join four instances of the Nums table, each representing a different octet. The length of each octet can vary in the range 1 through 3; therefore, the filter $n <= 3$ is used for each instance of Nums. The rest is done in the SELECT list. You generate the pattern made of underscores based on the octets' lengths, separated by dots. For each octet, you also calculate its length (ln) and starting position (sn), which you will later use in SUBSTRING functions to extract the actual octets. Table 1-12 shows the content of the view (abbreviated), with the different IP patterns, along with the length and starting position of each octet.

Table 1-12   IP Patterns (abbreviated)

Pattern	l1	l2	l3	l4	s1	s2	s3	s4
_._._._	1	1	1	1	1	3	5	7
_.__._._	1	2	1	1	1	3	6	8
_.___._._	1	3	1	1	1	3	7	9
_._.__._	1	1	2	1	1	3	5	8
_.__.__._	1	2	2	1	1	3	6	9
_.___.__._	1	3	2	1	1	3	7	10
_._.___._	1	1	3	1	1	3	5	9
_.__.___._	1	2	3	1	1	3	6	10
_.___.___._	1	3	3	1	1	3	7	11
_._._.__	1	1	1	2	1	3	5	7
...	...	...	...	...	...	...	...	...
___.___.___.__	3	3	3	2	1	5	9	13
___._._.___	3	1	1	3	1	5	7	9

Table 1-12   IP Patterns (abbreviated)

Pattern	l1	l2	l3	l4	s1	s2	s3	s4
__.__.__.__	3	2	1	3	1	5	8	10
__.__.__.__	3	3	1	3	1	5	9	11
__.__.__.__	3	1	2	3	1	5	7	10
__.__.__.__	3	2	2	3	1	5	8	11
__.__.__.__	3	3	2	3	1	5	9	12
__.__.__.__	3	1	3	3	1	5	7	11
__.__.__.__	3	2	3	3	1	5	8	12
__.__.__.__	3	3	3	3	1	5	9	13

Now, whenever you need to extract the individual octets, simply join the table containing the IP addresses with the IPPatterns auxiliary table or view, based on the join condition *ip LIKE pattern*. Each IP will be matched with the pattern that it follows, and you will have access to the lengths and starting positions of the octets for extraction. For example, the following query extracts the octets from the IP addresses stored in the IPs table, producing the output shown in Table 1-13:

```
SELECT ip,
  CAST(SUBSTRING(ip, s1, l1) AS TINYINT) AS o1,
  CAST(SUBSTRING(ip, s2, l2) AS TINYINT) AS o2,
  CAST(SUBSTRING(ip, s3, l3) AS TINYINT) AS o3,
  CAST(SUBSTRING(ip, s4, l4) AS TINYINT) AS o4
FROM dbo.IPs
  JOIN dbo.IPPatterns
    ON ip LIKE pattern
ORDER BY o1, o2, o3, o4;
```

Table 1-13   Parsed IPs

ip	o1	o2	o3	o4
3.107.2.4	3	107	2	4
3.107.3.169	3	107	3	169
3.107.104.172	3	107	104	172
22.20.2.77	22	20	2	77
22.107.202.123	22	107	202	123
22.156.9.91	22	156	9	91
22.156.89.32	22	156	89	32
131.33.2.201	131	33	2	201
131.33.2.202	131	33	2	202
131.107.2.201	131	107	2	201

Note   There are many other techniques to parse IP addresses, for example, using the PARSENAME built-in function, and others. But here I wanted to demonstrate a solution that requires thinking outside the box, and also, one that can be generalized beyond the IP addresses scenario.

Case-Sensitive Filters

Sensitivity of character-based data is dependent on the data's collation properties. Most environments use SQL Server default case-insensitive collation. However, you might sometimes need to apply case-sensitive filters to case-insensitive data. Keep in mind that regardless of the sensitivity of the data based on the effective collation, its binary representation is always case sensitive. That is, 'A' and 'a' have different binary representations, but are treated as equal for sorting, comparison, and uniqueness if the effective collation is case insensitive.

To apply a case-sensitive filter to case-insensitive data, you change the expression's collation. For example, the following query returns details about the customer N'ALFKI', using a case-sensitive filter:

```
USE Northwind;

SELECT CustomerID, CompanyName, Country
FROM dbo.Customers
WHERE CustomerID COLLATE Latin1_General_CS_AS = N'ALFKI';
```

The problem with this solution is that because you applied manipulation to the base column *CustomerID*, the filter is not a SARG and the optimizer cannot consider using an index. To "fix" the problem, you can also add the case-insensitive filter just to allow the optimizer to consider the index:

```
SELECT CustomerID, CompanyName, Country
FROM dbo.Customers
WHERE CustomerID COLLATE Latin1_General_CS_AS = N'ALFKI'
  AND CustomerID = N'ALFKI';
```

Rows matching the case-insensitive filter are a superset of those matching the case-sensitive one. An index can be used here to access the rows that match the case-insensitive filter. SQL Server can then inspect those rows to see whether they also match the case-sensitive filter. Figure 1-2 shows the execution plans of both queries. You can see that the plan for the first query basically applies a table scan (an unordered clustered index scan), while the plan for the second query efficiently uses an index seek.

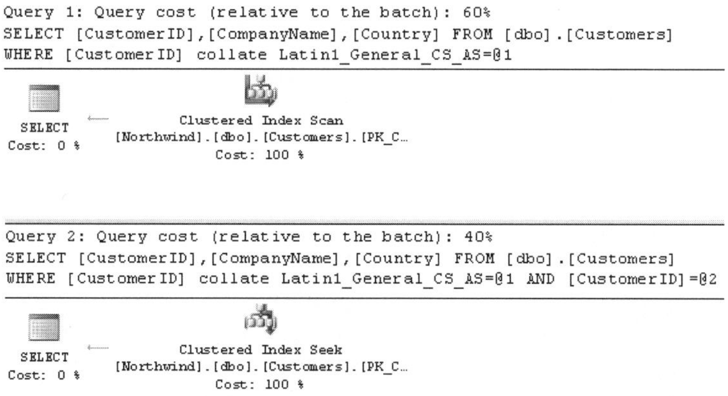

```
Query 1: Query cost (relative to the batch): 60%
SELECT [CustomerID],[CompanyName],[Country] FROM [dbo].[Customers]
WHERE [CustomerID] collate Latin1_General_CS_AS=@1
```

```
Query 2: Query cost (relative to the batch): 40%
SELECT [CustomerID],[CompanyName],[Country] FROM [dbo].[Customers]
WHERE [CustomerID] collate Latin1_General_CS_AS=@1 AND [CustomerID]=@2
```

Figure 1-2   Execution plan for case-sensitive filters

Large Objects

Large Object (LOB) support was enhanced significantly in SQL Server 2005. Support for LOBs in earlier versions of SQL Server was limited compared with regular datatypes, and their manipulation was awkward, to say the least. SQL Server 2005 introduces a unified programming model for regular datatypes and LOBs using a new MAX specifier for dynamic-length datatypes. The older LOB datatypes TEXT, NTEXT, and IMAGE are still supported for backward compatibility, but they will enter a deprecation process in a future version. SQL Server 2005 also introduces a new XML datatype (also a LOB) that allows you to store and manipulate XML data natively. Support for loading data from files is also enhanced with the introduction of the new BULK rowset provider. This new provider allows you to efficiently load file data as a row set using the BULK engine, and also to load file data into LOB columns.

MAX Specifier

You can indicate the MAX specifier instead of an actual size when you define a column, variable, or parameter using one of the dynamic-length datatypes: VARCHAR, NVARCHAR, or VARBINARY. By using the MAX specifier, you tell SQL Server that the stored values can potentially reach the maximum size supported by LOBs, which is currently 2 GB. SQL Server will determine how to store the values internally.

One of the more important aspects of this enhancement is that the programming model for regular types and LOBs is now unified. Namely, they can be used with column datatypes, local variables, input or output parameters, and so on. Also, unlike the older LOB datatypes, all functions that support regular datatypes now also support datatypes defined with the MAX specifier.

For example, the following code creates a table called CustomerData, with an INT *custid* column and *txt_data*, *ntxt_data*, and *binry_data* columns defined with the datatypes VARCHAR(MAX), NVARCHAR(MAX), and VARBINARY(MAX), respectively:

```
USE tempdb;
GO
IF OBJECT_ID('dbo.CustomerData') IS NOT NULL
  DROP TABLE dbo.CustomerData;
GO

CREATE TABLE dbo.CustomerData
(
  custid       INT             NOT NULL PRIMARY KEY,
  txt_data     VARCHAR(MAX)    NULL,
  ntxt_data    NVARCHAR(MAX)   NULL,
  binary_data  VARBINARY(MAX)  NULL
);
```

As I mentioned earlier, you can treat these datatypes as regular ones. For example, load a new customer row with the *custid* 102 and the character string '*Customer 102 text data*' in the *txt_data* column:

```
INSERT INTO dbo.CustomerData(custid, txt_data)
  VALUES(102, 'Customer 102 text data');
```

You can use the character string functions with which you're already familiar to manipulate character data stored in a dynamic MAX column. However, if you want to modify a certain section within such a value, using a character string function such as STUFF would result in overriding the entire string, which is inefficient with large values. Instead, SQL Server enhances the UPDATE statement by providing you with a WRITE method for dynamic MAX columns. The WRITE method allows you to modify only a section within the string and not override the whole thing.

Logically, the WRITE method is similar to the STUFF function. It accepts three arguments: *@expression*, *@offset*, and *@length*. The *@expression* argument replaces *@length* units (characters/bytes) starting from *@offset* position in the target value.

Note   Note that *@offset* is zero-based.

For example, the following code operates on the *txt_data* column value for customer 102. It replaces the string '*102*' located at offset *9* (zero-based) with the string '*one hundred and two*', resulting in the string '*Customer one hundred and two text data*':

```
UPDATE dbo.CustomerData
  SET txt_data.WRITE('one hundred and two', 9, 3)
WHERE custid = 102;
```

Note   If the target LOB is NULL, an update that uses WRITE will fail.

If *@expression* is NULL, *@length* is ignored, and the value is truncated at the *@offset* position. For example, the following code truncates the string at the 28th position, resulting in the string '*Customer one hundred and two*':

```
UPDATE dbo.CustomerData
  SET txt_data.WRITE(NULL, 28, 0)
WHERE custid = 102;
```

If *@length* is NULL, the string is truncated at the *@offset* position, and *@expression* is appended at the end. For example, the following code truncates the string at the ninth position, and appends '*102*' at the end, resulting in the string '*Customer 102*':

```
UPDATE dbo.CustomerData
  SET txt_data.WRITE('102', 9, NULL)
WHERE custid = 102;
```

If *@offset* is NULL and *@length* is 0, *@expression* is simply appended at the end. For example, the following code appends the string '* is discontinued*' at the end, resulting in the string '*Customer 102 is discontinued*':

```
UPDATE dbo.CustomerData
  SET txt_data.WRITE(' is discontinued', NULL, 0)
WHERE custid = 102;
```

If *@expression* is an empty string, no data is inserted; rather, you just remove a substring at the *@offset* position in the size of *@length*. For example, the following code removes 4 characters at the ninth position:

```
-- Removing 4 characters beginning at position 9
UPDATE dbo.CustomerData
  SET txt_data.WRITE('', 9, 4)
WHERE custid = 102;
```

If you query the data at this point, you will get the string '*Customer is discontinued*':

```
SELECT txt_data FROM dbo.CustomerData WHERE custid = 102;
```

BULK Rowset Provider

SQL Server 2005 introduces the BULK rowset provider, which allows you to use the BULK engine to load file data as a rowset or as a single LOB value. You specify BULK as the provider in the OPENROWSET function, along with other options that are relevant to your request.

For example, the following code returns the data from a file called shippers.txt as a row set, based on the format file shippers.fmt:

```
SELECT ShipperID, CompanyName, Phone
  FROM OPENROWSET(BULK 'c:\temp\shippers.txt',
        FORMATFILE = 'c:\temp\shippers.fmt') AS S;
```

> **More Info**   All files used in this section's examples can be downloaded from *http://www.insidetsql.com* as part of the book's source code download. For more information, see the Introduction.

The format file is the same format file you're familiar with when working with bcp.exe or BULK INSERT. In fact, you can generate it either manually or by using bcp.exe as you have used it thus far. Besides FORMATFILE, you can also specify other bulk options: CODEPAGE, ERRORFILE, FIRSTROW, LASTROW, MAXERRORS and ROWS_PER_BATCH.

You can also use the BULK provider to load file data as a row set into a target table using an INSERT statement. This way, you can efficiently utilize the BULK engine. In such an INSERT statement, you can control load options using table hints, including KEEPIDENTITY, KEEP-DEFAULTS, IGNORE_CONSTRAINTS, IGNORE_TRIGGERS and TABLOCK. To demonstrate loading a row set into a table using the BULK provider, first run the following code, which creates the Shippers table:

```
USE tempdb;
GO
IF OBJECT_ID('dbo.Shippers') IS NOT NULL
  DROP TABLE dbo.Shippers;
GO
```

```
CREATE TABLE dbo.Shippers
(
  ShipperID   INT          NOT NULL PRIMARY KEY,
  CompanyName NVARCHAR(40) NOT NULL,
  Phone       NVARCHAR(24) NOT NULL CHECK(Phone NOT LIKE '%[^0-9() ]%')
);
GO
```

The following code is an example for loading the content of a file called shippers.txt into the target Shippers table, using the shippers.fmt format file:

```
INSERT INTO dbo.Shippers WITH (IGNORE_CONSTRAINTS)
  SELECT ShipperID, CompanyName, Phone
    FROM OPENROWSET(BULK 'c:\temp\shippers.txt',
           FORMATFILE = 'c:\temp\shippers.fmt') AS S;
```

The table hint IGNORE_CONSTRAINTS tells SQL Server not to validate CHECK and FOREIGN KEY constraints when loading the data.

The BULK rowset provider can also be used to load the content of a file as a scalar LOB value in a SELECT, INSERT or UPDATE statement. You use the OPENROWSET function and specify the BULK option, the source file name, and one of three options for the type of data: SINGLE_CLOB for regular character data, SINGLE_NCLOB for Unicode data, and SINGLE_BLOB for binary data.

> **Note**   When you want to load XML data from a file, you use either SINGLE_CLOB or SINGLE_NCLOB depending on whether the XML file contains regular character data or Unicode data.

To demonstrate this capability, the following INSERT statement inserts a new customer into the CustomerData table, with *custid* 101, and an XML value loaded from the file xmlfile101.xml into the *xml_data* column:

```
INSERT INTO dbo.CustomerData(custid, xml_data)
  SELECT 101,
  (SELECT xml_data FROM OPENROWSET(
    BULK 'c:\temp\xmlfile101.xml', SINGLE_NCLOB) AS F(xml_data));
```

Similarly, the following UPDATE statement loads the three files: textfile101.txt, unicodefile101.txt and binaryfile101.jpg into customer 101's columns: *txt_data*, *ntxt_data* and *binary_data*, respectively:

```
UPDATE dbo.CustomerData
  SET txt_data  = (SELECT txt_data FROM OPENROWSET(
    BULK 'c:\temp\textfile101.txt', SINGLE_CLOB) AS F(txt_data)),
  ntxt_data  = (SELECT ntxt_data FROM OPENROWSET(
    BULK 'c:\temp\unicodefile101.txt', SINGLE_NCLOB) AS F(ntxt_data)),
  binary_data  = (SELECT binary_data FROM OPENROWSET(
    BULK 'c:\temp\binaryfile101.jpg', SINGLE_BLOB) AS F(binary_data))
WHERE custid = 101;
```

Implicit Conversions

This section describes how implicit conversions work in T-SQL, including the way SQL Server evaluates scalar and filter expressions.

Scalar Expressions

T-SQL expressions have a result datatype, which is determined by the datatype with the highest precedence among the participating operands in the expression. You can find the datatype precedence in Books Online under precedence [SQL Server] / data types / Datatype Precedence (Transact-SQL).

Expression evaluation rules might be a bit confusing in some cases if you're not aware of this behavior. For example, if you apply an AVG aggregate function to an integer column, the result datatype of the expression will be an integer. So, the average of the integers {2, 3} will be the integer 2 and not 2.5. To force a decimal evaluation, you should either explicitly cast the integer column to a decimal one: *AVG(CAST(col1 AS DECIMAL(12, 2)))*, or implicitly: *AVG(1. * col1)*.

A binary expression involving two operands with different datatypes will first implicitly convert the lower in precedence to the higher before evaluating the result. That's why in the expression *1. * col1*, where *col1* is an integer, *col1* is implicitly converted to a decimal datatype, and the result datatype of the expression is also decimal. Similarly, the expression *1 + '1'* evaluates to the integer 2 after implicitly converting the character string '1' to an integer, since a character string (VARCHAR) is lower in precedence than an integer (INT).

The same rules apply to CASE expressions. The result datatype of a CASE expression is determined by the highest datatype in precedence among the possible result expressions in the THEN clauses, regardless of which is going to be returned in practice. Take the following CASE expression, for example:

```
CASE
  WHEN <logical_expression1> THEN <int_expression>
  WHEN <logical_expression2> THEN <varchar_expression>
  WHEN <logical_expression3> THEN <decimal_expression>
END
```

Because the datatype with the highest precedence is DECIMAL, the result datatype of such a CASE expression is predetermined to be DECIMAL. If in practice the second logical expression evaluates to TRUE, SQL Server will attempt to implicitly convert <varchar_expression> to DECIMAL. If the value is not convertible, you will get a conversion error at run time. Try running the following expression and you will get a conversion error:

```
SELECT
  CASE
    WHEN 1 > 1 THEN 10
    WHEN 1 = 1 THEN 'abc'
    WHEN 1 < 1 THEN 10.
  END;
```

There are a couple of ways to deal with this problem. One option is to convert all return expressions explicitly to a common type that all can convert to—for example, a VARCHAR. However, such a conversion might cause loss or incorrect functionality—for example, in comparison, sorting, and so on. The other option is to convert all result expressions to SQL_VARIANT, which will be considered a common type, even though all base types will be preserved within it:

```
SELECT
  CASE
    WHEN 1 > 1 THEN CAST(10 AS SQL_VARIANT)
    WHEN 1 = 1 THEN CAST('abc' AS SQL_VARIANT)
    WHEN 1 < 1 THEN CAST(10. AS SQL_VARIANT)
  END;
```

To add to the confusion of implicit conversions, SQL_VARIANTs compare differently from regular datatypes. That is, if you compare two expressions with different regular datatypes, the lower in precedence is implicitly converted to the higher. So, the following statement returns 'Bigger':

```
-- Comparing regular types
IF 12.0 > 10E
  PRINT 'Bigger'
ELSE
  PRINT 'Smaller';
```

DECIMAL is considered lower than FLOAT, and is promoted before the comparison. However, with SQL_VARIANTs, if the "datatype family" is higher in the datatype hierarchy, that in itself is sufficient to determine that the value is greater, regardless of whether it really is. So, the following statement returns 'Smaller' because FLOAT is in the Approximate numeric datatype family, DECIMAL is in the Exact numeric family, and the former is higher in the hierarchy than the latter:

```
-- Comparing SQL_VARIANTs
IF CAST(12.0 AS SQL_VARIANT) > CAST(10E AS SQL_VARIANT)
  PRINT 'Bigger'
ELSE
  PRINT 'Smaller';
```

You can find the datatype family hierarchy order in Books Online under sql_variant comparisons.

Filter Expressions

In the last three versions of SQL Server, handling of implicit conversions in filter expressions changed with each version. Consider the following filter expression pattern: *col1* = *<scalar_expression>*.

When both sides of the expression have the same datatype, the expression is considered a Search Argument (SARG), and the optimizer can consider the potential of using an index on *col1*, assuming that one exists, based on the selectivity of the query. If you perform manipulation on the base column (*f(col1)* *<operator>* *<scalar_expression>*), it is no longer considered a SARG.

However, there are differences in behavior between the different versions of SQL Server if both sides of the expressions have different datatypes. SQL Server 7.0 always converted the scalar expression's datatype to the column's datatype to have a SARG, and allow utilizing an index on *col1*.

SQL Server 2000 changed the behavior to be more consistent with other implicit conversions. If the scalar expression's datatype was higher in precedence than the column's, the column's datatype was implicitly converted to the scalar expression's datatype. This could mean that the predicate was not a SARG and that an index could not be utilized, though in some cases the optimizer used Constant Scan and Nested Loops operators to allow using an index. But in a join condition, such as *T1.col1 = T2.col2*, in which the two sides had different datatypes (even if both were of the same family, such as Exact numerics INT and DECIMAL, and had good indexes), the optimizer could not assume that both indexes apply the same sort of behavior. So, for example, you couldn't get a Merge Join operator in such a case unless the side with the lower precedence was explicitly sorted with a Sort operator after its datatype was converted.

SQL Server 2005 is smarter with filter expressions. It realizes that within the same datatype family, indexes apply the same sorting behavior, so it can rely on indexes. For example, in a filter such as *<int_col>* = *<decimal_expression>*, it can utilize an index, and in a join condition such as *int_col = decimal_col*, it can utilize a Merge Join operator without explicitly sorting the lower side. For example, if you run the following code in both SQL Server 2000 and 2005:

```
SET NOCOUNT ON;
USE tempdb;
GO
DROP TABLE dbo.T1, dbo.T2;
GO
CREATE TABLE dbo.T1(col1 INT PRIMARY KEY);
CREATE TABLE dbo.T2(col1 NUMERIC(12, 2) PRIMARY KEY);

INSERT INTO dbo.T1(col1) VALUES(1);
INSERT INTO dbo.T1(col1) VALUES(2);
INSERT INTO dbo.T1(col1) VALUES(3);

INSERT INTO dbo.T2(col1) VALUES(1.);
INSERT INTO dbo.T2(col1) VALUES(2.);
INSERT INTO dbo.T2(col1) VALUES(3.);

SELECT T1.col1, T2.col1
FROM T1 INNER MERGE JOIN T2
  ON dbo.T1.col1 = dbo.T2.col1;
```

You will find that SQL Server 2000 must explicitly sort one of the inputs to get a Merge join, while SQL Server 2005 doesn't, as you can see in Figure 1-3 and Figure 1-4.

Figure 1-3   Execution plan for a join in SQL Server 2000

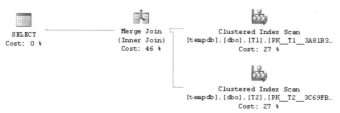

Figure 1-4   Execution plan for a join in SQL Server 2005

These changes in behavior also apply to constants. Each constant has a datatype, regardless of its context. There are two special cases where the datatype of a constant interpreted by SQL Server might not be what you would expect. These cases are:

```
<bit_col> = 1 -- or 0
<bigint_col> = <value greater than 2147483647>
```

Regarding the former, SQL Server treats the value as an INT and not as a BIT. In SQL Server 7.0, the BIT value was converted to an INT because that's how filters worked. This also meant that if the constant was different than 0, even when not 1, it was always converted to 1.

SQL Server 2000 had more consistent implicit conversions, and because BIT is considered lower than INT, the column was implicitly converted to INT, and the filter was not a SARG. Similarly, a value greater than a 4-byte integer was considered a DECIMAL and not a BIGINT. So, an expression such as the preceding one caused implicit conversion of the BIGINT column and not of the constant. A way around these issues in SQL Server 2000 was to convert the constant explicitly to the column's datatype, for example, *bit_col = CAST(1 AS BIT)*, *bigint_col = CAST(3000000000 AS BIGINT)*.

In SQL Server 2005, there's no need for such explicit conversions of the constants because, as I mentioned earlier, it's smarter in the handling of filter expressions.

SQL Server 2005 collects string summary statistics to improve cardinality estimations for LIKE predicates with arbitrary wildcards. It collects information about the frequency distribution of substrings for character columns. SQL Server 2000 could produce reasonable selectivity estimates when the LIKE pattern had a constant prefix (*col LIKE 'const%'*). SQL Server 2005 can now make more accurate selectivity estimations even when the pattern doesn't have a constant prefix (*col LIKE '%const%'*). The optimizer can now make better decisions in terms of when to use an index scan followed by lookups instead of opting for a table scan. As an example, the following query yields a plan with a Table Scan in SQL

Server 2000 and an Index Scan followed by Lookups in SQL Server 2005, as shown in Figure 1-5 and Figure 1-6:

```
USE Northwind;

SELECT OrderID, CustomerID, EmployeeID
FROM dbo.Orders
WHERE CustomerID LIKE N'%Z%';
```

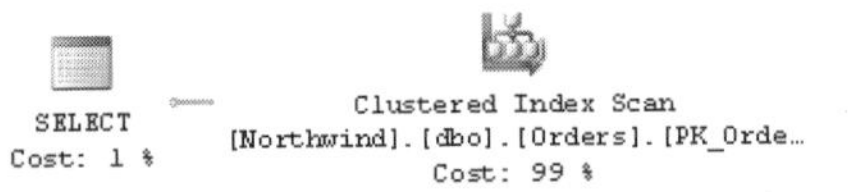

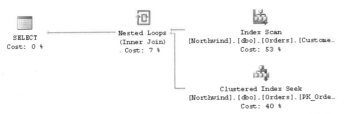

```
        SELECT            Clustered Index Scan
        Cost: 1 %    [Northwind].[dbo].[Orders].[PK_Orde...
                              Cost: 99 %
```

Figure 1-5   Execution plan for the LIKE filter in SQL Server 2000

```
                                              Index Scan
        SELECT       Nested Loops      [Northwind].[dbo].[Orders].[Custome...
        Cost: 0 %    (Inner Join)                Cost: 53 %
                     . Cost: 7 %

                                          Clustered Index Seek
                                   [Northwind].[dbo].[Orders].[PK_Orde...
                                              Cost: 40 %
```

Figure 1-6   Execution plan for the LIKE filter in SQL Server 2005

CLR-Based User-Defined Types

With the advent of .NET integration in SQL Server 2005, you can now create CLR-based User-Defined Types (UDTs) using a .NET language of your choice. Much has been debated on the subject already since Microsoft announced their plans for strong .NET integration in the product. The whole concept of .NET (as well as XML) integration in a relational database is controversial. I must admit that I had my concerns. I thought that the worlds would collide, and that they belonged to separate universes. I was especially concerned about the large potential for abuse of these new features if they were not used wisely. In this respect, my original opinion still stands, but I believe that it's the role of education to prevent such abuse. These features are integral parts of SQL Server 2005; so even though this book's focus is T-SQL programming, I thought it should give you enough background and tools to decide when to use CLR and XML and when to use T-SQL.

My main source of information on the subject was my good friend Dejan Sarka, a SQL Server MVP and a mentor with Solid Quality Learning. Relational theory and data modeling is Dejan's realm. While consulting with him, he made me realize that CLR and XML integration are actually in accord with the relational model. Their coexistence with T-SQL in SQL Server actually makes a lot of sense. I find his vision fascinating. To do justice to the subject, I asked Dejan to cover it, as well as the other parts of the book that discuss .NET and XML integration and their role in the relation model.

Theoretical Introduction to UDTs

Before showing you how to implement CLR UDTs, I'd first like to give you some theoretical background. This knowledge should help you decide how to implement CLR UDTs properly. A common question these days is whether SQL Server, with all this CLR (and XML) support, has become an object-relational or even an object database management system. I'll explain why I think this is not the case and that, rather, SQL Server is becoming a more complete relational database management system.

Domains and Relations

To have a unified object-relational world, you must answer a single crucial question: what concept is there in the relational world that is a counterpart to the concept *object class* in the object world? In object-oriented programming (OOP), the most important concept is a class used as a template for instantiating (creating) objects; objects are variables that physically live in computer memory. So what are the most important concepts in the relational world?

> **Note**   My views on the subject have been largely affected by the work of Chris J. Date and Hugh Darwen in their famous book *Foundation for Object/Relational Databases: The Third Manifesto* (Addison-Wesley Professional, 1998).

Relational databases contain relations. Table 1-14 is an example of a typical Employees relation, which is physically represented in the database as a table.

Table 1-14   Employees Relation

EmployeeID: posInt	Name: string	City: cityenum
17	Fernando	Alicante
19	Alejandro	Bogotá
24	Herbert	Vienna
20	Douglas	Atlanta

In every row, you can find a proposition. For example, the second row represents an employee with an ID of 19, with the name Alejandro, who lives in Bogotá, Colombia. In the table's header, you can find the predicates for the propositions: an employee with an ID that is a positive integer; a name that is an arbitrary string; and who lives in a city, which is included in some enumeration of cities. Notice the names of the domain components in the table's header. Domains limit the propositions. Because an employee ID is a positive integer, it cannot be lower than zero. You can have only cities from the city list. Domains constrain the universe of discourse—they constitute the things you can talk about. Relations constitute propositions— the truths you utter about those things. With domains and relations, you can describe the whole subsystem of employees. Therefore, domains and relations are necessary and also sufficient to represent reality. These are the most important concepts in the relational world.

I have to emphasize the constraining role of domains. Propositions are assertions of facts, and databases are structured collections of propositions. If propositions are not true, the database represents falsehoods, not facts. Therefore, integrity is fundamental for databases. Constraints help you maintain integrity. But what is integrity? You must have some concepts in place to define conceptual integrity. You should be aware of the fact that you usually do not know who the users (people, applications) of a database are. Those users can come from any part of the world, any culture, any religion. You have to carefully choose the concepts on which integrity will be based. Preferably, those concepts and their nature should be few in number and agreed upon.

Let me explain this theoretical part with an example: imagine that you have a domain called Spouse. You should define a constraint for this domain: a person can have one spouse only. By defining such a constraint, you already made a mistake because some cultures and religions don't limit this association to a one-to-one relationship! Still, a smart domain can include all possible constraints for an attribute. Whenever you try to manipulate the data, the system could check that the operands are of the correct types for the operation—for example, they have the correct domains. (A domain is a synonym for a data type.) For example, the system could allow a multiplication operation between the attributes *Quantity* and *Price* but not allow addition, which has no meaning in this context.

As you know, relational databases are based on set theory. A relation represents a set—that is, a set of propositions. A set consists of unique members; therefore, you need a way to distinguish between different propositions. You need to define candidate keys, out of which you will choose one as the primary key. Domains and keys are sufficient to implement all possible constraints. By the way, this is how the Domain-Key normal form (DKNF) is defined: a relation is in Domain/Key Normal Form if every constraint on the relation is a logical consequence of the definition of keys and domains. A relation in DKNF is free from all update anomalies. Of course, there is no simple algorithmic procedure to implement DKNF.

Relations and Classes

Developers commonly think of database relations the same way they think of classes in OOP. Object/relational mapping tools translate classes to relations. I'll try to prove that this common perception is wrong, although the practical implementation of the mapping is usually correct.

Starting with relations, remember this: a relation is a set. Set theory defines the Axiom of Extensionality, which states that sets formed by the same elements are equal. There's a corollary here: sets formed by different elements are different. What does this mean? If you insert, update or delete a proposition (a physical row), you are actually replacing one set (or relation) with a different one.

 Note   The Axiom of Extensionality comes from Zermelo-Fraenkel Set Theory, a version of set theory that is a formal system expressed in first-order predicate logic.

In programming, a variable is a holder of an encoded value. A value is an individual constant that has no location in time and space. A variable, on the other hand, has a strictly defined location in time and space. Many different variables can simultaneously contain an encoding of the same value. Updating a variable means replacing the value it holds with some other value.

Comparing the last two paragraphs, you can logically deduct that a relation is a variable! At a specific moment in a specific location, a relation contains a set; updating a relation means replacing its value with another set. Thinking of relations as variables can be quite confusing; in OOP, variables live in computer memory for a short time and are treated as transient, while relations live for a longer time on hard disk and are treated as persistent. But where exactly is the border between transience and persistence? Isn't persistence just another level of transience and vice versa? Considering the physical layer, with all the progress in hardware, there is no strict border between memory and persistent storage anymore as well. Also consider different collections in OOP languages; isn't a set just another collection with stricter rules?

As you can see, a relation is not the same thing as a class. To add more proofs, let's for a moment assume that a relation is a class. If a relation were a class, it could contain other relations because a class can contain subclasses. Table 1-15 shows an example of such a relation.

Table 1-15   A Relation with a Multivalued Column

EmployeeID: posInt	Name: string	City: cityenum	Hobbies: relation	
			Name: string	Type: string
17	Fernando	Alicante	Basketball	Sport
			Beer	NearlySport
19	Alejandro	Bogotá	...	
24	Herbert	Vienna	...	
20	Douglas	Atlanta	...	

But according to relational theory, a relation can contain scalar values only (first Normal Form). A subrelation is a collection, yielding multivalued attributes. Note that a scalar value does not mean that the value cannot be internally complex. It means that you are dealing with a single item, complex as it might be. Consider SQL Server's DATETIME data types covered earlier in the chapter. Remember that internally these datatypes consist of two parts—date and time—but we refer to a single timestamp; hence, DATETIME datatypes are scalar. Conversely, a collection of DATETIME values would be a multivalued attribute. Thus, if a relation is a class, it is no longer a relation.

To reinforce the point I'm trying to make, if a relation is a class, a row represents an object and a column represents a public instance of a variable. But in OOP, encapsulation is one of the most important concepts. Encapsulation means that internal members (variables) are hidden and accessible only through public operations (methods). Encapsulation proved to be very useful, so even special methods called properties evolved. Properties are merely standard methods that access (*accessors*) and replace (*mutators*) the values of a variable. So, starting with the assumption that a relation is a class and following the last two deductions, you get an absurd conclusion—a relation is neither a relation nor a class. Thus, a relation is not a class. QED.

I'd like to add a couple of words about entities. The term *entity* is very abstract and vague, and often used very loosely as a result of the difficulty in describing abstract things. There, I just had this difficulty myself, finishing the last sentence trying to describe the uses of this term and managing only the awkward "things." When you are designing a database, you are searching for entities and represent them as relations. When you are designing an OOP application, you are searching for entities and represent them as classes. So you could ask yourself: if you are searching for the same thing, aren't then relations and classes the same? The question is tricky. Let me ask another question: what exactly is an entity? Here's the definition from The Free Dictionary (*http://www.thefreedictionary.com*): "something that exists as a particular and discrete unit." It is a very abstract concept. We use the term *entity* to have a common dictionary for business objects, relational databases, and OOP applications. If things have a common abstract name, it does not mean they are the same!

Finally, if a relation is a class, where do domains fit in the picture?

Domains and Classes

According to Fabian Pascal (*Practical Issues in Database Management* [Addison-Wesley Professional, 2000]), a domain consists of the following:

- A name
- One or more named possible representations:
  - One is physically stored
  - At least one is declared to the users
- Type constraints
- A set of operators permissible on the type's values

Note the last bullet: the set of operators permissible on the type's values is actually what constrains us, besides explicit type constraints. Also, internal representations are hidden; you deal with presentations declared to the users. This definition does not deal with simple or complex types. It is correct for all types. Think of the integer type: addition, subtraction, and multiplication operations are defined on this domain, while integer division (DIV) does not have very nice properties. To summarize, a domain is a data type of arbitrary internal complexity, whose values are manipulable solely by means of the operators defined for the type; internal representations are hidden.

Now let's write the definition for a class: a class is a data type of arbitrary internal complexity, whose values are manipulable solely by means of the operators defined for the type; internal representations are hidden. The definitions for a class and a domain are the same. Therefore, the proper equation says a domain is a class. Or, stated differently, an object-relational system is nothing more than a true relational system.

Complex Domains

Now that you know that a domain is the same thing as a class, you can ask another question: why not use arbitrary complex domains? You could implement an Employees relation in different ways:

- Domain EmployeeDomain (EmployeeID, Name, City) and relation Employees (employee: EmployeeDomain)

- Domains PosInt, String and CityEnum and relation Employees (EmployeeId: PosInt, Name: String, City: CityEnum)

The problem with the first design is that it enforces a higher level of encapsulation. An employee has no visible components. It is less open to end users. (Developers are also end users in this context.) Re-creating propositions is very difficult work, if not nearly impossible. All possible constraints except the primary key are included in the domain. Operations allowed on EmployeeDomain values are not commonly known; the author of the domain has to explain them to the public. The number of operations that the creator of the domain has to define rises exponentially with the complexity. Remember, you usually don't know who the users of the domain are going to be. It is quite possible that the constraints will not be acceptable to all of them. You don't want to implement such a high level of encapsulation. Clearly, the second design is preferable.

You realize that simple domains are preferable for relational database design. But why do you call built-in types such as integers simple? Well, that's because it is simple for you to deal with values of those types. From school, you know what operations are allowed with integer types, how the operations are named, and how they should be implemented. You don't have to learn new concepts to handle integers. The producers of database management systems are implementing standard definitions. This is why you regard built-in types as simple. Even a small deviation from commonly accepted concepts, such as SQL Server's DATETIME data types, involves complexities that you have to learn and deal with. That's the main reason why the second design of a relation is preferable—the design with simple domains, where propositions are less encapsulated.

You can build constraints in many different places:

- Data types

- Database schemas (table structures), including data types, nullability, uniqueness

- Check and other constraints as explicit objects

- Lookup tables, which are actually check constraints using enumerations with any finite cardinality

- Triggers
- Stored procedures
- Data Access Layer (DAL) procedures
- Middle-tier code
- Client code
- Screen event handlers
- Code built dynamically from values in a database

Items at the top of the list are closer to the data. Going down the list, you're moving away from the data. The further you are from the data, the easier it is to circumvent a constraint. On the other hand, the higher you are in the list, the harder it is to change a constraint. This fact can be a problem if a constraint is volatile. A domain is the closest possible place to the data. Therefore, it is a suitable place to implement constraints that are not changing or are extremely important. If constraints are volatile or not agreed upon, it is not the right place for their implementation. Imagine what would happen if Microsoft suddenly decided to change the implementation of the integer data type! Again, you can clearly see that domains should not be too complex. Constraints built in domains cannot be easily relaxed, and that's just not practical.

That's why even primary keys are not strictly enforced by relational database management systems. Imagine how procedures that perform data cleansing on text files before importing them to tables would look like if primary keys were mandatory. It's much more practical to import the data first, cleanse it in a relational database, and finally create the constraints.

Besides logical reasons, there are important physical reasons for not using complex domains as well. The most important one is performance. If your data type is performing badly, your users cannot do much about it. Deployment is another issue. Client applications must know how to deal with your data type at the client side. Programming languages know how to deal with standard, or what we called simple, types. Code for your complex data type must be available to client applications; otherwise, they won't know how to manipulate the values of your domain at the client side. This means that you might face a situation where you would have to deploy the code for your domain to thousands of client computers. First-time deployment is usually not a problem; you can do it along with the application deployment, but what about upgrades?

I am not entirely against complex domains. If you're sure that your application is the sole user of a complex domain, and if constraints are so important for the business problem you are trying to solve, then a complex domain might be the right design. Another adequate use of complex types would be when you are sure that the knowledge and constraints are generally agreed upon. The question is, when do you know this? Well, if you invent a new format for storing some special kind of data, you can add a data type and make your format available in databases as well.

Why Do We Need Complex Classes?

After realizing that simple data types are preferable to complex ones inside a relational database, and equating domains and classes, you can turn the question around and ask: Why do you then need complex classes in OOP applications?

For a brief moment, imagine a classical factory. The factory has a warehouse with many production lines. The same item that is available openly in a warehouse (and is, by the way, maintained with set-oriented operations) changes its shape when it comes to a production line. In a warehouse, the item is stored in such a way that it can be used by any tool from any production line. While in a concrete production line, the item becomes more closed (that is, more encapsulated), and you do not want to make a mess by handling it with inappropriate tools.

Clearly, we need both designs: simple types with a lower level of encapsulation inside a database and more complex types in applications.

Finally, as I already mentioned, object-relational mapping tools typically map classes to relations, not to domains. You can now realize that this is the correct mapping in most of the cases, although a relation is not the same thing as a class. Anyway, in case you need to apply a more encapsulated approach, you can save data for an application using a complex domain as you sometimes have to save semi-finished products in a factory for a while. In an extreme case, you can save the state of an object (serialize it) in a binary data type column, such as VARBINARY(MAX), and thus make it unavailable to any application that does not know how to deserialize it properly.

Note that as mentioned earlier in the chapter, the XML datatype can be adequate to store the state of objects using XML serialization in a database as well. Because the XML datatype is well known, agreed upon and standardized, it opens objects that would otherwise be available only to applications that created them.

Language for Creating UDTs

When I was first introduced to the idea of supporting CLR UDTs inside SQL Server, I wondered why Microsoft hadn't implemented the ANSI standard CREATE DOMAIN command instead. After all, I liked the idea of implementing them in .NET languages.

Well, to implement a data type you need to implement many fine-grained methods. Nonprocedural languages, such as T-SQL, consist of larger building blocks of commands. Think of it; a UDT knows to do only things you define in its methods and properties (which are actually methods as well). Now, imagine how many different methods you would have to implement just for basic operations even for a very simple type! Also, your mutator methods should be resilient to input errors; therefore, you need to control and constrain the input. Regular expressions, for example, are very useful for this task. Programming all these fine-grained details would be very awkward in a nonprocedural language.

So my conclusion is that Microsoft's implementation of CLR-based UDTs is the correct way to go. My only disappointment is that SQL Server 2005 doesn't support operator overloading in UDTs. Such support would have raised the level of usability of UDTs significantly. Comparison, logical, and arithmetic operators are well known all over the world. Thus, for any UDT that should support such operators, they would have been directly applicable. The lack of support for operator overloading forces you to learn how operators are implemented through UDT-specific methods. It also forces you to create your own User-Defined Aggregates (UDAs) for calculations that would have otherwise been supported by built-in aggregates directly against UDTs (for example, SUM).

I've mentioned that I would use complex domains if I needed to store a semi-finished product or implement an extremely important business rule, or if I invented some specific format for storing data only. Simple UDTs can be useful for standard formats that don't need to support many operations. A good example is an IP address type—in many applications, you just need to store and read IP addresses. With operator overloading, implementing types such as complex numbers, which are very well known, with UDTs could have been much simpler.

Programming a UDT

After this long theoretical introduction, let's get down to business—creating a concrete UDT. You need to create a class or a structure (struct in C#, Structure in Microsoft Visual Basic .NET) in .NET code. Classes in .NET live in assemblies, and SQL Server loads the .NET code from its own databases, so you have to catalog the assembly. I'll show you how to create a complex number domain. Besides supporting basic operations (read and write), your complex numbers need to support comparisons, basic arithmetic operations, and a SUM aggregate function.

I'll use the Cartesian form of a complex number:

```
cn = a + bi
```

where $i = square\ root\ of\ -1$ (i.e. $i * i = -1$).

Basic arithmetic operations are defined as:

1. Addition: $(a + bi) + (c + di) = (a + c) + (b + d)i$
2. Subtraction: $(a + bi) - (c + di) = (a - c) + (b - d)i$
3. Multiplication: $(a + bi) \times (c + di) = (ac - bd) + (bc + ad)i$
4. Division: $(a + bi)/(c + di) = ((ac + bd) + (bc - ad)i)/(c^2 + d^2)$

UDT Requirements

Besides supporting operations intrinsic to the data type, a UDT must also support conversions to and from character strings to facilitate data input and presentation. Microsoft requires every UDT to implement default accessor and mutator specific methods for this:

ToString and *Parse*. The *ToString* method converts the UDT to a string value. The *Parse* method converts a string input to a UDT value. If you want it to be resilient to erroneous input, you should include in it some error-checking logic. .NET attributes define the UDT's behavior within SQL Server and provide information on which the deployment process in Visual Studio .NET relies. The most important attribute is *Microsoft.SqlServer.Server.SqlUserDefinedType-Attribute*, which defines the behavior of the type itself. This attribute is required. It defines the UDT's behavior inside SQL Server, like storage format (native or user-defined), and also helps in deployment from Visual Studio (for example, when Visual Studio sees this attribute, it knows that it has to use the CREATE TYPE command). For more details regarding UDT requirements please refer to Books Online.

All SQL Server data types, as opposed to .NET native types, should know how to deal with unknown values. A NULL instance of a UDT must be supported; you can choose how to represent it internally. If possible, represent it with a state of a UDT; otherwise, use a flag. The state of all NULL instances should be the same, so it is quite useful to create a class-level (static in C#, Shared in Visual Basic .NET), read-only variable that holds a NULL instance of your type. When you create a UDT, you have to implement the *System.Data.SqlTypes.INullable* interface and create a public static (Shared in Visual Basic .NET), read-only *Null* property. The interface consists of a single read-only *IsNull* property, which shows whether the value is unknown. The *Null* property is used to return an instance whose value is NULL.

Inheritance relationships are not recognized by SQL Server. You can use class hierarchies, but they are not defined in the SQL Server catalog and not used in T-SQL operations. In the CLR code, you can use class hierarchies; that is, use a base class and then define a subclass, which is your UDT. The subclass inherits all the methods of the base class. If the inherited methods are explicitly programmed in the subclass—and this means they are overridden (commonly you do this to change the behavior of the method, not just to repeat the code from the base class)—then SQL Server will recognize them. If not, SQL Server does not know how to go to the base class and execute the code from the base class. But at the client side, in a .NET application that has references to the assembly with the base class and the UDT class, you can use methods from the base class without explicitly overriding them, because .NET recognizes class hierarchies. So basically you would not use inheritance when you define a UDT, unless you want to have some additional functionality at the client side, and you don't want to have the same functionality at the server side.

You have to define how to persist your UDT, or in .NET jargon, how to serialize it. The type of the serialization is defined with the *Format* property of the attribute *SqlUserDefinedType-Attribute*. Possible formats are *Native* and *UserDefined*. *Native* means that the compiler will lay out the structure for you. You have to tell the compiler that you want to use compiler layout by specifying the *Serializable* and *StructLayout(LayoutKind.Sequential)* attributes. Sequential order means that variables defined first will be laid out first. (Persisting a state actually means saving the values of variables.) SQL Server takes care of normalizing the values in the variables, so you can specify that the *IsByteOrdered* property equals true. Normalization here means that SQL Server combines all variables of a class instance to a byte array of an arbitrary length, and transforms it into a byte array of a controllable length; such that no information will be lost in the transformation. The *IsByteOrdered* property means that values are ordered, so it is possible to use the column in an index, or in the ORDER BY clause of a query, and so on. You can use this property because SQL Server does the normalization. This way, values of your type can be compared, and you can use your type in a primary key, for example. With Native serialization, the *MaxByteSize* property should not be specified.

Native formatting is simple to implement, but it has a drawback—you can use only .NET value types in your UDT. The only really big problem is the string type, which is a reference type in .NET. To include a reference type in a UDT, you have to define your own serialization for the UDT. You have to specify *Format.UserDefined* and implement the *IBinarySerialize* interface, which has two methods: *Read* and *Write*. You can define the ordering of the values of your type in the *Write* method. A nice option would be, for example, to use the first 8 bytes for ordering and calculate them with your own algorithm. Then, when reading the value (*Read* method), you can skip these 8 bytes. If you don't define ordering, values of your type would not be comparable. You also have to specify the *MaxByteSize* property, which can be at most 8000.

The UDT should support XML serialization as well. It must implement the *System.Xml .IXmlSerializable* interface. Or all public fields and properties must be of types that are XML serializable, or they must be decorated with the *XmlIgnore* attribute if overriding standard serialization is required. Our UDT does not implement an explicit XML serialization and also does not use the *XmlIgnore* attribute, so we can use XML serialization from string representation only.

SQL Server and .NET native types do not match one-to-one. You should use .NET *SqlTypes* whenever possible because they correspond directly to SQL Server native types. The *System .Data.SqlTypes* namespace contains the classes that represent SQL Server native data types available to the assembly.

Finally, to get a list of all requirements of a CLR user-defined data type, please refer to the "User-Defined Type Requirements" topic in Books Online.

Note   You can find C# and Visual Basic .NET samples for a complex number UDT at C:\Program Files\Microsoft SQL Server\90\Samples\Engine\Programmability\CLR \UserDefinedDataType, if you installed the samples from the Microsoft SQL Server 2005 program group.

In this chapter, I'll develop my own complex number UDT using a basic .NET template, but I'll use things that I found good from the sample. You might wonder what's wrong with the sample and why I don't just use it as is. First of all, I want to show you the complete procedure for creating a UDT. As pointed out to me by Adam Machanic—a distinguished SQL Server MVP—another issue with the sample is that it includes overloaded comparison operators. This is misleading because SQL Server 2005 does not support operator overloading. Values of the sample type are comparable because the type is decorated with the *"IsByteOrdered = true"* property of the *SqlUserDefinedType* attribute, and SQL Server uses byte order to compare values. You can verify that comparisons still work even when you comment out all operator overloading code.

Creating a UDT

Visual Studio .NET 2005 has templates (skeletons) for creating CLR objects in SQL Server 2005 and also supports deployment of UDTs. Some editions of Visual Studio .NET 2005 don't support SQL Server CLR objects directly–for example, the Standard edition. If you're working with such an edition, you have to create a standard class library and then deploy the objects in SQL Server using T-SQL explicitly (via the CREATE ASSEMBLY | TYPE | AGGREGATE | FUNCTION | PROCEDURE | TRIGGER commands). In my examples, I'll take the longer route so that you'll be familiar with the whole process. But first let's develop a UDT in C# step by step. I'll present a code snippet in each step accompanied by explanations. Putting all code snippets together would give you a complete working UDT.

> **More Info**   The complete UDT code is available to you as part of the book's source code which you can download from *http://www.insidetsql.com*.

To create a UDT, first create a new project in Visual Studio 2005. Assuming that you are using Visual Studio 2005 Professional Edition or higher, choose the Visual C# project type, Database subtype, SQL Server project template. If you're using an earlier edition of Visual Studio, use the Class Library project template. Name the project ComplexNumberCS, specify the folder C:\, and confirm to create the solution.

> **Note**   You can specify any other folder that you like, but remember your choice because you will need to refer to the physical location of the assembly later when you deploy it in SQL Server.

Now that the solution has been created, add a new User-Defined Type item (relevant to SQL Server project template). Name the class *ComplexNumberCS.cs*. Feel free to examine the basic skeleton of the UDT that the IDE created. However, for our example, you'll replace the template code with what I'll provide here. If you used the Class Library project template, rename the existing class (Class1.cs) to *ComplexNumberCS.cs*.

The first part of our UDT declares the namespaces used by the assembly, the class name, and the attributes used:

```
using System;
using System.Data;
using System.Data.SqlClient;
using System.Data.SqlTypes;
using Microsoft.SqlServer.Server;
using System.Text.RegularExpressions;
using System.Globalization;

[Serializable]
[Microsoft.SqlServer.Server.SqlUserDefinedType(Format.Native,IsByteOrdered = true)]
public struct ComplexNumberCS : INullable
{
```

You're going to use *RegularExpressions* to split and check the input. The *Globalization* namespace is needed because you want to have a culture-invariant string representation of values of your type. You can see that the type uses native formatting and is byte ordered when persisted. It also implements the *INullable* interface. Next, define the variables you need:

```
//Regular expression used to parse values of the form (a,bi)
private static readonly Regex _parser
    = new Regex(@"\A\(\s*(?<real>\-?\d+(\.\d+)?)\s*,\s*(?<img>\-?\d+
    (\.\d+)?)\s*i\s*\)\Z",
                RegexOptions.Compiled | RegexOptions.ExplicitCapture);

// Real and imaginary parts
private double _real;
private double _imaginary;

// Internal member to show whether the value is null
private bool _isnull;

// Null value returned equal for all instances
private const string NULL = "<<null complex>>";
private static readonly ComplexNumberCS NULL_INSTANCE
    = new ComplexNumberCS(true);
```

For more details on regular expressions, please refer to the .NET documentation.

> **Note** The printed code is formatted to be more readable in the book; for example, in practice the complete regular expression should appear in a single line.

In the next step, you define two constructors (constructor methods can be overloaded), one for a known value and one for an unknown value:

```
// Constructor for a known value
public ComplexNumberCS(double real, double imaginary)
{
    this._real = real;
    this._imaginary = imaginary;
    this._isnull = false;
}

// Constructor for an unknown value
private ComplexNumberCS(bool isnull)
{
    this._isnull = isnull;
    this._real = this._imaginary = 0;
}
```

As mentioned earlier, you have to define a *ToString* method in your UDT to specify the default string representation. Because your type is derived from *System.Object*, which includes a *ToString* method, you must explicitly override the inherited method:

```
// Default string representation
public override string ToString()
```

```
{
    return this._isnull ? NULL : ("("
        + this._real.ToString(CultureInfo.InvariantCulture) + ","
        + this._imaginary.ToString(CultureInfo.InvariantCulture)
        + "i)");
}
```

Now you need two read-only properties to handle unknown values:

```
// Null handling
public bool IsNull
{
    get
    {
        return this._isnull;
    }
}

public static ComplexNumberCS Null
{
    get
    {
        return NULL_INSTANCE;
    }
}
```

And maybe the most important method, which will accept, check, and parse the input–the *Parse* method:

```
// Parsing input using regular expression
public static ComplexNumberCS Parse(SqlString sqlString)
{
    string value = sqlString.ToString();

    if (sqlString.IsNull || value == NULL)
        return new ComplexNumberCS(true);

    // Check whether the input value matches the regex pattern
    Match m = _parser.Match(value);

    // If the input's format is incorrect, throw an exception
    if (!m.Success)
        throw new ArgumentException(
            "Invalid format for complex number. "
            + "Format is ( n, mi ) where n and m are floating "
            + "point numbers in normal (not scientific) format "
            + "(nnnnnn.nn).");

    // If everything is OK, parse the value;
    // we will get two double type values
    return new ComplexNumberCS(double.Parse(m.Groups[1].Value,
        CultureInfo.InvariantCulture), double.Parse(m.Groups[2].Value,
        CultureInfo.InvariantCulture));
}
```

You've implemented the basic operations. All additional knowledge that the type should have can be added through additional methods and properties. So let's start with the two properties already from the Microsoft sample—*Real* and *Imaginary*; they will be the public properties that access and modify the real and imaginary parts of a complex number:

```
// Properties to deal with real and imaginary parts separately
public double Real
{
    get
    {
        if (this._isnull)
            throw new InvalidOperationException();

        return this._real;
    }
    set
    {
        this._real = value;
    }
}

public double Imaginary
{
    get
    {
        if (this._isnull)
            throw new InvalidOperationException();

        return this._imaginary;
    }
    set
    {
        this._imaginary = value;
    }
}
```

You have arrived at the last part—programming arithmetic operations. The use of #region and #endregion here allows you to collapse this section of code in the Visual Studio .NET interface.

```
// Region with arithmetic operations
#region arithmetic operations

// Addition
public ComplexNumberCS AddCN(ComplexNumberCS c)
{
    // null checking
    if (this._isnull || c._isnull)
        return new ComplexNumberCS(true);
    // addition
    return new ComplexNumberCS(this.Real + c.Real,
        this.Imaginary + c.Imaginary);
}

// Subtraction
public ComplexNumberCS SubCN(ComplexNumberCS c)
```

```
    {
        // null checking
        if (this._isnull || c._isnull)
            return new ComplexNumberCS(true);
        // subtraction
        return new ComplexNumberCS(this.Real - c.Real,
            this.Imaginary - c.Imaginary);
    }

    // Multiplication
    public ComplexNumberCS MulCN(ComplexNumberCS c)
    {
        // null checking
        if (this._isnull || c._isnull)
            return new ComplexNumberCS(true);
        // multiplication
        return new ComplexNumberCS(this.Real * c.Real - this.Imaginary * c.Imaginary,
            this.Imaginary * c.Real + this.Real * c.Imaginary);
    }

    // Division
    public ComplexNumberCS DivCN(ComplexNumberCS c)
    {
        // null checking
        if (this._isnull || c._isnull)
            return new ComplexNumberCS(true);
        // division
        return new ComplexNumberCS(
            (this.Real * c.Real + this.Imaginary * c.Imaginary)
              / (c.Real * c.Real + c.Imaginary * c.Imaginary),
            (this.Imaginary * c.Real - this.Real * c.Imaginary)
              / (c.Real * c.Real + c.Imaginary * c.Imaginary)
            );
    }
    #endregion
}
```

If you followed the example, stitching the code snippets one after the other, your UDT is now ready to be built. Choose the Build menu, and select the first option, Build ComplexNum-berCS. You could also deploy the UDT from Visual Studio .NET, and check the deployment options via the project's Properties dialog box. But as I mentioned earlier, I'd like to show you the T-SQL commands required for this task.

Deploying the UDT Using T-SQL

The next steps deploy the new UDT in SQL Server using T-SQL code. To follow this part, use SSMS. First you need to enable CLR, unless it's already enabled, and create a test database:

```
USE master;
EXEC sp_configure 'clr enabled', 1;
RECONFIGURE;
GO
CREATE DATABASE Clrtest;
GO
USE Clrtest;
```

Now you need to import the assembly to the database. To do so, use the CREATE ASSEMBLY command. The command has a PERMISSION_SET clause, which specifies a set of code access permissions that are granted to the assembly when it is accessed by SQL Server. If the clause is not specified, SAFE level is applied by default. I recommend using SAFE because it is the most restrictive permission set. Code executed by an assembly with SAFE permissions cannot access external system resources such as files, the network, environment variables, or the registry. EXTERNAL_ACCESS allows assemblies access to some external system resources. UNSAFE level allows unrestricted resource access, both within and outside the SQL Server instance, and calls to unmanaged code. Run the following code to import the assembly:

```
CREATE ASSEMBLY ComplexNumberCS
FROM ' \ComplexNumberCS\ComplexNumberCS\bin\Debug\ComplexNumberCS.dll'
WITH PERMISSION_SET = SAFE;
```

After you catalog the assembly, you can start using your new UDT. First you have to bind the SQL Server type to the .NET code using the CREATE TYPE command:

```
CREATE TYPE dbo.ComplexNumberCS
EXTERNAL NAME ComplexNumberCS.[ComplexNumberCS];
```

Then you simply use the UDT just like any other SQL Server native type. For example, the following code creates a table with a column of the new type:

```
CREATE TABLE dbo.CNUsage
(
  id INT IDENTITY(1,1) NOT NULL,
  cn ComplexNumberCS NULL
);
```

As you can see, the *cn* column allows NULLs. Now insert two rows with values in the format (*a, bi*), as expected by the *Parse* method. Then insert an incorrect value to show the error that you get:

```
-- Correct values
INSERT INTO dbo.CNUsage(cn) VALUES('(2,3i)');
INSERT INTO dbo.CNUsage(cn) VALUES('(1,7i)');
GO
-- Now an incorrect value
INSERT INTO dbo.CNUsage(cn) VALUES('(1i,7)');
```

You get the following output as the result of the last INSERT:

```
Msg 6522, Level 16, State 2, Line 1
A .NET Framework error occurred during execution of user defined routine or aggregate
'ComplexNumberCS':
System.ArgumentException: Invalid format for complex number. Format is ( n, mi ) where n and
 m are floating point numbers in normal (not scientific) format (nnnnnn.nn).
System.ArgumentException:
   at ComplexNumberCS.Parse(SqlString sqlString)
.
The statement has been terminated.
```

As you can see, you get a generic SQL Server error number 6522 and the message you defined when throwing an exception in the *Parse* method. Next, issue a SELECT statement, and notice the output that you get in Table 1-16.

```
SELECT * FROM dbo.CNUsage;
```

Table 1-16   Output from SELECT Query against *CNUsage*

id	cn
1	0xC000000000000000C00800000000000000
2	0xBFF0000000000000C01C00000000000000

SSMS displays each *cn* value as a simple byte stream. SSMS is a client tool; the UDT's code isn't transferred from the server to the client, not even the code implementing the *ToString* method.

> **Note**   If CNUsage is viewed with SSMS's "Open Table" command, the default string representation is shown; SSMS invokes *ToString* behind the scenes. You can easily see this for yourself by tracing the activity submitted from SSMS to SQL Server.

To get a proper string representation, you have to call *ToString* explicitly to force it to execute at the server. Or you can make the code available to the client by putting the assembly in the global assembly cache (GAC), for example. Dealing with the client side is outside the scope of this book, so I'll make calls to *ToString* and other methods explicitly:

```
SELECT id, cn.ToString() AS cn
FROM dbo. CNUsage;
```

This query generates the output shown in Table 1-17.

Table 1-17   Formatted Complex Numbers

id	cn
1	(2,3i)
2	(1,7i)

With an explicit call to *ToString*, the presentation is more readable. Ordering should follow a byte order of the serialization (remember *IsByteOrdered* = *true*?), starting with the first member, which in our case is the real component of the complex number. Issue the following query, which sorts the rows by *cn* and generates the output shown in Table 1-18:

```
SELECT id, cn.ToString() AS cn
FROM dbo.CNUsage
ORDER BY cn;
```

Table 1-18   Formatted and Sorted Complex Numbers

id	cn
2	(1,7i)
1	(2,3i)

You can see that the second complex number (2, 3i) is sorted before the first one (2, 3i) because its real component is smaller. If you have different ordering needs, you have to implement a user-defined serialization and use your own algorithm for the *Write* method.

> **Note**   When you implement an interface, you have to implement all methods defined in the interface; hence you will also have to implement the *Read* method.

Next, check whether the UDT can really accept NULLs:

```
INSERT INTO dbo.CNUsage(cn) VALUES(NULL);

SELECT id, cn.ToString() AS cn,
  cn.Real AS [Real part],
  cn.Imaginary AS [Imaginary part]
FROM dbo.CNUsage;
```

The output is shown in Table 1-19.

Table 1-19   NULL Complex Numbers

id	cn	Real part	Imaginary part
1	(2,3i)	2	3
2	(1,7i)	1	7
4	NULL	NULL	NULL

The NULL is accepted and returned without any problem.

> **Note**   By the way, can you tell why the *id* column of the unknown complex number shows the value 4, and not 3? The reason is that upon an INSERT statement, the IDENTITY value increments regardless of whether the INSERT succeeded or failed.

As you can see, I also checked the additional *Real* and *Imaginary* properties implemented in the type. Finally, you can check the four arithmetic operations. I'll do this using variables to show that a UDT works with variables just like any other data type. I'll also use an explicit conversion from a string to the UDT—again, just to show that it is possible; SQL Server 2005 supports casting and conversion of UDTs to strings and vice versa. Run the following code to check whether the results of the complex arithmetic are correct:

```
-- Arithmetic operations
-- Addition
DECLARE @cn1 ComplexNumberCS, @cn2 ComplexNumberCS, @cn3 ComplexNumberCS;
SET @cn1 = CAST('(8, 5i)' AS ComplexNumberCS);
SET @cn2 = '(2, 1i)';
SET @cn3 = @cn1.AddCN(@cn2);
SELECT @cn3.ToString(), CAST(@cn3 AS VARCHAR(MAX)), @cn3.Real, @cn3.Imaginary;
GO
```

```
-- Subtraction
DECLARE @cn1 ComplexNumberCS, @cn2 ComplexNumberCS, @cn3 ComplexNumberCS;
SET @cn1 = CAST('(3, 4i)' AS ComplexNumberCS);
SET @cn2 = '(1, 2i)';
SET @cn3 = @cn1.SubCN(@cn2);
SELECT @cn3.ToString(), CAST(@cn3 AS VARCHAR(MAX)), @cn3.Real, @cn3.Imaginary;
GO
-- Multiplication
DECLARE @cn1 ComplexNumberCS, @cn2 ComplexNumberCS, @cn3 ComplexNumberCS;
SET @cn1 = CAST('(3, 2i)' AS ComplexNumberCS);
SET @cn2 = '(1, 4i)';
SET @cn3 = @cn1.MulCN(@cn2);
SELECT @cn3.ToString(), CAST(@cn3 AS VARCHAR(MAX)), @cn3.Real, @cn3.Imaginary;
GO
-- Division
DECLARE @cn1 ComplexNumberCS, @cn2 ComplexNumberCS, @cn3 ComplexNumberCS;
SET @cn1 = CAST('(10, 5i)' AS ComplexNumberCS);
SET @cn2 = '(2, 4i)';
SET @cn3 = @cn1.DivCN(@cn2);
SELECT @cn3.ToString(), CAST(@cn3 AS VARCHAR(MAX)), @cn3.Real, @cn3.Imaginary;
GO
```

However, try running the following code using the plus (+) operator and SUM aggregate function:

```
DECLARE @cn1 ComplexNumberCS, @cn2 ComplexNumberCS, @cn3 ComplexNumberCS;
SET @cn1 = CAST('(10, 5i)' AS ComplexNumberCS);
SET @cn2 = '(2, 4i)';
SET @cn3 = @cn1 + @cn2;
SELECT SUM(cn) FROM dbo.CNUsage;
```

You will get the following errors:

```
Msg 403, Level 16, State 1, Line 4
Invalid operator for data type. Operator equals add, type equals ComplexNumberCS.
Msg 8117, Level 16, State 1, Line 5
Operand data type ComplexNumberCS is invalid for sum operator.
```

You can now realize how useful it would have been if SQL Server 2005 supported operator overloading with CLR user-defined types. You can overcome the plus operator problem by writing your own methods, as I demonstrated earlier. However, you can't use UDTs in aggregate functions that depend on arithmetic (like SUM, AVG), rather in functions that depend only on comparison or NULLability (like MAX, COUNT). Fortunately, SQL Server supports user-defined aggregate functions (UDA), which must be written in a .NET language, like user-defined types. If you need an aggregate function that would support your UDT, you have to create your own.

As background for creating UDAs, please refer to *Inside T-SQL Querying*. Let me quickly show an example. Add a new Aggregate item to the ComplexNumberCS project in Visual Studio .NET 2005, name it *ComplexNumberCS_SUM.cs*, substitute its body with the code in Listing 1-4, and rebuild the project.

Listing 1-4   C# .NET–based ComplexNumberCS UDA

```
C# ComplexNumberCS_SUM UDA
using System;
using System.Data;
using System.Data.SqlClient;
using System.Data.SqlTypes;
using Microsoft.SqlServer.Server;


[Serializable]
[Microsoft.SqlServer.Server.SqlUserDefinedAggregate(Format.Native)]
public struct ComplexNumberCS_SUM
{
    ComplexNumberCS cn;

    public void Init()
    {
        cn = ComplexNumberCS.Parse("(0, 0i)");
    }

    public void Accumulate(ComplexNumberCS Value)
    {
        cn = cn.AddCN(Value);
    }

    public void Merge(ComplexNumberCS_SUM Group)
    {
        Accumulate(Group.Terminate());
    }

    public ComplexNumberCS Terminate()
    {
        return cn;
    }

}
```

Next, you need to update the assembly in the database. To do so, use the ALTER ASSEMBLY command. You shouldn't have any problems because you're not changing the UDT you're already using. Remember, you have to catalog the aggregate function using the CREATE AGGREGATE command:

```
-- Alter assembly to add the ComplexNumberCS_SUM UDA
ALTER ASSEMBLY ComplexNumberCS
FROM 'C:\ComplexNumberCS\ComplexNumberCS\bin\Debug\ComplexNumberCS.dll';
GO

-- Create the aggregate function
CREATE AGGREGATE dbo.ComplexNumberCS_SUM(@input ComplexNumberCS)
RETURNS ComplexNumberCS
EXTERNAL NAME ComplexNumberCS.[ComplexNumberCS_SUM];
```

And finally, use the new aggregate function to calculate the sum of all non-NULL values in the table, and you will get (3, 10i) back:

```
SELECT dbo.ComplexNumberCS_SUM(cn).ToString() AS ComplexSum
FROM CNUsage
WHERE cn IS NOT NULL;
```

You can see that CLR UDAs can be written to support CLR UDTs.

In case your language of preference is Visual Basic .NET, for your convenience, Listings 1-5 and 1-6 have the code for the Visual Basic .NET–based UDT and UDA, respectively. Conceptually, all the discussion about UDTs and UDAs is language independent.

Listing 1-5   Visual Basic .NET–based ComplexNumberVB UDT

```vbnet
Imports System
Imports System.Data
Imports System.Data.SqlClient
Imports System.Data.SqlTypes
Imports Microsoft.SqlServer.Server
Imports System.Text.RegularExpressions
Imports System.Globalization


<Serializable()> _
<Microsoft.SqlServer.Server.SqlUserDefinedType(Format.Native, _
    IsByteOrdered:=True)> _
Public Structure ComplexNumberVB
    Implements INullable

    Private Shared ReadOnly parser As New Regex( _
  "\A\(\s*(?<real>\-?\d+(\.\d+)?)\s*,\s*(?<img>\-?\d+(\.\d+)?)\s*i\s*\)\Z", _
    RegexOptions.Compiled Or RegexOptions.ExplicitCapture)
    Private realValue As Double
    Private imaginaryValue As Double
    Private isNullValue As Boolean
    Private Const nullValue As String = "<<null complex>>"
    Private Shared ReadOnly NULL_INSTANCE As New ComplexNumberVB(True)

    Public Sub New(ByVal real As Double, ByVal imaginary As Double)
        Me.realValue = real
        Me.imaginaryValue = imaginary
        Me.isNullValue = False
    End Sub

    Private Sub New(ByVal isnull As Boolean)
        Me.isNullValue = isnull
        Me.realValue = 0
        Me.imaginaryValue = 0
    End Sub

    Public Overrides Function ToString() As String
        If Me.isNullValue = True Then
            Return nullValue
        Else
```

```vb
                Return "(" & Me.realValue.ToString(CultureInfo.InvariantCulture) _
                    & "," & Me.imaginaryValue.ToString( _
                    CultureInfo.InvariantCulture) _
                    & "i)"
            End If
        End Function

        Public ReadOnly Property IsNull() As Boolean Implements INullable.IsNull
            Get
                Return Me.isNullValue
            End Get
        End Property

        Public Shared ReadOnly Property Null() As ComplexNumberVB
            Get
                Return NULL_INSTANCE
            End Get
        End Property

        Public Shared Function Parse(ByVal sqlString As SqlString) _
          As ComplexNumberVB
            Dim value As String = sqlString.ToString()

            If sqlString.IsNull Or value = nullValue Then
                Return New ComplexNumberVB(True)
            End If

            Dim m As Match = parser.Match(value)

            If Not m.Success Then
                Throw New ArgumentException( _
                    "Invalid format for complex number. Format is " + _
                        "( n, mi ) where n and m are floating point numbers " + _
                        "in normal (not scientific) format (nnnnnn.nn).")
            End If

            Return New ComplexNumberVB(Double.Parse(m.Groups(1).Value, _
                CultureInfo.InvariantCulture), _
                Double.Parse(m.Groups(2).Value, CultureInfo.InvariantCulture))
        End Function

        Public Property Real() As Double
            Get
                If Me.isNullValue Then
                    Throw New InvalidOperationException()
                End If
                Return Me.realValue
            End Get
            Set(ByVal Value As Double)
                Me.realValue = Value
            End Set
        End Property
```

```vb
    Public Property Imaginary() As Double
        Get
            If Me.isNullValue Then
                Throw New InvalidOperationException()
            End If
            Return Me.imaginaryValue
        End Get
        Set(ByVal Value As Double)
            Me.imaginaryValue = Value
        End Set
    End Property

#Region "arithmetic operations"

    ' Addition
    Public Function AddCN(ByVal c As ComplexNumberVB) As ComplexNumberVB
        'Null(checking)
        If Me.isNullValue Or c.isNullValue Then
            Return New ComplexNumberVB(True)
        End If
        ' addition
        Return New ComplexNumberVB(Me.Real + c.Real, _
            Me.Imaginary + c.Imaginary)
    End Function

    ' Subtraction
    Public Function SubCN(ByVal c As ComplexNumberVB) As ComplexNumberVB
        'Null(checking)
        If Me.isNullValue Or c.isNullValue Then
            Return New ComplexNumberVB(True)
        End If
        ' addition
        Return New ComplexNumberVB(Me.Real - c.Real, _
            Me.Imaginary - c.Imaginary)
    End Function


    ' Multiplication
    Public Function MulCN(ByVal c As ComplexNumberVB) As ComplexNumberVB
        'Null(checking)
        If Me.isNullValue Or c.isNullValue Then
            Return New ComplexNumberVB(True)
        End If
        ' addition
        Return New ComplexNumberVB(Me.Real * c.Real - _
          Me.Imaginary * c.Imaginary, _
            Me.Imaginary * c.Real + Me.Real * c.Imaginary)
    End Function


    ' Division
    Public Function DivCN(ByVal c As ComplexNumberVB) As ComplexNumberVB
        'Null(checking)
```

```
        If Me.isNullValue Or c.isNullValue Then
            Return New ComplexNumberVB(True)
        End If
        ' addition
        Return New ComplexNumberVB( _
            (Me.Real * c.Real + Me.Imaginary * c.Imaginary) _
                / (c.Real * c.Real + c.Imaginary * c.Imaginary), _
            (Me.Imaginary * c.Real - Me.Real * c.Imaginary) _
                / (c.Real * c.Real + c.Imaginary * c.Imaginary) _
            )
    End Function

#End Region

End Structure
```

Listing 1-6   Visual Basic .NET–based ComplexNumberVB_SUM UDA

```
Imports System
Imports System.Data
Imports System.Data.SqlClient
Imports System.Data.SqlTypes
Imports Microsoft.SqlServer.Server


<Serializable()> _
<Microsoft.SqlServer.Server.SqlUserDefinedAggregate(Format.Native)> _
Public Structure ComplexNumberVB_SUM

    Dim cn As ComplexNumberVB

    Public Sub Init()
        cn = ComplexNumberVB.Parse("(0, 0i)")
    End Sub

    Public Sub Accumulate(ByVal value As ComplexNumberVB)
        cn = cn.AddCN(value)
    End Sub

    Public Sub Merge(ByVal value As ComplexNumberVB_SUM)
        Accumulate(value.Terminate())
    End Sub

    Public Function Terminate() As ComplexNumberVB
        Return cn
    End Function

End Structure
```

The T-SQL commands needed to deploy the UDT and UDA in SQL Server are the same ones you used earlier, of course.

Once you're done experimenting with the new UDT, run the following code for cleanup:

```
USE master;
DROP DATABASE Clrtest;
GO
EXEC sp_configure 'clr enabled', 0;
RECONFIGURE;
GO
```

XML Data Type

SQL Server 2005 introduces a native XML datatype and substantially enhanced XML support. Earlier versions of SQL Server had some support for XML data, but not as a native type and with limited functionality. You can now store XML data, constrain it with XML schemas, index it with specialized XML indexes, and manipulate it using the XQuery language, which follows the W3C standard. XQuery manipulation includes querying (query method), retrieving values (value method), existence checks (exists method), modifying sections within the XML data (modify method) as opposed to overriding the whole thing, shredding XML data into multiple rows in a result set (nodes method), and more. In the following section, I'll explain why you need the XML data type inside a database, when to use it, and when not to use it. I'll also provide code samples demonstrating the use of the XML data type. Still, this is a T-SQL programming book, so I won't go into all the details of XML technologies supported in SQL Server 2005.

> **More Info**   For more information on XML technologies, please refer to *Microsoft SQL Server 2005 XML* (Sams, 2006) by Michael Rys. Michael is the program manager in charge of XML technologies with the SQL Server development team.

XML Support in a Relational Database

The first question that came to my mind when I heard that SQL Server 2005 will support a native XML data type was: Why do I need such support in a relational database? I've been pondering the idea for months and have finally become convinced that such support is important and beneficial. XML is the lingua franca of exchanging data among different applications and different platforms. It is widely used, and almost all modern technologies support it. Databases simply have to deal with XML. Now, XML could be stored as simple text. But plain text representation means having no knowledge of the structure built into an XML document. You could decompose the text, store it in multiple relational tables, and use relational technologies to manipulate the data. But relational structures are quite static and not so easy to change. Think of dynamic or volatile XML structures. Storing XML data in a native XML data type solves these problems, enabling functionality attached to the type that can accommodate support for a wide variety of XML technologies.

Is the Relational Model Obsolete?

With the advent of XML and Object technologies, some people wonder whether the relational model is obsolete. Many developers looking for greater programmatic flexibility feel that their choices are very limited with the relational model. The world is constantly changing, and you need technologies to support these changes. Some people think that storing everything in XML format bridges the gap between object-oriented (OO) applications and relational databases. However, in many cases people are just reinventing the wheel.

I agree that the relational model is limiting, but it is intentionally so! The idea is simple—you need constraints to enforce data integrity. Constraints prevent chaos. When you're driving, you obey speed limits and traffic lights, allowing drivers to share the same roads and pass through the same crossroads. When you need to store items in real life, you do so in an organized, structured fashion. A pharmacy that keeps its medicines lying around in a muddle probably won't get many appreciative customers. But the XML data type is structured; in fact, its structure is more relaxed than relational data. So why not use Microsoft Office Word or Excel, which also support structured representation and are even more relaxed than XML, for business applications?

Are schemas really so volatile nowadays? Well, they are volatile for some business cases, but quite stable for the most part. Not being able to find a structure that suits a business problem does not mean that such a structure does not exist. I've seen an example in which a sales Orders table included a column with all order details (order lines) for the order as a single XML value. Come on, an order details schema is not volatile; it's actually so well known that it has a design pattern! I repeat; a relational schema constrains us deliberately. Consider the order details example again; when you are dealing with sales, data integrity is crucial; without it, your company can lose business.

Relational databases support many other constraints besides detailed schema. It's true that you can program them in a middle tier or in any other layer if you use a so-called XML database, but why reinvent the wheel? Why develop something that's already developed? In many cases, reinventing the wheel indicates a lack of knowledge. I've seen a system that started with an XML database without any constraints except schemas. The idea was to design a flexible system. Well, after a while the customer and the developers realized that they needed more constraints. As time passed, more and more constraints were built into the system. Eventually, the system had no flexibility, which in a sense is a good thing because it did in fact need a fixed schema. But with all the constraints that were built into the system, it was almost impossible for applications to use the data and for administrators to maintain the system, all of which made the system extremely expensive. Remember that data is usually used by more than one application—think of Customer Relationship Management (CRM) systems that need merged data from all possible sources and BI solutions, including reporting, OLAP cubes, and Data Mining models.

A couple of years ago I was in an Italian restaurant with some friends. Itzik wanted a pizza, but the restaurant didn't have it. The wait staff suggested the closest thing they had—a kind of meat loaf. Itzik asked for one but added, "As long as it looks like a pizza, smells like a pizza, and tastes like a pizza." Why am I recalling this event? Because if a problem needs a detailed schema and constraints, and the data must be available to many applications, I really don't care what kind of database and model you use—as long as it looks like the relational model, behaves like the relational model, and constrains like the relational model.

When Should You Use XML Instead of Relational Representation?

I hope that after the introduction, you won't think that I'm entirely opposed to having XML support inside a relational database. I can actually give many examples where it does make sense.

First of all, I have to admit, a schema sometimes is in fact volatile. Think about situations in which you have to support many different schemas for the same kind of event. There are many such cases within SQL Server itself. DDL triggers are a good example. There are dozens of different DDL events, and each event returns different event information—that is, data with a different schema. If DDL triggers used relational schemas to return event information (as DML triggers do), SQL Server would need to support dozens of different schemas, some of which would be very complicated. A conscious design choice was that DDL triggers will return event information in XML format via the *EventInfo* function. Event information in XML format is quite easy to manipulate. Furthermore, with this architecture, SQL Server will be able to extend support for new DDL events in future versions more easily.

Another interesting example of internal XML support in SQL Server 2005, and proof that Microsoft is practicing what it preaches, is XML showplans. You can now generate execution plan information in XML format using the SET SHOWPLAN_XML and SET STATISTICS XML statements. Think of the value for applications and tools that need execution plan information—it's easy to request and parse it now. You can even force the optimizer to use a given execution plan expressed in XML format by using the USE PLAN query hint.

The "XML Best Practices" section in Books Online says that you should use an XML model if your data is sparse (among other circumstances). This is true, though it's not the only solution. Your data is sparse, having many unknown values, if some columns are not applicable to all rows. Standard solutions for such a problem introduce subtypes or implement an open schema model in a relational environment. Still, a solution based on XML could be the easiest to implement. A solution that introduces subtypes can lead to many new tables. A solution that implements a relational open schema model can lead to complex, dynamic SQL statements.

There are other reasons mentioned in Books Online for using an XML model—for example, a changing structure, which I mentioned earlier. XML inherently supports hierarchical sorted data. This fact makes people wonder whether XML is more appropriate for representing hierarchical data than a relational model. A relational solution that has references among entities is cumbersome. However, a hierarchy can be represented in a relational model as an adjacency list (parent/child attributes) with a self-referencing foreign key constraint. You can then query the data using recursive common table expressions (CTEs). There are also other solutions to representing structures such as graphs, trees, and hierarchies in a relational model.

What if ordering is inherent in your data? I don't find this a good enough reason to justify using XML. You can have an attribute that defines the order; otherwise, you probably haven't done your business analysis well.

Finally, another scenario suggested for using XML representation is when you want to modify parts of the data based on its structure. I agree with this reasoning in some cases, and I'll explain and demonstrate why in the following section.

Objects in .NET applications can be persisted in one of two ways: using binary or XML serialization. Binary serialization is very encapsulated; only applications that know the structure (class) of the object and the way it's serialized can deserialize it. XML serialization is much more open. All you need to know is the XML schema, and even without it you can browse the data. Now think of objects in a wider sense. Everything you store in a computer is a kind of object. For example, take Microsoft Visio diagrams. They can be stored in internal Visio format or as XML. If they are stored in the internal format, you can open them only with Microsoft Visio. If they are stored in XML format, you can open them even with Notepad. And if you store them using XML format in a database, you can use T-SQL queries to search and manipulate the document data. That is valuable functionality! Imagine you are searching for all Visio documents that include a specific element. If they are stored in internal format, you have to open them one by one and visually check them. If they are stored as XML documents in a file system, you can use full-text indexes and search through them. But if they are stored in a database in an XML column, you can find all documents you need with a single SELECT statement.

As another example for using XML, consider a frequently asked question: "How do you pass an array as a parameter to a stored procedure?" The solution is not that easy. One option is to pass the array of values as a comma-separated string and then use T-SQL code to separate the elements. Another option is to pass the array as an XML parameter, and use the .nodes method to shred the values into a relational presentation.

After this introduction, you should have an idea of when the XML data type is appropriate and when you should stick to the relational model. Having the background covered, I can now discuss the new XQuery language, the XML data type methods, and some other XML enhancements. I'll also walk you through code samples that you're likely to find useful.

XML Serialized Objects in a Database

Note This section contains queries that require an active connection to the Internet. If you don't have one, simply read this section without running those queries yourself.

Figure 1-7 has four simple Visio diagrams: an Object-Role Modeling (ORM) diagram for products and their associated properties, an Entity-Relationship (ER) diagram for the product entity, a Unified Modeling Language (UML) class diagram for the product entity, and an ER diagram for customers.

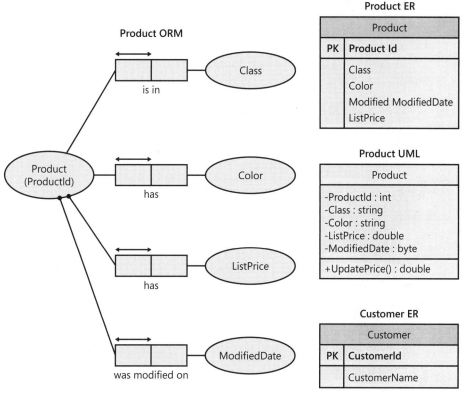

Figure 1-7   Visio diagrams

I saved all diagrams in XML format (.vsd Visio files). The XML schema (XSD) for Visio documents is published at *http://msdn.microsoft.com/library/default.asp?url=/library/en-us/ vissdk11/html/vixmlelemVisioDocument_HV01085731.asp*. The filenames of the four diagrams are ProductORM.vdx, ProductER.vdx, ProductUML.vdx, and CustomerER.vdx. These files are available for download at *http://www.insidetsql.com* as part of the book's source code download. I'll demonstrate how to import these files into XML column values in a table and manipulate them. To follow the demonstration, create the folder C:\VisioFiles and copy the .vsd files from the book's CD to that folder.

First prepare a new test database:

```
USE master;
CREATE DATABASE XMLtest;
GO
USE XMLtest;
```

Next, use the following code to create a table with an XML column and import the Visio documents into the table:

```
CREATE TABLE dbo.VisioDocs
(
  id  INT NOT NULL,
  doc XML NOT NULL
);
GO

INSERT INTO dbo.VisioDocs (id, doc)
 SELECT 1, *
 FROM OPENROWSET(BULK 'C:\VisioFiles\ProductORM.vdx',
   SINGLE_BLOB) AS x;
INSERT INTO dbo.VisioDocs (id, doc)
 SELECT 2, *
 FROM OPENROWSET(BULK 'C:\VisioFiles\ProductER.vdx',
   SINGLE_BLOB) AS x;
INSERT INTO dbo.VisioDocs (id, doc)
 SELECT 3, *
 FROM OPENROWSET(BULK 'C:\VisioFiles\ProductUML.vdx',
   SINGLE_BLOB) AS x;
INSERT INTO dbo.VisioDocs (id, doc)
 SELECT 4, *
 FROM OPENROWSET(BULK 'C:\VisioFiles\CustomerER.vdx',
   SINGLE_BLOB) AS x;
```

You can clearly see the advantage of loading file data using the new BULK rowset provider over the limited support for loading file data in earlier versions of SQL Server. It's so simple now!

It's time to check what you loaded:

```
SELECT id, doc FROM dbo.VisioDocs;
```

This simple SELECT statement produces the output shown in Table 1-20.

Table 1-20   Visio Documents Stored in an XML Column

id	doc
1	<VisioDocument xmlns="http://schemas.microsoft.co...
2	<VisioDocument xmlns="http://schemas.microsoft.co...
3	<VisioDocument xmlns="http://schemas.microsoft.co...
4	<VisioDocument xmlns="http://schemas.microsoft.co...

The XML data is shown in the table as a hyperlink. SSMS can, in contrast to SQL Server 2000's Query Analyzer (QA), properly parse and represent XML data. If you click the hyperlink in the row having *id* 1, you get the XML data in a new window. Here's a small snippet of what you get:

```
<VisioDocument xmlns="http://schemas.microsoft.com/visio/2003/core" key=
"6EBD363F713E11F015D5C3B92BA3B51614E0DDCD04221BE2E5746F025DB606135E3471EE1AFC2FE765E28213490
B60BAC4D061FC55E033D2B6396B8358AECEA0" start="190" metric="0" DocLangID="1033"
buildnum="5130" version="11.0" xml:space="preserve">
  <DocumentProperties>
    <Creator>Dejan Sarka</Creator>
    <Template>C:\Program Files\Microsoft Office\Visio11\1033\ORMSRC_U.VST</Template>
    <Company>Solid Quality Learning</Company>
    <BuildNumberCreated>738202634</BuildNumberCreated>
    <BuildNumberEdited>738202634</BuildNumberEdited>...
```

You can see that the document has an internal structure, and the structure of course complies with the published XML schema I mentioned earlier. You can now use the XQuery language within a SELECT statement to extract portions of the XML data. For example, the following query returns the company of the creator of each document, generating the output shown in Table 1-21:

```
SELECT id,
  doc.value('declare namespace VI=
    "http://schemas.microsoft.com/visio/2003/core";
    (/VI:VisioDocument/VI:DocumentProperties/VI:Company)[1]',
    'NVARCHAR(50)') AS company
FROM dbo.VisioDocs;
```

Table 1-21   Companies of Creators of Visio Documents

id	company
1	Solid Quality Learning
2	Solid Quality Learning
3	Solid Quality Learning
4	Unknown Company

I used the .value method of the XML data type. This method returns a scalar .value, so it can be specified in the SELECT list. Note that the .value method accepts an XQuery expression as input. It consists of two parts: prolog and body. In the prolog, you declare all namespaces used in the query. In our case, it is the namespace declared by Microsoft for Visio documents, which I copied out of the XML output from the previous example. Namespaces allow you to have elements with the same names describing different entities and attributes, similar to .NET namespaces. Elements inside different namespaces are treated as different elements. If you don't include the namespace, XQuery would not find any element, and the .value method would return NULL. A namespace is declared with a prefix—that is, an alias you use in the body of the query. In the XQuery expression, you define the path to the element you want to read. Starting from the root element (*<VisioDocument>*) and going through the second-level element (*<DocumentProperties>*), you arrive to the element you need (*<Company>*).

Notice the use of the index [1]. An untyped XML document (without a defined schema) supports multiple elements with the same name in the same level. The .value method must return a scalar value; therefore, you have to specify the exact index of the element in the level you are browsing, even if you know that there is only one. XQuery supports aggregate functions such as *Sum*, *Count*, *Avg*, *Min*, and *Max*. You can use those to aggregate multiple values and return the scalar result value. Finally, every column in the returned result set must have a data type, so the XQuery expression converts the returned value to NVARCHAR(50).

Next, suppose you want to find all database model diagrams (ER diagrams). All documents with database models are based on the DBMODL_U.VST template, and the template is included in the *<Template>* element of the XML schema for Visio documents. You can use the .value method in the WHERE clause like so, returning the output shown in Table 1-22:

```
SELECT id, 'ER DB Model' AS templatetype
FROM dbo.VisioDocs
WHERE doc.value(
  'declare namespace VI="http://schemas.microsoft.com/visio/2003/core";
  (/VI:VisioDocument/VI:DocumentProperties/VI:Template)[1]',
  'nvarchar(100)') LIKE N'%DBMODL_U.VST%';
```

Table 1-22   ER Diagrams

id	templatetype
2	ER DB Model
4	ER DB Model

Next, the .query method, as the name implies, is used to query XML data. It returns an instance of an untyped XML value. The method's input query can be as simple as an XPath expression returning some subelements of an XML value. Or it can be a complex query using a FLOWR statement. FLOWR is an acronym for For, Let, Order by, Where, and Return. The For clause binds one or more iterator variables to input sequences. It's similar to a standard ForEach loop in OOP languages. Input sequences are either sequences of nodes or sequences of atomic values. The Let clause binds a temporary variable to the result of a query expression. It is similar to the WITH clause in T-SQL used to define a CTE. The Let clause is not implemented in SQL Server 2005. The Where clause applies a filter predicate to the iteration and is similar to a T-SQL query filter. Similarly, the Order by clause is used to order the output similar to a T-SQL query's ORDER BY clause. The Return clause constructs the result of a FLOWR expression, shaping the XML output.

As an example for using the .query method, the following code invokes a FLOWR expression to iterate through subelements of the *<DocumentSettings>* element, generating the output shown in Table 1-23:

```
SELECT doc.query('
  declare namespace VI="http://schemas.microsoft.com/visio/2003/core";
  for $v in /VI:VisioDocument/VI:DocumentSettings
  return $v') AS settings
FROM dbo.VisioDocs;
```

Table 1-23   Document Settings Retrieved with the .query Method

settings
<VI:DocumentSettings xmlns:VI="http://schemas.microsoft.co...
<VI:DocumentSettings xmlns:VI="http://schemas.microsoft.co...
<VI:DocumentSettings xmlns:VI="http://schemas.microsoft.co...
<VI:DocumentSettings xmlns:VI="http://schemas.microsoft.co...

If you click one of the links, you get the settings for the selected document in XML format:

```
<VI:DocumentSettings xmlns:VI="http://schemas.microsoft.com/visio/2003/
core" TopPage="0" DefaultTextStyle="3" DefaultLineStyle="3" DefaultFillStyle="3"
DefaultGuideStyle="4">
  <VI:GlueSettings>9</VI:GlueSettings>
  <VI:SnapSettings>39</VI:SnapSettings>
  <VI:SnapExtensions>34</VI:SnapExtensions>
  <VI:DynamicGridEnabled>0</VI:DynamicGridEnabled>
  <VI:ProtectStyles>0</VI:ProtectStyles>
  <VI:ProtectShapes>0</VI:ProtectShapes>
  <VI:ProtectMasters>0</VI:ProtectMasters>
  <VI:ProtectBkgnds>0</VI:ProtectBkgnds>
</VI:DocumentSettings>
```

As I mentioned earlier, the Return clause can be used to shape the XML value returned. For example, the following query retrieves the *<Creator>* element, returning it as an attribute called *creatorname* of an element called *<Person>*:

```
SELECT doc.query('
  declare namespace VI="http://schemas.microsoft.com/visio/2003/core";
  for $v in /VI:VisioDocument/VI:DocumentProperties
  return element Person
    {
      attribute creatorname
                {$v/VI:Creator[1]/text()[1]}
    }')
FROM dbo.VisioDocs;
```

Here's the XML value this query returns in the first output row:

```
<Person creatorname="Dejan Sarka" />
```

Next, suppose that you want to find all Visio documents with an unknown creator company (*<Company>* element has "Unknown Company"). You might be thinking of using the .value method in the WHERE clause. However, remember that the XML data type is actually a LOB type. There can be up to 2 GB of data in every single column value. Scanning through the XML data sequentially is not a very efficient way of retrieving a simple scalar value. With relational data, you can create an index on a filtered column, allowing an index seek operation instead of a table scan. Similarly, you can index XML columns with specialized XML indexes. The first index you create on an XML column is the Primary XML index. This index contains a shredded persisted representation of the XML values. For each XML value in the column, the index creates several rows of data. The number of rows in the index is approximately the number of nodes in the XML value. Such an index can already speed up searches for a specific element (using the .exist method, which I'll describe later). After creating the Primary XML index, you can create up to three secondary XML indexes:

- Path, which is especially useful if your queries specify path expressions. It speeds up the .exist method better than the Primary XML index.

- Value, which is useful if queries are value based, and the path is not fully specified or it includes a wildcard.

- Property, which is very useful for queries that retrieve one or more values from individual XML instances (.value method).

The Primary XML index has to be created first. It can be created only on tables with a clustered primary key. The query you are going to use to find all unknown companies invokes the .value method in the WHERE clause, searching for a single value. The use of the .value method in this case is similar to using the .exist method; therefore, a secondary XML Path index is most appropriate. So you need to create a clustered primary key, then a Primary XML index, and then a secondary one:

```
ALTER TABLE dbo.VisioDocs
  ADD CONSTRAINT PK_VisioDocs PRIMARY KEY CLUSTERED (id);

CREATE PRIMARY XML INDEX idx_xml_primary ON dbo.VisioDocs(doc);

CREATE XML INDEX idx_xml_path ON VisioDocs(doc)
  USING XML INDEX idx_xml_primary
  FOR PATH;
```

Next, invoke the following three statements in a single batch, with Include Actual Execution Plan turned on in SSMS:

```
SELECT id, doc
FROM dbo.VisioDocs
WHERE doc.value(
  'declare namespace VI="http://schemas.microsoft.com/visio/2003/core";
  (/VI:VisioDocument/VI:DocumentProperties/VI:Company)[1]',
  'nvarchar(50)') LIKE N'Unknown%';

DROP INDEX idx_xml_primary ON dbo.VisioDocs;

SELECT id, doc
FROM dbo.VisioDocs
WHERE doc.value(
  'declare namespace VI="http://schemas.microsoft.com/visio/2003/core";
  (/VI:VisioDocument/VI:DocumentProperties/VI:Company)[1]',
  'nvarchar(50)') LIKE N'Unknown%';
```

Both SELECT statements are identical, retrieving documents with unknown companies. The first one uses XML indexes, while the second doesn't (because it's invoked after dropping the indexes).

> **Note**   When you drop the Primary XML index, all secondary XML indexes are dropped automatically.

If you look at the cost ratios of the queries in the plan, you will find the first has 3 percent cost out of the whole batch, and the second 97 percent. You realize that the substantial cost difference exists because the first query uses XML indexes while the second doesn't.

Using XML with Open Schema

You can use the XML data type to support an open schema environment. Suppose that you need to store contacts in a table. For domestic contacts, you need to store an ID and a foreign spoken language. For foreign contacts, you need to store the mother tongue and a flag that shows whether the contact speaks English or not. You could solve this problem with two subtypes: one for the domestic contacts and one for the foreign ones. You would use a separate table for the subtype-specific attributes; however, I'd like to show how you can implement a solution with a single table using the XML data type. First, create the following Contacts table:

```
CREATE TABLE dbo.Contacts
(
  contactid        INT           NOT NULL PRIMARY KEY,
  contactname      NVARCHAR(50)  NOT NULL,
  domestic         BIT           NOT NULL,
  otherattributes  XML           NOT NULL
);
```

Notice that the table contains a flag that specifies whether the contact is domestic or foreign. Before you start to insert data, you will constrain the input allowed in the *other-attributes* column. You can constrain the XML data with a schema collection. Values entered into the column will be validated against schemas in the collection and accepted only if they comply with any of the schemas in the collection. Validation against a collection of schemas enables support of different schemas for domestic and foreign contacts. If you wanted to validate XML values only against a single schema, you would define only a single schema in the collection.

You create the schema collection using the new CREATE XML SCHEMA COLLECTION T-SQL statement. You have to supply the XML schema as input—that is, the XSD document. Creating the schema is a task that should not be taken lightly. If you make an error in the schema, some invalid data might be accepted and some valid data might be rejected.

The easiest and safest way that I can suggest to create robust XML schemas is to create relational tables first, and then use the new XMLSCHEMA option of the FOR XML clause. Store the result XML value (the schema) in a variable, and provide the variable as input to the CREATE XML SCHEMA COLLECTION statement. Run the code in Listing 1-7 to create the schema collection *ContactOtherAttributes* with the Domestic and Foreigns schemas.

Listing 1-7   Creation script for the *ContactOtherAttributes* schema collection

```
CREATE TABLE dbo.Domestic
(
  ID              NVARCHAR(15),
  ForeignLanguage NVARCHAR(50)
);

CREATE TABLE dbo.Foreigns
(
  NativeLanguage NVARCHAR(50),
  SpeaksEnglish  BIT
);
GO

-- Store the Schemas in a Variable and Create the Collection
DECLARE @mySchema NVARCHAR(MAX);

SET @mySchema = N'';

SET @mySchema = @mySchema +
  (SELECT *
   FROM Domestic
   FOR XML AUTO, ELEMENTS, XMLSCHEMA('Domestic'));

SET @mySchema = @mySchema +
  (SELECT *
   FROM Foreigns
   FOR XML AUTO, ELEMENTS, XMLSCHEMA('Foreign'));

-- Create Schema Collection
CREATE XML SCHEMA COLLECTION dbo.ContactOtherAttributes AS @mySchema;
GO

-- Drop Tables
DROP TABLE dbo.Domestic, dbo.Foreigns;
```

You can get information about schema collections by querying the catalog views: sys.xml_schema_collections, sys.xml_schema_namespaces, sys.xml_schema_components and some others:

```
-- Retrieve information about the schema collection
SELECT *
FROM sys.xml_schema_collections
WHERE name = 'ContactOtherAttributes';

-- Retrieve information about the namespaces in the schema collection
SELECT N.*
FROM sys.xml_schema_namespaces AS N
  JOIN sys.xml_schema_collections AS C
    ON N.xml_collection_id = C.xml_collection_id
```

```
WHERE C.name = 'ContactOtherAttributes';

-- Retrieve information about the components in the schema collection
SELECT CP.*
FROM sys.xml_schema_components AS CP
  JOIN sys.xml_schema_collections AS C
    ON CP.xml_collection_id = C.xml_collection_id
WHERE C.name = 'ContactOtherAttributes';
```

By executing these queries against the metadata info, you will notice that schema collections are shredded in relational tables. Now you need to alter the XML column from a well-formed state to a schema-validated one:

```
ALTER TABLE dbo.Contacts
  ALTER COLUMN otherattributes XML(dbo.ContactOtherAttributes);
```

> **Note**   When you change an XML column from well-formed to schema-validated, all values in that column are validated, so the alteration can take a while.

Now insert some valid data:

```
INSERT INTO dbo.Contacts VALUES(1, N'Mike', 1, N'
<Domestic xmlns="Domestic">
  <ID>012345678901234</ID>
  <ForeignLanguage>Spanish</ForeignLanguage>
</Domestic>');
INSERT INTO dbo.Contacts VALUES(2, N'Herbert', 0, N'
<Foreigns xmlns="Foreign">
  <NativeLanguage>German</NativeLanguage>
  <SpeaksEnglish>1</SpeaksEnglish>
</Foreigns>');
INSERT INTO dbo.Contacts VALUES(3, N'Richard', 1, N'
<Domestic xmlns="Domestic">
  <ID>012345678901234</ID>
  <ForeignLanguage>German</ForeignLanguage>
</Domestic>');
INSERT INTO dbo.Contacts VALUES(4, N'Gianluca', 0, N'
<Foreigns xmlns="Foreign">
  <NativeLanguage>Italian</NativeLanguage>
  <SpeaksEnglish>1</SpeaksEnglish>
</Foreigns>');
```

Next try to insert some invalid data:

```
INSERT INTO dbo.Contacts VALUES(5, N'Tibor', 0, N'
<Foreigns xmlns="Foreign">
  <Hobbie>Beer</Hobbie>
  <SpeaksEnglish>1</SpeaksEnglish>
</Foreigns>');
GO
```

```
INSERT INTO dbo.Contacts VALUES(5, N'Kalen', 1, N'
<Domestic xmlns="Domestic">
  <ID>012345678901234</ID>
  <ForeignLanguage>Spanish</ForeignLanguage>
  <ForeignLanguage>German</ForeignLanguage>
</Domestic>');
GO
```

Of course, you get errors:

```
Msg 6965, Level 16, State 1, Line 1
XML Validation: Invalid content. Expected element(s):Foreign:NativeLanguage,Foreign:Speaks
English where element 'Foreign:Hobbie' was specified. Location: /*:Foreigns[1]/*:Hobbie[1]
Msg 6923, Level 16, State 1, Line 4
XML Validation: Unexpected element(s): Domestic:ForeignLanguage. Location: /*:Domestic[1]
/*:ForeignLanguage[2]
```

The last error was generated because you tried to insert a contact who speaks two foreign languages but the schema supports only one. As you can see, validation against the schema collection is working.

To explain other aspects of the XML data type, I'll need to insert a contact who speaks two foreign languages. Therefore, you will change the *OtherAttributes* XML column from schema-validated back to well-formed. Before doing so, try to answer the following question: "Would SQL Server currently prevent me from storing an XML value for a domestic contact (domestic column = 1) who adheres to a foreign contact schema and not a domestic one?" The answer is, actually, no. To further constrain the input, you could add a CHECK constraint verifying the existence of an element corresponding to the input contact type (for example, domestic column = 1, and the XML value contains the *<ID>* element).

If you need to constrain the XML data beyond schema validation, maybe it is time to rethink your design. Maybe the solution implementing each subtype in a separate table would be more appropriate!

Moving forward, run the following code to remove the schema validation and retry the last insert:

```
ALTER TABLE dbo.Contacts ALTER COLUMN otherattributes XML;
GO

INSERT INTO dbo.Contacts VALUES(5, N'Kalen', 1, N'
<Domestic xmlns="Domestic">
  <ID>012345678901234</ID>
  <ForeignLanguage>Spanish</ForeignLanguage>
  <ForeignLanguage>German</ForeignLanguage>
</Domestic>');
```

Suppose you want to get a single row for every foreign language spoken by domestic contacts. Currently, there are three domestic contacts, together speaking four foreign languages; therefore, you expect four rows in the output. Your first attempt might be to use the .query method, without any formatting of the output. In this case, you will get a linear sequence of the values as shown in Table 1-24:

```
SELECT contactid, contactname,
  otherattributes.query('
    declare namespace D="Domestic";
    /D:Domestic/D:ForeignLanguage/text()') AS languagespoken
FROM dbo.Contacts
WHERE domestic = CAST(1 AS BIT);
```

Table 1-24   Output of the .query Method

contactid	contactname	languagespoken
1	Mike	Spanish
3	Richard	German
5	Kalen	SpanishGerman

However, you get a single row for Kalen, while she deserves two. Also, the data type returned for the *languagespoken* column is XML (which is the datatype returned by the .query method), while you want a character type. You might also attempt to use the .value method as follows:

```
SELECT contactid, contactname,
  otherattributes.value('
    declare namespace D="Domestic";
    /D:Domestic/D:ForeignLanguage/text()',
    'NVARCHAR(50)') AS languagespoken
FROM dbo.Contacts
WHERE domestic = CAST(1 AS BIT);
```

This time, you get an error because the .value method requires a singleton sequence—and you know that Kalen speaks two foreign languages. You have to split the query into two parts: one for the first foreign language, and one for the second. Then you need to combine the two result sets into a single one by using the UNION ALL set operation. But you don't want to return rows with NULLs in the second foreign language, so you have to check whether the second language exists before returning it. You can achieve this by using the .exists method in the WHERE clause of the second SELECT statement. The .exist method simply checks whether the element specified by the path exists, returning 1 if it does and 0 if it doesn't. Here's the solution query, returning the output shown in Table 1-25:

```
SELECT contactid, contactname,
  otherattributes.value('
    declare namespace D="Domestic";
    (/D:Domestic/D:ForeignLanguage/text())[1]',
    'NVARCHAR(50)') AS languagespoken
FROM dbo.Contacts
WHERE domestic = CAST(1 AS BIT)

UNION ALL
```

```
SELECT contactid, contactname,
  otherattributes.value('
    declare namespace D="Domestic";
    (/D:Domestic/D:ForeignLanguage/text())[2]',
    'NVARCHAR(50)')
FROM dbo.Contacts
WHERE domestic = CAST(1 AS BIT)
  AND otherattributes.exist('
    declare namespace D="Domestic";
    (/D:Domestic/D:ForeignLanguage)[2]') = 1;
```

Table 1-25 Output of the .value and .exist Methods

contactid	contactname	languagespoken
1	Mike	Spanish
3	Richard	German
5	Kalen	Spanish
5	Kalen	German

Although the result is correct, you might not be satisfied with the solution. What if you don't know the maximum number of foreign languages in advance? Considering that the number can be very high, imagine how long the query would become.

It's time to introduce the .nodes method. This method is useful when you want to shred an XML value into relational data. The result of the .nodes method is a result set that contains logical copies of the original XML instances. In those logical copies, the context node of every row instance is set to one of the nodes identified by the XQuery expression—meaning that you get a row for every single node from the starting point defined by the XQuery expression. The .nodes method returns copies of the XML values, so you have to use additional methods to extract the scalar values out of them. The .nodes method has to be invoked for every row in the table. Do you remember which new T-SQL feature allows you to invoke a right table expression for every row of a left table expression? Of course, it's the APPLY table operator.

The solution query invokes the .nodes method in the FROM clause for each row in the base table using the CROSS APPLY operator. The .nodes method's input XQuery expression returns a row for any foreign language spoken. To start simply, the following code will invoke the .query method to return the output of the .nodes method with no manipulation, generating the output shown in Table 1-26:

```
SELECT contactid, contactname, N.c1.query('.') AS languagespoken
  FROM dbo.Contacts
    CROSS APPLY
      otherattributes.nodes('
        declare namespace D="Domestic";
        (/D:Domestic/D:ForeignLanguage)') AS N(c1);
```

Table 1-26 Output of the .nodes and .query Methods

contactid	contactname	languagespoken
1	Mike	`<p1:ForeignLanguage xmlns:p1="Domestic">Spanish </p1:ForeignLanguage>`
3	Richard	`<p1:ForeignLanguage xmlns:p1="Domestic">German </p1:ForeignLanguage>`
5	Kalen	`<p1:ForeignLanguage xmlns:p1="Domestic">Spanish </p1:ForeignLanguage>`
5	Kalen	`<p1:ForeignLanguage xmlns:p1="Domestic">German </p1:ForeignLanguage>`

Finally, you can extract the scalar values from the XML result by using the .value method, generating the desired output shown in Table 1-25:

```
SELECT contactid, contactname,
  N.c1.value('(./text())[1]','NVARCHAR(50)') AS languagespoken
FROM dbo.Contacts
  CROSS APPLY
    otherattributes.nodes('
      declare namespace D="Domestic";
      (/D:Domestic/D:ForeignLanguage)') AS N(c1);
```

XML Data Type as a Parameter of a Stored Procedure

Suppose you want to create a stored procedure that would accept a list of names as a parameter and return all contacts with a name that appears in the input list. Of course, you could use a delimited list and then separate the elements using T-SQL code. However, using an XML input and applying the .nodes method seems simpler to me. Here's the code implementing the stored procedure:

```
CREATE PROCEDURE dbo.GetContacts
  @inplist XML
AS

SELECT C.*
FROM dbo.Contacts AS C
  JOIN (SELECT D1.c1.value('(./text())[1]','NVARCHAR(50)') AS nameneeded
          FROM @inplist.nodes('/Names/NameNeeded') AS D1(c1)) AS D2
    ON C.contactname = D2.nameneeded;
GO
```

The procedure uses the .nodes and .value methods to extract the elements from the input list. You create the input list in XML format by using the FOR XML clause extensions. The RAW mode of the FOR XML clause in SQL Server 2005 can now produce named elements (as opposed to just producing a predefined element named "row"). The FOR XML clause can also return element-centric XML instead of attribute-centric XML by using the ELEMENTS keyword, just like the AUTO mode. The FOR XML clause is invalid in views, inline functions, derived tables, and subqueries when they contain a set operation. But you want to get the list of the names by performing a UNION ALL operation between multiple SELECT statements with scalar values. To circumvent the limitation, use a derived table. Here's sample code to invoke the stored procedure:

```
DECLARE @inplist AS XML;

SET @inplist=
  (SELECT * FROM
     (SELECT N'Gianluca' AS NameNeeded
      UNION ALL
      SELECT N'Mike') AS D
  FOR XML RAW('Names'), ELEMENTS);

EXEC dbo.GetContacts @inplist;
```

XQuery Modification Statements

As mentioned earlier, the XML data type is a LOB. The amount of data stored in a column of this type can be very large. It would not be very practical to replace the complete value when all you need is just to change a small portion of it—for example, a scalar value of some subelement. SQL Server provides you with a .modify method, similar in concept to the .WRITE method for VARCHAR(MAX) and the other MAX types.

Note   You might have noticed that I'm strictly using lowercase for XML data type methods. That's because they are case sensitive, just like everything in XML.

The W3C standard doesn't support data modification with XQuery. However, SQL Server 2005 provides its own language extensions to support data modification with XQuery. XQuery supports the following keywords for data modification:

- insert
- delete
- replace value of

As the last XML example, here's an UPDATE statement that invokes the .modify method and demonstrates all three types of modification:

```
-- insert a subelement
UPDATE dbo.Contacts
  SET otherattributes.modify('
    declare namespace D="Domestic";
    insert <D:Hobbie>Cigar</D:Hobbie>
    into /D:Domestic[1]')
WHERE contactid = 1;
```

```
-- Delete 2nd language for Kalen
UPDATE dbo.Contacts
  SET otherattributes.modify('
    declare namespace D="Domestic";
    delete /D:Domestic/D:ForeignLanguage[2]')
WHERE contactid = 5;

-- change the value of an element
UPDATE dbo.Contacts
 SET otherattributes.modify('
    declare namespace D="Domestic";
    replace value of
      /D:Domestic[1]/D:ForeignLanguage[1]/text()[1]
      with "Russian" ')
WHERE contactid = 3;

-- Show Table Content after Modifications
SELECT * FROM dbo.Contacts;
```

To clean up, drop the XMLtest database:

```
USE master;
DROP DATABASE XMLtest;
```

This concludes the introduction of XML support in SQL Server 2005. Sure, there's a lot more that can be said; but I hope this chapter gave you sufficient tools to decide when it is appropriate to use XML and when it isn't, plus a taste of this distinctive world through the examples I provided.

Conclusion

Datatypes design and implementation choices are not to be taken lightly. These are the foundations upon which your databases will be built, and they will reflect on all database users and applications.

I spent a lot of space discussing DATETIME datatypes because these involve a lot of complexity and are commonly used.

XML and CLR also received substantial coverage. There are three reasons for this: they are new to SQL Server 2005, they have great potential for enhancing the productivity of your database, and they have great potential for misuse and abuse. I hope you were convinced that CLR and XML fit well in the relational model if you use them wisely. That's the key—using them wisely. Education will play a vital role in determining whether XML and CLR support will ultimately succeed or fail.

Chapter 2

Temporary Tables and Table Variables

T-SQL programming often involves the need to materialize data temporarily. *Temporary tables* are just one solution; other ways for handling an independent physical or logical materialization of a set include table variables and table expressions such as views, inline user-defined functions (UDFs), derived tables, and common table expressions (CTEs).

You might need to physically persist interim states of your data for performance reasons, or just as a staging area. Examples of such scenarios include:

- Materializing aggregated data to some level of granularity (for example, employee and month), and issuing running, sliding, and other statistical reports against that data

- Materializing a result of a query for paging purposes

- Materializing result sets of interim queries, and querying the materialized data

- Materializing the result of a CUBE/ROLLUP query, and issuing queries against that data

- Walking through the output of a cursor and saving information you read or calculate per row for further manipulation

- Pivoting data from an Open Schema environment to a more traditional form, and issuing queries against the pivoted data

- Creating a result set that contains a hierarchy with additional attributes such as materialized paths or levels, and issuing reports against the result

- Hold data that needs to be scrubbed before it can be inserted

One of the benefits of materializing data in a temporary table is that it can be more compact than the base data, with preprocessed calculations, and you can index it when it might be inefficient or impractical to index all the base data. Performancewise, you benefit from materializing the data when you need to access it multiple times, but in some cases, even when all you have is a single query against the data, you benefit.

You might also need to materialize interim sets logically in virtual temporary tables (table expressions) to develop solutions in a modular approach. I'll show examples in this chapter that address this need as well. Either way, there are many cases in which using temporary tables, table variables, or table expressions makes sense.

There's a lot of confusion around choosing the appropriate type of temporary object for a given task, and there are many myths regarding the differences between temporary tables and table variables. Furthermore, temporary tables and table variables are often abused because of lack of knowledge of efficient set-based programming. This is one area in which programming maturity comes into play, just as maturity helps you decide between using cursors or set-based solutions and between using dynamic execution or static code.

In this chapter, I will try to provide you with a clear picture of how the different temporary object types behave, in which circumstances you should use each, and whether you should use them at all. At the end of the chapter, I'll provide a summary table (Table 2-4) that contrasts and compares the different types. This table will cover the factors you should take into consideration before making your choice.

Temporary Tables

SQL Server supports two types of temporary tables: local and global. For the most part, I'll focus on local temporary tables because this is the type you would typically consider in the same situations as table variables and table expressions. I'll also describe global temporary tables, but these typically have completely different uses than local temporary tables.

Local Temporary Tables

I'll start with some fundamentals of local temporary tables before showing examples, and I'll do the same whenever discussing a new temporary object type. When referring to temporary tables in this section, assume that the discussion pertains to local ones.

You create and manipulate a temporary table just as you would a permanent one, for the most part. I'll point out the aspects of temporary tables that are different from permanent ones, or aspects that are often misunderstood.

tempdb

Temporary tables are created in tempdb, regardless of the database context of your session. They have physical representation in tempdb, although when they're small enough and Microsoft SQL Server has enough memory to spare, their pages will reside in cache. SQL

Server will persist the temporary table's pages on disk when there is too little free memory. Furthermore, tempdb's recovery model is SIMPLE and cannot be changed. This means that all bulk operations involved with temporary tables are always minimally logged. Unlike user databases, there's no recovery process in tempdb. There are many other issues you need to consider with regard to tempdb. I'll cover some of these issues later in the chapter in a dedicated section.

So one reason to use a temporary table is to take the load off of a user database when you need to persist temporary data. You can also enjoy the fact that tempdb is treated differently from user databases.

> **Tip**   My preferred method for checking whether an object already exists is to use the OBJECT_ID function. If the function returns a NULL, the object doesn't exist. If you want to check whether a temporary table already exists, make sure you specify the tempdb database prefix; otherwise, SQL Server will look for it in the current database, won't find one, and will always return a NULL. For example, to check whether #T1 exists, use *OBJECT_ID('tempdb..#T1')* and not *OBJECT_ID('#T1')*.
>
> Also, SQL Server 2005 now supports a second argument for OBJECT_ID, where you can specify the object type you're looking for (for example, *'U'* for User table). The second argument's value must match the type column in sys.objects. This second argument was available in SQL Server 2000 as well, but it just wasn't documented until now.

Scope and Visibility

Temporary table names are prefixed with a number symbol (#). A temporary table is owned by the creating session and visible only to it. However, SQL Server allows different sessions to create a temporary table with the same name. Internally, SQL Server adds underscores and a unique numeric suffix to the table name to distinguish between temporary tables with the same name across sessions. For example, suppose that you created a temporary table called #T1. If you query the table sys.objects (dbo.sysobjects in SQL Server 2000) in tempdb looking for a table with name LIKE '#T1%', you will find a table with a name similar to the following (the suffix will vary): #T1_____
_____0000000001E. Although this is the table's internal name, you refer to it in your code by the name you used when you created it—#T1.

Within the session, the temporary table is visible only to the creating level in the call stack and also inner levels, not to outer ones. For example, if you create a temp table in the session's outermost level, it's available anywhere within the session, across batches, and even in inner levels—for example, dynamic batch, stored procedure, and trigger. As long as you don't close the connection, you can access the temporary table. If it's created within a stored procedure, it's visible to the stored procedure and inner levels invoked by that procedure (for example, a nested procedure or a trigger). You can rely on the visibility behavior of temporary tables— for example, when you want to pass data between different levels in your session, or even just signal something to an inner level and that inner level doesn't support input parameters (for example, a trigger). However, in some cases, you can pass such information through the *context_info* feature, which is visible across the session. (See SET CONTEXT_INFO in Books Online for details.)

Once its creating level gets out of scope (terminates), a temporary table is automatically destroyed. If a temporary table was created in the outermost level, it is destroyed when the session is terminated. If it's created within a stored procedure, it is automatically dropped as soon as the stored procedure is finished.

Remember that a temporary table is not visible to levels outside of the creating one in the call stack. That's why, for example, you can't use a temporary table created in a dynamic batch in the calling batch. Once the dynamic batch is out of scope, the temporary table is gone. Later in the chapter, I'll suggest alternatives to use when such a need occurs. The next part, regarding the scope, is a bit tricky. You can, in fact, create multiple temporary tables with the same name within the same session, as long as you create them in different levels—although doing so might lead to trouble. I'll elaborate on this point in the "Temporary Table Name Resolution" section later in the chapter.

The scope and visibility of a temporary table are very different than they are with both permanent tables and table variables and can be major factors in choosing one type of temporary object over another.

Transaction Context

A temporary table is an integral part of an outer transaction if it's manipulated in one (with DML or DDL). This fact has consequences for logging and locking. Logging has to support rollback operations only, not roll-forward ones. (Remember, there is no recovery process in tempdb.) As for locking, because the temporary table is visible only to the creating session, less locking is involved than with permanent tables, which can be accessed from multiple sessions.

So, one of the factors you should consider when choosing a temporary object type is whether you want manipulation against it to be part of an outer transaction.

Statistics

The optimizer creates and maintains distribution statistics (column value histograms) for temporary tables and keeps track of their cardinality, much as it does for permanent ones. This capability is especially important when you index the temporary table. Distribution information is available to the optimizer when it needs to estimate selectivity, and you will get optimized plans that were generated based on this information. This is one of the main areas in which temporary tables differ from table variables in terms of performance.

Also, because statistics are maintained for temporary tables, your code will be recompiled if a sufficient number of rows of a referenced table has changed since the last compilation (the recompilation threshold is reached). The recompilation threshold (RT) is based on the table type and the number of rows. For permanent tables, if $n <= 500$, then $RT = 500$ (n = table's cardinality when a query plan is compiled). If $n > 500$, then $RT = 500 + 0.20 * n$. For temporary tables, if $n < 6$, then $RT = 6$. If $6 <= n <= 500$, then $RT = 500$. If $n > 500$, then $RT = 500 + 0.20 * n$. You realize that, for example, after loading six rows into a temporary table, adding a seventh will trigger a recompile, whereas with permanent tables the first trigger will occur much later. If you want queries against temporary tables to use the same recompilation thresholds as against permanent ones, use the KEEP PLAN query hint.

> **Note**   SQL Server 2005 uses a statement-level recompilation model, as opposed to the procedure-level model in SQL Server 2000. I urge you to read the white paper "Batch Compilation, Recompilation, and Plan Caching Issues in SQL Server 2005" by Arun Marathe for details about the subject, including relevance to temporary tables. You can link to this paper at *http://www.microsoft.com/technet/prodtechnol/sql/2005/recomp.mspx*.

The fact that the optimizer maintains distribution statistics for temporary tables and the aforementioned implications are the most crucial aspects of choosing a temporary object type. These factors are especially important when choosing between temporary tables and table variables, for which the optimizer doesn't create or maintain distribution statistics. Rowcount information is maintained for table variables (in sysindexes in SQL Server 2000, and in sys.partitions in SQL Server 2005) but this information is often inaccurate. Table variables themselves do not trigger recompiles, and recompiles are required to update the rowcount information. You can force a recompile for a query involving table variables in SQL Server 2005 using the RECOMPILE query hint. In short, table variables don't involve optimality-based recompilations.

There are two main questions you must ask yourself:

1. Does the optimizer need distribution statistics or accurate cardinality estimations to generate an efficient plan, and if so, what's the cost of using an inefficient plan when statistics are not available?

2. What's the cost of recompilations if you do use temporary tables?

There are cases in which the optimizer doesn't need statistics to figure out an optimal plan—for example, given a query requesting all rows from a table, a point query filtering a column on which a unique index is defined, a range query that utilizes a clustered or covering index, and so on. In such cases, regardless of the table's size, there's no benefit in having statistics because you will only suffer from the cost of recompilations. In such cases, consider using a table variable.

Also, if the table is tiny (say, a couple of pages), the alternatives are 1) using a table variable resulting in complete scans and few or no recompilations and 2) use a temporary table resulting in index seeks and more recompilations. The advantage of seeks versus scans may be outweighed by the disadvantage of recompiles. That's another case for which you should consider using table variables.

On the other hand, if the optimizer does need statistics to generate an efficient plan and you're not dealing with tiny tables, the cost of using an inefficient plan might well be substantially higher than the cost of the recompilations involved. That's a case in which you should consider using temporary tables. In the "Table Variables" section, I'll provide examples related to these scenarios in which I'll also demonstrate execution plans.

Temporary Table Name Resolution

As I mentioned earlier, technically you're allowed to create multiple local temporary tables with the same name within the same session, as long as you create them in different levels. However, you should avoid doing this because of name-resolution considerations that might cause your code to break.

When a batch is resolved, the schema of a temporary table that is created within that batch is not available. So resolution of code that refers to the temporary table is deferred to run time. However, if a temporary table name you refer to already exists within the session (for example, it has been created by a higher level in the call stack), that table name will resolve to the existing temporary table. However, the code will always run against the innermost temporary table with the referenced name.

This resolution architecture can cause your code to break when you least expect it; this can happen when temporary tables with the same name exist in different levels with different schemas.

This part is very tricky and is probably best explained by using an example. Run the following code to create the stored procedures proc1 and proc2:

```
SET NOCOUNT ON;
USE tempdb;
GO
IF OBJECT_ID('dbo.proc1') IS NOT NULL
  DROP PROC dbo.proc1;
GO
IF OBJECT_ID('dbo.proc2') IS NOT NULL
  DROP PROC dbo.proc2;
GO

CREATE PROC dbo.proc1
AS

CREATE TABLE #T1(col1 INT NOT NULL);
INSERT INTO #T1 VALUES(1);
SELECT * FROM #T1;

EXEC dbo.proc2;
GO

CREATE PROC dbo.proc2
AS
```

```
CREATE TABLE #T1(col1 INT NULL);
INSERT INTO #T1 VALUES(2);
SELECT * FROM #T1;
GO
```

proc1 creates a temporary table called #T1 with a single integer column, loads a row with the value 1, returns #T1's contents, and invokes proc2. proc2 also creates a temporary table called #T1 with a single integer column, loads a row with the value 2, and returns #T1's contents. Both #T1 tables have the same schema. Now, invoke proc1:

```
EXEC dbo.proc1;
```

The output is what you probably expected:

```
col1
-----------
1

col1
-----------
2
```

Both procedures returned the contents of the #T1 table they created. Being oblivious to the resolution process I described earlier doesn't really affect you in this case. After all, you did get the expected result, and the code ran with no errors. However, things change if you alter *proc2* in such a way that it creates #T1 with a different schema than in *proc1*:

```
ALTER PROC dbo.proc2
AS

CREATE TABLE #T1(col1 INT NULL, col2 INT NOT NULL);
INSERT INTO #T1 VALUES(2, 2);
SELECT * FROM #T1;
GO
```

Run *proc1* again:

```
EXEC dbo.proc1;
```

And notice the error you get in the output:

```
col1
-----------
1

Msg 213, Level 16, State 1, Procedure proc2, Line 5
Insert Error: Column name or number of supplied values does not match table definition.
```

Can you explain the error? Admittedly, the problem in the resolution process I described is very elusive, and you might not have realized it after the first read. Try to read the paragraph describing the resolution process again, and then see whether you can explain the error. Essentially, when *proc2* was invoked by *proc1*, a table called #T1 already existed. So even though *proc2*'s code creates a table called #T2 with two columns and loads a row with two values, when the INSERT statement is resolved, *proc2*'s #T1 does not exist yet, but *proc1*'s does. Therefore, SQL Server reports a resolution error—you attempt to load a row with two values to a table with one column (as if).

If you invoke *proc2* alone, there's no reason for the code to fail because no other #T1 table exists in the session—and it doesn't fail:

```
EXEC dbo.proc2;
```

You get an output with the row loaded to *proc2*'s #T1:

```
col1         col2
----------- -----------
2            2
```

The execution plan for *proc2* now resides in cache. Ironically, if you now run *proc1* again, the code will complete with no errors. *proc2* will not go through a resolution process again (neither will it go through parsing or optimization); rather, SQL Server will simply reuse the plan from cache:

```
EXEC dbo.proc1;
```

And now you get the output you probably expected to begin with:

```
col1
-----------
1

col1         col2
----------- -----------
2            2
```

However, if *proc2*'s plan will be removed from cache and you run *proc1*, you're code will break.

In short, hopefully you realize that it's wise to avoid naming temporary tables the same in different stored procedures/levels. A way to avoid such issues is to add a unique *proc* identifier to the names of temporary tables. For example, you could name the temporary table in proc1 #T1_proc1, and in proc2 name the temporary table #T1_proc2.

Schema Changes to Temporary Tables in Dynamic Batches

Remember that a local temporary table created in a certain level is not visible to outer levels in the call stack. Occasionally, programmers look for ways around this limitation, especially when working with dynamic execution. That is, you want to construct the schema of the temporary table dynamically and populate it based on some user input, and then access it from an outer level. Frankly, insisting on using local temporary tables in such a scenario is very problematic. The solution involves ugly code, as is the nature of dynamic execution in general, plus recompilations resulting from schema changes and data modifications. You should consider other alternatives to provide for the original need. Still, I want to show you a way around the limitations.

Here's an initial algorithm that attempts to provide a solution for this request:

1. In the outer level, create temporary table #T with a single dummy column.

2. Within a dynamic batch, perform the following tasks:

    2.1. Alter #T, adding the columns you need.

    2.2. Alter #T, dropping the dummy column.

    2.3. Populate #T.

3. Back in the outer level, access #T in a new batch.

The problem with this algorithm lies in the last item within the dynamic batch. References to #T will be resolved against the outer #T's schema. Remember that when the batch is resolved, #T's new schema is not available yet. The solution is to populate #T within another dynamic batch, in a level inner to the dynamic batch that alters #T's schema. You do this by performing the following tasks:

1. In the outer level, create temporary table #T with a single dummy column.

2. Within a dynamic batch, perform the following tasks:

    2.1. Alter #T, adding the columns you need.

    2.2. Alter #T, dropping the dummy column.

    2.3. Open another level of dynamic execution.

        2.3.1. Populate #T.

3. Back in the outer level, access #T in a new batch.

Here's some sample code that implements this algorithm and generates the output shown in Table 2-1:

```
-- Assume @schema and @insert were constructed dynamically
DECLARE @schema AS VARCHAR(1000), @insert AS VARCHAR(1000);
SET @schema = 'col1 INT, col2 DECIMAL(10, 2)';
SET @insert = 'INSERT INTO #T42 VALUES(10, 20.30)';

-- In the outer level, create temp table #T with a single dummy column
CREATE TABLE #T42(dummycol INT);

-- Within a dynamic batch:
--     Alter #T adding the columns you need
--     Alter #T dropping the dummy column
--     Open another level of dynamic execution
--         Populate #T
EXEC('
ALTER TABLE #T42 ADD ' + @schema + ';
ALTER TABLE #T42 DROP COLUMN dummycol;
```

```
EXEC(''' + @insert + ''')');
GO

-- Back in the outer level, access #T in a new batch
SELECT * FROM #T42;

-- Cleanup
DROP TABLE #T42;
```

Table 2-1   Output of Code that Dynamically Alters the Schema of a Temporary Table

col1	col2
10	20.30

Global Temporary Tables

Global temporary tables differ from local ones mainly in their scope and visibility. They are accessible by all sessions, with no security limitations whatsoever. Any session can even drop the table. So when you design your application, you should factor in security and consider whether you really want temporary tables or just permanent ones. You create global temporary tables by prefixing their names with two number symbols (##), and like local temporary tables, they are also created in tempdb. However, because global temporary tables are accessible to all sessions, you cannot create multiple ones with the same name; neither in the same session, nor across sessions. So typical scenarios for using global temporary tables are when you want to share temporary data among sessions and don't care about security.

Unlike local temporary tables, global ones persist until the creating session—not the creating level—terminates. For example, if you create such a table in a stored procedure and the stored procedure goes out of scope, the table is not destroyed. SQL Server will automatically attempt to drop the table when the creating session terminates, all statements issued against it from other sessions finish, and any locks they hold are released.

I'll walk you through a simple example to demonstrate the accessibility and termination of a global temporary table. Open two connections to SQL Server (call them Connection 1 and Connection 2). In Connection 1, create and populate the table ##T1:

```
CREATE TABLE ##T1(col1 INT);
INSERT INTO ##T1 VALUES(1);
```

In Connection 2, open a transaction, and modify the table:

```
BEGIN TRAN
  UPDATE ##T1 SET col1 = col1 + 1;
```

Then close Connection 1. If it weren't for the open transaction that still holds locks against the table, SQL Server would have dropped the table at this point. However, because Connection 2 still holds locks against the table, it's not dropped yet. Next, in Connection 2, query the table and commit the transaction:

```
  SELECT * FROM ##T1;
COMMIT
```

At this point, SQL Server drops the table because there are no active statements accessing it, and no locks are held against it. If you try to query it again from any session, you will get an error saying that the table doesn't exist:

```
SELECT * FROM ##T1;
```

There's a special case where you might want to have a global temporary table available but not owned by any session. In this case, it will always exist, regardless of which sessions are open or closed, and eliminated only if someone explicitly drops it. To achieve this, you create the table within a special procedure (using the sp_ prefix, created in the master) and mark the stored procedure with the "startup" procedure option. SQL Server invokes a startup procedure every time it starts. Furthermore, SQL Server always maintains a reference counter greater than zero for a global temporary table created within a startup procedure. This ensures that SQL Server will not attempt to drop it automatically.

Here's some sample code that creates a startup procedure called sp_Globals, which in turn creates a global temporary table called ##Globals.

```
USE master;
GO
IF OBJECT_ID('dbo.sp_Globals') IS NOT NULL
  DROP PROC dbo.sp_Globals
GO
CREATE PROC dbo.sp_Globals
AS

CREATE TABLE ##Globals
(
  varname sysname NOT NULL PRIMARY KEY,
  val     SQL_VARIANT NULL
);
GO

EXEC dbo.sp_procoption 'sp_Globals', 'startup', 'true';
```

After restarting SQL Server, the global temporary table will be created automatically and persist until someone explicitly drops it. To test the procedure, restart SQL Server and then run the following code:

```
SET NOCOUNT ON;
INSERT INTO ##Globals VALUES('var1', CAST('abc' AS VARCHAR(10)));
SELECT * FROM ##Globals;
```

You probably guessed already that ##Globals is a shared global temporary table where you can logically maintain cross-session global variables. This can be useful, for example, when you need to maintain temporary counters or other "variables" that are globally accessible by all sessions. The preceding code creates a new global variable called *var1*, initializes it with the character string *'abc'*, and queries the table. The output of this code is shown in Table 2-2.

Table 2-2   Contents of ##Globals

varname	val
var1	abc

When you're done, run the following code for cleanup:

```
USE master;
GO
DROP PROC dbo.sp_Globals;
DROP TABLE ##Globals;
```

Table Variables

Table variables are probably among the least understood T-SQL elements. Many myths and misconceptions surround them, and these are embraced even by experienced T-SQL pro-grammers. One widespread myth is that table variables are memory-resident only with no physical representation. Another is that table variables are always preferable to temporary tables. In this section, I'll dispel these myths and explain the scenarios in which table vari-ables are preferable to temporary tables as well as scenarios in which they aren't preferable. I'll do so by first going through the fundamentals of table variables, just as I did with temporary tables, and follow with tangible examples.

You create a table variable using a DECLARE statement, followed by the variable name and the schema definition. You then refer to it as you do with permanent tables. Here's a very basic example:

```
DECLARE @T1 TABLE(col1 INT);
INSERT @T1 VALUES(1);
SELECT * FROM @T1;
```

Limitations

Many limitations apply to table variables but not to temporary tables. In this section, I'll describe some of them, while others will be described in dedicated sections.

- You cannot create explicit indexes on table variables, only PRIMARY KEY and UNIQUE constraints, which create unique indexes underneath the covers. You cannot create non-unique indexes. If you need an index on a non-unique column, you must add attributes that make the combination unique and create a PRIMARY KEY or UNIQUE constraint on the combination.

- You cannot alter the definition of a table variable once it is declared. This means that everything you need in the schema must be included in the original DECLARE statement. This fact is limiting on one hand, but it also results in fewer recompilations. Remember that one of the triggers of recompilations is schema changes.

- You cannot issue SELECT INTO and INSERT EXEC statements against a table variable in SQL Server 2000. SQL Server 2005 supports INSERT EXEC with table variables.

- You cannot qualify a column name with a table variable name. This is especially an issue when referring to a table variable's column in correlated subqueries with column name ambiguity.

- In queries that modify table variables, parallel plans will not be used.

tempdb

To dispel what probably is the most widespread myth involving table variables, let me state that they do have physical representation in tempdb, very similar to temporary tables. As proof, run the following code that shows which temporary tables currently exist in tempdb by querying metadata info, creates a table variable, and queries metadata info again:

```
SELECT TABLE_NAME FROM tempdb.INFORMATION_SCHEMA.TABLES
WHERE TABLE_NAME LIKE '%#%';
GO
DECLARE @T TABLE(col1 INT);
INSERT INTO @T VALUES(1);
SELECT TABLE_NAME FROM tempdb.INFORMATION_SCHEMA.TABLES
WHERE TABLE_NAME LIKE '%#%';
```

When I ran this code, the first batch returned no output, while the second returned #0CBAE877, which is the name of the temporary table in tempdb that represents the table variable @T. Of course, you will probably get a different name when you run this code. But the point is to show that there is a hidden temporary table created behind the scenes. Just like temporary tables, a table variable's pages will reside in cache when the table is small enough and when SQL Server has enough memory to spare. So the discussion about aspects of working with temporary tables with regard to tempdb applies to table variables as well.

Scope and Visibility

The scope of a table variable is well defined. It is defined as the current level, and within it the current batch only, just as with any other variable. That is, a table variable is not accessible to inner levels, and not even to other batches within the same level. In short, you can use it only within the same batch it was created. This scope is much more limited than that of a local temporary table and is typically an important factor in choosing a temporary object type.

Transaction Context

Unlike a temporary table, a table variable is not part of an outer transaction; rather, its transaction scope is limited to the statement level to support statement rollback capabilities only. If you modify a table variable and the modification statement is aborted, the changes of that particular statement will be undone. However, if the statement is part of an outer transaction that is rolled back, changes against the table variable that finished will not be undone. Table variables are unique in this respect.

You can rely on this behavior to your advantage. For example, suppose that you need to write an audit trigger that audits changes against some table. If some logical condition is met, you want to roll back the change; however, you still want to audit the attempted change. If you copy data from inserted/deleted to your audit tables, a rollback in the trigger will also undo the audit writes. If you first roll back the change and then try to audit it, deleted and inserted are empty. It's a Catch-22 situation.

To solve the problem, you first copy data from inserted/deleted to table variables, issue a rollback, and then in a new transaction within the trigger, copy the data from the table variables to your audit tables. There's no other simpler way around the problem.

The unique transaction context of table variables has performance advantages over temporary tables because less logging and locking are involved.

Statistics

As I mentioned earlier, the optimizer doesn't create distribution statistics or maintain accurate cardinality information for table variables as it does for temporary tables. This is one of the main factors you should consider when choosing a type of temporary object for a given task. The downside is that you might get inefficient plans when the optimizer needs to consult histograms to determine selectivity. This is especially a problem with big tables, where you might end up with excessive I/O. The upside is that table variables, for the very same reason, involve much fewer recompilations. Before making your choice, you need to figure out which is more expensive in the particular task you're designating the temporary object for.

To explain the statistics aspect of table variables in a more tangible way, I'll show you some queries, their execution plans, and their I/O costs.

Examine the following code, and request an estimated execution plan for it from SQL Server Management Studio (SSMS):

```
DECLARE @T TABLE
(
  col1 INT NOT NULL PRIMARY KEY,
  col2 INT NOT NULL,
  filler CHAR(200) NOT NULL DEFAULT('a'),
  UNIQUE(col2, col1)
);

INSERT INTO @T(col1, col2)
  SELECT n, (n - 1) % 100000 + 1 FROM dbo.Nums
  WHERE n <= 100000;

SELECT * FROM @T WHERE col1 = 1;
SELECT * FROM @T WHERE col1 <= 50000;
```

```
SELECT * FROM @T WHERE col2 = 1;
SELECT * FROM @T WHERE col2 <= 2;
SELECT * FROM @T WHERE col2 <= 5000;
```

You can find the code to create and populate the Nums table in Chapter 1.

The estimated execution plans generated for these queries are shown in Figure 2-1.

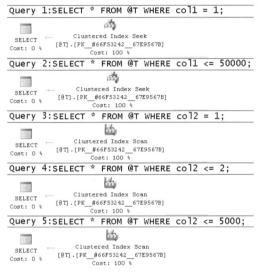

Figure 2-1   Estimated execution plans for queries against a table variable

The code creates a table variable called *@T* with two columns. The values in *col1* are unique, and each value in *col2* appears ten times. The code creates two unique indexes underneath the covers: one on *col1*, and one on (*col2, col1*).

The first important thing to notice in the estimated plans is the number of rows the optimizer estimates to be returned from each operator—1 in all five cases, even when looking for a non-unique value or ranges. You realize that unless you filter a unique column, the optimizer simply cannot estimate the selectivity of queries for lack of statistics. So it assumes 1 row. This hard-coded assumption is based on the fact that SQL Server assumes that you use table variables only with small sets of data.

As for the efficiency of the plans, the first two queries get a good plan (seek, followed by a partial scan in the second query). But that's because you have a clustered index on the filtered column, and the optimizer doesn't need statistics to figure out what the optimal plan is in this case. However, with the third and fourth queries you get a table scan (an unordered clustered index scan) even though both queries are very selective and would benefit from using the index on (*col2, col1*), followed by a small number of lookups. The fifth query would benefit from a table scan because it has low selectivity. Fortunately, it got an adequate plan, but that's by chance. To analyze I/O costs, run the code after turning on the SET STATISTICS IO option. The amount of I/O involved with each of the last three queries is 2,713 reads, which is equivalent to the number of pages consumed by the table.

Next, go through the same analysis process with the following code, which uses a temporary table instead of a table variable:

```
SELECT n AS col1, (n - 1) % 100000 + 1 AS col2,
  CAST('a' AS CHAR(200)) AS filler
INTO #T
FROM dbo.Nums
WHERE n <= 100000;

ALTER TABLE #T ADD PRIMARY KEY(col1);
CREATE UNIQUE INDEX idx_col2_col1 ON #T(col2, col1);
GO

SELECT * FROM #T WHERE col1 = 1;
SELECT * FROM #T WHERE col1 <= 50000;

SELECT * FROM #T WHERE col2 = 1;
SELECT * FROM #T WHERE col2 <= 2;
SELECT * FROM #T WHERE col2 <= 5000;
```

The estimated execution plans generated for these queries are shown in Figures 2-2 and 2-3.

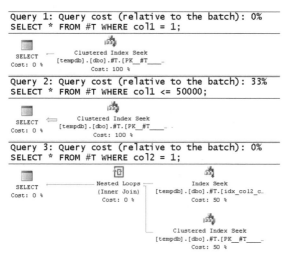

Figure 2-2   Estimated execution plans for queries 1, 2, 3 against a temporary table

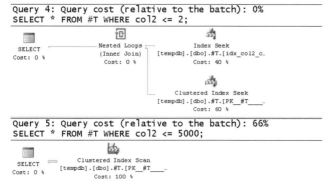

Figure 2-3   Estimated execution plans for queries 4, 5 against a temporary table

Now that statistics are available, the optimizer can make educated estimations. You can see that the estimated number of rows returned from each operator is more reasonable. You can also see that high-selectivity queries 3 and 4 use the index on *(col2, col1)*, and the low selectivity query 5 does a table scan, as it should.

STATISTICS IO reports dramatically reduced I/O costs for queries 3 and 4. These are 5 and 8 reads, respectively, against the temporary table versus 2,713 for both queries against the table variable.

When you're done, drop #T for cleanup:

```
DROP TABLE #T;
```

tempdb Considerations

Remember that temporary tables and table variables are physically stored in tempdb. SQL Server also stores data in tempdb for many implicit activities that take place behind the scenes. Examples for such activities include: spooling data as part of an execution plan of a query, sorting, and maintaining row versions (SQL Server 2005). You realize that tempdb can become a bottleneck, and you should give it focused tuning attention so that it will accommodate the workload against your server.

Here are some important points you should consider when tuning tempdb:

- In systems where tempdb is heavily used (explicitly or implicitly), consider placing tempdb on its own disk array, and not on the same drives where other databases are located. Also, stripe the data portion to multiple drives to increase I/O throughput. The more spindles, the better. Ideally, use RAID 10 for the data portion and RAID 1 for the log.

- Every time you restart SQL Server, tempdb is re-created, and its size reverts to the effective defined size. If you made no changes to the original size configuration after installing SQL Server, tempdb's size will default to 8 MB and its growth increment will default to 10 percent. In most production environments, these values might not be practical. Whenever a process needs to store data in tempdb and tempdb is full, SQL Server will initiate an autogrow operation. The process will have to wait for the space to be allocated. Also, when the database is small, 10 percent is a very small unit. The small fragments will most probably be allocated in different places on disk, resulting in a high level of file-system fragmentation. And if that's not enough, remember that every time SQL Server restarts, tempdb's size will revert to its defined size (8 MB). This means that the whole process will start again, where tempdb will keep on autogrowing until it reaches a size appropriate to your environment's workload. Until it reaches that point, processes will suffer as they wait while tempdb autogrows.

- You can figure out the appropriate size for tempdb by observing its actual size after a period of activity with no restarts. You then alter the database and change the SIZE parameter of tempdb's files so that tempdb's size will be appropriate. Whenever SQL

Server is restarted, tempdb will just start out at the defined size. If you do this, there won't be a need for autogrowth until tempdb gets full, which should occur only with irregular and excessive tempdb activity.

■ Remember that logically tempdb is re-created whenever SQL Server restarts. Like any other new database, tempdb is created as a copy of the model database. This means that if you create permanent objects in tempdb (permanent tables, user defined types, database users, and so on), they're erased in the next restart. If you need objects to exist in tempdb after restarts, you have two options. One is to create them in model. They will appear in tempdb after a restart. However, this option will also affect new user databases you create. Another option is to encapsulate code that creates all objects in a startup procedure. (See information on startup procedures earlier in the chapter in the "Global Temporary Tables" section.) Remember that a startup procedure is invoked whenever SQL Server is restarted. Essentially, the objects will be re-created every time upon restart, but this will be transparent to users.

■ With regard to temporary tables, obviously dealing with very large volumes of data can cause performance problems. However, you might face performance problems with tempdb even when working with small temporary tables. When many concurrent sessions create temporary tables, SQL Server might experience contention when it tries to allocate pages. This was mainly an issue with SQL Server 2000 SP3 and earlier service packs, but some aspects of the problem are still relevant in later versions. I urge you to read Microsoft Knowledge Base article 328551, "FIX: Concurrency enhancements for the tempdb database," which discusses the problem and suggests solutions. You can access it at the following URL: *http://support.microsoft.com/default.aspx?scid= kb;en-us;328551.*

Table Expressions

In this chapter's opening paragraphs, I mentioned that there might be cases in which you need "logical" temporary tables—that is, only virtual materialization of interim sets, as opposed to physical materialization in temporary tables and table variables. Table expressions give you this capability. These include derived tables, CTEs, views, and inline table-valued UDFs. Here I'll point out the scenarios in which these are preferable compared with other temporary objects and provide an example.

You should use table expressions in cases where you need a temporary object mainly for simplification—for example, when developing a solution in a modular approach, a step at a time. Also, use table expressions when you need to access the temporary object only once or a very small number of times and you don't need to index interim result sets. SQL Server doesn't physically materialize a table expression. The optimizer actually merges the outer query and the inner one, and it generates one plan for the query accessing the underlying tables directly. So I'm mainly talking about simplification, and I showed and will continue

to show many such examples throughout the book. But even beyond simplification, in some cases you will be able to improve performance of solutions by using table expressions. There might be cases where the optimizer will generate a better plan for your query compared to alternative queries.

In terms of scope and visibility, derived tables and CTEs are available only to the current statement, while views and inline UDFs are available globally to users that have permissions to access them. I'll discuss views and inline UDFs later in this book in Chapters 5 and 6. For details on derived tables and CTEs, please refer to *Inside T-SQL Querying*.

As an example of using a table expression to solve a problem, suppose you want to return from the Orders table in the Northwind database, the row with the highest *OrderID* for each employee. Here's a solution that uses a derived table, generating the output shown in Table 2-3:

```
USE Northwind;

SELECT O.OrderID, O.EmployeeID, O.CustomerID, O.OrderDate
FROM dbo.Orders AS O
  JOIN (SELECT EmployeeID, MAX(OrderID) AS MaxOid
        FROM dbo.Orders
        GROUP BY EmployeeID) AS D
    ON O.OrderID = D.MaxOid;
```

Table 2-3   Row with the Highest *OrderID* for Each Employee

OrderID	EmployeeID	CustomerID	OrderDate
11077	1	RATTC	1998-05-06 00:00:00.000
11073	2	PERIC	1998-05-05 00:00:00.000
11063	3	HUNGO	1998-04-30 00:00:00.000
11076	4	BONAP	1998-05-06 00:00:00.000
11043	5	SPECD	1998-04-22 00:00:00.000
11045	6	BOTTM	1998-04-23 00:00:00.000
11074	7	SIMOB	1998-05-06 00:00:00.000
11075	8	RICSU	1998-05-06 00:00:00.000
11058	9	BLAUS	1998-04-29 00:00:00.000

Comparison Summary

Table 2-4 contains a summary of the functionality and behavior of the different object types. Note that I didn't include global temporary tables because typically you use those for different purposes than the other types of temporary objects. You might find this table handy as a reference when you need to choose the appropriate temporary object type for a given task.

Table 2-4 Comparison Summary

Functionality/Object Type	Local Temp Table	Table Variable	Table Expression
Scope/Visibility	Current and inner levels	Local Batch	Derived Table/CTE: Current statement View/Inline UDF: Global
Physical representation in tempdb	Yes	Yes	No
Part of outer transaction /Affected by outer transaction rollback	Yes	No	Yes
Logging	To support transaction rollback	To support statement rollback	Yes
Locking	Yes	No	Yes
Statistics/recompilations/ efficient plans	Yes	No	Yes
Table size	Any	Typically recommended for small tables	Any

Summary Exercise—Relational Division

As a summary exercise, you're given the following task for cases in which you might want to consider using temporary objects: in the Northwind database, you need to determine which customers have orders handled by the same set of employees. The result set should contain a row for each customer, with the customer ID, and a value representing the group of employees. The latter is expressed as the minimum customer ID out of all customers that share the same set of employees. That is, if customers A, B, and C were handled by the same set of employees (for example, 3, 7, 9), the result set would contain {(A, A), (B, A), (C, A)}. Return NULL for customers that have no orders. The desired result is shown in Table 2-5 (abbreviated).

Table 2-5 Desired Result of Summary Exercise (Abbreviated)

CustomerID	Grp
FISSA	NULL
PARIS	NULL
ALFKI	ALFKI
ANATR	ANATR
THECR	ANATR
ANTON	ANTON
TRADH	ANTON

Table 2-5   Desired Result of Summary Exercise (Abbreviated)

CustomerID	Grp
AROUT	AROUT
BERGS	BERGS
HANAR	BERGS
BLAUS	BLAUS
BLONP	BLONP
...	...

You can observe, for example, that ANATR and THECR were handled by the same set of employees. Note that you should use the sample tables in the Northwind database only to check the accuracy of your result. For performance estimations, you need to create your own tables with substantially more rows to reflect realistic production environments. For example, you can run the code in Listing 2-1 to create in tempdb a Customers table with 10,000 customers and an Orders table with 1,000,000 orders. The run times that I will mention were measured against these benchmark tables on my system.

Listing 2-1   Code that creates realistic table sizes for summary exercise benchmark

```
SET NOCOUNT ON;
USE tempdb;
GO

IF OBJECT_ID('dbo.Orders') IS NOT NULL
  DROP TABLE dbo.Orders;
GO
IF OBJECT_ID('dbo.Customers') IS NOT NULL
  DROP TABLE dbo.Customers;
GO

SELECT n AS CustomerID
INTO dbo.Customers
FROM dbo.Nums
WHERE n <= 10000;

ALTER TABLE dbo.Customers ADD PRIMARY KEY(CustomerID);

SELECT n AS OrderID,
  1 + ABS(CHECKSUM(NEWID())) % 10000 AS CustomerID,
  1 + ABS(CHECKSUM(NEWID())) % 40    AS EmployeeID
INTO dbo.Orders
FROM dbo.Nums
WHERE n <= 1000000;

ALTER TABLE dbo.Orders ADD PRIMARY KEY(OrderID);
CREATE INDEX idx_cid_eid ON dbo.Orders(CustomerID, EmployeeID);
```

The first solution doesn't make any use of temporary objects; rather, it implements a classic relational division approach applying reverse logic with subqueries:

```
SELECT CustomerID,
    CASE WHEN EXISTS(SELECT * FROM dbo.Orders AS O
                    WHERE O.CustomerID = C1.CustomerID)
      THEN COALESCE(
        (SELECT MIN(C2.CustomerID)
          FROM dbo.Customers AS C2
          WHERE C2.CustomerID < C1.CustomerID
           AND NOT EXISTS
             (SELECT * FROM dbo.Orders AS O1
               WHERE O1.CustomerID = C1.CustomerID
                AND NOT EXISTS
                  (SELECT * FROM dbo.Orders AS O2
                    WHERE O2.CustomerID = C2.CustomerID
                     AND O2.EmployeeID = O1.EmployeeID))
            AND NOT EXISTS
             (SELECT * FROM dbo.Orders AS O2
               WHERE O2.CustomerID = C2.CustomerID
                AND NOT EXISTS
                  (SELECT * FROM dbo.Orders AS O1
                    WHERE O1.CustomerID = C1.CustomerID
                     AND O1.EmployeeID = O2.EmployeeID))),
        CustomerID) END AS Grp
FROM dbo.Customers AS C1
ORDER BY Grp, CustomerID;
```

The query invokes a CASE expression for every customer from the Customers table (C1). The CASE expression invokes the COALESCE function for customers who placed orders, and returns NULL for customers who placed no orders. If the customer placed orders, COALESCE will substitute a NULL returned by the input expression with the current *CustomerID*. The input expression will return the result of the following:

- Return the minimum *CustomerID* from a second instance of Customers (C2)

- Where *C2.CustomerID* (*Cust2*) is smaller than *C1.CustomerID* (*Cust1*)

- And you cannot find an employee in *Cust1*'s orders that does not appear in *Cust2*'s orders

- And you cannot find an employee in *Cust2*'s orders that does not appear in *Cust1*'s orders

Logically, you could do without filtering *Cust2* < *Cust1*, but this expression is used to avoid wasting resources. Anyway, you need to return the minimum *CustomerID* out of the ones with the same employee list. If customer A has the same employee list as customer B, both will end up with a *Grp* value of A. For customer B, there's a point in comparing it to customer A (smaller ID), but for customer A there's no point in comparing it to customer B (higher ID). Naturally, the minimum *CustomerID* within the group will not find customers with smaller IDs. In such a case, the expression will return a NULL, and the outer COALESCE will substitute the NULL with the current *CustomerID*. As for the rest, it's a classical phrasing of relational division with reverse logic.

This solution is expensive because of the excessive scan count, which has to do with the large number of invocations of the correlated subqueries. To give you a sense, this solution ran over an hour before I gave up waiting for it to finish and stopped it. Most standard set-based solutions you can come up with for this problem that don't use temporary objects will typically be expensive.

If you devise a solution in which you generate an interim set that can benefit from an index, you might want to consider using temporary tables. For example, you can materialize the distinct list of *CustomerID*, *EmployeeID* values; index the temporary table; and continue from there. The materialized data would substantially reduce the number of rows in the set you'll query. Still, you won't be dealing with a tiny set, and most probably your solution will access the table multiple times. You want efficient plans to be generated based on distribution statistics and accurate cardinality information. All this should lead you to use a local temporary table and not a table variable.

Listing 2-2 has a solution that first creates the suggested local temporary table, indexes it, and then queries it.

Listing 2-2   Solution based on temporary tables

```
SELECT DISTINCT CustomerID, EmployeeID
INTO #CustsEmps
FROM dbo.Orders;

CREATE UNIQUE CLUSTERED INDEX idx_cid_eid
  ON #CustsEmps(CustomerID, EmployeeID);
GO

WITH Agg AS
(
  SELECT CustomerID,
    MIN(EmployeeID) AS MN,
    MAX(EmployeeID) AS MX,
    COUNT(*)        AS CN,
    SUM(EmployeeID) AS SM,
    CHECKSUM_AGG(EmployeeID) AS CS
  FROM #CustsEmps
  GROUP BY CustomerID
),
AggJoin AS
(
  SELECT A1.CustomerID AS Cust1, A2.CustomerID AS Cust2, A1.CN
  FROM Agg AS A1
    JOIN Agg AS A2
      ON  A2.CustomerID <= A1.CustomerID
      AND A2.MN = A1.MN
      AND A2.MX = A1.MX
      AND A2.CN = A1.CN
      AND A2.SM = A1.SM
      AND A2.CS = A1.CS
),
```

```
CustGrp AS
(
  SELECT Cust1, MIN(Cust2) AS Grp
  FROM AggJoin AS AJ
  WHERE CN = (SELECT COUNT(*)
              FROM #CustsEmps AS C1
                JOIN #CustsEmps AS C2
                  ON C1.CustomerID = AJ.Cust1
                  AND C2.CustomerID = AJ.Cust2
                  AND C2.EmployeeID = C1.EmployeeID)
  GROUP BY Cust1
)
SELECT CustomerID, Grp
FROM dbo.Customers AS C
  LEFT OUTER JOIN CustGrp AS G
    ON C.CustomerID = G.Cust1
ORDER BY Grp, CustomerID;
GO

DROP TABLE #CustsEmps;
```

I also used table expressions here to build the solution in a modular approach. I used CTEs, but the solution can be easily revised to use derived tables in SQL Server 2000.

The first CTE (*Agg*) groups the data from the temporary table by *CutomerID*, and returns a bunch of aggregates based on *EmployeeID* for each customer (MIN, MAX, COUNT, SUM, CHECKSUM_AGG).

The second CTE (*AggJoin*) joins two instances of *Agg* (*A1* and *A2*)—matching for each customer in *A1*, all customers from *A2* with a lower *CustomerID* and the same values in all aggregates. The purpose of comparing aggregates is to return, for each customer, smaller than or equal to customer IDs that potentially share the same list of employees. The reasoning behind the use of the smaller than or equal to (<=) filter is the similar to the one in the previous solution. That is, comparing sets of employees between customers when *A2.CustomerID* (*Cust2*) is greater than *A1.CustomerID* (*Cust1*) is superfluous.

The third CTE (*CustGrp*), filters from *AggJoin* only pairs that are proven to share the exact list of employees, by verifying that the count of matching employees in both is identical to the count of employees in each. The query groups the filtered rows by *Cust1*, returning the minimum *Cust2* for each *Cust1*. At this point, *CustGrp* contains the correct *Grp* value for each customer.

Finally the outer query performs a left outer join that adds customers with no orders.

This solution runs for 7 seconds. Note that you could use a CTE with the set of distinct *CustomerID, EmployeeID* combinations instead of the temporary table #CustEmps. This way, you could avoid using temporary tables altogether. I tested such a solution and it ran for about 12 seconds—almost twice the runtime of the solution that utilizes a temporary table. The advantage in the temporary table approach was that you could index it.

Considering the fastest solution we had so far—the one utilizing a temporary table—is this really the best you can get? Apparently not. You can use the FOR XML PATH option to concatenate all distinct *EmployeeID* values per customer. You can then group the data by the concatenated string, and return for each customer the minimum *CustomerID* within the group using the OVER clause. The fast and nifty concatenation technique was devised by Michael Rys, a program manager with the Microsoft SQL Server development team in charge of SQL Server XML technologies, and Eugene Kogan, a technical lead on the Microsoft SQL Server Engine team. The PATH mode provides an easier way to mix elements and attributes than the EXPLICIT directive. Here's the complete solution:

```
WITH CustGroups AS
(
  SELECT CustomerID,
    (SELECT CAST(EmployeeID AS VARCHAR(10)) + ';' AS [text()]
     FROM (SELECT DISTINCT EmployeeID
           FROM dbo.Orders AS O
           WHERE O.CustomerID = C.CustomerID) AS D
     ORDER BY EmployeeID
     FOR XML PATH('')) AS CustEmps
  FROM dbo.Customers AS C
)
SELECT CustomerID,
  CASE WHEN CustEmps IS NULL THEN NULL
    ELSE MIN(CustomerID) OVER(PARTITION BY CustEmps) END AS Grp
FROM CustGroups
ORDER BY Grp, CustomerID;
```

The solution is short and slick, doesn't use temporary tables at all, and runs for 7 seconds as well! This is to prove that you should revisit slow-running solutions from time to time; especially with new functionality available in SQL Server 2005.

Conclusion

I hope this chapter helped you realize that there are significant differences between the different types of temporary objects supported by SQL Server. I had to dispel a few widespread myths, especially with regard to table variables. Remember that it's typically advisable to use table variables for small tables and to compare table variables against temporary tables for the most critical queries. You realize that there's a time and place for each type and that there's no one type that is always preferable to the others. I gave you a summary table with the aspects and functionality of each type, which should help you make the right choices based on your needs. Also, remember to pay special focus to tempdb, which can become a bottleneck in your system, especially when working extensively with temporary tables.

Chapter 3
Cursors

You probably won't find many database professionals arguing about the necessity for SELECT statements, but many argue about whether cursors are necessary. Arguments also arise about the use of temporary tables; dynamic code; and integrated XML, XQuery, and CLR. There must be a reason why database professionals are in complete agreement about some aspects of Microsoft SQL Server 2005 but have conflicting opinions about other aspects (call the constructs under conflicting opinions *arguable constructs*). Let me offer my two cents' worth on the subject.

These arguable constructs have a high potential for misuse because database professionals often lack knowledge and experience in set-based querying and the relational model. Such misuse can lead to very poor implementations. Defenders of these arguable constructs would argue that any construct can be abused because of lack of knowledge and experience. Still, I think that there is a difference between these constructs and many others. Knives and matches are very useful tools, but only in the hands of responsible people. You wouldn't want those devices in the hands of children. Even with no bad intentions on the part of the users, the potential for catastrophe is high. A child could also do damage with crayons and books, but the likelihood of that happening is much lower and the damage wouldn't be as severe.

I didn't say that I side with those who oppose the arguable constructs, or that I'm on any side for that matter. But I do think that placing such tools in the hands of programmers who lack adequate knowledge of set-based querying and the relational model can yield bad results. The key is having the maturity to recognize the appropriate time and place to use each construct (static set-based queries, dynamic SQL, cursors, XML, CLR, table expressions, temporary tables, and so on). This book tries to guide you to that level of maturity.

I hope you will forgive me for the philosophical approach to this subject, but for me SQL is a "way" that has important philosophical aspects. In my mind—and you don't have to agree—I separate the careers of T-SQL programmers into three typical phases:

1. **Procedural.** This is the phase in which programmers have just started to work with databases. They have insufficient experience working with the relational model

and set-based thinking. In this phase, it's common to see misuse of tools such as cursors, temporary tables, dynamic execution, and procedural coding in general. Programmers at this stage are usually oblivious to the damage that they're causing.

2. **Becoming sober.** This is the phase in which programmers realize there's more to database programming—that SQL is not a nuisance that interferes with writing procedural code but, rather, it's based on the strong foundations of set theory and the relational model. In this phase, programmers tend to believe "experts" who say cursors, temporary tables, and dynamic execution are evil and should never be used. At this point, programmers either avoid using such constructs altogether or really feel bad about the code they write. There's usually lack of confidence at this stage.

3. **Maturity.** This stage is characterized by the void or Zen mindset. In this phase, programmers have deep knowledge and understanding, and they feel confident about their code. This doesn't mean they stop pursuing deeper knowledge or improving fundamental techniques. In this phase, programmers apply set-based thinking for the most part, but they realize that there's a time and place for other constructs as well. I refer to this phase as the "void" in the positive and abstract sense—that is, programmers develop intuition regarding the type of solution that would fit a given task and don't need to spend much time determining which technique is appropriate.

Developing the intuition described in phase three involves knowing when the typical approach of using pure static SQL programming will not do the job. Although pure static SQL programming is typically the way to go, it will only get you so far in some cases. There are cases where using temporary tables can substantially improve performance; where dynamic execution actually overcomes complex problems; where the use of procedural languages such as C# and Visual Basic allows more flexibility without conflicting with the relational model; and where storing states of data in XML format makes sense. This book explores these cases in dedicated chapters and sections.

Using Cursors

In this chapter, I'll explain the types of problems for which cursors are a reasonable solution, even though such cases are not common. The goal of the chapter is to show you how to use them wisely.

I'll assume that you have sufficient technical knowledge of the various cursor types and know the syntax for declaring and using them. If you don't, you can find a lot of information about cursors in Books Online. My focus is to explain why cursors are typically not the right choice and to present the cases in which cursors do make sense.

So why should you avoid using cursors for the most part?

For one, cursors conflict with the main premise of the relational model. Using cursors, you apply procedural logic rather than set-based logic. That is, you write a lot of code with iterations, where you mainly focus on "how" to deal with data. When you apply set-based logic, you typically write substantially less code, as you focus on "what" you want and not how to get it. You need to be able to recognize the cases where a problem is procedural/iterative in nature—where you truly need to process one row at a time. In these cases, you should consider using a cursor. For example, you have a table that contains user information along with e-mail addresses, and you need to send e-mail to all users. Or you need to invoke a stored procedure per each row in some table and provide the stored procedure with column values from each row as arguments.

Cursors also have a lot of overhead involved with the row-by-row manipulation and are typically substantially slower than set-based code (queries). I demonstrate the use of set-based solutions throughout the book. You need to be able to measure and estimate the cursor overhead and identify the few scenarios where cursors will yield better performance than set-based code. In some cases, data distribution will determine whether a cursor or a set-based solution will yield better performance.

There's another very important aspect of cursors—they can request and assume ordered data as input, whereas queries can accept only a relational input, which by definition cannot assume a particular order. This difference is important in identifying scenarios in which cursors might actually be faster—such as problems that are tightly based on ordered access to the data. Examples of such problems are running aggregations and ranking calculations, resolving some temporal problems, and so on. The I/O cost involved with the cursor activity plus the cursor overhead might end up being lower than a set-based solution that performs substantially more I/O.

ANSI recognizes the practical need for manipulation of ordered data and provides some standards for addressing this need. In extensions to the ANSI SQL:1999 standard and in the ANSI SQL:2003 standard, you can find several query constructs that inherently rely on ordering—for example, the ANSI OVER(ORDER BY ...) clause, which determines the calculation order for ranking and aggregate calculations, or the SEARCH clause defined with recursive CTEs, which determines the order of traversal of trees.

SQL Server 2005 implements the OVER clause with support for ORDER BY only for ranking functions, and SQL Server 2005's engine was, of course, enhanced to support the rapid performance of such calculations. As a result, ranking calculations using queries are now substantially faster than cursor-based solutions. With aggregate functions in SQL Server 2005, however, the OVER clause does not support ORDER BY. Therefore, set-based solutions to compute running aggregations with large groups of data are slower than cursor-based solutions. I'll demonstrate this in the section Running Aggregations later in this chapter. The SEARCH clause for recursive common table expressions (CTEs) has not been implemented in SQL Server 2005.

Another kind of problem where cursor solutions are faster than query solutions is matching problems, which I'll also demonstrate. With those, I haven't found set-based solutions that perform nearly as well as cursor solutions. But I haven't given up. One of my goals is to find set-based solutions for problems that are not procedural. Some of those problems could have set-based solutions if newer ANSI constructs had been supported in SQL Server. I hope that SQL Server will implement those in future versions. And when the ANSI standard doesn't have answers, I believe there will be vendor-specific product extensions, followed by motions to the ANSI committee to add them to the standard.

Cursor Overhead

In this chapter's introduction, I talked about the benefits that set-based solutions have over cursor-based ones. I mentioned both logical and performance benefits. For the most part, efficiently written set-based solutions will outperform cursor-based solutions for two reasons.

First, you empower the optimizer to do what it's so good at—generating multiple valid execution plans, and choosing the most efficient one. When you apply a cursor-based solution, you're basically forcing the optimizer to go with a rigid plan that doesn't leave much room for optimization—at least not as much room as with set-based solutions.

Second, row-by-row manipulation creates a lot of overhead. You can run some simple tests to witness and measure this overhead—for example, just scanning a table with a simple query and comparing the results to scanning it with a cursor. To compare apples to apples, make sure you're scanning the same amount of data as you did with the cursor-based query. You can eliminate the actual disk I/O cost by running the code twice. (The first run will load the data to cache.) To eliminate the time it takes to generate the output, you should run your code with the Discard Results After Execution option in SQL Server Management Studio (SSMS) turned on. The difference in performance between the set-based code and the cursor code will then be the cursor's overhead.

I will now demonstrate how to compare scanning the same amount of data with set-based code versus with a cursor. Run the following code to generate a table called T1, with a million rows, each containing slightly more than 200 bytes:

```
SET NOCOUNT ON;
USE tempdb;
GO
IF OBJECT_ID('dbo.T1') IS NOT NULL
  DROP TABLE dbo.T1;
GO
SELECT n AS keycol, CAST('a' AS CHAR(200)) AS filler
INTO dbo.T1
FROM dbo.Nums;

CREATE UNIQUE CLUSTERED INDEX idx_keycol ON dbo.T1(keycol);
```

You can find the code to create and populate the Nums table in Chapter 1.

Turn on the Discard Results After Execution option in SSMS (under Tools|Options|Query Results|SQL Server|Results to Grid or Results to Text). Now clear the cache:

```
DBCC DROPCLEANBUFFERS;
```

Run the following set-based code twice—the first run will measure performance against cold cache, and the second will measure it against warm cache:

```
SELECT keycol, filler FROM dbo.T1;
```

On my system, this query ran for 4 seconds against cold cache and 2 seconds against warm cache. Clear the cache again, and then run the cursor code twice:

```
DECLARE @keycol AS INT, @filler AS CHAR(200);
DECLARE C CURSOR FAST_FORWARD FOR SELECT keycol, filler FROM dbo.T1;
OPEN C
FETCH NEXT FROM C INTO @keycol, @filler;
WHILE @@fetch_status = 0
BEGIN
  -- Process data here
  FETCH NEXT FROM C INTO @keycol, @filler;
END
CLOSE C;
DEALLOCATE C;
```

This code ran for 22 seconds against cold cache and 20 seconds against warm cache. Considering the warm cache example, in which there's no physical I/O involved, the cursor code ran ten times more slowly than the set-based code, and notice that I used the fastest cursor you can get—FAST_FORWARD. Both solutions scanned the same amount of data. Besides the performance overhead, you also have the development and maintenance overhead of your code. This is a very basic example involving little code; in production environments with more complex code, the problem is, of course, much worse.

Dealing with Each Row Individually

Remember that cursors can be useful when the problem is a procedural one, and you must deal with each row individually. I provided examples of such scenarios earlier. Here I want to show an alternative to cursors that programmers may use to apply iterative logic, and compare its performance with the cursor code I just demonstrated in the previous section. Remember that the cursor code that scanned a million rows took approximately 20 seconds to complete. Another common technique to iterate through a table's rows is to loop through the keys and use a set-based query for each row. To test the performance of such a solution, make sure the Discard Results After Execution option in SSMS is still turned on. Then run the following code:

```
DECLARE @keycol AS INT, @filler AS CHAR(200);

SELECT @keycol = keycol, @filler = filler
FROM (SELECT TOP (1) keycol, filler
      FROM dbo.T1
      ORDER BY keycol) AS D;

WHILE @@rowcount = 1
BEGIN
  -- Process data here
```

```
-- Get next row
SELECT @keycol = keycol, @filler = filler
FROM (SELECT TOP (1) keycol, filler
      FROM dbo.T1
      WHERE keycol > @keycol
      ORDER BY keycol) AS D;
END
```

This implementation is a bit "cleaner" than dealing with a cursor, and that's the aspect of it that I like. You use a TOP (1) query to grab the first row (based on key order). Within a loop, when a row was found in the previous iteration, you process the data and request the next row (the row with the next key). This code ran for about 90 seconds—several times slower than the cursor code. I created a clustered index on *keycol* to improve performance by accessing the desired row in each iteration with minimal I/O. Without that index, this code would run substantially slower because each invocation of the query would need to rescan large portions of data. A cursor solution based on sorted data would also benefit from an index and would run substantially slower without one because it would need to sort the data after scanning it. With large tables and no index on the sort columns, the sort operation can be very expensive because sorting in terms of complexity is $O(n \log n)$, while scanning is only $O(n)$.

Before you proceed, make sure you turn off the "Discard Results After Execution" option in SSMS.

Order-Based Access

In the introduction, I mentioned that cursors have the potential to yield better performance than set-based code when the problem is inherently order based. In this section, I'll show some examples. Where relevant, I'll discuss query constructs that ANSI introduces to allow for "cleaner" code that performs well without the use of cursors. However, some of these ANSI constructs have not been implemented in SQL Server 2005.

Custom Aggregates

In *Inside T-SQL Querying*, I discussed custom aggregates by describing problems that require you to aggregate data even though SQL Server doesn't provide such aggregates as built-in functions—for example, product of elements, string concatenation, and so on. I described four classes of solutions and demonstrated three of them: pivoting, which is limited to a small number of elements in a group; user-defined aggregates (UDAs) written in a .NET language, which force you to write in a language other than T-SQL and enable CLR support in SQL Server; and specialized solutions, which can be very fast but are applicable to specific cases and are not suited to generic use. Another approach to solving custom aggregate problems is using cursors. This approach is not very fast; nevertheless, it is straightforward, generic, and not limited to situations in which you have a small number of elements in a group. To see a demonstration of a cursor-based solution for custom aggregates, run the code in Listing 3-1 to create and populate the Groups table, which I also used in my examples in *Inside T-SQL Querying.*

Listing 3-1   Creating and populating the Groups table

```
USE tempdb;
GO
IF OBJECT_ID('dbo.Groups') IS NOT NULL
  DROP TABLE dbo.Groups;
GO

CREATE TABLE dbo.Groups
(
  groupid  VARCHAR(10) NOT NULL,
  memberid INT         NOT NULL,
  string   VARCHAR(10) NOT NULL,
  val      INT         NOT NULL,
  PRIMARY KEY (groupid, memberid)
);

INSERT INTO dbo.Groups(groupid, memberid, string, val)
  VALUES('a', 3, 'stra1', 6);
INSERT INTO dbo.Groups(groupid, memberid, string, val)
  VALUES('a', 9, 'stra2', 7);
INSERT INTO dbo.Groups(groupid, memberid, string, val)
  VALUES('b', 2, 'strb1', 3);
INSERT INTO dbo.Groups(groupid, memberid, string, val)
  VALUES('b', 4, 'strb2', 7);
INSERT INTO dbo.Groups(groupid, memberid, string, val)
  VALUES('b', 5, 'strb3', 3);
INSERT INTO dbo.Groups(groupid, memberid, string, val)
  VALUES('b', 9, 'strb4', 11);
INSERT INTO dbo.Groups(groupid, memberid, string, val)
  VALUES('c', 3, 'strc1', 8);
INSERT INTO dbo.Groups(groupid, memberid, string, val)
  VALUES('c', 7, 'strc2', 10);
INSERT INTO dbo.Groups(groupid, memberid, string, val)
  VALUES('c', 9, 'strc3', 12);
```

Listing 3-2 shows cursor code that calculates the aggregate product of the *val* column for each group represented by the *groupid* column, and it generates the output shown in Table 3-1.

Listing 3-2   Cursor code for custom aggregate

```
DECLARE
  @Result TABLE(groupid VARCHAR(10), product BIGINT);
DECLARE
  @groupid AS VARCHAR(10), @prvgroupid AS VARCHAR(10),
  @val AS INT, @product AS BIGINT;

DECLARE C CURSOR FAST_FORWARD FOR
  SELECT groupid, val FROM dbo.Groups ORDER BY groupid;
```

```
OPEN C

FETCH NEXT FROM C INTO @groupid, @val;
SELECT @prvgroupid = @groupid, @product = 1;

WHILE @@fetch_status = 0
BEGIN
  IF @groupid <> @prvgroupid
  BEGIN
    INSERT INTO @Result VALUES(@prvgroupid, @product);
    SELECT @prvgroupid = @groupid, @product = 1;
  END

  SET @product = @product * @val;

  FETCH NEXT FROM C INTO @groupid, @val;
END

IF @prvgroupid IS NOT NULL
  INSERT INTO @Result VALUES(@prvgroupid, @product);

CLOSE C;

DEALLOCATE C;

SELECT groupid, product FROM @Result;
```

Table 3-1 Aggregate Product

Groupid	product
A	42
B	693
C	960

The algorithm is straightforward: scan the data in *groupid* order; while traversing the rows in the group, keep multiplying by *val*; and whenever the *groupid* value changes, store the result of the product for the previous group aside in a table variable. When the loop exits, you still hold the aggregate product for the last group, so store it in the table variable as well unless the input was empty. Finally, return the aggregate products of all groups as output.

Running Aggregations

The previous problem, which discussed custom aggregates, used a cursor-based solution that scanned the data only once, but so did the pivoting solution, the UDA solution, and some of the specialized set-based solutions. If you consider that cursors incur more overhead than set-based solutions that scan the same amount of data, you can see that the cursor-based solutions are bound to be slower. On the other hand, set-based solutions for running aggregation problems in SQL Server 2005 involve rescanning portions of the data multiple times, whereas the cursor-based solutions scan the data only once.

I covered Running Aggregations in *Inside T-SQL Querying*. Here, I'll demonstrate cursor-based solutions. Run the following code, which creates and populates the EmpOrders table:

```
USE tempdb;
GO

IF OBJECT_ID('dbo.EmpOrders') IS NOT NULL
  DROP TABLE dbo.EmpOrders;
GO

CREATE TABLE dbo.EmpOrders
(
  empid    INT      NOT NULL,
  ordmonth DATETIME NOT NULL,
  qty      INT      NOT NULL,
  PRIMARY KEY(empid, ordmonth)
);

INSERT INTO dbo.EmpOrders(empid, ordmonth, qty)
  SELECT O.EmployeeID,
    CAST(CONVERT(CHAR(6), O.OrderDate, 112) + '01'
      AS DATETIME) AS ordmonth,
    SUM(Quantity) AS qty
  FROM Northwind.dbo.Orders AS O
    JOIN Northwind.dbo.[Order Details] AS OD
    ON O.OrderID = OD.OrderID
  GROUP BY EmployeeID,
    CAST(CONVERT(CHAR(6), O.OrderDate, 112) + '01'
      AS DATETIME);
```

This is the same table and sample data I used in *Inside T-SQL Querying* to demonstrate set-based solutions.

The cursor-based solution is straightforward. In fact, it's similar to calculating custom aggregates except for a simple difference: the code calculating custom aggregates set aside in a table variable only the final aggregate for each group, while the code calculating running aggregations sets aside the accumulated aggregate value for each row. Listing 3-3 shows the code that calculates running total quantities for each employee and month and yields the output shown in Table 3-2 (abbreviated).

Listing 3-3   Cursor code for custom aggregate

```
DECLARE @Result
  TABLE(empid INT, ordmonth DATETIME, qty INT, runqty INT);
DECLARE
  @empid AS INT,@prvempid AS INT, @ordmonth DATETIME,
  @qty AS INT, @runqty AS INT;

DECLARE C CURSOR FAST_FORWARD FOR
  SELECT empid, ordmonth, qty
  FROM dbo.EmpOrders
  ORDER BY empid, ordmonth;

OPEN C
```

```
FETCH NEXT FROM C INTO @empid, @ordmonth, @qty;
SELECT @prvempid = @empid, @runqty = 0;

WHILE @@fetch_status = 0
BEGIN
  IF @empid <> @prvempid
    SELECT @prvempid = @empid, @runqty = 0;

  SET @runqty = @runqty + @qty;

  INSERT INTO @Result VALUES(@empid, @ordmonth, @qty, @runqty);

  FETCH NEXT FROM C INTO @empid, @ordmonth, @qty;
END

CLOSE C;

DEALLOCATE C;

SELECT empid, CONVERT(VARCHAR(7), ordmonth, 121) AS ordmonth,
  qty, runqty
FROM @Result
ORDER BY empid, ordmonth;
```

Table 3-2   Running Aggregations (Abbreviated)

empid	Ordmonth	qty	runqty
1	1996-07	121	121
1	1996-08	247	368
1	1996-09	255	623
1	1996-10	143	766
1	1996-11	318	1084
1	1996-12	536	1620
1	1997-01	304	1924
1	1997-02	168	2092
1	1997-03	275	2367
1	1997-04	20	2387
...	...	...	...
2	1996-07	50	50
2	1996-08	94	144
2	1996-09	137	281
2	1996-10	248	529
2	1996-11	237	766
2	1996-12	319	1085
2	1997-01	230	1315
2	1997-02	36	1351

Table 3-2   Running Aggregations (Abbreviated)

empid	Ordmonth	qty	runqty
2	1997-03	151	1502
2	1997-04	468	1970
...	...	...	...

The cursor solution scans the data only once, meaning that it has linear performance degradation with respect to the number of rows in the table. The set-based solution suffers from an n^2 performance issue, in which n refers to the number of rows per group. If you have g groups with n number of rows per group, you scan $g \times (n + n^2)/2$ rows. This formula assumes that you have an index on (groupid, val). Without an index, you simply have n^2 rows scanned, where n is the number of rows in the table. If the group size is small enough (for example, a dozen rows), the set-based solution that uses an index would typically be faster than the cursor solution. The cursor's overhead is still higher than the set-based solution's extra work of scanning more data. However, the set-based solution scans substantially more data (unless there are only a few rows per group), resulting in a slower solution where performance degrades in an n^2 manner with respect to the group size.

To gain a sense of these performance differences, look at Figure 3-1, which has the result of a benchmark.

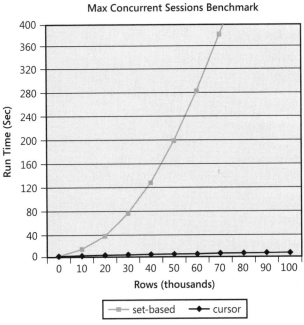

Figure 3-1   Benchmark for running calculations

You can see the run time of the solutions with respect to the number of rows in the table, assuming a single group—that is, by calculating running aggregations for the whole table. The horizontal axis has the number of rows in the table divided by 1000, ranging from 0 through

100,000 rows. The y axis ranges from 0 through 400 seconds. You can see a linear graph for the cursor solution, and a nice n^2 parabola for the set-based one. You can also notice clearly that beyond a very small number of rows the cursor solution performs dramatically faster.

This is one of the problems that ANSI already provided an answer for in the form of query constructs; however, SQL Server has not yet implemented it. According to ANSI, you would write the following solution:

```
SELECT empid, CONVERT(VARCHAR(7), ordmonth, 121) AS ordmonth, qty,
  SUM(qty) OVER(PARTITION BY empid ORDER BY ordermonth) AS runqty
FROM dbo.EmpOrders;
```

As mentioned earlier, SQL Server 2005 already introduced the infrastructure to support the OVER clause. It currently implements it with both the PARTITION BY and ORDER BY clauses for ranking functions, but only with the PARTITION BY clause for aggregate functions. Hopefully, future versions of SQL Server will enhance the support for the OVER clause. Queries such as the one just shown have the potential to run substantially faster than the cursor solution; the infrastructure added to the product relies on a single scan of the data to perform such calculations.

Maximum Concurrent Sessions

The Maximum Concurrent Sessions problem is yet another example of calculations based on ordered data. You record data for user sessions against different applications in a table called Sessions. Run the code in Listing 3-4 to create and populate the Sessions table.

Listing 3-4   Creating and populating the Sessions table

```
USE tempdb;
GO
IF OBJECT_ID('dbo.Sessions') IS NOT NULL
  DROP TABLE dbo.Sessions;
GO

CREATE TABLE dbo.Sessions
(
  keycol    INT         NOT NULL IDENTITY PRIMARY KEY,
  app       VARCHAR(10) NOT NULL,
  usr       VARCHAR(10) NOT NULL,
  host      VARCHAR(10) NOT NULL,
  starttime DATETIME    NOT NULL,
  endtime   DATETIME    NOT NULL,
  CHECK(endtime > starttime)
);

INSERT INTO dbo.Sessions
  VALUES('app1', 'user1', 'host1', '20030212 08:30', '20030212 10:30');
INSERT INTO dbo.Sessions
  VALUES('app1', 'user2', 'host1', '20030212 08:30', '20030212 08:45');
INSERT INTO dbo.Sessions
  VALUES('app1', 'user3', 'host2', '20030212 09:00', '20030212 09:30');
```

```
INSERT INTO dbo.Sessions
  VALUES('app1', 'user4', 'host2', '20030212 09:15', '20030212 10:30');
INSERT INTO dbo.Sessions
  VALUES('app1', 'user5', 'host3', '20030212 09:15', '20030212 09:30');
INSERT INTO dbo.Sessions
  VALUES('app1', 'user6', 'host3', '20030212 10:30', '20030212 14:30');
INSERT INTO dbo.Sessions
  VALUES('app1', 'user7', 'host4', '20030212 10:45', '20030212 11:30');
INSERT INTO dbo.Sessions
  VALUES('app1', 'user8', 'host4', '20030212 11:00', '20030212 12:30');
INSERT INTO dbo.Sessions
  VALUES('app2', 'user8', 'host1', '20030212 08:30', '20030212 08:45');
INSERT INTO dbo.Sessions
  VALUES('app2', 'user7', 'host1', '20030212 09:00', '20030212 09:30');
INSERT INTO dbo.Sessions
  VALUES('app2', 'user6', 'host2', '20030212 11:45', '20030212 12:00');
INSERT INTO dbo.Sessions
  VALUES('app2', 'user5', 'host2', '20030212 12:30', '20030212 14:00');
INSERT INTO dbo.Sessions
  VALUES('app2', 'user4', 'host3', '20030212 12:45', '20030212 13:30');
INSERT INTO dbo.Sessions
  VALUES('app2', 'user3', 'host3', '20030212 13:00', '20030212 14:00');
INSERT INTO dbo.Sessions
  VALUES('app2', 'user2', 'host4', '20030212 14:00', '20030212 16:30');
INSERT INTO dbo.Sessions
  VALUES('app2', 'user1', 'host4', '20030212 15:30', '20030212 17:00');

CREATE INDEX idx_app_st_et ON dbo.Sessions(app, starttime, endtime);
```

The request is to calculate, for each application, the maximum number of sessions that were open at the same point in time. Such types of calculations are required to determine the cost of a type of service license that charges by the maximum number of concurrent sessions.

Try to develop a set-based solution that works; then try to optimize it; and then try to estimate its performance potential. Later I'll discuss a cursor-based solution and show a benchmark that compares the set-based solution with the cursor-based solution.

One way to solve the problem is to generate an auxiliary table with all possible points in time during the covered period, use a subquery to count the number of active sessions during each such point in time, create a derived table/CTE from the result table, and finally group the rows from the derived table by application, requesting the maximum count of concurrent sessions for each application. Such a solution is extremely inefficient. Assuming you create the optimal index for it—one on (*app, starttime, endtime*)—the total number of rows you end up scanning just in the leaf level of the index is huge. It's equal to the number of rows in the auxiliary table multiplied by the average number of active sessions at any point in time. To give you a sense of the enormity of the task, if you need to perform the calculations for a month's worth of activity, the number of rows in the auxiliary table will be: 31 (days) × 24 (hours) × 60 (minutes) × 60 (seconds) × 300 (units within a second). Now multiply the result of this calculation by the average number of active sessions at any given point in time (say 20 as an example), and you get 16,070,400,000.

Of course there's room for optimization. There are periods in which the number of concurrent sessions doesn't change, so why calculate the counts for those? The count changes only when a new session starts (increased by 1) or an existing session ends (decreased by 1). Furthermore, because a start of a session increases the count and an end of a session decreases it, a start event of one of the sessions is bound to be the point at which you will find the maximum you're looking for. Finally, if two sessions start at the same time, there's no reason to calculate the counts for both. So you can apply a DISTINCT clause in the query that returns the start times for each application, although with an accuracy level of 3 ⅓ milliseconds (ms), the number of duplicates would be very small—unless you're dealing with very large volumes of data.

In short, you can simply use as your auxiliary table a derived table or CTE that returns all distinct start times of sessions per application. From there, all you need to do is follow logic similar to that mentioned earlier. Here's the optimized set-based solution, yielding the output shown in Table 3-3:

```
SELECT app, MAX(concurrent) AS mx
FROM (SELECT app,
        (SELECT COUNT(*)
         FROM dbo.Sessions AS S2
         WHERE S1.app = S2.app
           AND S1.ts >= S2.starttime
           AND S1.ts < S2.endtime) AS concurrent
      FROM (SELECT DISTINCT app, starttime AS ts
            FROM dbo.Sessions) AS S1) AS C
GROUP BY app;
```

Table 3-3   Maximum Concurrent Sessions Set-Based Solution

app	mx
app1	4
app2	3

Notice that instead of using a BETWEEN predicate to determine whether a session was active at a certain point in time (*ts*), I used *ts >= starttime AND ts < endtime*. If a session ends at the *ts* point in time, I don't want to consider it as active.

The execution plan for this query is shown in Figure 3-2.

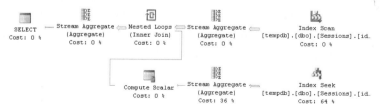

Figure 3-2 Execution plan for Maximum Concurrent Sessions, set-based solution

First, the index I created on (*app, starttime, endtime*) is scanned and duplicates are removed (by the stream aggregate operator). Unless the table is huge, you can assume that the number of rows returned will be very close to the number of rows in the table. For each *app, starttime* (call it *ts*) returned after removing duplicates, a Nested Loops operator initiates activity that calculates the count of active sessions (by a seek within the index, followed by a partial scan to count active sessions). The number of pages read in each iteration of the Nested Loops operator is the number of levels in the index plus the number of pages consumed by the number of active sessions. To make my point, I'll focus on the number of rows scanned at the leaf level because this number varies based on active sessions. Of course, to do adequate performance estimations, you should take page counts (logical reads) as well as many other factors into consideration. If you have *n* rows in the table, assuming that most of them have unique *app, starttime* values and there are *o* overlapping sessions at any given point in time, you're looking at the following: $n \times o$ rows scanned in total at the leaf level, beyond the pages scanned by the seek operations that got you to the leaf.

You now need to figure out how this solution scales when the table grows larger. Typically, such reports are required periodically—for example, once a month, for the most recent month. With the recommended index in place, the performance shouldn't change as long as the traffic doesn't increase for a month's worth of activity—that is, if it's related to $n \times o$ (where *n* is the number of rows for the recent month). But suppose that you anticipate traffic increase by a factor of *f*? If traffic increases by a factor of f, both total rows and number of active sessions at a given time grow by that factor; so in total, the number of rows scanned at the leaf level becomes $(n \times f)(o \times f) = n \times o \times f^2$. You see, as the traffic grows, performance doesn't degrade linearly; rather, it degrades much more drastically.

Next let's talk about a cursor-based solution. The power of a cursor-based solution is that it can scan data in order. Relying on the fact that each session represents two events—one that increases the count of active sessions, and one that decreases the count—I'll declare a cursor for the following query:

```
SELECT app, starttime AS ts, 1 AS event_type FROM dbo.Sessions
UNION ALL
SELECT app, endtime, -1 FROM dbo.Sessions
ORDER BY app, ts, event_type;
```

This query returns the following for each session start or end event: the application (*app*), the timestamp (*ts*); an event type (*event_type*) of +1 for a session start event or −1 for a session end event. The events are sorted by *app, ts,* and *event_type*. The reason for sorting by *app, ts* is obvious. The reason for adding *event_type* to the sort is to guarantee that if a session ends at the same time another session starts, you will take the end event into consideration first (because sessions are considered to have ended at their end time). Other than that, the cursor code is straightforward—simply scan the data in order and keep adding up the +1s and −1s for each application. With every new row scanned, check whether the cumulative value to that point is greater than the current maximum for that application, which you store in a variable. If it is, store it as the new maximum. When done with an application, insert a row containing the application ID and maximum into a table variable. That's about it. You can find the complete cursor solution in Listing 3-5.

Listing 3-5 Cursor code for Maximum Concurrent Sessions, cursor-based solution

```
DECLARE
  @app AS VARCHAR(10), @prevapp AS VARCHAR (10), @ts AS datetime,
  @event_type AS INT, @concurrent AS INT, @mx AS INT;

DECLARE @Result TABLE(app VARCHAR(10), mx INT);

DECLARE C CURSOR FAST_FORWARD FOR
  SELECT app, starttime AS ts, 1 AS event_type FROM dbo.Sessions
  UNION ALL
  SELECT app, endtime, -1 FROM dbo.Sessions
  ORDER BY app, ts, event_type;

OPEN C;

FETCH NEXT FROM C INTO @app, @ts, @event_type;
SELECT @prevapp = @app, @concurrent = 0, @mx = 0;

WHILE @@fetch_status = 0
BEGIN
  IF @app <> @prevapp
  BEGIN
    INSERT INTO @Result VALUES(@prevapp, @mx);
    SELECT @prevapp = @app, @concurrent = 0, @mx = 0;
  END

  SET @concurrent = @concurrent + @event_type;
  IF @concurrent > @mx SET @mx = @concurrent;

  FETCH NEXT FROM C INTO @app, @ts, @event_type;
END

IF @prevapp IS NOT NULL
  INSERT INTO @Result VALUES(@prevapp, @mx);

CLOSE C

DEALLOCATE C

SELECT * FROM @Result;
```

The cursor solution scans the leaf of the index only twice. You can represent its cost as $n \times 2 \times v$, where v is the cursor overhead involved with each single row manipulation. Also, if the traffic grows by a factor of f, the performance degrades linearly to $n \times 2 \times v \times f$. You realize that unless you're dealing with a very small input set, the cursor solution has the potential to perform much faster, and as proof, you can use the code in Listing 3-6 to conduct a benchmark test. Change the value of the *@numrows* variable to determine the number of rows in the table. I ran this code with numbers varying from 10,000 through 100,000 in steps of 10,000. Figure 3-3 shows a graphical depiction of the benchmark test I ran.

Listing 3-6   Benchmark code for Maximum Concurrent Sessions problem

```
SET NOCOUNT ON;
USE tempdb;
GO
IF OBJECT_ID('dbo.Sessions') IS NOT NULL
  DROP TABLE dbo.Sessions
GO

DECLARE @numrows AS INT;
SET @numrows = 10000;
-- Test with 10K - 100K

SELECT
  IDENTITY(int, 1, 1) AS keycol,
  D.*,
  DATEADD(
    second,
    1 + ABS(CHECKSUM(NEWID())) % (20*60),
    starttime) AS endtime
INTO dbo.Sessions
FROM
(
  SELECT
    'app' + CAST(1 + ABS(CHECKSUM(NEWID())) % 10 AS VARCHAR(10)) AS app,
    'user1' AS usr,
    'host1' AS host,
    DATEADD(
      second,
      1 + ABS(CHECKSUM(NEWID())) % (30*24*60*60),
      '20040101') AS starttime
  FROM dbo.Nums
  WHERE n <= @numrows
) AS D;

ALTER TABLE dbo.Sessions ADD PRIMARY KEY(keycol);
CREATE INDEX idx_app_st_et ON dbo.Sessions(app, starttime, endtime);

DBCC FREEPROCCACHE WITH NO_INFOMSGS;
DBCC DROPCLEANBUFFERS WITH NO_INFOMSGS;

DECLARE @dt1 AS DATETIME, @dt2 AS DATETIME,
  @dt3 AS DATETIME, @dt4 AS DATETIME;
SET @dt1 = GETDATE();

-- Set-Based Solution
SELECT app, MAX(concurrent) AS mx
FROM (SELECT app,
         (SELECT COUNT(*)
          FROM dbo.Sessions AS S2
          WHERE S1.app = S2.app
            AND S1.ts >= S2.starttime
            AND S1.ts < S2.endtime) AS concurrent
      FROM (SELECT DISTINCT app, starttime AS ts
            FROM dbo.Sessions) AS S1) AS C
```

```
GROUP BY app;

SET @dt2 = GETDATE();

DBCC FREEPROCCACHE WITH NO_INFOMSGS;
DBCC DROPCLEANBUFFERS WITH NO_INFOMSGS;

SET @dt3 = GETDATE();

-- Cursor-Based Solution
DECLARE
  @app AS VARCHAR(10), @prevapp AS VARCHAR (10), @ts AS datetime,
  @event_type AS INT, @concurrent AS INT, @mx AS INT;

DECLARE @Result TABLE(app VARCHAR(10), mx INT);

DECLARE C CURSOR FAST_FORWARD FOR
  SELECT app, starttime AS ts, 1 AS event_type FROM dbo.Sessions
  UNION ALL
  SELECT app, endtime, -1 FROM dbo.Sessions
  ORDER BY app, ts, event_type;

OPEN C;

FETCH NEXT FROM C INTO @app, @ts, @event_type;
SELECT @prevapp = @app, @concurrent = 0, @mx = 0;

WHILE @@fetch_status = 0
BEGIN
  IF @app <> @prevapp
  BEGIN
    INSERT INTO @Result VALUES(@prevapp, @mx);
    SELECT @prevapp = @app, @concurrent = 0, @mx = 0;
  END

  SET @concurrent = @concurrent + @event_type;
  IF @concurrent > @mx SET @mx = @concurrent;

  FETCH NEXT FROM C INTO @app, @ts, @event_type;
END

IF @prevapp IS NOT NULL
  INSERT INTO @Result VALUES(@prevapp, @mx);

CLOSE C

DEALLOCATE C

SELECT * FROM @Result;

SET @dt4 = GETDATE();

PRINT CAST(@numrows AS VARCHAR(10)) + ' rows, set-based: '
  + CAST(DATEDIFF(ms, @dt1, @dt2) / 1000. AS VARCHAR(30))
  + ', cursor: '
  + CAST(DATEDIFF(ms, @dt3, @dt4) / 1000. AS VARCHAR(30))
  + ' (sec)';
```

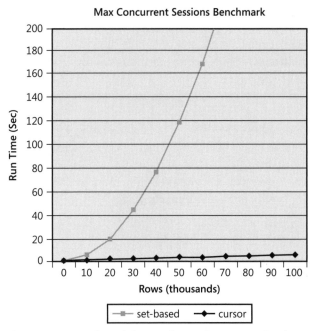

Figure 3-3 Benchmark for Maximum Concurrent Sessions solutions

Again, you can see a nicely shaped parabola in the set-based solution's graph, and now you know how to explain it: remember—if traffic increases by a factor of f, the number of leaf-level rows inspected by the set-based query grows by a factor of f^2.

> **Tip** It might seem that all the cases in which I show cursor code that performs better than set-based code have to do with problems where cursor code has a complexity of $O(n)$ and set-based code has a complexity of $O(n^2)$, where n is the number of rows in the table. These are just convenient problems to demonstrate performance differences. However, you might face problems for which the solutions have different complexities. The important point is to be able to estimate complexity and performance. If you want to learn more about algorithmic complexity, visit the Web site of the National Institute for Standards and Technologies. Go to *http://www.nist.gov/dads/*, and search for complexity, or access the definition directly at *http://www.nist.gov/dads/HTML/complexity.html*.

Interestingly, this is yet another type of problem where a more complete implementation of the OVER clause would have allowed for a set-based solution to perform substantially faster than the cursor one. Here's what the set-based solution would have looked like if SQL Server supported ORDER BY in the OVER clause for aggregations:

```
SELECT app, MAX(concurrent) AS mx
FROM (SELECT app, SUM(event_type)
        OVER(PARTITION BY app ORDER BY ts, event_type) AS concurrent
      FROM (SELECT app, starttime AS ts, 1 AS event_type FROM dbo.Sessions
            UNION ALL
            SELECT app, endtime, -1 FROM dbo.Sessions) AS D1) AS D2
GROUP BY app;
```

Before I proceed to the next class of problems, I'd like to stress the importance of using good sample data in your benchmarks. Too often I have seen programmers simply duplicate data from a small table many times to generate larger sets of sample data. With our set-based solution, remember the derived table query that generates the timestamps:

```
SELECT DISTINCT app, starttime AS ts
FROM dbo.Sessions
```

If you simply duplicate the small sample data that I provided in Listing 3-4 (16 rows) many times, you will not increase the number of DISTINCT timestamps accordingly. So the sub-query that counts rows will end up being invoked only 16 times regardless of how many times you duplicated the set. The results that you will get when measuring performance won't give you a true indication of cost for production environments where, obviously, you have almost no duplicates in the data.

The solution to the problem can be even more elusive if you don't have any DISTINCT applied to remove duplicates. To demonstrate the problem, first rerun the code in Listing 3-4 to repopulate the Sessions table with 16 rows.

Next, run the following query, which is similar to the solution I showed earlier, but run it without removing duplicates first. Then examine the execution plan shown in Figure 3-4:

```
SELECT app, MAX(concurrent) AS mx
FROM (SELECT app,
        (SELECT COUNT(*)
         FROM dbo.Sessions AS S2
         WHERE S1.app = S2.app
           AND S1.starttime >= S2.starttime
           AND S1.starttime < S2.endtime) AS concurrent
      FROM dbo.Sessions AS S1) AS C
GROUP BY app;
```

Figure 3-4   Execution plan for revised Maximum Concurrent Sessions solution, small data set

Here the problem is not yet apparent because there are no duplicates. The plan is, in fact, almost identical to the one generated for the solution that does remove duplicates. The only difference is that here there's no stream aggregate operator that removes duplicates, naturally.

Next, populate the table with 10,000 duplicates of each row:

```
INSERT INTO dbo.Sessions
  SELECT app, usr, host, starttime, endtime
  FROM dbo.Sessions, dbo.Nums
  WHERE n <= 10000;
```

Rerun the solution query, and examine the execution plan shown in Figure 3-5.

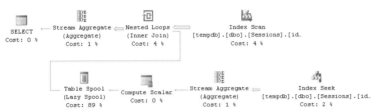

Figure 3-5   Execution plan for revised Maximum Concurrent Sessions solution, large data set with high density

If you have a keen eye, you will find an interesting difference between this plan and the previous one, even though the query remained the same and only the data density changed. This plan spools, instead of recalculating, row counts that were already calculated for a given *app, ts*. Before counting rows, the plan first looks in the spool to check whether the count has already been calculated. If the count has been calculated, the plan will grab the count from the spool instead of scanning rows to count. The Index Seek and Stream Aggregate operations took place here only 16 times—once for each unique *app, ts* value, and not once for each row in the table as might happen in production. Again, you see how a bad choice of sample data can yield a result that is not representative of your production environment. Using this sample data and being oblivious to the discrepancy might lead you to believe that this set-based solution scales linearly. But of course, if you use more realistic sample data, such as the data I used in my benchmark, you won't fall into that trap. I used random calculations for the start times within the month and added a random value of up to 20 minutes for the end time, assuming that this represents the average session duration in my production environment.

Matching Problems

The algorithms for the solutions that I have discussed so far, both set-based and cursor-based, had simple to moderate complexity levels. This section covers a class of problems that are algorithmically much more complex, known as *matching problems*. In a matching problem, you have a specific set of items of different values and volumes and one container of a given size, and you must find the subset of items with the greatest possible value that will fit into the container. I have yet to find reasonable set-based solutions that are nearly as good as cursor-based solutions, both in terms of performance and simplicity. I won't even bother to provide the set-based solutions I devised because they're very complex and slow. Instead, I'll focus on cursor-based solutions.

I'll introduce a couple of simple variations of the problem. You're given the tables Events and Rooms, which you create and populate by running the code in Listing 3-7.

Listing 3-7 Code that creates and populates the Events and Rooms tables

```
USE tempdb;
GO
IF OBJECT_ID('dbo.Events') IS NOT NULL
  DROP TABLE dbo.Events;
GO
IF OBJECT_ID('dbo.Rooms') IS NOT NULL
  DROP TABLE dbo.Rooms;
GO

CREATE TABLE dbo.Rooms
(
  roomid VARCHAR(10) NOT NULL PRIMARY KEY,
  seats INT NOT NULL
);

INSERT INTO dbo.Rooms(roomid, seats) VALUES('C001', 2000);
INSERT INTO dbo.Rooms(roomid, seats) VALUES('B101', 1500);
INSERT INTO dbo.Rooms(roomid, seats) VALUES('B102', 100);
INSERT INTO dbo.Rooms(roomid, seats) VALUES('R103', 40);
INSERT INTO dbo.Rooms(roomid, seats) VALUES('R104', 40);
INSERT INTO dbo.Rooms(roomid, seats) VALUES('B201', 1000);
INSERT INTO dbo.Rooms(roomid, seats) VALUES('R202', 100);
INSERT INTO dbo.Rooms(roomid, seats) VALUES('R203', 50);
INSERT INTO dbo.Rooms(roomid, seats) VALUES('B301', 600);
INSERT INTO dbo.Rooms(roomid, seats) VALUES('R302', 55);
INSERT INTO dbo.Rooms(roomid, seats) VALUES('R303', 55);

CREATE TABLE dbo.Events
(
  eventid INT NOT NULL PRIMARY KEY,
  eventdesc VARCHAR(25) NOT NULL,
  attendees INT NOT NULL
);

INSERT INTO dbo.Events(eventid, eventdesc, attendees)
  VALUES(1, 'Adv T-SQL Seminar', 203);
INSERT INTO dbo.Events(eventid, eventdesc, attendees)
  VALUES(2, 'Logic Seminar',    48);
INSERT INTO dbo.Events(eventid, eventdesc, attendees)
  VALUES(3, 'DBA Seminar',      212);
INSERT INTO dbo.Events(eventid, eventdesc, attendees)
  VALUES(4, 'XML Seminar',       98);
INSERT INTO dbo.Events(eventid, eventdesc, attendees)
  VALUES(5, 'Security Seminar', 892);
INSERT INTO dbo.Events(eventid, eventdesc, attendees)
  VALUES(6, 'Modeling Seminar',  48);
GO

CREATE INDEX idx_att_eid_edesc
  ON dbo.Events(attendees, eventid, eventdesc);
CREATE INDEX idx_seats_rid
  ON dbo.Rooms(seats, roomid);
```

The Events table holds information for seminars that you're supposed to run on a given date. Typically, you will need to keep track of events on many dates, but our task here will be one that we would have to perform separately for each day of scheduled events. Assume that this data represents one day's worth of events; for simplicity's sake, I didn't include a date column because all its values would be the same. The Rooms table holds room capacity information. To start with a simple task, assume that you have reserved a conference center with the guarantee that there will be enough rooms available to host all your seminars. You now need to match events to rooms with as few empty seats as possible, because the cost of renting a room is determined by the room's seating capacity, not by the number of seminar attendees.

A naïve algorithm that you can apply is somewhat similar to a merge join algorithm that the optimizer uses to process joins. Figure 3-6 has a graphical depiction of it, which you might find handy when following the verbal description of the algorithm. Listing 3-8 has the code implementing the algorithm.

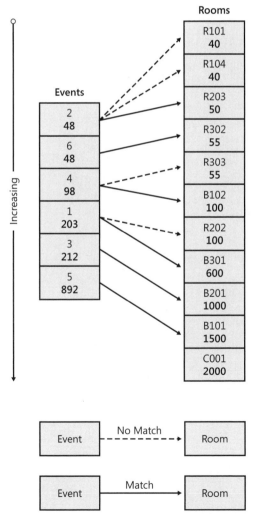

Figure 3-6   Matching algorithm for guaranteed solution scenario

Listing 3-8 Cursor code for matching problem (guaranteed solution)

```
DECLARE
  @roomid AS VARCHAR(10), @seats AS INT,
  @eventid AS INT, @attendees AS INT;

DECLARE @Result TABLE(roomid  VARCHAR(10), eventid INT);

DECLARE CRooms CURSOR FAST_FORWARD FOR
  SELECT roomid, seats FROM dbo.Rooms
  ORDER BY seats, roomid;
DECLARE CEvents CURSOR FAST_FORWARD FOR
  SELECT eventid, attendees FROM dbo.Events
  ORDER BY attendees, eventid;

OPEN CRooms;
OPEN CEvents;

FETCH NEXT FROM CEvents INTO @eventid, @attendees;
WHILE @@FETCH_STATUS = 0
BEGIN
  FETCH NEXT FROM CRooms INTO @roomid, @seats;

  WHILE @@FETCH_STATUS = 0 AND @seats < @attendees
    FETCH NEXT FROM CRooms INTO @roomid, @seats;

  IF @@FETCH_STATUS = 0
    INSERT INTO @Result(roomid, eventid) VALUES(@roomid, @eventid);
  ELSE
  BEGIN
    RAISERROR('Not enough rooms for events.', 16, 1);
    BREAK;
  END

  FETCH NEXT FROM CEvents INTO @eventid, @attendees;
END

CLOSE CRooms;
CLOSE CEvents;

DEALLOCATE CRooms;
DEALLOCATE CEvents;

SELECT roomid, eventid FROM @Result;
```

Here's a description of the algorithm as it's implemented with cursors:

- Declare two cursors, one on the list of rooms (*CRooms*) sorted by increasing capacity (number of seats), and one on the list of events (*CEvents*) sorted by increasing number of attendees.

- Fetch the first (smallest) event from the *CEvents* cursor.

- While the fetch returned an actual event that needs a room:

  ❏ Fetch the smallest unrented room from *CRooms*. If there was no available room, or if the room you fetched is too small for the event, fetch the next smallest room from *CRooms*, and continue fetching as long as you keep fetching actual rooms and they are too small for the event. You will either find a big enough room, or you will run out of rooms without finding one.

  ❏ If you did not run out of rooms, and the last fetch yielded a room and the number of seats in that room is smaller than the number of attendees in the current event:

    ● If you found a big enough room, schedule the current event in that room. If you did not, then you must have run out of rooms, so generate an error saying that there are not enough rooms to host all the events, and break out of the loop.

    ● Fetch another event.

- Return the room/event pairs you stored aside.

Notice that you scan both rooms and events in order, never backing up; you merge matching pairs until you either run out of events to find rooms for or you run out of rooms to accommodate events. In the latter case—you run out of rooms, generating an error, because the algorithm used was guaranteed to find a solution if one existed.

Next, let's complicate the problem by assuming that even if there aren't enough rooms for all events, you still want to schedule something. This will be the case if you remove rooms with a number of seats greater than 600:

```
DELETE FROM dbo.Rooms WHERE seats > 600;
```

Assume you need to come up with a *greedy* algorithm that finds seats for the highest possible number of attendees (to increase revenue) and for that number of attendees, involves the lowest cost. The algorithm I used for this case is graphically illustrated in Figure 3-7 and implemented with cursors in Listing 3-9.

Listing 3-9 Cursor code for matching problem (nonguaranteed solution)

```
DECLARE
  @roomid AS VARCHAR(10), @seats AS INT,
  @eventid AS INT, @attendees AS INT;

DECLARE @Events TABLE(eventid INT, attendees INT);
DECLARE @Result TABLE(roomid  VARCHAR(10), eventid INT);

-- Step 1: Descending
DECLARE CRoomsDesc CURSOR FAST_FORWARD FOR
  SELECT roomid, seats FROM dbo.Rooms
  ORDER BY seats DESC, roomid DESC;
DECLARE CEventsDesc CURSOR FAST_FORWARD FOR
  SELECT eventid, attendees FROM dbo.Events
  ORDER BY attendees DESC, eventid DESC;
```

```
OPEN CRoomsDesc;
OPEN CEventsDesc;

FETCH NEXT FROM CRoomsDesc INTO @roomid, @seats;
WHILE @@FETCH_STATUS = 0
BEGIN
  FETCH NEXT FROM CEventsDesc INTO @eventid, @attendees;

  WHILE @@FETCH_STATUS = 0 AND @seats < @attendees
    FETCH NEXT FROM CEventsDesc INTO @eventid, @attendees;

  IF @@FETCH_STATUS = 0
    INSERT INTO @Events(eventid, attendees)
      VALUES(@eventid, @attendees);
  ELSE
    BREAK;

  FETCH NEXT FROM CRoomsDesc INTO @roomid, @seats;
END

CLOSE CRoomsDesc;
CLOSE CEventsDesc;

DEALLOCATE CRoomsDesc;
DEALLOCATE CEventsDesc;

-- Step 2: Ascending
DECLARE CRooms CURSOR FAST_FORWARD FOR
  SELECT roomid, seats FROM Rooms
  ORDER BY seats, roomid;
DECLARE CEvents CURSOR FAST_FORWARD FOR
  SELECT eventid, attendees FROM @Events
  ORDER BY attendees, eventid;

OPEN CRooms;
OPEN CEvents;

FETCH NEXT FROM CEvents INTO @eventid, @attendees;
WHILE @@FETCH_STATUS = 0
BEGIN
  FETCH NEXT FROM CRooms INTO @roomid, @seats;

  WHILE @@FETCH_STATUS = 0 AND @seats < @attendees
    FETCH NEXT FROM CRooms INTO @roomid, @seats;

  IF @@FETCH_STATUS = 0
    INSERT INTO @Result(roomid, eventid) VALUES(@roomid, @eventid);
  ELSE
  BEGIN
    RAISERROR('Not enough rooms for events.', 16, 1);
    BREAK;
  END

  FETCH NEXT FROM CEvents INTO @eventid, @attendees;
END
```

```
CLOSE CRooms;
CLOSE CEvents;

DEALLOCATE CRooms;
DEALLOCATE CEvents;

SELECT roomid, eventid FROM @Result;
```

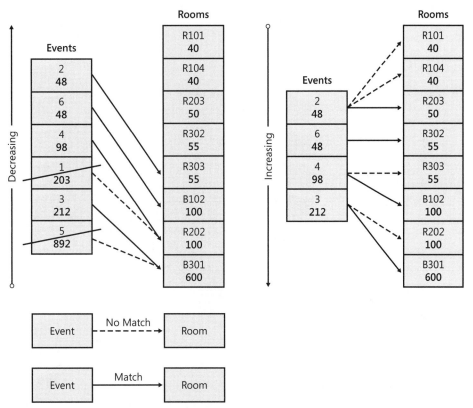

Figure 3-7   Greedy matching algorithm for nonguaranteed solution scenario

The algorithm has two phases:

1. Use logic similar to the previous algorithm to match events to rooms, but scan both in descending order to assure the largest events can find rooms. Store the *eventid*s that found a room in a table variable (*@Events*). At this point, you have the list of events you can fit that produce the highest revenue, but you also have the least efficient room utilization, meaning the highest possible costs. However, the purpose of the first step was merely to figure out the most profitable events that you can accommodate.

2. The next step is identical to the algorithm in the previous problem with one small revision: declare the *CEvents* cursor against the *@Events* table variable and not against the real Events table. By doing this, you end up with the most efficient room utilization for this set of events.

I'd like to thank my good friend, SQL Server MVP Fernando G. Guerrero, who is the CEO of Solid Quality Learning. Fernando suggested ways to improve and optimize the algorithms for this class of problems.

If you're up for challenges, try to look for ways to solve these problems with set-based solutions. Also, try to think of solutions when adding another layer of complexity. Suppose each event has a revenue value stored with it that does not necessarily correspond to the number of attendees. Each room has a cost stored with it that does not necessarily correspond to its capacity. Again, you have no guarantee that there will be enough rooms to host all events. The challenge is to find the most profitable solution.

Conclusion

Throughout the book, I try to stress the advantages set-based solutions have over cursor-based ones. I show many examples of tuned set-based solutions that outperform the cursor alternatives. In this chapter, I explained why that's the case for most types of problems. Nevertheless, I tried giving you the tools to identify the classes of problems that are exceptions—where currently SQL Server 2005 doesn't provide a better solution than using cursors. Some of the problems would have better set-based answers if SQL Server implemented additional ANSI constructs, whereas others don't even have proper answers in the ANSI standard yet. The point is that there's a time and place for cursors if they are used wisely and if a set-based means of solving the problem cannot be found.

Chapter 4
Dynamic SQL

Dynamic SQL (code that is executed dynamically), like cursors and temporary tables, is another area of T-SQL that should be used with care and wisdom. It has the potential to be used in an unsafe way and could lead to serious security breaches and code that performs badly and is difficult to maintain. On the other hand, when used wisely, dynamic SQL can help you achieve things that would be difficult to achieve any other way. And there are cases in which it is the only way you can provide good performance. In short, using dynamic SQL requires programmatic maturity.

Note   I'll discuss some of the potential security breaches involved with dynamic SQL later in the chapter under the section "SQL Injection." SQL Injection is a hacking technique that is used to "plant" malicious code through strings that are later parsed and executed by SQL Server. I strongly recommend that you research the subject thoroughly before using dynamic SQL in both production and test or development environments. A lot of information about the subject is available on the Internet and in other resources. There's also a short but excellent article about dynamic SQL in Books Online under "Security Considerations for SQL Server /SQL Injection," also available via the following URL:

http://msdn2.microsoft.com/en-us/library/ms161953(SQL.90).aspx.

Dynamic SQL is typically required when you must construct sections of your code based on user input. This is exactly why it is so dangerous; it is like allowing customers in a store to use the cash register themselves to ring up their own purchases and make their own change. Using dynamic SQL where you concatenate your code strings based on user inputs amounts to letting users write your code, and it is extremely difficult to do it safely. I've made the effort to demonstrate some techniques to protect against security breaches involved with SQL Injection; but even if you let security experts review your code, they will tell you that it's almost impossible to protect against SQL Injection attempts when incorporating user input in your code. Static code can have some dynamic elements, but only when the dynamic part is an expression that returns a scalar value. For example, you can incorporate an input parameter for a filter expression in a static query. In other words, parameterization, handled correctly, encapsulates and type-checks the user inputs.

Microsoft SQL Server provides you with two commands that invoke code strings that you construct dynamically—EXEC (short for EXECUTE) and sp_executesql.

> **Note**   Note that the EXEC command has two uses; one to invoke a stored procedure: *EXEC <procedure name and arguments>*, and the other to invoke dynamic code: *EXEC(<string>)*. When discussing EXEC in this chapter, I'll be referring to the latter unless explicitly stated otherwise.

As a rule, sp_executesql is preferable because it has an interface (input/output parameters) and EXEC doesn't. With sp_executesql, you are more likely to reuse execution plans because you can more easily generate a query string that you invoke repeatedly—the same query string with different input values as arguments in each invocation. Also with sp_executesql you can write safer code, as I will explain later in the chapter. Still, EXEC is more flexible in certain cases, which I will describe in this chapter. So remember that unless you have a compelling reason to use EXEC, stick with using sp_executesql.

Before I delve into EXEC, sp_executesql, and their characteristics and applications, I'd like to briefly mention some important aspects of working with dynamic SQL in general:

- Dynamic SQL requires that the user executing the code have direct permissions to execute it even if the code is within a stored procedure. That is, if you provide a user with EXECUTE permissions on a routine and the routine invokes dynamic code, the user is still required to have direct permissions to run the code that is invoked dynamically. This limitation is relaxed in SQL Server 2005 because in that version of SQL Server you can impersonate the user and allow the code to run under any security context that you like, and that context will apply to all activities. This is achieved by using the new EXECUTE AS clause, which I will describe in Chapter 7.

- Dynamic SQL operates in a batch that is separate from the calling batch. This means that the dynamic batch is parsed, resolved, and optimized as a separate unit. This aspect of dynamic SQL can be a drawback because you end up with another unit of compilation. But when used wisely, it can actually be beneficial to you. I'll demonstrate how you can take advantage of this behavior later in the chapter.

- Environmental settings of the calling batch—such as the database context, session options, and the like—are in effect for all inner levels in the call stack (dynamic batch, stored procedure call, and so on). For example, if you change the database context of a calling batch with the USE *<database_name>* command, the new database context is in effect for a dynamic batch. However, changes made to environmental settings within a dynamic batch are not in effect for outer levels once the dynamic batch goes out of context. I'll demonstrate this behavior later in the chapter.

- Very similar to environmental settings, a local temporary table created in a calling batch is visible to inner levels, including a dynamic batch. However, a local temporary table created in an inner level is not visible to outer levels. As soon as the creating level goes out of scope, the local temporary table is automatically destroyed. For details about this behavior, please refer to Chapter 2.

- Unlike environmental settings and temporary tables, a local variable is visible only to the batch where it was declared. They are not visible to inner levels. I'll also demonstrate this behavior later in the chapter.

So without further ado, let's delve into EXEC, sp_executesql, and the uses of dynamic SQL.

EXEC

The EXEC command (short for EXECUTE) has two uses: one is to execute a stored procedure, and the other is to execute a dynamic batch. The latter gets a character string within parentheses as an input and invokes the code within that character string. In the following section, I'll describe EXEC(<*string*>) and some interesting enhancements introduced in SQL Server 2005 that increase its functionality.

A Simple EXEC Example

As a simple example of using EXEC, the following code returns the count of rows from a given variable table name:

```
SET NOCOUNT ON;
USE Northwind;

DECLARE @schemaname AS NVARCHAR(128), @tablename AS NVARCHAR(128);
SET @schemaname = N'dbo';
SET @tablename = N'Orders';

DECLARE @objectname AS NVARCHAR(517);
SET @objectname = QUOTENAME(@schemaname) + N'.' + QUOTENAME(@tablename);
EXEC(N'SELECT COUNT(*) FROM ' + @objectname + N';');
```

Given the Orders table name as input in the Northwind database, this code returns 830. I constructed the code within the parentheses of the EXEC command, but note that only a string variable, a string literal, or a concatenation of string variables and/or string literals are allowed within the parentheses. You're not allowed to invoke functions or use a CASE expression. For example, the following code, which attempts to invoke the QUOTENAME function within the parentheses to quote object names, fails:

```
DECLARE @schemaname AS NVARCHAR(128), @tablename AS NVARCHAR(128);
SET @schemaname = N'dbo';
SET @tablename = N'Order Details';
EXEC(N'SELECT COUNT(*) FROM '
    + QUOTENAME(@schemaname) + N'.' + QUOTENAME(@tablename) + N';');
```

This code produces the following error:

```
Msg 102, Level 15, State 1, Line 5
Incorrect syntax near 'QUOTENAME'.
```

So it's a good practice to always construct the code in a variable, where such limitations don't apply, and then provide the variable name as input to the EXEC command, as in:

```
DECLARE
  @schemaname AS NVARCHAR(128),
  @tablename AS NVARCHAR(128),
  @sql AS NVARCHAR(539);
SET @schemaname = N'dbo';
SET @tablename = N'Order Details';
SET @sql = N'SELECT COUNT(*) FROM '
  + QUOTENAME(@schemaname) + N'.' + QUOTENAME(@tablename) + N';';
EXEC(@sql);
```

This code returns the output 2155.

EXEC Has No Interface

As I mentioned earlier, EXEC(<*string*>) has no interface. Its only input is a character string with the code that you want to invoke. Remember that a dynamic batch has no access to local variables defined in the calling batch. For example, the following code attempts to access a variable defined in the calling batch and fails:

```
DECLARE @i AS INT;
SET @i = 10248;

DECLARE @sql AS VARCHAR(52);
SET @sql = 'SELECT * FROM dbo.Orders WHERE OrderID = @i;';
EXEC(@sql);
```

This code produces the following error:

```
Msg 137, Level 15, State 2, Line 1
Must declare the scalar variable "@i".
```

Using EXEC, if you want to access the variable, you have to concatenate its contents to the code string you're constructing dynamically:

```
DECLARE @i AS INT;
SET @i = 10248;

DECLARE @sql AS VARCHAR(52);
SET @sql = 'SELECT * FROM dbo.Orders WHERE OrderID = '
  + CAST(@i AS VARCHAR(10)) + N';';
EXEC(@sql);
```

Concatenating the contents of a variable to a code string imposes a security risk (SQL Injection) if the variable contains a character string. One of the measures that you can take to protect against SQL Injection is to limit the size of the code string you're constructing to the minimum required length (52 in this example). Of course, in practice you don't need dynamic SQL at all in such a situation. You could simply use static code and refer to @i in the filter, as in:

```
SELECT * FROM dbo.Orders WHERE OrderID = @i;
```

I've used this simple example just for demonstration purposes. Imagine that other sections of the code are constructed dynamically and cannot be used in a static query.

Concatenating the contents of a variable has its performance drawbacks. SQL Server will create a new ad-hoc execution plan for each unique query string even though the query pattern is the same. To demonstrate this, first clear the execution plans from cache:

```
DBCC FREEPROCCACHE;
```

Then run the dynamic code three times, assigning a different value to @i every time. Use the following three values: 10248, 10249, and 10250. Next query sys.syscacheobjects (or master.dbo.syscacheobjects in SQL Server 2000) using the following code, and then examine the execution plan information you get back, which is shown in Table 4-1:

```
SELECT cacheobjtype, objtype, usecounts, sql
FROM sys.syscacheobjects
WHERE sql NOT LIKE '%cache%'
  AND sql NOT LIKE '%sys.%';
```

Table 4-1   Cached Plans for EXEC

cacheobjtype	objtype	usecounts	sql
Compiled Plan	Adhoc	1	SELECT * FROM dbo.Orders WHERE OrderID = 10250;
Compiled Plan	Adhoc	1	SELECT * FROM dbo.Orders WHERE OrderID = 10249;
Compiled Plan	Adhoc	1	SELECT * FROM dbo.Orders WHERE OrderID = 10248;
Compiled Plan	Prepared	3	(@1 smallint)SELECT * FROM [dbo].[Orders] WHERE [OrderID]=@1

The code invoked dynamically is safe for autoparameterization because the query filters a unique column. Hence, a parameterized plan was created (in the fourth row in the table) and reused. Nevertheless, a separate ad hoc plan was created for each different input so that it can be reused if an identical query string is invoked again. Generating multiple plans has its cost, of course.

In addition to supporting no input parameters in the dynamic batch, EXEC doesn't support output parameters. By default, EXEC returns the output of a query to the caller. For example, the following code returns the distinct count of values in a given column of a given table:

```
DECLARE
  @schemaname AS NVARCHAR(128),
  @tablename  AS NVARCHAR(128),
  @colname    AS NVARCHAR(128),
  @sql        AS NVARCHAR(805);

SET @schemaname = N'dbo';
SET @tablename  = N'Orders';
SET @colname    = N'CustomerID';
SET @sql = N'SELECT COUNT(DISTINCT '
  + QUOTENAME(@colname) + N') FROM '
  + QUOTENAME(@schemaname)
  + N'.'
  + QUOTENAME(@tablename)
  + N';';

EXEC(@sql);
```

Given the *CustomerID* column and the Orders table in the Northwind database as inputs, the output you get is 89. However, things are trickier when you want to return the output to a variable in the calling batch. To achieve this, you must first insert the output to a target table using the INSERT EXEC syntax, and then retrieve the value from the table into the variable, as in:

```
DECLARE
  @schemaname AS NVARCHAR(128),
  @tablename  AS NVARCHAR(128),
  @colname    AS NVARCHAR(128),
  @sql        AS NVARCHAR(805),
  @cnt        AS INT;

SET @schemaname = N'dbo';
SET @tablename  = N'Orders';
SET @colname    = N'CustomerID';
SET @sql = N'SELECT COUNT(DISTINCT '
  + QUOTENAME(@colname) + N') FROM '
  + QUOTENAME(@schemaname)
  + N'.'
  + QUOTENAME(@tablename)
  + N';';

CREATE TABLE #T(cnt INT);
INSERT INTO #T
  EXEC(@sql);
SET @cnt = (SELECT cnt FROM #T);
SELECT @cnt;
DROP TABLE #T;
```

Remember that if you create a temporary table in a calling batch, it is visible to an inner dynamic batch. So you could also create a temporary table first, and insert the value into the temporary table within the dynamic batch using a plain INSERT statement:

```
DECLARE
  @schemaname AS NVARCHAR(128),
  @tablename  AS NVARCHAR(128),
  @colname    AS NVARCHAR(128),
  @sql        AS NVARCHAR(825),
  @cnt        AS INT;

SET @schemaname = N'dbo';
SET @tablename  = N'Orders';
SET @colname    = N'CustomerID';
SET @sql = N'INSERT INTO #T(cnt) SELECT COUNT(DISTINCT '
  + QUOTENAME(@colname) + N') FROM '
  + QUOTENAME(@schemaname)
  + N'.'
  + QUOTENAME(@tablename)
  + N';';

CREATE TABLE #T(cnt INT);
EXEC(@sql);
SET @cnt = (SELECT cnt FROM #T);
SELECT @cnt;
DROP TABLE #T;
```

Concatenating Variables

In SQL Server 2000, EXEC had an advantage over sp_executesql in terms of supporting longer input code. Even though technically sp_executesql's input code string was of an NTEXT datatype, you typically wanted to construct the code string in a local variable. However, you couldn't declare a local variable with a large object type, so practically, query strings executed with sp_executesql were limited to the largest supported length of a Unicode character string (NVARCHAR), which was 4,000 characters. EXEC, on the other hand, supported a regular character (VARCHAR) input code string, allowing up to 8000 characters. Furthermore, EXEC supports a special functionality that allows you to concatenate multiple variables within the parentheses, each up to the maximum supported size of 8000 characters. For example, the following code constructs and invokes a code string that is longer than 8000 characters by concatenating three variables, generating an output with 7999 *A* characters and one *B* character:

```
DECLARE @sql1 AS VARCHAR(8000), @sql2 AS VARCHAR(8000), @sql3 AS VARCHAR(8000);
SET @sql1 = 'PRINT ''';
SET @sql2 = REPLICATE('A', 7999) + 'B';
SET @sql3 = ''';';
EXEC(@sql1 + @sql2 + @sql3);
```

However, this technique is very awkward, and it requires some acrobatics to construct code strings that are longer than 8000 characters. In SQL Server 2005, this technique is no longer necessary because you can provide the EXEC command with a variable defined as VAR-CHAR(MAX) or NVARCHAR(MAX) as input. Now the input string can be up to 2 GB in size, meaning over two billion characters in a VARCHAR(MAX) value, and one billion characters in NVARCHAR(MAX). For example, the following code generates a code string with 10,000 PRINT statements within it, producing a printout of all numbers in the range 1 through 10,000, each in a separate output line:

```
DECLARE @sql AS VARCHAR(MAX), @i AS INT;
SET @sql = '';
SET @i = 1;
WHILE @i <= 10000
BEGIN
  SET @sql = @sql + 'PRINT ' + CAST(@i AS VARCHAR(10))
    + CHAR(13) + CHAR(10);
  SET @i = @i + 1;
END
EXEC(@sql);
```

EXEC AT

SQL Server 2005 introduces the EXEC AT syntax, which allows you to invoke dynamic pass-through code against a linked server. This enhancement addresses several shortcomings of SQL Server 2000 in terms of support for linked servers. In SQL Server 2000, if you wanted to invoke pass-through code against a linked server, using the target server's dialect, you had to use the OPENQUERY table function. OPENQUERY has several limitations: the input query string must be static—it can't be a variable, and it can't accept input arguments. Furthermore, you invoke OPENQUERY in the FROM clause of an outer query, so the function must represent a table. This requirement is very limiting when you just want to invoke executable code against the target server; for example, DDL statements. Similar limitations apply to the OPEN-ROWSET table function. For details about the OPENQUERY and OPENROWSET functions, please refer to Books Online.

All these limitations were addressed by the EXEC command in SQL Server 2005 by using the AT clause. To see the new capabilities, from a SQL Server 2005 instance, create a linked server to another SQL Server instance to which you have access, for example, a local instance of SQL Server Express. I will use a linked server called Dojo in my examples:

```
EXEC sp_addlinkedserver [Dojo], 'SQL Server';
```

The following example shows how you can use input parameters in the input string:

```
EXEC
(
 'SELECT ProductID, ProductName, UnitPrice
FROM Northwind.dbo.Products
WHERE ProductID = ?;', 3
) AT [Dojo];
```

I'm assuming in this example that the Northwind database exists in the target server, and permissions were set to allow access to the target linked server.

EXEC invokes a query against Dojo, which returns the product details of a specified product ID (3 in this case), producing the output shown in Table 4-2.

Table 4-2   Product 3 Details

ProductID	ProductName	UnitPrice
3	Aniseed Syrup	10.00

The question mark is replaced with the specified input value. The input value doesn't have to be a constant; it can be a variable:

```
DECLARE @pid AS INT;
SET @pid = 3;
EXEC
(
 'SELECT ProductID, ProductName, UnitPrice
FROM Northwind.dbo.Products
WHERE ProductID = ?;', @pid
) AT [Dojo];
```

In fact, even the input code string can be a variable, which you construct dynamically:

```
DECLARE @sql AS NVARCHAR(MAX), @pid AS INT;

SET @sql =
 'SELECT ProductID, ProductName, UnitPrice
FROM Northwind.dbo.Products
WHERE ProductID = ?;'
SET @pid = 3;

EXEC(@sql, @pid) AT [Dojo];
```

Furthermore, EXEC doesn't have to return a table result. The following example creates a table called T1 in tempdb at Dojo:

```
EXEC
(
 'USE tempdb;
IF OBJECT_ID(''dbo.T1'') IS NOT NULL
  DROP TABLE dbo.T1;
CREATE TABLE dbo.T1
(
  keycol INT NOT NULL PRIMARY KEY,
  datacol VARCHAR(10) NOT NULL
);'
) AT [Dojo];
```

Remember that the AT clause allows you to invoke pass-through code at a specified linked server. The pass-through code is in the target server's dialect, and the target server type is not limited to SQL Server. It can be any OLEDB or ODBC provider supported as a linked server.

To demonstrate code invoked against a non–SQL Server provider, apply the following:

- Use the sp_addlinkedserver stored procedure to create a linked server called Access-Northwind against a Microsoft Access database.

- For security reasons, use the sp_droplinkedsrvlogin stored procedure to remove the default self-mapping added for all local logins.

- Use the sp_droplinkedsrvlogin stored procedure to map local logins to a security account on the remote server.

- Use the sp_serveroption stored procedure to allow remote procedure calls (RPCs) against the linked server.

> **Note** Note that by enabling RPC, you're increasing the attackable surface area of the target server. I'm turning this setting on for the AccessNorthwind linked server so that the code samples that I'll be demonstrating will work. For details about enabling RPC, please refer to the section "Security for Remote Servers" in Books Online (URL: *ms-help://MS.SQLCC.v9/ MS.SQLSVR.v9.en/udb9/html/03bb3e21-f917-4463-892c-10b1dc13c53a.htm*).

(I'll assume you have the target database installed in the specified folder.) The following code demonstrates this:

```
EXEC sp_addlinkedserver
    @server = 'AccessNorthwind',
    @provider = 'Microsoft.Jet.OLEDB.4.0',
    @srvproduct = 'OLE DB Provider for Jet',
    -- @datasrc may wrap; should appear in one line
    @datasrc = 'c:\program files\microsoft office\office11\samples\northwind.mdb';
GO
-- Remove default self-mapping added for all local logins
EXEC sp_droplinkedsrvlogin 'AccessNorthwind', NULL;
-- Add login mappings
EXEC sp_addlinkedsrvlogin
  'AccessNorthwind', 'false', '<specify_local_login_name_here>', Admin, NULL;
-- Allow RPC out
EXEC sp_serveroption 'AccessNorthwind', 'rpc out', true;
```

The following code invokes a TRANSFORM query against the AccessNorthwind linked server. The query pivots monthly counts of orders per year, including a filter on the *EmployeeID* column based on an input parameter, and it generates the output shown in Table 4-3:

```
EXEC
(
 'TRANSFORM Count(*) AS CountOfOrders
  SELECT  YEAR(OrderDate) AS OrderYear
  FROM Orders
  WHERE EmployeeID = ?
  GROUP BY YEAR(OrderDate)
  PIVOT MONTH(OrderDate);', 3
) AT AccessNorthwind;
```

Table 4-3 Output of TRANSFORM Query Against an Access Database

Order Year	1	2	3	4	5	6	7	8	9	10	11	12
1996	NULL	NULL	NULL	NULL	NULL	NULL	4	2	1	3	4	4
1997	7	9	3	5	5	6	2	4	4	7	8	11
1998	10	6	12	10	NULL	NULL	NULL	NULL	NULL	NULL	NULL	NULL

If you'll allow me to digress a bit, this reminds me of one of Steve Kass's intriguing tricks for overcoming the fact that pivoting in SQL Server is not dynamic. Steve is the technical editor of this book and is well-versed in the principles of logic. Steve once suggested creating a linked server to an Access database, which in turn has a linked table pointing to a SQL Server table. You then issue a TRANSFORM pass-through query against the linked server, which queries your SQL Server table using full dynamic pivoting capabilities. I thought this was quite nifty and original!

Once you're done, remember to drop the T1 table and the linked servers created in this section:

```
EXEC
(
 'USE tempdb;
IF OBJECT_ID(''dbo.T1'') IS NOT NULL
  DROP TABLE dbo.T1;'
) AT [Dojo];
EXEC sp_dropserver [Dojo];
EXEC sp_dropserver [AccessNorthwind];
```

sp_executesql

The sp_executesql command was introduced in SQL Server later than the EXEC command, mainly to provide better support for reusing execution plans. In this section, I'll describe sp_executesql and its enhanced support in SQL Server 2005.

The sp_executesql Interface

The sp_executesql command is more flexible than EXEC(<*string*>) because it has an interface, which supports both input and output parameters. This capability allows you to create query strings with arguments that can reuse execution plans more efficiently than EXEC. The components of sp_executesql are very similar to those of a stored procedure, with the difference being that you construct the code dynamically. Those components include: a batch of code; parameter declaration section; parameter assignment section. The syntax for using sp_executesql is as follows:

```
EXEC sp_executesql
  @stmt = <statement>, -- similar to proc's body
  @params = <params>,  -- similar to proc's params declaration
  <params assignment> -- like in a procedure call
```

The *@stmt* parameter is the input dynamic batch, which can refer to input and output parameters. This section is similar to a stored procedure's body except that *@stmt* can be constructed dynamically, whereas a stored procedure's body is static. In fact, you might want to invoke sp_executesql from a stored procedure's code, whereby you construct the dynamic batch based on user inputs to the stored procedure. The *@params* parameter is similar to the header of a stored procedure, where you define input/output parameters. In fact, the syntax for *@params* is identical to that of a stored procedure's declaration section. You can even define default values to the parameters just as you can with a stored procedure. The *@params* string can also be constructed dynamically. Finally, the *<params assignment>* section is similar to the EXEC part of invoking a stored procedure, in which you assign values to the input/output parameters.

To demonstrate that sp_executesql plan management is superior to that of EXEC, I'll use the same example I showed earlier when discussing EXEC:

```
DECLARE @i AS INT;
SET @i = 10248;

DECLARE @sql AS NVARCHAR(46);
SET @sql = 'SELECT * FROM dbo.Orders WHERE OrderID = @oid;';

EXEC sp_executesql
  @stmt = @sql,
  @params = N'@oid AS INT',
  @oid = @i;
```

Notice that now, instead of concatenating the contents of *@i*, this code defines an input parameter called *@oid*. The code defines *@oid* as an integer input in the *@params* section, and it assigns the contents of *@i* from the calling batch to *@oid* in the *<params assignment>* section.

Before you invoke this code and examine the execution plans it generates, clear the execution plans from cache:

```
DBCC FREEPROCCACHE;
```

Run the dynamic code three times with the following three inputs to the *@i* variable: 10248, 10249, and 10250. Next, query *sys.syscacheobjects* and notice in the output shown in Table 4-4 that only one prepared plan was created and that it was reused three times:

```
SELECT cacheobjtype, objtype, usecounts, sql
FROM sys.syscacheobjects
WHERE sql NOT LIKE '%cache%'
  AND sql NOT LIKE '%sys.%'
  AND sql NOT LIKE '%sp_executesql%';
```

As a reminder, EXEC created three separate ad hoc plans in the same scenario. Now imagine production environments in which the same query pattern is invoked thousands or tens of thousands of times a day, or even more.

Table 4-4   Cached Plans for sp_executesql

cacheobjtype	objtype	usecounts	sql
Compiled Plan	Prepared	3	(@oid AS INT)SELECT * FROM dbo.Orders WHERE OrderID = @oid

Another powerful capability of sp_executesql related to its support for an interface is that it lets you use output parameters to return values to a variable defined in the calling batch. This capability avoids the need to return data through temporary tables, and it results in more efficient code and fewer recompilations. The syntax for defining and using output parameters is identical to that of stored procedures. Namely, you need to declare the parameter specifying the OUTPUT clause and also specify the OUTPUT clause when assigning the parameter with a pointer to a variable defined in the calling batch. For example, the following simplistic code sample demonstrates how to return a value from the dynamic batch, through the output parameter @p to the outer batch's variable @i:

```
DECLARE @sql AS NVARCHAR(12), @i AS INT

SET @sql = N'SET @p = 10;';

EXEC sp_executesql
  @stmt   = @sql,
  @params = N'@p AS INT OUTPUT',
  @p      = @i OUTPUT;

SELECT @i;
```

This code returns the output 10.

You can use sp_executesql's output parameters in many interesting ways. For example, here's a nifty trick I learned from Ron Talmage, who is a SQL Server MVP, a mentor, and a founder of Solid Quality Learning. Suppose that you have a character string stored in a variable called @s that holds hex digits that represent a binary string. You want to convert the character string to a real binary value and store it in a variable called @b. The task is actually much trickier than it seems. If you use simple conversions, you get the binary representation of each character, which is not really what you're after. However, as Ron figured out, you can use sp_executesql's output parameter to assign the string as if it were a binary value to a binary parameter, as demonstrated by the following code:

```
DECLARE @sql AS NVARCHAR(4000),
  @b AS VARBINARY(1000), @s AS VARCHAR(2002);
SET @s = '0x0123456789abcdef';

IF @s NOT LIKE '0x%' OR @s LIKE '0x%[^0-9a-fA-F]%'
BEGIN
  RAISERROR('Possible SQL Injection attempt.', 16, 1);
  RETURN;
END
```

```
SET @sql = N'SET @o = ' + @s + N';';
EXEC sp_executesql
  @stmt = @sql,
  @params = N'@o AS VARBINARY(1000) OUTPUT',
  @o = @b OUTPUT;

SELECT @b;
```

This code first checked for a possible SQL Injection attempt (the input string must be a valid binary string). The code then converted the character string ('0x0123456789ABCDEF' in this example) to the binary value 0x0123456789ABCDEF. Unfortunately, you cannot use this technique to convert a binary value to a character string. SQL Server provides you with a scalar user-defined function (UDF) called fn_varbintohexstr to achieve this:

```
DECLARE @sql AS NVARCHAR(4000),
  @b AS VARBINARY(1000), @s AS VARCHAR(2002);
SET @b = 0x0123456789ABCDEF;
SET @s = sys.fn_varbintohexstr(@b);
SELECT @s;
```

> **Note**   Note that the fn_varbintohexstr function is undocumented and unsupported.

This code converted the binary value 0x0123456789ABCDEF to the character string '0x0123456789ABCDEF'.

Statement Limit

As I mentioned earlier, one of the limitations of sp_executesql in SQL Server 2000 was that the input code string was practically limited to 4000 characters. This limitation is not relevant anymore because you can now provide sp_executesql with an NVARCHAR(MAX) value as input. Note that sp_executesql supports only Unicode input—unlike EXEC which supports both regular character and Unicode input. Earlier I showed code using the EXEC command to construct 10,000 PRINT statements. Here's code that accomplishes the same thing using sp_executesql:

```
DECLARE @sql AS NVARCHAR(MAX), @i AS INT;
SET @sql = N'';
SET @i = 1;
WHILE @i <= 10000
BEGIN
  SET @sql = @sql + N'PRINT ' + CAST(@i AS NVARCHAR(10))
    + NCHAR(13) + NCHAR(10);
  SET @i = @i + 1;
END
EXEC sp_executesql @sql;
```

This code prints numbers in the range 1 through 10,000, each on a separate line.

Environmental Settings

As I mentioned in this chapter's opening section, environmental settings (such as database context and SET options) that are set in a calling batch are in effect for a dynamic batch, but not the other way around. To demonstrate this aspect of environmental settings, the following code sets the database context of a calling batch to Northwind; it invokes a dynamic batch, which changes the database context to an input database name (pubs in this case); and finally, it outputs the database context of the outer batch after the dynamic batch is invoked:

```
USE Northwind;
DECLARE @db AS NVARCHAR(258);
SET @db = QUOTENAME(N'pubs');
EXEC(N'USE ' + @db + ';');
SELECT DB_NAME();
```

Because a change in database context in the inner batch has no effect on an outer batch, the output is Northwind and not pubs. On the other hand, environmental changes in the dynamic batch are in effect for the dynamic batch itself. Therefore, the following code returns the output pubs:

```
USE Northwind;
DECLARE @db AS NVARCHAR(258);
SET @db = QUOTENAME(N'pubs');
EXEC(N'USE ' + @db + N' SELECT DB_NAME();');
```

Similarly, such changes are in effect for levels inner to the dynamic batch, such as a nested level of dynamic SQL:

```
USE Northwind;
DECLARE @db AS NVARCHAR(258);
SET @db = QUOTENAME(N'pubs');
EXEC(N'USE ' + @db + N'; EXEC(''SELECT DB_NAME();'');');
```

The output of this code is also pubs.

Uses of Dynamic SQL

Now that the fundamentals of dynamic SQL, EXEC, and sp_executesql have been covered, this section will demonstrate several ways to apply dynamic SQL.

Dynamic Maintenance Activities

One of the main uses of dynamic SQL is to construct code dynamically for automated maintenance activities such as performing index defragmentation, backups, and the like. You need to query metadata and environmental information and use it to construct the code.

 Caution   Be aware that metadata should be carefully checked for potential SQL Injection attempts (for example, through maliciously named objects).

A classic scenario for automated maintenance code that is constructed dynamically is index defragmentation. You inspect fragmentation information using either DBCC SHOWCONTIG in SQL Server 2000 or *sys.dm_db_index_physical_stats* in SQL Server 2005. You then rebuild or reorganize indexes with a higher level of fragmentation than a certain threshold that you determine as high enough to justify defragmentation. Listing 4-1 has sample code for defragmentation in SQL Server 2005, adapted from Books Online.

Listing 4-1 Dealing with fragmentation, adapted from Books Online

```
-- ensure a USE <databasename> statement has been executed first.
SET NOCOUNT ON;
DECLARE @objectid int;
DECLARE @indexid int;
DECLARE @partitioncount bigint;
DECLARE @schemaname nvarchar(258);
DECLARE @objectname nvarchar(258);
DECLARE @indexname nvarchar(258);
DECLARE @partitionnum bigint;
DECLARE @partitions bigint;
DECLARE @frag float;
DECLARE @command varchar(8000);
-- ensure the temporary table does not exist
IF EXISTS (SELECT name FROM sys.objects WHERE name = 'work_to_do')
    DROP TABLE work_to_do;
-- conditionally select from the function, converting object and index IDs
-- to names.
SELECT
    object_id AS objectid,
    index_id AS indexid,
    partition_number AS partitionnum,
    avg_fragmentation_in_percent AS frag
INTO work_to_do
FROM sys.dm_db_index_physical_stats (DB_ID(), NULL, NULL , NULL, 'LIMITED')
WHERE avg_fragmentation_in_percent > 10.0 AND index_id > 0;
-- Declare the cursor for the list of partitions to be processed.
DECLARE partitions CURSOR FOR SELECT * FROM work_to_do;

-- Open the cursor.
OPEN partitions;

-- Loop through the partitions.
FETCH NEXT
    FROM partitions
    INTO @objectid, @indexid, @partitionnum, @frag;

WHILE @@FETCH_STATUS = 0
    BEGIN;
        SELECT @objectname = QUOTENAME(o.name),
          @schemaname = QUOTENAME(s.name)
        FROM sys.objects AS o
        JOIN sys.schemas as s ON s.schema_id = o.schema_id
        WHERE o.object_id = @objectid;
```

```
        SELECT @indexname = QUOTENAME(name)
        FROM sys.indexes
        WHERE  object_id = @objectid AND index_id = @indexid;

        SELECT @partitioncount = count (*)
        FROM sys.partitions
        WHERE object_id = @objectid AND index_id = @indexid;

-- 30 is an arbitrary decision point at which to switch
-- between reorganizing and rebuilding
IF @frag < 30.0
    BEGIN;
    SELECT @command = 'ALTER INDEX ' + @indexname + ' ON '
        + @schemaname + '.' + @objectname + ' REORGANIZE';
    IF @partitioncount > 1
        SELECT @command = @command + ' PARTITION='
            + CONVERT (CHAR, @partitionnum);
    EXEC (@command);
    END;

IF @frag >= 30.0
    BEGIN;
    SELECT @command = 'ALTER INDEX ' + @indexname +' ON ' + @schemaname
        + '.' + @objectname + ' REBUILD';
    IF @partitioncount > 1
        SELECT @command = @command + ' PARTITION='
            + CONVERT (CHAR, @partitionnum);
    EXEC (@command);
    END;
PRINT 'Executed ' + @command;

FETCH NEXT FROM partitions INTO @objectid, @indexid, @partitionnum, @frag;
END;
-- Close and deallocate the cursor.
CLOSE partitions;
DEALLOCATE partitions;

-- drop the temporary table
IF EXISTS (SELECT name FROM sys.objects WHERE name = 'work_to_do')
    DROP TABLE work_to_do;
GO
```

 Note This code uses EXEC and not sp_executesql. Remember that sp_executesql is mainly beneficial for better reuse of execution plans. Because the maintenance activities invoked dynamically here don't involve querying, plan reuse is not really an issue.

This code defragments indexes in the current database that have a fragmentation level (expressed in code as *avg_fragmentation_in_percent*) greater than 10 percent. If the fragmentation level is greater than 10 percent and less than 30 percent, this code constructs and invokes an index reorganize operation. If the fragmentation level is greater than or equal to 30 percent, it invokes a full index rebuild operation. These are arbitrary numbers that were chosen for demonstration purposes. You should use your own thresholds based on the performance of the queries and the maintenance window that you have available.

> **Note** In SQL Server 2005, you can issue online index operations.

Storing Computations

The support that sp_executesql has for output parameters allows you to create very interesting applications. For example, a customer of mine who develops software for salary calculations once asked me to evaluate T-SQL expression strings dynamically. The company had a table that contained several inputs for a calculation in several columns, and they had a T-SQL expression that referred to those inputs in another column. Each row represented the salary computation of a particular employee, and the row could contain a salary computation that was different from other rows based on the employee's contract.

To provide for this need, you can create a trigger on the table for INSERT and UPDATE statements. The trigger will read the input arguments and the computation from the inserted view for each row, run sp_executesql to return the result of the computation through an output parameter to a local variable defined in the trigger, and use an UPDATE statement to store the result in a result column in the table. Taking this approach would make the table resemble a Microsoft Office Excel spreadsheet.

Here I'll represent the problem in more generic terms. To demonstrate the technique, first run the code in Listing 4-2 to create the Computations table.

Listing 4-2   Creating the Computations table

```
USE tempdb;
GO
IF OBJECT_ID('dbo.Computations') IS NOT NULL
  DROP TABLE dbo.Computations;
GO

CREATE TABLE dbo.Computations
(
  keycol      INT           NOT NULL IDENTITY PRIMARY KEY,
  arg1        INT           NULL,
  arg2        INT           NULL,
  arg3        INT           NULL,
  computation VARCHAR(4000) NOT NULL,
  result      INT           NULL,
  CONSTRAINT CHK_Computations_SQL_Injection
    CHECK (REPLACE(computation,'@arg','') NOT LIKE '%[^0-9.+/* -]%')
);
```

The columns *arg1*, *arg2*, and *arg3* will hold the input arguments for the computation. The *computation* column will hold T-SQL expressions that refer to the inputs using an @ symbol in front of each argument (for example, *@arg1* would stand for the value in *arg1*). Examples of expressions are as follows: '*@arg1* + *@arg2* + *@arg3*', '*@arg1* * *@arg2* − *@arg3*', ' 2. * *@arg2* / *@arg1*', or any other valid T-SQL expression that yields a scalar value as a result. A CHECK constraint is defined on the *computation* column to protect against SQL Injection attempts. The constraint allows only arguments (@arg), digits, dots and basic arithmetic operations; you may want to revise the constraint based on your needs, but bear in mind that the more you "relax" the constraint, the greater is the risk that SQL Injection attempts will succeed. The trigger should evaluate the expression from each modified row and store the result value in the result column.

Run the code in Listing 4-3 to create the trg_Computations_iu_calc_result trigger.

Listing 4-3   Trigger that calculates the result of the computations

```
CREATE TRIGGER trg_Computations_iu_calc_result
  ON dbo.Computations FOR INSERT, UPDATE
AS

DECLARE @rc AS INT;
SET @rc = @@rowcount;

-- If no rows affected, return
IF @rc = 0 RETURN;

-- If none of the columns: arg1, arg2, arg3, computation
-- were updated, return
IF COLUMNS_UPDATED() & 30 /* 00011110 binary */ = 0 RETURN;

-- Not allowed to update result
IF    EXISTS(SELECT * FROM inserted)
  AND EXISTS(SELECT * FROM deleted)
  AND UPDATE(result)
BEGIN
  RAISERROR('Not allowed to update result.', 16, 1);
  ROLLBACK;
  RETURN;
END

DECLARE
  @key        AS INT,                 -- keycol
  @in_arg1    AS INT,                 -- arg1
  @in_arg2    AS INT,                 -- arg2
  @in_arg3    AS INT,                 -- arg3
  @out_result AS INT,                 -- result of computation
  @comp       AS NVARCHAR(4000), -- computation
  @params     AS NVARCHAR(100);  -- parameter's list for sp_executesql

-- If only one row was inserted, don't use a cursor
IF @rc = 1
BEGIN
  -- Grab values from inserted
  SELECT @key = keycol, @in_arg1 = arg1, @in_arg2 = arg2,
    @in_arg3 = arg3, @comp = N'SET @result = ' + computation
  FROM inserted;
```

```
  -- Generate a string with the in/out parameters
  SET @params = N'@result INT output, @arg1 INT, @arg2 INT, @arg3 INT';

  -- Calculate computation and store the result in @out_result
  EXEC sp_executesql
    @comp,
    @params,
    @result = @out_result output,
    @arg1   = @in_arg1,
    @arg2   = @in_arg2,
    @arg3   = @in_arg3;

  -- Update the result column in the row with the current key
  UPDATE dbo.Computations
    SET result = @out_result
  WHERE keycol = @key;
END
-- If only multiple rows were inserted, use a cursor
ELSE
BEGIN
  -- Loop through all keys in inserted
  DECLARE CInserted CURSOR FAST_FORWARD FOR
    SELECT keycol, arg1, arg2, arg3, N'SET @result = ' + computation
    FROM inserted;

  OPEN CInserted;

  -- Get first row from inserted
  FETCH NEXT FROM CInserted
    INTO @key, @in_arg1, @in_arg2, @in_arg3, @comp ;

  WHILE @@fetch_status = 0
  BEGIN

    -- Generate a string with the in/out parameters
    SET @params = N'@result INT output, @arg1 INT, @arg2 INT, @arg3 INT';

    -- Calculate computation and store the result in @out_result
    EXEC sp_executesql
      @comp,
      @params,
      @result = @out_result output,
      @arg1   = @in_arg1,
      @arg2   = @in_arg2,
      @arg3   = @in_arg3;

    -- Update the result column in the row with the current key
    UPDATE dbo.Computations
      SET result = @out_result
    WHERE keycol = @key;

    -- Get next row from inserted
    FETCH NEXT FROM CInserted
      INTO @key, @in_arg1, @in_arg2, @in_arg3, @comp;
END
```

```
    CLOSE CInserted;
    DEALLOCATE CInserted;
  END
  GO
```

The trigger first evaluates the number of rows that were affected by the firing statement (INSERT or UPDATE). If zero rows were modified, the trigger simply terminates. It has nothing to do in such a case. The trigger then checks whether one of the four relevant columns (*arg1, arg2, arg3, computation*) was modified using the COLUMNS_UPDATED() function. I will describe this function in more detail in Chapter 8. This function returns a bitmap with a representative bit for each column. For an UPDATE statement, the bit is turned on if the corresponding column was specified in the SET clause, and it's turned off if the corresponding column wasn't specified in the SET clause. For an INSERT statement, all column bits are turned on. If none of the relevant columns were modified, the trigger simply terminates. It has no reason to reevaluate the computation if neither the inputs nor the computation changed. If the statement that fired the trigger was an UPDATE statement, and the column *result* was modified, the trigger generates an error message and rolls back the update.

The trigger defines local variables to host the input arguments, the computation, and the result value. Each row must be handled separately, so a cursor is needed if there is more than one row.

For each modified row, the trigger reads the inputs and the computation into its local variables. Notice that the trigger adds a prefix to the computation: *N'SET @result = '+ computation*. This is a very important trick that allows you to return the result of the computation back to the trigger's local variable (*@out_result*) through an output parameter (*@result*). After reading the inputs and the computation from the current row into the trigger's local variables, the code invokes sp_executesql to evaluate the expression and store it in *@out_result* through the output parameter *@result*:

```
EXEC sp_executesql
  @comp,
  @params,
  @result = @out_result output,
  @arg1   = @in_arg1,
  @arg2   = @in_arg2,
  @arg3   = @in_arg3;
```

Now that the result is stored in the *@result* variable, the trigger updates the corresponding row in the Computations table with the result value.

To test the trigger, issue the following INSERT statements and query the Computations table:

```
INSERT INTO dbo.Computations(arg1, arg2, arg3, computation)
  VALUES(1, 2, 3, '@arg1 + @arg2 + @arg3');
INSERT INTO dbo.Computations(arg1, arg2, arg3, computation)
  VALUES(4, 5, 6, '@arg1 * @arg2 - @arg3');
INSERT INTO dbo.Computations(arg1, arg2, computation)
  VALUES(7, 8, '2. * @arg2 / @arg1');
SELECT * FROM dbo.Computations;
```

You get the output shown in Table 4-5.

Table 4-5   Contents of Computations Table After Inserts

keycol	arg1	arg2	arg3	computation	result
1	1	2	3	@arg1 + @arg2 + @arg3	6
2	4	5	6	@arg1 * @arg2 - @arg3	14
3	7	8	NULL	2. * @arg2 / @arg1	2

Next issue an UPDATE statement that changes the *arg1* values in all rows, and then query the table again:

```
UPDATE dbo.Computations SET arg1 = arg1 * 2;
SELECT * FROM dbo.Computations;
```

You can see the contents of Computations after the update in Table 4-6, and observe that the change is reflected correctly in the result column.

Table 4-6   Contents of Computations Table After Inserts

keycol	arg1	arg2	arg3	computation	result
1	2	2	3	@arg1 + @arg2 + @arg3	7
2	8	5	6	@arg1 * @arg2 - @arg3	34
3	14	8	NULL	2. * @arg2 / @arg1	1

Bear in mind that dynamic SQL is used to run code that is constructed, among other things, from the *computation* column values. I added a CHECK constraint to guard against common strings used in SQL Injection; but as I mentioned earlier, it's almost impossible to guarantee that all cases are covered. There are alternatives to this solution that do not use dynamic SQL. For strings with limited complexity, this can be done in a UDF as shown at *http:// www.users.drew.edu/skass/sql/infix.sql.txt*. A CLR function could also be used to evaluate the expression. If the expression result is given by a UDF, then this example can be much less complex, because the result can be defined as a persisted computed column, and no trigger will be required. It will also not be a security risk from dynamic SQL. Allowing complete flexibility to include SQL expressions in the calculation string is a priority that competes with security, because validation that a string represents only an expression can be done with a T-SQL parser.

Dynamic Filters

Another important use of dynamic SQL is supporting applications that allow users to choose dynamic filters and sorting, which is very typical of many Web applications. For example, paging applications typically need to support dynamic filtering and sorting requests. You can achieve this by using dynamic SQL, but of course you should consider seriously the risk of SQL Injection in your solutions.

Note that static query solutions are available for dynamic filtering and sorting; however, these typically produce very inefficient plans that result in slow-running queries. By using dynamic SQL wisely, you can get efficient plans, and if you define the inputs as parameters, you can even get efficient reuse of execution plans.

In my examples, for simplicity's sake I'll demonstrate dynamic filters based on equality operators. Of course, you can apply more complex filtering logic with other operators, and you can also accomplish dynamic sorting in a similar manner by constructing the ORDER BY clause dynamically.

Suppose that you're given a task to write a stored procedure that returns orders from the Orders table, providing optional filters on various order attributes. You create and populate the Orders table by running the code in Listing 4-4.

Listing 4-4   Script that creates and populates the Orders table

```
SET NOCOUNT ON;
USE tempdb;
GO
IF OBJECT_ID('dbo.usp_GetOrders') IS NOT NULL
  DROP PROC dbo.usp_GetOrders;
IF OBJECT_ID('dbo.Orders') IS NOT NULL
  DROP TABLE dbo.Orders;
GO

CREATE TABLE dbo.Orders
(
  OrderID    INT        NOT NULL,
  CustomerID NCHAR(5)   NOT NULL,
  EmployeeID INT        NOT NULL,
  OrderDate  DATETIME   NOT NULL,
  filler     CHAR(2000) NOT NULL DEFAULT('A')
)

INSERT INTO dbo.Orders(OrderID, CustomerID, EmployeeID, OrderDate)
  SELECT OrderID, CustomerID, EmployeeID, OrderDate
  FROM Northwind.dbo.Orders;

CREATE CLUSTERED INDEX idx_OrderDate ON dbo.Orders(OrderDate);
CREATE UNIQUE INDEX idx_OrderID ON dbo.Orders(OrderID);
CREATE INDEX idx_CustomerID ON dbo.Orders(CustomerID);
CREATE INDEX idx_EmployeeID ON dbo.Orders(EmployeeID);
```

Write a stored procedure that queries and filters orders based on user inputs. The stored procedure should have a parameter for each of the order attributes: *OrderID*, *CustomerID*, *EmployeeID*, and *OrderDate*. All parameters should have a default value NULL. If a parameter was assigned with a value, your stored procedure should filter the rows in which the corresponding column is equal to the parameter's value; otherwise (parameter is NULL), the parameter should simply be ignored. Note that all four columns in the Orders table were defined as NOT

NULL, so you can rely on this fact in your solutions. Here's one common solution that uses static code:

```
CREATE PROC dbo.usp_GetOrders
  @OrderID    AS INT      = NULL,
  @CustomerID AS NCHAR(5) = NULL,
  @EmployeeID AS INT      = NULL,
  @OrderDate  AS DATETIME = NULL
WITH RECOMPILE
AS

SELECT OrderID, CustomerID, EmployeeID, OrderDate, filler
FROM dbo.Orders
WHERE (OrderID    = @OrderID    OR @OrderID    IS NULL)
  AND (CustomerID = @CustomerID OR @CustomerID IS NULL)
  AND (EmployeeID = @EmployeeID OR @EmployeeID IS NULL)
  AND (OrderDate  = @OrderDate  OR @OrderDate  IS NULL);
GO
```

I created the stored procedure with the RECOMPILE option to generate a new execution plan whenever the code is run. Without the RECOMPILE option, regardless of the inputs, the stored procedure would reuse the cached execution plan generated for the first invocation, which is not a good idea in this case.

The main trick here is to use the following expression for each input:

```
(<col> = <@parameter> OR <@parameter> IS NULL)
```

If a value is specified for *<@parameter>*, then *<@parameter> IS NULL* is false, and the expression is equivalent to *<col> = <@parameter>* alone. If a value is not specified for *<@parameter>*, it will be NULL, and *<@parameter> IS NULL* will be true, making the whole expression true.

The problem with this implementation is that it produces inefficient plans. The optimizer doesn't have the capability to create different branches of a plan, where each branch represents a completely different course of action based on whether a parameter contains a known value or a NULL. Remember that the stored procedure was created with the RECOMPILE option, meaning that for each invocation of the stored procedure the optimizer generated a plan that it perceived as adequate for the given inputs. Still, the plans that the optimizer generated were inefficient. Run the following code, which invokes the stored procedure with different arguments:

```
EXEC dbo.usp_GetOrders @OrderID = 10248;
EXEC dbo.usp_GetOrders @OrderDate = '19970101';
EXEC dbo.usp_GetOrders @CustomerID = N'CENTC';
EXEC dbo.usp_GetOrders @EmployeeID = 5;
```

Of course, you can specify more than one argument. The optimizer generates the plans shown in Figure 4-1 for the above invocations of the procedure.

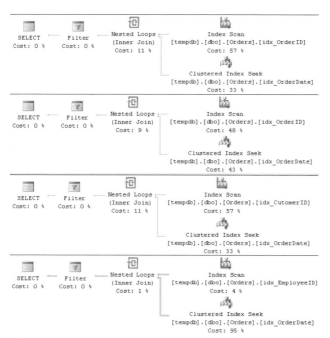

Figure 4-1   Execution plans for stored procedure usp_GetOrders, static version 1

For the first invocation of the stored procedure where the *OrderID* column is being filtered, you would expect the plan to show an Index Seek operation in the index *idx_OrderID*, followed by a lookup. For the second invocation of the stored procedure where the *OrderDate* column is being filtered, you would expect to see an Index Seek operation within the index *idx_OrderDate*. But that's not what you get; rather, all plans follow similar logic. First, instead of performing an efficient seek operation within the index created on the column that is being filtered, the plans perform a full scan of the leaf level of an index that contains the filtered value specified. It then performs seek operations to look up the qualifying rows within the clustered index. Finally, the plan filters the rows based on the rest of the filters. If you run this code against a much larger test table, you'll see a high I/O cost due to the index scans.

Here's another common implementation of dynamic filters using static code:

```
ALTER PROC dbo.usp_GetOrders
  @OrderID    AS INT       = NULL,
  @CustomerID AS NCHAR(5) = NULL,
  @EmployeeID AS INT       = NULL,
  @OrderDate  AS DATETIME = NULL
WITH RECOMPILE
AS

SELECT OrderID, CustomerID, EmployeeID, OrderDate, filler
FROM dbo.Orders
WHERE OrderID    = COALESCE(@OrderID,    OrderID)
  AND CustomerID = COALESCE(@CustomerID, CustomerID)
  AND EmployeeID = COALESCE(@EmployeeID, EmployeeID)
  AND OrderDate  = COALESCE(@OrderDate,  OrderDate);
GO
```

The trick here is to use the following expression for each parameter:

```
<col> = COALESCE(<@parameter>, <col>)
```

If a value is specified, COALESCE returns that value. If a value isn't specified, COALESCE returns <col>, in which case the expression <col> = COALESCE(<@parameter>, <col>) will be true (assuming that the column doesn't allow NULLs). If you rerun the test code, which invokes the stored procedure four times, you will see that all invocations get the same plan, which is shown in Figure 4-2.

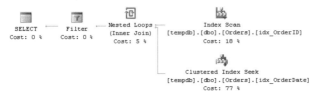

Figure 4-2   Execution plan for stored procedure usp_GetOrders, static version 2

This plan is even worse than the previous one. It follows similar logic as the previous plan, but this time it always: scans the index on *OrderID* and applies the *OrderDate* and *OrderID* filters during that scan, looks up the qualifying rows in the clustered index, and applies the rest of the filters. Again, the index scan operation plus a large number of lookups before further filtering yield a high I/O cost and result in poorly performing code.

By using dynamic SQL, you address two problems. First, you will get efficient plans. Second, the dynamic batch will be able to reuse execution plans when given the same combination of arguments. Listing 4-5 shows a stored procedure implementation that uses dynamic SQL.

Listing 4-5   Stored procedure *usp_GetOrders*, dynamic code

```
ALTER PROC dbo.usp_GetOrders
   @OrderID    AS INT      = NULL,
   @CustomerID AS NCHAR(5) = NULL,
   @EmployeeID AS INT      = NULL,
   @OrderDate  AS DATETIME = NULL
AS

DECLARE @sql AS NVARCHAR(4000);

SET @sql =
    N'SELECT OrderID, CustomerID, EmployeeID, OrderDate, filler'
  + N' FROM dbo.Orders'
  + N' WHERE 1 = 1'
  + CASE WHEN @OrderID IS NOT NULL THEN
       N' AND OrderID = @oid' ELSE N'' END
  + CASE WHEN @CustomerID IS NOT NULL THEN
       N' AND CustomerID = @cid' ELSE N'' END
  + CASE WHEN @EmployeeID IS NOT NULL THEN
       N' AND EmployeeID = @eid' ELSE N'' END
  + CASE WHEN @OrderDate IS NOT NULL THEN
       N' AND OrderDate = @dt' ELSE N'' END;
```

```
EXEC sp_executesql
  @sql,
  N'@oid AS INT, @cid AS NCHAR(5), @eid AS INT, @dt AS DATETIME',
  @oid = @OrderID,
  @cid = @CustomerID,
  @eid = @EmployeeID,
  @dt  = @OrderDate;
GO
```

You can see that an expression involving a filter on a certain column is concatenated only if a value was specified in the corresponding parameter. The expression 1=1 prevents you from needing to determine dynamically whether to specify a WHERE clause at all when no input is specified. This expression has no effect on performance because the optimizer realizes that it always evaluates to TRUE, and therefore, it's neutral. Notice that the procedure was not created with the RECOMPILE option. There's no need for it here because the dynamic batch will naturally reuse a plan when given the same list of arguments. It does this because the query string that will be constructed is the same. You can easily observe the efficient plan reuse here by querying sys.syscacheobjects.

Run the test code, which invokes the stored procedure four times, and observe the desired efficient plans shown in Figure 4-3.

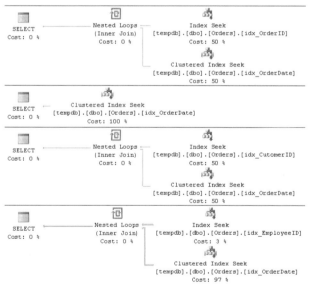

Figure 4-3   Execution plan for stored procedure usp_GetOrders, dynamic version

Each plan is different and is optimal for the given inputs. And, as I mentioned earlier, multiple invocations with the same argument list will efficiently reuse previously cached parameterized execution plans.

Tip Another solution to dynamic filters is to generate multiple stored procedures that invoke static code—one for each possible set of filtered columns. This solution is actually ideal in that it has no security risks, produces efficient plans, and reuses execution plans. In fact, you can use dynamic SQL to generate the different static stored procedures. The number of procedures you need to generate for n parameters is 2^n. This solution is realistic when you have a small number of parameters. For example, with four parameters you must create 16 procedures. However, with a large number of parameters, you'll end up with an unwieldy number of stored procedures.

Dynamic PIVOT/UNPIVOT

Pivot queries rotate data from a state of rows to columns, and unpivot queries rotate data from a state of columns to rows. I covered pivoting and unpivoting techniques in *Inside T-SQL Querying*. In both SQL Server 2000 and 2005, static pivot and unpivot queries could not handle an unknown number of elements that must be rotated. I'll show you how to deal with an unknown number of elements by using dynamic SQL. In my examples, I'll use a table called Orders. Run the code in Listing 4-6 to create the Orders table and populate it with sample data.

Listing 4-6 Creating and populating the Orders table

```
USE tempdb;
GO

IF OBJECT_ID('dbo.Orders') IS NOT NULL
  DROP TABLE dbo.Orders;
GO

CREATE TABLE dbo.Orders
(
  orderid   int        NOT NULL PRIMARY KEY NONCLUSTERED,
  orderdate datetime   NOT NULL,
  empid     int        NOT NULL,
  custid    varchar(5) NOT NULL,
  qty       int        NOT NULL
);

CREATE UNIQUE CLUSTERED INDEX idx_orderdate_orderid
  ON dbo.Orders(orderdate, orderid);

INSERT INTO dbo.Orders(orderid, orderdate, empid, custid, qty)
  VALUES(30001, '20020802', 3, 'A', 10);
INSERT INTO dbo.Orders(orderid, orderdate, empid, custid, qty)
  VALUES(10001, '20021224', 1, 'A', 12);
INSERT INTO dbo.Orders(orderid, orderdate, empid, custid, qty)
  VALUES(10005, '20021224', 1, 'B', 20);
INSERT INTO dbo.Orders(orderid, orderdate, empid, custid, qty)
  VALUES(40001, '20030109', 4, 'A', 40);
INSERT INTO dbo.Orders(orderid, orderdate, empid, custid, qty)
  VALUES(10006, '20030118', 1, 'C', 14);
```

```
INSERT INTO dbo.Orders(orderid, orderdate, empid, custid, qty)
  VALUES(20001, '20030212', 2, 'B', 12);
INSERT INTO dbo.Orders(orderid, orderdate, empid, custid, qty)
  VALUES(40005, '20040212', 4, 'A', 10);
INSERT INTO dbo.Orders(orderid, orderdate, empid, custid, qty)
  VALUES(20002, '20040216', 2, 'C', 20);
INSERT INTO dbo.Orders(orderid, orderdate, empid, custid, qty)
  VALUES(30003, '20040418', 3, 'B', 15);
INSERT INTO dbo.Orders(orderid, orderdate, empid, custid, qty)
  VALUES(30004, '20020418', 3, 'C', 22);
INSERT INTO dbo.Orders(orderid, orderdate, empid, custid, qty)
  VALUES(30007, '20020907', 3, 'D', 30);
GO
```

The following static PIVOT query returns yearly total order quantities per customer, returning a row for each customer and a column for each year, and it generates the output shown in Table 4-7:

```
SELECT custid,
  SUM(CASE WHEN orderyear = 2002 THEN qty END) AS [2002],
  SUM(CASE WHEN orderyear = 2003 THEN qty END) AS [2003],
  SUM(CASE WHEN orderyear = 2004 THEN qty END) AS [2004]
FROM (SELECT custid, YEAR(orderdate) AS orderyear, qty
      FROM dbo.Orders) AS D
GROUP BY custid;
```

Table 4-7   Result of PIVOT Query

custid	2002	2003	2004
A	22	40	10
B	20	12	15
C	22	14	20
D	30	NULL	NULL

The preceding solution is SQL Server 2000 compatible. When using a static query, you have to know in advance which items you want to rotate. Listing 4-7 shows the dynamic solution that rotates all years that exist in the Orders table without knowing them in advance.

Listing 4-7   Dynamic pivot, pre-2005

```
DECLARE @T AS TABLE(y INT NOT NULL PRIMARY KEY);

DECLARE
  @cols AS NVARCHAR(MAX),
  @y    AS INT,
  @sql  AS NVARCHAR(MAX);

-- Populate @T with distinct list of years (result columns)
INSERT INTO @T SELECT DISTINCT YEAR(orderdate) FROM dbo.Orders;
```

```
-- Construct the expression list for the SELECT clause
SET @y = (SELECT MIN(y) FROM @T);
SET @cols = N' ';
WHILE @y IS NOT NULL
BEGIN
  SET @cols = @cols
    + N',' + NCHAR(13) + NCHAR(10)
    + N'  SUM(CASE WHEN orderyear = '
    + CAST(@y AS NVARCHAR(4))
    + N' THEN qty END) AS ' + QUOTENAME(@y);

  SET @y = (SELECT MIN(y) FROM @T WHERE y > @y);
END
SET @cols = SUBSTRING(@cols, 2, LEN(@cols));

-- Check @cols for possible SQL Injection attempt
-- Use when example is extended to concatenating strings
-- (not required in this particular example
--   since concatenated elements are integers)
IF   UPPER(@cols) LIKE UPPER(N'%0x%')
  OR UPPER(@cols) LIKE UPPER(N'%;%')
  OR UPPER(@cols) LIKE UPPER(N'%''%')
  OR UPPER(@cols) LIKE UPPER(N'%--%')
  OR UPPER(@cols) LIKE UPPER(N'%/*%*/%')
  OR UPPER(@cols) LIKE UPPER(N'%EXEC%')
  OR UPPER(@cols) LIKE UPPER(N'%xp_%')
  OR UPPER(@cols) LIKE UPPER(N'%sp_%')
  OR UPPER(@cols) LIKE UPPER(N'%SELECT%')
  OR UPPER(@cols) LIKE UPPER(N'%INSERT%')
  OR UPPER(@cols) LIKE UPPER(N'%UPDATE%')
  OR UPPER(@cols) LIKE UPPER(N'%DELETE%')
  OR UPPER(@cols) LIKE UPPER(N'%TRUNCATE%')
  OR UPPER(@cols) LIKE UPPER(N'%CREATE%')
  OR UPPER(@cols) LIKE UPPER(N'%ALTER%')
  OR UPPER(@cols) LIKE UPPER(N'%DROP%')
  -- look for other possible strings used in SQL Injection here
BEGIN
  RAISERROR('Possible SQL Injection attempt.', 16, 1);
  RETURN;
END

-- Construct the full T-SQL statement
-- and execute dynamically
SET @sql = N'SELECT custid' + @cols + N'
FROM (SELECT custid, YEAR(orderdate) AS orderyear, qty
      FROM dbo.Orders) AS D
GROUP BY custid;';

EXEC sp_executesql @sql;
```

The trick here is to construct the series of CASE expressions in the SELECT list dynamically based on a loop against the table variable (@T) to which you loaded the distinct list of years.

> **Caution**   Note that whenever constructing code from user input—be it direct user input, or data from a table (like in our case)—such code is susceptible to SQL Injection attacks. In our example, we're constructing code from integer values (years), so the risk is lower; but bear in mind that when you extend this technique to concatenate character strings, the risk is great. I added validation of the string generated in *@cols* assuming that you might extend the example to character strings. Still, remember that sophisticated hackers will always find ways to circumvent your validations, so never assume that your code is completely safe.

As for SQL Server 2005, following is the static query version of the solution using the native PIVOT operator:

```
SELECT *
FROM (SELECT custid, YEAR(orderdate) AS orderyear, qty
      FROM dbo.Orders) AS D
  PIVOT(SUM(qty) FOR orderyear IN([2002],[2003],[2004])) AS P;
```

To support an unknown list of years, you must construct the list of columns served as input to the IN clause dynamically, as shown in Listing 4-8.

Listing 4-8   Dynamic PIVOT, 2005

```
DECLARE @T AS TABLE(y INT NOT NULL PRIMARY KEY);

DECLARE
  @cols AS NVARCHAR(MAX),
  @y    AS INT,
  @sql  AS NVARCHAR(MAX);

-- Construct the column list for the IN clause
-- e.g., [2002],[2003],[2004]
SET @cols = STUFF(
  (SELECT N',' + QUOTENAME(y) AS [text()]
   FROM (SELECT DISTINCT YEAR(orderdate) AS y FROM dbo.Orders) AS Y
   ORDER BY y
   FOR XML PATH('')),
  1, 1, N'');

-- Check @cols for possible SQL Injection attempt
-- Use when example is extended to concatenating strings
-- (not required in this particular example
--  since concatenated elements are integers)
IF   UPPER(@cols) LIKE UPPER(N'%0x%')
  OR UPPER(@cols) LIKE UPPER(N'%;%')
  OR UPPER(@cols) LIKE UPPER(N'%''%')
  OR UPPER(@cols) LIKE UPPER(N'%--%')
  OR UPPER(@cols) LIKE UPPER(N'%/*%*/%')
  OR UPPER(@cols) LIKE UPPER(N'%EXEC%')
  OR UPPER(@cols) LIKE UPPER(N'%xp_%')
  OR UPPER(@cols) LIKE UPPER(N'%sp_%')
  OR UPPER(@cols) LIKE UPPER(N'%SELECT%')
  OR UPPER(@cols) LIKE UPPER(N'%INSERT%')
  OR UPPER(@cols) LIKE UPPER(N'%UPDATE%')
```

```
    OR UPPER(@cols) LIKE UPPER(N'%DELETE%')
    OR UPPER(@cols) LIKE UPPER(N'%TRUNCATE%')
    OR UPPER(@cols) LIKE UPPER(N'%CREATE%')
    OR UPPER(@cols) LIKE UPPER(N'%ALTER%')
    OR UPPER(@cols) LIKE UPPER(N'%DROP%')
    -- look for other possible strings used in SQL Injection here
BEGIN
    RAISERROR('Possible SQL Injection attempt.', 16, 1);
    RETURN;
END

-- Construct the full T-SQL statement
-- and execute dynamically
SET @sql = N'SELECT *
FROM (SELECT custid, YEAR(orderdate) AS orderyear, qty
      FROM dbo.Orders) AS D
  PIVOT(SUM(qty) FOR orderyear IN(' + @cols + N')) AS P;';

EXEC sp_executesql @sql;
```

Notice also that I used an improved technique to concatenate strings using the FOR XML PATH option. I described this efficient technique in Chapter 2.

In a similar manner, you can support dynamic unpivoting. To see how the technique works, first run the code in Listing 4-9, which creates and populates the PvtCustOrders table with pivoted total yearly quantities per customer.

Listing 4-9   Creating and populating the PvtCustOrders table

```
USE tempdb;
GO
IF OBJECT_ID('dbo.PvtCustOrders') IS NOT NULL
  DROP TABLE dbo.PvtCustOrders;
GO

SELECT *
INTO dbo.PvtCustOrders
FROM (SELECT custid, YEAR(orderdate) AS orderyear, qty
      FROM dbo.Orders) AS D
  PIVOT(SUM(qty) FOR orderyear IN([2002],[2003],[2004])) AS P;
```

I will show a solution in SQL Server 2005 because the concept is similar in both versions. The only significant difference is that you construct different expressions dynamically since SQL Server 2005 now has a native UNPIVOT operator. Here's the static query that unpivots the rows in such a way that the result will contain a row for each customer and year, and that generates the output shown in Table 4-8:

```
SELECT custid, orderyear, qty
FROM dbo.PvtCustOrders
  UNPIVOT(qty FOR orderyear IN([2002],[2003],[2004])) AS U;
```

Table 4-8   **Result of UNPIVOT Query**

custid	orderyear	qty
A	2002	22
A	2003	40
A	2004	10
B	2002	20
B	2003	12
B	2004	15
C	2002	22
C	2003	14
C	2004	20
D	2002	30

To make the solution dynamic, you use code similar to the pivoting code shown in Listing 4-10.

Listing 4-10   Dynamic UNPIVOT, SQL Server 2005 version

```
DECLARE @T AS TABLE(y INT NOT NULL PRIMARY KEY);

DECLARE
  @cols AS NVARCHAR(MAX),
  @sql  AS NVARCHAR(MAX);

-- Construct the column list for the IN clause
-- e.g., [2002],[2003],[2004]
SET @cols = STUFF(
  (SELECT N','+ QUOTENAME(y) AS [text()]
   FROM (SELECT COLUMN_NAME AS y
         FROM INFORMATION_SCHEMA.COLUMNS
         WHERE TABLE_SCHEMA = N'dbo'
           AND TABLE_NAME = N'PvtCustOrders'
           AND COLUMN_NAME NOT IN(N'custid')) AS Y
   ORDER BY y
   FOR XML PATH('')),
  1, 1, N'');

-- Construct the full T-SQL statement
-- and execute dynamically
SET @sql = N'SELECT custid, orderyear, qty
FROM dbo.PvtCustOrders
  UNPIVOT(qty FOR orderyear IN(' + @cols + N')) AS U;';

EXEC sp_executesql @sql;
```

Here, instead of querying the attribute list from the data table, you query the column list from the INFORMATION_SCHEMA.COLUMNS view.

SQL Injection

One of the greatest security risks and causes of great damage to computerized systems is a hacking technique called SQL injection. By using SQL injection, hackers inject their own malicious code into statements you execute dynamically on your SQL Servers, often from accounts with elevated privileges. An attacker can launch a SQL injection attack when you construct code by concatenating strings. I'll explain and demonstrate SQL injection techniques by presenting examples of both client-based attacks and server-based attacks. I'll then explain what measures you can take to block some of the attacks. But bear in mind that sophisticated attackers have very innovative minds; if you construct code that concatenates strings based on user input or stored data or metadata, it's almost impossible to block SQL Injection attacks altogether. In this section I'll demonstrate a couple of examples for SQL Injection attacks and provide a few suggestions regarding protective measures that you can take. This section is by no means complete. As I mentioned earlier, you can find a lot of information about the subject on the Internet and in other resources, and I also pointed out an excellent article on the subject that appears in Books Online.

SQL Injection: Code Constructed Dynamically at Client

Suppose that you provide a login screen in your client Visual Basic application that is designed to collect a username and password in two input text boxes (call them *InputUserName* and *InputPass*). You construct a query that verifies this information against a Users table, which you have in your database to determine whether to allow or reject the login attempt. Run the code in Listing 4-11 to create the Users table and populate it with two sample users.

Listing 4-11   Creating and populating the Users table

```
USE tempdb;
GO

IF OBJECT_ID('dbo.Users') IS NOT NULL
  DROP TABLE Users;
GO

CREATE TABLE dbo.Users
(
  username VARCHAR(30) NOT NULL PRIMARY KEY,
  pass     VARCHAR(16) NOT NULL
);

INSERT INTO Users(username, pass) VALUES('user1', '123');
INSERT INTO Users(username, pass) VALUES('user2', '456');
```

Suppose that you're using the following Visual Basic code at the client application to construct a query and verify the user credentials:

```
sql = "SELECT COUNT(*) AS cnt FROM dbo.Users WHERE username = '" _
  & InputUserName & "' AND pass = '" & InputPass & "';"
```

Suppose that *user1* enters the following information in the input boxes:

```
InputUserName = "user1"
InputPass     = "123"
```

Your code constructs the following query, and executing it returns a count of 1:

```
SELECT COUNT(*) AS cnt FROM dbo.Users WHERE username = 'user1' AND pass = '123';
```

Your code checks whether the count is greater than 0. If it is, as is the case here, you allow the user to log in, and if it is 0, you reject the login attempt. A hacker versed in SQL injection will very likely try to enter the following inputs:

```
InputUserName = "' OR 1 = 1 --"
InputPass = ""
```

Your Visual Basic code then constructs the following query:

```
SELECT COUNT(*) AS cnt FROM dbo.Users WHERE username = '' OR 1 = 1 --' AND pass = '';
```

The trick here is that the hacker closed the quote you opened in front of the user name, added the expression 1=1, which will become part of the filter expression, and then added the two dashes (–) to make the rest of the original code, which is now invalid SQL, into a comment so that it won't generate an error. This query will always return a count greater than 0, thereby allowing the hacker to log in without having the right credentials. Note that if you use a member of the sysadmin role or another privileged user to connect to SQL Server and invoke this query, a hacker will be able to create havoc and mayhem in your system. In addition to gaining the ability to log in, a hacker can inject additional code beyond the original query—for example, *" OR 1 = 1 DROP DATABASE <db_name> --"* or *"' OR 1 = 1 EXEC master.dbo.xp_cmdshell "format d:" --"*.

> **Note** Note that in SQL Server 2005 xp_cmdshell is disabled by default for security reasons. If you enable it, bear in mind that you increase SQL Server's attackable surface area.

SQL Injection: Code Constructed Dynamically at Server

This section will introduce an example for a SQL injection attack that exploits code constructed dynamically at the server. Consider the very common technique of passing SQL Server a dynamic list of arguments using a single input string with a comma-separated list of values. For example, the following stored procedure accepts such an input array with order IDs called *@orders*, and it returns the *OrderID* (integer) and *CustomerID* (character) for matching orders:

```
USE Northwind;
GO

IF OBJECT_ID('dbo.usp_getorders') IS NOT NULL
  DROP PROC dbo.usp_getorders;
GO
```

```
CREATE PROC dbo.usp_getorders
  @orders AS VARCHAR(1000)
AS

DECLARE @sql AS NVARCHAR(4000);

SET @sql = 'SELECT OrderID, CustomerID FROM dbo.Orders WHERE OrderID IN('
  + @orders + ');';

EXEC sp_executesql @sql;
GO
```

The procedure constructs the query string dynamically, concatenating the input array of orders in the parentheses of the IN predicate. The user enters a string with a list of orders and gets back the *OrderID* and *CustomerID* of the input orders. For example, the following code returns the output shown in Table 4-9:

```
EXEC dbo.usp_getorders '10248,10249,10250';
```

Table 4-9 Customer Information

OrderID	CustomerID
10248	VINET
10249	TOMSP
10250	HANAR

A hacker will know how to communicate with SQL Server by testing various code strings to check whether you constructed the code dynamically. If the code wasn't developed with security in mind, the application probably doesn't hide error messages generated by SQL Server from the user. By default, such error messages will simply show up in the browser. Imagine that you're the hacker. You will first test whether the code is constructed dynamically by specifying two dashes in the input box. Here is the stored procedure call that is submitted by the client to SQL Server:

```
EXEC dbo.usp_getorders ' --';
```

And here is the code that is executed by the stored procedure at the server:

```
SELECT OrderID, CustomerID FROM dbo.Orders WHERE OrderID IN( --);
```

You get the following error message:

```
Msg 102, Level 15, State 1, Line 1
Incorrect syntax near '('.
```

The error tells you that there's unclosed parentheses, meaning that there's dynamic code that concatenates the input after an opening parenthesis. That's actually what you (the hacker) wanted to see, and at this point you already know that the server is yours.

Next you want to examine the format of the output of the stored procedure, so you specify '-1) --' as the input. Here's the code that is executed by the stored procedure:

```
SELECT OrderID, CustomerID FROM dbo.Orders WHERE OrderID IN(-1) --);
```

You get an empty set back:

```
OrderID     CustomerID
----------- ----------
```

but you can see that the output contains an integer column and a character one. Now you use a UNION ALL operator to return table information from the database instead of order information, as shown in the following code:

```
EXEC dbo.usp_getorders '-1) UNION ALL SELECT id, name FROM sysobjects --';
```

The stored procedure will execute the following code:

```
SELECT OrderID, CustomerID FROM dbo.Orders WHERE OrderID IN(-1)
UNION ALL SELECT id, name FROM sysobjects --);
```

It is important to look at this code to realize how easy it is for a hacker to obtain information from your database that you did not intend to expose. For example, running this code in the Northwind database produces the output (abbreviated) shown in Table 4-10.

Table 4-10   Table Information (Abbreviated)

OrderID	CustomerID
4	sysrowsetcolumns
5	sysrowsets
7	sysallocunits
...	...
21575115	Customers
...	...

Suppose that you're interested in customer information. You have the object ID of the Customers table, so now you use UNION ALL to return column information by using the following code:

```
EXEC dbo.usp_getorders '-1) UNION ALL
SELECT colorder, name FROM syscolumns WHERE id = 21575115 --';
```

The following code is executed at the server, generating the output shown in Table 4-11:

```
SELECT OrderID, CustomerID FROM dbo.Orders WHERE OrderID IN(-1) UNION ALL
SELECT colorder, name FROM syscolumns WHERE id = 21575115 --);
```

Table 4-11   Column Information

OrderID	CustomerID
1	CustomerID
2	CompanyName
3	ContactName
4	ContactTitle
5	Address
6	City
7	Region
8	PostalCode
9	Country
10	Phone
11	Fax

Now that you have the full column list from the Customers table, you use the following code to request customer data by specifying a placeholder under the integer column and concatenate the customer attributes you need under the character column:

```
EXEC dbo.usp_getorders '-1) UNION ALL SELECT 1, CustomerID + '';'' +
CompanyName + '';'' + Phone FROM dbo.Customers --';
```

The following code is executed at the server, generating the output shown in Table 4-12:

```
SELECT OrderID, CustomerID FROM dbo.Orders WHERE OrderID IN(-1)
UNION ALL SELECT 1, CustomerID + ';' + CompanyName + ';' + Phone FROM dbo.Customers --);
```

Table 4-12   Column Information (Abbreviated)

OrderID	CustomerID
1	ALFKI;Alfreds Futterkiste;030-0074321
1	ANATR;Ana Trujillo Emparedados y helados;(5) 555-4729
1	ANTON;Antonio Moreno Taquería;(5) 555-3932
1	AROUT;Around the Horn;(171) 555-7788
1	BERGS;Berglunds snabbköp;0921-12 34 65
...	...

Imagine, you get customer IDs, company names, and phone numbers, and you could request more information!

Now the real "fun" begins as you inject changes and destructive commands—for example, suppose you supplied this parameter to the procedure: '-1) UPDATE dbo.Customers SET Phone = "9999999" WHERE CustomerID = "ALFKI" –'. The code that would run behind the scenes looks like this (don't run it):

```
SELECT OrderID, CustomerID FROM dbo.Orders WHERE OrderID
IN(-1) UPDATE dbo.Customers SET Phone = '9999999' WHERE CustomerID = 'ALFKI' --);
```

To experiment and observe which code strings the stored procedure generates based on various inputs, use a version with a *PRINT @sql* command instead of *EXEC sp_executesql @sql*.

Protecting Against SQL Injection

Following are examples for measures you can take to provide some level of protection (though not complete) for your environment against SQL injection attacks:

- In order to reduce the surface area for attack, do not enable functionality that is not needed like xp_cmdshell, the SQL Server Agent service, and so on.

- Provide minimal permissions to the executing user. For example, in the login scenario I presented, there's no reason to connect to the database using a powerful user. Create a user that has access only to the Users table and has no other permissions. This will prevent hackers from modifying data, but they might still be able to read it. In SQL Server 2005, you can impersonate users, so the new credentials will even apply to code invoked dynamically at the server. This opens a whole new window of opportunities for hackers. Dynamic SQL can now run under impersonated user credentials and not even require direct permissions from the user executing the stored procedure.

- Inspect user input thoroughly and use stored procedures. For example, the input to the *usp_getorders* stored procedure should contain only digits and commas. If you inspect the input and find that it contains other characters, don't run the code. Instead, send an alert to notify an administrator of a potential SQL injection attempt:

```
IF @Orders LIKE '%[^0-9,]%'
BEGIN
  -- Raise an error
  -- Send an alert
  RETURN;
END
```

  If other characters are allowed, use pattern matching to check whether common SQL injection constructs—such as a single quote, two dashes, EXEC, sp_, xp_, UNION, and so on—exist in the input. Note though, that this technique is not bulletproof since there are so many possible attacks.

- Limit the length of the inputs when possible. For example, a user name or password should not be hundreds or thousands of characters long. Such limitations are an effortless way to prevent many SQL injection attempts. Note though, that some hacking techniques rely on truncation of the inputs; for example, if you set a variable defined as NVARCHAR(128) with a value that is longer than 128 characters, SQL Server will truncate the input beyond the 128th character. Such techniques and ways to block them are described in the article I cited earlier from Books Online.

- Use stored procedures. Stored procedures help by encapsulating input, type-checking it (good for integers and date inputs), allowing permissions settings, and so on.

- Avoid using dynamic SQL when possible. Static code is safe, especially if your write it yourself giving attention to security issues. For example, I will discussed techniques to split an array of elements into multiple rows using a static query in Chapter 6. You can create a function that accepts an array and invokes a static query that splits it into elements, returning a table with the different elements in separate rows. You can then use this function, joining its result table with the data table to return the order attributes. Such an implementation will not only prevent SQL injection attacks, it will also reuse the same execution plan for multiple invocations of the code. The current implementation of the stored procedure will produce a different execution plan for each unique input. Imagine the performance effect of invoking such a stored procedure thousands of times a day. You can use thousands of plans or one plan. I will provide the static function implementation in Chapter 6. Also be careful with CLR routines, which could have dynamic SQL hidden in them.

- When you need to quote inputs, don't do it explicitly. Rather, use the QUOTENAME function for this purpose, or even safer, replace CHAR(39) with CHAR(39)+CHAR(39). QUOTENAME has some limitations which you can read about in the SQL Injection article in Books Online. The function will double each explicit quote that a hacker specifies, practically ensuring that the input will be treated as an input string argument and not as part of your code. To demonstrate this, I'll use PRINT to return the code string that is generated. In practice, there will be an EXEC or sp_executesql invocation. The following code doesn't use the QUOTENAME function to quote the input value:

```
DECLARE @lastname AS NVARCHAR(40), @sql AS NVARCHAR(200);
SET @lastname = N'Davolio';
SET @sql = N'SELECT * FROM dbo.Employees WHERE LastName = '''
  + @lastname + ''';';
PRINT @sql;
```

With innocent input such as Davolio, this code produces the following query:

```
SELECT * FROM dbo.Employees WHERE LastName = 'Davolio';
```

But a hacker can easily inject code like so:

```
DECLARE @lastname AS NVARCHAR(40), @sql AS NVARCHAR(200);
SET @lastname = N''' DROP TABLE dbo.Employees --';
SET @sql = N'SELECT * FROM dbo.Employees WHERE LastName = '''
  + @lastname + ''';';
PRINT @sql;
```

And that code injection will produce the following code:

```
SELECT * FROM dbo.Employees WHERE LastName = '' DROP TABLE dbo.Employees --';
```

Now use QUOTENAME instead of explicitly adding single quotes to the last name:

```
DECLARE @lastname AS NVARCHAR(40), @sql AS NVARCHAR(200);
SET @lastname = N''' DROP TABLE dbo.Employees --';
SET @sql = N'SELECT * FROM dbo.Employees WHERE LastName = '
  + QUOTENAME(@lastname, '''') + ';';
PRINT @sql;
```

By doing this, you get the following harmless query:

```
SELECT * FROM dbo.Employees WHERE LastName = ''' DROP TABLE dbo.Employees --';
```

Here I tried to make a point regarding user input strings you concatenate to your code. Of course your code would be much safer if you do not concatenate the last name at all, rather use sp_executesql with an input parameter defined for last name:

```
DECLARE @entered_lastname AS NVARCHAR(40), @sql AS NVARCHAR(200);
-- user input
SET @entered_lastname = N''' DROP TABLE dbo.Employees --';

SET @sql = N'SELECT * FROM dbo.Employees WHERE LastName = @lastname;'

EXEC sp_executesql
  @stmt = @sql,
  @params = N'@lastname AS NVARCHAR(40)',
  @lastname = @entered_lastname;
```

Or even better, don't use dynamic SQL at all in such cases, rather static SQL:

```
DECLARE @lastname AS NVARCHAR(40);
-- user input
SET @lastname = N''' DROP TABLE dbo.Employees --';

SELECT * FROM dbo.Employees WHERE LastName = @lastname;
```

Conclusion

By now, you probably have realized that dynamic SQL holds within it great power and, at the same time, great risk. By using dynamic SQL wisely, you can get great performance benefits and flexible solutions. Using it unwisely often leads to lengthy, inefficient code that is open to attacks that can cause havoc in your system.

Chapter 5
Views

This chapter starts with a brief description of views and their uses. As the chapter progresses, I'll discuss details of working with views. Among other things, I'll cover the use of views to simplify your queries, and indexed views to improve the performance of your database.

What Are Views?

A view is a named virtual table that is defined by a query and used as a table. Unlike permanent tables, a view has no physical representation of its data unless you create an index on it. Whenever you issue a query against a nonindexed view, SQL Server in practice has to access the underlying tables. Unless specified otherwise, the discussions in this chapter involve nonindexed views.

When you create a view, you specify a name for the view and a query. Microsoft SQL Server stores only metadata information about the view, describing the object, its columns, security, dependencies, and so on. When you query a view—by retrieving or modifying data—the query processor replaces a view reference with its definition; in other words, the query processor "expands" the view definition and generates an execution plan accessing the underlying objects.

Views play important roles in the database. One of the more valuable uses of views is as an abstraction mechanism. For example, you can use views to make it easier to provide a more or less normalized picture of the underlying data, where appropriate, without changing the normalization of the actual data. You can use them to simplify your solutions by applying a modular approach—solving complex problems one step at a time. You can use views as a security layer (to some degree) by granting access to filtered or manipulated data only through views, and not directly against the base tables (provided that the schema of the view and the schema of the underlying objects are the same).

Views can also play a performance role if you create an index on them. Creating a clustered index on the view materializes its data on disk, giving the view a physical dimension, as opposed to its normal virtual role. I'll describe indexed views later in the chapter in a dedicated section. For now, the important point is that without an index, a view typically has no special performance impact—negative or positive.

As with any other table expression (such as a derived table, common table expression [CTE], or inline table-valued user-defined function [UDF]), the query defining the view must meet three requirements:

- ORDER BY cannot be used in the view's query unless there is also a TOP or FOR XML specification in the definition.

- All result columns must have names.

- All result column names must be unique.

An ORDER BY clause without TOP or FOR XML specification is not allowed in the query defining the view because a view is supposed to represent a table. A table is a logical entity that has no order to its rows—as opposed to a cursor, which is a physical object that does have order to its records. Naturally, all columns must have names in a valid table, and the names must be unique. You can assign column names to the target columns of a view either in parentheses following the view name or as inline column aliases following the individual expressions.

As an example, run the following code to create the VCustsWithOrders view:

```
SET NOCOUNT ON;
USE Northwind;
GO
IF OBJECT_ID('dbo.VCustsWithOrders') IS NOT NULL
  DROP VIEW dbo.VCustsWithOrders;
GO
CREATE VIEW dbo.VCustsWithOrders
AS

SELECT CustomerID, CompanyName, ContactName, ContactTitle,
  Address, City, Region, PostalCode, Country, Phone, Fax
FROM Customers AS C
WHERE EXISTS
  (SELECT * FROM dbo.Orders AS O
   WHERE O.CustomerID = C.CustomerID);
GO
```

This view contains customers that placed orders.

Note   If you attempt to run this code in SQL Server 2000, it will fail because of the exist-ence of the semicolon at the end of the CREATE VIEW statement. To create the view in SQL Server 2000, simply drop the semicolon. The semicolon is an ANSI requirement, though T-SQL never required it in the past. In SQL Server 2005, you're required to use a semicolon only in particular cases, for example, before a WITH clause that defines a CTE to avoid ambiguity (because the WITH clause can be used for other purposes as well). Otherwise, the use of a semicolon is optional. However, because a semicolon is an ANSI requirement, it might be a good idea to start getting used to it.

The view's query uses the EXISTS predicate to return customers that have at least one order in the Orders table.

Tip   As an aside, even though the use of * is generally a bad practice, you can use it safely with the EXISTS predicate. The optimizer knows that the EXISTS predicate does not refer to a particular attribute from the row. Rather, it cares only about existence; therefore, it ignores the SELECT list altogether. You can deduce this by examining execution plans for such que-ries and noticing that if there's an index on the filtered column (*O.CustomerID* in the preced-ing example), it will be used and there won't be additional lookup operations. Another way to demonstrate that the SELECT list is completely ignored is by specifying expressions that would normally cause an error, for example:

```
IF EXISTS(SELECT 1/0) PRINT 'no error';
```

This code runs with no error, demonstrating that SQL Server didn't evaluate the expression. If SQL Server had evaluated the expression, you would have received an error.

The following sections will explore various aspects of views in more detail, starting with the reasoning behind disallowing an ORDER BY clause without a TOP or FOR XML specification in the view's query.

ORDER BY in a View

As I mentioned earlier, there is a reason behind disallowing an ORDER BY clause in the view's query. A view is similar to a table in the sense that it represents a logical entity with no prede-termined order to its rows—unlike a cursor that has order to its records.

Try running the following code, which attempts to introduce an ORDER BY clause in the VCustsWithOrders view:

```
ALTER VIEW dbo.VCustsWithOrders
AS

SELECT Country, CustomerID, CompanyName, ContactName, ContactTitle,
  Address, City, Region, PostalCode, Phone, Fax
FROM Customers AS C
```

```
WHERE EXISTS
  (SELECT * FROM dbo.Orders AS O
   WHERE O.CustomerID = C.CustomerID)
ORDER BY Country;
GO
```

The attempt fails, generating the following error:

```
Msg 1033, Level 15, State 1, Procedure VCustsWithOrders, Line 10
The ORDER BY clause is invalid in views, inline functions, derived tables, subqueries, and
common table expressions, unless TOP or FOR XML is also specified.
```

Notice that the error doesn't say that ORDER BY is disallowed altogether; rather, it says that there are a couple of exceptions where it is allowed—when TOP or FOR XML is also specified. Remember that both TOP and FOR XML are T-SQL extensions, not standard SQL elements. TOP and ORDER BY or ORDER BY and FOR XML are part of the result set specification, whereas ORDER BY alone is not, and only specifies a detail of presentation. Hence, TOP and ORDER BY or ORDER BY and FOR XML are allowed in a view definition while ORDER BY alone is not.

If you need to return sorted data to the client, you can always specify an ORDER BY clause in the outer query against the view:

```
SELECT Country, CustomerID, CompanyName
FROM dbo.VCustsWithOrders
ORDER BY Country;
```

Allowing an ORDER BY clause in a query against the view makes sense because obviously the client expects to get a physical object back—a record set. And for the client, there is a reason for wanting the data sorted.

Note that when using the TOP option in an outer query, the ORDER BY clause serves two functions: one is to determine which rows to pick, and the second is to determine the order of the records in the result cursor. However, when used with the TOP option in a table expression (for example, in a view's query), the ORDER BY clause serves only one function—determining which rows to pick. In such a case, the view still represents a valid table (a set). When querying the view, there's no guarantee that the rows would be returned in any particular order unless the outer query against the view has an ORDER BY clause as well. When TOP is also specified, the ORDER BY clause is allowed within a view (or other table expressions) because it serves only a logical function and not a physical one. Understanding this detail can help you develop correct code and avoid using table expressions in ways they really weren't designed to work.

For example, an attempt to create a "sorted" view is wrong to begin with because a view is a table and a table has no order to its rows. It was common in SQL Server 2000 for programmers who were after "sorted" views to exploit what would seem to be a loophole in the system.

The loophole involved creating an absurd view in which you specify TOP 100 PERCENT and an ORDER BY clause, as in:

```
ALTER VIEW dbo.VCustsWithOrders
AS

SELECT TOP (100) PERCENT
  Country, CustomerID, CompanyName, ContactName, ContactTitle,
  Address, City, Region, PostalCode, Phone, Fax
FROM Customers AS C
WHERE EXISTS
  (SELECT * FROM dbo.Orders AS O
   WHERE O.CustomerID = C.CustomerID)
ORDER BY Country;
GO
```

> **Note**   The preceding code assumes you are using SQL Server 2005. Therefore, the use of a semicolon to terminate the ALTER VIEW statement, and the use of parentheses with the TOP option. If you want to test this code in SQL Server 2000, remove the parentheses and the semicolon.

So what is the meaning of the ORDER BY clause in the view's query? Things are fuzzy here because the TOP option is not standard. But if you try to think in terms of sets, the ORDER BY clause is meaningless because you're selecting all rows that meet the filter expression. When querying the view, SQL Server does not have to guarantee any order of the output unless the outer query has an ORDER BY clause. SQL Server 2005's Books Online now has a helpful statement describing this behavior: "The ORDER BY clause is used only to determine the rows that are returned by the TOP clause in the view definition. The ORDER BY clause does not guarantee ordered results when the view is queried, unless ORDER BY is also specified in the query itself."

Even if the optimizer does not ignore the ORDER BY clause and returns the data sorted, you shouldn't rely on this behavior. Interestingly, when I ran the following query in SQL Server 2000, I got the data sorted as shown in Table 5-1:

```
SELECT Country, CustomerID, CompanyName
FROM dbo.VCustsWithOrders;
```

Table 5-1   Output of Query Against View with ORDER BY in SQL Server 2000 (Abbreviated)

Country	CustomerID	CompanyName
Argentina	RANCH	Rancho grande
Argentina	CACTU	Cactus Comidas para llevar
Argentina	OCEAN	Océano Atlántico Ltda.
Austria	ERNSH	Ernst Handel

Table 5-1 Output of Query Against View with ORDER BY in SQL Server 2000 (Abbreviated)

Country	CustomerID	CompanyName
Austria	PICCO	Piccolo und mehr
Belgium	SUPRD	Suprêmes délices
Belgium	MAISD	Maison Dewey
Brazil	TRADH	Tradição Hipermercados
Brazil	WELLI	Wellington Importadora
Brazil	QUEDE	Que Delícia
...	...	...

However, when I ran the query in SQL Server 2005, I got the unsorted output shown in Table 5-2.

Table 5-2 Output of Query Against View with ORDER BY in SQL Server 2005 (Abbreviated)

Country	CustomerID	CompanyName
Germany	ALFKI	Alfreds Futterkiste
Mexico	ANATR	Ana Trujillo Emparedados y helados
Mexico	ANTON	Antonio Moreno Taquería
UK	AROUT	Around the Horn
Sweden	BERGS	Berglunds snabbköp
Germany	BLAUS	Blauer See Delikatessen
France	BLONP	Blondesddsl père et fils
Spain	BOLID	Bólido Comidas preparadas
France	BONAP	Bon app'
Canada	BOTTM	Bottom-Dollar Markets
...	...	...

Examining the execution plans in both versions explains what happened. Figure 5-1 shows the execution plan I got in SQL Server 2000, and Figure 5-2 shows the execution plan in SQL Server 2005.

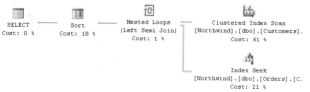

Figure 5-1 Execution plan for a query against a view with ORDER BY in SQL Server 2000

Figure 5-2   Execution plan for a query against a view with ORDER BY in SQL Server 2005

You can see that the plan in SQL Server 2000 uses a sort operator, sorting the data by *Country*. On the other hand, SQL Server 2005's optimizer completely ignored the combination of TOP (100) PERCENT and the ORDER BY clause. The optimizer realized that TOP and ORDER BY are meaningless here; therefore, it didn't bother to sort the data. Unfortunately, programmers accustomed to the SQL Server 2000 behavior will consider this change in behavior a bug, even though the whole premise for creating such a view is wrong.

> **Note**   The view designer in SQL Server 2000's Enterprise Manager had a place to specify the order of a view, yielding a view definition with a TOP 100 PERCENT specification and an ORDER by clause. This might have been how programmers discovered this loophole. Unfortunately, the SQL Server Management Studio (SSMS) view designer in SQL Server 2005 also has a place to specify the order of a view. Although the SQL Server 2005 query processor may treat TOP 100 PERCENT .. ORDER BY differently from how the SQL Server 2000 processor did, this unfortunate usage will probably continue, because the SSMS view designer encourages it. It will simply create more confusion. Hopefully, you will realize that such use is absurd and refrain from it altogether.

When you're done, run the following code to drop the VCustsWithOrders view:

```
IF OBJECT_ID('dbo.VCustsWithOrders') IS NOT NULL
  DROP VIEW dbo.VCustsWithOrders;
```

Refreshing Views

When you create a view, SQL Server stores metadata information describing the view, its columns, security, dependencies, and so on. Schema changes in underlying objects are not reflected in the view's metadata information. After applying such schema changes, it's a good practice to refresh the view's metadata information using the sp_refreshview stored procedure so that the changes will be reflected in the view.

To demonstrate what can happen when you make schema changes and don't refresh the view's metadata information, first run the following code, which creates the table T1 and the view V1:

```
USE tempdb;
GO
IF OBJECT_ID('dbo.V1') IS NOT NULL
  DROP VIEW dbo.V1;
```

```
GO
IF OBJECT_ID('dbo.T1') IS NOT NULL
  DROP TABLE dbo.T1;
GO
CREATE TABLE dbo.T1(col1 INT, col2 INT);
INSERT INTO dbo.T1(col1, col2) VALUES(1, 2);
GO
CREATE VIEW dbo.V1
AS

SELECT * FROM dbo.T1;
GO
```

As a practice, avoid using * in your SELECT statements. I'm using it here just for demonstration purposes. When V1 was initially created, SQL Server stored metadata information about the columns that existed at that point in time—*col1* and *col2*. If you query the view, you get the output shown in Table 5-3 returning both columns:

```
SELECT * FROM dbo.V1;
```

Table 5-3 Output of Query Against V1 Before Adding Column to T1

col1	col2
1	2

Next add a column to T1:

```
ALTER TABLE dbo.T1 ADD col3 INT;
```

The schema change in T1 was not reflected in the view's metadata information. As far as SQL Server is concerned, the view still has just two columns. If you query the view again, you still get the output shown in Table 5-3:

```
SELECT * FROM dbo.V1;
```

To refresh the view's metadata information, run the sp_refreshview stored procedure against V1:

```
EXEC sp_refreshview 'dbo.V1';
```

Query V1 again, and you will get the output shown in Table 5-4, which includes the new column—*col3*:

```
SELECT * FROM dbo.V1;
```

Table 5-4 Output of Query Against V1 After Metadata Refresh

col1	col2	col3
1	2	NULL

This is just one example where a schema change in the underlying objects is not reflected in the view's metadata information. You might find it to be a good practice to refresh all views' metadata information after applying schema changes to objects in the database. To avoid the tedious process of writing the sp_refreshview statements you can use the following query:

```
SELECT N'EXEC sp_refreshview '
    + QUOTENAME(VIEW_NAME, '''') + ';' AS cmd
FROM (SELECT QUOTENAME(TABLE_SCHEMA)
        + N'.' + QUOTENAME(TABLE_NAME) AS VIEW_NAME
    FROM INFORMATION_SCHEMA.VIEWS) AS V
WHERE OBJECTPROPERTY(OBJECT_ID(VIEW_NAME), 'IsSchemaBound') = 0;
```

The query will generate as its output the lines of code with the sp_refreshview statements against all views in the database that are not schema-bound.

> **Warning**   Make sure that you examine the output carefully before running it. Someone with permission to create views can maliciously plant specially crafted view names to subvert this maintenance code into doing damage.

When you're done, drop V1 and T1:

```
USE tempdb;
GO
IF OBJECT_ID('dbo.V1') IS NOT NULL
  DROP VIEW dbo.V1;
GO
IF OBJECT_ID('dbo.T1') IS NOT NULL
  DROP TABLE dbo.T1;
GO
```

Modular Approach

Views can be used to develop solutions in a modular way. You solve each step of the problem with a query, and define a view based on that query. This process simplifies the solution by allowing you to focus on a single step at a time.

I'll demonstrate a modular approach through an example. First, run the code in Listing 5-1 to create and populate the Sales table:

Listing 5-1   Creating and populating the Sales table

```
SET NOCOUNT ON;
USE tempdb;
GO
IF OBJECT_ID('dbo.Sales') IS NOT NULL
  DROP TABLE dbo.Sales;
GO
```

```
CREATE TABLE dbo.Sales
(
  mnth DATETIME NOT NULL PRIMARY KEY,
  qty  INT      NOT NULL
);

INSERT INTO dbo.Sales(mnth, qty) VALUES('20041201', 100);
INSERT INTO dbo.Sales(mnth, qty) VALUES('20050101', 110);
INSERT INTO dbo.Sales(mnth, qty) VALUES('20050201', 120);
INSERT INTO dbo.Sales(mnth, qty) VALUES('20050301', 130);
INSERT INTO dbo.Sales(mnth, qty) VALUES('20050401', 140);
INSERT INTO dbo.Sales(mnth, qty) VALUES('20050501', 140);
INSERT INTO dbo.Sales(mnth, qty) VALUES('20050601', 130);
INSERT INTO dbo.Sales(mnth, qty) VALUES('20050701', 120);
INSERT INTO dbo.Sales(mnth, qty) VALUES('20050801', 110);
INSERT INTO dbo.Sales(mnth, qty) VALUES('20050901', 100);
INSERT INTO dbo.Sales(mnth, qty) VALUES('20051001', 110);
INSERT INTO dbo.Sales(mnth, qty) VALUES('20051101', 100);
INSERT INTO dbo.Sales(mnth, qty) VALUES('20051201', 120);
INSERT INTO dbo.Sales(mnth, qty) VALUES('20060101', 130);
INSERT INTO dbo.Sales(mnth, qty) VALUES('20060201', 140);
INSERT INTO dbo.Sales(mnth, qty) VALUES('20060301', 100);
INSERT INTO dbo.Sales(mnth, qty) VALUES('20060401', 100);
INSERT INTO dbo.Sales(mnth, qty) VALUES('20060501', 100);
INSERT INTO dbo.Sales(mnth, qty) VALUES('20060601', 110);
INSERT INTO dbo.Sales(mnth, qty) VALUES('20060701', 120);
INSERT INTO dbo.Sales(mnth, qty) VALUES('20060801', 110);
INSERT INTO dbo.Sales(mnth, qty) VALUES('20060901', 120);
INSERT INTO dbo.Sales(mnth, qty) VALUES('20061001', 130);
INSERT INTO dbo.Sales(mnth, qty) VALUES('20061101', 140);
INSERT INTO dbo.Sales(mnth, qty) VALUES('20061201', 100);
```

The table contains one row per month with the sales quantity (column *qty*) and month (column *mnth*). Notice that I used the DATETIME datatype to store a month to support datetime-related calculations. Even though I care only about the year and month elements of the value, I had to specify something in the day portion. So I specified the first day of each month as the day and midnight is assumed by default as the time. When you need to present the data, you can always extract the relevant elements from the full datetime value.

The task at hand is to return groups of consecutive months that have the same sales trend. That is, identify ranges of months with the same trend (up, same, down, or unknown). The trend for a given month is based on its *qty* value minus the *qty* value of the previous month. If the difference is positive, the trend is '*up*'; if it's negative, the trend is '*down*'; if it's zero, the trend is '*same*'; otherwise, the trend is '*unknown*'. Table 5-5 shows the desired result.

Table 5-5   Ranges of Months with the Same Sales Trend

start_range	end_range	trend
200412	200412	unknown
200501	200504	up
200505	200505	same

Table 5-5   Ranges of Months with the Same Sales Trend

start_range	end_range	trend
200506	200509	down
200510	200510	up
200511	200511	down
200512	200602	up
200603	200603	down
200604	200605	same
200606	200607	up
200608	200608	down
200609	200611	up
200612	200612	down

Trying to develop a single query to solve the problem can be too complex. Instead, break the solution into steps. I'll first show a solution that will work in SQL Server 2000 and then optimize it by using features available in SQL Server 2005.

First calculate the sign of the difference between the current month's *qty* and the previous month's. This can be achieved by creating the VSgn view as follows:

```
IF OBJECT_ID('dbo.VSgn') IS NOT NULL
  DROP VIEW dbo.VSgn;
GO
CREATE VIEW dbo.VSgn
AS

SELECT mnth, qty,
  SIGN((S1.qty -
        (SELECT TOP 1 qty
         FROM dbo.Sales AS S2
         WHERE S2.mnth < S1.mnth
         ORDER BY S2.mnth DESC))) AS sgn
FROM dbo.Sales AS S1
GO
```

Remember that in SQL Server 2000 a semicolon terminating the CREATE VIEW statement is not allowed, nor are parentheses for TOP's input.

The contents of the VSgn view are shown in Table 5-6.

Table 5-6   Contents of VSgn

mnth	qty	sgn
2004-12-01 00:00:00.000	100	NULL
2005-01-01 00:00:00.000	110	1
2005-02-01 00:00:00.000	120	1
2005-03-01 00:00:00.000	130	1

Table 5-6   Contents of VSgn

mnth	qty	sgn
2005-04-01 00:00:00.000	140	1
2005-05-01 00:00:00.000	140	0
2005-06-01 00:00:00.000	130	−1
2005-07-01 00:00:00.000	120	−1
2005-08-01 00:00:00.000	110	−1
2005-09-01 00:00:00.000	100	−1
2005-10-01 00:00:00.000	110	1
2005-11-01 00:00:00.000	100	−1
2005-12-01 00:00:00.000	120	1
2006-01-01 00:00:00.000	130	1
2006-02-01 00:00:00.000	140	1
2006-03-01 00:00:00.000	100	−1
2006-04-01 00:00:00.000	100	0
2006-05-01 00:00:00.000	100	0
2006-06-01 00:00:00.000	110	1
2006-07-01 00:00:00.000	120	1
2006-08-01 00:00:00.000	110	−1
2006-09-01 00:00:00.000	120	1
2006-10-01 00:00:00.000	130	1
2006-11-01 00:00:00.000	140	1
2006-12-01 00:00:00.000	100	−1

The SIGN function returns 1 for a positive input, 0 for when zero is input, −1 for a negative input, and NULL for a NULL input. The *sgn* column actually represents the sales trend of the current month. At this point, you want to group all consecutive months that have the same sales trend. To do so, you first need to calculate a grouping factor—a value that will identify the group. One option for the grouping factor is the earliest future month in which the trend is different from the current month's trend. If you think about it, you'll see that such a value will be the same for all consecutive months that have the same trend.

Run the following code to create the VGrp view, which calculates the grouping factor:

```
IF OBJECT_ID('dbo.VGrp') IS NOT NULL
  DROP VIEW dbo.VGrp;
GO
CREATE VIEW dbo.VGrp
AS

SELECT mnth, sgn,
  (SELECT MIN(mnth) FROM dbo.VSgn AS V2
   WHERE V2.sgn <> V1.sgn
     AND V2.mnth > V1.mnth) AS grp
FROM dbo.VSgn AS V1
GO
```

The contents of the VGrp view is shown in Table 5-7.

Table 5-7   Contents of VGrp

mnth	sgn	Grp
2004-12-01 00:00:00.000	NULL	NULL
2005-01-01 00:00:00.000	1	2005-05-01 00:00:00.000
2005-02-01 00:00:00.000	1	2005-05-01 00:00:00.000
2005-03-01 00:00:00.000	1	2005-05-01 00:00:00.000
2005-04-01 00:00:00.000	1	2005-05-01 00:00:00.000
2005-05-01 00:00:00.000	0	2005-06-01 00:00:00.000
2005-06-01 00:00:00.000	−1	2005-10-01 00:00:00.000
2005-07-01 00:00:00.000	−1	2005-10-01 00:00:00.000
2005-08-01 00:00:00.000	−1	2005-10-01 00:00:00.000
2005-09-01 00:00:00.000	−1	2005-10-01 00:00:00.000
2005-10-01 00:00:00.000	1	2005-11-01 00:00:00.000
2005-11-01 00:00:00.000	−1	2005-12-01 00:00:00.000
2005-12-01 00:00:00.000	1	2006-03-01 00:00:00.000
2006-01-01 00:00:00.000	1	2006-03-01 00:00:00.000
2006-02-01 00:00:00.000	1	2006-03-01 00:00:00.000
2006-03-01 00:00:00.000	−1	2006-04-01 00:00:00.000
2006-04-01 00:00:00.000	0	2006-06-01 00:00:00.000
2006-05-01 00:00:00.000	0	2006-06-01 00:00:00.000
2006-06-01 00:00:00.000	1	2006-08-01 00:00:00.000
2006-07-01 00:00:00.000	1	2006-08-01 00:00:00.000
2006-08-01 00:00:00.000	−1	2006-09-01 00:00:00.000
2006-09-01 00:00:00.000	1	2006-12-01 00:00:00.000
2006-10-01 00:00:00.000	1	2006-12-01 00:00:00.000
2006-11-01 00:00:00.000	1	2006-12-01 00:00:00.000
2006-12-01 00:00:00.000	−1	NULL

You can observe that the *grp* column values are unique for each consecutive group of months that have the same trend. The only exception is the two NULLs. You received a NULL for December 2004 because that month showed an unknown trend. You received a NULL for December 2006 because there is no data after that date. The two NULLs belong to two different consecutive trend groups, but you can easily solve the problem by using both *sgn* (representing the trend) and *grp* to define the group.

The last part is straightforward—group the data by *sgn* and *grp*, return *MIN(mnth)* as the start of the range, and return *MAX(mnth)* as the end of the range. Also, use a CASE expression to convert the *sgn* value to a more descriptive representation of the trend.

Run the following code to create the VTrends view implementing this step:

```
IF OBJECT_ID('dbo.VTrends') IS NOT NULL
  DROP VIEW dbo.VTrends;
GO
CREATE VIEW dbo.VTrends
AS

SELECT
  CONVERT(VARCHAR(6), MIN(mnth), 112) AS start_range,
  CONVERT(VARCHAR(6), MAX(mnth), 112) AS end_range,
  CASE sgn
    WHEN -1 THEN 'down'
    WHEN  0 THEN 'same'
    WHEN  1 THEN 'up'
    ELSE         'unknown'
  END AS trend
FROM dbo.VGrp
GROUP BY sgn, grp
GO
```

If you query VTrends as shown in the following code, you will get the desired results shown earlier in Table 5-5:

```
SELECT start_range, end_range, trend
FROM dbo.VTrends
ORDER BY start_range;
```

In SQL Server 2005, you have new features that allow you to optimize the solution. First create a view called VSalesRN with row numbers assigned to the rows from Sales based on the order of *mnth*:

```
IF OBJECT_ID('dbo.VSalesRN') IS NOT NULL
  DROP VIEW dbo.VSalesRN;
GO
CREATE VIEW dbo.VSalesRN
AS

SELECT mnth, qty, ROW_NUMBER() OVER(ORDER BY mnth) AS rn
FROM dbo.Sales;
GO
```

The contents of the view are shown in Table 5-8.

Table 5-8   Contents of VSalesRN

mnth	qty	rn
2004-12-01 00:00:00.000	100	1
2005-01-01 00:00:00.000	110	2
2005-02-01 00:00:00.000	120	3
2005-03-01 00:00:00.000	130	4
2005-04-01 00:00:00.000	140	5
2005-05-01 00:00:00.000	140	6

Table 5-8   Contents of VSalesRN

mnth	qty	rn
2005-06-01 00:00:00.000	130	7
2005-07-01 00:00:00.000	120	8
2005-08-01 00:00:00.000	110	9
2005-09-01 00:00:00.000	100	10
2005-10-01 00:00:00.000	110	11
2005-11-01 00:00:00.000	100	12
2005-12-01 00:00:00.000	120	13
2006-01-01 00:00:00.000	130	14
2006-02-01 00:00:00.000	140	15
2006-03-01 00:00:00.000	100	16
2006-04-01 00:00:00.000	100	17
2006-05-01 00:00:00.000	100	18
2006-06-01 00:00:00.000	110	19
2006-07-01 00:00:00.000	120	20
2006-08-01 00:00:00.000	110	21
2006-09-01 00:00:00.000	120	22
2006-10-01 00:00:00.000	130	23
2006-11-01 00:00:00.000	140	24
2006-12-01 00:00:00.000	100	25

In the VSgn view, you join two instances of VSalesRN to match each current row with the row for the previous month. You then have access to both the current month's and previous month's *qty* values, and you calculate the sign of their difference. Here's the code for the SQL Server 2005 version of the VSgn view:

```
IF OBJECT_ID('dbo.VSgn') IS NOT NULL
  DROP VIEW dbo.VSgn;
GO
CREATE VIEW dbo.VSgn
AS

SELECT Cur.mnth, Cur.qty, SIGN(Cur.qty - Prv.qty) AS sgn
FROM dbo.VSalesRN AS Cur
  JOIN dbo.VSalesRN AS Prv
    ON Cur.rn = Prv.rn + 1;
GO
```

You can further optimize the solution by revising the VGrp view, which calculates the grouping factor as follows:

```
IF OBJECT_ID('dbo.VGrp') IS NOT NULL
  DROP VIEW dbo.VGrp;
GO
CREATE VIEW dbo.VGrp
AS
```

```
SELECT mnth, sgn,
  DATEADD(month,
    -ROW_NUMBER() OVER(PARTITION BY sgn ORDER BY mnth),
    mnth) AS grp
FROM dbo.VSgn;
GO
```

The logic behind the calculation of the grouping factor here is a bit tricky. You calculate a row number (*rn*) based on the order of *mnth*, partitioned by *sgn* (trend). This means that, for each trend, you can have multiple consecutive groups, naturally with gaps between them. Now try to think of the way the *mnth* value increments within a particular trend versus how *rn* increments. Both continue to increment by one unit as long as you're still in the same consecutive group. Once you have a gap, *mnth* increments by more than one unit, while *rn* keeps incrementing by one. You can conclude that if you subtract *rn* months from *mnth*, the result for each consecutive group will be constant and unique. As I mentioned, the logic here is tricky and can be hard to grasp. To better understand it, I suggest that you pull VGrp's query aside and play with it. For example, return the row number itself (as opposed to using it in a calculation), and so on.

Finally, create the VTrends view to group the data by *sgn* and *grp*, returning the ranges of consecutive months with the same trend.

```
IF OBJECT_ID('dbo.VTrends') IS NOT NULL
  DROP VIEW dbo.VTrends;
GO
CREATE VIEW dbo.VTrends
AS

SELECT
  CONVERT(VARCHAR(6), MIN(mnth), 112) AS start_range,
  CONVERT(VARCHAR(6), MAX(mnth), 112) AS end_range,
  CASE sgn
    WHEN -1 THEN 'down'
    WHEN  0 THEN 'same'
    WHEN  1 THEN 'up'
    ELSE          'unknown'
  END AS trend
FROM dbo.VGrp
GROUP BY sgn, grp;
GO
```

Query the VTrends view and you will get the desired result:

```
SELECT start_range, end_range, trend
FROM dbo.VTrends
ORDER BY start_range;
```

Remember that SQL Server 2005 supports CTEs, which also allow you to develop solutions applying a modular approach. In fact, you can think of CTEs as inline views that exist only in the scope of the outer query. If you think about it, other than allowing a modular development approach, there's no real reason to create the intermediate views in the solution. Instead, you should just create the final one (VTrends). So why create these as objects in the database? In SQL Server 2000, you didn't have better options, but in SQL Server 2005 you can create just one view (VTrends), which will be defined by a CTE developed using a modular approach. Run the code in Listing 5-2 to alter the VTrends view, implementing it with multiple CTEs defined in the same WITH statement instead of defining multiple views.

Listing 5-2   Implementing VTrends with a CTE

```
ALTER VIEW dbo.VTrends
AS

WITH CSalesRN AS
(
  SELECT mnth, qty, ROW_NUMBER() OVER(ORDER BY mnth) AS rn
  FROM dbo.Sales
),
CSgn AS
(
  SELECT Cur.mnth, Cur.qty, SIGN(Cur.qty - Prv.qty) AS sgn
  FROM CSalesRN AS Cur
    JOIN CSalesRN AS Prv
      ON Cur.rn = Prv.rn + 1
),
CGrp AS
(
  SELECT mnth, sgn,
    DATEADD(month,
      -ROW_NUMBER() OVER(PARTITION BY sgn ORDER BY mnth),
      mnth) AS grp
  FROM CSgn
)
SELECT
  CONVERT(VARCHAR(6), MIN(mnth), 112) AS start_range,
  CONVERT(VARCHAR(6), MAX(mnth), 112) AS end_range,
  CASE sgn
    WHEN -1 THEN 'down'
    WHEN  0 THEN 'same'
    WHEN  1 THEN 'up'
    ELSE         'unknown'
  END AS trend
FROM CGrp
GROUP BY sgn, grp;
GO
```

If you query VTrends using the following code, you will get the desired output shown earlier in Table 5-5:

```
SELECT start_range, end_range, trend
FROM dbo.VTrends
ORDER BY start_range;
```

In short, developing solutions with the modular approach simplifies the process and reduces the chances of bugs and errors.

When you're done, run the following cleanup code:

```
IF OBJECT_ID('dbo.VTrends') IS NOT NULL
  DROP VIEW dbo.VTrends;
GO
IF OBJECT_ID('dbo.VGrp') IS NOT NULL
  DROP VIEW dbo.VGrp;
GO
IF OBJECT_ID('dbo.VSgn') IS NOT NULL
  DROP VIEW dbo.VSgn;
GO
IF OBJECT_ID('dbo.VSalesRN') IS NOT NULL
  DROP VIEW dbo.VSalesRN;
GO
IF OBJECT_ID('dbo.Sales') IS NOT NULL
  DROP TABLE dbo.Sales;
GO
```

Updating Views

Remember that a view is a virtual table, and remember that when you submit a query against a view, SQL Server expands the view's select statement and issues the query against the underlying tables. A view is not limited to being a target of SELECT queries; it can be a target for modifications, too. When you submit a modification against a view, SQL Server will modify the underlying tables. The view in such a case acts as an agent or a vehicle. Of course, you can limit the data that you're exposing through the view by allowing modifications through the view but not directly against the underlying tables. This way, the view can play a security role to some degree in terms of privacy and disclosure.

For example, one way to achieve row-level security is by using views.

Caution   In this section, I'll show the simple use of views to provide row-level security. Note that the technique I will demonstrate is imperfect and might be useful for applications in which security is not a firm requirement. For details about row-level security and the disclosure risk of this security mechanism, please refer to the following white paper: *http://www.microsoft.com/technet/prodtechnol/sql/2005/multisec.mspx*.

The code in Listing 5-3 creates a table called UserData with a column called *loginname* that accepts a default value from the SUSER_SNAME function (current login name). The code creates a view that exposes all attributes except *loginname* only to the current user by using the filter *loginname = SUSER_SNAME()*. The code denies data manipulation language (DML) permissions against the table to public, and it grants permissions against the view to public. With these restrictions in place, users can access and manipulate only their own data.

Listing 5-3   Creating UserData and VUserData and setting permissions

```
USE tempdb;
GO
IF OBJECT_ID('dbo.VUserData') IS NOT NULL
  DROP VIEW dbo.VUserData;
GO
IF OBJECT_ID('dbo.UserData') IS NOT NULL
  DROP TABLE dbo.UserData;
GO
CREATE TABLE dbo.UserData
(
  keycol    INT        NOT NULL IDENTITY PRIMARY KEY,
  loginname sysname    NOT NULL DEFAULT (SUSER_SNAME()),
  datacol   VARCHAR(20) NOT NULL,
  /* ... other columns ... */
);
GO
CREATE VIEW dbo.VUserData
AS

SELECT keycol, datacol
FROM dbo.UserData
WHERE loginname = SUSER_SNAME()
GO

DENY SELECT, INSERT, UPDATE, DELETE ON dbo.UserData TO public;
GRANT SELECT, INSERT, UPDATE, DELETE ON dbo.VUserData TO public;
GO
```

Modifications against views have the following limitations:

- You cannot insert data through a view if the view includes even one column that doesn't get its value implicitly. A column can get a value implicitly if it allows NULLs, has a default value, has an IDENTITY property, or is typed as ROWVERSION.

- If the view is defined by a join query, an UPDATE or INSERT statement is allowed to affect only one side of the join. That is, an INSERT statement must specify a target column list that belongs only to one side of the join. Similarly, the columns that an UPDATE statement modifies must all belong to one side of the join. However, you are allowed to refer to any column you want to elsewhere in the query—on the right side of an assignment, in the query's filter, and so on. You cannot delete data from a view defined by a join query.

- You cannot modify a column that is a result of a calculation. This limitation includes both scalar expressions and aggregates. SQL Server doesn't make an attempt to reverse engineer the calculation.

- If WITH CHECK OPTION was specified when the view was created or altered, INSERT or UPDATE statements that conflict with the view's query filter will be rejected. I will elaborate on this point later in the "View Options" section.

Data modification statements in violation of these limitations can be issued if there is an INSTEAD OF trigger on the view. An INSTEAD OF trigger replaces the original modification with your own code. For example, you can write your own code to reverse engineer modifications of columns that result from a calculation and issue the modification directly against the underlying tables. I will discuss triggers in Chapter 8.

Be especially careful when you allow modifications against a view defined by a join query. Users who are not aware that the target object for their modifications is a view and not a table might find the effect of their modifications surprising in some cases—for example, when they modify the "one" side of a one-to-many join.

As an example, run the code in Listing 5-4 to create the Customers and Orders tables and the VCustOrders view that joins the two.

Listing 5-4   Creating Customers, Orders, and VCustOrders

```
SET NOCOUNT ON;
USE tempdb;
GO
IF OBJECT_ID('dbo.VCustOrders') IS NOT NULL
  DROP VIEW dbo.VCustOrders;
GO
IF OBJECT_ID('dbo.Orders') IS NOT NULL
  DROP TABLE dbo.Orders;
GO
IF OBJECT_ID('dbo.Customers') IS NOT NULL
  DROP TABLE dbo.Customers;
GO

CREATE TABLE dbo.Customers
(
  cid   INT        NOT NULL PRIMARY KEY,
  cname VARCHAR(25) NOT NULL,
  /* other columns */
)
INSERT INTO dbo.Customers(cid, cname) VALUES(1, 'Cust 1');
INSERT INTO dbo.Customers(cid, cname) VALUES(2, 'Cust 2');

CREATE TABLE dbo.Orders
(
  oid INT NOT NULL PRIMARY KEY,
  cid INT NOT NULL REFERENCES dbo.Customers,
  /* other columns */
)
INSERT INTO dbo.Orders(oid, cid) VALUES(1001, 1);
INSERT INTO dbo.Orders(oid, cid) VALUES(1002, 1);
INSERT INTO dbo.Orders(oid, cid) VALUES(1003, 1);
INSERT INTO dbo.Orders(oid, cid) VALUES(2001, 2);
INSERT INTO dbo.Orders(oid, cid) VALUES(2002, 2);
INSERT INTO dbo.Orders(oid, cid) VALUES(2003, 2);
GO
```

```
CREATE VIEW dbo.VCustOrders
AS

SELECT C.cid, C.cname, O.oid
FROM dbo.Customers AS C
  JOIN dbo.Orders AS O
    ON O.cid = C.cid;
GO
```

Query the view, and examine its contents, which are shown in Table 5-9.

```
SELECT cid, cname, oid FROM dbo.VCustOrders;
```

Table 5-9   Contents of VCustOrders

cid	cname	oid
1	Cust 1	1001
1	Cust 1	1002
1	Cust 1	1003
2	Cust 2	2001
2	Cust 2	2002
2	Cust 2	2003

Notice that customer attributes, such as the company name (*cname*), are duplicated for each matching order.

Suppose that a user who was granted UPDATE permissions against the view wants to modify the company name to '*Cust 42*', where the order ID (*oid*) is equal to 1001. The user submits the following update:

```
UPDATE dbo.VCustOrders
  SET cname = 'Cust 42'
WHERE oid = 1001;
```

Of course, if the target of the update was a table and not a view, you would have seen only one row with '*Cust 42*' in *cname* when querying the table. However, the target of the update is a view, and SQL Server modifies the Customers table underneath the covers. In practice, *cname* is modified for customer 1. Now query the VCustOrders view using the following code and examine the output shown in Table 5-10:

```
SELECT cid, cname, oid FROM dbo.VCustOrders;
```

Table 5-10   Contents of VCustOrders After Update

cid	cname	oid
1	Cust 42	1001
1	Cust 42	1002
1	Cust 42	1003

Table 5-10   Contents of VCustOrders After Update

cid	cname	oid
2	Cust 2	2001
2	Cust 2	2002
2	Cust 2	2003

What happened was that the *cname* value was changed for order 1001. The view's *cname* value for order 1001 was the *cname* value from the Customers table associated with order 1001's customer (customer number 1, as stored in the Orders table). The view returned customer number 1's *cname* value for all three of customer number 1's orders.

When you're done, run the following cleanup code:

```
USE tempdb;
GO
IF OBJECT_ID('dbo.VUserData') IS NOT NULL
  DROP VIEW dbo.VUserData;
GO
IF OBJECT_ID('dbo.UserData') IS NOT NULL
  DROP TABLE dbo.UserData;
GO
IF OBJECT_ID('dbo.VCustOrders') IS NOT NULL
  DROP VIEW dbo.VCustOrders;
GO
IF OBJECT_ID('dbo.Orders') IS NOT NULL
  DROP TABLE dbo.Orders;
GO
IF OBJECT_ID('dbo.Customers') IS NOT NULL
  DROP TABLE dbo.Customers;
GO
```

View Options

When you create or alter a view, you can specify options that will control the view's behavior and functionality. The options ENCRYPTION, SCHEMABINDING, and VIEW_METADATA are specified in the view's header, and the CHECK OPTION is specified after the query.

ENCRYPTION

The ENCRYPTION option is available for views, UDFs, stored procedures, and triggers. If you don't specify the ENCRYPTION option, SQL Server stores the text defining the body of the object/routine as clear text in *sys.sql.modules* (or in *syscomments* in SQL Server 2000). If you specify the ENCRYPTION option, the object's text will be converted to an obfuscated format. But don't rely on this option as an encryption mechanism to protect your intellectual property. People have found ways to decrypt text stored for objects created with the ENCRYPTION option. Even in SQL Server 2005 the object's text will be accessible to privileged users through the dedicated administrator connection (DAC), direct access to the database files or

from memory using a debugger. For details on the ENCRYPTION option, please refer to
Books Online.

SCHEMABINDING

The SCHEMABINDING option binds the schema of the view or UDF to the schema of the
underlying objects. If you create a view with the SCHEMABINDING option, SQL Server will
reject attempts to drop underlying objects or make any schema modification to referenced columns. This option has two syntactical requirements in terms of the query defining the view:
two-part names must be used for all objects (for example, dbo.Orders, not just Orders), and
the use of * is not allowed in the SELECT list—rather, all column names must be specified
explicitly.

As an example of using both ENCRYPTION and SCHEMABINDING, the following code
re-creates the VCustsWithOrders view, which I used earlier in my examples:

```
USE Northwind;
GO
IF OBJECT_ID('dbo.VCustsWithOrders') IS NOT NULL
  DROP VIEW dbo.VCustsWithOrders;
GO
CREATE VIEW dbo.VCustsWithOrders WITH ENCRYPTION, SCHEMABINDING
AS

SELECT CustomerID, CompanyName, ContactName, ContactTitle,
  Address, City, Region, PostalCode, Country, Phone, Fax
FROM dbo.Customers AS C
WHERE EXISTS
  (SELECT 1 FROM dbo.Orders AS O
   WHERE O.CustomerID = C.CustomerID);
GO
```

Note   If the view already exists, it's wiser to use ALTER VIEW than to drop and re-create the
view, because ALTER VIEW preserves permissions.

Notice that I substituted the * I used originally in the subquery's SELECT list with the constant 1 to meet the requirements of the SCHEMABINDING option.

Try to get the text of the view:

```
EXEC sp_helptext 'dbo.VCustsWithOrders';
```

You will get the following output:

```
The text for object 'dbo.VCustsWithOrders' is encrypted.
```

Try to alter one of the referenced columns:

```
ALTER TABLE dbo.Customers DROP COLUMN Address;
```

You will get the following error:

```
Msg 5074, Level 16, State 1, Line 1
The object 'VCustsWithOrders' is dependent on column 'Address'.
Msg 4922, Level 16, State 9, Line 1
ALTER TABLE DROP COLUMN Address failed because one or more objects access this column.
```

CHECK OPTION

Specifying WITH CHECK OPTION when creating a view prevents INSERT and UPDATE statements that conflict with the view's query filter. Without this option, a view normally accepts modifications that do not meet the query's filter. For example, the VCustsWithOrders view accepts the following INSERT, even though it inserts a new customer that has no orders yet:

```
INSERT INTO dbo.VCustsWithOrders(CustomerID, CompanyName)
  VALUES(N'ABCDE', N'Company ABCDE');
```

The new customer was added to the Customers table, but obviously when you query the view, you won't see the new customer because the view contains only customers with orders:

```
SELECT CustomerID, CompanyName
FROM dbo.VCustsWithOrders
WHERE CustomerID = N'ABCDE';
```

This query returns an empty set.

If you query the Customers table directly, you will see the new customer:

```
SELECT CustomerID, CompanyName
FROM dbo.Customers
WHERE CustomerID = N'ABCDE';
```

This query returns information about customer ABCDE.

Next run the following code to add the CHECK OPTION to the view's definition:

```
ALTER VIEW dbo.VCustsWithOrders WITH ENCRYPTION, SCHEMABINDING
AS

SELECT CustomerID, CompanyName, ContactName, ContactTitle,
  Address, City, Region, PostalCode, Country, Phone, Fax
FROM dbo.Customers AS C
WHERE EXISTS
  (SELECT 1 FROM dbo.Orders AS O
   WHERE O.CustomerID = C.CustomerID)
WITH CHECK OPTION;
GO
```

Note When altering the view, you must specify again all options that you want to preserve—in our case, ENCRYPTION and SCHEMABINDING. If you don't mention them in the ALTER statement, they will no longer be in effect.

Now try to insert a row that conflicts with the filter:

```
INSERT INTO dbo.VCustsWithOrders(CustomerID, CompanyName)
  VALUES(N'FGHIJ', N'Company FGHIJ');
```

You will get the following error:

```
Msg 550, Level 16, State 1, Line 1
The attempted insert or update failed because the target view either specifies WITH CHECK
OPTION or spans a view that specifies WITH CHECK OPTION and one or more rows resulting from
the operation did not qualify under the CHECK OPTION constraint.
The statement has been terminated.
```

VIEW_METADATA

SQL Server can control client requests to query or modify data through a view only when the request ends up generating T-SQL code with the view as the target. However, clients that request browse-mode metadata through the DB-Library, ODBC, or OLEDB APIs might cause trouble. Browse-mode metadata is additional metadata about the base tables and columns in the result set that SQL Server returns to these client-side APIs. Of course, if the client chooses to construct statements with the base table as the target instead of the view, user requests might not work as expected.

Suppose that a user was granted permission against a view but not against the underlying tables. The user tries to perform some activity against the view. If the client tool constructs a statement against the base table because it requested browse-mode metadata, such a statement will fail on a security violation. On the other hand, if a user attempts to modify data through a view, and the modification conflicts with a CHECK OPTION defined with the view, such a modification might succeed if submitted directly against the underlying table.

Enterprise Manager (EM) in SQL Server 2000 is one of those tools that requests browse-mode metadata information when you manipulate data through a view graphically (after right-clicking a view name and choosing "Open View" and then "Return all rows"). If you trace the activity that EM submits to SQL Server when you manipulate a view's data, you will find that the activity is actually submitted with the underlying tables as the target. For example, try to insert a new customer through the VCustsWithOrders view using EM. Specify *FGHIJ* in the *CustomerID* column and company *FGHIJ* as the *CompanyName* column. You'll find that although this attempt was supposed to fail on a CHECK OPTION violation, it is accepted, and the row is added to the Customers table. If you trace EM's activity against SQL Server, you will realize why this attempt was successful. The following statement will show up in the trace:

```
exec sp_executesql N'INSERT INTO "Northwind"."dbo"."Customers" ("CustomerID","CompanyName")
VALUES (@P1,@P2)', N'@P1 nvarchar(5),@P2 nvarchar(40)',
N'FGHIJ', N'Company FGHIJ'
```

EM constructed a statement directly against the Customers table instead of against the view. SQL Server Management Studio (SSMS) addressed this problem partially. A similar attempt will still be successful if done in the view/query designer results pane. It will fail if done in the results pane generated by "Open View". For the latter, you will find the following statement in the trace showing that the activity was submitted against the view:

```
exec sp_executesql N'INSERT INTO VCustsWithOrders(CustomerID, CompanyName) VALUES (@Customer
ID, @CompanyName)',N'@CustomerID
nvarchar(5),@CompanyName nvarchar(13)',@CustomerID=N'FGHIJ',@CompanyName=N'Company FGHIJ'
```

If you want SQL Server to send metadata information about the view and not the underlying tables when browse mode metadata is requested by the client APIs, specify the VIEW_METADATA option when you create or alter the view, as in:

```
ALTER VIEW dbo.VCustsWithOrders
  WITH ENCRYPTION, SCHEMABINDING, VIEW_METADATA
AS

SELECT CustomerID, CompanyName, ContactName, ContactTitle,
  Address, City, Region, PostalCode, Country, Phone, Fax
FROM dbo.Customers AS C
WHERE EXISTS
  (SELECT 1 FROM dbo.Orders AS O
   WHERE O.CustomerID = C.CustomerID)
WITH CHECK OPTION;
GO
```

When you're done, issue the following cleanup code:

```
USE Northwind;
GO
DELETE FROM dbo.Customers
WHERE CustomerID IN(N'ABCDE', N'FGHIJ');
GO
IF OBJECT_ID('dbo.VCustsWithOrders') IS NOT NULL
  DROP VIEW dbo.VCustsWithOrders;
GO
```

Indexed Views

Remember that without an index, a view does not have any physical representation of its data—rather, it just has metadata information pointing to the underlying objects. However, SQL Server will physically materialize a view's data if you create a unique clustered index on the view. SQL Server will keep the indexed view in sync with modifications against the underlying tables. You cannot request to synchronize the view's contents on demand or on scheduled basis. An indexed view is very much like a table index in terms of data integrity.

Indexed views can give you great performance benefits for queries that retrieve data. Indexed views can substantially reduce the amount of I/O required to return data and the processing time required for expensive calculations. Substantial performance gains can be achieved, for example, for data aggregation queries or expensive joins. However, keep in mind that modifications to an indexed view's underlying tables will require changes to the indexed (and therefore materialized) view, degrading the performance of your modifications.

There's a long list of requirements and restrictions for creating an indexed view, often preventing indexed views from being a viable option. The requirement list in SQL Server 2005 did not get much shorter.

The first index that you create on a view must be unique and clustered. After creating a clustered index on a view, you can create additional nonclustered indexes. The view must be created with the SCHEMABINDING option; therefore, you must use the two-part naming convention for object names and explicitly specify column names in the SELECT list. If the view's query aggregates data, its select list must include the COUNT_BIG(*) aggregate function. COUNT_BIG is the same as COUNT, except that its result type is BIGINT. This count allows SQL Server to keep track of the number of rows that were aggregated in each group, and it is also used to calculate other aggregates. Some SET options in the session must be in a certain state. The list of requirements and restrictions goes on. Please refer to Books Online for the gory details.

As an example, suppose that you want to optimize queries that request aggregated data from the Orders and Order Details tables for employees. One way to do this is to create a materialized view containing the aggregates you expect to request. The following code creates the VEmpOrders indexed view based on a query that joins Orders and Order Details, groups the data by *EmployeeID*, and calculates the sum of *Quantity* and the count of rows for each employee:

```
USE Northwind;
GO
IF OBJECT_ID('dbo.VEmpOrders') IS NOT NULL
  DROP VIEW dbo.VEmpOrders;
GO
CREATE VIEW dbo.VEmpOrders WITH SCHEMABINDING
AS

SELECT O.EmployeeID, SUM(OD.Quantity) AS TotalQty, COUNT_BIG(*) AS Cnt
FROM dbo.Orders AS O
  JOIN dbo.[Order Details] AS OD
    ON OD.OrderID = O.OrderID
GROUP BY O.EmployeeID;
GO
CREATE UNIQUE CLUSTERED INDEX idx_uc_empid ON dbo.VEmpOrders(EmployeeID);
GO
```

Notice that the view was created with the SCHEMABINDING option, the tables are referenced with two-part names, the COUNT_BIG function is used because it's a query that calculates aggregates, and the index created on the view is both clustered and unique.

SQL Server doesn't regenerate the whole index whenever the underlying tables are modified; rather, it maintains the index in a smarter manner. When you insert data, SQL Server will identify the affected row of the view and increment the aggregate values *TotalQty* and *Cnt* for that row. When you delete data, SQL Server will decrement these values. When you update data in the underlying tables, SQL Server will update the aggregate values accordingly.

To observe the performance benefit indexed views can give you, run the following query after turning on the STATISTICS IO option and the Include Actual Execution Plan in SSMS:

```
SELECT EmployeeID, TotalQty, Cnt FROM dbo.VEmpOrders;
```

The output of this query is shown in Table 5-11, and the execution plan is shown in Figure 5-3.

Table 5-11 Contents of VEmpOrders

EmployeeID	TotalQty	Cnt
1	7812	345
2	6055	241
3	7852	321
4	9798	420
5	3036	117
6	3527	168
7	4654	176
8	5913	260
9	2670	107

Figure 5-3 Execution plan for a query against the VEmpOrders view

The plan shows that the view's clustered index was scanned. For this small view, which contains only nine rows, the total I/O was two logical reads. If you're using the Enterprise edition of SQL Server (or the Developer edition, which is equivalent in its feature set), the query optimizer will consider using the indexed view for queries against the view without specifying any hints, and for queries against the base tables. For example, the following query generates the execution plan shown in Figure 5-4:

```
SELECT O.EmployeeID, SUM(OD.Quantity) AS TotalQty, AVG(OD.Quantity) AS AvgQty, COUNT_BIG(*)
AS Cnt
FROM dbo.Orders AS O
  JOIN dbo.[Order Details] AS OD
    ON OD.OrderID = O.OrderID
GROUP BY O.EmployeeID;
```

Figure 5-4 Execution plan for a query against the Orders and Order Details tables

As you can see, the indexed view was used, and again the I/O cost was only two logical reads. Interestingly, the query requested the aggregate *AVG(OD.Quantity)*, which was not part of the view, yet the indexed view was used. Remember that the sum and the count were calculated. If you expand the properties of the Compute Scalar operator in the plan, you will find the following expression, which calculates the average from the sum and the count:

```
[Expr1005] = CASE WHEN [Northwind].[dbo].[VEmpOrders].[Cnt]=(0) THEN NULL ELSE [Northwind].[
dbo].[VEmpOrders].[TotalQty]/
CONVERT_IMPLICIT(int,[Northwind].[dbo].[VEmpOrders].[Cnt],0) END, [[Northwind].[dbo].[VEmpOr
ders].Cnt] = [Northwind].[dbo].[VEmpOrders].[Cnt]
```

Note   If you're not working with the Enterprise or Developer edition of SQL Server, an indexed view will not be considered by default even when you query the view directly. To use the index, you must specify the NOEXPAND hint.

As I mentioned earlier, the requirements and restrictions list for creating an indexed view did not get much shorter in SQL Server 2005. The optimizer was enhanced in the sense that it uses indexed views in more cases. For example, SQL Server 2000 did not use an indexed view when the outer query specified a subinterval of the view's query filter. That is, if the view's query had the filter *col1 > 5* and the outer query had the filter *col1 > 10*, the indexed view was not considered at all. SQL Server 2005 now supports subintervals. Similarly, SQL Server 2000 did not consider the index when the outer query used a logically equivalent filter expression as the view's expression, but not an exact one. For example, if the view's query had the filter *col1 = 5* and the outer query had *5 = col1*, SQL Server 2000's optimizer did not consider using the indexed view. SQL Server 2005's optimizer does.

More Info   For detailed information about indexed views in SQL Server 2005 and improvements over SQL Server 2000, please refer to the white paper "Improving Performance with SQL Server 2005 Indexed Views" by Eric Hanson, which can be found at *http://www.microsoft.com/technet/prodtechnol/sql/2005/ipsql05iv.mspx*.

You can use indexed views for other purposes besides performance. For example, T-SQL's UNIQUE constraint treats two NULLs as equal. If you create a UNIQUE constraint on a nullable column, the constraint will allow only one instance of a NULL in that column. Suppose that you want to enforce uniqueness for known (that is, NOT NULL) values only, but allow multiple NULLs. You can achieve this by using a trigger, but such a trigger has a cost. If the trigger rolls back, it's as if the modification that fired it was done twice—or, more accurately, done and then undone. Instead of using a trigger, you can enforce such an integrity rule by using an indexed view. Create an indexed view based on a query that filters only the non-NULL values from the source column. Remember that the clustered index created on a view must be unique. Such an index will prevent duplicate known values from entering the base table, but it will allow multiple NULLs because NULLs are not part of the unique index.

To demonstrate this, run the following code, which creates the table T1 with the column *keycol*, and an indexed view based on a query that filters only known *keycol* values from T1:

```
USE tempdb;
GO
IF OBJECT_ID('dbo.V1') IS NOT NULL
  DROP VIEW dbo.V1;
GO
IF OBJECT_ID('dbo.T1') IS NOT NULL
  DROP TABLE dbo.T1;
GO
CREATE TABLE dbo.T1
(
  keycol  INT         NULL,
  datacol VARCHAR(10) NOT NULL
);
GO
CREATE VIEW dbo.V1 WITH SCHEMABINDING
AS

SELECT keycol FROM dbo.T1 WHERE keycol IS NOT NULL;
GO
CREATE UNIQUE CLUSTERED INDEX idx_uc_keycol ON dbo.V1(keycol);
```

Next, issue the following INSERT statements:

```
INSERT INTO dbo.T1(keycol, datacol) VALUES(1,    'a');
INSERT INTO dbo.T1(keycol, datacol) VALUES(1,    'b'); -- fails
INSERT INTO dbo.T1(keycol, datacol) VALUES(NULL, 'c');
INSERT INTO dbo.T1(keycol, datacol) VALUES(NULL, 'd');
```

Notice that the second attempt to insert a row with the value 1 in *keycol* fails, but both NULLs are accepted. Query T1 and observe in the output shown in Table 5-12 that both NULLs reached the table:

```
SELECT keycol, datacol FROM dbo.T1;
```

Table 5-12 Contents of T1

keycol	datacol
1	a
NULL	c
NULL	d

When done, run the following code for cleanup:

```
USE Northwind;
GO
IF OBJECT_ID('dbo.VEmpOrders') IS NOT NULL
  DROP VIEW dbo.VEmpOrders;
GO
USE tempdb;
```

```
GO
IF OBJECT_ID('dbo.V1') IS NOT NULL
  DROP VIEW dbo.V1;
GO
IF OBJECT_ID('dbo.T1') IS NOT NULL
  DROP TABLE dbo.T1;
GO
```

Conclusion

Views give you great power. They give you some degree of security enforcement, allow you to develop simpler solutions in a modular approach, and can help you improve the performance of your queries when you index them. Keep in mind that a view represents a table and, as such, does not have any guaranteed order to its rows. Do not attempt to produce a "sorted" view because the entire premise for adopting such an approach is wrong. If you need to send data from a view to the client in a particular order, specify an ORDER BY clause in the outer query. Remember to refresh views' metadata information after applying schema changes to underlying objects in the database.

Chapter 6
User-Defined Functions

User-defined functions (UDFs) are routines that perform calculations/computations and return a value—scalar (singular) or table. Microsoft SQL Server 2000 introduced UDFs, which you developed with T-SQL and could incorporate in queries, computed columns, and constraints. SQL Server 2005 introduces common language runtime (CLR) integration, allowing you to develop UDFs—as well as other routines and objects—using a .NET language of your choice.

This chapter explores the types of UDFs that are supported by SQL Server: scalar-valued UDFs, which return a single value, and table-valued UDFs (inline and multiple-statement), which return a table. I'll provide sample code for CLR UDFs in both C# and Microsoft Visual Basic.

All the .NET routines in this book were developed by Dejan Sarka.

Note This chapter is the first of three chapters (6, 7, and 8) that cover CLR routines. Some of the steps involved in building and deploying CLR code into a database are common to any type of CLR routine that you create in SQL Server and also very technical. To avoid repetition of such technical steps in the text and to allow you to focus on the code of the routines, I compiled all the relevant information about CLR routines into Appendix A.

In Appendix A, you will find instructions for creating a test database called CLRUtilities, which you will use to test all CLR routines covered in these three chapters. You will also find step-by-step instructions required to develop, build, deploy, and test all the CLR routines.

The appendix also gathers in one place all the code of CLR routines that is scattered throughout these three chapters. I recommend that, before reading the remainder of this chapter, you follow the instructions in Appendix A, which will have you create in advance all the routines you will use in these three chapters. Then return to this chapter and continue reading, focusing on the code of the CLR routines instead of on the common technical steps.

Some Facts About UDFs

UDFs can be embedded in queries, constraints, and computed columns. The code that defines a UDF may not cause side effects that affect the database state outside the scope of the function—that is, the UDF's code is not allowed to modify data in tables or to invoke a function that has side effects (for example, RAND). In addition, the UDF's code can only create table variables and cannot create or access temporary tables. Also, the UDF's code is not allowed to use dynamic execution.

When creating or altering a UDF, you can specify function options in the header. T-SQL UDFs support the ENCRYPTION and SCHEMABINDING options, which I described in the previous chapter when discussing views. Both T-SQL and CLR UDFs can be created with a new EXECUTE AS clause, which lets you define the security context of the execution of the function. This option is not available to inline table-valued UDFs. An inline table-valued UDF is very similar to a view with the exception that it can accept arguments. It consists of a single query that defines the table returned by the function. With scalar UDFs (both T-SQL and CLR), you can now also specify one of the options: RETURNS NULL ON NULL INPUT or CALLED ON NULL INPUT (the default). The former option tells SQL Server not to invoke the function at all if a parameter value is NULL; in this case, the function result will be NULL. The latter option tells SQL Server that you want it to invoke the function even when one of the input parameters is NULL.

It is a good practice to create all your UDFs with both the SCHEMABINDING and RETURNS NULL ON NULL INPUT options when it is the desired behavior. SCHEMABINDING will prevent dropping underlying objects and schema changes to referenced columns. RETURNS NULL ON NULL INPUT can improve the performance of your code by bypassing the function logic and returning NULL when one of the inputs is NULL. Where this is the desired behavior, and the option is used, it may eliminate the need to check for NULL input with explicit code in the body of the function. In the code samples in this chapter, for the sake of brevity, I will not specify these options.

Scalar UDFs

Scalar UDFs return a single (scalar) value. They can be specified where scalar expressions are allowed—for example, in a query, constraint, computed column, and so on. Scalar UDFs have several syntactical requirements. Scalar UDFs:

- Must have a BEGIN/END block defining their body.
- Must be schema qualified when invoked (unless invoked as stored procedures with EXEC, as in *EXEC myFunction 3, 4*).
- Do not allow omitting optional parameters (ones that have default values) when invoked; rather, you must at least specify the DEFAULT keyword for those.

The following sections explore both T-SQL and CLR UDFs.

T-SQL Scalar UDFs

T-SQL UDFs are typically faster than CLR UDFs when the main cost of their activity pertains to set-based data manipulation, as opposed to procedural logic and computations. This is the case with any type of routine—not just UDFs. In the function's header you specify its name, define the input parameters, and define the datatype of the returned value. As an example of a scalar UDF, the following code creates the fn_ConcatOrders function, which accepts a customer ID as input and returns a string with the concatenated *OrderID*s for the input customer:

```
SET NOCOUNT ON;
USE Northwind;
GO
IF OBJECT_ID('dbo.fn_ConcatOrders') IS NOT NULL
  DROP FUNCTION dbo.fn_ConcatOrders;
GO

CREATE FUNCTION dbo.fn_ConcatOrders
  (@cid AS NCHAR(5)) RETURNS VARCHAR(8000)
AS
BEGIN
  DECLARE @orders AS VARCHAR(8000);
  SET @orders = '';
  SELECT @orders = @orders + CAST(OrderID AS VARCHAR(10)) + ';'
  FROM dbo.Orders
  WHERE CustomerID = @cid;

  RETURN @orders;
END
GO
```

The function declares the *@orders* variable and initializes it with an empty string. The query in the function uses a special T-SQL assignment SELECT syntax. It scans the qualifying rows, and for each row it assigns a value to the *@orders* variable. The value is the current content of *@orders* concatenated with the current *OrderID* and a semicolon as the separator.

> **Important**   This query does not guarantee any order of concatenation. The *OrderID*s will be concatenated in the order in which SQL Server happened to physically scan the data. In such a query, be careful not to rely on an ORDER BY clause. SQL Server will not produce an error if you specify ORDER BY, but it won't guarantee that the data is sorted before the assignments take place.
>
> Also, there's no official documentation from Microsoft describing this aggregate concatenation technique (with or without an ORDER BY clause). The behavior described here is based on observation alone—I haven't yet seen it fail without ORDER BY. But remember that there's no official guarantee that the elements from all qualifying rows will be concatenated, so you may prefer to refrain from relying on this technique in production code altogether.

To test the fn_ConcatOrders function, run the following query, which generates the output shown in abbreviated form in Table 6-1:

```
SELECT CustomerID, dbo.fn_ConcatOrders(CustomerID) AS Orders
FROM dbo.Customers;
```

Table 6-1 Concatenated *OrderID*s per Customer (Abbreviated)

CustomerID	*Orders*
ALFKI	10643;10692;10702;10835;10952;11011;
ANATR	10308;10625;10759;10926;
ANTON	10365;10507;10535;10573;10677;10682;10856;
AROUT	10355;10383;10453;10558;10707;10741;10743;10768;10793;10864;10920; 10953;11016;
BERGS	10278;10280;10384;10444;10445;10524;10572;10626;10654;10672;10689;107 33;10778;10837;10857;10866;10875;10924;
BLAUS	10501;10509;10582;10614;10853;10956;11058;
BLONP	10265;10297;10360;10436;10449;10559;10566;10584;10628;10679;10826;
BOLID	10326;10801;10970;
BONAP	10331;10340;10362;10470;10511;10525;10663;10715;10730;10732;10755;108 27;10871;10876;10932;10940;11076;
BSBEV	10289;10471;10484;10538;10539;10578;10599;10943;10947;11023;
...	...

In SQL Server 2005, you don't really need such techniques to achieve string concatenation. You can use the FOR XML PATH option, which I described earlier in the book, providing an empty string as an input, as in:

```
SET NOCOUNT ON;
USE Northwind;
GO

SELECT CustomerID,
  (SELECT CAST(OrderID AS VARCHAR(10)) + ';' AS [text()]
   FROM dbo.Orders AS O
   WHERE O.CustomerID = C.CustomerID
   ORDER BY OrderID
   FOR XML PATH('')) AS Orders
FROM dbo.Customers AS C;
```

Here you can fully control the order of concatenation.

User-defined aggregates (UDAs) in SQL Server 2005 can also solve this problem. Although with a UDA you won't be able to control the order of concatenation, and the concatenated string will be limited to 8000 bytes. For more info about UDAs, please refer to *Inside T-SQL Querying*.

When you're done, run the following code for cleanup:

```
IF OBJECT_ID('dbo.fn_ConcatOrders') IS NOT NULL
  DROP FUNCTION dbo.fn_ConcatOrders;
```

Performance Issues

You should be aware that invoking scalar UDFs in queries has a high cost when you provide the function with attributes from the outer table as inputs. Even when the function only has a return clause with a scalar expression, it is not considered inline. The overhead of the function call per-row involves a high cost. You can run a simple performance test to realize the high cost involved with UDFs compared to inline expressions in a query.

Before you run the performance test, make sure you have the Nums table in the database. I provided the code to create and populate Nums in Chapter 1.

Turn on the Discard Results After Execution option in SQL Server Management Studio (SSMS) so that your measurements will not include the time it takes to generate the output.

Start by running a query against a million rows from Nums, with an inline expression that adds 1 to *n*:

```
SELECT n, n+1 AS n2 FROM dbo.Nums WHERE n <= 1000000;
```

The first invocation of the code might have had to scan the data physically. Now that the data is loaded in to cache, run the query a second time and measure the run time. When I ran this code on my system, it finished in less than a second.

Next create the fn_add1 UDF:

```
IF OBJECT_ID('dbo.fn_add1') IS NOT NULL
  DROP FUNCTION dbo.fn_add1;
GO
CREATE FUNCTION dbo.fn_add1(@i AS INT) RETURNS INT
AS
BEGIN
  RETURN @i + 1;
END
GO
```

Now run the query using fn_add1:

```
SELECT n, dbo.fn_add1(n) AS n2 FROM dbo.Nums WHERE n <= 1000000;
```

This query ran for 3 seconds.

The high cost of the last query has to do with the overhead of each function call. You can easily observe the multiple invocations of the UDF by running a SQL Server Profiler trace with the *SP:Completed* (or *SP:Starting*) event while the query is running. To limit the size of the trace, you might want to test the query against fewer rows—for example, with the filter $n <= 10$. Figure 6-1 shows the events I got when I traced this query.

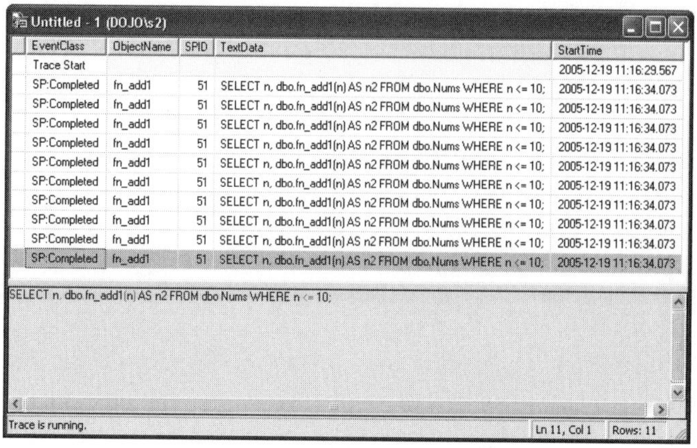

Figure 6-1 Profiler trace of multiple scalar UDF invocations

At this point, you can turn off the Discard Results After Execution option in SSMS.

There are many benefits to using UDFs in terms of code simplicity and maintenance; though in terms of performance, typically you'll be better off if you manage to express your calculations as inline expressions in the query and avoid using UDFs. You might be surprised at times that some calculations that seem to require iterative or procedural logic can be achieved with inline expressions.

For example, the following query counts the number of occurrences of the string stored in the variable *@find* in the *Customers.CompanyName* column:

```
DECLARE @find AS NVARCHAR(40);
SET @find = N'n';

SELECT CompanyName,
  (LEN(CompanyName+'*') - LEN(REPLACE(CompanyName, @find, '')+'*'))
    / LEN(@find) AS Cnt
FROM dbo.Customers;
```

Table 6-2 shows, in abbreviated form, the output this query produces.

Table 6-2   Occurrences of *'n'* in Customer Company Names (Abbreviated)

CompanyName	Cnt
Alfreds Futterkiste	0
Ana Trujillo Emparedados y helados	1
Antonio Moreno Taquería	3
Around the Horn	2
Berglunds snabbköp	2

Table 6-2   Occurrences of 'n' in Customer Company Names (Abbreviated)

CompanyName	*Cnt*
Blauer See Delikatessen	1
Blondesddsl père et fils	1
Bólido Comidas preparadas	0
Bon app'	1
Bottom-Dollar Markets	0
...	...

The expression uses the REPLACE function to calculate this count. The logic is that you can figure out how many times @*find* appears in a string by seeing how much shorter the string would get if each instance were removed (that is, replaced with "). Notice that '*' is added to both strings before their lengths are measured to avoid getting an incorrect length when the string has trailing spaces.

UDFs Used in Constraints

Scalar UDFs can be used in constraints. The following sections discuss and demonstrate how you can use UDFs in DEFAULT, CHECK, PRIMARY KEY, and UNIQUE constraints.

DEFAULT Constraints

Scalar UDFs can be used in DEFAULT constraints. The only limitation that you should be aware of is that a UDF cannot accept columns from the table as inputs when used in a DEFAULT constraint. As an example, the code in Listing 6-1 creates a table called T1 and a UDF called fn_T1_getkey, which returns the minimum missing key in T1.

Listing 6-1   Creating table T1 and the fn_T1_getkey UDF

```
IF OBJECT_ID('dbo.T1') IS NOT NULL
  DROP TABLE dbo.T1;
GO
CREATE TABLE dbo.T1
(
  keycol INT NOT NULL CONSTRAINT PK_T1 PRIMARY KEY CHECK (keycol > 0),
  datacol VARCHAR(10) NOT NULL
);
GO

IF OBJECT_ID('dbo.fn_T1_getkey') IS NOT NULL
  DROP FUNCTION dbo.fn_T1_getkey;
GO
CREATE FUNCTION dbo.fn_T1_getkey() RETURNS INT
AS
BEGIN
  RETURN
    CASE
      WHEN NOT EXISTS(SELECT * FROM dbo.T1 WHERE keycol = 1) THEN 1
```

```
        ELSE (SELECT MIN(keycol + 1)
              FROM dbo.T1 AS A
              WHERE NOT EXISTS
                (SELECT *
                 FROM dbo.T1 AS B
                 WHERE B.keycol = A.keycol + 1))
    END;
  END
  GO
```

The following code adds a DEFAULT constraint to *keycol*, which invokes the fn_T1_getkey function:

```
ALTER TABLE dbo.T1 ADD DEFAULT(dbo.fn_T1_getkey()) FOR keycol;
```

> **Note** Note that this DEFAULT constraint will do its job only for single row inserts, not for multiple-row inserts. Also, reusing key values is almost never advisable in actual business scenarios. I'm using this example here for demonstration purposes.

The following code inserts three rows, generating the keys 1, 2, and 3; deletes the row with the key 2; and inserts another row, generating the key 2:

```
INSERT INTO dbo.T1(datacol) VALUES('a');
INSERT INTO dbo.T1(datacol) VALUES('b');
INSERT INTO dbo.T1(datacol) VALUES('c');
DELETE FROM dbo.T1 WHERE keycol = 2;
INSERT INTO dbo.T1(datacol) VALUES('d');
```

Query the table by using the following code, and notice in Table 6-3 (which shows the output) that key 2 was assigned to the row that was inserted last (*datacol* = '*d*'), because the row with the key 2 was previously deleted:

```
SELECT * FROM dbo.T1;
```

Table 6-3 Contents of T1

keycol	datacol
1	a
2	d
3	C

CHECK Constraints

Unlike UDFs used in DEFAULT constraints, UDFs used in CHECK constraints are allowed to refer to columns from the table as inputs. CHECK constraints with UDFs give you great power in enforcing integrity rules, allowing you in some cases to avoid using triggers, which are typically more expensive. Later in this chapter I will demonstrate using UDFs that match input strings based on regular expressions in CHECK constraints.

PRIMARY KEY and UNIQUE Constraints

You can create a UNIQUE or PRIMARY KEY constraint on a computed column that invokes a UDF. Keep in mind that both constraints create a unique index underneath the covers. This means that the target computed column and the UDF it invokes must meet indexing guidelines. For example, the UDF must be schema bound (created with the SCHEMABINDING option); the computed column must be deterministic and precise or deterministic and persisted, and so on. You can find the details about indexing guidelines for computed columns and UDFs in Books Online.

The following code attempts to add to T1 a computed column called *col1*, which invokes the fn_add1 UDF, and create a UNIQUE constraint on that column:

```
ALTER TABLE dbo.T1
  ADD col1 AS dbo.fn_add1(keycol) CONSTRAINT UQ_T1_col1 UNIQUE;
```

The attempt fails with the following error:

```
Msg 2729, Level 16, State 1, Line 1
Column 'col1' in table 'dbo.T1' cannot be used in an index or statistics or as a partition
key because it is non-deterministic.
Msg 1750, Level 16, State 0, Line 1
Could not create constraint. See previous errors.
```

The reason for the error is that the function doesn't meet one of the requirements for indexing, which says that the function must be schema bound. As you can see, the error message itself is not too helpful in indicating the cause of the error or in suggesting how to fix it. You need to realize that in order to fix the problem, you should alter the function by adding the SCHEMABINDING option:

```
ALTER FUNCTION dbo.fn_add1(@i AS INT) RETURNS INT
  WITH SCHEMABINDING
AS
BEGIN
  RETURN @i + 1;
END
GO
```

Try adding the computed column with the UNIQUE constraint again, and this time your code will run successfully:

```
ALTER TABLE dbo.T1
  ADD col1 AS dbo.fn_add1(keycol) CONSTRAINT UQ_T1_col1 UNIQUE;
```

It's a bit trickier when you try to create a PRIMARY KEY constraint on such a computed column. To see how this works, first drop the existing PRIMARY KEY from T1:

```
ALTER TABLE dbo.T1 DROP CONSTRAINT PK_T1;
```

Next attempt to add another computed column called *col2* with a PRIMARY KEY constraint:

```
ALTER TABLE dbo.T1
  ADD col2 AS dbo.fn_add1(keycol)
    CONSTRAINT PK_T1 PRIMARY KEY;
```

The attempt will fail, generating the following error:

```
Msg 1711, Level 16, State 1, Line 1
Cannot define PRIMARY KEY constraint on column 'col2' in table 'T1'. The computed column has
 to be persisted and not nullable.
Msg 1750, Level 16, State 0, Line 1
Could not create constraint. See previous errors.
```

You must explicitly guarantee that *col2* will never end up with a NULL. You can achieve this by defining the column as PERSISTED and NOT NULL, as in:

```
ALTER TABLE dbo.T1
  ADD col2 AS dbo.fn_add1(keycol) PERSISTED NOT NULL
    CONSTRAINT PK_T1 PRIMARY KEY;
```

The PERSISTED option is new to SQL Server 2005; in SQL Server 2000, to successfully create a primary key constraint on the computed column, you must encapsulate the UDF invocation within the ISNULL function, as in:

```
ALTER TABLE dbo.T1
  ADD col2 AS ISNULL(dbo.fn_add1(keycol), 0)
    CONSTRAINT PK_T1 PRIMARY KEY;
```

When you're done, run the following code for cleanup:

```
IF OBJECT_ID('dbo.T1') IS NOT NULL
  DROP TABLE dbo.T1;
GO
IF OBJECT_ID('dbo.fn_T1_getkey') IS NOT NULL
  DROP FUNCTION dbo.fn_T1_getkey;
GO
IF OBJECT_ID('dbo.fn_T1_datacol_count') IS NOT NULL
  DROP FUNCTION dbo.fn_T1_datacol_count;
```

CLR Scalar UDFs

This section covers CLR scalar UDFs and compares them with T-SQL UDFs where relevant. Remember that Appendix A provides the instructions you need to follow to develop, build, deploy, and test the CLR routines. In this chapter, as well as in other sections in the book where I cover CLR routines, I'll focus only on the routines' code. The appendix provides the namespace definitions and the *CLRUtilities* class that contains the routines. Here's the C# version of the namespace definitions and the header of the *CLRUtilities* class:

```
using System;
using System.Data;
using System.Data.SqlClient;
```

```
using System.Data.SqlTypes;
using Microsoft.SqlServer.Server;
using System.Text;
using System.Text.RegularExpressions;
using System.Collections;
using System.Collections.Generic;
using System.Diagnostics;
using System.Reflection;

public partial class CLRUtilities
{
    ... routine definitions go here ...
}
```

And here's the Visual Basic version:

```
Imports System
Imports System.Data
Imports System.Data.SqlClient
Imports System.Data.SqlTypes
Imports Microsoft.SqlServer.Server
Imports System.Text
Imports System.Text.RegularExpressions
Imports System.Collections
Imports System.Collections.Generic
Imports System.Diagnostics
Imports System.Reflection
Imports System.Runtime.InteropServices

Partial Public Class CLRUtilities
    ... routine definitions go here ...
End Class
```

I won't repeat the definition of the namespaces and the class. I also won't provide instructions that are as detailed as those in the appendix for the common technical steps involved.

CLR Routines

The ability to develop CLR routines in SQL Server gives you great power, but at the same time it introduces great risk. .NET gives you a richer programming vocabulary and better performance than T-SQL in areas that T-SQL was never designed to cope with efficiently. These areas include complex calculations, iterative and procedural logic, string manipulation, external access to operating system resources, and so on. T-SQL is a declarative language. It's much more powerful and better performing than .NET when the task at hand is data manipulation with set-based queries. The danger with .NET integration is that it is also a vehicle for programmers who have not yet adopted a SQL mindset, enabling them to introduce poorly performing code with inappropriate tools. In this book, I'll give examples of where routines should be developed with .NET.

 More Info   For information about set-based querying and efficient set-based solutions, please refer to *Inside T-SQL Querying*, which covers those topics in great detail.

Regular Expressions

Regular expressions give you a powerful way to match patterns of text with concise and flexible notation. *Regular expression* is a standard and meaningful term that has been around a long time. ANSI SQL defines a SIMILAR TO predicate that provides support for regular expressions, but unfortunately SQL Server 2005 hasn't yet implemented this predicate in T-SQL. However, you can take good advantage of regular expressions in .NET code. For example, the following C# code defines a function called fn_RegExMatch:

```
// Validate input string against regular expression
[SqlFunction(IsDeterministic = true, DataAccess = DataAccessKind.None)]
public static SqlBoolean fn_RegExMatch(SqlString inpStr,
  SqlString regExStr)
{
    if (inpStr.IsNull || regExStr.IsNull)
        return SqlBoolean.Null;
    else
        return (SqlBoolean)Regex.IsMatch(inpStr.Value, regExStr.Value ,
          RegexOptions.CultureInvariant);
}
```

The attributes in the header will tell SQL Server that the function is deterministic and that there's no data access involved. Note the usage of *RegexOptions.CultureInvariant* option to get a culture-independent match. If the match would be culture-dependent, the function would not be deterministic. (See *http://msdn2.microsoft.com/en-us/library/z0sbec17.aspx* for details.)

The function accepts a string (*inpStr*) and a regular expression (*regExStr*) as inputs. The return type of this function is *SqlBoolean*, which has three possible values: 0, 1, and Null; the return value is Null if *regExStr* or *inpStr* is null, 1 if the pattern *regExStr* was found in *inpStr*, and 0 otherwise. As you can see, the function's code is very simple. The code first tests for NULL input parameters and returns NULL if either parameter is NULL. If neither input parameter is NULL, the function returns the result of the *Regex.IsMatch* method. This method checks whether the string provided as the first parameter contains the pattern provided as the second parameter. The *RegEx.IsMatch* method returns a .NET *System.Boolean* value, which must be explicitly converted to *SqlBoolean*.

Here's the function's code using Visual Basic, in case that's your language of preference:

```
' Validate input string against regular expression
<SqlFunction(IsDeterministic:=True, DataAccess:=DataAccessKind.None)> _
Public Shared Function fn_RegExMatch(ByVal inpStr As SqlString, _
  ByVal regExStr As SqlString) As SqlBoolean
    If (inpStr.IsNull Or regExStr.IsNull) Then
        Return SqlBoolean.Null
    Else
        Return CType(Regex.IsMatch(inpStr.Value, regExStr.Value, _
          RegexOptions.CultureInvariant), SqlBoolean)
    End If
End Function
```

If you followed all the instructions described in Appendix A, you're ready to test and use the function. Those instructions include: enabling CLR in SQL Server (disabled by default), creating a test database called CLRUtilities, developing your code in Microsoft Visual Studio 2005, building an assembly in a .dll file on disk, loading the Intermediate Language (IL) code from the assembly into a SQL Server database, and registering routines from the assembly in the database. Here's the code you need to run to enable CLR in SQL Server and create the CLRUtilities test database, in case you haven't yet done so:

```
SET NOCOUNT ON;
USE master;
EXEC sp_configure 'clr enabled', 1;
RECONFIGURE;
GO
IF DB_ID('CLRUtilities') IS NOT NULL
  DROP DATABASE CLRUtilities;
GO
CREATE DATABASE CLRUtilities;
GO
USE CLRUtilities;
GO
```

Note   Note that by turning on the 'clr enabled' server configuration option (disabled by default) you specify that user assemblies can be run by Microsoft SQL Server at the instance level. You cannot control this option at a more granular level, so by enabling this option, you enable it for the whole SQL Server instance. Enabling this option might impose a security risk. The level of risk depends on what you will allow each individual assembly to do. When creating assemblies with the CREATE ASSEMBLY command, you can control code access permissions by setting the PERMISSION_SET option to *SAFE, EXTERNAL_ACCESS* or *UNSAFE*. Here's a security note from Books Online describing the three:

SAFE is the recommended permission setting for assemblies that perform computation and data management tasks without accessing resources outside an instance of SQL Server.

We recommend using EXTERNAL_ACCESS *for assemblies that access resources outside of an instance of SQL Server.* EXTERNAL_ACCESS *assemblies include the reliability and scalability protections of* SAFE *assemblies, but from a security perspective are similar to* UNSAFE *assemblies. This is because code in* EXTERNAL_ACCESS *assemblies runs by default under the SQL Server service account and accesses external resources under that account, unless the code explicitly impersonates the caller. Therefore, permission to create* EXTERNAL_ACCESS *assemblies should be granted only to logins that are trusted to run code under the SQL Server service account. For more information about impersonation, see CLR Integration Security.*

Specifying UNSAFE *enables the code in the assembly complete freedom to perform operations in the SQL Server process space that can potentially compromise the robustness of SQL Server.* UNSAFE *assemblies can also potentially subvert the security system of either SQL Server or the common language runtime.* UNSAFE *permissions should be granted only to highly trusted assemblies. Only members of the sysadmin fixed server role can create and alter UNSAFE assemblies.*

None of the functions that will be discussed in this chapter requires external access, so the assembly will be created with a SAFE permission set. In the following chapters, I will demonstrate a stored procedure that requires EXTERNAL_ACCESS permission set and a trigger that requires UNSAFE permission set, but I'll do so only for demonstration purposes. When demonstrating those routines, I'll alter the assembly to support the required permission set. Bear in mind the security risk involved in allowing external access to your assembly.

In all the following examples in the book, I'll assume that the CLRUtilities database exists and that you already built the assembly from Visual Studio.

Next run the following code to load the assembly into the database if you haven't done so yet:

```
USE CLRUtilities;
GO
CREATE ASSEMBLY CLRUtilities
FROM 'C:\CLRUtilities\CLRUtilities\bin\Debug\CLRUtilities.dll'
WITH PERMISSION_SET = SAFE;
-- If no Debug folder, use instead:
-- FROM 'C:\CLRUtilities\CLRUtilities\bin\CLRUtilities.dll'
```

Of course, if the CLRUtilities.dll file containing the assembly was created in a different folder, specify the relevant folder instead. The CREATE ASSEMBLY command loads the IL code from the .dll file into the database. Once it's loaded, you no longer need the external file. Note that if you rebuild the assembly later after adding routines and do not use the automatic deployment option from Visual Studio Professional edition, you will need to issue an ALTER ASSEMBLY or DROP and CREATE ASSEMBLY commands manually to reload the IL code into the database. This step is not necessary if you followed the instructions in Appendix A and already created all routines that are discussed in the book. I will not refer further to this step.

Whenever I discuss a new routine, I will provide the T-SQL code required to register it in the database (CREATE FUNCTION | PROCEDURE | TRIGGER command), although you don't actually need to run such code if you followed the instructions in Appendix A fully.

Here's the code you need to run to register the C# version of the fn_RegExMatch function in the CLRUtilities database:

```
USE CLRUtilities;
GO
IF OBJECT_ID('dbo.fn_RegExMatch') IS NOT NULL
  DROP FUNCTION dbo.fn_RegExMatch;
GO
CREATE FUNCTION dbo.fn_RegExMatch
  (@inpstr AS NVARCHAR(MAX), @regexstr AS NVARCHAR(MAX))
RETURNS BIT
EXTERNAL NAME CLRUtilities.CLRUtilities.fn_RegExMatch;
```

And here's the code that registers the Visual Basic version:

```
CREATE FUNCTION dbo.fn_RegExMatch
  (@inpstr AS NVARCHAR(MAX), @regexstr AS NVARCHAR(MAX))
RETURNS BIT
EXTERNAL NAME CLRUtilities.[CLRUtilities.CLRUtilities].fn_RegExMatch;
```

Note   Notice the discrepancy between the external name specified when registering a function developed with C# compared to one developed with Visual Basic (*CLRUtilities .CLRUtilities.fn_RegExMatch* vs. *CLRUtilities.[CLRUtilities.CLRUtilities].fn_RegExMatch*). This is quite confusing. In previous .NET versions (2002, 2003), whenever you created a class library, C# added a root namespace with the same name as the class, and Visual Basic didn't. Now the behavior is different: Visual Basic creates a root namespace, and C# does not. To make the T-SQL code consistent regardless of the .NET language you used, you must prevent the creation of the root namespace when programming with Visual Basic. In Visual Studio, right-click the project, select Properties, Application page. Clear the "Root namespace" textbox. In this book I will assume that you did not clear this option, hence when registering objects you will see a discrepancy in the specified external names.

At this point, you can start using the fn_RegExMatch function.

More Info   You can find many useful regular expressions on the Internet—for example, at this "library": *http://www.regexlib.com*.

As an example of using your new function, suppose that you want to check whether a certain e-mail address is valid. To do so, use the regular expression: $N'^([\w-]+\.)*?[\w-]+@[\w-]+ \.([\w-]+\.)*?[\w]+\$'$.

The regular expression checks whether the address starts with a word, contains the "at" (@) symbol, and has at least two words delimited with a dot (.) after the @ symbol. It can have additional dot-separated words before and after the @ symbol. Note that this regular expression is simplistic and is provided here for demonstration purposes. To learn how to write more robust and complete regular expressions, I suggest that you visit *http:// www.regularexpressions.info/*.

The following code returns 1 because the e-mail address provided is valid:

```
SELECT dbo.fn_RegExMatch(
  N'dejan@solidqualitylearning.com',
  N'^([\w-]+\.)*?[\w-]+@[\w-]+\.([\w-]+\.)*?[\w]+$');
```

And the following code returns 0 because the address is invalid:

```
SELECT dbo.fn_RegExMatch(
  N'dejan#solidqualitylearning.com',
  N'^([\w-]+\.)*?[\w-]+@[\w-]+\.([\w-]+\.)*?[\w]+$');
```

You can also use the function in a CHECK constraint. For example, the following code creates the table TestRegEx with a CHECK constraint that limits the values of the *jpgfilename* column to file names with an extension "jpg":

```
IF OBJECT_ID('dbo.TestRegEx') IS NOT NULL
  DROP TABLE dbo.TestRegEx;
GO
```

```
CREATE TABLE dbo.TestRegEx
(
  jpgfilename NVARCHAR(4000) NOT NULL
  CHECK(dbo.fn_RegExMatch(jpgfilename,
    N'^(([a-zA-Z]:)|(\\{2}\w+)\$?)(\\(\w[\w ]*.*))+\.(jpg|JPG)$')
      = CAST(1 As BIT))
);
```

The values in the *jpgfilename* column must meet the following pattern: the value must start with either a letter in the range A through Z followed by a colon (drive letter), or with two backslashes and a word (network share). Then the value must have at least one backslash denoting the root folder of the drive or the share. After that, the value can have additional backslash-word combinations denoting multiple subfolders. Finally, after the last word there must be a dot followed by the letters "jpg" (uppercase or lowercase).

The following INSERT containing a valid JPEG file name is accepted:

```
INSERT INTO dbo.TestRegEx(jpgfilename) VALUES(N'C:\Temp\myFile.jpg');
INSERT INTO dbo.TestRegEx(jpgfilename) VALUES(N'\\MyShare\Temp\myFile.jpg');
INSERT INTO dbo.TestRegEx(jpgfilename) VALUES(N'\\MyShare\myFile.jpg');
INSERT INTO dbo.TestRegEx(jpgfilename) VALUES(N'C:\myFile.jpg');
```

The following INSERT containing a .txt file name is rejected:

```
INSERT INTO dbo.TestRegEx(jpgfilename) VALUES(N'C:\Temp\myFile.txt');
INSERT INTO dbo.TestRegEx(jpgfilename) VALUES(N'\\MyShare\\Temp\myFile.jpg');
INSERT INTO dbo.TestRegEx(jpgfilename) VALUES(N'\\myFile.jpg');
INSERT INTO dbo.TestRegEx(jpgfilename) VALUES(N'C:myFile.jpg');
```

When you're done, run the following code for cleanup:

```
IF OBJECT_ID('dbo.TestRegEx') IS NOT NULL
  DROP TABLE dbo.TestRegEx;
GO
IF OBJECT_ID('dbo.fn_RegExMatch') IS NOT NULL
  DROP FUNCTION dbo.fn_RegExMatch;
```

Explicit vs. Implicit Conversions

When you develop CLR objects in SQL Server 2005, you might think that you can use either .NET native types or .NET SQL types for your input/output parameters and variables. .NET SQL types map more accurately to SQL Server types. Using .NET native types in the routines' interfaces will cause implicit casting of the values when passed from or to SQL Server. Some programmers prefer to stick to .NET SQL types because they believe that there's overhead in the implicit conversions. Such a choice limits you in some cases because .NET SQL types are not as rich as .NET native types in their functionality. For example, the .NET native *System.String* type (*string* in C#, *String* in Visual Basic) has the *Substring* method, while the .NET SQL type *SqlString* doesn't.

It is not performance that makes a real difference. Usage of SQL types in .NET code for CLR objects inside a database is highly recommended because native .NET types do not support NULL values. For example, if you would implement the fn_RegExMatch function with the .NET *string* native type instead of the *SqlString* type for the parameters, you would get a compile error where the code tests whether any of the parameters is NULL (the first if statement in the function's body). If you use the .NET string type and skip NULL testing, the function returns an exception when you call it with NULL arguments. And if you need additional functionality provided by .NET native types, you will have to do some explicit casting. Additionally, you can get the value in .NET native type using the *Value* property of a SQL type variable, store this value in another variable of the native .NET type, and then all the normal properties and methods of a native type will be available. In the fn_RegExMatch function, the *RegEx.IsMatch* method expects native .NET string types as input; therefore, the *Value* property of the .NET SQL types is used. The return type of the method is a .NET native Boolean value, so the code casts it explicitly to *SqlBoolean*.

This section will show you that the performance difference between implicit and explicit casting is not significant. The following C# code defines the functions fn_ImpCast, which uses .NET native types and implicit conversion, and fn_ExpCast, which uses .NET SQL types and explicit conversion:

```
// Compare implicit vs. explicit casting
[SqlFunction(IsDeterministic = true, DataAccess = DataAccessKind.None)]
public static string fn_ImpCast(string inpStr)
{
    return inpStr.Substring(2, 3);
}

[SqlFunction(IsDeterministic = true, DataAccess = DataAccessKind.None)]
public static SqlString fn_ExpCast(SqlString inpStr)
{
    return (SqlString)inpStr.ToString().Substring(2, 3);
}
```

And here's the Visual Basic code that defines the functions:

```
' Compare implicit vs. explicit casting
<SqlFunction(IsDeterministic:=True, DataAccess:=DataAccessKind.None)> _
Public Shared Function fn_ImpCast(ByVal inpStr As String) As String
    Return inpStr.Substring(2, 3)
End Function

<SqlFunction(IsDeterministic:=True, DataAccess:=DataAccessKind.None)> _
Public Shared Function fn_ExpCast(ByVal inpStr As SqlString) As SqlString
    Return CType(inpStr.ToString().Substring(2, 3), SqlString)
End Function
```

Here's code that registers the C# functions in the database:

```
IF OBJECT_ID('dbo.fn_ImpCast') IS NOT NULL
  DROP FUNCTION dbo.fn_ImpCast;
GO
IF OBJECT_ID('dbo.fn_ExpCast') IS NOT NULL
  DROP FUNCTION dbo.fn_ExpCast;
GO
-- Create fn_ImpCast function
CREATE FUNCTION dbo.fn_ImpCast(@inpstr AS NVARCHAR(4000))
RETURNS NVARCHAR(4000)
EXTERNAL NAME CLRUtilities.CLRUtilities.fn_ImpCast;
GO
-- Create fn_ExpCast function
CREATE FUNCTION dbo.fn_ExpCast(@inpstr AS NVARCHAR(4000))
RETURNS NVARCHAR(4000)
EXTERNAL NAME CLRUtilities.CLRUtilities.fn_ExpCast;
```

Here's code that registers the Visual Basic functions:

```
-- Create fn_ImpCast function
CREATE FUNCTION dbo.fn_ImpCast(@inpstr AS NVARCHAR(4000))
RETURNS NVARCHAR(4000)
EXTERNAL NAME CLRUtilities.[CLRUtilities.CLRUtilities].fn_ImpCast;
GO
-- Create fn_ExpCast function
CREATE FUNCTION dbo.fn_ExpCast(@inpstr AS NVARCHAR(4000))
RETURNS NVARCHAR(4000)
EXTERNAL NAME CLRUtilities.[CLRUtilities.CLRUtilities].fn_ExpCast;
```

The following code invokes the fn_ImpCast function a million times in a loop, running for 16 seconds:

```
SET NOCOUNT ON;
GO
DECLARE @a AS NVARCHAR(4000);
DECLARE @i AS INT;
SET @i = 1;
WHILE @i <= 1000000
BEGIN
  SET @a = dbo.fn_ImpCast(N'123456');
  SET @i = @i + 1;
END
```

The following code invokes the fn_ExpCast function, running for 17 seconds:

```
DECLARE @a AS NVARCHAR(4000);
DECLARE @i AS INT;
SET @i = 1;
WHILE @i <= 1000000
BEGIN
  SET @a = dbo.fn_ExpCast(N'123456');
  SET @i = @i + 1;
END
```

As you can see, the difference is not significant, and in this test the implicit casting method even performs a bit better than the explicit casting method.

When you're done, run the following code for cleanup:

```
IF OBJECT_ID('dbo.fn_ImpCast') IS NOT NULL
  DROP FUNCTION dbo.fn_ImpCast;
GO
IF OBJECT_ID('dbo.fn_ExpCast') IS NOT NULL
  DROP FUNCTION dbo.fn_ExpCast;
```

SQL Signature

The following section provides T-SQL and CLR implementations of a function that returns a signature of a query string. The idea is to receive a query string as an input and return a string that represents the query "signature" or "template." In that signature, all literals that appeared in the input query string are replaced with a common symbol (in our case, #). For example, assume you are using the following query string:

```
N'SELECT * FROM dbo.T1 WHERE col1 = 3 AND col2 > 78;'
```

You want to get the following string back:

```
N'SELECT * FROM dbo.T1 WHERE col1 = # AND col2 > #'
```

Such a function can be very handy when you want to aggregate query performance data from traces after inserting the trace data to a table. If you group the data by the original query string, queries that are logically the same will end up in different groups. Aggregating performance data by the query signature will give you more useful and valuable information.

T-SQL SQL Signature UDF

You can find the T-SQL implementation of the SQL Signature function in Listing 6-2. I'd like to thank Stuart Ozer, who authored the function, for allowing me to cover it in this book. Stuart is with the Microsoft SQL Server Customer Advisory Team.

Listing 6-2   Creation script for the fn_SQLSigTSQL UDF

```
IF OBJECT_ID('dbo.fn_SQLSigTSQL') IS NOT NULL
  DROP FUNCTION dbo.fn_SQLSigTSQL;
GO

CREATE FUNCTION dbo.fn_SQLSigTSQL
  (@p1 NTEXT, @parselength INT = 4000)
RETURNS NVARCHAR(4000)


--
-- This function is provided "AS IS" with no warranties,
-- and confers no rights.
```

```
-- Use of included script samples are subject to the terms specified at
-- http://www.microsoft.com/info/cpyright.htm
--
-- Strips query strings
AS
BEGIN
  DECLARE @pos AS INT;
  DECLARE @mode AS CHAR(10);
  DECLARE @maxlength AS INT;
  DECLARE @p2 AS NCHAR(4000);
  DECLARE @currchar AS CHAR(1), @nextchar AS CHAR(1);
  DECLARE @p2len AS INT;

  SET @maxlength = LEN(RTRIM(SUBSTRING(@p1,1,4000)));
  SET @maxlength = CASE WHEN @maxlength > @parselength
                        THEN @parselength ELSE @maxlength END;
  SET @pos = 1;
  SET @p2 = '';
  SET @p2len = 0;
  SET @currchar = '';
  set @nextchar = '';
  SET @mode = 'command';

  WHILE (@pos <= @maxlength)
  BEGIN
    SET @currchar = SUBSTRING(@p1,@pos,1);
    SET @nextchar = SUBSTRING(@p1,@pos+1,1);
    IF @mode = 'command'
    BEGIN
      SET @p2 = LEFT(@p2,@p2len) + @currchar;
      SET @p2len = @p2len + 1 ;
      IF @currchar IN (',','(',' ','=','<','>','!')
        AND @nextchar BETWEEN '0' AND '9'
      BEGIN
        SET @mode = 'number';
        SET @p2 = LEFT(@p2,@p2len) + '#';
        SET @p2len = @p2len + 1;
      END
      IF @currchar = ''''
      BEGIN
        SET @mode = 'literal';
        SET @p2 = LEFT(@p2,@p2len) + '#''';
        SET @p2len = @p2len + 2;
      END
    END
    ELSE IF @mode = 'number' AND @nextchar IN (',',')',' ','=','<','>','!')
      SET @mode= 'command';
    ELSE IF @mode = 'literal' AND @currchar = ''''
      SET @mode= 'command';

    SET @pos = @pos + 1;
  END
  RETURN @p2;
END
GO
```

The fn_SQLSigTSQL function accepts two input parameters: *@p1* is the input query string, and *@parselength* is the maximum number of characters that you want to parse. If *@parselength* is smaller than the length of the query string stored in *@p1*, the function will parse only the *@parselength* leftmost characters. The function iterates through the characters of the string one at a time. It keeps a state value in a variable called *@mode*, which can be set to one of the following values: *'command'*, *'number'*, or *'literal'*.

Command is the default state, and it simply means that the current character will be concatenated to the output string as is. *Number* means that a number literal is identified, in which case the # symbol will be concatenated. A *number* literal is identified when a digit follows a comma, an opening parenthesis, a space, or an operator. The state changes from *number* to *command* when the next character is a comma, a closing parenthesis, a space, or an operator. *Literal* means that a character string literal is identified, in which case the string #' will be concatenated. A character string literal is identified when an opening quote is detected. The state changes from *literal* to *command* when a closing quote is detected.

To test the fn_SQLSigTSQL function, run the following code:

```
SELECT dbo.fn_SQLSigTSQL
  (N'SELECT * FROM dbo.T1 WHERE col1 = 3 AND col2 > 78', 4000);
```

You will get the following output:

```
SELECT * FROM dbo.T1 WHERE col1 = # AND col2 > #
```

CLR SQL Signature UDF

Listings 6-3 and 6-4 have the C# and Visual Basic implementations of the SQL Signature function. The .NET versions of the function are adaptations of Stuart's algorithm. These adaptations were developed by Andrew J. Kelly and Dejan Sarka, both of whom are mentors with Solid Quality Learning and distinguished SQL Server MVPs. The .NET versions of the function described here are logically similar to the T-SQL version in Listing 6-2 and are provided for performance testing and comparison purposes only. They do not represent good CLR writing. Later in this chapter, I'll describe a much more powerful CLR-based solution using regular expressions to produce query signatures.

Listing 6-3   The fn_SQLSigCLR function, C# version

```csharp
// SQL Signature
[SqlFunction(IsDeterministic = true, DataAccess = DataAccessKind.None)]
public static SqlString fn_SQLSigCLR(SqlString inpRawString,
  SqlInt32 inpParseLength)
{
    if (inpRawString.IsNull)
        return SqlString.Null;
    int pos = 0;
    string mode = "command";
```

```
string RawString = inpRawString.Value;
int maxlength = RawString.Length;
StringBuilder p2 = new StringBuilder();
char currchar = ' ';
char nextchar = ' ';
int ParseLength = RawString.Length;
if (!inpParseLength.IsNull)
    ParseLength = inpParseLength.Value;
if (RawString.Length > ParseLength)
{
    maxlength = ParseLength;
}
while (pos < maxlength)
{
    currchar = RawString[pos];
    if (pos < maxlength - 1)
    {
        nextchar = RawString[pos + 1];
    }
    else
    {
        nextchar = RawString[pos];
    }
    if (mode == "command")
    {
        p2.Append(currchar);
        if ((",( =<>!".IndexOf(currchar) >= 0)
            &&
            (nextchar >= '0' && nextchar <= '9'))
        {
            mode = "number";
            p2.Append('#');
        }
        if (currchar == '\'')
        {
            mode = "literal";
            p2.Append("#'");
        }
    }
    else if ((mode == "number")
            &&
            (",( =<>!".IndexOf(nextchar) >= 0))
    {
        mode = "command";
    }
    else if ((mode == "literal") && (currchar == '\''))
    {
        mode = "command";
    }
    pos++;
}
return p2.ToString();
}
```

Listing 6-4   The fn_SQLSigCLR function, Visual Basic version

```vb
' SQL Signature
<SqlFunction(IsDeterministic:=True, DataAccess:=DataAccessKind.None)> _
Public Shared Function fn_SQLSigCLR(ByVal inpRawString As SqlString, _
  ByVal inpParseLength As SqlInt32) As SqlString
    If inpRawString.IsNull Then
        Return SqlString.Null
    End If
    Dim pos As Integer = 0
    Dim mode As String = "command"
    Dim RawString As String = inpRawString.Value
    Dim maxlength As Integer = RawString.Length
    Dim p2 As StringBuilder = New StringBuilder()
    Dim currchar As Char = " "c
    Dim nextchar As Char = " "c
    Dim ParseLength As Integer = RawString.Length
    If (Not inpParseLength.IsNull) Then
        ParseLength = inpParseLength.Value
    End If
    If (RawString.Length > ParseLength) Then
        maxlength = ParseLength
    End If
    While (pos < maxlength)
        currchar = RawString(pos)
        If (pos < maxlength - 1) Then
            nextchar = RawString(pos + 1)
        Else
            nextchar = RawString(pos)
        End If
        If (mode = "command") Then
            p2.Append(currchar)
            If ((",( =<>!".IndexOf(currchar) >= 0) _
                And _
                (nextchar >= "0"c And nextchar <= "9"c)) Then
                mode = "number"
                p2.Append("#")
            End If
            If (currchar = "'"c) Then
                mode = "literal"
                p2.Append("#")
            End If
        ElseIf ((mode = "number") And _
                (",( =<>!".IndexOf(nextchar) >= 0)) Then
            mode = "command"
        ElseIf ((mode = "literal") And _
                (currchar = "'"c)) Then
            mode = "command"
        End If
        pos = pos + 1
    End While
    Return p2.ToString
End Function
```

Use the following code to register the C# version of the fn_SQLSigCLR function:

```
IF OBJECT_ID('dbo.fn_SQLSigCLR') IS NOT NULL
  DROP FUNCTION dbo.fn_SQLSigCLR;
GO
CREATE FUNCTION dbo.fn_SQLSigCLR
  (@rawstring AS NVARCHAR(4000), @parselength AS INT)
RETURNS NVARCHAR(4000)
EXTERNAL NAME CLRUtilities.CLRUtilities.fn_SQLSigCLR;
```

And use the following code if you implemented the function with Visual Basic:

```
CREATE FUNCTION dbo.fn_SQLSigCLR
  (@rawstring AS NVARCHAR(4000), @parselength AS INT)
RETURNS NVARCHAR(4000)
EXTERNAL NAME CLRUtilities.[CLRUtilities.CLRUtilities].fn_SQLSigCLR;
```

Run the following code to test the fn_SQLSigCLR function:

```
SELECT dbo.fn_SQLSigCLR
  (N'SELECT * FROM dbo.T1 WHERE col1 = 3 AND col2 > 78', 4000);
```

You will get the following output:

```
SELECT * FROM dbo.T1 WHERE col1 = # AND col2 > #
```

Compare Performance of T-SQL and CLR SQL Signature UDFs

Remember that .NET code is much faster than T-SQL in string manipulation. The SQL Signature function is a perfect example for demonstrating the performance difference, especially because both versions implement the same algorithm. You will be able to observe the net performance difference in string manipulation.

First, run the following code to create the table Queries and populate it with 100,000 query strings:

```
IF OBJECT_ID('dbo.Queries') IS NOT NULL
  DROP TABLE dbo.Queries;
GO
SELECT CAST(N'SELECT * FROM dbo.T1 WHERE col1 = 3 AND col2 > 78'
         AS NVARCHAR(MAX)) AS query
INTO dbo.Queries
FROM dbo.Nums
WHERE n <= 100000;
```

Turn on the Discard Results After Execution option in SSMS.

When I ran the following code with the T-SQL version of the function, it took almost 100 seconds to finish:

```
SELECT dbo.fn_SQLSigTSQL(query, 4000) FROM dbo.Queries;
```

The CLR C# version finished in 1 second, and the Visual Basic version finished in 2 seconds:

```
SELECT dbo.fn_SQLSigCLR(query, 4000) FROM dbo.Queries;
```

Turn off the Discard Results After Execution option in SSMS.

As you can see, the CLR version of the function is about 100 times faster than the T-SQL version.

As I mentioned earlier, the fn_SQLSigCLR function implements the same algorithm implemented by the fn_SQLSigTSQL function and is provided mainly for performance comparison purposes. You can implement a much more powerful CLR-based solution using regular expressions. Earlier I showed how you can use regular expressions to do pattern matching; that is, to check whether a certain string matches a certain pattern. You can also use regular expressions to do pattern-based replacement; that is, you can replace all occurrences of a pattern within a string with another pattern. Here's the C# definition of the fn_RegExReplace function, which invokes the *Replace* method of a *Regex* object:

```
// fn_RegExReplace - for generic use of RegEx-based replace
[SqlFunction(IsDeterministic = true, DataAccess = DataAccessKind.None)]
public static SqlString fn_RegExReplace(
    SqlString input, SqlString pattern, SqlString replacement)
{
    if (input.IsNull || pattern.IsNull || replacement.IsNull)
        return SqlString.Null;
    else
        return (SqlString)Regex.Replace(
        input.Value, pattern.Value, replacement.Value);
}
```

And here's the Visual Basic definition of the function:

```
' fn_RegExReplace - for generic use of RegEx-based replace
<SqlFunction(IsDeterministic:=True, DataAccess:=DataAccessKind.None)> _
Public Shared Function fn_RegExReplace( _
  ByVal input As SqlString, ByVal pattern As SqlString, _
  ByVal replacement As SqlString) As SqlString
    If (input.IsNull Or pattern.IsNull Or replacement.IsNull) Then
        Return SqlString.Null
    Else
        Return CType(Regex.Replace( _
            input.Value, pattern.Value, replacement.Value), SqlString)
    End If
End Function
```

The function accepts three input arguments: *input, pattern,* and *replacement.* The function first checks whether one of the inputs is Null, and if so, returns a Null. If none of the inputs is Null, the function invokes the *Regex.Replace* method, which substitutes each occurrence of *pattern* within the string *input* with the *replacement* pattern. Here I'll demonstrate how you can use the fn_RegExReplace function to generate query signatures, but of course you can use the function for general pattern-based string replacement purposes.

Use the following code to register the C# version of the fn_RegExReplace function:

```
IF OBJECT_ID('dbo.fn_RegExReplace') IS NOT NULL
  DROP FUNCTION dbo.fn_RegExReplace;
GO
CREATE FUNCTION dbo.fn_RegExReplace(
  @input       AS NVARCHAR(MAX),
  @pattern     AS NVARCHAR(MAX),
  @replacement AS NVARCHAR(MAX))
RETURNS NVARCHAR(MAX)
WITH RETURNS NULL ON NULL INPUT
EXTERNAL NAME CLRUtilities.CLRUtilities.fn_RegExReplace;
```

And use the following code if you implemented the function with Visual Basic:

```
CREATE FUNCTION dbo.fn_RegExReplace(
  @input       AS NVARCHAR(MAX),
  @pattern     AS NVARCHAR(MAX),
  @replacement AS NVARCHAR(MAX))
RETURNS NVARCHAR(MAX)
WITH RETURNS NULL ON NULL INPUT
EXTERNAL NAME CLRUtilities.[CLRUtilities.CLRUtilities].fn_RegExReplace;
```

Here's an example of how you can use the function to generate query signatures out of the query strings stored in the Queries table:

```
SELECT
  dbo.fn_RegExReplace(query,
    N'([\s,(=<>!](?![^\]]+[\]]))(?:(?:(?:(?#      expression coming
    )(?:([N])?('')(?:[^'']|'''')*(''))(?#         character
    )|(?:0x[\da-fA-F]*)(?#                         binary
    )|(?:[-+]?(?:(?:[\d]*\.[\d]*|[\d]+)(?#         precise number
    )(?:[eE]?[\d]*)))(?#                           imprecise number
    )|(?:[~]?[-+]?(?:[\d]+))(?#                    integer
    ))(?:[\s]?[\+\-\*\/\%\&\|\^][\s]?)?)+(?#       operators
    ))',
    N'$1$2$3#$4')
FROM dbo.Queries;
```

The pattern is self-documented with inline comments. It identifies (and substitutes with a # symbol) more types of literals than the fn_SQLSigCLR did. It identifies character literals, binary ones, precise numbers, imprecise numbers, and even folds expressions involving literals and substitutes them with a # symbol. This solution has another advantage over the fn_SQLSigCLR function—you can maintain the regular expressions yourself and enhance them to support more cases without having to alter the definition of the function. However, the enhanced capabilities you get from regular expressions do come at a certain cost; the above query ran in about 12 seconds—12 times slower than the fn_SQLSigCLR function, but still 8 times faster than the fn_SQLSigTSQL function.

> **Tip**   You might want to create functions that serve a generic purpose such as making the fn_RegExReplace function accessible in all databases without the need to database-qualify the function name (CLRUtilities.dbo.fn_RegExReplace). To achieve this, create a synonym to the function in each database where you want to make it available. For example, to make the function available in the Northwind database, run the following code:
>
> ```
> USE Northwind;
> GO
> CREATE SYNONYM dbo.fn_RegExReplace
>   FOR CLRUtilities.dbo.fn_RegExReplace;
> ```
>
> If you create a synonym in the model database, the synonym will be created in every new database that you create in the future because a new database is created as a copy of the model. This also applies to the tempdb database, which is created every time you restart SQL Server.

When you're done, run the following code for cleanup:

```
USE Northwind;
GO
IF OBJECT_ID('dbo.fn_RegExReplace', 'SN') IS NOT NULL
  DROP SYNONYM dbo.fn_RegExReplace;
GO
USE CLRUtilities;
GO
IF OBJECT_ID('dbo.fn_SQLSigTSQL') IS NOT NULL
  DROP FUNCTION dbo.fn_SQLSigTSQL;
GO
IF OBJECT_ID('dbo.fn_SQLSigCLR') IS NOT NULL
  DROP FUNCTION dbo.fn_SQLSigCLR;
GO
IF OBJECT_ID('dbo.fn_RegExReplace') IS NOT NULL
  DROP FUNCTION dbo.fn_RegExReplace;
GO
```

Table-Valued UDFs

Table-valued UDFs are UDFs that return a table and are typically specified in the FROM clause of an outer query. This section will describe inline table-valued UDFs, multistatement table-valued UDFs, and CLR table-valued UDFs.

Inline Table-Valued UDFs

Inline table-valued UDFs are similar to views in the sense that their returned table is defined by a query specification. However, the UDF's query can refer to input parameters, while a view cannot. So you can think of an inline UDF as a "parameterized view." SQL Server actually treats inline UDFs very similarly to views. The query processor replaces an Inline UDF reference with its definition; in other words, the query processor "expands" the UDF definition and generates an execution plan accessing the underlying objects.

Unlike scalar and multistatement table-valued UDFs, you don't specify a BEGIN/END block in an inline UDF's body. All you specify is a RETURN clause and a query. In the function's header, you simply state that it returns a table. As an example, the following code creates in Northwind the fn_GetCustOrders function, which accepts a customer ID as an input, and returns the input customer's orders:

```
SET NOCOUNT ON;
USE Northwind;
GO
IF OBJECT_ID('dbo.fn_GetCustOrders') IS NOT NULL
  DROP FUNCTION dbo.fn_GetCustOrders;
GO
CREATE FUNCTION dbo.fn_GetCustOrders
  (@cid AS NCHAR(5)) RETURNS TABLE
AS
RETURN
  SELECT OrderID, CustomerID, EmployeeID, OrderDate, RequiredDate,
    ShippedDate, ShipVia, Freight, ShipName, ShipAddress, ShipCity,
    ShipRegion, ShipPostalCode, ShipCountry
  FROM dbo.Orders
  WHERE CustomerID = @cid;
GO
```

Run the following query to match the orders of customer ALFKI (returned by the function) with their order details and generate the output shown in Table 6-4:

```
SELECT O.OrderID, O.CustomerID, OD.ProductID, OD.Quantity
FROM dbo.fn_GetCustOrders(N'ALFKI') AS O
  JOIN [Order Details] AS OD
    ON O.OrderID = OD.OrderID;
```

Table 6-4   Customer ALFKI's Orders and Order Details

OrderID	CustomerID	ProductID	Quantity
10643	ALFKI	28	15
10643	ALFKI	39	21
10643	ALFKI	46	2
10692	ALFKI	63	20
10702	ALFKI	3	6
10702	ALFKI	76	15
10835	ALFKI	59	15
10835	ALFKI	77	2
10952	ALFKI	6	16
10952	ALFKI	28	2
11011	ALFKI	58	40
11011	ALFKI	71	20

Like views, inline UDFs can be a target of a modification statement. You can assign any DML permission on the function to users. Of course, the underlying tables will absorb the actual modification. For example, the following code sets *ShipVia* (shipper ID) in all of ALFKI's orders to 2 and shows you the state of the orders before and after the update:

```
BEGIN TRAN
  SELECT OrderID, ShipVia FROM fn_GetCustOrders(N'ALFKI') AS O;
  UPDATE fn_GetCustOrders(N'ALFKI') SET ShipVia = 2;
  SELECT OrderID, ShipVia FROM fn_GetCustOrders(N'ALFKI') AS O;
ROLLBACK
```

The code is invoked in a transaction and then rolled back just for demonstration purposes, to avoid applying the change permanently in the Northwind sample database. Tables 6-5 and 6-6 show the state of ALFKI's orders before and after the update, respectively.

Table 6-5   Customer ALFKI's Orders Before Update

OrderID	ShipVia
10643	1
10692	2
10702	1
10835	3
10952	1
11011	1

Table 6-6   Customer ALFKI's Orders After Update

OrderID	ShipVia
10643	2
10692	2
10702	2
10835	2
10952	2
11011	2

Similarly, you can delete data through the function, assuming that you have appropriate permissions. For example, the following code (don't run it) would delete ALFKI's orders placed in 1997:

```
DELETE FROM fn_GetCustOrders(N'ALFKI') WHERE YEAR(OrderDate) = 1997;
```

Don't run this code because it will fail with a foreign key violation. I just wanted to provide you with a code sample.

When you're done, run the following code for cleanup:

```
IF OBJECT_ID('dbo.fn_GetCustOrders') IS NOT NULL
  DROP FUNCTION dbo.fn_GetCustOrders;
```

Split Array

This section provides both T-SQL and CLR implementations of a function that accepts a string containing an array of elements as input and returns a table with the individual elements, each in a separate result row.

T-SQL Split UDF

Run the following code to create the fn_SplitTSQL inline table-valued function:

```
USE CLRUtilities;
GO
IF OBJECT_ID('dbo.fn_SplitTSQL') IS NOT NULL
  DROP FUNCTION dbo.fn_SplitTSQL;
GO
CREATE FUNCTION dbo.fn_SplitTSQL
  (@string NVARCHAR(MAX), @separator NCHAR(1) = N',') RETURNS TABLE
AS
RETURN
  SELECT
    n - LEN(REPLACE(LEFT(s, n), @separator, '')) + 1 AS pos,
    SUBSTRING(s, n,
      CHARINDEX(@separator, s + @separator, n) - n) AS element
  FROM (SELECT @string AS s) AS D
    JOIN dbo.Nums
      ON n <= LEN(s)
      AND SUBSTRING(@separator + s, n, 1) = @separator;
GO
```

The function accepts two input parameters: *@string* and *@separator*. The *@string* parameter holds the input array, and *@separator* holds the character used to separate the elements in the array. The function queries a derived table called D that has a single row and a single column called *array*, which represents the input array. The function joins D with the Nums auxiliary table to generate as many copies of *array* as the number of elements. The join finds a match for each *@separator* value that appears in *@separator* + *array*. In other words, *array* will be duplicated once for each element, and n from Nums will represent the starting position of an element.

The SELECT list has an expression invoking the SUBSTRING function to extract the element starting at the nth character up until the next occurrence of *@separator* in *array*. The SELECT list has another expression that uses the technique I described earlier in the chapter to count occurrences of a substring within a string. In our case, the technique is used to count the number of occurrences of *@separator* in the first n characters within *array*. This count plus one is in fact the position of the current element within *array*.

To test the fn_SplitTSQL function, run the following code, which generates the output shown in Table 6-7:

```
SELECT pos, element FROM dbo.fn_SplitTSQL(N'a,b,c', N',') AS F;
```

Table 6-7   Array Split into Its Elements

pos	element
1	a
2	b
3	c

You can use the function in interesting ways. For example, suppose that a client application needs to send SQL Server a comma-separated list of order IDs and expects to get back information about orders whose keys appear in the list. Typically, programmers implement such logic in a stored procedure using dynamic execution. I discussed both security and performance downsides of such an approach in Chapter 4. With your new function, you can answer such a need with a static query that will be able to reuse a previously cached execution plan:

```
DECLARE @arr AS NVARCHAR(MAX);
SET @arr = N'10248,10249,10250';

SELECT O.OrderID, O.CustomerID, O.EmployeeID, O.OrderDate
FROM dbo.fn_SplitTSQL(@arr, N',') AS F
  JOIN Northwind.dbo.Orders AS O
    ON CAST(F.element AS INT) = O.OrderID;
```

This query generates the output shown in Table 6-8.

Table 6-8   Output of Query Joining fn_SplitTSQL UDF and Orders Table

OrderID	CustomerID	EmployeeID	OrderDate
10248	VINET	5	1996-07-04 00:00:00.000
10249	TOMSP	6	1996-07-05 00:00:00.000
10250	HANAR	4	1996-07-08 00:00:00.000

CLR Split UDF

The CLR implementation of the split function is simpler, although it actually uses two methods. Here's the C# definition of the fn_SplitCLR function:

```
// Struct used in string split functions
struct row_item
{
    public string item;
    public int pos;
}

// Split array of strings and return a table
// FillRowMethodName = "ArrSplitFillRow"
[SqlFunction(FillRowMethodName = "ArrSplitFillRow",
 DataAccess = DataAccessKind.None,
 TableDefinition = "pos INT, element NVARCHAR(4000) ")]
public static IEnumerable fn_SplitCLR(SqlString inpStr,
    SqlString charSeparator)
```

```
{
    string locStr;
    string[] splitStr;
    char[] locSeparator = new char[1];
    locSeparator[0] = (char)charSeparator.Value[0];
    if (inpStr.IsNull)
        locStr = "";
    else
        locStr = inpStr.Value;
    splitStr = locStr.Split(locSeparator,
        StringSplitOptions.RemoveEmptyEntries);
    //locStr.Split(charSeparator.ToString()[0]);
    List<row_item> SplitString = new List<row_item>();
    int i = 1;
    foreach (string s in splitStr)
    {
        row_item r = new row_item();
        r.item = s;
        r.pos = i;
        SplitString.Add(r);
        ++i;
    }
    return SplitString;
}

public static void ArrSplitFillRow(
   Object obj, out int pos, out string item)
{
    pos = ((row_item)obj).pos;
    item = ((row_item)obj).item;
}
```

The function's header sets the *FillRowMethodName* attribute to *"ArrSplitFillRow"*. *ArrSplitFill-Row* is a method (defined after the fn_SplitCLR function's definition) that simply converts the input object to a string. The header also defines the schema of the output table in the *Table-Definition* attribute. This attribute is needed only if you deploy the function automatically using Visual Studio. If you deploy the function manually using T-SQL, you don't need to specify this attribute.

The function simply invokes the built-in *Split* method of the *string* type to split the input array (after converting the input array from a .NET SQL type *SqlString* to a .NET native type *string*). It uses the *StringSplitOptions.RemoveEmptyEntries Split* method option, so the return value does not include array elements that contain an empty string.

Here's the Visual Basic version of the fn_SplitCLR function:

```
'Struct used in string split functions
Structure row_item
    Dim item As String
    Dim pos As Integer
End Structure
```

```
' Split array of strings and return a table
' FillRowMethodName = "ArrSplitFillRow"
<SqlFunction(FillRowMethodName:="ArrSplitFillRow", _
    DataAccess:=DataAccessKind.None, _
    TableDefinition:="pos INT, element NVARCHAR(4000) ")> _
Public Shared Function fn_SplitCLR(ByVal inpStr As SqlString, _
    ByVal charSeparator As SqlString) As IEnumerable
    Dim locStr As String
    Dim splitStr() As String
    Dim locSeparator(0) As Char
    locSeparator(0) = CChar(charSeparator.Value(0))
    If (inpStr.IsNull) Then
        locStr = ""
    Else
        locStr = inpStr.Value
    End If
    splitStr = locStr.Split(locSeparator, _
        StringSplitOptions.RemoveEmptyEntries)
    Dim SplitString As New List(Of row_item)
    Dim i As Integer = 1
    For Each s As String In splitStr
        Dim r As New row_item
        r.item = s
        r.pos = i
        SplitString.Add(r)
        i = i + 1
    Next
    Return SplitString
End Function

Public Shared Sub ArrSplitFillRow( _
ByVal obj As Object, <Out()> ByRef pos As Integer, _
  <Out()> ByRef item As String)
    pos = CType(obj, row_item).pos
    item = CType(obj, row_item).item
End Sub
```

Use the following code to register the C# version of the function in the database:

```
IF OBJECT_ID('dbo.fn_SplitCLR') IS NOT NULL
  DROP FUNCTION dbo.fn_SplitCLR;
GO
CREATE FUNCTION dbo.fn_SplitCLR
  (@string AS NVARCHAR(4000), @separator AS NCHAR(1))
RETURNS TABLE(pos INT, element NVARCHAR(4000))
EXTERNAL NAME CLRUtilities.CLRUtilities.fn_SplitCLR;
```

Use the following code to register the Visual Basic version:

```
CREATE FUNCTION dbo.fn_SplitCLR
  (@string AS NVARCHAR(4000), @separator AS NCHAR(1))
RETURNS TABLE(pos INT, element NVARCHAR(4000))
EXTERNAL NAME CLRUtilities.[CLRUtilities.CLRUtilities].fn_SplitCLR;
```

Run the following query to test the fn_SplitCLR function, and produce the output shown earlier in Table 6-7:

```
SELECT pos, element FROM dbo.fn_SplitCLR(N'a,b,c', N',');
```

To test the function against a table of arrays, first run the following code, which creates the Arrays table and populates it with some sample arrays:

```
IF OBJECT_ID('dbo.Arrays') IS NOT NULL
  DROP TABLE dbo.Arrays;
GO
CREATE TABLE dbo.Arrays
(
  arrid INT          NOT NULL IDENTITY PRIMARY KEY,
  arr   NVARCHAR(4000) NOT NULL
);

INSERT INTO dbo.Arrays(arr) VALUES(N'20,220,25,2115,14');
INSERT INTO dbo.Arrays(arr) VALUES(N'30,330,28');
INSERT INTO dbo.Arrays(arr) VALUES(N'12,10,8,8,122,13,2,14,10,9');
INSERT INTO dbo.Arrays(arr) VALUES(N'-4,-6,1050,-2');
```

Use the following query to apply the function to each array from the Arrays table, and generate the output shown in Table 6-9:

```
SELECT arrid, pos, element
FROM dbo.Arrays AS A
  CROSS APPLY dbo.fn_SplitCLR(arr, N',') AS F;
```

Table 6-9   Strings from the Arrays Table Split into Elements

arrid	pos	element
1	1	20
1	2	220
1	3	25
1	4	2115
1	5	14
2	1	30
2	2	330
2	3	28
3	1	12
3	2	10
3	3	8
3	4	8
3	5	122
3	6	13

Table 6-9   Strings from the Arrays Table Split into Elements

arrid	pos	element
3	7	2
3	8	14
3	9	10
3	10	9
4	1	–4
4	2	–6
4	3	1050
4	4	–2

Compare Performance of T-SQL and CLR Split

To compare the performance between the T-SQL and CLR splitting techniques, first duplicate the current contents of Arrays 100,000 times by running the following code:

```
INSERT INTO dbo.Arrays
  SELECT arr
  FROM dbo.Arrays, dbo.Nums
  WHERE n <= 100000;
```

The Arrays table is now populated with 400,004 rows.

Use the following query (with results discarded) to apply the T-SQL splitting technique:

```
SELECT
  n - LEN(REPLACE(LEFT(arr, n), ',', '')) + 1 AS pos,
  SUBSTRING(arr, n, CHARINDEX(',', arr + ',', n) - n) AS element
FROM Arrays
  JOIN dbo.Nums
    ON n <= LEN(arr)
    AND SUBSTRING(',' + arr, n, 1) = ',';
```

Notice that I didn't use the fn_SplitTSQL UDF here because you can use the same technique directly against the Arrays table. This code ran for 17 seconds on my system.

As for the CLR version, it ran for 8 seconds—twice faster than the T-SQL version.

When you're done, run the following code for cleanup:

```
IF OBJECT_ID('dbo.Arrays') IS NOT NULL
  DROP TABLE dbo.Arrays;
GO
IF OBJECT_ID('dbo.fn_SplitTSQL') IS NOT NULL
  DROP FUNCTION dbo.fn_SplitTSQL;
GO
IF OBJECT_ID('dbo.fn_SplitCLR') IS NOT NULL
  DROP FUNCTION dbo.fn_SplitCLR;
```

Multistatement Table-Valued UDFs

A multistatement table-valued UDF is a function that returns a table variable. The function has a body with the sole purpose of populating the table variable. You develop a multistatement table-valued UDF when you need a routine that returns a table, and the implementation of the routine cannot be expressed as a single query, rather requires multiple statements; for example, flow elements like loops, and so on.

A multistatement table-valued UDF used in a similar manner to an inline table-valued UDF, but it cannot be a target of a modification statement. That is, it can be used only in the FROM clause of a SELECT query. Internally, SQL Server treats the two completely differently. Although an inline UDF is treated more like a view, a multistatement table-valued UDF is treated more like a stored procedure. As with other UDFs, a multistatement table-valued UDF is not allowed to have side effects.

As an example of a multistatement table-valued UDF, you will create a function that accepts an employee ID as input and returns details about the input employee and its subordinates in all levels. First run the code in Listing 6-5 to create the Employees table and populate it with some sample data.

Listing 6-5 Data definition language (DDL) and sample data for the Employees table

```
SET NOCOUNT ON;
USE tempdb;
GO
IF OBJECT_ID('dbo.Employees') IS NOT NULL
  DROP TABLE dbo.Employees;
GO
CREATE TABLE dbo.Employees
(
  empid   INT       NOT NULL PRIMARY KEY,
  mgrid   INT       NULL     REFERENCES dbo.Employees,
  empname VARCHAR(25) NOT NULL,
  salary  MONEY     NOT NULL
);

INSERT INTO dbo.Employees(empid, mgrid, empname, salary)
  VALUES(1, NULL, 'David', $10000.00);
INSERT INTO dbo.Employees(empid, mgrid, empname, salary)
  VALUES(2, 1, 'Eitan', $7000.00);
INSERT INTO dbo.Employees(empid, mgrid, empname, salary)
  VALUES(3, 1, 'Ina', $7500.00);
INSERT INTO dbo.Employees(empid, mgrid, empname, salary)
  VALUES(4, 2, 'Seraph', $5000.00);
INSERT INTO dbo.Employees(empid, mgrid, empname, salary)
  VALUES(5, 2, 'Jiru', $5500.00);
INSERT INTO dbo.Employees(empid, mgrid, empname, salary)
  VALUES(6, 2, 'Steve', $4500.00);
INSERT INTO dbo.Employees(empid, mgrid, empname, salary)
  VALUES(7, 3, 'Aaron', $5000.00);
```

```
INSERT INTO dbo.Employees(empid, mgrid, empname, salary)
  VALUES(8, 5, 'Lilach', $3500.00);
INSERT INTO dbo.Employees(empid, mgrid, empname, salary)
  VALUES(9, 7, 'Rita', $3000.00);
INSERT INTO dbo.Employees(empid, mgrid, empname, salary)
  VALUES(10, 5, 'Sean', $3000.00);
INSERT INTO dbo.Employees(empid, mgrid, empname, salary)
  VALUES(11, 7, 'Gabriel', $3000.00);
INSERT INTO dbo.Employees(empid, mgrid, empname, salary)
  VALUES(12, 9, 'Emilia' , $2000.00);
INSERT INTO dbo.Employees(empid, mgrid, empname, salary)
  VALUES(13, 9, 'Michael', $2000.00);
INSERT INTO dbo.Employees(empid, mgrid, empname, salary)
  VALUES(14, 9, 'Didi', $1500.00);

CREATE UNIQUE INDEX idx_unc_mgrid_empid ON dbo.Employees(mgrid, empid);
GO
```

Run the code in Listing 6-6 to create the SQL Server 2000–compatible version of the fn_subordinates UDF.

Listing 6-6   Creation script for the function fn_subordinates, SQL Server 2000

```
IF OBJECT_ID('dbo.fn_subordinates') IS NOT NULL
  DROP FUNCTION dbo.fn_subordinates;
GO
CREATE FUNCTION dbo.fn_subordinates(@mgrid AS INT) RETURNS @Subs Table
(
  empid   INT NOT NULL PRIMARY KEY NONCLUSTERED,
  mgrid   INT NULL,
  empname VARCHAR(25) NOT NULL,
  salary  MONEY       NOT NULL,
  lvl     INT NOT NULL,
  UNIQUE CLUSTERED(lvl, empid)
)
AS
BEGIN
  DECLARE @lvl AS INT;
  SET @lvl = 0;                  -- Init level counter with 0

  -- Insert root node to @Subs
  INSERT INTO @Subs(empid, mgrid, empname, salary, lvl)
    SELECT empid, mgrid, empname, salary, @lvl
    FROM dbo.Employees WHERE empid = @mgrid;

  WHILE @@rowcount > 0           -- while prev level had rows
  BEGIN
    SET @lvl = @lvl + 1;         -- Increment level counter

    -- Insert next level of subordinates to @Subs
    INSERT INTO @Subs(empid, mgrid, empname, salary, lvl)
      SELECT C.empid, C.mgrid, C.empname, C.salary, @lvl
```

```
        FROM @Subs AS P            -- P = Parent
          JOIN dbo.Employees AS C -- C = Child
            ON P.lvl = @lvl - 1    -- Filter parents from prev level
            AND C.mgrid = P.empid;
    END

    RETURN;
  END
  GO
```

The function accepts the *@mgrid* input parameter, which is the ID of the input manager. The function returns the @Subs table variable, with details about the input manager and all its subordinates in all levels. In addition to the employee attributes, @Subs also has a column called *lvl* that keeps track of the level distance from the input manager (0 for the input manager, and increasing by one unit for each level).

The function keeps track of the current level in the *@lvl* local variable, which is initialized with zero.

The function first inserts into @Subs the row from Employees with ID equal to *@mgrid*.

Then, in a loop, if the last insert affected more than zero rows, the code increments the *@lvl* variable's value by one and inserts the next level of employees—in other words, direct subordinates of the managers found in the previous level—into @Subs.

The *lvl* column is important because it allows you to isolate the employees who were inserted into @Subs in the last iteration. To return only subordinates of the employees found in the previous level, the join condition filters from @Subs only rows where the *lvl* column is equal to the previous level (*@lvl − 1*).

To test the function, run the following code, which returns information about employee 3 and her subordinates. The output is shown in Table 6-10:

```
SELECT empid, mgrid, empname, salary, lvl
FROM dbo.fn_subordinates(3) AS S;
```

Table 6-10 Employee 3 and Subordinates in All Levels

empid	mgrid	empname	salary	lvl
3	1	Ina	7500.00	0
7	3	Aaron	5000.00	1
9	7	Rita	3000.00	2
11	7	Gabriel	3000.00	2
12	9	Emilia	2000.00	3
13	9	Michael	2000.00	3
14	9	Didi	1500.00	3

Run the code in Listing 6-7 to create the SQL Server 2005 version of the fn_subordinates UDF.

Listing 6-7   Creation script for the function fn_subordinates, SQL Server 2005

```
IF OBJECT_ID('dbo.fn_subordinates') IS NOT NULL
  DROP FUNCTION dbo.fn_subordinates;
GO
CREATE FUNCTION dbo.fn_subordinates(@mgrid AS INT) RETURNS TABLE
AS
RETURN
  WITH SubsCTE
  AS
  (
    -- Anchor member returns a row for the input manager
    SELECT empid, mgrid, empname, salary, 0 AS lvl
    FROM dbo.Employees
    WHERE empid = @mgrid

    UNION ALL

    -- Recursive member returns next level of subordinates
    SELECT C.empid, C.mgrid, C.empname, C.salary, P.lvl + 1
    FROM SubsCTE AS P
      JOIN dbo.Employees AS C
        ON C.mgrid = P.empid
  )
  SELECT * FROM SubsCTE;
GO
```

The SQL Server 2005 version of the UDF applies logic similar to the SQL Server 2000 version, except that it uses the new recursive common table expressions (CTEs). As you can see, it can be implemented as an inline tabled-valued UDF. It's simpler in the sense that you don't need to define the returned table explicitly or filter the previous level's managers.

The first query in the CTE's body returns the row from Employees for the given root employee. It also returns zero as the level of the root employee. In a recursive CTE, a query that doesn't have any recursive references is known as an *anchor member*.

The second query in the CTE's body (following the UNION ALL set operation) has a recursive reference to itself. This makes it a *recursive member*, and it is treated in a special manner. The recursive reference to the CTE's name (*SubsCTE*) represents the result set returned previously. The recursive member query joins the previous result set representing the managers in the previous level with the Employees table to return the next level of employees. The recursive query also calculates the level value as the employee's manager level plus one. The first time that the recursive member is invoked, *SubsCTE* stands for the result set returned by the anchor member (root employee). There's no explicit termination check for the recursive member. Rather, it is invoked repeatedly until it returns an empty set. Thus, the first time it is invoked, it returns direct subordinates of the subtree's root employee. The second time it is invoked, *SubsCTE* represents the result set of the first invocation of the recursive member (first level of subordinates), so it returns the second level of subordinates. The recursive member is invoked repeatedly until there are no more subordinates, in which case it will return an empty set and recursion will stop.

The reference to the CTE name in the outer query represents the UNION ALL of all the result sets returned by the invocation of the anchor member and all the invocations of the recursive member.

To test the function, run the following query, which generates the output shown earlier in Table 6-10:

```
SELECT empid, mgrid, empname, salary, lvl
FROM dbo.fn_subordinates(3) AS S;
```

> **More Info**   For more details about querying hierarchical data such as an employee organizational chart, please refer to *Inside T-SQL Querying*.

When you're done, run the following code for cleanup:

```
USE tempdb;
GO
IF OBJECT_ID('dbo.Employees') IS NOT NULL
  DROP TABLE dbo.Employees;
GO
IF OBJECT_ID('dbo.fn_subordinates') IS NOT NULL
  DROP FUNCTION dbo.fn_subordinates;
```

Per-Row UDFs

Nondeterministic functions are functions that are not guaranteed to return the same output when invoked multiple times with the same input. When you invoke nondeterministic built-in functions in a query (such as RAND and GETDATE), those functions are invoked once for the whole query and not once per row. The only exception to this rule is the NEWID function, which generates a globally unique identifier (GUID). NEWID is the only nondeterministic built-in function that will be invoked once per row.

To demonstrate this behavior of nondeterministic functions, run the following code, which queries the Orders table in the Northwind database; invokes the functions RAND, GETDATE, and NEWID; and generates the output shown in abbreviated form in Table 6-11:

```
USE Northwind;

SELECT RAND() AS rnd, GETDATE() AS dt, NEWID() AS guid, OrderID AS oid
FROM dbo.Orders;
```

Table 6-11   Output of Query Invoking Nondeterministic Functions (Abbreviated)

rnd	dt	guid	oid
0.23575580157313	2005-12-19 14:18:00.157	52BCB19F-DDA0-4890-AE1C-B7387E2D9E07	10249
0.23575580157313	2005-12-19 14:18:00.157	7D3AAE2B-003F-4DD9-9E2E-F52C108F1ACE	10251
0.23575580157313	2005-12-19 14:18:00.157	A8FFDE94-0160-4AB5-B5B0-5A4A39A05B2F	10258
0.23575580157313	2005-12-19 14:18:00.157	335322D2-16E4-4966-80C0-83C176A86911	10260
0.23575580157313	2005-12-19 14:18:00.157	3AA95970-9AC9-45A6-863F-8E70AD25F5D7	10265
0.23575580157313	2005-12-19 14:18:00.157	3C4A3925-1E37-4617-BC54-B36C66819E6B	10267
0.23575580157313	2005-12-19 14:18:00.157	2730F1A0-222C-4FA9-92B9-3CD7C304C7A7	10269
0.23575580157313	2005-12-19 14:18:00.157	8306A132-9D00-4218-835D-6CCFA07A82A8	10270
0.23575580157313	2005-12-19 14:18:00.157	8D9292A2-3CA5-4A2B-B504-9431C96CA2A6	10274
0.23575580157313	2005-12-19 14:18:00.157	7E59D1A0-ADE6-4DB5-AC53-92CFCA192247	10275
...	...	...	...

You can observe that both RAND and GETDATE were invoked only once for the whole query, and their result values were copied to all rows. On the other hand, NEWID was invoked once per row, generating a different value in each row.

Suppose that you had the need to invoke the RAND function for each row. You might have thought of invoking RAND from a UDF and then invoking the UDF in an outer query, knowing that a UDF is invoked once per row. Here's an attempt to create such a UDF called fn_rand:

```
IF OBJECT_ID('dbo.fn_rand') IS NOT NULL
  DROP FUNCTION dbo.fn_rand;
GO
CREATE FUNCTION dbo.fn_rand() RETURNS FLOAT
AS
BEGIN
  RETURN RAND();
END
GO
```

However, this attempt fails and produces the following error:

```
Msg 443, Level 16, State 1, Procedure fn_rand, Line 6
Invalid use of side-effecting or time-dependent operator in 'rand' within a function.
```

The error tells you that your function is not allowed to have side effects, and the RAND function does change an internal state.

There's a back door that allows you to implicitly invoke RAND from a UDF. Create a view that invokes RAND, and query the view from the UDF, like so:

```
IF OBJECT_ID('dbo.fn_rand') IS NOT NULL
  DROP FUNCTION dbo.fn_rand;
GO
IF OBJECT_ID('dbo.VRand') IS NOT NULL
  DROP VIEW dbo.VRand;
GO
CREATE VIEW dbo.VRand AS SELECT RAND() AS r;
GO
CREATE FUNCTION dbo.fn_rand() RETURNS FLOAT
AS
BEGIN
  RETURN (SELECT r FROM dbo.VRand);
END
GO
```

You can test the fn_rand UDF by invoking it in a query against the Orders table, which will generate the output shown in abbreviated form in Table 6-12:

```
SELECT dbo.fn_rand() AS rnd, OrderID AS oid FROM dbo.Orders;
```

Table 6-12   Output of Query Invoking the fn_rand UDF (Abbreviated)

rnd	oid
0.126413837261193	10248
0.222567782284458	10249
0.475723707976473	10250
0.57880518253848	10251
0.169390263927576	10252
0.337301740768919	10253
0.489646055111808	10254
0.826464402198423	10255
0.232679419042244	10256
0.152765690787598	10257
...	...

SQL Server 2000 disallowed the invocation of nondeterministic functions from UDFs. SQL Server 2005 is more lenient in the sense that it inspects more properties of a UDF and distinguishes between functions that have side effects and functions that don't. For example, in

SQL Server 2000 you couldn't invoke the GETDATE function from a UDF, but in SQL Server 2005 you can:

```
IF OBJECT_ID('dbo.fn_getdate') IS NOT NULL
  DROP FUNCTION dbo.fn_getdate;
GO
CREATE FUNCTION dbo.fn_getdate() RETURNS DATETIME
AS
BEGIN
  RETURN GETDATE();
END
GO
```

When you're done, run the following code for cleanup:

```
IF OBJECT_ID('dbo.fn_rand') IS NOT NULL
  DROP FUNCTION dbo.fn_rand;
GO
IF OBJECT_ID('dbo.VRand') IS NOT NULL
  DROP VIEW dbo.VRand;
GO
IF OBJECT_ID('dbo.fn_getdate') IS NOT NULL
  DROP FUNCTION dbo.fn_getdate;
GO
```

Conclusion

User-defined functions can be embedded in queries, constraints, and computed columns. This capability allows you to enhance the functionality of your queries while still preserving a high level of readability and simplicity. SQL Server 2005 introduces .NET integration and the ability to create functions with CLR code. You can create both scalar and table-valued CLR UDFs. Remember to use CLR UDFs wisely, though. They are especially good for tasks that T-SQL is not built to cope with efficiently, including procedural logic, complex calculations, string manipulation, and so on. On the other hand, .NET code should not be the choice when the task mainly involves set-based data manipulation. T-SQL will typically be simpler and perform much better for such tasks.

Chapter 7
Stored Procedures

Stored procedures are executable server-side routines. They give you great power and performance benefits if used wisely. Unlike user-defined functions (UDFs), stored procedures are allowed to have side effects. That is, they are allowed to change data in tables, and even the schema of objects. Stored procedures can be used as a security layer. You can control access to objects by granting execution permissions on stored procedures and not to underlying objects. You can perform input validation in stored procedures, and you can use stored procedures to allow activities only if they make sense as a whole unit, as opposed to allowing users to perform activities directly against objects.

Stored procedures also give you the benefits of encapsulation; if you need to change the implementation of a stored procedure because you developed a more efficient way to achieve a task, you can issue an ALTER PROCEDURE statement. As long as the procedure's interface remains the same, the users and the applications are not affected. On the other hand, if you implement your business logic in the client application, the impact of a change can be very painful.

Stored procedures also provide many important performance benefits. By default, a stored procedure will reuse a previously cached execution plan, saving the CPU resources and the time it takes to parse, resolve, and optimize your code. Network traffic is minimized by shortening the code strings that the client submits to Microsoft SQL Server—the client submits only the stored procedure's name and its arguments, as opposed to the full code. Moreover, all the activity is performed at the server, avoiding multiple roundtrips between the client and the server. The stored procedure will pass only the final result to the client through the network.

This chapter explores stored procedures. It starts with brief coverage of the different types of stored procedures supported by SQL Server 2005 and then delves into details. The chapter covers the stored procedure's interface, resolution process, compilation, recompilations and execution plan reuse, the EXECUTE AS clause, and the new common language runtime (CLR) stored procedures. You will have a couple of chances in the chapter to practice what you've learned by developing stored procedures that serve common practical needs.

Types of Stored Procedures

SQL Server 2005 supports different types of stored procedures: user-defined, system, and extended. You can develop user-defined stored procedures with T-SQL or with the CLR. This section briefly covers the different types.

User-Defined Stored Procedures

A user-defined stored procedure is created in a user database and typically interacts with the database objects. When you invoke a user-defined stored procedure, you specify the EXEC (or EXECUTE) command and the stored procedure's schema-qualified name, and arguments:

```
EXEC dbo.usp_Proc1 <arguments>;
```

As an example, run the code in Listing 7-1 to create the usp_GetSortedShippers stored procedure in the Northwind database:

Listing 7-1   Creation Script for usp_GetSortedShippers

```
USE Northwind;
GO
IF OBJECT_ID('dbo.usp_GetSortedShippers') IS NOT NULL
  DROP PROC dbo.usp_GetSortedShippers;
GO
-- Stored procedure usp_GetSortedShippers
-- Returns shippers sorted by requested sort column
CREATE PROC dbo.usp_GetSortedShippers
  @colname AS sysname = NULL
AS

DECLARE @msg AS NVARCHAR(500);

-- Input validation
IF @colname IS NULL
BEGIN
  SET @msg = N'A value must be supplied for parameter @colname.';
  RAISERROR(@msg, 16, 1);
  RETURN;
END
```

```
IF @colname NOT IN(N'ShipperID', N'CompanyName', N'Phone')
BEGIN
  SET @msg =
    N'Valid values for @colname are: '
    + N'N''ShipperID'', N''CompanyName'', N''Phone''.';
  RAISERROR(@msg, 16, 1);
  RETURN;
END

-- Return shippers sorted by requested sort column
IF @colname = N'ShipperID'
  SELECT ShipperID, CompanyName, Phone
  FROM dbo.Shippers
  ORDER BY ShipperID;
ELSE IF @colname = N'CompanyName'
  SELECT ShipperID, CompanyName, Phone
  FROM dbo.Shippers
  ORDER BY CompanyName;
ELSE IF @colname = N'Phone'
  SELECT ShipperID, CompanyName, Phone
  FROM dbo.Shippers
  ORDER BY Phone;
GO
```

The stored procedure accepts a column name from the Shippers table in the Northwind database as input (*@colname*); after input validation, it returns the rows from the Shippers table sorted by the specified column name. Input validation here involves verifying that a column name was specified, and that the specified column name exists in the Shippers table. Later in the chapter, I will discuss the subject of parameterizing sort order in more detail; for now, I just wanted to provide a simple example of a user-defined stored procedure. Run the following code to invoke usp_GetSortedShippers specifying *N'CompanyName'* as input, generating the output shown in Table 7-1:

```
USE Northwind;
EXEC dbo.usp_GetSortedShippers @colname = N'CompanyName';
```

Table 7-1   Shippers Sorted by *CompanyName*

ShipperID	CompanyName	Phone
3	Federal Shipping	(503) 555-9931
1	Speedy Express	(503) 555-9831
2	United Package	(503) 555-3199

You can leave out the keyword EXEC if the stored procedure is the first statement of a batch, but I recommend using it all the time. You can also omit the stored procedure's schema name (*dbo* in our case), but when you neglect to specify it, SQL Server must resolve the schema. The resolution in SQL Server 2005 occurs in the following order (adapted from Books Online):

■   The sys schema of the current database.

- The caller's default schema if executed in a batch or in dynamic SQL. Or, if the nonqualified procedure name appears inside the body of another procedure definition, the schema containing this other procedure is searched next.

- The dbo schema in the current database.

As an example, suppose that you connect to the Northwind database and your user's default schema in Northwind is called schema1. You invoke the following code in a batch:

```
EXEC usp_GetSortedShippers @colname = N'CompanyName';
```

The resolution takes place in the following order:

- Look for usp_GetSortedShippers in the sys schema of Northwind (sys.usp_GetSortedShippers). If found, execute it; if not, proceed to the next step (as in our case).

- If invoked in a batch (as in our case) or dynamic SQL, look for usp_GetSortedShippers in schema1 (schema1.usp_GetSortedShippers). Or, if invoked in another procedure (say, schema2.usp_AnotherProc), look for usp_GetSortedShippers in schema2 next. If found, execute it; if not, proceed to the next step (as in our case).

- Look for usp_GetSortedShippers in the dbo schema (dbo.usp_GetSortedShippers). If found (as in our case), execute it; if not, generate a resolution error.

Besides the potential for confusion and ambiguity when not specifying the schema, there's also an important performance reason to always specify it. When many connections are simultaneously running the same stored procedure, they may begin to block each other due to compile locks that they need to obtain when the schema name is not specified.

> **More Info**   For more information about this problem, please refer to Knowledge Base Article ID 263889, "Description of SQL blocking caused by compile locks," at *http://support.microsoft.com/?id=263889*.

As I mentioned earlier, stored procedures can be used as a security layer. You can control access to objects by granting execution permissions on stored procedures and not to underlying objects. For example, suppose that there's a database user called user1 in the Northwind database. You want to allow user1 to invoke the usp_GetSortedShippers procedure, but you want to deny user1 from accessing the Shippers table directly. You can achieve this by granting the user with EXECUTE permissions on the procedure, and denying SELECT (and possibly other) permissions on the table, as in:

```
DENY SELECT ON dbo.Shippers TO user1;
GRANT EXECUTE ON dbo.usp_GetSortedShippers TO user1;
```

SQL Server will allow user1 to execute the stored procedure. However, if user1 attempts to query the Shippers table directly:

```
SELECT ShipperID, CompanyName, Phone
FROM dbo.Shippers;
```

SQL Server will generate the following error:

```
Msg 229, Level 14, State 5, Line 1
SELECT permission denied on object 'Shippers', database 'Northwind', schema 'dbo'.
```

This security model gives you a high level of control over the activities that users will be allowed to perform.

I'd like to point out other aspects of stored procedure programming through the usp_GetSortedShippers sample procedure:

- Notice that I explicitly specified column names in the query and didn't use SELECT *. Using SELECT * is a bad practice. In the future, the table might undergo schema changes that cause your application to break. Also, if you really need only a subset of the table's columns and not all of them, the use of SELECT * prevents the optimizer from utilizing covering indexes defined on that subset of columns.

- The query is missing a filter. This is not a bad practice by itself; this is perfectly valid if you really need all rows from the table. But you might be surprised to learn that in per-formance-tuning projects at Solid Quality Learning, we still find production applications that need filtered data but filter it only at the client. Such an approach introduces extreme pressure on both SQL Server and the network. Filters allow the optimizer to consider using indexes, which minimizes the I/O cost. Also, by filtering at the server, you reduce network traffic. If you need filtered data, make sure you filter it at the server; use a WHERE clause (or ON, HAVING where relevant)!

- Notice the use of a semicolon (;) to suffix statements. Although not a requirement of T-SQL for all statements, the semicolon suffix is an ANSI requirement. In SQL Server 2000, a semicolon is not required at all but is optional. In SQL Server 2005, you are required to suffix some statements with a semicolon to avoid ambiguity of your code. For example, the WITH keyword is used for different purposes—to define a CTE, to spec-ify a table hint, and others. SQL Server requires you to suffix the statement preceding the CTE's WITH clause to avoid ambiguity. Getting used to suffixing all statements with a semicolon is a good practice.

Now let's get back to the focus of this section—user-defined stored procedures.

As I mentioned earlier, to invoke a user-defined stored procedure, you specify EXEC, the schema-qualified name of the procedure, and the parameter values for the invocation if there are any. References in the stored procedure to system and user object names that are not fully qualified (that is, without the database prefix) are always resolved in the database in which the procedure was created. If you want to invoke a user-defined procedure created in another database, you must database-qualify its name. For example, if you are connected to a database called db1 and want to invoke a stored procedure called usp_Proc1, which resides in db2, you would use the following code:

```
USE db1;
EXEC db2.dbo.usp_Proc1 <arguments>;
```

Invoking a procedure from another database wouldn't change the fact that object names that are not fully qualified would be resolved in the database in which the procedure was created (db2, in this case).

If you want to invoke a remote stored procedure residing in another instance of SQL Server, you would use the fully qualified stored procedure name, including the linked server name: server.database.schema.proc.

When done, run the following code for cleanup:

```
USE Northwind;
GO
IF OBJECT_ID('dbo.usp_GetSortedShippers') IS NOT NULL
  DROP PROC dbo.usp_GetSortedShippers;
```

Special Stored Procedures

By "special stored procedure," I mean a stored procedure created with a name beginning with *sp_* in the master database. A stored procedure created in this way has special behavior.

> **Important**   Note that Microsoft strongly recommends against creating your own stored procedures with the *sp_* prefix. This prefix is used by SQL Server to designate system stored procedures. In this section, I will create stored procedures with the *sp_* prefix to demonstrate their special behavior.

As an example, the following code creates the special procedure sp_Proc1, which prints the database context and queries the INFORMATION_SCHEMA.TABLES view—first with dynamic SQL, then with a static query:

```
SET NOCOUNT ON;
USE master;
GO

IF OBJECT_ID('dbo.sp_Proc1') IS NOT NULL
  DROP PROC dbo.sp_Proc1;
GO

CREATE PROC dbo.sp_Proc1
AS
PRINT 'master.dbo.sp_Proc1 executing in ' + DB_NAME();
```

```
-- Dynamic query
EXEC('SELECT TABLE_CATALOG, TABLE_SCHEMA, TABLE_NAME
FROM INFORMATION_SCHEMA.TABLES
WHERE TABLE_TYPE = ''BASE TABLE'';');

-- Static query
SELECT TABLE_CATALOG, TABLE_SCHEMA, TABLE_NAME
FROM INFORMATION_SCHEMA.TABLES
WHERE TABLE_TYPE = 'BASE TABLE';
GO
```

One of the unique aspects of a special procedure is that you don't need to database-qualify its name when connected to another database. For example, you can be connected to Northwind and still be able to run it without database-qualifying its name:

```
USE Northwind;
EXEC dbo.sp_Proc1;
```

The PRINT command returns *'master.dbo.sp_Proc1 executing in Northwind'*. The database name in the printed message was obtained by the DB_NAME function. It seems that DB_NAME "thinks" that the database context is Northwind (the current database) and not master. Similarly, dynamic SQL also assumes the context of the current database; so the EXEC command (which invokes a query against INFORMATION_SCHEMA.TABLES) returns table names from the Northwind database. In contrast to the previous two statements, the static query against INFORMATION_SCHEMA.TABLES seems to "think" that it is running in master—it returns table names from the master database and not Northwind. Similarly, if you refer with static code to user objects (for example, a table called T1), SQL Server will look for them in master. If that's not confusing enough, in SQL Server 2000, static code referring to system tables (for example, sysobjects) was resolved in the current database. SQL Server 2005 preserves this behavior with the corresponding backward compatibility views (for example, sys.sysobjects)—but not with the new catalog views (for example, sys.objects).

Interestingly, the *sp_* prefix works magic also with other types of objects besides stored procedures.

> **Caution**   The behavior described in the following section is undocumented, and you should not rely on it in production environments.

For example, the following code creates a table with the *sp_* prefix in master:

```
USE master;
GO
IF OBJECT_ID('dbo.sp_Globals') IS NOT NULL
  DROP TABLE dbo.sp_Globals;
GO

CREATE TABLE dbo.sp_Globals
(
  var_name sysname      NOT NULL PRIMARY KEY,
  val      SQL_VARIANT NULL
);
```

And the following code switches between database contexts, and it always manages to find the table even though the table name is not database-qualified.

```
USE Northwind;
INSERT INTO dbo.sp_Globals(var_name, val)
  VALUES('var1', 10);
USE pubs;
INSERT INTO dbo.sp_Globals(var_name, val)
  VALUES('var2', CAST(1 AS BIT));
USE tempdb;
SELECT var_name, val FROM dbo.sp_Globals;
```

The last query produces the output shown in Table 7-2.

Table 7-2   Contents of sp_Globals Table

var_name	Val
var1	10
var2	1

For cleanup, run the following code:

```
USE master;
GO
IF OBJECT_ID('dbo.sp_Globals') IS NOT NULL
  DROP TABLE dbo.sp_Globals;
```

Do not drop sp_Proc1 yet because it is used in the following section.

System Stored Procedures

System stored procedures are procedures that were shipped by Microsoft. In SQL Server 2000, system stored procedures resided in the master database, had the *sp_* prefix, and were marked with the *"system"* (MS Shipped) flag. In SQL Server 2005, system stored procedures reside physically in an internal hidden Resource database, and they exist logically in every database.

A special procedure (*sp_* prefix, created in master) that is also marked as a system procedure gets additional unique behavior. When the installation scripts that are run by SQL Server's setup program create system procedures, they mark those procedures as system using the undocumented procedure *sp_MS_marksystemobject*.

Caution   You should not use the *sp_MS_marksystemobject* stored procedure in production because you won't get any support if you run into trouble with them. Also, there's no guarantee that the behavior you get by marking your procedures as system will remain the same in future versions of SQL Server, or even future service packs. Here, I'm going to use it for demonstration purposes to show additional behaviors that system procedures have.

Run the following code to mark the special procedure sp_Proc1 also as a system procedure:

```
USE master;
EXEC sp_MS_marksystemobject 'dbo.sp_Proc1';
```

If you now run sp_Proc1 in databases other than master, you will observe that all code statements within the stored procedure assume the context of the current database:

```
USE Northwind;
EXEC dbo.sp_Proc1;
USE pubs;
EXEC dbo.sp_Proc1;
EXEC Northwind.dbo.sp_Proc1;
```

As a practice, avoid using the *sp_* prefix for user-defined stored procedures. Remember that if a local database has a stored procedure with the same name and schema as a special procedure in master, the user-defined procedure will be invoked. To demonstrate this, create a procedure called sp_Proc1 in Northwind as well:

```
USE Northwind;
GO
IF OBJECT_ID('dbo.sp_Proc1') IS NOT NULL
  DROP PROC dbo.sp_Proc1;
GO

CREATE PROC dbo.sp_Proc1
AS
PRINT 'Northwind.dbo.sp_Proc1 executing in ' + DB_NAME();
GO
```

If you run the following code, you will observe that when connected to Northwind, sp_Proc1 from Northwind was invoked:

```
USE Northwind;
EXEC dbo.sp_Proc1;
USE pubs;
EXEC dbo.sp_Proc1;
```

Drop the Northwind version because it would interfere with the following examples:

```
USE Northwind;
GO
IF OBJECT_ID('dbo.sp_Proc1') IS NOT NULL
  DROP PROC dbo.sp_Proc1;
```

Interestingly, system procedures have an additional unique behavior. They also resolve user objects in the current database, not just system objects. To demonstrate this, run the following code to re-create the sp_Proc1 special procedure, which queries a user table called Orders, and to mark the procedure as system:

```
USE master;
GO
IF OBJECT_ID('dbo.sp_Proc1') IS NOT NULL
  DROP PROC dbo.sp_Proc1;
GO

CREATE PROC dbo.sp_Proc1
AS
PRINT 'master.dbo.sp_Proc1 executing in ' + DB_NAME();
SELECT OrderID FROM dbo.Orders;
GO

EXEC sp_MS_marksystemobject 'dbo.sp_Proc1';
```

Run sp_Proc1 in Northwind, and you will observe that the query ran successfully against the Orders table in Northwind:

```
USE Northwind;
EXEC dbo.sp_Proc1;
```

Make a similar attempt in pubs:

```
USE pubs;
EXEC dbo.sp_Proc1;
master.dbo.sp_Proc1 executing in pubs
Msg 208, Level 16, State 1, Procedure sp_Proc1, Line 5
Invalid object name 'dbo.Orders'.
```

The error tells you that SQL Server looked for an Orders table in pubs but couldn't find one.

When you're done, run the following code for cleanup:

```
USE master;
GO
IF OBJECT_ID('dbo.sp_Proc1') IS NOT NULL
  DROP PROC dbo.sp_Proc1;
GO
USE Northwind
GO
IF OBJECT_ID('dbo.sp_Proc1') IS NOT NULL
  DROP PROC dbo.sp_Proc1;
```

Other Types of Stored Procedures

SQL Server also supports other types of stored procedures:

- **Temporary stored procedures** You can create temporary procedures by prefixing their names with a single number symbol or a double one (# or ##). A single number symbol would make the procedure a local temporary procedure, and two number symbols would make it a global one. Local and global temporary procedures behave in terms of visibility and scope like local and global temporary tables, respectively.

> **More Info**   For details about local and global temporary tables, please refer to Chapter 2.

- **Extended stored procedures**   These procedures allow you to create external routines with a programming language such as C using the Open Data Services (ODS) API. These were used in prior versions of SQL Server to extend the functionality of the product. External routines were written using the ODS API, compiled to a .dll file, and registered as extended stored procedures in SQL Server. They were used like user-defined stored procedures with T-SQL. In SQL Server 2005, extended stored procedures are supported for backward compatibility and will be removed in a future version of SQL Server. Now you can rely on the .NET integration in the product and develop CLR stored procedures, as well as other types of routines. I'll cover CLR procedures later in the chapter.

The Stored Procedure Interface

This section covers the interface (that is, the input and output parameters) of stored procedures.

Input Parameters

You can define input parameters for a stored procedure in its header. An input parameter must be provided with a value when the stored procedure is invoked unless you assign the parameter with a default value. As an example, the following code creates the usp_GetCustOrders procedure, which accepts a customer ID and datetime range boundaries as inputs, and returns the given customer's orders in the given datetime range:

```
USE Northwind;
GO

IF OBJECT_ID('dbo.usp_GetCustOrders') IS NOT NULL
  DROP PROC dbo.usp_GetCustOrders;
GO

CREATE PROC dbo.usp_GetCustOrders
  @custid   AS NCHAR(5),
  @fromdate AS DATETIME = '19000101',
  @todate   AS DATETIME = '99991231'
AS

SET NOCOUNT ON;

SELECT OrderID, CustomerID, EmployeeID, OrderDate
FROM dbo.Orders
WHERE CustomerID = @custid
  AND OrderDate >= @fromdate
  AND OrderDate < @todate;
GO
```

> **Tip** The SET NOCOUNT ON option tells SQL Server not to produce the message saying how many rows were affected for data manipulation language (DML) statements. Some client database interfaces, such as OLEDB, absorb this message as a row set. The result is that when you expect to get a result set of a query back to the client, instead you get this message of how many rows were affected as the first result set. By issuing SET NOCOUNT ON, you avoid this problem in those interfaces, so you might want to adopt the practice of specifying it.

When invoking a stored procedure, you must specify inputs for those parameters that were not given default values in the definition (for *@custid* in our case). There are two formats for assigning values to parameters when invoking a stored procedure: *unnamed* and *named*. In the unnamed format, you just specify values without specifying the parameter names. Also, you must specify the inputs by declaration order of the parameters. You can omit inputs only for parameters that have default values and that were declared at the end of the parameter list. You cannot omit an input between two parameters for which you do specify values. If you want such parameters to use their default values, you would need to specify the DEFAULT keyword for those.

As an example, the following code invokes the procedure without specifying the inputs for the two last parameters, which will use their default values, and produces the output shown in Table 7-3:

```
EXEC dbo.usp_GetCustOrders N'ALFKI';
```

Table 7-3   Customer ALFKI's Orders

OrderID	CustomerID	EmployeeID	OrderDate
10643	ALFKI	6	1997-08-25 00:00:00.000
10692	ALFKI	4	1997-10-03 00:00:00.000
10702	ALFKI	4	1997-10-13 00:00:00.000
10835	ALFKI	1	1998-01-15 00:00:00.000
10952	ALFKI	1	1998-03-16 00:00:00.000
11011	ALFKI	3	1998-04-09 00:00:00.000

If you want to specify your own value for the third parameter but use the default for the second, specify the DEFAULT keyword for the second parameter:

```
EXEC dbo.usp_GetCustOrders N'ALFKI', DEFAULT, '20060212';
```

This code also produces the output in Table 7-3.

And, of course, if you want to specify your own values for all parameters, just specify them in order, as in:

```
EXEC dbo.usp_GetCustOrders N'ALFKI', '19970101', '19980101';
```

which produces the output shown in Table 7-4:

Table 7-4   Customer ALFKI's Orders in 1997

OrderID	CustomerID	EmployeeID	OrderDate
10643	ALFKI	6	1997-08-25 00:00:00.000
10692	ALFKI	4	1997-10-03 00:00:00.000
10702	ALFKI	4	1997-10-13 00:00:00.000

These are the basics of stored procedures. You're probably already familiar with them, but I decided to include this coverage to lead to a recommended practice. There are many maintenance-related issues that can arise when using the unnamed assignment format. You must specify the arguments in order; you must not omit an optional parameter; and by looking at the code, it might not be clear what the inputs actually mean and to which parameter they relate. Therefore, it's a good practice to use the named assignment format, where you specify the name of the argument and assign it with an input value, as in:

```
EXEC dbo.usp_GetCustOrders
  @custid   = N'ALFKI',
  @fromdate = '19970101',
  @todate   = '19980101';
```

The code is much more readable; you can play with the order in which you specify the inputs; and you can omit any parameter that you like if it has a default value.

Output Parameters

Output parameters allow you to return output values from a stored procedure. A change made to the output parameter within the stored procedure is reflected in the variable from the calling batch that was assigned to the output parameter. The concept is similar to a pointer in C or a *ByRef* parameter in Visual Basic.

As an example, the following code alters the definition of the usp_GetCustOrders procedure, adding to it the output parameter *@numrows*:

```
ALTER PROC dbo.usp_GetCustOrders
  @custid   AS NCHAR(5),
  @fromdate AS DATETIME = '19000101',
  @todate   AS DATETIME = '99991231',
  @numrows  AS INT OUTPUT
AS

SET NOCOUNT ON;
DECLARE @err AS INT;

SELECT OrderID, CustomerID, EmployeeID, OrderDate
FROM dbo.Orders
WHERE CustomerID = @custid
  AND OrderDate >= @fromdate
  AND OrderDate < @todate;
```

```
SELECT @numrows = @@rowcount, @err = @@error;

RETURN @err;
GO
```

@numrows will return the number of rows affected by the query. Notice that the stored procedure also uses a RETURN clause to return the value of the *@@error* function after the invocation of the query.

To get the output parameter back from the stored procedure when invoking it, you will need to assign it with a variable defined in the calling batch and mention the keyword OUTPUT. To get back the return status, you will also need to provide a variable from the calling batch right before the procedure name and an equal sign. Here's an example:

```
DECLARE @myerr AS INT, @mynumrows AS INT;

EXEC @myerr = dbo.usp_GetCustOrders
  @custid   = N'ALFKI',
  @fromdate = '19970101',
  @todate   = '19980101',
  @numrows  = @mynumrows OUTPUT;

SELECT @myerr AS err, @mynumrows AS rc;
```

The stored procedure returns the output shown in Table 7-4, plus it assigns the return status *0* to *@myerr* and the number of affected rows (in this case, 3) to the *@mynumrows* variable.

If you want to manipulate the row set returned by the stored procedure with T-SQL, you will need to create a table first and use the INSERT/EXEC syntax, as shown in Listing 7-2.

Listing 7-2   Send output of *usp_GetCustOrders* to a table

```
IF OBJECT_ID('tempdb..#CustOrders') IS NOT NULL
  DROP TABLE #CustOrders;
GO
CREATE TABLE #CustOrders
(
  OrderID    INT       NOT NULL PRIMARY KEY,
  CustomerID NCHAR(5) NOT NULL,
  EmployeeID INT       NOT NULL,
  OrderDate  DATETIME NOT NULL
);

DECLARE @myerr AS INT, @mynumrows AS INT;

INSERT INTO #CustOrders(OrderID, CustomerID, EmployeeID, OrderDate)
  EXEC @myerr = dbo.usp_GetCustOrders
    @custid   = N'ALFKI',
    @fromdate = '19970101',
    @todate   = '19980101',
    @numrows  = @mynumrows OUTPUT;
```

```
SELECT OrderID, CustomerID, EmployeeID, OrderDate
FROM #CustOrders;

SELECT @myerr AS err, @mynumrows AS rc;
GO
```

A client will accept output from a stored procedure into client objects. For example, in ADO programming you define items in a *Parameters* collection for input parameters, output parameters, and return status. A stored procedure can return more than one result set if within it you invoke multiple queries. In the client code, you will absorb the result sets, moving from one record set to another—for example, using the *.NextRecordset* property of the *Recordset* object in ADO. A stored procedure can generate other types of outputs as well, including the output of PRINT and RAISERROR commands. Both would be received by the client through the client interface's structures—for example, the *Errors* collection in ADO.

ADO.NET allows you to accept any possible output from a SQL Server stored procedure at the client side. Of course, in order to accept some output, as the first step, you have to execute the procedure. You execute a stored procedure by using the *SqlCommand* object. To denote you are executing a stored procedure, you have to set the *CommandType* property of the *SqlCommand* object to *CommandType.StoredProcedure*. To define which procedure to execute, you have to insert the name of the procedure to the *CommandText* property. To actually execute the procedure, use the *ExecuteScalar*, *ExecuteNonQuery*, *ExecuteReader*, or *ExecuteXmlReader* methods of the *SqlCommand* object, depending on the output(s) of the stored procedure. Following are the different types of output of stored procedures needed to get the output:

- **A single row set**   A single row set can be accepted to an object of the *SqlDataReader* class for the connected environment (connected means that your application maintains a permanent connection to the SQL Server—that is, the connection is always available), and an object of the *SqlDataAdapter* class. If you want to fill an object of the *DataTable* class, which is a member of an object of the *DataSet* class for the disconnected scenario (disconnected here means that after you read the data in the DataTable, in your application, you can disconnect from SQL Server, and you can still use the data read in your application from the DataTable object).

- **Multiple row sets**   The *SqlDataReader* class. Use the *NextResult* method of a data reader object to loop through all row sets returned by a stored procedure.

- **Output parameters**   Accept output parameters in the *Parameters* collection of a *SqlCommand* object. A *SqlParameter* object in ADO.NET can have four possible directions: *Input*, *Output*, *InputOutput*, or *ReturnValue*. Of course, a single parameter can have a single direction selected at a time. For *ReturnValue* direction, please see the next bullet. Input parameters can be used for input only, and output parameters can be used for output only. SQL Server stored procedure output parameters are actually input/output parameters, so you can pass a value through an output parameter when executing a stored procedure. Therefore, you can specify the *InputOutput* direction of a *SqlParameter* object in ADO.NET, but you have to assign the input value to it before executing the stored procedure or you will get a compile error.

- **Return value**   Accept it in a *SqlParameter* object with the *ReturnValue* direction. The return value parameter has to be the first one in the *Parameters* collection of a *SqlCommand* object.

- **Number of rows affected**   This can be tricky. You can't rely on the output of SQL Server here, because the developer could add the SET NOCOUNT ON statement to the stored procedure. *SqlDataReader* objects have the *RecordsAffected* property, which gets the number of rows updated, inserted, or deleted. For a SELECT statement, this property can't be used. But there is a problem also with INSERT, UPDATE, and DELETE statements: the *RecordAffected* property gets only the total number of rows affected by all DML statements in the stored procedure. What if you need the number of rows for each DML statement separately? In this case, you can define as many output parameters as the number of DML statements in the procedure, and then store the @@*rowcount* value in every output parameter after every DML statement. This way you can easily get the number of rows affected by SELECT statements as well.

- **Errors**   All your .NET code should use a *Try..Catch* block for every risky operation. In the *Catch* block, you can trap real errors—that is, errors with severity levels greater than 10, meaning significant errors, not just warnings or info messages. You run the statements that can produce an error, like executing a stored procedure by using a *SqlCommand* object, in the *Try* block. When an error occurs in the *Try* block, the control of the application is transferred immediately to the *Catch* block, where you can access a *SqlException* object that describes the error. This *SqlException* object has an *Errors* collection. In the collection, you get objects of *SqlError* type, a single object for any error of severity level from 11 through 16 thrown by your SQL Server. You can loop through the collection and read all errors returned by SQL Server. Among the properties of the *SqlError* are a *Number* property, which holds the error number, and a *Message* property, which holds the error message.

- **Warnings**   This can be tricky as well. Warnings in SQL Server are error messages with a severity level of 10 or lower. If there is no real error in your code, you can get the warnings in the procedure that handles the *InfoMessage* event of the *SqlConnection* object. The InfoMessage event receives a *SqlInfoMessageEventArgs* object. *SqlInfoMessageEventArgs* has an *Errors* collection, which is similar to previously mentioned Errors collection of the *SQLException* object—it is a collection of objects of *SqlError* type, this time with SQL Server errors of severity level 10 or lower. Again, you can loop through the collection and get all the information from SQL Server warnings that you need. But if there were a real error in the stored procedure, you could catch all the warnings as well as the errors in the *Catch* block, and the *InfoMessage* event would never occur.

- **T-SQL PRINT statement output**   You handle this output in the same way that you handle warnings. Read the output using the *InfoMessage* event handler of a *SqlConnection*, or read it in a *Catch* block if there was a real error in the stored procedure.

- **DBCC statement output**   Some DBCC commands support the TABLERESULTS option. If you use this option, you can read the output using the *SqlDataReader* object just as you would read any other row set. If the output of the DBCC statement is textual and not a table, you can get it by using the *InfoMessage* event of the *SqlConnection* object. Again, the same rules apply as for warnings and PRINT output.

■ **XML output**   ADO.NET 2.0 fully supports the new XML data type, so you can simply use a *SqlDataReader* object to get the results in table format, including XML data type columns. XML output from a SELECT statement with the FOR XML clause can be retrieved into an *XmlReader* object, and you have to use the *ExecuteXmlReader* method of the *SqlCommand* object, of course.

■ **User-defined data types (UDTs)**   ADO.NET fully supports UDTs as well, so you can fetch values of UDT columns the same way you fetch values of columns of native types. Note that SQL Server sends only the values, not the code for the UDT; therefore, to use any of the UDT's methods at the client side, the code must be available at the client side as well.

■ **Schema of a row set retrieved with a *SqlDataReader***   *SqlDataReader* in ADO.NET 2.0 has a new method called *GetSchemaTable*. This method can be used to get a *DataTable* that describes the column metadata of the *SqlDataReader*.

For examples and more details about ADO.NET, please refer to *ADO.NET Examples and Best Practices for C# Programmers* (Apress, 2002) by William R. Vaughn and Peter Blackburn.

When you're done, run the following code for cleanup:

```
USE Northwind;
GO
IF OBJECT_ID('dbo.usp_GetCustOrders') IS NOT NULL
  DROP PROC dbo.usp_GetCustOrders;
GO
IF OBJECT_ID('tempdb..#CustOrders') IS NOT NULL
  DROP TABLE #CustOrders;
GO
```

Resolution

When you create a stored procedure, SQL Server first parses the code to check for syntax errors. If the code passes the parsing stage, successfully, SQL Server attempts to resolve the names it contains. The resolution process verifies the existence of object and column names, among other things. If the referenced objects exist, the resolution process will take place fully—that is, it will also check for the existence of the referenced column names.

If an object name exists but a column within it doesn't, the resolution process will produce an error and the stored procedure will not be created. However, if the object doesn't exist at all, SQL Server will create the stored procedure and defer the resolution process to run time, when the stored procedure is invoked. Of course, if a referenced object or a column is still missing when you execute the stored procedure, the code will fail. This process of postponing name resolution until run time is called *deferred name resolution*.

I'll demonstrate the resolution aspects I just described. First run the following code to make sure that the usp_Proc1 procedure, the usp_Proc2 procedure, and the table T1 do not exist within tempdb:

```
USE tempdb;
GO
IF OBJECT_ID('dbo.usp_Proc1') IS NOT NULL
  DROP PROC dbo.usp_Proc1;
GO
IF OBJECT_ID('dbo.usp_Proc2') IS NOT NULL
  DROP PROC dbo.usp_Proc2;
GO
IF OBJECT_ID('dbo.T1') IS NOT NULL
  DROP TABLE dbo.T1;
```

Run the following code to create the stored procedure usp_Proc1, which refers to a table named T1, which doesn't exist:

```
CREATE PROC dbo.usp_Proc1
AS

SELECT col1 FROM dbo.T1;
GO
```

Because table T1 doesn't exist, resolution was deferred to run time, and the stored procedure was created successfully. If T1 does not exist when you invoke the procedure, it fails at run time. Run the following code:

```
EXEC dbo.usp_Proc1;
```

You will get the following error:

```
Msg 208, Level 16, State 1, Procedure usp_Proc1, Line 6
Invalid object name 'dbo.T1'.
```

Next create table T1 with a column called *col1*:

```
CREATE TABLE dbo.T1(col1 INT);
INSERT INTO dbo.T1(col1) VALUES(1);
```

Invoke the stored procedure again:

```
EXEC dbo.usp_Proc1;
```

This time it will run successfully.

Next, attempt to create a stored procedure called usp_Proc2, referring to a nonexistent column (*col2*) in the existing T1 table:

```
CREATE PROC dbo.usp_Proc2
AS

SELECT col2 FROM dbo.T1;
GO
```

Here, the resolution process was not deferred to run time because T1 exists. The stored procedure was not created, and you got the following error:

```
Msg 207, Level 16, State 1, Procedure usp_Proc2, Line 4
Invalid column name 'col2'.
```

When you're done, run the following code for cleanup:

```
USE tempdb;
GO
IF OBJECT_ID('dbo.usp_Proc1') IS NOT NULL
  DROP PROC dbo.usp_Proc1;
GO
IF OBJECT_ID('dbo.usp_Proc2') IS NOT NULL
  DROP PROC dbo.usp_Proc2;
GO
IF OBJECT_ID('dbo.T1') IS NOT NULL
  DROP TABLE dbo.T1;
```

Compilations, Recompilations, and Reuse of Execution Plans

Earlier I mentioned that when you create a stored procedure, SQL Server parses your code and then attempts to resolve it. If resolution was deferred, it will take place at first invocation. Upon first invocation of the stored procedure, if the resolution phase finished successfully, SQL Server analyzes and optimizes the queries within the stored procedure and generates an execution plan. An execution plan holds the instructions to process the query. These instructions include which order to access the tables in; which indexes, access methods, and join algorithms to use; whether to spool interim sets; and so on. SQL Server typically generates multiple permutations of execution plans and will choose the one with the lowest cost out of the ones that it generated.

Note that SQL Server won't necessarily create all possible permutations of execution plans; if it did, the optimization phase might take too long. SQL Server will limit the optimizer by calculating a threshold for optimization, which is based on the sizes of the tables involved as well as other factors.

Stored procedures can reuse a previously cached execution plan, thereby saving the resources involved in generating a new execution plan. This section will discuss the reuse of execution plans, cases when a plan cannot be reused, and a specific issue relating to plan reuse called the "parameter sniffing problem."

Reuse of Execution Plans

The process of optimization requires mainly CPU resources. SQL Server will, by default, reuse a previously cached plan from an earlier invocation of a stored procedure, without investigating whether it actually is or isn't a good idea to do so.

To demonstrate plan reuse, first run the following code, which creates the usp_GetOrders stored procedure:

```
USE Northwind;
GO
IF OBJECT_ID('dbo.usp_GetOrders') IS NOT NULL
  DROP PROC dbo.usp_GetOrders;
GO

CREATE PROC dbo.usp_GetOrders
  @odate AS DATETIME
AS

SELECT OrderID, CustomerID, EmployeeID, OrderDate
FROM dbo.Orders
WHERE OrderDate >= @odate;
GO
```

The stored procedure accepts an order date as input (*@odate*) and returns orders placed on or after the input order date.

Turn on the STATISTICS IO option to get back I/O information for your session's activity:

```
SET STATISTICS IO ON;
```

Run the stored procedure for the first time, providing an input with *high selectivity* (that is, an input for which a small percentage of rows will be returned); it will generate the output shown in Table 7-5:

```
EXEC dbo.usp_GetOrders '19980506';
```

Table 7-5   Output of EXEC *dbo.usp_GetOrders '19980506'*

OrderID	CustomerID	EmployeeID	OrderDate
11074	SIMOB	7	1998-05-06 00:00:00.000
11075	RICSU	8	1998-05-06 00:00:00.000
11076	BONAP	4	1998-05-06 00:00:00.000
11077	RATTC	1	1998-05-06 00:00:00.000

Examine the execution plan produced for the query, shown in Figure 7-1.

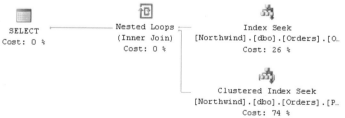

Figure 7-1   Execution plan showing that the index on *OrderDate* is used

Because this is the first time the stored procedure is invoked, SQL Server generated an execution plan for it based on the selective input value and cached that plan.

The optimizer uses cardinality and density information to estimate the cost of the access methods that it considers applying, and the selectivity of filters is an important factor. For example, a query with a highly selective filter can benefit from a nonclustered, noncovering index, while a *low selectivity* filter (that is, one that returns a high percentage of rows) would not justify using such an index.

For highly selective input such as that provided to our stored procedure, the optimizer chose a plan that uses a nonclustered noncovering index on the *OrderDate* column. The plan first performed a seek within that index (Index Seek operator), reaching the first index entry that matches the filter at the leaf level of the index. This seek operation caused two page reads, one at each of the two levels in the index. In a larger table, such an index might contain three or four levels.

Following the seek operation, the plan performed a partial ordered forward scan within the leaf level of the index (which is not seen in the plan but is part of the Index Seek operator). The partial scan fetched all index entries that match the query's filter (that is, all *OrderDate* values greater than or equal to the input *@odate*). Because the input was very selective, only four matching *OrderDate* values were found. In this particular case, the partial scan did not need to access additional pages at the leaf level beyond the leaf page that the seek operation reached, so it did not incur additional I/O.

The plan used a Nested Loops operator, which invoked a series of Clustered Index Seek operations to look up the data row for each of the four index entries that the partial scan found. Because the clustered index on this small table has two levels, the lookups cost eight page reads: $2 \times 4 = 8$. In total, there were 10 page reads: 2 (*seek*) $+ 2 \times 4$ (*lookups*) $= 10$. This is the value reported by STATISTICS IO as logical reads.

That's the optimal plan for this selective query with the existing indexes.

Remember that I mentioned earlier that stored procedures will, by default, reuse a previously cached plan? Now that you have a plan stored in cache, additional invocations of the stored procedure will reuse it. That's fine if you keep invoking the stored procedure with a highly selective input. You will enjoy the fact that the plan is reused, and SQL Server will not waste resources on generating new plans. That's especially important with systems that invoke stored procedures very frequently.

However, imagine that the stored procedure's inputs vary considerably in selectivity—some invocations have high selectivity while others have very low selectivity. For example, the following code invokes the stored procedure with an input that has low selectivity:

```
EXEC dbo.usp_GetOrders '19960101';
```

Because there is a plan in cache, it will be reused, which is unfortunate in this case. I provided the minimum *OrderDate* that exists in the table as input. This means that all rows in the table (830) qualify. The plan will require a clustered index lookup for each qualifying row. This invocation generated 1,664 logical reads, even though the whole Orders table resides on 22 data pages. Keep in mind that the Orders table is very small and that in production environments such a table would typically have millions of rows. The cost of reusing such a plan would then be much more dramatic, given a similar scenario. Take a table with 1,000,000 orders, for example, residing on about 25,000 pages. Suppose that the clustered index contains three levels. Just the cost of the lookups would then be 3,000,000 reads: *1,000,000 × 3 = 3,000,000.*

Obviously, in a case such as this, in which a lot of data access is involved and there are large variations in selectivity, it's a very bad idea to reuse a previously cached execution plan.

Similarly, if you invoked the stored procedure for the first time with a low selectivity input, you would get a plan that is optimal for that input—one that issues a table scan (unordered clustered index scan)—and that plan would be cached. Then, in later invocations, the plan would be reused even when the input has high selectivity.

At this point, you can turn off the STATISTICS IO option:

```
SET STATISTICS IO OFF;
```

You can observe the fact that an execution plan was reused by querying the *sys.syscacheobjects* system view (or *master.dbo.syscacheobjects* in SQL Server 2000), which contains information about execution plans:

```
SELECT cacheobjtype, objtype, usecounts, sql
FROM sys.syscacheobjects
WHERE sql NOT LIKE '%cache%'
  AND sql LIKE '%usp_GetOrders%';
```

This query generates the output shown in Table 7-6.

Table 7-6   Execution Plan for usp_GetOrders in sys.syscacheobjects

cacheobjtype	objtype	usecounts	sql
Compiled Plan	Proc	2	CREATE PROC dbo.usp_GetOrders ...

Notice that one plan was found for the usp_GetOrders procedure in cache, and that it was used twice (*usecounts* = 2).

One way to solve the problem is to create two stored procedures—one for requests with high selectivity, and a second for low selectivity. You create another stored procedure with flow logic, examining the input and determining which procedure to invoke based on the input's selectivity that your calculations estimate. The idea is nice in theory, but it's very difficult to implement in practice. It can be very complex to calculate the boundary point dynamically without consuming additional resources. Furthermore, this stored procedure accepts only one input, so imagine how complex things would become with multiple inputs.

Another way to solve the problem is to create (or alter) the stored procedure with the RECOMPILE option, as in:

```
ALTER PROC dbo.usp_GetOrders
  @odate AS DATETIME
WITH RECOMPILE
AS

SELECT OrderID, CustomerID, EmployeeID, OrderDate
FROM dbo.Orders
WHERE OrderDate >= @odate;
GO
```

The RECOMPILE option tells SQL Server to create a new execution plan every time it is invoked. It is especially useful when the time it takes to generate a plan is a small portion of the run time of the stored procedure, and the implications of running the procedure with an inadequate plan would increase the run time substantially.

First run the altered procedure specifying an input with high selectivity:

```
EXEC dbo.usp_GetOrders '19980506';
```

You will get the plan shown in Figure 7-1, which is optimal in this case and generates an I/O cost of 10 logical reads.

Next run it specifying an input with low selectivity:

```
EXEC dbo.usp_GetOrders '19960101';
```

You will get the plan in Figure 7-2, showing a table scan (unordered clustered index scan), which is optimal for this input. The I/O cost in this case is 22 logical reads.

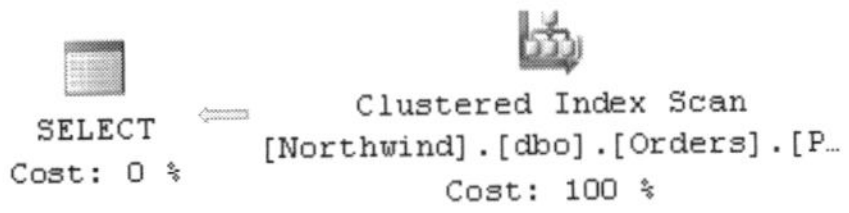

```
                                    Clustered Index Scan
    SELECT     ⟸       [Northwind].[dbo].[Orders].[P...
    Cost: 0 %                       Cost: 100 %
```

Figure 7-2 Execution plan showing a table scan (unordered clustered index scan)

Note that when creating a stored procedure with the RECOMPILE option, SQL Server doesn't even bother to keep the execution plan for it in cache. If you now query sys.syscacheobjects, you will get no plan back for the usp_GetOrders procedure:

```
SELECT * FROM sys.syscacheobjects
WHERE sql NOT LIKE '%cache%'
  AND sql LIKE '%usp_GetOrders%';
```

In SQL Server 2000, the unit of compilation was the whole stored procedure. So even if you wanted just one particular query to be recompiled, you couldn't request it. If you created the stored procedure with the RECOMPILE option, the whole procedure went through recompilation every time you invoked it.

SQL Server 2005 supports statement-level recompile. Instead of having all queries in the stored procedure recompiled, SQL Server can now recompile individual statements. You're provided with a new RECOMPILE query hint that allows you to explicitly request a recompilation of a particular query. This way, other queries can benefit from reusing previously cached execution plans if there's no reason to recompile them every time the stored procedure is invoked.

Run the following code to alter the procedure, specifying the RECOMPILE query hint:

```
ALTER PROC dbo.usp_GetOrders
  @odate AS DATETIME
AS

SELECT OrderID, CustomerID, EmployeeID, OrderDate
FROM dbo.Orders
WHERE OrderDate >= @odate
OPTION(RECOMPILE);
GO
```

In our case, there's only one query in the stored procedure, so it doesn't really matter whether you specify the RECOMPILE option at the procedure or the query level. But try to think of the advantages of this hint when you have multiple queries in one stored procedure.

To see that you get good plans, first run the procedure specifying an input with high selectivity:

```
EXEC dbo.usp_GetOrders '19980506';
```

You will get the plan in Figure 7-1, and an I/O cost of 10 logical reads.

Next run it specifying an input with low selectivity:

```
EXEC dbo.usp_GetOrders '19960101';
```

You will get the plan in Figure 7-2 and an I/O cost of 22 logical reads.

Don't get confused by the fact that syscacheobjects shows a plan with the value 2 as the *usecounts*:

```
SELECT cacheobjtype, objtype, usecounts, sql
FROM sys.syscacheobjects
WHERE sql NOT LIKE '%cache%'
  AND sql LIKE '%usp_GetOrders%';
```

The output is the same as in Table 7-6. Remember that if there were other queries in the stored procedure, they could potentially reuse the execution plan.

Recompilations

As I mentioned earlier, a stored procedure will reuse a previously cached execution plan by default. There are exceptions that would trigger a recompilation. Remember that in SQL Server 2000, a recompilation occurs at the whole procedure level, whereas in SQL Server 2005, it occurs at the statement level.

Such exceptions might be caused by issues related to plan correctness or plan optimality. Plan correctness issues include schema changes in underlying objects (for example, adding/dropping a column, adding/dropping an index, and so on) or changes to SET options that can affect query results (for example, ANSI_NULLS, CONCAT_NULL_YIELDS_NULL, and so on). Plan optimality issues that cause recompilation include making data changes in referenced objects to the extent that a new plan might be more optimal–for example, as a result of a statistics update.

Both types of causes for recompilations have many particular cases. At the end of this section, I will provide you with a resource that describes them in great detail.

Naturally, if a plan is removed from cache after a while for lack of reuse, SQL Server will generate a new one when the procedure is invoked again.

To see an example of a cause of a recompilation, first run the following code, which creates the stored procedure usp_CustCities:

```
IF OBJECT_ID('dbo.usp_CustCities') IS NOT NULL
  DROP PROC dbo.usp_CustCities;
GO

CREATE PROC dbo.usp_CustCities
AS

SELECT CustomerID, Country, Region, City,
  Country + '.' + Region + '.' + City AS CRC
FROM dbo.Customers
ORDER BY Country, Region, City;
GO
```

The stored procedure queries the Customers table, concatenating the three parts of the customer's geographical location: *Country*, *Region*, and *City*. By default, the SET option CONCAT_NULL_YIELDS_NULL is turned ON, meaning that when you concatenate a NULL with any string, you get a NULL as a result.

Run the stored procedure for the first time, and you will get the output shown in abbreviated form in Table 7-7:

```
EXEC dbo.usp_CustCities;
```

Table 7-7   Output of *usp_CustCities* when CONCAT_NULL_YIELDS_NULL Is ON (Abbreviated)

CustomerID	Country	Region	City	CRC
CACTU	Argentina	NULL	Buenos Aires	NULL
OCEAN	Argentina	NULL	Buenos Aires	NULL
RANCH	Argentina	NULL	Buenos Aires	NULL
ERNSH	Austria	NULL	Graz	NULL
PICCO	Austria	NULL	Salzburg	NULL
MAISD	Belgium	NULL	Bruxelles	NULL
SUPRD	Belgium	NULL	Charleroi	NULL
QUEDE	Brazil	RJ	Rio de Janeiro	Brazil.RJ.Rio de Janeiro
RICAR	Brazil	RJ	Rio de Janeiro	Brazil.RJ.Rio de Janeiro
HANAR	Brazil	RJ	Rio de Janeiro	Brazil.RJ.Rio de Janeiro
GOURL	Brazil	SP	Campinas	Brazil.SP.Campinas
WELLI	Brazil	SP	Resende	Brazil.SP.Resende
TRADH	Brazil	SP	Sao Paulo	Brazil.SP.Sao Paulo
FAMIA	Brazil	SP	Sao Paulo	Brazil.SP.Sao Paulo
COMMI	Brazil	SP	Sao Paulo	Brazil.SP.Sao Paulo
...	...	...	...	...

As you can see, whenever *Region* was NULL, the concatenated string became NULL. SQL Server cached the execution plan of the stored procedure for later reuse. Along with the plan, SQL Server also stored the state of all SET options that can affect query results. You can observe those in a bitmap called *setopts* in sys.syscacheobjects.

Set the CONCAT_NULL_YIELDS_NULL option to OFF, telling SQL Server to treat a NULL in concatenation as an empty string:

```
SET CONCAT_NULL_YIELDS_NULL OFF;
```

And rerun the stored procedure, which will produce the output shown in abbreviated form in Table 7-8:

```
EXEC dbo.usp_CustCities;
```

Table 7-8   Output of *usp_CustCities* when CONCAT_NULL_YIELDS_NULL Is OFF (Abbreviated)

CustomerID	Country	Region	City	CRC
CACTU	Argentina	NULL	Buenos Aires	Argentina..Buenos Aires
OCEAN	Argentina	NULL	Buenos Aires	Argentina..Buenos Aires
RANCH	Argentina	NULL	Buenos Aires	Argentina..Buenos Aires
ERNSH	Austria	NULL	Graz	Austria..Graz

Table 7-8   Output of *usp_CustCities* when CONCAT_NULL_YIELDS_NULL Is OFF (Abbreviated)

CustomerID	Country	Region	City	CRC
PICCO	Austria	NULL	Salzburg	Austria..Salzburg
MAISD	Belgium	NULL	Bruxelles	Belgium..Bruxelles
SUPRD	Belgium	NULL	Charleroi	Belgium..Charleroi
QUEDE	Brazil	RJ	Rio de Janeiro	Brazil.RJ.Rio de Janeiro
RICAR	Brazil	RJ	Rio de Janeiro	Brazil.RJ.Rio de Janeiro
HANAR	Brazil	RJ	Rio de Janeiro	Brazil.RJ.Rio de Janeiro
GOURL	Brazil	SP	Campinas	Brazil.SP.Campinas
WELLI	Brazil	SP	Resende	Brazil.SP.Resende
TRADH	Brazil	SP	Sao Paulo	Brazil.SP.Sao Paulo
FAMIA	Brazil	SP	Sao Paulo	Brazil.SP.Sao Paulo
COMMI	Brazil	SP	Sao Paulo	Brazil.SP.Sao Paulo
...	...	...	...	...

You can see that when *Region* was NULL, it was treated as an empty string, and as a result, you didn't get a NULL in the *CRC* column. Changing the session option in this case changed the meaning of a query. When you ran this stored procedure, SQL Server first checked whether there was a cached plan that also has the same state of SET options. SQL Server didn't find one, so it had to generate a new plan. Note that regardless of whether the change in the SET option does or doesn't affect the query's meaning, SQL Server looks for a match in the set options state in order to reuse a plan.

Query sys.syscacheobjects, and you will find two plans for usp_CustCities, with two different *setopts* bitmaps, as shown in Table 7-9:

```
SELECT cacheobjtype, objtype, usecounts, setopts, sql
FROM sys.syscacheobjects
WHERE sql NOT LIKE '%cache%'
  AND sql LIKE '%usp_CustCities%';
```

Table 7-9   Execution Plans for *usp_CustCities* in *sys.syscacheobjects*

cacheobjtype	objtype	usecounts	setopts	sql
Compiled Plan	Proc	1	4347	CREATE PROC dbo.usp_CustCities ...
Compiled Plan	Proc	1	4339	CREATE PROC dbo.usp_CustCities ...

Why should you care? Client interfaces and tools typically change the state of some SET options whenever you make a new connection to the database. Different client interfaces change different sets of options, yielding different execution environments. If you're using multiple database interfaces and tools to connect to the database and they have different execution environments, they won't be able to reuse each other's plans. You can easily identify the SET options that each client tool changes by running a trace while the applications connect to the database. If you see discrepancies in the execution environment, you can code explicit SET commands in all applications, which will be submitted whenever a new connection is made. This way, all applications will have sessions with the same execution environment and be able to reuse one another's plans.

When you're done experimenting, turn the CONCAT_NULL_YIELDS_NULL option back ON:

```
SET CONCAT_NULL_YIELDS_NULL ON;
```

This is just one case in which an execution plan is not reused. There are many others. At the end of the following section, I'll provide a resource where you can find more.

Parameter Sniffing Problem

As I mentioned earlier, SQL Server will generate a plan for a stored procedure based on the inputs provided to it upon first invocation, for better or worse. "First invocation" also refers to the first invocation after a plan was removed from cache for lack of reuse or for any other reason. The optimizer "knows" what the values of the input parameters are, and it generates an adequate plan for those inputs. However, things are different when you refer to local variables in your queries. And for the sake of our discussion, it doesn't matter if these are local variables of a plain batch or of a stored procedure. The optimizer cannot "sniff" the content of the variables; therefore, when it optimizes the query, it must make a guess. Obviously, this can lead to poor plans if you're not aware of the problem and don't take corrective measures.

To demonstrate the problem, first insert a new order to the Orders table, specifying the GETDATE function for the *OrderDate* column:

```
INSERT INTO dbo.Orders(OrderDate, CustomerID, EmployeeID)
  VALUES(GETDATE(), N'ALFKI', 1);
```

Alter the usp_GetOrders stored procedure so that it will declare a local variable and use it in the query's filter:

```
ALTER PROC dbo.usp_GetOrders
  @d AS INT = 0
AS

DECLARE @odate AS DATETIME;
SET @odate = DATEADD(day, -@d, CONVERT(VARCHAR(8), GETDATE(), 112));

SELECT OrderID, CustomerID, EmployeeID, OrderDate
FROM dbo.Orders
WHERE OrderDate >= @odate;
GO
```

The procedure defines the integer input parameter *@d* with a default value *0*. It declares a datetime local variable called *@odate*, which is set to today's date minus *@d* days. The stored procedure then issues a query returning all orders with an *OrderDate* greater than or equal to *@odate*. Invoke the stored procedure using the default value of *@d*, which will generate the output shown in Table 7-10:

```
EXEC dbo.usp_GetOrders;
```

Table 7-10   Output of usp_GetOrders

OrderID	CustomerID	EmployeeID	OrderDate
11079	ALFKI	1	2006-02-12 01:23:53.210

> **Note**   The output that you get will have a value in *OrderDate* that reflects the GETDATE value of when you inserted the new order.

The optimizer didn't know what the value of *@odate* was when it optimized the query. So it used a conservative hard-coded value that is 30 percent of the number of rows in the table. For such a low-selectivity estimation, the optimizer naturally chose a table scan, even though the query in practice is highly selective and would be much better off using the index on *OrderDate*.

You can observe the optimizer's estimation and chosen plan by requesting an estimated execution plan (not actual). The estimated execution plan you get for this invocation of the stored procedure is shown in Figure 7-3.

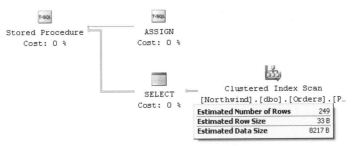

Figure 7-3   Execution plan showing estimated number of rows

You can see that the optimizer chose a table scan (unordered clustered index scan), due to its selectivity estimation of 30 percent (249 rows / 830 total number of rows).

There are several ways to tackle the problem. One is to use, whenever possible, inline expressions in the query that refer to the input parameter instead of a variable. In our case, it is possible:

```
ALTER PROC dbo.usp_GetOrders
  @d AS INT = 0
AS
```

```
SELECT OrderID, CustomerID, EmployeeID, OrderDate
FROM dbo.Orders
WHERE OrderDate >= DATEADD(day, -@d, CONVERT(VARCHAR(8), GETDATE(), 112));
GO
```

Run usp_GetOrders again, and notice the use of the index on *OrderDate* in the execution plan:

```
EXEC dbo.usp_GetOrders;
```

The plan that you will get is similar to the one shown earlier in Figure 7-1. The I/O cost here is just four logical reads.

Another way to deal with the problem is to use a stub procedure. That is, create two procedures. The first procedure accepts the original parameter, assigns the result of the calculation to a local variable, and invokes a second procedure providing it with the variable as input. The second procedure accepts an input order date passed to it and invokes the query that refers directly to the input parameter. When a plan is generated for the procedure that actually invokes the query (the second procedure), the value of the parameter will, in fact, be known at optimization time.

Run the code in Listing 7-3 to implement this solution.

Listing 7-3   Using a stub procedure

```
IF OBJECT_ID('dbo.usp_GetOrdersQuery') IS NOT NULL
  DROP PROC dbo.usp_GetOrdersQuery;
GO

CREATE PROC dbo.usp_GetOrdersQuery
  @odate AS DATETIME
AS

SELECT OrderID, CustomerID, EmployeeID, OrderDate
FROM dbo.Orders
WHERE OrderDate >= @odate;
GO

ALTER PROC dbo.usp_GetOrders
  @d AS INT = 0
AS

DECLARE @odate AS DATETIME;
SET @odate = DATEADD(day, -@d, CONVERT(VARCHAR(8), GETDATE(), 112));

EXEC dbo.usp_GetOrdersQuery @odate;
GO
```

Invoke the usp_GetOrders procedure:

```
EXEC dbo.usp_GetOrders;
```

You will get an optimal plan for the input similar to the one shown earlier in Figure 7-1, yielding an I/O cost of only four logical reads.

Don't forget the issues I described in the previous section regarding the reuse of execution plans. The fact that you got an efficient execution plan for this input doesn't necessarily mean that you would want to reuse it in following invocations. It all depends on whether the inputs are typical or atypical. Make sure you follow the recommendations I gave earlier in case the inputs are atypical.

Finally, there's a new tool provided to you in SQL Server 2005 to tackle the problem—the OPTIMIZE FOR query hint. This hint allows you to provide SQL Server with a literal that reflects the selectivity of the variable, in case the input is typical. For example, if you know that the variable will typically end up with a highly selective value, as you did in our example, you can provide the literal '99991231', which reflects that:

```
ALTER PROC dbo.usp_GetOrders
  @d AS INT = 0
AS

DECLARE @odate AS DATETIME;
SET @odate = DATEADD(day, -@d, CONVERT(VARCHAR(8), GETDATE(), 112));

SELECT OrderID, CustomerID, EmployeeID, OrderDate
FROM dbo.Orders
WHERE OrderDate >= @odate
OPTION(OPTIMIZE FOR(@odate = '99991231'));
GO
```

Run the stored procedure:

```
EXEC dbo.usp_GetOrders;
```

You will get an optimal plan for a highly selective *OrderDate* similar to the one shown earlier in Figure 7-1, yielding an I/O cost of four logical reads.

Note that you might face similar problems when changing the values of input parameters before using them in queries. For example, say you define an input parameter called *@odate* and assign it with a default value of NULL. Before using the parameter in the query's filter, you apply the following code:

```
SET @odate = COALESCE(@odate, '19000101');
```

The query then filters orders where *OrderDate* >= *@odate*. When the query is optimized, the optimizer is not aware of the fact that *@odate* has undergone a change, and it optimizes the query with the original input (NULL) in mind. You will face a similar problem to the one I described with variables, and you should tackle it using similar logic.

More Info   For more information on the subject, please refer to the white paper "Batch Compilation, Recompilation, and Plan Caching Issues in SQL Server 2005," by Arun Marathe, which can be accessed at *http://www.microsoft.com/technet/prodtechnol/sql/2005/recomp.mspx*.

When you're done, run the following code for cleanup:

```
DELETE FROM dbo.Orders WHERE OrderID > 11077;
GO
IF OBJECT_ID('dbo.usp_GetOrders') IS NOT NULL
  DROP PROC dbo.usp_GetOrders;
GO
IF OBJECT_ID('dbo.usp_CustCities') IS NOT NULL
  DROP PROC dbo.usp_CustCities;
GO
IF OBJECT_ID('dbo.usp_GetOrdersQuery') IS NOT NULL
  DROP PROC dbo.usp_GetOrdersQuery;
GO
```

EXECUTE AS

Stored procedures can play an important security role. You can grant users EXECUTE permissions on the stored procedure without granting them direct access to the underlying objects, thus giving you more control over resource access. However, there are exceptions that would require the caller to have direct permissions on underlying objects. To avoid requiring direct permissions from the caller, all following must be true:

- The stored procedure and the underlying objects belong to the same schema.
- The activity is static (as opposed to using dynamic SQL).
- The activity is DML (SELECT, INSERT, UPDATE, or DELETE), or it is an execution of another stored procedure.

If any listed item is not true, the caller will be required to have direct permissions against the underlying objects. Otherwise, the statements in the stored procedure that do not meet the requirements will fail on a security violation.

That's the behavior in SQL Server 2000, which cannot be changed. That's also the behavior in SQL Server 2005, only now you can set the security context of the stored procedure to that of another user, as if the other user was running the stored procedure. When you create the stored procedure, you can specify an EXECUTE AS clause with one of the following options:

- **CALLER (default)** Security context of the caller
- **SELF** Security context of the user creating or altering the stored procedure
- **OWNER** Security context of the owner of the stored procedure
- **'user_name'** Security context of the specified user name

Remember, all chaining rules and requirements not to have direct permissions for underlying objects still apply, but they apply to the effective user, not the calling user (unless CALLER was specified, of course).

In addition, a user that has impersonation rights can issue an independent EXECUTE AS <option> command to impersonate another entity (login or user). If this is done, it's as if the session changes its security context to that of the impersonated entity.

Parameterizing Sort Order

To practice what you've learned so far, try to provide a solution to the following task: write a stored procedure called usp_GetSortedShippers that accepts a column name from the Shippers table in the Northwind database as one of the inputs (*@colname*), and that returns the rows from the table sorted by the input column name. Assume also that you have a sort direction as input (*@sortdir*), with the value *'A'* representing ascending order and *'D'* representing descending order. The stored procedure should be written with performance in mind—that is, it should use indexes when appropriate (for example, a clustered or nonclustered covering index on the sort column).

Listing 7-4 shows the first suggested solution for the task.

Listing 7-4   Parameterizing sort order, solution 1

```
USE Northwind;
GO
IF OBJECT_ID('dbo.usp_GetSortedShippers') IS NOT NULL
  DROP PROC dbo.usp_GetSortedShippers;
GO
CREATE PROC dbo.usp_GetSortedShippers
  @colname AS sysname, @sortdir AS CHAR(1) = 'A'
AS

IF @sortdir = 'A'
  SELECT ShipperID, CompanyName, Phone
  FROM dbo.Shippers
  ORDER BY
    CASE @colname
      WHEN N'ShipperID'    THEN CAST(ShipperID AS SQL_VARIANT)
      WHEN N'CompanyName'  THEN CAST(CompanyName AS SQL_VARIANT)
      WHEN N'Phone'        THEN CAST(Phone AS SQL_VARIANT)
    END
ELSE
  SELECT ShipperID, CompanyName, Phone
  FROM dbo.Shippers
  ORDER BY
    CASE @colname
      WHEN N'ShipperID'    THEN CAST(ShipperID AS SQL_VARIANT)
      WHEN N'CompanyName'  THEN CAST(CompanyName AS SQL_VARIANT)
      WHEN N'Phone'        THEN CAST(Phone AS SQL_VARIANT)
    END DESC;
GO
```

The solution uses an IF statement to determine which of two queries to run based on the requested sort direction. The only difference between the queries is that one uses an ascending order for the sort expression and the other a descending one. Each query uses a single CASE expression that returns the appropriate column value based on the input column name.

> **Note**   SQL Server determines the datatype of the result of a CASE expression based on the datatype with the highest precedence among the possible result values of the expression; not by the datatype of the actual returned value. This means, for example, that if the CASE expression returns a VARCHAR(30) value in one of the THEN clauses and an INT value in another, the result of the expression will always be INT, because INT is higher in precedence than VARCHAR. If in practice the VARCHAR(30) value is returned, SQL Server will attempt to convert it. If the value is not convertible, you get a runtime error. If it is convertible, it becomes an INT and, of course, might have a different sort behavior than the original value.

To avoid such issues, I simply converted all the possible return values to SQL_VARIANT. SQL Server will set the datatype of the CASE expression to SQL_VARIANT, but it will preserve the original base types within that SQL_VARIANT.

Run the following code to test the solution, requesting to sort the shippers by *ShipperID* in descending order, and it will generate the output shown in Table 7-11:

```
EXEC dbo.usp_GetSortedShippers N'ShipperID', N'D';
```

Table 7-11   Output of usp_GetSortedShippers

ShipperID	CompanyName	Phone
3	Federal Shipping	(503) 555-9931
2	United Package	(503) 555-3199
1	Speedy Express	(503) 555-9831

The output is logically correct, but notice the plan generated for the stored procedure, shown in Figure 7-4.

Figure 7-4   Execution plan showing a table scan (unordered clustered index scan) and a sort operator

Remember that the optimizer cannot rely on the sort that the index maintains if you performed manipulation on the sort column. The plan shows a table scan (unordered clustered index scan) followed by an explicit sort operation. For the problem the query was intended to solve, an optimal plan would have performed an ordered scan operation in the clustered index defined on the *ShipperID* column—eliminating the need for an explicit sort operation.

Listing 7-5 shows the second solution for the task.

Listing 7-5   Parameterizing sort order, solution 2

```
ALTER PROC dbo.usp_GetSortedShippers
  @colname AS sysname, @sortdir AS CHAR(1) = 'A'
AS

SELECT ShipperID, CompanyName, Phone
FROM dbo.Shippers
ORDER BY
  CASE WHEN @colname = N'ShipperID'   AND @sortdir = 'A'
    THEN ShipperID   END,
  CASE WHEN @colname = N'CompanyName' AND @sortdir = 'A'
    THEN CompanyName END,
  CASE WHEN @colname = N'Phone'       AND @sortdir = 'A'
    THEN Phone       END,
  CASE WHEN @colname = N'ShipperID'   AND @sortdir = 'D'
    THEN ShipperID   END DESC,
  CASE WHEN @colname = N'CompanyName' AND @sortdir = 'D'
    THEN CompanyName END DESC,
  CASE WHEN @colname = N'Phone'       AND @sortdir = 'D'
    THEN Phone       END DESC;
GO
```

This solution uses CASE expressions in a more sophisticated way. Each column and sort direction combination is treated with its own CASE expression. Only one of the CASE expressions will yield TRUE for all rows, given the column name and sort direction that particular CASE expression is looking for. All other CASE expressions will return NULL for all rows. This means that only one of the CASE expressions—the one that looks for the given column name and sort direction—will affect the order of the output.

Run the following code to test the stored procedure:

```
EXEC dbo.usp_GetSortedShippers N'ShipperID', N'D';
```

Though this stored procedure applies an interesting logical manipulation, it doesn't change the fact that you perform manipulation on the column and don't sort by it as is. This means that you will get a similar nonoptimal plan to the one shown earlier in Figure 7-4.

Listing 7-6 shows the third solution for the task.

Listing 7-6   Parameterizing sort order, solution 3

```
ALTER PROC dbo.usp_GetSortedShippers
  @colname AS sysname, @sortdir AS CHAR(1) = 'A'
AS

IF @colname NOT IN (N'ShipperID', N'CompanyName', N'Phone')
BEGIN
  RAISERROR('Possible SQL injection attempt.', 16, 1);
  RETURN;
END
```

```
DECLARE @sql AS NVARCHAR(4000);

SET @sql = N'SELECT ShipperID, CompanyName, Phone
FROM dbo.Shippers
ORDER BY '
  + QUOTENAME(@colname)
  + CASE @sortdir WHEN 'D' THEN N' DESC' ELSE '' END
  + ';';

EXEC sp_executesql @sql;
GO
```

This solution simply uses dynamic execution, concatenating the input column name and sort direction to the ORDER BY clause of the query. In terms of performance the solution achieves our goal—namely, it will use an index efficiently if an appropriate one exists. To see that it does, run the following code:

```
EXEC dbo.usp_GetSortedShippers N'ShipperID', N'D';
```

Observe in the execution plan shown in Figure 7-5 that the plan performs an ordered backward clustered index scan with no sort operator, which is optimal for these inputs.

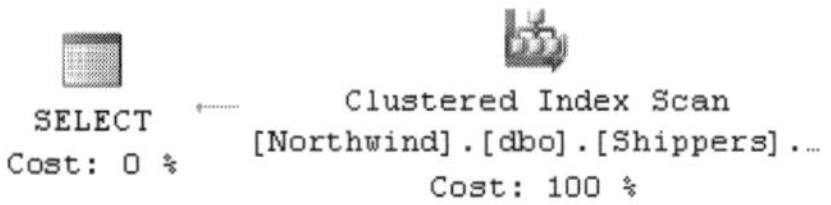

```
SELECT              Clustered Index Scan
Cost: 0 %       [Northwind].[dbo].[Shippers].…
                          Cost: 100 %
```

Figure 7-5 Execution plan showing ordered backward clustered index scan

Another advantage of this solution is that it's easy to maintain. The downside of this solution is the use of dynamic execution, which involves many security-related issues (for example, ownership chaining and SQL injection if the inputs are not validated). For details about security issues related to dynamic execution, please refer to Chapter 4.

The fourth solution that I'll cover is shown in Listing 7-7.

Listing 7-7 Parameterizing sort order, solution 4

```
CREATE PROC dbo.usp_GetSortedShippers_ShipperID_A
AS
  SELECT ShipperID, CompanyName, Phone
  FROM dbo.Shippers
  ORDER BY ShipperID;
GO
CREATE PROC dbo.usp_GetSortedShippers_CompanyName_A
AS
  SELECT ShipperID, CompanyName, Phone
  FROM dbo.Shippers
  ORDER BY CompanyName;
GO
CREATE PROC dbo.usp_GetSortedShippers_Phone_A
```

```
AS
  SELECT ShipperID, CompanyName, Phone
  FROM dbo.Shippers
  ORDER BY Phone;
GO
CREATE PROC dbo.usp_GetSortedShippers_ShipperID_D
AS
  SELECT ShipperID, CompanyName, Phone
  FROM dbo.Shippers
  ORDER BY ShipperID   DESC;
GO
CREATE PROC dbo.usp_GetSortedShippers_CompanyName_D
AS
  SELECT ShipperID, CompanyName, Phone
  FROM dbo.Shippers
  ORDER BY CompanyName DESC;
GO
CREATE PROC dbo.usp_GetSortedShippers_Phone_D
AS
  SELECT ShipperID, CompanyName, Phone
  FROM dbo.Shippers
  ORDER BY Phone       DESC;
GO

ALTER PROC dbo.usp_GetSortedShippers
  @colname AS sysname, @sortdir AS CHAR(1) = 'A'
AS

IF @colname = N'ShipperID'      AND @sortdir = 'A'
  EXEC dbo.usp_GetSortedShippers_ShipperID_A;
ELSE IF @colname = N'CompanyName' AND @sortdir = 'A'
  EXEC dbo.usp_GetSortedShippers_CompanyName_A;
ELSE IF @colname = N'Phone'       AND @sortdir = 'A'
  EXEC dbo.usp_GetSortedShippers_Phone_A;
ELSE IF @colname = N'ShipperID'   AND @sortdir = 'D'
  EXEC dbo.usp_GetSortedShippers_ShipperID_D;
ELSE IF @colname = N'CompanyName' AND @sortdir = 'D'
  EXEC dbo.usp_GetSortedShippers_CompanyName_D;
ELSE IF @colname = N'Phone'       AND @sortdir = 'D'
  EXEC dbo.usp_GetSortedShippers_Phone_D;
GO
```

This solution might seem childish at first glance. You create a separate stored procedure with a single static query for each possible combination of inputs. Then, usp_GetSortedShippers can act as a redirector. Simply use a series of IF / ELSE IF statements to check for each possible combination of inputs, and you explicitly invoke the appropriate stored procedure for each. Sure, it is a bit long and requires more maintenance than the previous solution, but it uses static queries that generate optimal plans. Note that each query will get its own plan and will be able to reuse a previously cached plan for the same query.

To test the procedure, run the following code:

```
EXEC dbo.usp_GetSortedShippers N'ShipperID', N'D';
```

You will get the optimal plan for the given inputs, similar to the plan shown earlier in Figure 7-5.

When you're done, run the following code for cleanup:

```
IF OBJECT_ID('dbo.usp_GetSortedShippers') IS NOT NULL
  DROP PROC dbo.usp_GetSortedShippers;
IF OBJECT_ID('dbo.usp_GetSortedShippers_ShipperID_A') IS NOT NULL
  DROP PROC dbo.usp_GetSortedShippers_ShipperID_A;
IF OBJECT_ID('dbo.usp_GetSortedShippers_CompanyName_A') IS NOT NULL
  DROP PROC dbo.usp_GetSortedShippers_CompanyName_A;
IF OBJECT_ID('dbo.usp_GetSortedShippers_Phone_A') IS NOT NULL
  DROP PROC dbo.usp_GetSortedShippers_Phone_A;
IF OBJECT_ID('dbo.usp_GetSortedShippers_ShipperID_D') IS NOT NULL
  DROP PROC dbo.usp_GetSortedShippers_ShipperID_D;
IF OBJECT_ID('dbo.usp_GetSortedShippers_CompanyName_D') IS NOT NULL
  DROP PROC dbo.usp_GetSortedShippers_CompanyName_D;
IF OBJECT_ID('dbo.usp_GetSortedShippers_Phone_D') IS NOT NULL
  DROP PROC dbo.usp_GetSortedShippers_Phone_D;
```

Dynamic Pivot

As another exercise, assume that you're given the task of writing a stored procedure that produces a dynamic pivot in the database you are connected to. The stored procedure accepts the following parameters (all Unicode character strings): *@query*, *@on_rows*, *@on_cols*, *@agg_func* and *@agg_col*. Based on the inputs, you're supposed to construct a PIVOT query string and execute it dynamically. Here's the description of the input parameters:

- **@query** Query or table/view name given to the PIVOT operator as input
- **@on_rows** Column/expression list that will be used as the grouping columns
- **@on_cols** Column or expression to be pivoted; the distinct values from this column will become the target column names
- **@agg_func** Aggregate function (MIN, MAX, SUM, COUNT, and so on)
- **@agg_col** Column/expression given to the aggregate function as input

If you're still confused regarding the requirements and the meaning of each input, skip the solution in Listing 7-8. Instead, examine the invocation examples and the outputs that follow the listing and the explanation of the solution. Then try to provide your own solution before looking at this one.

> **Important** Note that the solution in Listing 7-8 follows bad programming practices and is insecure. I'll use this solution to discuss flaws in its implementation and then suggest a more robust and secure alternative.

Listing 7-8 shows a suggested solution for the task.

Listing 7-8   Creation script for the sp_pivot stored procedure

```
USE master;
GO

IF OBJECT_ID('dbo.sp_pivot') IS NOT NULL
  DROP PROC dbo.sp_pivot;
GO

CREATE PROC dbo.sp_pivot
  @query    AS NVARCHAR(MAX),
  @on_rows  AS NVARCHAR(MAX),
  @on_cols  AS NVARCHAR(MAX),
  @agg_func AS NVARCHAR(MAX) = N'MAX',
  @agg_col  AS NVARCHAR(MAX)
AS

DECLARE
  @sql     AS NVARCHAR(MAX),
  @cols    AS NVARCHAR(MAX),
  @newline AS NVARCHAR(2);

SET @newline = NCHAR(13) + NCHAR(10);

-- If input is a valid table or view
-- construct a SELECT statement against it
IF COALESCE(OBJECT_ID(@query, N'U'),
            OBJECT_ID(@query, N'V')) IS NOT NULL
  SET @query = N'SELECT * FROM ' + @query;

-- Make the query a derived table
SET @query = N'( ' + @query + @newline + N'        ) AS Query';

-- Handle * input in @agg_col
IF @agg_col = N'*'
  SET @agg_col = N'1';

-- Construct column list
SET @sql =
  N'SET @result = '                                + @newline +
  N'  STUFF('                                      + @newline +
  N'    (SELECT N'','' + '                         + @newline +
  N'       + N''QUOTENAME(pivot_col) AS [text()]''  + @newline +
  N'     FROM (SELECT DISTINCT('                   + @newline +
  N'       + @on_cols + N') AS pivot_col'          + @newline +
  N'          FROM' + @query + N') AS DistinctCols' + @newline +
  N'     ORDER BY pivot_col'                       + @newline +
  N'     FOR XML PATH('''''')),'                   + @newline +
  N'  1, 1, N'''''');'

EXEC sp_executesql
  @stmt   = @sql,
  @params = N'@result AS NVARCHAR(MAX) OUTPUT',
  @result = @cols OUTPUT;
```

```
-- Create the PIVOT query
SET @sql =
  N'SELECT *'                                    + @newline +
  N'FROM'                                        + @newline +
  N'  ( SELECT '                                 + @newline +
  N'      ' + @on_rows + N','                    + @newline +
  N'      ' + @on_cols + N' AS pivot_col,'       + @newline +
  N'      ' + @agg_col + N' AS agg_col'          + @newline +
  N'    FROM '                                   + @newline +
  N'      ' + @query                             + @newline +
  N'  ) AS PivotInput'                           + @newline +
  N'  PIVOT'                                     + @newline +
  N'    ( ' + @agg_func + N'(agg_col)'           + @newline +
  N'      FOR pivot_col'                         + @newline +
  N'        IN(' + @cols + N')'                  + @newline +
  N'    ) AS PivotOutput;'

EXEC sp_executesql @sql;
GO
```

I'm using this exercise both to explain how to achieve dynamic pivoting and to discuss bad programming practices and security flaws. I'll start by discussing the logic behind the code, and then I'll describe the bad programming practices and flaws and present a more robust and secure solution.

The stored procedure is created as a special procedure in master to allow running it in any database. Remember that dynamic execution is invoked in the context of the current database. This means that the stored procedure's code will effectively run in the context of the current database, interacting with local user objects.

The code checks whether the input parameter *@query* contains a valid table or view. If it does, the code constructs a SELECT statement against the object, storing the statement back in *@query*. If *@query* doesn't contain an existing table/view name, the code assumes that it already contains a query.

The code then makes the query a derived table by adding surrounding parentheses and a derived table alias (*AS Query*). The result string is stored back in *@query*. This derived table will be used both to determine the distinct values that need to be pivoted (from the column/expression stored in the *@on_cols* input parameter) and as the input table expression for the PIVOT operator.

Because the PIVOT operator doesn't support * as an input for the aggregate function—for example, COUNT(*)—the code substitutes a * input in *@agg_col* with the constant *1*.

The code continues by constructing a dynamic query string within the *@sql* variable. This string has code that constructs the column list that will later be served to PIVOT's IN clause. The column list is constructed by a FOR XML PATH query. The query concatenates the distinct list of values from the column/expression stored in the *@on_cols* input parameter.

The concatenation query string (stored in *@sql*) is invoked dynamically. The dynamic code returns through an output parameter a string with the column list, and it assigns it to the variable *@cols*.

The next section of code constructs the actual PIVOT query string in the *@sql* variable. It constructs an outer query against the derived table (aliased as Query), which is currently stored in *@query*. The outer query creates another derived table called PivotInput. The SELECT list in the outer query includes the following items:

- The grouping column/expression list stored in *@on_rows*, which is the part that the PIVOT operator will use in its implicit grouping activity

- The columns/expression to be pivoted (currently stored in *@on_cols*), aliased as *pivot_col*

- The column that will be used as the aggregate function's input (currently stored in *@agg_col*), aliased as *agg_col*

The PIVOT operator works on the derived table PivotInput. Within PIVOT's parentheses, the code embeds the following items: the aggregate function (*@agg_func*) with the aggregate column as its input (*agg_col*), and the column list (*@cols*) within the parentheses of the IN clause. The outermost query simply uses a SELECT * to grab all columns returned from the PIVOT operation.

Finally, the PIVOT query constructed in the *@sql* variable is invoked dynamically.

> **More Info**   For in-depth discussion of the PIVOT operator, refer to *Inside T-SQL Querying*.

The sp_pivot stored procedure is extremely flexible, though this flexibility comes at a high security cost, which I'll describe later. To demonstrate its flexibility, I'll provide three examples of invoking it with different inputs. Make sure you study and understand all the inputs carefully.

The following code produces the count of orders per employee and order year, pivoted by order month, and it generates the output shown in Table 7-12:

```
EXEC Northwind.dbo.sp_pivot
  @query    = N'dbo.Orders',
  @on_rows  = N'EmployeeID AS empid, YEAR(OrderDate) AS order_year',
  @on_cols  = N'MONTH(OrderDate)',
  @agg_func = N'COUNT',
  @agg_col  = N'*';
```

Table 7-12   Count of Orders per Employee and Order Year Pivoted by Order Month

empid	order_year	1	2	3	4	5	6	7	8	9	10	11	12
1	1996	0	0	0	0	0	0	1	5	5	2	4	9
2	1996	0	0	0	0	0	0	1	2	5	2	2	4
3	1996	0	0	0	0	0	0	4	2	1	3	4	4

Table 7-12   Count of Orders per Employee and Order Year Pivoted by Order Month

empid	order_year	1	2	3	4	5	6	7	8	9	10	11	12
4	1996	0	0	0	0	0	0	7	5	3	8	5	3
5	1996	0	0	0	0	0	0	3	0	1	2	2	3
6	1996	0	0	0	0	0	0	2	4	3	0	3	3
7	1996	0	0	0	0	0	0	0	1	2	5	3	0
8	1996	0	0	0	0	0	0	2	6	3	2	2	4
9	1996	0	0	0	0	0	0	2	0	0	2	0	1
1	1997	3	2	5	1	5	4	7	3	8	7	3	7
2	1997	4	1	4	3	3	4	3	1	7	1	5	5
3	1997	7	9	3	5	5	6	2	4	4	7	8	11
4	1997	8	6	4	8	5	5	6	11	5	7	6	10
5	1997	0	0	3	0	2	2	1	3	2	3	1	1
6	1997	2	2	2	4	2	2	2	2	1	4	5	5
7	1997	3	1	2	6	5	1	5	3	5	1	1	3
8	1997	5	8	6	2	4	3	6	5	3	7	2	3
9	1997	1	0	1	2	1	3	1	1	2	1	3	3
1	1998	9	9	11	8	5	0	0	0	0	0	0	0
2	1998	7	3	9	18	2	0	0	0	0	0	0	0
3	1998	10	6	12	10	0	0	0	0	0	0	0	0
4	1998	6	14	12	10	2	0	0	0	0	0	0	0
5	1998	4	6	2	1	0	0	0	0	0	0	0	0
6	1998	3	4	7	5	0	0	0	0	0	0	0	0
7	1998	4	6	4	9	2	0	0	0	0	0	0	0
8	1998	7	2	10	9	3	0	0	0	0	0	0	0
9	1998	5	4	6	4	0	0	0	0	0	0	0	0

The following code produces the sum of the value (quantity * unit price) per employee, pivoted by order year, and it generates the output shown in Table 7-13:

```
EXEC Northwind.dbo.sp_pivot
  @query    = N'
SELECT O.OrderID, EmployeeID, OrderDate, Quantity, UnitPrice
FROM dbo.Orders AS O
  JOIN dbo.[Order Details] AS OD
    ON OD.OrderID = O.OrderID',
  @on_rows  = N'EmployeeID AS empid',
  @on_cols  = N'YEAR(OrderDate)',
  @agg_func = N'SUM',
  @agg_col  = N'Quantity*UnitPrice';
```

Table 7-13   Sum of Value per Employee Pivoted by Order Year

empid	1996	1997	1998
3	19231.80	111788.61	82030.89
6	17731.10	45992.00	14475.00
9	11365.70	29577.55	42020.75
7	18104.80	66689.14	56502.05
1	38789.00	97533.58	65821.13
4	53114.80	139477.70	57594.95
2	22834.70	74958.60	79955.96
5	21965.20	32595.05	21007.50
8	23161.40	59776.52	50363.11

The following code produces the sum of the quantity per store, pivoted by order year and month, and it generates the output shown in Table 7-14:

```
EXEC pubs.dbo.sp_pivot
  @query    = N'
SELECT stor_id, YEAR(ord_date) AS oy, MONTH(ord_date) AS om, qty
FROM dbo.sales',
  @on_rows  = N'stor_id',
  @on_cols  = N'
CAST(oy AS VARCHAR(4)) + ''_''
  + RIGHT(''0'' + CAST(om AS VARCHAR(2)), 2)',
  @agg_func = N'SUM',
  @agg_col  = N'qty';
```

Table 7-14   Sum of Quantity per Store Pivoted by Order Year and Month

stor_id	1992_06	1993_02	1993_03	1993_05	1993_10	1993_12	1994_09
6380	NULL	NULL	NULL	NULL	NULL	NULL	8
7066	NULL	NULL	NULL	50	NULL	NULL	75
7067	80	NULL	NULL	NULL	NULL	NULL	10
7131	NULL	NULL	NULL	85	NULL	NULL	45
7896	NULL	35	NULL	NULL	15	10	NULL
8042	NULL	NULL	25	30	NULL	NULL	25

The implementation of the stored procedure sp_pivot suffers from bad programming practices and security flaws. As I mentioned earlier in the chapter, Microsoft strongly advises against using the *sp_* prefix for user-defined procedure names. On one hand, creating this procedure as a special procedure allows flexibility; on the other hand, by doing so you're relying on behavior that is not supported. It is advisable to forgo the flexibility obtained by creating the procedure with the *sp_* prefix and create it with another prefix as a user-defined stored procedure in the user databases where you need it.

The code defines all input parameters with a virtually unlimited size (using the MAX specifier) and doesn't have any input validation. Because the stored procedure invokes dynamic execution based on user input strings, it's very important to limit the sizes of the inputs and to check those for potential SQL injection attacks. With the existing implementation it's very easy for hackers to inject code that will do havoc and mayhem in your system. You can find discussions about SQL injection in Chapter 4 and in Books Online (URL: *http://msdn2 .microsoft.com/en-us/library/ms161953(SQL.90).aspx*). As an example for injecting malicious code through user inputs, consider the following invocation of the stored procedure:

```
EXEC Northwind.dbo.sp_pivot
  @query    = N'dbo.Orders',
  @on_rows  = N'1 AS dummy_col ) DummyTable;
PRINT ''So easy to inject code here!
This could have been a DROP TABLE or xp_cmdshell command!'';
SELECT * FROM (select EmployeeID AS empid',
  @on_cols  = N'MONTH(OrderDate)',
  @agg_func = N'COUNT',
  @agg_col  = N'*';
```

The query string generated by the stored procedure looks like this:

```
SELECT *
FROM
  ( SELECT
      1 AS dummy_col ) DummyTable;
PRINT 'So easy to inject code here!
This could have been a DROP TABLE or xp_cmdshell command!';
SELECT * FROM (select EmployeeID AS empid,
      MONTH(OrderDate) AS pivot_col,
      1 AS agg_col
    FROM
      ( SELECT * FROM dbo.Orders
      ) AS Query
  ) AS PivotInput
  PIVOT
    ( COUNT(agg_col)
      FOR pivot_col
        IN([1],[2],[3],[4],[5],[6],[7],[8],[9],[10],[11],[12])
    ) AS PivotOutput;
```

When this code is executed, the injected PRINT statement executes without any problem. I used a harmless PRINT statement just to demonstrate that code can be easily injected here, but obviously the malicious code could be any valid T-SQL code; for example, a DROP TABLE statement, invocation of xp_cmdshell, and so on. In short, it is vital here to take protective measures against SQL injection attempts, as I will demonstrate shortly.

Besides SQL injection attempts, input validation is not performed at all; for example, to verify the validity of input object and column names. The stored procedure also doesn't incorporate exception handling. I discuss exception handling in Chapter 10, so I won't demonstrate it here in the revised solution. I will demonstrate input validation, though.

Before presenting the revised solution, first get rid of the existing sp_pivot implementation:

```
USE master;
GO
IF OBJECT_ID('dbo.sp_pivot') IS NOT NULL
  DROP PROC dbo.sp_pivot;
```

Listing 7-9 shows a suggested revised solution for the task.

Listing 7-9   Creation script for the usp_pivot stored procedure

```
USE Northwind;
GO

IF OBJECT_ID('dbo.usp_pivot') IS NOT NULL
  DROP PROC dbo.usp_pivot;
GO

CREATE PROC dbo.usp_pivot
  @schema_name AS sysname      = N'dbo', -- schema of table/view
  @object_name AS sysname      = NULL,   -- name of table/view
  @on_rows     AS sysname      = NULL,   -- group by column
  @on_cols     AS sysname      = NULL,   -- rotation column
  @agg_func    AS NVARCHAR(12) = N'MAX', -- aggregate function
  @agg_col     AS sysname      = NULL    -- aggregate column
AS


DECLARE
  @object  AS NVARCHAR(600),
  @sql     AS NVARCHAR(MAX),
  @cols    AS NVARCHAR(MAX),
  @newline AS NVARCHAR(2),
  @msg     AS NVARCHAR(500);

SET @newline = NCHAR(13) + NCHAR(10);
SET @object  = QUOTENAME(@schema_name) + N'.' + QUOTENAME(@object_name);

-- Check for missing input
IF    @schema_name IS NULL
   OR @object_name IS NULL
   OR @on_rows     IS NULL
   OR @on_cols     IS NULL
   OR @agg_func    IS NULL
   OR @agg_col     IS NULL
BEGIN
  SET @msg = N'Missing input parameters: '
    + CASE WHEN @schema_name IS NULL THEN N'@schema_name;' ELSE N'' END
    + CASE WHEN @object_name IS NULL THEN N'@object_name;' ELSE N'' END
    + CASE WHEN @on_rows     IS NULL THEN N'@on_rows;'     ELSE N'' END
    + CASE WHEN @on_cols     IS NULL THEN N'@on_cols;'     ELSE N'' END
    + CASE WHEN @agg_func    IS NULL THEN N'@agg_func;'    ELSE N'' END
    + CASE WHEN @agg_col     IS NULL THEN N'@agg_col;'     ELSE N'' END
  RAISERROR(@msg, 16, 1);
  RETURN;
END
```

```
-- Allow only existing table or view name as input object
IF COALESCE(OBJECT_ID(@object, N'U'),
            OBJECT_ID(@object, N'V')) IS NULL
BEGIN
  SET @msg = N'%s is not an existing table or view in the database.';
  RAISERROR(@msg, 16, 1, @object);
  RETURN;
END

-- Verify that column names specified in @on_rows, @on_cols, @agg_col exist
IF  COLUMNPROPERTY(OBJECT_ID(@object), @on_rows, 'ColumnId') IS NULL
  OR COLUMNPROPERTY(OBJECT_ID(@object), @on_cols, 'ColumnId') IS NULL
  OR COLUMNPROPERTY(OBJECT_ID(@object), @agg_col, 'ColumnId') IS NULL
BEGIN
  SET @msg = N'%s, %s and %s must'
    + N' be existing column names in %s.';
  RAISERROR(@msg, 16, 1, @on_rows, @on_cols, @agg_col, @object);
  RETURN;
END

-- Verify that @agg_func is in a known list of functions
-- Add to list as needed and adjust @agg_func size accordingly
IF @agg_func NOT IN
  (N'AVG', N'COUNT', N'COUNT_BIG', N'SUM', N'MIN', N'MAX',
   N'STDEV', N'STDEVP', N'VAR', N'VARP')
BEGIN
  SET @msg = N'%s is an unsupported aggregate function.';
  RAISERROR(@msg, 16, 1, @agg_func);
  RETURN;
END

-- Construct column list
SET @sql =
  N'SET @result = '                                    + @newline +
  N'  STUFF('                                          + @newline +
  N'    (SELECT N'','' + '
         + N'QUOTENAME(pivot_col) AS [text()]'         + @newline +
  N'     FROM (SELECT DISTINCT('
         + QUOTENAME(@on_cols) + N') AS pivot_col'     + @newline +
  N'           FROM ' + @object + N') AS DistinctCols' + @newline +
  N'     ORDER BY pivot_col'                           + @newline +
  N'     FOR XML PATH('''')),'                         + @newline +
  N'    1, 1, N'''');';

EXEC sp_executesql
  @stmt   = @sql,
  @params = N'@result AS NVARCHAR(MAX) OUTPUT',
  @result = @cols OUTPUT;

-- Check @cols for possible SQL injection attempt
IF  UPPER(@cols) LIKE UPPER(N'%0x%')
  OR UPPER(@cols) LIKE UPPER(N'%;%')
  OR UPPER(@cols) LIKE UPPER(N'%''%')
  OR UPPER(@cols) LIKE UPPER(N'%--%')
  OR UPPER(@cols) LIKE UPPER(N'%/*%*/%')
```

```
    OR UPPER(@cols) LIKE UPPER(N'%EXEC%')
    OR UPPER(@cols) LIKE UPPER(N'%xp_%')
    OR UPPER(@cols) LIKE UPPER(N'%sp_%')
    OR UPPER(@cols) LIKE UPPER(N'%SELECT%')
    OR UPPER(@cols) LIKE UPPER(N'%INSERT%')
    OR UPPER(@cols) LIKE UPPER(N'%UPDATE%')
    OR UPPER(@cols) LIKE UPPER(N'%DELETE%')
    OR UPPER(@cols) LIKE UPPER(N'%TRUNCATE%')
    OR UPPER(@cols) LIKE UPPER(N'%CREATE%')
    OR UPPER(@cols) LIKE UPPER(N'%ALTER%')
    OR UPPER(@cols) LIKE UPPER(N'%DROP%')
    -- look for other possible strings used in SQL injection here
  BEGIN
    SET @msg = N'Possible SQL injection attempt.';
    RAISERROR(@msg, 16, 1);
    RETURN;
  END

  -- Create the PIVOT query
  SET @sql =
    N'SELECT *'                                      + @newline +
    N'FROM'                                          + @newline +
    N'  ( SELECT '                                   + @newline +
    N'       ' + QUOTENAME(@on_rows) + N','          + @newline +
    N'       ' + QUOTENAME(@on_cols) + N' AS pivot_col,'  + @newline +
    N'       ' + QUOTENAME(@agg_col) + N' AS agg_col'     + @newline +
    N'    FROM ' + @object                           + @newline +
    N'  ) AS PivotInput'                             + @newline +
    N'  PIVOT'                                       + @newline +
    N'    ( ' + @agg_func + N'(agg_col)'             + @newline +
    N'      FOR pivot_col'                           + @newline +
    N'        IN(' + @cols + N')'                    + @newline +
    N'  ) AS PivotOutput;';

  EXEC sp_executesql @sql;
  GO
```

This implementation of the stored procedure follows good programming practices and addresses the security flaws mentioned earlier. Keep in mind, however, that when constructing code based on user inputs and stored data/metadata, it is extremely difficult (if at all possible) to achieve complete protection against SQL injection.

The stored procedure usp_pivot is created as a user-defined procedure in the Northwind database with the *usp_* prefix. This means that it isn't as flexible as the previous implementation in the sense that it interacts only with tables and views from Northwind. Note that you can create a view in Northwind that queries objects from other databases, and provide this view as input to the stored procedure.

The usp_pivot stored procedure's code takes several measures to try and prevent SQL injection attempts:

■   The sizes of the input parameters are limited.

■ Instead of allowing any query as input, the stored procedure accepts only a valid table or view name that exists in the database. Similarly, instead of allowing any T-SQL expression for the arguments @on_rows, @on_cols and @agg_col, the stored procedure accepts only valid column names that exist in the input table/view. Note that you can create a view with any query that you like and serve it as input to the stored procedure.

■ The code uses QUOTENAME where relevant to quote object and column names with square brackets.

■ The stored procedure's code inspects the @cols variable for possible code strings injected to it through data stored in the rotation column values that are being concatenated.

The code also performs input validation to verify that all parameters were supplied; that the table/view and column names exist; and that the aggregate function appears in the list of functions that you want to support. As I mentioned, I discuss exception handling in Chapter 10.

The usp_pivot stored procedure might seem much less flexible than sp_pivot, but remember that you can always create a view to prepare the data for usp_pivot. For example, consider the following code used earlier to return the sum of value (quantity * unit price) per employee, pivoted by order year:

```
EXEC Northwind.dbo.sp_pivot
  @query    = N'
SELECT O.OrderID, EmployeeID, OrderDate, Quantity, UnitPrice
FROM dbo.Orders AS O
  JOIN dbo.[Order Details] AS OD
    ON OD.OrderID = O.OrderID',
  @on_rows  = N'EmployeeID AS empid',
  @on_cols  = N'YEAR(OrderDate)',
  @agg_func = N'SUM',
  @agg_col  = N'Quantity*UnitPrice';
```

You can achieve the same with usp_pivot by first creating a view that prepares the data:

```
USE Northwind;
GO
IF OBJECT_ID('dbo.ViewForPivot') IS NOT NULL
  DROP VIEW dbo.ViewForPivot;
GO

CREATE VIEW dbo.ViewForPivot
AS

SELECT
  O.OrderID       AS orderid,
  EmployeeID      AS empid,
  YEAR(OrderDate) AS order_year,
  Quantity * UnitPrice AS val
FROM dbo.Orders AS O
  JOIN dbo.[Order Details] AS OD
    ON OD.OrderID = O.OrderID;
GO
```

Then invoke usp_pivot, as in:

```
EXEC dbo.usp_pivot
  @object_name = N'ViewForPivot',
  @on_rows  = N'empid',
  @on_cols  = N'order_year',
  @agg_func = N'SUM',
  @agg_col  = N'val';
```

You will get the output shown earlier in Table 7-13.

If you think about it, that's a small price to pay compared to compromising the security of your system.

When you're done, run the following code for cleanup:

```
USE Northwind;
GO
IF OBJECT_ID('dbo.ViewForPivot') IS NOT NULL
  DROP VIEW dbo.ViewForPivot;
GO
IF OBJECT_ID('dbo.usp_pivot') IS NOT NULL
  DROP PROC dbo.usp_pivot;
```

CLR Stored Procedures

SQL Server 2005 allows you to develop CLR stored procedures (as well as other routines) using a .NET language of your choice. The previous chapter provided the background about CLR routines, gave advice on when to develop CLR routines versus T-SQL ones, and described the technicalities of how to develop CLR routines. Remember to read Appendix A for instructions on developing, building, deploying, and testing your .NET code. Here I'd just like to give a couple of examples of CLR stored procedures that apply functionality outside the reach of T-SQL code.

The first example is a CLR procedure called usp_GetEnvInfo. This stored procedure collects information from environment variables and returns it in table format. The environment variables that this procedure will return include: Machine Name, Processors, OS Version, CLR Version.

Note that, to collect information from environment variables, the assembly needs external access to operating system resources. By default assemblies are created (using the CREATE ASSEMBLY command) with the most restrictive PERMISSION_SET option – SAFE; meaning that they're limited to accessing database resources only. This is the recommended option to obtain maximum security and stability. The permission set options EXTERNAL_ACCESS and UNSAFE (specified in the CREATE ASSEMBLY or ALTER ASSEMBLY commands, or in the *Project* | *Properties* dialog in Visual Studio under the *Database* tab) allow external access to system resources such as files, the network, environment variables, or the registry. To allow

EXTERNAL_ACCESS and UNSAFE assemblies to run, you also need to set the database option TRUSTWORTHY to ON. Allowing EXTERNAL_ACCESS or UNSAFE assemblies to run represents a security risk and should be avoided. I will describe a safer alternative shortly, but first I'll demonstrate this option. To set the TRUSTWORTHY option of the CLRUtilities database to ON and to change the permission set of the CLRUtilities assembly to EXTERNAL_ACCESS you would run the following code:

```
-- Database option TRUSTWORTHY needs to be ON for EXTERNAL_ACCESS
ALTER DATABASE CLRUtilities SET TRUSTWORTHY ON;
GO
-- Alter assembly with PERMISSION_SET = EXTERNAL_ACCESS
ALTER ASSEMBLY CLRUtilities
WITH PERMISSION_SET = EXTERNAL_ACCESS;
```

At this point you will be able to run the usp_GetEnvInfo stored procedure. Keep in mind though, that UNSAFE assemblies have complete freedom and can compromise the robustness of SQL Server and the security of the system. EXTERNAL_ACCESS assemblies get the same reliability and stability protection as SAFE assemblies, but from a security perspective they're like UNSAFE assemblies.

A more secure alternative is to sign the assembly with a strong-named key file or Authenticode with a certificate. This strong name (or certificate) is created inside SQL Server as an asymmetric key (or certificate) and has a corresponding login with EXTERNAL ACCESS ASSEMBLY permission (for external access assemblies) or UNSAFE ASSEMBLY permission (for unsafe assemblies). For example, suppose that you have code in the CLRUtilities assembly that needs to run with the EXTERNAL_ACCESS permission set. You can sign the assembly with a strong-named key file from the *Project | Properties* dialog in Visual Studio under the *Signing* tab. Then run the following code to create an asymmetric key from the executable .dll file and a corresponding login with the EXTERNAL_ACCESS ASSEMBLY permission.

```
-- Create an asymmetric key from the signed assembly
-- Note: you have to sign the assembly using a strong name key file
USE master
GO
CREATE ASYMMETRIC KEY CLRUtilitiesKey
  FROM EXECUTABLE FILE =
    'C:\CLRUtilities\CLRUtilities\bin\Debug\CLRUtilities.dll'
-- Create login and grant it with external access permission
CREATE LOGIN CLRUtilitiesLogin FROM ASYMMETRIC KEY CLRUtilitiesKey
GRANT EXTERNAL ACCESS ASSEMBLY TO CLRUtilitiesLogin
GO
```

For more details about securing your assemblies, please refer to Books Online and to the following URL: *http://msdn2.microsoft.com/en-us/library/ms345106.aspx*.

Listing 7-10 shows the definition of the *usp_GetEnvInfo* stored procedure using C# code.

Listing 7-10   CLR usp_GetEnvInfo stored procedure, C# version

```
// Stored procedure that returns environment info in tabular format
[SqlProcedure]
public static void usp_GetEnvInfo()
{
    // Create a record - object representation of a row
    // Include the metadata for the SQL table
    SqlDataRecord record = new SqlDataRecord(
        new SqlMetaData("EnvProperty", SqlDbType.NVarChar, 20),
        new SqlMetaData("Value", SqlDbType.NVarChar, 256));
    // Marks the beginning of the result set to be sent back to the client
    // The record parameter is used to construct the metadata
    // for the result set
    SqlContext.Pipe.SendResultsStart(record);
    // Populate some records and send them through the pipe
    record.SetSqlString(0, @"Machine Name");
    record.SetSqlString(1, Environment.MachineName);
    SqlContext.Pipe.SendResultsRow(record);
    record.SetSqlString(0, @"Processors");
    record.SetSqlString(1, Environment.ProcessorCount.ToString());
    SqlContext.Pipe.SendResultsRow(record);
    record.SetSqlString(0, @"OS Version");
    record.SetSqlString(1, Environment.OSVersion.ToString());
    SqlContext.Pipe.SendResultsRow(record);
    record.SetSqlString(0, @"CLR Version");
    record.SetSqlString(1, Environment.Version.ToString());
    SqlContext.Pipe.SendResultsRow(record);
    // End of result set
    SqlContext.Pipe.SendResultsEnd();
}
```

In this procedure, you can see the usage of some specific extensions to ADO.NET for usage within SQL Server CLR routines. These are defined in the *Microsoft.SqlServer.Server* namespace in .NET 2.0.

When you call a stored procedure from SQL Server, you are already connected. You don't have to open a new connection; you need access to the caller's context from the code running in the server. The caller's context is abstracted in a *SqlContext* object. Before using the *SqlContext* object, you should test whether it is available by using its *IsAvailable* property.

The procedure retrieves some environmental data from the operating system. The data can be retrieved by the properties of an *Environment* object, which can be found in the *System* namespace. But the data you get is in text format. In the CLR procedure, you can see how to generate a row set for any possible format. The routine's code stores data in a *SqlDataRecord* object, which represents a single row of data. It defines the schema for this single row by using the *SqlMetaData* objects.

SELECT statements in a T-SQL stored procedure send the results to the connected caller's "pipe." This is the most effective way of sending results to the caller. The same technique is exposed to CLR routines running in SQL Server. Results can be sent to the connected pipe using the send methods of the *SqlPipe* object. You can instantiate the *SqlPipe* object with the *Pipe* property of the *SqlContext* object.

Listing 7-11 shows the definition of the usp_GetEnvInfo stored procedure using Visual Basic code.

Listing 7-11   CLR usp_GetEnvInfo stored procedure, Visual Basic version

```vb
' Stored procedure that returns environment info in tabular format
<SqlProcedure()> _
Public Shared Sub usp_GetEnvInfo()
    ' Create a record - object representation of a row
    ' Include the metadata for the SQL table
    Dim record As New SqlDataRecord( _
        New SqlMetaData("EnvProperty", SqlDbType.NVarChar, 20), _
        New SqlMetaData("Value", SqlDbType.NVarChar, 256))
    ' Marks the beginning of the result set to be sent back to the client
    ' The record parameter is used to construct the metadata for
    ' the result set
    SqlContext.Pipe.SendResultsStart(record)
    '' Populate some records and send them through the pipe
    record.SetSqlString(0, "Machine Name")
    record.SetSqlString(1, Environment.MachineName)
    SqlContext.Pipe.SendResultsRow(record)
    record.SetSqlString(0, "Processors")
    record.SetSqlString(1, Environment.ProcessorCount.ToString())
    SqlContext.Pipe.SendResultsRow(record)
    record.SetSqlString(0, "OS Version")
    record.SetSqlString(1, Environment.OSVersion.ToString())
    SqlContext.Pipe.SendResultsRow(record)
    record.SetSqlString(0, "CLR Version")
    record.SetSqlString(1, Environment.Version.ToString())
    SqlContext.Pipe.SendResultsRow(record)
    ' End of result set
    SqlContext.Pipe.SendResultsEnd()
End Sub
```

Run the following code to register the C# version of the usp_GetEnvInfo stored procedure in the CLRUtilities database:

```sql
USE CLRUtilities;
GO
IF OBJECT_ID('dbo.usp_GetEnvInfo') IS NOT NULL
  DROP PROC usp_GetEnvInfo;
GO
CREATE PROCEDURE dbo.usp_GetEnvInfo
AS EXTERNAL NAME CLRUtilities.CLRUtilities.usp_GetEnvInfo;
```

Use the following code to register the stored procedure in case you used Visual Basic to develop it:

```sql
CREATE PROCEDURE dbo.usp_GetEnvInfo
AS EXTERNAL NAME
  CLRUtilities.[CLRUtilities.CLRUtilities].usp_GetEnvInfo;
```

Run the following code to test the usp_GetEnvInfo procedure, generating the output shown in Table 7-15:

```
EXEC dbo.usp_GetEnvInfo;
```

Table 7-15   Output of usp_GetEnvInfo Stored Procedure

EnvProperty	Value
Machine Name	DOJO
Processors	1
OS Version	Microsoft Windows NT 5.1.2600 Service Pack 2
CLR Version	2.0.50727.42

The second example for a CLR procedure creates the usp_GetAssemblyInfo stored procedure, which returns information about an input assembly.

Listing 7-12 shows the definition of the usp_GetAssemblyInfo stored procedure using C# code.

Listing 7-12   CLR usp_GetAssemblyInfo stored procedure, C# version

```csharp
// Stored procedure that returns assembly info
// uses Reflection
[SqlProcedure]
public static void usp_GetAssemblyInfo(SqlString asmName)
{
    // Retrieve the clr name of the assembly
    String clrName = null;
    // Get the context
    using (SqlConnection connection =
            new SqlConnection("Context connection = true"))
    {
        connection.Open();
        using (SqlCommand command = new SqlCommand())
        {
            // Get the assembly and load it
            command.Connection = connection;
            command.CommandText =
                "SELECT clr_name FROM sys.assemblies WHERE name = @asmName";
            command.Parameters.Add("@asmName", SqlDbType.NVarChar);
            command.Parameters[0].Value = asmName;
            clrName = (String)command.ExecuteScalar();
            if (clrName == null)
            {
                throw new ArgumentException("Invalid assembly name!");
            }
            Assembly myAsm = Assembly.Load(clrName);
            // Create a record - object representation of a row
            // Include the metadata for the SQL table
            SqlDataRecord record = new SqlDataRecord(
                new SqlMetaData("Type", SqlDbType.NVarChar, 50),
                new SqlMetaData("Name", SqlDbType.NVarChar, 256));
```

```
                                    // Marks the beginning of the result set to be sent back
                                    // to the client
                                    // The record parameter is used to construct the metadata
                                    // for the result set
                                    SqlContext.Pipe.SendResultsStart(record);
                                    // Get all types in the assembly
                                    Type[] typesArr = myAsm.GetTypes();
                                    foreach (Type t in typesArr)
                                    {
                                        // Type in a SQL database should be a class or
                                        // a structure
                                        if (t.IsClass == true)
                                        {
                                            record.SetSqlString(0, @"Class");
                                        }
                                        else
                                        {
                                            record.SetSqlString(0, @"Structure");
                                        }
                                        record.SetSqlString(1, t.FullName);
                                        SqlContext.Pipe.SendResultsRow(record);
                                        // Find all public static methods
                                        MethodInfo[] miArr = t.GetMethods();
                                        foreach (MethodInfo mi in miArr)
                                        {
                                            if (mi.IsPublic && mi.IsStatic)
                                            {
                                                record.SetSqlString(0, @"  Method");
                                                record.SetSqlString(1, mi.Name);
                                                SqlContext.Pipe.SendResultsRow(record);
                                            }
                                        }
                                    }
                                    // End of result set
                                    SqlContext.Pipe.SendResultsEnd();
                                }
                            }
                        }
```

A DBA could have a problem finding out exactly what part of a particular .NET assembly is loaded to the database. Fortunately, this problem can be easily mitigated. All .NET assemblies include metadata, describing all types (classes and structures) defined within it, including all public methods and properties of the types. In .NET, the *System.Reflection* namespace contains classes and interfaces that provide a managed view of loaded types.

For a very detailed overview of a .NET assembly stored in the file system, you can use the Reflector for .NET, a very sophisticated tool created by Lutz Roeder. Because it is download-able for free from his site at *http://www.aisto.com/roeder/dotnet/*, it is very popular among .NET developers. Also, Miles Trochesset wrote in his blog at *http://blogs.msdn.com/sqlclr/ archive/2005/11/21/495438.aspx* a SQL Server CLR DDL trigger that is fired on the CREATE ASSEMBLY statement. The trigger automatically registers all CLR objects from the assembly, including UDTs, UDAs, UDFs, SPs and triggers. I guess it is going to be very popular among database developers. I used both tools as a starting point to create my simplified version of a SQL Server CLR stored procedure. I thought that a DBA might prefer to read the assembly metadata from a stored procedure, not from an external tool, like Lutz Roeder's Reflector for .NET is, and also that a DBA might want just to read the metadata first, not immediately to register all CLR objects from the assembly, like Miles Trochesset's trigger does.

The usp_GetAssemblyInfo procedure has to load an assembly from the sys.*assemblies* catalog view. To achieve this task, it has to execute a *SqlCommand*. *SqlCommand* needs a connection. In the usp_GetEnvInfo procedure's code you saw the usage of the *SqlContext* class; now you need an explicit *SqlConnection* object. You can get the context of the caller's connection by using a new connection string option, *"Context connection = true"*.

As in the usp_GetEnvInfo procedure, you want to get the results in tabular format. Again you use the *SqlDataRecord* and *SqlMetaData* objects to shape the row returned. Remember that the *SqlPipe* object gives you the best performance to return the row to the caller.

Before you can read the metadata of an assembly, you have to load it. The rest is quite easy. The *GetTypes* method of a loaded assembly can be used to retrieve a collection of all types defined in the assembly. The code retrieves this collection in an array. Then it loops through the array, and for each type it uses the *GetMethods* method to retrieve all public methods in an array of the *MethodInfo* objects. This procedure retrieves type and method names only. The *Reflection* classes allow you to get other metadata information as well—for example, the names and types of input parameters. Listing 7-13 shows the definition of the usp_GetAssemblyInfo stored procedure using Visual Basic code.

Listing 7-13   CLR usp_GetAssemblyInfo stored procedure, Visual Basic version

```
' Stored procedure that returns assembly info
' uses Reflection
<SqlProcedure()> _
Public Shared Sub usp_GetAssemblyInfo(ByVal asmName As SqlString)
    ' Retrieve the clr name of the assembly
    Dim clrName As String = Nothing
    ' Get the context
    Using connection As New SqlConnection("Context connection = true")
        connection.Open()
        Using command As New SqlCommand
            ' Get the assembly and load it
            command.Connection = connection
            command.CommandText = _
              "SELECT clr_name FROM sys.assemblies WHERE name = @asmName"
            command.Parameters.Add("@asmName", SqlDbType.NVarChar)
            command.Parameters(0).Value = asmName
            clrName = CStr(command.ExecuteScalar())
            If (clrName = Nothing) Then
                Throw New ArgumentException("Invalid assembly name!")
            End If
            Dim myAsm As Assembly = Assembly.Load(clrName)
            ' Create a record - object representation of a row
            ' Include the metadata for the SQL table
```

```
                    Dim record As New SqlDataRecord( _
                        New SqlMetaData("Type", SqlDbType.NVarChar, 50), _
                        New SqlMetaData("Name", SqlDbType.NVarChar, 256))
                    ' Marks the beginning of the result set to be sent back
                    ' to the client
                    ' The record parameter is used to construct the metadata
                    ' for the result set
                    SqlContext.Pipe.SendResultsStart(record)
                    ' Get all types in the assembly
                    Dim typesArr() As Type = myAsm.GetTypes()
                    For Each t As Type In typesArr
                        ' Type in a SQL database should be a class or a structure
                        If (t.IsClass = True) Then
                            record.SetSqlString(0, "Class")
                        Else
                            record.SetSqlString(0, "Structure")
                        End If
                        record.SetSqlString(1, t.FullName)
                        SqlContext.Pipe.SendResultsRow(record)
                        ' Find all public static methods
                        Dim miArr() As MethodInfo = t.GetMethods
                        For Each mi As MethodInfo In miArr
                            If (mi.IsPublic And mi.IsStatic) Then
                                record.SetSqlString(0, " Method")
                                record.SetSqlString(1, mi.Name)
                                SqlContext.Pipe.SendResultsRow(record)
                            End If
                        Next
                    Next
                    ' End of result set
                    SqlContext.Pipe.SendResultsEnd()
                End Using
            End Using
        End Sub
```

Run the following code to register the C# version of the usp_GetAssemblyInfo stored procedure in the CLRUtilities database:

```
IF OBJECT_ID('dbo.usp_GetAssemblyInfo') IS NOT NULL
  DROP PROC usp_GetAssemblyInfo;
GO
CREATE PROCEDURE usp_GetAssemblyInfo
  @asmName AS sysname
AS EXTERNAL NAME CLRUtilities.CLRUtilities.usp_GetAssemblyInfo;
```

And in case you used Visual Basic to develop the stored procedure, use the following code to register it:

```
CREATE PROCEDURE usp_GetAssemblyInfo
  @asmName AS sysname
AS EXTERNAL NAME
  CLRUtilities.[CLRUtilities.CLRUtilities].usp_GetAssemblyInfo;
```

Run the following code to test the usp_GetAssemblyInfo procedure, providing it with the CLRUtilities assembly name as input:

```
EXEC usp_GetAssemblyInfo N'CLRUtilities';
```

You get the output shown in Table 7-16 with the assembly name and the names of all methods (routines) defined within it. You should recognize the routine names except for one—trg_GenericDMLAudit—a CLR trigger that I'll describe in the next chapter.

Table 7-16   Output of usp_GetAssemblyInfo Stored Procedure

Type	Name
Class	CLRUtilities
Method	fn_RegExMatch
Method	fn_SQLSigCLR
Method	fn_ImpCast
Method	fn_ExpCast
Method	fn_SplitCLR
Method	ArrSplitFillRow
Method	usp_GetEnvInfo
Method	usp_GetAssemblyInfo
Method	trg_GenericDMLAudit

When you're done, run the following code for cleanup:

```
USE CLRUtilities;
GO
IF OBJECT_ID('dbo.usp_GetEnvInfo') IS NOT NULL
  DROP PROC dbo.usp_GetEnvInfo;
GO
IF OBJECT_ID('dbo.usp_GetAssemblyInfo') IS NOT NULL
  DROP PROC dbo.usp_GetAssemblyInfo;
```

Conclusion

Stored procedures are one of the most powerful tools that SQL Server provides you. Understanding them well and using them wisely will result in robust, secure, and well-performing databases. Stored procedures give you a security layer, encapsulation, reduction in network traffic, reuse of execution plans, and much more. SQL Server 2005 introduces the ability to develop CLR routines, eliminating the need to develop extended stored procedures and enhancing the functionality of your database.

Chapter 8
Triggers

Triggers are routines that fire automatically as a result of an event in the database server. Microsoft SQL Server supports data-manipulation language (DML) and data-definition language (DDL) triggers, which can be developed either with T-SQL or with .NET code and can fire AFTER or INSTEAD OF the triggering event. In this chapter, I'll describe in detail the different types of triggers, first describing DML AFTER triggers and later, in a dedicated section, DDL AFTER triggers. I'll also focus on AFTER triggers that you write with T-SQL, and in a dedicated section, I'll describe triggers that you develop with .NET code (CLR triggers).

Triggers are first and foremost stored procedures in terms of how SQL Server treats them internally. They undergo similar processing phases to stored procedures (parsing, resolution, and optimization). However, triggers do not have an interface (input and output parameters), and you cannot invoke them explicitly. They fire automatically as a result of a statement submitted against the database server.

Triggers are part of the transaction that fired them. That is, the transaction is not considered complete until the trigger also finishes running. If you issue a ROLLBACK TRAN within the trigger's code, you effectively roll back the trigger's activity as well as all the activity of the transaction to which the trigger belongs. The rollback will undo all activity as of the outermost BEGIN TRAN statement, if one was explicitly issued. If the firing statement was not issued in an explicit transaction, a rollback in a trigger will undo all activity issued within the trigger until the ROLLBACK TRAN statement, as well as the activity of the firing statement.

Keep in mind that if you issue a rollback within the trigger (just as with any transaction), it's as if the activity were performed twice—done and then undone. If your trigger is intended to enforce an integrity rule and you can achieve the task by prevention rather than reaction, you should do so to get better performance. For example, if you can enforce the integrity rule with a constraint, use the constraint. If you cannot enforce it with a constraint, see whether you can enforce it with a stored procedure that first performs validation before it determines whether to apply the change. Use triggers only if you can't enforce the rules with constraints.

Triggers allow you to automate the process of reacting to statements issued by users and applications (AFTER triggers) or substituting the original statement with your own code (INSTEAD OF triggers). You can react to or substitute DML activities (INSERT, UPDATE, and DELETE) or react to DDL activities (CREATE, ALTER, and DROP). You can develop triggers with T-SQL or with .NET code. SQL Server 2005 does not support SELECT triggers, row-level triggers or BEFORE triggers. INSTEAD OF triggers are the closest you can get in SQL Server to BEFORE triggers.

You can use triggers to enforce complex integrity rules, to audit changes, and to do much more.

AFTER Triggers

AFTER triggers fire after the firing statement has already taken place. You use these triggers to react to changes against the database server.

DML AFTER triggers can be created only on permanent tables. They cannot be created on views or temporary tables. You create such triggers on a specific table and for a specific DML statement or statement list, including INSERT, UPDATE, and DELETE.

If a constraint defined on a table rejects a modification, a trigger defined on that table will not fire.

AFTER triggers are fired per statement, not per row. Regardless of how many rows were affected by the firing statement (zero, one, or multiple), an AFTER trigger will fire only once.

You can create multiple AFTER triggers (both DML and DDL) on each object for each statement type. If you have multiple triggers on the same table for the same type of statement, they will fire synchronously (one after the other). SQL Server allows you to mark the trigger that will fire first and the one that will fire last by using the *sp_settriggerorder* stored procedure. The order in which triggers between the first and last are fired is undefined.

AFTER triggers are useful for automated reactive activities that you want to issue as a result of the firing statement—for example, enforcing integrity rules that you cannot enforce with constraints, auditing, maintaining denormalized data, and so on.

The *inserted* and *deleted* Special Tables

Within DML triggers you can access the old and new image of the affected rows through special tables called *inserted* and *deleted*. The *inserted* table contains the new image of the affected rows, and *deleted* contains the old image. Naturally, *inserted* will contain rows only for INSERT and UPDATE triggers, and it will be empty for DELETE triggers. Similarly, *deleted* will contain rows only for DELETE and UPDATE triggers, and it will be empty for INSERT triggers.

The *inserted* and *deleted* tables are structured the same as the table on which the trigger was defined—that is, they have the same columns as the base table. Note that these tables are not indexed; therefore, every time you query them, you're scanning the whole thing. There are some exceptions, of course. For example, if you use the EXISTS predicate or a TOP query with no ORDER BY clause, SQL Server won't need to scan the whole table.

These special tables are implemented in completely different ways in SQL Server 2000 and SQL Server 2005.

In SQL Server 2000, these tables are actually views built against the section of the transaction log that contains the log records for the statement that fired the trigger. This fact has many performance implications. Whenever you query *inserted* or *deleted*, you're scanning a portion of the transaction log. Remember that the transaction log is written sequentially, and that it is typically a bottleneck in online transaction processing (OLTP) systems. Any interference with the transaction log's activity ultimately postpones the flushing of changes to the data portion of the database. Intensive trigger activity might very well cause the transaction log to become even a more serious bottleneck in the system.

Typically, it's sufficient to place the transaction log on a RAID 1 disk system, which doesn't provide striping of the data, because the transaction log writes sequentially and will not benefit from striping. However, if you have intensive activities (such as triggers or transaction log replication) that read from the log, it's a good idea to stripe the log on multiple disk drives using a RAID 10 controller. By taking this approach, you can have different disk arms working on the different read/write activities.

In SQL Server 2005, *inserted* and *deleted* point to row-versioned data in tempdb. Row versioning is a new technology in SQL Server 2005 supporting various aspects of the product, including new snapshot isolation levels, triggers, online index operations, and multiple active result sets (MARS). This technology allows storing earlier versions of a row in tempdb. Regarding triggers, SQL Server stores row versions for both data changed by the statement firing the trigger and data changed by the trigger. The *inserted* and *deleted* tables now point to row-versioned data and not to a section in the transaction log.

When you upgrade your system from SQL Server 2000 to SQL Server 2005, you have an immediate change in internal activity for triggers. The load is removed from the transaction log, but it shifts to tempdb. This change in the architecture is very interesting because the transaction log writes sequentially and you remove interference with the log activity. Multiple activities against tempdb can be performed in parallel, enjoying striping of the data. However, it is important to be aware of this architectural change and be prepared with sufficient storage and a sufficient RAID system for tempdb before you upgrade to SQL Server 2005.

In both SQL Server 2005 and earlier versions of SQL Server, intensive trigger activity can cause performance issues. In both versions, *inserted* and *deleted* are not indexed, so you might end up scanning large portions of data when querying those. In SQL Server 2000, triggers place tension on the transaction log, and in SQL Server 2005, they place tension on tempdb. If you really need to scan *inserted* or *deleted* completely and you can obtain the data you need with a single scan (for example, a set-based join between *inserted* or *deleted* and the base table), there's not much that you would need to do to improve performance. However, if you need to access *inserted* or *deleted* with multiple iterations—for example, if you need to treat each row individually—it would be wise to spool the data and put it aside in a temporary table that you can index, as in:

```
SELECT * INTO #I FROM inserted
  CREATE UNIQUE CLUSTERED INDEX idx_keycol ON #I(keycol);
```

Understanding the way *inserted* and *deleted* work is the key to developing robust and efficient triggers. On the other hand, misunderstanding them could lead to serious performance problems.

Identifying the Number of Affected Rows

Remember that triggers are fired per statement, not per row. This means that a trigger will fire once for zero, one, or multiple affected rows. In most cases, if a trigger was fired for zero affected rows, you don't want it to react to the statement that fired it. If one row was affected, you can typically apply simple logic and query *inserted* or *deleted* directly, knowing that they contain only one row. For example, you can safely use an assignment SELECT like the following one to grab data from that row:

```
SELECT @var1 = col1, @var2 = col2, … FROM inserted;
```

However, you will face logical issues with such a statement if zero or multiple rows were affected. With zero affected rows, such a statement does not perform any assignment at all, so the variables will have the values they had earlier. With multiple affected rows, this statement will perform multiple assignments—one for each row. However, the variables will have the values assigned to them in the last assignment performed. If you just assume that your triggers will fire only for single-row modifications, but they don't, you'll end up with logical bugs.

Suppose that you use a SET command to assign a value from *inserted* or *deleted* to a variable:

```
SET @var1 = (SELECT col1 FROM inserted);
```

If one row was affected, this assignment will work perfectly fine. With zero affected rows, the subquery will return NULL. With multiple affected rows, this code will break, generating an error.

You need to take these things into consideration when programming triggers so that you can avoid bugs and realize good performance. You can save the value returned by the @@*rowcount* function in a local variable. A DECLARE statement will not cause a change in the value that @@*rowcount* returns, so you have the opportunity to declare a local variable and assign it with the return value of the function. If you do so right at the beginning of the trigger, @@*rowcount* will return the number of rows affected by the firing statement. You can then inspect the value in the local variable and determine a course of action based on the number of rows affected by the firing statement.

With zero affected rows, you typically just want to return from the trigger—there's no point in wasting resources if you need not do anything. If more than zero rows were affected, the course of action you should take depends on the type of activity you want to issue from the trigger. If you can achieve the activity by using a set-based join between *inserted* or *deleted* and the base table, you can apply the same code for both single and multiple affected rows. For example, suppose that you're writing an INSERT trigger for a table called T1 that is supposed to modify an attribute called *col1* in the new rows. You can achieve this by joining *inserted* and T1:

```
WITH C AS
(
  SELECT T1.col1 AS T1_col1 -- plus other columns of interest
  FROM inserted AS I
    JOIN T1
      ON T1.keycol = I.keycol
)
UPDATE C
  SET T1_col1 = <expression>;
```

The purpose of the join is just to filter the new rows added to T1.

However, suppose that you need to deal with each new row individually using iterative logic. You need to retrieve values from each row individually and take some action. Remember that if only one row was affected, you can safely use an assignment SELECT to grab values from the row in *inserted* or *deleted*:

```
SELECT @var1 = col1, @var2 = col2, … FROM inserted;
```

So you can check the number of affected rows, and if it is one, use such logic. Otherwise, you need to apply iterative logic. Remember that *inserted* and *deleted* are not indexed. You can copy the data from the special table into a temporary table, index it, and then iterate through the rows in the temporary table using a loop. A more efficient solution is to use a cursor based on a query against *inserted* or *deleted*. I feel more comfortable with the former approach, in which I copy the data to my own temporary table and index it; so if performance is not an issue I typically apply this approach (for example, with a small number of rows). Of course, you can benchmark both approaches for a given task before you decide which to use. In this section, I'll demonstrate the approach using a temporary table, and later in the chapter, I'll demonstrate the approach using a cursor.

To demonstrate the flow handling based on the number of affected rows, first run the following code to create the table T1:

```
SET NOCOUNT ON;
USE tempdb;
GO
IF OBJECT_ID('dbo.T1') IS NOT NULL
  DROP TABLE dbo.T1;
GO

CREATE TABLE dbo.T1
(
  keycol  INT         NOT NULL PRIMARY KEY,
  datacol VARCHAR(10) NOT NULL
);
```

Run the code in Listing 8-1 to create the trigger *trg_T1_i*.

Listing 8-1 Creation script for *trg_T1_i* trigger

```
CREATE TRIGGER trg_T1_i ON T1 FOR INSERT
AS

DECLARE @rc AS INT;
SET @rc = @@rowcount;

IF @rc = 0 RETURN;

DECLARE @keycol AS INT, @datacol AS VARCHAR(10);

IF @rc = 1 -- single row
BEGIN
  SELECT @keycol = keycol, @datacol = datacol FROM inserted;
  PRINT 'Handling keycol: '
    + CAST(@keycol AS VARCHAR(10))
    + ', datacol: ' + @datacol;
END
ELSE -- multi row
BEGIN
  SELECT * INTO #I FROM inserted;
  CREATE UNIQUE CLUSTERED INDEX idx_keycol ON #I(keycol);

  SELECT @keycol = keycol, @datacol = datacol
  FROM (SELECT TOP (1) keycol, datacol
        FROM #I
        ORDER BY keycol) AS D;

  WHILE @@rowcount > 0
  BEGIN
    PRINT 'Handling keycol: '
      + CAST(@keycol AS VARCHAR(10))
      + ', datacol: ' + @datacol;

    SELECT @keycol = keycol, @datacol = datacol
    FROM (SELECT TOP (1) keycol, datacol
          FROM #I
          WHERE keycol > @keycol
          ORDER BY keycol) AS D;
  END
END
GO
```

Note You can use either the keyword FOR or the keyword AFTER to define an AFTER trigger.

This trigger simply prints the values provided in each new row loaded by the firing INSERT statement. It demonstrates how to deal with each row individually.

The trigger first stores the value returned by the *@@rowcount* function in the local variable *@rc*. If zero rows were affected, the trigger returns. If one row was affected, the code uses an assignment SELECT to grab the values from the row inserted into local variables. If multiple rows were affected, the code copies the rows from *inserted* into the temporary table #I and creates a clustered index on *#I.keycol*. The code then grabs the values from the row with the minimum key by using a TOP (1) query. The code then enters a loop that continues for as long as the last statement found a row. In each iteration, the code prints the values from the current row and grabs the values from the next row (the row with the first key that is greater than the current one).

To test the trigger, first run the following code, which loads zero rows:

```
INSERT INTO dbo.T1 SELECT 1, 'A' WHERE 1 = 0;
```

As expected, you will get no output from the trigger.

Next load a single row:

```
INSERT INTO dbo.T1 SELECT 1, 'A';
```

You will get the following output:

```
Handling keycol: 1, datacol: A
```

Finally, load multiple rows:

```
INSERT INTO dbo.T1
  SELECT 2, 'B'
  UNION ALL
  SELECT 3, 'C'
  UNION ALL
  SELECT 4, 'D';
```

You will get the following output:

```
Handling keycol: 2, datacol: B
Handling keycol: 3, datacol: C
Handling keycol: 4, datacol: D
```

When you're done, run the following code for cleanup:

```
IF OBJECT_ID('dbo.T1') IS NOT NULL
  DROP TABLE dbo.T1;
```

Identifying the Type of Trigger

There might be cases in which you'd rather create one trigger for multiple statement types but still be able to identify the type of statement that fired the trigger. For example, for auditing purposes, you want to use the same code for INSERT, UPDATE, and DELETE to audit the fact that a change took place, but you want to also audit the type of change.

To identify the type of statement that fired the trigger, you can inspect *inserted* and *deleted*. Of course, if zero rows were affected, both tables will be empty, but in such a case you'd typically rather do nothing. If at least one row was affected, you can check which table contains rows to determine the type of change. As a result of an INSERT statement, you will find rows only in *inserted*; for a DELETE statement, you will find rows only in *deleted*; for an UPDATE statement, you will find rows in both tables.

To demonstrate this, first create the table T1 by running the following code:

```
IF OBJECT_ID('dbo.T1') IS NOT NULL
  DROP TABLE dbo.T1;
GO

CREATE TABLE dbo.T1
(
  keycol  INT         NOT NULL PRIMARY KEY,
  datacol VARCHAR(10) NOT NULL
);
```

Run the code in Listing 8-2 to create the trigger *trg_T1_iud*:

Listing 8-2   Creation script for *trg_T1_iud* trigger

```
CREATE TRIGGER trg_T1_iud ON dbo.T1 FOR INSERT, UPDATE, DELETE
AS

DECLARE @rc AS INT;
SET @rc = @@rowcount;

IF @rc = 0
BEGIN
  PRINT 'No rows affected';
  RETURN;
END

IF EXISTS(SELECT * FROM inserted)
BEGIN
  IF EXISTS(SELECT * FROM deleted)
  BEGIN
    PRINT 'UPDATE identified';
  END
  ELSE
  BEGIN
    PRINT 'INSERT identified';
  END
END
ELSE
BEGIN
  PRINT 'DELETE identified';
END
GO
```

The trigger's code first checks whether zero rows were affected. If that is the case, it simply returns. If at least one row was affected, the code uses the EXISTS predicate to determine which type of statement fired the trigger by examining which tables contain rows. Remember that the optimizer supports a short-circuiting capability when optimizing the EXISTS predicate. Once a row is identified, there's no reason to scan other rows to determine whether the table contains rows or not.

> **Tip**   In SQL Server 2000, if you used the COUNT(*) aggregate to check for existence of rows—for example, *IF (SELECT COUNT(*) FROM Table) > 0*—the technique was typically expensive. The optimizer typically used a full scan of the leaf level of the narrowest index created on the table to determine that count. This meant that it was always a better idea to use the EXISTS predicate. The optimizer in SQL Server 2005 does a much better job of optimizing logical expressions, such as the one just shown. It typically produces the same plan for *IF (SELECT COUNT(*)...) >0* to the one it generates for a logically equivalent expression based on the EXISTS predicate, by applying short-circuiting.

To test the trigger, run the following INSERT statement that loads zero rows:

```
INSERT INTO T1 SELECT 1, 'A' WHERE 1 = 0;
```

You will get the output:

```
No rows affected
```

Insert one row:

```
INSERT INTO T1 SELECT 1, 'A';
```

You will get the output:

```
INSERT identified
```

Issue an UPDATE statement:

```
UPDATE T1 SET datacol = 'AA' WHERE keycol = 1;
```

You will get the output:

```
UPDATE identified
```

Finally, issue a DELETE statement:

```
DELETE FROM T1 WHERE keycol = 1;
```

You will get the output:

```
DELETE identified
```

When you're done, run the following code for cleanup:

```
IF OBJECT_ID('dbo.T1') IS NOT NULL
  DROP TABLE dbo.T1;
```

Not Firing Triggers for Specific Statements

There's no built-in way to suppress a trigger for a particular statement. You can only disable a trigger completely using an ALTER TABLE DISABLE TRIGGER command. If you want to prevent a trigger from firing for a particular statement, you have to develop your own programmatic solution. You need to somehow signal the trigger that you don't want it to run its code.

One way to achieve this is by creating a temporary table with a particular name in the calling batch. Remember that a local temporary table is visible only to the creating session, in the calling level, and all levels inner to it. The trigger can first check whether a temporary table with that particular name exists and, if it does, return. Otherwise, the code can continue running normally. Back in the calling batch, you can drop the temporary table when you don't want to prevent the trigger from running its code anymore.

To demonstrate this solution, first run the following code, which creates the table T1:

```
USE tempdb;
GO
IF OBJECT_ID('dbo.T1') IS NOT NULL
  DROP TABLE dbo.T1;
GO
CREATE TABLE dbo.T1(col1 INT);
```

Next run the following code to create the trigger *trg_T1_i*:

```
CREATE TRIGGER trg_T1_i ON dbo.T1 FOR INSERT
AS

IF OBJECT_ID('tempdb..#do_not_fire_trg_T1_i') IS NOT NULL RETURN;

PRINT 'trg_T1_i in action...';
GO
```

The trigger uses the OBJECT_ID function to determine whether a temporary table called *#do_not_fire_trg_T1_i* exists. If the table does exist, it returns. If the table doesn't exist, the code continues running normally.

> **Note** Remember that temporary tables are created in tempdb. Make sure that when using the OBJECT_ID function to determine whether a temporary table exists, you database-qualify the object name. If you are connected to another database and invoke the function without the tempdb prefix, you'll always get a NULL back.

If you don't want to prevent the trigger's code from running, just submit your usual modifications. For example, run the following INSERT statement:

```
INSERT INTO dbo.T1 VALUES(1);
```

You will get the output:

```
trg_T1_i in action...
```

This output tells you that the trigger's code ran fully.

If you want to prevent the trigger's code from running in full, signal it by creating the temporary table with the expected name:

```
-- Setting signal
CREATE TABLE #do_not_fire_trg_T1_i(col1 INT);
INSERT INTO T1 VALUES(2);
-- Clearing signal
DROP TABLE #do_not_fire_trg_T1_i;
```

This solution works, but it does have an impact on tempdb's activity.

Another solution that you can implement uses the session's *context info*. Logically, context info is a VARBINARY(128) variable owned by the session. At any point in the session, you can change it by using the SET CONTEXT_INFO command or query it by using the CONTEXT_INFO function.

> **Note**   The CONTEXT_INFO function is new in SQL Server 2005. To acquire the session's context info in SQL Server 2000, use the following query:
>
> ```
> SELECT context_info FROM master.dbo.sysprocesses WHERE spid = @@spid
> ```

You can rely on the session's context info to communicate between different levels of code—in our case, between the calling batch and the trigger. Think of context info as a global session variable. For example, a batch can store a specific GUID in a section of the session's context info when it wants to send a signal to the trigger. The trigger will look for that particular GUID to determine whether or not to continue running the code.

To generate the GUID that you will use as your signal, you can use the NEWID() function, as in:

```
SELECT CAST(NEWID() AS BINARY(16));
```

The GUID is converted to a binary value because you want to store it in the session's context info, which is binary. You invoke this code only once to acquire a GUID, and then specify it explicitly in your code. When I invoked this code, I got the value *0x7EDBCEC5E165E749BF1261A655F52C48*. I will use this GUID in my examples. Of course, you should use the one you get. If you're using the session's context info for multiple tasks (for example, to send signals to multiple different triggers), make sure that you dedicate a different section within it for each task. Whenever you set the value of context info, make sure that you don't override it completely. Rather, just substitute the relevant section within it dedicated to the task at hand.

For encapsulation purposes, I'll create three stored procedures: one that sets the signal, one that clears it, and one that returns it. I'll create the stored procedures as special ones so that they can be used in all databases without database-qualifying the procedure name.

In our example, let's assume that we dedicate the first 16 bytes of the context info (starting at position 1) for our trigger's signal.

Run the following code to create the *sp_TrgSignal_Set* stored procedure, which sets the signal:

```
USE master;
GO
IF OBJECT_ID('dbo.sp_TrgSignal_Set') IS NOT NULL
  DROP PROC dbo.sp_TrgSignal_Set;
GO
CREATE PROC dbo.sp_TrgSignal_Set
  @guid AS BINARY(16),
  @pos  AS INT
AS

DECLARE @ci AS VARBINARY(128);
SET @ci =
  ISNULL(SUBSTRING(CONTEXT_INFO(), 1, @pos-1),
         CAST(REPLICATE(0x00, @pos-1) AS VARBINARY(128)))
  + @guid +
  ISNULL(SUBSTRING(CONTEXT_INFO(), @pos+16, 128-16-@pos+1), 0x);
SET CONTEXT_INFO @ci;
GO
```

The stored procedure accepts two inputs; *@guid* is the 16-byte GUID used as the signal, and *@pos* is the starting position (byte number) in which you want to store the signal in context info (in our case, 1). Notice that the procedure doesn't override the whole value stored in context info, rather just the relevant 16 bytes. It achieves this by querying the CONTEXT_INFO function. The code extracts the surrounding sections from the existing context info, concatenates the signal between the preceding and following sections, and then stores the concatenated string back in the session's context info.

In a similar manner, the following *sp_TrgSignal_Clear* stored procedure clears the signal from the section dedicated to it by zeroing the relevant bits:

```
IF OBJECT_ID('dbo.sp_TrgSignal_Clear') IS NOT NULL
  DROP PROC dbo.sp_TrgSignal_Clear;
GO
CREATE PROC dbo.sp_TrgSignal_Clear
  @pos  AS INT
AS

DECLARE @ci AS VARBINARY(128);
SET @ci =
  ISNULL(SUBSTRING(CONTEXT_INFO(), 1, @pos-1),
         CAST(REPLICATE(0x00, @pos-1) AS VARBINARY(128)))
  + CAST(REPLICATE(0x00, 16) AS VARBINARY(128)) +
  ISNULL(SUBSTRING(CONTEXT_INFO(), @pos+16, 128-16-@pos+1), 0x);
SET CONTEXT_INFO @ci;
GO
```

And finally, the following *sp_TrgSignal_Get* stored procedure returns the signal by querying the CONTEXT_INFO function:

```
IF OBJECT_ID('dbo.sp_TrgSignal_Get') IS NOT NULL
  DROP PROC dbo.sp_TrgSignal_Get;
GO
CREATE PROC dbo.sp_TrgSignal_Get
  @guid AS BINARY(16) OUTPUT,
  @pos  AS INT
AS

SET @guid = SUBSTRING(CONTEXT_INFO(), @pos, 16);
GO
```

Now you can alter the *trg_T1_i* trigger to look for the signal in the session's context info instead of using the temporary table technique:

```
USE tempdb;
GO
ALTER TRIGGER trg_T1_i ON dbo.T1 FOR INSERT
AS

DECLARE @signal AS BINARY(16);
EXEC dbo.sp_TrgSignal_Get
  @guid = @signal OUTPUT,
  @pos  = 1;
IF @signal = 0x7EDBCEC5E165E749BF1261A655F52C48 RETURN;

PRINT 'trg_T1_i in action...';
GO
```

To test the trigger, first issue an INSERT statement without setting the signal:

```
INSERT INTO dbo.T1 VALUES(1);
```

The trigger's code will run in full, and you will get the output:

```
trg_T1_i in action...
```

To prevent the trigger's code from firing, set the signal:

```
EXEC dbo.sp_TrgSignal_Set
  @guid = 0x7EDBCEC5E165E749BF1261A655F52C48,
  @pos = 1;
```

Now issue an INSERT statement:

```
INSERT INTO T1 VALUES(2);
```

You will get no output, telling you that the trigger got the signal and aborted.

When you want to clear the signal, issue the following code:

```
EXEC dbo.sp_TrgSignal_Clear @pos = 1;
```

Now that the signal is cleared, issue an INSERT statement:

```
INSERT INTO T1 VALUES(3);
```

The trigger's code will run in full again, producing the output:

```
trg_T1_i in action...
```

When you're done, run the following code for cleanup:

```
USE tempdb;
GO
IF OBJECT_ID('dbo.T1') IS NOT NULL
  DROP TABLE dbo.T1;
GO
USE master;
GO
IF OBJECT_ID('dbo.sp_TrgSignal_Set') IS NOT NULL
  DROP PROC dbo.sp_TrgSignal_Set;
GO
IF OBJECT_ID('dbo.sp_TrgSignal_Clear') IS NOT NULL
  DROP PROC dbo.sp_TrgSignal_Clear;
GO
IF OBJECT_ID('dbo.sp_TrgSignal_Get') IS NOT NULL
  DROP PROC dbo.sp_TrgSignal_Get;
```

Nesting and Recursion

SQL Server supports both nesting and recursion of triggers. Nesting of triggers takes place when a statement issued from one trigger causes another trigger to fire. Recursion takes place when a trigger ends up firing itself, either directly or through a series of other triggers. Nesting of triggers is controlled at the server level via the *'nested triggers'* server configuration option and is turned on by default. Recursion of triggers is controlled at the database level via the *RECURSIVE_TRIGGERS* database option and is turned off by default. Suppose that you want to allow trigger recursion in a database called HR; you would use the following code:

```
ALTER DATABASE HR SET RECURSIVE_TRIGGERS ON;
```

Recursion in general needs a termination check to stop the recursion from going infinitely. With triggers, of course, recursion won't be able to go infinitely because SQL Server has a hard-coded limit of 32 nesting levels of routines. However, once you reach that limit, the attempt to fire the 33rd trigger instance will break and all activity will be rolled back. Remember that triggers also fire for zero affected rows. If within the trigger you issue a modification that fires itself recursively, and you have no termination check, the trigger will continue firing recursively until it breaks the nesting limit. In short, make sure that you introduce a recursion termination check where you first verify whether you really need to issue a modification.

For example, suppose that you have an Employees table in the HR database. You want to write a trigger that will, upon a deletion of employees, delete direct subordinates of the deleted employees. You want the trigger to fire recursively so that all subordinates of the deleted employees in all levels will be deleted. The code for such a trigger involves a simple join between *deleted* and the Employees table. As the recursion termination check, you can inspect the value of *@@rowcount*. If the value is zero, abort the procedure. The result of this approach is that as soon as the previous invocation of the trigger deletes no employees, the trigger will abort and recursion will stop. Here's an example of what such a trigger might look like:

```
CREATE TRIGGER trg_Employees_d ON dbo.Employees FOR DELETE
AS

IF @@rowcount = 0 RETURN; -- recursion termination check

DELETE E
FROM dbo.Employees AS E
  JOIN deleted AS M
    ON E.mgrid = M.empid;
GO
```

Remember that if a constraint defined on the table rejects a modification, the trigger will not have a chance to fire. This would be the case for this trigger if you had a self-referencing foreign key defined on the *mgrid* column pointing to the *empid* column. Such a foreign key will reject any attempt to delete an employee who has subordinates, and the trigger will not have a chance to fire. To allow the trigger to fire, you would have to remove or disable the foreign key. But then, you will need to enforce referential integrity with your own code—for example, by using other triggers.

UPDATE and COLUMNS_UPDATED

When writing a trigger for an UPDATE statement, you sometimes want to react to the change only if certain columns were modified. For example, if you want to reject an attempt to modify a primary key value, you want to react only if the primary key column was specified as the target column in the SET clause of the firing UPDATE statement. SQL Server gives you two tools that allow you to identify whether certain columns were modified—the UPDATE predicate and the COLUMNS_UPDATED function.

The UPDATE predicate accepts a column name as input and returns TRUE if the input column was specified in the SET clause of the firing UPDATE statement. For example, to check whether a column called *empid* was modified, you would use the following:

```
IF UPDATE(empid) …
```

The UPDATE function will return TRUE for any column if you use it in an INSERT trigger.

The COLUMNS_UPDATED function returns a binary string with a bit for each column. You typically use it when you need to inspect multiple columns and you don't want to specify the UPDATE predicate many times. A bit representing a column will be turned on (1) if the column was modified and off (0) if it wasn't. The bytes within the string are organized from left to right—that is, the leftmost byte represents the first 8 columns (columns with ordinal positions 1 through 8), the second byte from the left represents the next 8 columns (columns with ordinal positions 9 through 16), and so on. Within each byte, the bits are organized from right to left—that is, the rightmost bit in the leftmost byte represents the first column, the second bit from the right represents the second column, and so on.

This organization of the bits might seem strange, but in practice, it makes a lot of sense. To check whether a certain column was modified, you need to use the bitwise AND (&) operator between the bitmap returned by COLUMNS_UPDATED and your own bitmask, which contains only the relevant bits turned on. However, bitwise operators in SQL Server require integer inputs (or inputs that can be implicitly converted to integers). COLUMNS_UPDATED might be longer than 8 bytes (the size of the largest supported integer—BIGINT). In that case, you would need to extract portions of the return value of COLUMNS_UPDATED using the SUBSTRING function. And for the SUBSTRING function, you specify an offset from the left of the input string. Thus, it's convenient that the bytes are organized from left to right.

For example, suppose that you want to isolate the byte containing the bit that represents a column with an ordinal position @i. The byte number (from the left) holding the relevant bit is this: $(@i - 1) / 8 + 1$. To extract that byte, you would use the following expression:

```
SUBSTRING(COLUMNS_UPDATED(),(@i - 1) / 8 + 1, 1)
```

As for the mask that you need to prepare for checking whether a certain bit is turned on, you generate it by raising 2 to the power that is one less than the bit position within the byte ($2^{bitpos-1}$). The expression calculating the bit position from the right within the byte (*bitpos*) for a column with an ordinal position @i is the following: $(@i - 1) \% 8 + 1$. So the expression generating the mask would be this: $POWER(2, (@i - 1) \% 8)$. To check whether that bit is actually turned on, you perform a bitwise AND (&) operation between the relevant byte and your mask. If the result is greater than zero, that bit is turned on. Here's the full test:

```
IF SUBSTRING(COLUMNS_UPDATED(),(@i - 1) / 8 + 1, 1) & POWER(2,(@i-1)%8) > 0
```

As a more tangible example, run the code in Listing 8-3 to create a table called T1 with 100 columns in addition to the key column, and query that table.

Listing 8-3 Create the table T1 with 100 columns

```
USE tempdb;
GO
IF OBJECT_ID('dbo.T1') IS NOT NULL
  DROP TABLE dbo.T1;
GO

DECLARE @cmd AS NVARCHAR(4000), @i AS INT;

SET @cmd =
  N'CREATE TABLE dbo.T1(keycol INT NOT NULL IDENTITY PRIMARY KEY';
```

```
SET @i = 1;
WHILE @i <= 100
BEGIN
  SET @cmd =
    @cmd + N',col' + CAST(@i AS nvarchar(10)) +
    N' INT NOT NULL DEFAULT 0';
  SET @i = @i + 1;
END

SET @cmd = @cmd + N');'

EXEC sp_executesql @cmd;

INSERT INTO dbo.T1 DEFAULT VALUES;

SELECT * FROM T1;
GO
```

The last query in Listing 8-3 produces the output shown in abbreviated form in Table 8-1.

Table 8-1   Contents of T1 with 100 Columns (Abbreviated)

keycol	col1	col2	col3	col4	col5	...	col100
1	0	0	0	0	0	...	0

Suppose that you need to write an UPDATE trigger that identifies which columns were modified (or more accurately, which columns were specified as the target for the modification in the SET clause of the UPDATE statement). You might need this information for auditing or other purposes. For the sake of our example, our trigger will simply return the set of modified columns to show that it could identify them. Run the code in Listing 8-4 to create the *trg_T1_u_identify_updated_columns*, which achieves this task.

Listing 8-4   Trigger that identifies which columns were updated

```
CREATE TRIGGER trg_T1_u_identify_updated_columns ON dbo.T1 FOR UPDATE
AS
SET NOCOUNT ON;

DECLARE @i AS INT, @numcols AS INT;
DECLARE @UpdCols TABLE(ordinal_position INT NOT NULL PRIMARY KEY);

SET @numcols =
 (SELECT COUNT(*)
  FROM INFORMATION_SCHEMA.COLUMNS
  WHERE TABLE_SCHEMA = 'dbo'
    AND TABLE_NAME = 'T1');

SET @i = 1;
WHILE @i <= @numcols
BEGIN
  IF (SUBSTRING(COLUMNS_UPDATED(),(@i - 1) / 8 + 1, 1))
      & POWER(2, (@i - 1) % 8) > 0
```

```
    INSERT INTO @UpdCols VALUES(@i);
  SET @i = @i + 1;
END

SELECT COLUMN_NAME AS updated_column
FROM INFORMATION_SCHEMA.COLUMNS AS C JOIN @UpdCols AS U
  ON C.ORDINAL_POSITION = U.ordinal_position
WHERE TABLE_SCHEMA = 'dbo'
  AND TABLE_NAME = 'T1'
ORDER BY C.ORDINAL_POSITION;
GO
```

The trigger defines a few local variables first. The variable @i will be used as a loop iterator, and it also represents the ordinal position of the current column being handled. The variable @numcols will hold the number of columns in the table. And @UpdCols is a table variable that will hold the set of ordinal positions representing the modified columns.

Following the variable declaration section, the trigger's code queries the INFORMATION_SCHEMA.COLUMNS view to acquire the number of columns in the table, and it then assigns that number to @numcols. The code then sets the variable @i to 1, enters a loop that iterates once per column, and increments @i by 1 in each iteration. Within the loop's body, the code checks whether the column with the ordinal position represented by @i was modified by using the expression that I described earlier. If the column was modified, the code inserts a row with the current value of @i to the @UpdCols table variable.

Finally, the trigger's code joins INFORMATION_SCHEMA.COLUMNS with @UpdCols based on ordinal position match, returning the names of the modified columns.

To test the trigger, issue the following UPDATE statement, and you will get the output shown in Table 8-2:

```
UPDATE dbo.T1
  SET col4 = 2, col8 = 2, col90 = 2, col6 = 2
WHERE keycol = 1;
```

Table 8-2   Set of Modified Columns

updated_column
col4
col6
col8
col90

When you're done, run the following code for cleanup:

```
IF OBJECT_ID('dbo.T1') IS NOT NULL
  DROP TABLE dbo.T1;
```

Auditing Example

In the previous example, in which I discussed the COLUMNS_UPDATED function, I provided a technique to identify which columns appeared as the target for the modification in the SET clause of the firing UPDATE statement. I mentioned that you might want to use that technique for auditing. However, you might want to audit actual changes in column values and not just the fact that a column was a target of a modification. To demonstrate the technique that will allow you to achieve such auditing, first run the code in Listing 8-5. This code creates a table called T1 and an audit table called T1Audit, in which you will store audit information about updates against T1.

Listing 8-5   Creation script for the T1 table and audit table

```
SET NOCOUNT ON;
USE tempdb;
GO

IF OBJECT_ID('dbo.T1') IS NOT NULL
  DROP TABLE dbo.T1;
GO
IF OBJECT_ID('dbo.T1Audit') IS NOT NULL
  DROP TABLE dbo.T1Audit;
GO

CREATE TABLE dbo.T1
(
  keycol INT NOT NULL PRIMARY KEY,
  intcol INT NULL,
  varcharcol VARCHAR(10) NULL
);
GO

CREATE TABLE dbo.T1Audit
(
  lsn     INT        NOT NULL IDENTITY PRIMARY KEY, -- log serial number
  keycol  INT        NOT NULL,
  colname sysname    NOT NULL,
  oldval  SQL_VARIANT NULL,
  newval  SQL_VARIANT NULL
);
GO
```

Run the code in Listing 8-6 to create the trigger *trg_T1_U_Audit*, which records audit information about updates against T1 in T1Audit.

Listing 8-6   Creation script for the *trg_T1_U_Audit* trigger

```
CREATE TRIGGER trg_T1_u_audit ON dbo.T1 FOR UPDATE
AS

-- If 0 affected rows, do nothing
```

```
    IF @@rowcount = 0 RETURN;

    INSERT INTO dbo.T1Audit(keycol, colname, oldval, newval)
      SELECT *
      FROM (SELECT I.keycol, colname,
              CASE colname
                WHEN N'intcol' THEN CAST(D.intcol AS SQL_VARIANT)
                WHEN N'varcharcol' THEN CAST(D.varcharcol AS SQL_VARIANT)
              END AS oldval,
              CASE colname
                WHEN N'intcol' THEN CAST(I.intcol AS SQL_VARIANT)
                WHEN N'varcharcol' THEN CAST(I.varcharcol AS SQL_VARIANT)
              END AS newval
            FROM inserted AS I
              JOIN deleted AS D
                ON I.keycol = D.keycol
              CROSS JOIN
                (SELECT N'intcol' AS colname
                 UNION ALL SELECT N'varcharcol') AS C) AS D
      WHERE oldval <> newval
         OR (oldval IS NULL AND newval IS NOT NULL)
         OR (oldval IS NOT NULL AND newval IS NULL);
    GO
```

The trigger's code first checks whether zero rows were affected by the firing UPDATE statement. If that is the case, it aborts. There's nothing to audit if nothing changed.

The code then uses a query that joins *inserted* and *deleted* by matching their *keycol* values. The query uses an unpivoting technique to rotate each column value from both *inserted* and *deleted* to its own row.

> **More Info** For details about unpivoting techniques, please refer to my book *Inside Microsoft SQL Server 2005: T-SQL Querying* (Microsoft Press, 2006).

The query filters only rows where the new value is different than the old value, taking NULLs into consideration as well. An INSERT statement loads the result of the query into the audit table.

To test the audit trigger, first load a few rows to T1:

```
INSERT INTO dbo.T1(keycol, intcol, varcharcol) VALUES(1, 10, 'A');
INSERT INTO dbo.T1(keycol, intcol, varcharcol) VALUES(2, 20, 'B');
INSERT INTO dbo.T1(keycol, intcol, varcharcol) VALUES(3, 30, 'C');
```

Then issue the following UPDATE:

```
UPDATE dbo.T1
  SET varcharcol = varcharcol + 'X',
      intcol = 40 - intcol
WHERE keycol < 3;
```

Query the tables T1Audit and T1A, and you will get the results shown in Tables 8-3 and 8-4, respectively:

```
SELECT * FROM dbo.T1;
SELECT * FROM dbo.T1Audit;
```

Table 8-3   Contents of T1Audit

keycol	intcol	varcharcol
1	30	AX
2	20	BX
3	30	C

Table 8-4   Contents of T1

lsn	keycol	colname	oldval	newval
1	2	varcharcol	B	BX
2	1	Intcol	10	30
3	1	varcharcol	A	AX

As you can see, only column values that actually changed were audited.

> **Tip**   Suppose that your trigger performs an integrity check and issues a rollback if the integrity rule is violated. And suppose that you still want to audit the attempt even though you're rolling it back. Of course, a rollback issued after the auditing activity will also roll back the auditing activity. On the other hand, if the rollback is issued before the auditing activity, *inserted* and *deleted* will be empty after the rollback, and you'll be left with no data to audit. It's sort of a Catch-22 situation.
>
> Remember from Chapter 2 that table variables—like any other variables—are not affected by a rollback, as they are not considered part of an external transaction. You can use this behavior to your advantage. Upon detection of the integrity rule violation, copy the content of *inserted* and *deleted* into your own table variables; issue the rollback; and then, in a new transaction within the trigger, audit that data.

When you're done, run the following code for cleanup:

```
IF OBJECT_ID('dbo.T1') IS NOT NULL
   DROP TABLE dbo.T1;
GO
IF OBJECT_ID('dbo.T1Audit') IS NOT NULL
   DROP TABLE dbo.T1Audit;
```

INSTEAD OF Triggers

INSTEAD OF triggers fire instead of the original modification that was issued against the target object. The concept is a bit tricky: these are not BEFORE triggers that fire before the original statement actually runs; rather, they run instead of it. The original statement never reaches the target object. Rather, the trigger's code replaces it. If the trigger is supposed to apply some integrity check and the modification passes the check, you will need to write your own code that "resubmits" the original activity. You can do so by querying the *inserted* or *deleted* table. Note that in an INSTEAD OF trigger, *inserted* and *deleted* hold the data that was supposed to be changed, as opposed to holding the data that actually changed.

If you don't take any course of action in an INSTEAD OF trigger, the original change simply evaporates. If you're fond of practical jokes, create an INSTEAD OF INSERT, UPDATE, DELETE trigger on some table where the trigger doesn't perform any activity. The trigger's body still needs some code within it to be valid, so declare a variable or issue any other statement that has no visibility. Now wait. It can be really perplexing for people who try to issue a modification against the table when their attempt has no effect whatsoever on the data. Of course, I must add the caution: DO NOT DO THIS IN PRODUCTION. You can do this as a puzzle to test your colleagues—create a table with such a trigger and ask them to figure out why changes do not have any effect.

Unlike AFTER triggers, INSTEAD OF triggers can be created on views, not just tables. You can create only one such trigger for each statement type on each object. INSTEAD OF triggers do not fire recursively.

One of the nice things about INSTEAD OF triggers is that they fire before constraints are checked. This means that you can identify activities that would normally fail on a constraint violation and replace them with code that will not fail. For example, a multirow insert that attempts to introduce a duplicate key would normally be rolled back completely because the whole insert is considered a transaction. If you want to allow the rows that do not introduce duplicate keys to be inserted, and you can't change the source code, you can create an INSTEAD OF trigger to insert into the table only rows from *inserted* with distinct keys not already in the table. Another option is to specify the IGNORE_DUP_KEY option when creating the index.

INSTEAD OF triggers can also be used to circumvent limitations of modifications against views. I described those limitations in Chapter 5. For example, you're not allowed to update a column in a view that is a result of a calculation. With an INSTEAD OF trigger, you can reverse-engineer such a modification and issue a modification to the underlying table.

The following sections demonstrate a few scenarios where INSTEAD OF triggers can come in handy.

Per-Row Triggers

Suppose that you have a table with an AFTER trigger that works well only for single-row modifications and breaks for multirow ones. You need to support multirow modifications, but you're not allowed to modify the trigger's code. Maybe the code was developed by a third party with the ENCRYPTION option and you don't have access to the source code. Or maybe the trigger was created by another developer and you're not allowed to change it.

To demonstrate an example for a trigger that would work well only for single-row modifications, first run the following code, which creates the table T1:

```
USE tempdb;
GO
IF OBJECT_ID('dbo.T1') IS NOT NULL
  DROP TABLE dbo.T1;
GO

CREATE TABLE dbo.T1
(
  keycol  INT NOT NULL PRIMARY KEY,
  datacol INT NOT NULL
);
```

Run the following code to create an AFTER INSERT trigger called *trg_T1_i* on T1:

```
CREATE TRIGGER trg_T1_i ON T1 AFTER INSERT
AS

DECLARE @msg AS VARCHAR(100);
SET @msg = 'Key: '
  + CAST((SELECT keycol FROM inserted) AS VARCHAR(10)) + ' inserted.';
PRINT @msg;
GO
```

The trigger constructs a message with the *keycol* value of the row that was inserted and prints it. It uses a subquery to fetch the *keycol* value from *inserted*.

If you load a single row to the table, the trigger works well:

```
INSERT INTO dbo.T1(keycol, datacol) VALUES(1, 10);
```

You get the output:

```
Key: 1 inserted.
```

However, when you issue a multirow insert, the trigger fails:

```
INSERT INTO dbo.T1(keycol, datacol)
  SELECT 2, 20
  UNION ALL
  SELECT 3, 30
  UNION ALL
  SELECT 4, 40;
```

The trigger produces the following error:

```
Server: Msg 512, Level 16, State 1, Procedure trg_T1_i, Line 7
Subquery returned more than 1 value. This is not permitted when the subquery follows =, !=,
<, <= , >, >= or when the subquery is used as an expression.
The statement has been terminated.
```

The error was generated because a subquery that was used where a scalar value was expected produced multiple values. Assuming that you're not allowed to alter the trigger's code, you can tackle the problem by creating an INSTEAD OF INSERT trigger. You can use the technique I showed earlier to iterate through the rows in *inserted* to collect the values from each row and issue a single row insert for each source row against the target table. Each insert will cause a different instance of the AFTER trigger to fire, but it will fire for a row at a time. Run the code in Listing 8-7 to create such an INSTEAD OF trigger.

Listing 8-7   Creation script for the *trg_T1_ioi_perrow* trigger

```
CREATE TRIGGER trg_T1_ioi_perrow ON dbo.T1 INSTEAD OF INSERT
AS

DECLARE @rc AS INT;
SET @rc = @@rowcount;
IF @rc = 0 RETURN;

IF @rc = 1
  INSERT INTO dbo.T1 SELECT * FROM inserted;
ELSE
BEGIN
  DECLARE @keycol AS INT, @datacol AS INT;

  DECLARE Cinserted CURSOR FAST_FORWARD FOR
    SELECT keycol, datacol FROM inserted;
  OPEN Cinserted;

  FETCH NEXT FROM Cinserted INTO @keycol, @datacol;
  WHILE @@fetch_status = 0
  BEGIN
    INSERT INTO dbo.T1(keycol, datacol)
      VALUES(@keycol, @datacol);
    FETCH NEXT FROM Cinserted INTO @keycol, @datacol;
  END

  CLOSE Cinserted;
  DEALLOCATE Cinserted;
END
GO
```

The trigger's code uses the technique I described earlier to apply a course of action that depends on the number of affected rows, only this time using a cursor to iterate through the rows in *inserted*. If zero rows were affected, the trigger exits. If one row was affected, the trigger loads the row from *inserted* into T1, causing the AFTER trigger to fire for that row. If multiple rows were affected, the trigger uses a cursor to iterate through the rows in *inserted*, one at a time, collecting the values from the current row in each iteration, and it then inserts a row to T1 with those values. As a result, the AFTER trigger will fire once for each row.

To test the trigger, first issue the following INSERT statement, which loads a single row to T1:

```
INSERT INTO dbo.T1(keycol, datacol) VALUES(5, 50);
```

You will get the output:

```
Key: 5 inserted.
```

Try loading multiple rows using a single INSERT statement:

```
INSERT INTO dbo.T1(keycol, datacol)
  SELECT 6, 60
  UNION ALL
  SELECT 7, 70
  UNION ALL
  SELECT 8, 80;
```

The statement will run successfully, producing the following output:

```
Key: 6 inserted.
Key: 7 inserted.
Key: 8 inserted.
```

When you're done, run the following code for cleanup:

```
IF OBJECT_ID('dbo.T1') IS NOT NULL
  DROP TABLE dbo.T1;
```

Used with Views

The following example will demonstrate how to use an INSTEAD OF TRIGGER to support UPDATE statements against a view that would have not been supported otherwise.

Suppose that you have a table with order details and a view that aggregates order detail quantities per order. Run the code in Listing 8-8 to create the OrderDetails table, populate it with sample data, and create the *VOrderTotals* view, which calculates the sum of the quantity for each order.

Listing 8-8   Creation script for OrderDetails table and *VOrderTotals* view

```
USE tempdb;
GO
IF OBJECT_ID('dbo.VOrderTotals') IS NOT NULL
  DROP VIEW dbo.VOrderTotals;
GO
IF OBJECT_ID('dbo.OrderDetails') IS NOT NULL
  DROP TABLE dbo.OrderDetails;
GO

CREATE TABLE dbo.OrderDetails
(
  oid  INT NOT NULL,
```

```
    pid INT NOT NULL,
    qty INT NOT NULL,
    PRIMARY KEY(oid, pid)
);

INSERT INTO dbo.OrderDetails(oid, pid, qty) VALUES(10248, 1, 10);
INSERT INTO dbo.OrderDetails(oid, pid, qty) VALUES(10248, 2, 20);
INSERT INTO dbo.OrderDetails(oid, pid, qty) VALUES(10248, 3, 30);
INSERT INTO dbo.OrderDetails(oid, pid, qty) VALUES(10249, 1, 5);
INSERT INTO dbo.OrderDetails(oid, pid, qty) VALUES(10249, 2, 10);
INSERT INTO dbo.OrderDetails(oid, pid, qty) VALUES(10249, 3, 15);
INSERT INTO dbo.OrderDetails(oid, pid, qty) VALUES(10250, 1, 20);
INSERT INTO dbo.OrderDetails(oid, pid, qty) VALUES(10250, 2, 20);
INSERT INTO dbo.OrderDetails(oid, pid, qty) VALUES(10250, 3, 20);
GO

CREATE VIEW dbo.VOrderTotals
AS

SELECT oid, SUM(qty) AS totalqty
FROM dbo.OrderDetails
GROUP BY oid;
GO
```

Suppose that you want to allow updating the *totalqty* column and distribute the new value between the order details of the affected order by the same proportions that they had before the update. The trigger shown in Listing 8-9 achieves this task.

Listing 8-9   Creation script for *trg_VOrderTotals_ioi* trigger

```
CREATE TRIGGER trg_VOrderTotals_ioi ON dbo.VOrderTotals INSTEAD OF UPDATE
AS

IF @@rowcount = 0 RETURN;

IF UPDATE(oid)
BEGIN
  RAISERROR('Updates to the OrderID column are not allowed.', 16, 1);
  ROLLBACK TRAN;
  RETURN;
END;

WITH UPD_CTE AS
(
  SELECT qty, ROUND(1.*OD.qty / D.totalqty * I.totalqty, 0) AS newqty
  FROM dbo.OrderDetails AS OD
    JOIN inserted AS I
      ON OD.oid = I.oid
    JOIN deleted AS D
      ON I.oid = D.oid
)
UPDATE UPD_CTE
  SET qty = newqty;
GO
```

The trigger's code exits if no rows were updated. It then checks whether there was an attempt to update the order ID (*oid* column). If there was such an attempt, the trigger generates an error and rolls back the activity. The trigger then creates a common table expression (CTE) that joins *inserted*, *deleted*, and the OrderDetails table. The *deleted* view holds the value of *totalqty* before the update, and *inserted* holds the value after the update. The OrderDetails table is added to the join to gain access to the original quantity of each order detail row, and it will also end up being the actual target of the modification. The CTE's query calculates the portion each order detail row should get based on the original proportions (original quantity / original total quantity × new total quantity, rounded). The outer UPDATE statement updates the *qty* column in OrderDetails with the newly calculated quantity.

Run the following code to test the trigger:

```
SELECT oid, pid, qty FROM dbo.OrderDetails;
SELECT oid, totalqty FROM dbo.VOrderTotals;

UPDATE dbo.VOrderTotals
  SET totalqty = totalqty * 2;

SELECT oid, pid, qty FROM dbo.OrderDetails;
SELECT oid, totalqty FROM dbo.VOrderTotals;
```

The code first queries both OrderDetails and *VOrderTotals*, then it issues an UPDATE statement, and then it queries OrderDetails and *VOrderTotals* again. Tables 8-5 and 8-6 show the contents of the table and view, respectively, before the change. Tables 8-7 and 8-8 show the contents of the table and view, respectively, after the change.

Table 8-5   Contents of OrderDetails Before Update

oid	pid	qty
10248	1	10
10248	2	20
10248	3	30
10249	1	5
10249	2	10
10249	3	15
10250	1	20
10250	2	20
10250	3	20

Table 8-6   Contents of *VOrderTotals* Before Update

oid	totalqty
10248	60
10249	30
10250	60

Table 8-7   Contents of OrderDetails After Update

oid	pid	qty
10248	1	20
10248	2	40
10248	3	60
10249	1	10
10249	2	20
10249	3	30
10250	1	40
10250	2	40
10250	3	40

Table 8-8   Contents of *VOrderTotals* After Update

oid	totalqty
10248	120
10249	60
10250	120

When you're done, run the following code for cleanup:

```
IF OBJECT_ID('dbo.VOrderTotals') IS NOT NULL
  DROP VIEW dbo.VOrderTotals;
GO
IF OBJECT_ID('dbo.OrderDetails') IS NOT NULL
  DROP TABLE dbo.OrderDetails;
```

Automatic Handling of Sequences

Suppose that you maintain your own custom sequence instead of relying on the IDENTITY column property to generate numbers that will be used as keys in a table called T1. You achieve this by holding a value in a table called Sequence, and the value represents the last assigned sequence value. Whenever you need a new sequence value, you increment the value in the Sequence table and use it as the new key in T1.

Run the following code to create the table T1:

```
SET NOCOUNT ON;
USE tempdb;
GO
IF OBJECT_ID('dbo.T1') IS NOT NULL
  DROP TABLE dbo.T1;
GO
CREATE TABLE dbo.T1
(
  keycol  INT NOT NULL PRIMARY KEY,
  datacol VARCHAR(10) NOT NULL
);
```

Then run the following code to create and initialize the Sequence table:

```
IF OBJECT_ID('dbo.Sequence') IS NOT NULL
  DROP TABLE dbo.Sequence;
GO
CREATE TABLE dbo.Sequence(val INT NOT NULL);
INSERT INTO dbo.Sequence VALUES(0);
```

When you need a new sequence value, you can issue the following code:

```
DECLARE @key AS INT;
UPDATE dbo.Sequence SET @key = val = val + 1;
```

This code declares a local variable called *@key*, issues a specialized UPDATE statement that increments the *val* column value by one, and stores the result in the variable *@key*. You're effectively both updating and selecting the sequence value at the same time in an atomic operation. Suppose that you want to automate the process of assigning keys to new rows using a trigger, and you also want to support multirow inserts. An AFTER trigger would not be a good choice because the primary key will reject an attempt to load multiple rows where the key values are not specified.

Remember that an INSTEAD OF trigger is fired instead of the original modification; therefore, such a trigger will allow a multirow insert where the keys weren't specified. All rows will get the default value *0*, and the trigger can generate a different key for each row. The trigger will then insert rows into T1 with newly generated keys, while the rest of the columns (only *datacol* in our case) can be grabbed from *inserted*.

Here's the code of the INSTEAD OF trigger that will achieve the task—generating new keys and loading them along with the other attributes from the original INSERT statement:

```
CREATE TRIGGER trg_T1_ioi_assign_key ON dbo.T1 INSTEAD OF INSERT
AS

DECLARE @rc AS INT, @key AS INT;
SET @rc = @@rowcount;

IF @rc = 0 RETURN; -- if 0 affected rows, exit

-- Update sequence
UPDATE dbo.Sequence SET @key = val, val = val + @rc;

INSERT INTO dbo.T1(keycol, datacol)
  SELECT @key + ROW_NUMBER() OVER(ORDER BY const), datacol
  FROM (SELECT 1 AS const, datacol FROM inserted) AS I;
GO
```

The trigger's code first checks whether zero rows were loaded. If that's the case, it exits. The code then uses an UPDATE statement to assign the current value of the sequence to the variable *@key* and increment the sequence value by the number of affected rows—that is, it acquires a whole block of sequence values in one shot. Next, the trigger issues an INSERT statement that loads all rows from *inserted* into T1, generating new key values by adding a row number value to @*key*. The ORDER BY clause of the ROW_NUMBER function has no effect on the assignment order of the row numbers. The value of *const* will be 1 in all rows anyway. The reason for using this ORDER BY clause is that it's not optional in the ROW_NUMBER function. Of course, if you want to assign keys based on some specific order, specify the relevant attribute in the ORDER BY clause.

To test the trigger, issue the following INSERT statement:

```
INSERT INTO dbo.T1(datacol)
  SELECT LastName FROM Northwind.dbo.Employees;
```

If you query T1, you will get the output shown in Table 8-9:

```
SELECT keycol, datacol FROM dbo.T1;
```

Table 8-9   Contents of T1

keycol	datacol
1	Buchanan
2	Callahan
3	Davolio
4	Dodsworth
5	Fuller
6	King
7	Leverling
8	Peacock
9	Suyama

When you're done, run the following code for cleanup:

```
IF OBJECT_ID('dbo.T1') IS NOT NULL
  DROP TABLE dbo.T1;
GO
IF OBJECT_ID('dbo.Sequence') IS NOT NULL
  DROP TABLE dbo.Sequence;
```

DDL Triggers

DDL triggers allow you to respond to DDL events issued against the database server. You can use these triggers to roll back schema changes that don't meet rules that you want to enforce, audit schema changes, or react to a schema change in a form that makes sense for your environment.

> **Note**   SQL Server supports only AFTER triggers for DDL. If you want a trigger to reject the schema change that caused it to fire you must issue a ROLLBACK TRAN command in the trigger.

You can create DDL triggers either at the database level or at the server (instance) level. You can create those for particular DDL statements (for example, CREATE TABLE) or for statement groups (for example, DDL_DATABASE_LEVEL_EVENTS). Please consult Books Online for the gory details about the hierarchy of statements and statement groups for which you can define DDL triggers.

Within the trigger, you can get information about the event that fired it via the *eventdata* function. This function returns an XML value with the event information. For different types of statements, you will get different information from the *eventdata* function. As an example, here's the XML value returned by the *eventdata* function for a CREATE TABLE statement:

```
<EVENT_INSTANCE>
  <EventType>CREATE_TABLE</EventType>
  <PostTime>2006-08-28T19:52:34.250</PostTime>
  <SPID>51</SPID>
  <ServerName>DOJO\S2</ServerName>
  <LoginName>DOJO\itzik</LoginName>
  <UserName>dbo</UserName>
  <DatabaseName>testdb</DatabaseName>
  <SchemaName>dbo</SchemaName>
  <ObjectName>T1</ObjectName>
  <ObjectType>TABLE</ObjectType>
  <TSQLCommand>
    <SetOptions ANSI_NULLS="ON" ANSI_NULL_DEFAULT="ON" ANSI_PADDING="ON" QUOTED_IDENTIFIER=
      "ON" ENCRYPTED="FALSE" />
    <CommandText>CREATE TABLE dbo.T1(col1 INT NOT NULL PRIMARY KEY);
</CommandText>
  </TSQLCommand>
</EVENT_INSTANCE>
```

As you can see, you get a lot of useful information about the event, including the event type, when it was posted, the server process ID of the session, the instance name, the login name, the user name, the database name, the schema name of the object, the object name, the object type, the state of SET options, and even the actual T-SQL statement that caused the trigger to fire.

You can query the event information from the XML value by using XQuery.

> **More Info**   For information about XML and XQuery, please refer to Chapter 1.

To extract a particular attribute from the XML value, you use the following XQuery expression: *xml_value.query('data(//attribute_name)')*. *xml_value* will typically be a variable to which you assigned the XML value returned by the *eventdata* function, and *attribute_name* is the name of the attribute you want to extract. That's about all you need to know about XML and XQuery to grab the attributes out of the XML value. All the rest is just code that implements the logic you want your trigger to apply.

In the following sections, I will provide examples of both database-level DDL triggers and server-level ones.

Database-Level Triggers

Database-level DDL triggers allow you to react to database-level events, such as creating, altering, or dropping objects. Here's the syntax for the header of a database-level DDL trigger:

```
CREATE TRIGGER <trigger name>
  ON DATABASE
  FOR <one or more statements or statement groups>
```

You must be connected to the target database when creating the trigger.

In my examples, I will use a database called testdb, which you create by running the following code:

```
USE master;
GO
IF DB_ID('testdb') IS NOT NULL
  DROP DATABASE testdb;
GO
CREATE DATABASE testdb;
GO
USE testdb;
```

Suppose that you want to enforce a company policy in the testdb database that says that when you create a table you must define a primary key. You create the trigger shown in Listing 8-10 to achieve this task.

Listing 8-10   Creation script for *trg_create_table_with_pk* trigger

```
CREATE TRIGGER trg_create_table_with_pk ON DATABASE FOR CREATE_TABLE
AS

DECLARE @eventdata AS XML, @objectname AS NVARCHAR(257),
  @msg AS NVARCHAR(500);

SET @eventdata = eventdata();
SET @objectname =
  + QUOTENAME(CAST(@eventdata.query('data(//SchemaName)') AS sysname))
  + N'.' +
  QUOTENAME(CAST(@eventdata.query('data(//ObjectName)') AS sysname));

IF COALESCE(
    OBJECTPROPERTY(OBJECT_ID(@objectname), 'TableHasPrimaryKey'),
    0) = 0
BEGIN
  SET @msg = N'Table ' + @objectname + ' does not contain a primary key.'
    + CHAR(10) + N'Table creation rolled back.';
  RAISERROR(@msg, 16, 1);
  ROLLBACK;
  RETURN;
END
GO
```

The trigger is naturally created for CREATE_TABLE statements. The trigger's code first assigns the return XML value from the *eventdata* function to a local variable called *@eventdata*. The code then extracts the event attributes *SchemaName* and *ObjectName*, using XQuery expressions, and it constructs a schema-qualified table name in the *@objectname* variable. Finally, the code uses the OBJECTPROPERTY function to check whether the table contains a primary key. If it doesn't, the code generates an error message and rolls back the table creation.

To test the trigger, first try to create a table without a primary key:

```
CREATE TABLE dbo.T(col1 INT NOT NULL);
```

You will get the following error:

```
Server: Msg 50000, Level 16, State 1, Procedure trg_create_table_with_pk, Line 19
Table [dbo].[T] does not contain a primary key.
Table creation rolled back.
Server: Msg 3609, Level 16, State 1, Line 1
The transaction ended in the trigger. The batch has been aborted.
```

Then try to create a table with a primary key, and your code will run successfully:

```
CREATE TABLE dbo.T(col1 INT NOT NULL PRIMARY KEY);
```

As I mentioned earlier, DDL triggers can be used to audit DDL events—finally! The trigger's implementation is straightforward: use XQuery expressions to query the individual event attributes that you want to audit and load them to the audit table. That's all there is to it. As an example, run the code in Listing 8-11 to create the AuditDDLEvents table and the *trg_audit_ddl_events* trigger.

Listing 8-11   Creation script for AuditDDLEvents table and *trg_audit_ddl_events* trigger

```
IF OBJECT_ID('dbo.AuditDDLEvents') IS NOT NULL
  DROP TABLE dbo.AuditDDLEvents;
GO

CREATE TABLE dbo.AuditDDLEvents
(
  lsn              INT      NOT NULL IDENTITY,
  posttime         DATETIME NOT NULL,
  eventtype        sysname  NOT NULL,
  loginname        sysname  NOT NULL,
  schemaname       sysname  NOT NULL,
  objectname       sysname  NOT NULL,
  targetobjectname sysname  NOT NULL,
  eventdata        XML      NOT NULL,
  CONSTRAINT PK_AuditDDLEvents PRIMARY KEY(lsn)
);
GO


CREATE TRIGGER trg_audit_ddl_events ON DATABASE FOR DDL_DATABASE_LEVEL_EVENTS
AS
```

```
DECLARE @eventdata AS XML;
SET @eventdata = eventdata();

INSERT INTO dbo.AuditDDLEvents(
  posttime, eventtype, loginname, schemaname,
  objectname, targetobjectname, eventdata)
  VALUES(
    CAST(@eventdata.query('data(//PostTime)')         AS VARCHAR(23)),
    CAST(@eventdata.query('data(//EventType)')        AS sysname),
    CAST(@eventdata.query('data(//LoginName)')        AS sysname),
    CAST(@eventdata.query('data(//SchemaName)')       AS sysname),
    CAST(@eventdata.query('data(//ObjectName)')       AS sysname),
    CAST(@eventdata.query('data(//TargetObjectName)') AS sysname),
    @eventdata);
GO
```

The trigger is so simple that all it has is an assignment of the *eventdata* value to a local XML variable and a single INSERT statement that loads the event attributes into the audit table. Note that it also loads the full XML value in case you want to query attributes that were not extracted individually.

To test the trigger, issue the following DDL events:

```
CREATE TABLE dbo.T1(col1 INT NOT NULL PRIMARY KEY);
ALTER TABLE dbo.T1 ADD col2 INT NULL;
ALTER TABLE dbo.T1 ALTER COLUMN col2 INT NOT NULL;
CREATE NONCLUSTERED INDEX idx1 ON dbo.T1(col2);
```

Then query the audit table, and you will get the output shown in abbreviated form in Table 8-10:

```
SELECT * FROM dbo.AuditDDLEvents;
```

Table 8-10   Contents of AuditDDLEvents (Abbreviated)

lsn	posttime	eventtype	loginname	schema-name	object-name	target-object	event-data
1	2006-08-28 20:51:19.943	CREATE_TABLE	DOJO\itzik	dbo	T1		XML value
2	2006-08-28 20:51:20.123	ALTER_TABLE	DOJO\itzik	dbo	T1		XML value
3	2006-08-28 20:51:20.173	ALTER_TABLE	DOJO\itzik	dbo	T1		XML value
4	2006-08-28 20:51:20.183	CREATE_INDEX	DOJO\itzik	dbo	idx1	T1	XML value

Of course, you will get different values in *posttime* and *loginname* attributes.

Suppose that you come to work next morning and realize that schema changes took place against a table called T1. You realize this after users keep calling you complaining that the application breaks. You ask around to see whether someone applied a schema change to T1 in the last 24 hours, but naturally everyone is silent, choosing to exercise their Fifth Amendment rights. Fortunately (for you), you can query the audit table. You can even use an XQuery expression to extract event attributes that were not recorded individually. Here's the query that you would use, producing the output shown in Table 8-11:

```
SELECT posttime, eventtype, loginname,
  CAST(eventdata.query('data(//TSQLCommand)') AS NVARCHAR(2000))
  AS tsqlcommand
FROM dbo.AuditDDLEvents
WHERE schemaname = N'dbo' AND N'T1' IN(objectname, targetobjectname)
  AND posttime > GETDATE() - 1
ORDER BY posttime;
```

Table 8-11   Audit Events in the Last 24 Hours

posttime	eventtype	loginname	tslcommand
2006-08-28 20:51:19.943	CREATE_TABLE	DOJO\itzik	CREATE TABLE dbo.T1(col1 INT NOT NULL PRIMARY KEY);
2006-08-28 20:51:20.123	ALTER_TABLE	DOJO\itzik	ALTER TABLE dbo.T1 ADD col2 INT NULL;
2006-08-28 20:51:20.173	ALTER_TABLE	DOJO\itzik	ALTER TABLE dbo.T1 ALTER COLUMN col2 INT NOT NULL;
2006-08-28 20:51:20.183	CREATE_INDEX	DOJO\itzik	CREATE NONCLUSTERED INDEX idx1 ON dbo.T1(col2);

Now you know exactly which schema changes took place and who submitted them—in some cases, you see that it was you who applied the change and that you suffered from a slight case of amnesia.

> **Caution**   XML quoting of certain characters creates a security problem. Hackers can inject XML elements through object names or even character strings in the statement that fires the trigger. For example, if you create a table called [>], the XML value returned by the eventdata() function will have the object name: *>*, and the command text *CREATE TABLE [>](c int);*.

Note that SQL Server Management Studio (SSMS) provides solutions to some of the needs that I discussed in this section. For example, one of the reports on the SSMS summary page is "Schema change history," so a DDL trigger is not the only option for this.

When you're done, run the following code for cleanup:

```
USE master;
GO
IF DB_ID('testdb') IS NOT NULL
  DROP DATABASE testdb;
```

Server-Level Triggers

Server-level DDL triggers can be defined for server-level events. Examples of such events are creation of databases, changes to logins, and so on. You develop server-level triggers in a similar manner to database-level ones. In the trigger's header, you specify the following: ON ALL SERVER instead of ON DATABASE.

As an example, suppose that you want to audit CREATE, ALTER, and DROP statements for logins. Run the code in Listing 8-12 to create the AuditDDLLogins table and the *trg_audit_ddl_logins* trigger.

Listing 8-12   Creation script for AuditDDLLogins table and *trg_audit_ddl_logins* trigger

```
USE master;
GO
IF OBJECT_ID('dbo.AuditDDLLogins') IS NOT NULL
  DROP TABLE dbo.AuditDDLLogins;
GO

CREATE TABLE dbo.AuditDDLLogins
(
  lsn            INT      NOT NULL IDENTITY,
  posttime       DATETIME NOT NULL,
  eventtype      sysname  NOT NULL,
  loginname      sysname  NOT NULL,
  objectname     sysname  NOT NULL,
  logintype      sysname  NOT NULL,
  eventdata      XML      NOT NULL,
  CONSTRAINT PK_AuditDDLLogins PRIMARY KEY(lsn)
);
GO

CREATE TRIGGER trg_audit_ddl_logins ON ALL SERVER
  FOR DDL_LOGIN_EVENTS
AS
DECLARE @eventdata AS XML;
SET @eventdata = eventdata();

INSERT INTO master.dbo.AuditDDLLogins(
  posttime, eventtype, loginname,
  objectname, logintype, eventdata)
  VALUES(
    CAST(@eventdata.query('data(//PostTime)')    AS VARCHAR(23)),
    CAST(@eventdata.query('data(//EventType)')   AS sysname),
    CAST(@eventdata.query('data(//LoginName)')   AS sysname),
    CAST(@eventdata.query('data(//ObjectName)')  AS sysname),
    CAST(@eventdata.query('data(//LoginType)')   AS sysname),
    @eventdata);
GO
```

This audit trigger's code is almost identical to the audit trigger you created earlier; it just has different event attributes, which are relevant to login-related DDL events.

> **Caution**   Note that this trigger suffers from the same security problem as before with characters that XML must quote. Try, for example, to create a login called *[l<gin]*, and you will find that the login name that appears in the audit table is *l<gin*.

To test the trigger, issue the following login-related statements for creating, altering, and dropping a login:

```
CREATE LOGIN login1 WITH PASSWORD = '123';
ALTER LOGIN login1 WITH PASSWORD = 'xyz';
DROP LOGIN login1;
```

Next query the audit table, and you will get the output shown in abbreviated form in Table 8-12:

```
SELECT * FROM master.dbo.AuditDDLLogins;
```

Table 8-12   Contents of AuditDDLLogins (Abbreviated)

lsn	posttime	eventtype	loginname	objectname	logintype	eventdata
1	2005-08-28 21:01:54.083	CREATE_LOGIN	DOJO\itzik	login1	SQL Login	XML Value
2	2005-08-28 21:01:54.203	ALTER_LOGIN	DOJO\itzik	login1	SQL Login	XML Value
3	2005-08-28 21:01:54.257	DROP_LOGIN	DOJO\itzik	login1	SQL Login	XML Value

When you're done, run the following code for cleanup:

```
DROP TRIGGER trg_audit_ddl_logins ON ALL SERVER;
GO
IF OBJECT_ID('dbo.AuditDDLLogins') IS NOT NULL
  DROP TABLE dbo.AuditDDLLogins;
```

CLR Triggers

As it does with other types of routines, SQL Server 2005 allows you to use a .NET language of your choice to develop common language runtime (CLR) triggers. This capability is especially useful when you want your routines to perform activity for which T-SQL is weak at, such as complex calculations, procedural logic, or access to external resources. In this section, I will provide an example for a CLR trigger, though I have to say that I find the whole idea of developing triggers with CLR code moot.

As an example, you will be provided with a trigger that audits the data from *inserted* and *deleted* for DML triggers in the Microsoft Windows event application log. Auditing to the Windows event log gives you similar functionality as auditing to a table variable—you still have the audited information, even if the transaction is later rolled back.

When I was thinking about an example for a CLR trigger, I wanted to create a trigger that would send an e-mail at first. But then I realized this would be a bad example. Remember that a trigger is part of the transaction, and resources are locked during the transaction. Depending on the action issued and isolation level used, locks can be held until the end of the transaction. Sending e-mail can take a while. Also, if you want to send an e-mail from a trigger, you should also be prepared for different kinds of problems—for example, an SMTP of MAPI server could be stopped. The local event log should always be available or otherwise full, and writing to it is faster than sending e-mail. Keep in mind though, that writing to the local event log may still cause performance problems.

Note the importance of the previous paragraph. Because a trigger is part of a transaction, you should be very careful with the code you issue from the trigger; it should always run as fast as possible. I prefer to have only Transact-SQL statements in the body of a trigger. This way you have more control and you can test the performance easier. Imagine there is a performance bottleneck somewhere in the CLR trigger code, and you are a DBA without enough CLR programming knowledge, or you simply don't have access to the code. There is not much that you can do.

Possible performance problems are not the only drawback of auditing in the local event log. The event log can get full, and the auditing trigger would not be able to write to it in such a case, so it would roll back the transaction. You can manually clear the log, but until the log is cleared you would not be able to modify the data. Another possibility would be that the trigger would clear the log, but then what's the purpose of auditing, if you simply recycle the previously audited information? I tried to mitigate this problem by limiting the auditing info to the first 200 characters only. Even this solution doesn't make much sense, because you could simply use the T-SQL command RAISERROR ... WITH LOG, which can accomplish the same task easily—the errors logged with RAISERROR are currently limited to 440 bytes. Writing to the event log, whether you use RAISERROR or CLR code, needs permissions of quite a high level.

In short, my advice would be to avoid developing triggers with CLR code. Still, I wanted to provide an example for a CLR trigger to demonstrate the technicalities involved, and to discuss the drawbacks of doing so.

The trigger writes to a resource external to the database. In Chapter 7, I explained how to set up the environment to allow external access to assemblies, and the security and stability issues involved. Make sure you go over that section first if you haven't done so already. To allow the trigger that is described in this section to run, you have two options:

- The less secure and therefore less recommended option is to set the TRUSTWORTHY option of the database to ON, and to create (or alter) the assembly with the EXTERNAL_ACCESS permission set (UNSAFE would be needed to write to a remote machine event log):

```
-- Database option TRUSTWORTHY needs to be ON for EXTERNAL_ACCESS
ALTER DATABASE CLRUtilities SET TRUSTWORTHY ON;
GO
-- Alter assembly with PERMISSION_SET = EXTERNAL_ACCESS
ALTER ASSEMBLY CLRUtilities
WITH PERMISSION_SET = EXTERNAL_ACCESS;
```

■ As mentioned in Chapter 7, the more secure option is to sign the assembly with a strong name key file. Then run the following code to create an asymmetric key from the executable .dll file and a corresponding login with the EXTERNAL ACCESS (or UNSAFE) ASSEMBLY permission:

```
USE master;
GO
CREATE ASYMMETRIC KEY CLRUtilitiesKey
  FROM EXECUTABLE FILE =
    'C:\CLRUtilities\CLRUtilities\bin\Debug\CLRUtilities.dll';
-- Create login and grant it with unsafe permission level
CREATE LOGIN CLRUtilitiesLogin FROM ASYMMETRIC KEY CLRUtilitiesKey
GRANT EXTERNAL ACCESS ASSEMBLY TO CLRUtilitiesLogin;
```

CLR code inside SQL Server is always invoked in the context of the process account. If you would like to use the calling user's identity instead for your CLR code that performs an action outside SQL Server, you have to obtain an impersonation token through the *WindowsIdentity* property of the *SqlContext* object. The *WindowsIdentity* property returns a *WindowsIdentity* object instance. It represents the Windows (OS) identity of the caller (or null if the client was authenticated using SQL Server Authentication). To be able to access this property, an assembly has to be marked with the EXTERNAL_ACCESS or UNSAFE permission set.

You should be aware of all implications of setting the permission set for the assembly to EXTERNAL_ACCESS or UNSAFE and setting the database option THRUSTWORTHY to ON. Going deeper with security would be outside the scope of this book, but just be aware: the UNSAFE permission set allows assemblies unrestricted access to resources, both within and outside SQL Server, and also calling unmanaged code. From the example in this section, you can learn the technicalities of creating CLR triggers, but you can also get an impression of the implications of using CLR code inside a database imprudently.

Remember that Appendix A provides the instructions required to develop, build, deploy, and test your .NET code. Here you will be provided with the trigger's code, including explanations, and instructions to register the trigger in the database and test it.

Listing 8-13 has the C# code that defines the trg_GenericDMLAudit trigger.

Listing 8-13   C# code for trg_GenericDMLAudit trigger

```
    // Generic trigger for auditing DML statements
    // trigger will write first 200 characters from all columns
    // in an XML format to App Event Log
    [SqlTrigger(Name = @"trg_GenericDMLAudit", Target = "T1",
        Event = "FOR INSERT, UPDATE, DELETE")]
    public static void trg_GenericDMLAudit()
    {
        // Get the trigger context to get info about the action type
        SqlTriggerContext triggContext = SqlContext.TriggerContext;
        // Prepare the command and pipe objects
        SqlCommand command;
        SqlPipe pipe = SqlContext.Pipe;
```

```
            // Check whether the action is Insert
            switch (triggContext.TriggerAction)
            {
                case TriggerAction.Insert:
                    // Retrieve the connection that the trigger is using
                    using (SqlConnection connection
                        = new SqlConnection(@"context connection=true"))
                    {
                        connection.Open();
                        // Collect all columns into an XML type, cast it
                        // to nvarchar and select only a substring from it
                        // Info from Inserted
                        command = new SqlCommand(
                          @"SELECT 'New data: '
                            + SUBSTRING(CAST(a.InsertedContents AS NVARCHAR(MAX))
                                ,1,200) AS InsertedContents200
                              FROM (SELECT * FROM Inserted FOR XML AUTO, TYPE)
                                  AS a(InsertedContents);",
                            connection);
                        // Store info collected to a string variable
                        string msg;
                        msg = (string)command.ExecuteScalar();
                        // Write the audit info to the event log
                        EventLogEntryType entry = new EventLogEntryType();
                        entry = EventLogEntryType.SuccessAudit;
                        // Note: if the following line would use
                        // Environment.MachineName instead of "." to refer to
                        // the local machine event log, the assembly would need
                        // the UNSAFE permission set
                        EventLog ev = new EventLog(@"Application",
                          ".", @"GenericDMLAudit Trigger");
                        ev.WriteEntry(msg, entry);
                        // send the audit info to the user
                        pipe.Send(msg);
                    }
                    break;
                case TriggerAction.Update:
                    // Retrieve the connection that the trigger is using
                    using (SqlConnection connection
                        = new SqlConnection(@"context connection=true"))
                    {
                        connection.Open();
                        // Collect all columns into an XML type,
                        // cast it to nvarchar and select only a substring from it
                        // Info from Deleted
                        command = new SqlCommand(
                          @"SELECT 'Old data: '
                            + SUBSTRING(CAST(a.DeletedContents AS NVARCHAR(MAX))
                                ,1,200) AS DeletedContents200
                              FROM (SELECT * FROM Deleted FOR XML AUTO, TYPE)
                                  AS a(DeletedContents);",
                            connection);
                        // Store info collected to a string variable
                        string msg;
                        msg = (string)command.ExecuteScalar();
```

```
                                // Info from Inserted
                                command.CommandText =
                                  @"SELECT ' // New data: '
                                    + SUBSTRING(CAST(a.InsertedContents AS NVARCHAR(MAX))
                                        ,1,200) AS InsertedContents200
                                      FROM (SELECT * FROM Inserted FOR XML AUTO, TYPE)
                                          AS a(InsertedContents);";
                                msg = msg + (string)command.ExecuteScalar();
                                // Write the audit info to the event log
                                EventLogEntryType entry = new EventLogEntryType();
                                entry = EventLogEntryType.SuccessAudit;
                                EventLog ev = new EventLog(@"Application",
                                  ".", @"GenericDMLAudit Trigger");
                                ev.WriteEntry(msg, entry);
                                // send the audit info to the user
                                pipe.Send(msg);
                            }
                        break;
                case TriggerAction.Delete:
                    // Retrieve the connection that the trigger is using
                    using (SqlConnection connection
                        = new SqlConnection(@"context connection=true"))
                    {
                        connection.Open();
                        // Collect all columns into an XML type,
                        // cast it to nvarchar and select only a substring from it
                        // Info from Deleted
                        command = new SqlCommand(
                          @"SELECT 'Old data: '
                            + SUBSTRING(CAST(a. DeletedContents AS NVARCHAR(MAX))
                                ,1,200) AS DeletedContents200
                              FROM (SELECT * FROM Deleted FOR XML AUTO, TYPE)
                                  AS a(DeletedContents);",
                            connection);
                        // Store info collected to a string variable
                        string msg;
                        msg = (string)command.ExecuteScalar();
                        // Write the audit info to the event log
                        EventLogEntryType entry = new EventLogEntryType();
                        entry = EventLogEntryType.SuccessAudit;
                        EventLog ev = new EventLog(@"Application",
                          ".", @"GenericDMLAudit Trigger");
                        ev.WriteEntry(msg, entry);
                        // send the audit info to the user
                        pipe.Send(msg);
                    }
                    break;
                default:
                    // Just to be sure - this part should never fire
                    pipe.Send(@"Nothing happened");
                    break;
            }
        }
    }
```

Note that the header of the trigger in Listing 8-13 contains the attribute *Target = "T1"*. This attribute specifies the table on which you want to define the trigger. It is required only when deploying the trigger automatically from Microsoft Visual Studio. The trigger is written as a generic trigger that can be attached to any table. You can remove this attribute and use manual registration of the trigger to attach it to any table you like.

Using the *SqlContext* object, you can get the context of the current caller. The trigger's code uses a context connection, which should be familiar to you by now from the coverage of CLR stored procedures in the previous chapter. This is good enough for stored procedures, but inside a trigger you need a context in a much finer-grained level. You can gain the required context via the *SqlContext.TriggerContext* object (*SqlTriggerContext* class). This object provides context information about the trigger. This information includes the type of the DML action that caused the trigger to fire and which columns were modified if an UPDATE statement was issued. If this is a DDL trigger, you can get information about the event that fired the trigger from an XML *EventData* structure.

The trigger uses the *EventLogEntryType* enumeration and *EventLog* class from the *System. Diagnostics* namespace. It is also important that the trigger uses "." to refer to the current machine (remember that you want to write the auditing information to the local machine's event log). If it would use the *Environment* class from the *System* namespace to get the current machine name (*Environment.MachineName*), then the assembly would need the UNSAFE permission set. I have to thank Nicole Calinoiu, an extremely knowledgeable and friendly Visual Developer – Security MVP from Montreal, Canada, for pointing out this detail to me.

A small trick is used in the T-SQL part of the code embedded in the trigger (in the *Command- Text* property of the *SqlCommand* object). If you want to create a generic trigger that can be used with any table, you don't want to specify an explicit column list from *inserted* or *deleted*. Also, you need to collect information from all columns of all possible data types to generate a result string, because you write messages to the event log as strings. So the trigger's code uses SELECT * to get all the columns no matter what the structure of the table is, although gener- ally using SELECT * is a bad practice. It also uses the FOR XML clause to convert all informa- tion to XML in the inner SELECT (in the derived table). You can use the FOR XML clause in the derived table because it returns a table result. This is achieved by using the new TYPE directive of the FOR XML clause. You get back a table with a single column of the XML data type; without the TYPE directive, you would get the result in textual form. The code converts the value of the XML type column to the NVARCHAR type in the outer query and writes the first 200 characters to the event log.

Listing 8-14 shows the Microsoft Visual Basic code that defines the trg_GenericDMLAudit trigger.

Listing 8-14   Visual Basic code for trg_GenericDMLAudit trigger

```vb
' Generic trigger for auditing DML statements
' trigger will write first 200 characters from all columns
' in an XML format to App Event Log
<SqlTrigger(Name:="trg_GenericDMLAudit", Target:="T1", _
  Event:="FOR INSERT, UPDATE, DELETE")> _
Public Shared Sub trg_GenericDMLAudit()
    ' Get the trigger context to get info about the action type
    Dim triggContext As SqlTriggerContext = SqlContext.TriggerContext
    ' Prepare the command and pipe objects
    Dim command As SqlCommand
    Dim pipe As SqlPipe = SqlContext.Pipe

    ' Check whether the action is Insert
    Select Case triggContext.TriggerAction
        Case TriggerAction.Insert
            ' Retrieve the connection that the trigger is using
            Using connection _
              As New SqlConnection("Context connection = true")
                connection.Open()
                ' Collect all columns into an XML type,
                ' cast it to nvarchar and select only a substring from it
                ' Info from Inserted
                command = New SqlCommand( _
                  "SELECT 'New data: ' + " & _
                  "SUBSTRING(CAST(a.InsertedContents AS NVARCHAR(MAX)" & _
                  "),1,200) AS InsertedContents200 " & _
                  "FROM (SELECT * FROM Inserted FOR XML AUTO, TYPE) " & _
                  "AS a(InsertedContents);", _
                    connection)
                ' Store info collected to a string variable
                Dim msg As String
                msg = CStr(command.ExecuteScalar())
                ' Write the audit info to the event log
                Dim entry As EventLogEntryType
                entry = EventLogEntryType.SuccessAudit
                ' Note: if the following line would use
                ' Environment.MachineName instead of "." to refer to
                ' the local machine event log, the assembly would need
                ' the UNSAFE permission set
                Dim ev As New EventLog("Application", _
                  ".", "GenericDMLAudit Trigger")
                ev.WriteEntry(msg, entry)
                ' send the audit info to the user
                pipe.Send(msg)
            End Using
        Case TriggerAction.Update
            ' Retrieve the connection that the trigger is using
            Using connection _
              As New SqlConnection("Context connection = true")
                connection.Open()
                ' Collect all columns into an XML type,
                ' cast it to nvarchar and select only a substring from it
                ' Info from Deleted
                command = New SqlCommand( _
                  "SELECT 'Old data: ' + " & _
```

```vb
                    "SUBSTRING(CAST(a.DeletedContents AS NVARCHAR(MAX)" & _
                    "),1,200) AS DeletedContents200 " & _
                    "FROM (SELECT * FROM Deleted FOR XML AUTO, TYPE) " & _
                    "AS a(DeletedContents);", _
                     connection)
                    ' Store info collected to a string variable
                    Dim msg As String
                    msg = CStr(command.ExecuteScalar())
                    ' Info from Inserted
                    command.CommandText = _
                      "SELECT ' // New data: ' + " & _
                      "SUBSTRING(CAST(a.InsertedContents AS NVARCHAR(MAX)" & _
                      "),1,200) AS InsertedContents200 " & _
                      "FROM (SELECT * FROM Inserted FOR XML AUTO, TYPE) " & _
                      "AS a(InsertedContents);"
                    msg = msg + CStr(command.ExecuteScalar())
                    ' Write the audit info to the event log
                    Dim entry As EventLogEntryType
                    entry = EventLogEntryType.SuccessAudit
                    Dim ev As New EventLog("Application", _
                      ".", "GenericDMLAudit Trigger")
                    ev.WriteEntry(msg, entry)
                    ' send the audit info to the user
                    pipe.Send(msg)
                End Using
            Case TriggerAction.Delete
                ' Retrieve the connection that the trigger is using
                Using connection _
                  As New SqlConnection("Context connection = true")
                    connection.Open()
                    ' Collect all columns into an XML type,
                    ' cast it to nvarchar and select only a substring from it
                    ' Info from Deleted
                    command = New SqlCommand( _
                      "SELECT 'Old data: ' + " & _
                      "SUBSTRING(CAST(a.DeletedContents AS NVARCHAR(MAX)" & _
                      "),1,200) AS DeletedContents200 " & _
                      "FROM (SELECT * FROM Deleted FOR XML AUTO, TYPE) " & _
                      "AS a(DeletedContents);", _
                       connection)
                    ' Store info collected to a string variable
                    Dim msg As String
                    msg = CStr(command.ExecuteScalar())
                    ' Write the audit info to the event log
                    Dim entry As EventLogEntryType
                    entry = EventLogEntryType.SuccessAudit
                    Dim ev As New EventLog("Application", _
                      ".", "GenericDMLAudit Trigger")
                    ev.WriteEntry(msg, entry)
                    ' send the audit info to the user
                    pipe.Send(msg)
                End Using
            Case Else
                ' Just to be sure - this part should never fire
                pipe.Send("Nothing happened")
        End Select
    End Sub
```

Run the following code to create a test table called T1:

```
USE ClrUtilities;
GO
IF OBJECT_ID('dbo.T1') IS NOT NULL
  DROP TABLE dbo.T1;
GO
CREATE TABLE dbo.T1
(
  keycol  INT         NOT NULL PRIMARY KEY,
  datacol VARCHAR(10) NOT NULL
);
```

Use the following code to register the C# version of the trigger in the database and attach it to the table T1:

```
CREATE TRIGGER trg_T1_iud_GenericDMLAudit
 ON dbo.T1 FOR INSERT, UPDATE, DELETE
AS
EXTERNAL NAME CLRUtilities.CLRUtilities.trg_GenericDMLAudit;
```

Use the following code to register the trigger if you used Visual Basic to develop it:

```
CREATE TRIGGER trg_T1_iud_GenericDMLAudit
 ON dbo.T1 FOR INSERT, UPDATE, DELETE
AS
EXTERNAL NAME
  CLRUtilities.[CLRUtilities.CLRUtilities].trg_GenericDMLAudit;
```

Issue the following modifications against T1:

```
INSERT INTO dbo.T1(keycol, datacol) VALUES(1, N'A');
UPDATE dbo.T1 SET datacol = N'B' WHERE keycol = 1;
DELETE FROM dbo.T1 WHERE keycol = 1;
```

The trigger will produce the following output:

```
New data: <Inserted keycol="1" datacol="A"/>
Old data: <Deleted keycol="1" datacol="A"/> // New data: <Inserted keycol="1" datacol="B"/>
Old data: <Deleted keycol="1" datacol="B"/>
```

> **Tip**   You can clear the root namespace in a Visual Basic project, and this way the T-SQL code required to create/alter assemblies and register routines would be the same for Visual Basic and C# assemblies. To clear the root namespace, in Visual Studio select the Project | Properties menu item, go to the Application tab, and clear the "Root namespace" text box.

If you examine the Windows application log, you will find that the changes were audited there as well, as shown in Figure 8-1.

If you don't see the events in the Windows application log, make sure that it's not full or that you allow recycling it.

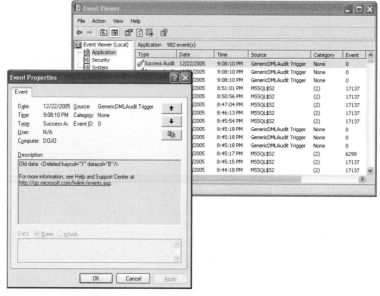

Figure 8-1   Application log

When you're done, run the following code for cleanup:

```
IF OBJECT_ID('dbo.T1') IS NOT NULL
  DROP TABLE dbo.T1;
```

Conclusion

Triggers allow you to automate processes. Process automation means less manual work and fewer chances to make mistakes and errors. You can use triggers to enforce complex integrity checks, audit changes, maintain denormalized data, and much more. SQL Server 2005 allows you to create triggers for DML statements and for DDL ones. You can use either T-SQL or .NET as your coding language.

Anyone can program triggers, but not everyone can program triggers efficiently. To program triggers efficiently, you need to understand the aspects of working with the *inserted* and *deleted* tables, the architecture of the product, the transaction log, the row versioning technology, and potential bottlenecks in the system.

Chapter 9
Transactions

Transactions allow you to define a unit of activity that will be considered *atomic*–all or nothing. The data will be considered *consistent* at the beginning of the transaction and at the end. Locks are obtained to *isolate* data resources, preventing (blocking) other processes from performing incompatible activities against those resources. You can control the degree of isolation of your transaction by specifying an *isolation level*. I will describe isolation levels in more detail later in the chapter. The database's transaction log guarantees that a committed transaction recorded within it is *durable*–that is, the change will reach the database. The aforementioned aspects of transactions are known as *ACID* (Atomicity, Consistency, Isolation, and Durability).

One aspect of database programming that determines whether a project rises or falls is the application's treatment of concurrency–multiple processes interacting with the same data. You have to understand the vision of the designers of the database product in terms of concurrency to develop well-behaving applications.

For example in Oracle, writers never block readers unless the reader requests that behavior explicitly. This functionality is supported because the product is able to construct an earlier consistent (committed) version of the data. In the past, Microsoft SQL Server maintained only one image of each row. An uncommitted change applied by a process to a row rendered an inconsistent state of the row. Another process attempting to read the row could not obtain an earlier consistent version. Rather, it could either wait for the other process to commit, or it could request the inconsistent state of the row (commonly referred to as a dirty read).

I will not get into the argument of which vision is better than the other–both have pros and cons. My take on the subject comes from a pragmatic point of view–you can develop successful projects with either vision, but you have to understand it. Programmers that are used to one vision and then start developing in a new one might find the shift in mindset hard, and they don't always make it. That's a recipe for a project that is doomed to fail.

For example, imagine that you're used to programming in an environment where you're never blocked when you read data—that is, the database platform can construct an earlier consistent version of rows. And then you start developing in an environment where the database platform maintains only one image of a row. Suddenly you're blocked when you try to read data that has been changed by an uncommitted transaction. You're not familiar with the concept of being blocked when you read data, and you don't know quite how to handle the situation yet. The easiest way to cope with the situation is to change all your reads to dirty reads. You might not be aware of the implications of such a request—that you might be getting data in an inconsistent state. The data might be in an intermediate state within a transaction, and it might even end up not being committed at all. In short, you need to understand the vision behind concurrency control in the database platform you are working with to develop successful projects.

SQL Server 2005 introduces new ways to handle concurrency via two new isolation levels, based on the ability to construct an earlier consistent version of a row. This ability is achieved thanks to a new *row versioning* technology incorporated within the engine, which serves other aspects of the product as well. Now you can choose the model you want to work with. Later in the chapter, I will describe the new isolation levels and the circumstances in which you would benefit from using them.

> **More Info**   Concurrency, transactions, and row versioning are described in great depth in *Inside Microsoft SQL Server 2005: The Storage Engine* by Kalen Delaney (Microsoft Press, 2006). Though Kalen covers the subject in depth, I found the idea of not covering the subject in a book that focuses on T-SQL programming unthinkable. So here I'll provide an overview of the subject, and I'll give you the fundamentals you need to program transactions with T-SQL.

What Are Transactions?

Transactions allow you to define the boundaries of activity that will be considered atomic. You do so by enclosing the statements that you want to participate in the transaction in a BEGIN TRAN/COMMIT TRAN block. Note that in SQL Server the default behavior is to consider a statement that does not appear in an explicit transaction block to be its own transaction—as if you enclosed that statement alone in a BEGIN TRAN/COMMIT TRAN block.

Whenever you submit a change to the database, SQL Server first checks whether the pages that need to be affected already reside in cache. If they do, the pages are modified in cache. If they don't, they're first loaded from disk into the cache and modified there. SQL Server records the changes in the database's transaction log. Once in a while, a process called *checkpoint* flushes changed pages ("dirty pages") from cache to the data portion of the database on disk. However, SQL Server will flush only changed pages for which the change was already recorded in the transaction log.

This architecture allows SQL Server to maintain transactions. If a transaction is rolled back—either explicitly or as a result of a failure—SQL Server has in the transaction log all the information it needs to undo the changes that were not committed. SQL Server might also use the information from the transaction log for roll-forward *recovery* capabilities, not just rollback operations. During a roll forward recovery phase, SQL Server replays committed transactions that were recorded in the transaction log but that had not been applied to the data portion of the database yet. This activity takes place, for example, when SQL Server starts up. For every database, SQL Server looks for the last checkpoint recorded in the transaction log. All transactions that were committed after the last checkpoint was recorded will be rolled forward (which is known as the *redo* phase). All open transactions for which a COMMIT TRAN was not recorded in the transaction log will be rolled back (which is known as the *undo* phase). Note that in SQL Server 2000 the database becomes available only after both phases are finished. SQL Server 2005 makes the database available as soon as the redo phase finishes.

To demonstrate the different aspects of working with transactions in this chapter, I'll use the tables T1 and T2, which you create and populate in the testdb database by running the code in Listing 9-1.

Listing 9-1 Creating and populating tables T1 and T2

```
SET NOCOUNT ON;
IF DB_ID('testdb') IS NULL
  CREATE DATABASE testdb;
GO
USE testdb;
GO
IF OBJECT_ID('dbo.T1') IS NOT NULL
  DROP TABLE dbo.T1;
IF OBJECT_ID('dbo.T2') IS NOT NULL
  DROP TABLE dbo.T2;
GO

CREATE TABLE dbo.T1
(
  keycol INT         NOT NULL PRIMARY KEY,
  col1   INT         NOT NULL,
  col2   VARCHAR(50) NOT NULL
);

INSERT INTO dbo.T1(keycol, col1, col2) VALUES(1, 101, 'A');
INSERT INTO dbo.T1(keycol, col1, col2) VALUES(2, 102, 'B');
INSERT INTO dbo.T1(keycol, col1, col2) VALUES(3, 103, 'C');

CREATE TABLE dbo.T2
(
  keycol INT         NOT NULL PRIMARY KEY,
  col1   INT         NOT NULL,
  col2   VARCHAR(50) NOT NULL
);

INSERT INTO dbo.T2(keycol, col1, col2) VALUES(1, 201, 'X');
INSERT INTO dbo.T2(keycol, col1, col2) VALUES(2, 202, 'Y');
INSERT INTO dbo.T2(keycol, col1, col2) VALUES(3, 203, 'Z');
GO
```

The contents of T1 and T2 are shown in Tables 9-1 and 9-2, respectively.

Table 9-1   Contents of T1

keycol	col1	col2
1	101	A
2	102	B
3	103	C

Table 9-2   Contents of T2

keycol	col1	col2
1	201	X
2	202	Y
3	203	Z

As a basic example, the following code issues two INSERT statements in a single transaction:

```
BEGIN TRAN
  INSERT INTO dbo.T1(keycol, col1, col2) VALUES(4, 101, 'C');
  INSERT INTO dbo.T2(keycol, col1, col2) VALUES(4, 201, 'X');
COMMIT TRAN
```

You enclose the two statements in a single transaction if you want the whole unit to be atomic—either both must succeed or both must fail. If your server fails for some reason, and only the first INSERT statement is recorded in the transaction log, the recovery process will roll back the partial transaction. On the other hand, if the transaction is recorded in the transaction log in full but not yet flushed to the data portion of the database (committed after the last checkpoint), the recovery process will redo it.

Note that SQL Server doesn't automatically roll back a transaction as a result of any failure. For example, constraint violations or lock timeout expirations leave a transaction open by default. You can write exception-handling code to determine whether you want to explicitly roll the transaction back or commit it. If you want all errors to cause a rollback of a transaction, set the XACT_ABORT session option to ON. Note that when exception handling is used, the XACT_ABORT option has a different effect. I'll discuss exception handling in the next chapter.

Locks

Locks provide the *isolation* aspect of transactions. They are acquired on data resources to prevent data inconsistency problems. SQL Server allows you to control the level of consistency you will get from your data by setting the isolation level of your session or query. I'll cover isolation levels later in the chapter. In this section, I'll focus on locks.

Locks can be obtained on resources at different granularity levels of data. The smallest granularity of data is the row level. If a row of a heap is locked (a heap is a table without a clustered index), the locked resource is a *row identifier (RID)*. If a row in an index is locked, the locked resource is a *key*. A lock can also be obtained on a page, an extent, a table, and on other types of resources as well. SQL Server automatically chooses which resource type to lock. In your queries, you can specify a table hint where you mention the resource type that you want to be locked (ROWLOCK, PAGLOCK, TABLOCK). SQL Server might choose not to adhere to your request if it doesn't have enough resources to satisfy it or if your request conflicts with other locks.

Lock *modes* determine how resources can be accessed by concurrent transactions. That is, if a process is granted a certain lock mode on a resource, another process attempting to acquire an incompatible lock mode on the same resource will be blocked. When you modify data, your transaction needs to acquire an *exclusive* (X) lock on the resource. If granted, the transaction will keep the exclusive lock until it is committed or rolled back. When you read data, by default (in the default isolation level) your transaction will need to acquire a *shared* (S) lock on the resource. If a shared lock is granted, your transaction will keep it only until the resource has been read.

Exclusive locks are incompatible with all lock modes. Similarly, all lock modes are incompatible with exclusive locks. That is, if one process holds a lock of any mode on a resource, another process cannot obtain an exclusive lock on that resource. Similarly, if one process holds an exclusive lock on a resource, another process cannot obtain a lock of any mode on that resource—thus the mode name *exclusive*. Shared locks, on the other hand, can be obtained while other processes hold shared locks on the same resource—thus the mode name *shared*.

SQL Server also supports other lock modes. An *update* (U) lock is used on resources that can be updated. Only one process at a time can hold an update lock on a resource. You can use an update lock to prevent deadlocks that can take place when processes are reading, locking (and maintaining the locks), and later updating the resource.

When SQL Server intends to acquire a lock on a resource, it first requests *Intent* locks on resources higher in the lock hierarchy (row → page → table). This lock mode is used to "signal" the intent to lock a resource lower in the lock hierarchy, and to simplify the lock incompatibility detection between different levels of granularity. For example, suppose your process requests to lock a row exclusively. SQL Server will first request *intent exclusive* (IX) locks at the table and page levels. Assume your process obtained all locks it requested. If another process attempts to acquire an incompatible lock on the same row, page, or table, SQL Server will detect the conflict immediately thanks to the intent locks.

Schema locks are acquired by processes that either change or depend on the schema of an object. A *schema modification* (Sch-M) lock is obtained when a data-definition-language (DDL) activity takes place against an object, and it blocks all activities against the object issued by other processes. *Schema stability* (Sch-S) locks are used when SQL Server compiles queries to block other processes from performing schema changes against the object.

Bulk update (BU) locks are used to allow multiple sessions to bulk load data into a table, while blocking processes from performing activities against the table other than bulk loads.

Finally, *key-range* locks protect ranges of rows. These are used by the serializable isolation level. I'll elaborate on this lock mode later in the chapter when discussing isolation levels.

For your convenience, Table 9-3 has a summary adapted from Books Online of lock compatibilities between some different lock modes.

Table 9-3   Lock Compatibility

	Granted Mode				
Requested Mode	**IS**	**S**	**U**	**IX**	**X**
Intent shared (IS)	Yes	Yes	Yes	Yes	No
Shared (S)	Yes	Yes	Yes	No	No
Update (U)	Yes	Yes	No	No	No
Intent exclusive (IX)	Yes	No	No	Yes	No
Exclusive (X)	No	No	No	No	No

As it does with lock resource types, SQL Server determines lock modes automatically. You can use a table hint to request that SQL Server use a specific lock mode (for example, XLOCK or UPDLOCK).

To demonstrate a blocking scenario, open three connections, and call them connections 1, 2, and 3.

Run the following code in connection 1 to open a transaction and update a row in table T1:

```
SET NOCOUNT ON;
USE testdb;
GO
BEGIN TRAN
  UPDATE dbo.T1 SET col2 = 'BB' WHERE keycol = 2;
```

The UPDATE transaction was granted with an exclusive lock, and the change was applied. Update locks are held until the end of a transaction, and because this transaction remains open, the process preserves the lock.

Run the following code in connection 2 to attempt to select all rows from T1:

```
SET NOCOUNT ON;
USE testdb;
GO
SELECT keycol, col1, col2 FROM dbo.T1;
```

Connection 2 needs a shared lock to read the data, but it cannot obtain one because an exclusive lock is held by connection 1 on one of the rows. Connection 2 is blocked. By default, SQL Server does not set any lock timeout, so if connection 1 will not release the lock, connection 2 will just keep on waiting.

To troubleshoot blocking scenarios, SQL Server 2005 gives you a whole array of new dynamic management views (DMV) and functions (DMF). For example, the sys.dm_tran_locks view gives you information about locks. Run the following query in connection 3, which generates the output shown in Table 9-4:

```
SET NOCOUNT ON;
USE testdb;
GO
-- Lock info
SELECT
    request_session_id              AS spid,
    resource_type                   AS restype,
    resource_database_id            AS dbid,
    resource_description            AS res,
    resource_associated_entity_id   AS resid,
    request_mode                    AS mode,
    request_status                  AS status
FROM sys.dm_tran_locks;
```

Table 9-4   Lock Info

spid	restype	dbid	res	resid	mode	status
55	DATABASE	12		0	S	GRANT
54	DATABASE	12		0	S	GRANT
53	DATABASE	12		0	S	GRANT
51	DATABASE	12		0	S	GRANT
54	OBJECT	12		1013578649	IS	GRANT
53	OBJECT	12		1013578649	IX	GRANT
54	PAGE	12	1:90	72057594040614912	IS	GRANT
53	PAGE	12	1:90	72057594040614912	IX	GRANT
53	OBJECT	12		821577965	IX	GRANT
53	KEY	12	(020068e8b274)	72057594040614912	X	GRANT
54	KEY	12	(020068e8b274)	72057594040614912	S	WAIT

You can observe that processes 53 and 54 are in conflict (of course, you might get different session IDs). Process 53 was granted an exclusive key lock, while process 54 is waiting for a shared lock on the same resource (last row in Table 9-4). To get similar information in SQL Server 2000, use the stored procedure sp_lock or the system table syslockinfo.

Query the sys.dm_exec_connections view to obtain information about the connections involved in the conflict (*connect_time*, *last_read*, *last_write*, *most_recent_sql_handle*, etc.):

```
SELECT * FROM sys.dm_exec_connections
WHERE session_id IN(53, 54);
```

In SQL Server 2000, the terms *connection* and *session* were synonymous; however, SQL Server 2005 supports multiple active result sets (MARS), where a single connection can have multiple active sessions running asynchronously. Therefore, SQL Server 2005 separates them into two views: sys.dm_exec_connections for connections, and sys.dm_exec_sessions for each session. Query the sys.dm_exec_sessions view to obtain information about the sessions involved in the conflict (*login_time*, *host_name*, *program_name*, *login_name*, *last_request_start_time*, *last_request_end_time*, state of set options, *transaction_isolation_level*, etc.):

```
SELECT * FROM sys.dm_exec_sessions
WHERE session_id IN(53, 54);
```

To get similar information in SQL Server 2000, use the sp_who/sp_who2 stored procedure or the sysprocesses system table.

SQL Server 2005 also provides you with the sys.dm_exec_requests view, which gives you information about currently executing requests. For a blocked session, the *blocking_session_id* attribute of the view will give you the session ID of the blocking session. Query the view to obtain information about blocked requests (blocked *session_id*, *blocking_session_id*, *wait_type*, *wait_time*, *wait_resource*, state of set options, etc.):

```
SELECT * FROM sys.dm_exec_requests
WHERE blocking_session_id > 0;
```

The sys.dm_exec_connections view contains a binary handle that you can provide to the function sys.dm_exec_sql_text to get the code text of the last request. For example, to get the code text for sessions 53 and 54, issue the following query, which generates the output shown in Table 9-5:

```
SELECT session_id, text
FROM sys.dm_exec_connections
  CROSS APPLY sys.dm_exec_sql_text(most_recent_sql_handle) AS ST
WHERE session_id IN(53, 54);
```

Table 9-5 Code Text of Last Request Issued by Sessions

session_id	text
53	BEGIN TRAN
	UPDATE dbo.T1 SET col2 = 'BB' WHERE keycol = 2;
54	SELECT keycol, col1, col2 FROM dbo.T1;

In SQL Server 2000, you use the DBCC INPUTBUFFER command or the fn_get_sql function to get the code buffer of a session.

There are other dynamic management objects that give you valuable concurrency-related information, as well as information about other aspects of the product. Please refer to Books Online for details.

Back to our blocking scenario—remember that by default a blocked session will wait for the blocking session to relinquish the resource, with no time limit. If you want to set a limit for waiting, use the LOCK_TIMEOUT session setting, specifying a value in milliseconds. If the timeout value you specified in LOCK_TIMEOUT expires and your session did not get the desired lock, SQL Server will generate error 1222.

> **Note**   When a lock timeout expires and SQL Server generates the error 1222, you know what the cause of the error was. SQL Server terminates the activity, and it tells you why. On the other hand, if you set a client timeout value (for example, command timeout), the client initiates the termination of the activity, and it doesn't care why the activity did not finish in the allotted time. In such a case, you can't tell what the reason for the error was. It might be blocking, it might just be a slow-running query, or it could be something else.

As an example of setting a lock timeout, first cancel the executing query in connection 2, which should still be waiting. The transaction in connection 1 is still open, holding an exclusive lock on a row in T1. Then run the following code in connection 2, which sets the lock timeout value to 5 seconds and then queries T1:

```
SET LOCK_TIMEOUT 5000;
SELECT keycol, col1, col2 FROM dbo.T1;
```

After 5 seconds, you will get the following error:

```
Msg 1222, Level 16, State 51, Line 2
Lock request time out period exceeded.
```

To reset the lock timeout setting to its default (no timeout, or wait forever), set the LOCK_TIMEOUT value to −1:

```
SET LOCK_TIMEOUT -1;
```

To terminate the transaction in connection 1 without committing the change, issue a rollback:

```
ROLLBACK TRAN;
```

If transactions are kept open for a long time, they might be keeping locks and preventing access to the data from other processes. To improve concurrency, you should try to keep your transactions as short as possible.

SQL Server maintains a memory block for each lock. If there is no limit on the number of locks that a single transaction can acquire, SQL Server could potentially suffer from memory starvation. Therefore, when SQL Server deems a transaction as holding too many locks (typically, a total in the area of thousands), it will attempt to escalate the fine-grained locks to a single table lock. Such an attempt will fail if there are conflicting locks on the table, in which case SQL Server will keep attempting to achieve lock escalation after each additional 1,250 acquired locks. Lock escalation attempts to reduce lock overhead, but of course results in reduced concurrency, because SQL Server ends up locking more data than is logically needed.

> **Tip**   When you set the database option to READ_ONLY, SQL Server does not bother to acquire shared locks for SELECT queries. It knows that changes cannot be applied to the database, meaning that SELECT queries can never be in conflict with any other activity. This means that queries produce less overhead and you get better performance. In systems where you only read data from the database—for example, data warehouses—consider setting the database update option to READ_ONLY. You can set the database to READ_WRITE just before invoking the extract, transform, and load (ETL) process that periodically loads changes to the data warehouse. When the ETL process finishes, set the database mode back to READ_ONLY. You can automate the changes to the database option as part of the ETL process.

Isolation Levels

Isolation levels allow you to control the consistency level that you will get when manipulating data, bearing in mind that multiple processes might be running concurrently. SQL Server 2000 gave you four isolation levels (*read uncommitted, read committed, repeatable read*, and *serializable*). SQL Server 2005 adds two new isolation levels (*snapshot* and *read committed snapshot*).

The different isolation levels control the level of consistency that you will get when manipulating data mainly by controlling the way readers behave. You can improve consistency at the cost of worsening concurrency, and vice versa. Technically, isolation levels improve consistency by increasing the duration of locks. Of course, the other side of the coin is that processes will need to wait longer.

Your choice of isolation level will determine which of the following types of consistency-related problems can or cannot happen:

- **Dirty reads**   A read of uncommitted data. One process changes data but does not commit the change before another process reads the same data. The second process ends up reading an inconsistent state of the data.

- **Lost updates**   One process reads data, makes some calculations based on the data, and later updates the data based on those calculations. If two processes first read the data and later update it based on what they read, one process might overwrite the other's update.

- **Nonrepeatable reads (also known as inconsistent analysis)**   In two separate reads within the same transaction, the process gets different values when reading the same resource. This can happen if a second process changed the data in between the reads made by the first process.

- **Phantoms**   Phantoms have to do with one process performing an action against a range of rows, while another process performs an incompatible action on rows in the same range. For example, one process deletes all rows based on some filter, and during the delete transaction (call it Tran1), another process inserts a new row that satisfies that filter. The new row is considered to be a *phantom row*. Issuing a SELECT query in the same transaction (Tran 1) with the same filter as the delete filter will return that phantom row—such a read is considered a *phantom read*.

Another aspect of concurrency that is determined by your choice of isolation level is the concurrency model, which can be either pessimistic or optimistic. In a pessimistic concurrency model, you lock a resource to guarantee that you will be able to perform an action you're planning later. In between the time you lock the resource and the time you perform the action later, no one can perform an incompatible action against the data. Obviously, this mode has the potential to hurt concurrency.

In an optimistic model, you don't lock the resource. Rather, you have the means to identify whether an incompatible action took place in between your activities. This model can potentially improve concurrency.

In the following sections, I'll describe the different isolation levels supported by SQL Server 2005 and which concurrency problems each does or doesn't allow.

SQL Server allows you to set the isolation level either at the session level or at the query level. You set the isolation level at the session level by issuing the following statement:

```
SET TRANSACTION ISOLATION LEVEL <isolation level>;
```

In this statement, *<isolation level>* can be one of the following: READ UNCOMMITTED, READ COMMITTED, REPEATABLE READ, SERIALIZABLE, or SNAPSHOT.

Or you can set the isolation level of a query by using a table hint (READUNCOMMITTED, READCOMMITTED, REPEATABLEREAD, or SERIALIZABLE). The hint NOLOCK is equivalent to READUNCOMMITTED.

> **Tip**   SQL Server also provides you with a table hint called READPAST. This hint causes your process to skip locked rows rather than being blocked or getting dirty reads. Make sure, though, that it makes sense for your application to use this hint. SQL Server 2000 supported this hint only for queries that retrieve data. SQL Server 2005 supports it also with queries that modify data.

SQL Server's default isolation level is read committed.

Read Uncommitted

When working with the read uncommitted isolation level, readers do not request shared locks. Thus, they're never in conflict with sessions that modify data. That is, they can read data that is locked exclusively, and they do not interfere with processes that modify data. Of course, at this level readers might get uncommitted changes. In other words, dirty reads can happen, as well as all other concurrency-related problems I described earlier. Read uncommitted is the worst isolation level in terms of consistency but the best in terms of concurrency.

To demonstrate a dirty read, first issue the following UPDATE statement to change the value of *T1.col2* to the string *'Version 1'* in the row where *keycol* is equal to 2:

```
UPDATE dbo.T1 SET col2 = 'Version 1' WHERE keycol = 2;
```

Open two connections, and call them connection 1 and connection 2. From connection 1, issue the following code, which updates *col2* to *'Version 2'* within a transaction and retrieves the modified column values, keeping the transaction open:

```
BEGIN TRAN
  UPDATE dbo.T1 SET col2 = 'Version 2' WHERE keycol = 2;
  SELECT col2 FROM dbo.T1 WHERE keycol = 2;
```

You get *'Version 2'* as the output, showing you the new state of the value your own transaction changed.

From connection 2, set the session's isolation level to read uncommitted, and read the data:

```
SET TRANSACTION ISOLATION LEVEL READ UNCOMMITTED;
SELECT col2 FROM dbo.T1 WHERE keycol = 2;
```

Even though another transaction changed the data and had not committed yet, you are able to see the uncommitted change—you get the output *'Version 2'*. Note that the modifying transaction still maintains an exclusive lock on the data, but if a process that reads the data doesn't request a shared lock, it cannot get a refusal.

From connection 1, issue a rollback:

```
ROLLBACK TRAN
```

If at this point you read the *col2* value from the row where *keycol* is equal to 2, you will get *'Version 1'* back. You realize that *'Version 2'* was never committed and that processes working with the read uncommitted isolation level might have relied on a state of the data that was never "approved."

Read Committed

Read committed is the default isolation level of SQL Server. In this isolation level, processes request a shared lock to read data and release it as soon as the data has been read—not when the transaction terminates. This means that dirty reads cannot happen; rather, the only changes you can read are those that have been committed. However, all other concurrency-related problems can happen with this isolation level.

To demonstrate the fact that a dirty read will not occur when working with the read committed isolation level, first run the following code in connection 1, changing the value of *col2* from *'Version 1'* to *'Version 2'*:

```
BEGIN TRAN
  UPDATE dbo.T1 SET col2 = 'Version 2' WHERE keycol = 2;
  SELECT col2 FROM dbo.T1 WHERE keycol = 2;
```

You get the output *'Version 2'*, because you can read your own changes, of course.

Now try to read the data from connection 2, working in the read committed isolation level, and you will be blocked:

```
SET TRANSACTION ISOLATION LEVEL READ COMMITTED;
SELECT col2 FROM dbo.T1 WHERE keycol = 2;
```

Commit the change in connection 1:

```
COMMIT TRAN
```

Connection 1 will release the exclusive lock, and connection two will get 'Version 2' back, which is the committed state of the value after the change.

For cleanup, change the value back to 'Version 1':

```
UPDATE dbo.T1 SET col2 = 'Version 1' WHERE keycol = 2;
```

Repeatable Read

Processes working with the repeatable read isolation level also request a shared lock when reading data, meaning that dirty reads cannot occur at this level. But unlike with read committed, at the repeatable read level transactions keep shared locks until they are terminated. You are guaranteed to get repeatable reads (consistent analysis) because no other process will be able to obtain an exclusive lock in between your reads.

Lost updates cannot happen at this level as well. If two processes that read data preserve shared locks until the end of the transaction, an attempt to modify that data by both will cause a deadlock, because each will request an exclusive lock that will be blocked by the other. When SQL Server detects a deadlock, it chooses a victim—typically, the process that performed less work—and rolls the victim's transaction back. The victim process will get the infamous error 1205 and can reissue the transaction. Although lost updates cannot happen in repeatable read, phantoms are still possible.

To demonstrate a case where you get consistent analysis when working at the repeatable read level, run the following code from connection 1:

```
SET TRANSACTION ISOLATION LEVEL REPEATABLE READ;
BEGIN TRAN
  SELECT col2 FROM dbo.T1 WHERE keycol = 2;
```

You get the output 'Version 2', and the process keeps a shared lock on the data because the transaction is still open.

If you attempt to modify the data from connection 2, you will be blocked:

```
UPDATE dbo.T1 SET col2 = 'Version 3' WHERE keycol = 2;
```

Read the data again in connection 1, and then commit:

```
  SELECT col2 FROM dbo.T1 WHERE keycol = 2;
COMMIT TRAN
```

You still get 'Version 2' back, meaning you got a repeatable read even though another process attempted to change the data in between your reads. Once the transaction committed, the shared lock was released, and connection 2 could obtain the exclusive lock it needed to update the data.

For cleanup, change the value back to 'Version 1':

```
UPDATE dbo.T1 SET col2 = 'Version 1' WHERE keycol = 2;
```

Serializable

The serializable isolation level is similar to repeatable read, with an additional facet—active transactions acquire key-range locks (placed on indexes) based on query filters. This applies not only to readers, but also to writers. Obtaining a key-range lock means that it's as if you logically lock all data that meets the query's filter. You not only lock whatever data was physically found when you accessed it, but you also lock data that does not exist yet that would happen to meet your query's filter. This level adds the prevention of phantoms to the list of problems that the repeatable read level's list doesn't handle.

To demonstrate the prevention of phantoms with the serializable isolation level, first create an index on *T1.col1*:

```
CREATE INDEX idx_col1 ON dbo.T1(col1);
```

Then run the following code from connection 1:

```
SET TRANSACTION ISOLATION LEVEL SERIALIZABLE;
BEGIN TRAN
  UPDATE dbo.T1 SET col2 = 'Version 2'
  WHERE col1 = 102;
```

Your transaction modifies the rows where *col1* = *102* (currently, there's only one such row in the table) and obtains an exclusive key-range lock in the index *idx_col1* based on the filter.

Next, from connection 2, attempt to introduce a phantom row—a row that meets the filter of the modification submitted by connection 1:

```
INSERT INTO dbo.T1(keycol, col1, col2) VALUES(5, 102, 'D');
```

You will be blocked. If you make a similar attempt in any other isolation level, the insert will be accepted.

To terminate the open transaction, commit the change from connection 1:

```
COMMIT TRAN;
```

Connection 1 releases the key-range lock, and connection 2 can insert the new row.

Before you continue, issue the following code to drop the index *idx_col1*, and to change the value of *col2* in the row where *keycol* = 2 back to '*Version 1*':

```
DROP INDEX dbo.T1.idx_col1;
GO
UPDATE dbo.T1 SET col2 = 'Version 1' WHERE keycol = 2;
```

Also, set all connections to work under the default read committed isolation level:

```
SET TRANSACTION ISOLATION LEVEL READ COMMITTED;
```

New Isolation Levels

SQL Server 2005 introduces a new *row versioning* technology that allows it to maintain older images (versions) of rows that resulted from committed transactions by using linked lists in tempdb. A source row can point to a linked list in tempdb, potentially containing multiple consistent versions of the row that were available in previous points in time, from newest to oldest.

The row versioning technology supports different aspects of the product, including: two new isolation levels, which I'll describe here; constructing the *inserted* and *deleted* tables in triggers, as described in the previous chapter; online index operations; and MARS.

The two new isolation levels that rely on row versioning are *snapshot* and *read committed snapshot*. In both isolation levels, a process does not request shared locks when reading data and is never in conflict with other processes modifying data. When reading data, if a requested row is locked, SQL Server uses the row versioning store to return an older consistent state of the row. Both of the snapshot-related isolation levels provide an optimistic concurrency model.

The following sections describe the two new isolation levels.

Snapshot

When a process reads data during a transaction running at the snapshot isolation level, the process will get the latest consistent version of the data that was available when the *transaction* started. A transaction is technically considered to have started when the first statement within the transaction is issued. Whenever a transaction modifies a row while at least one other transaction is running at the snapshot isolation level, SQL Server needs to store a consistent version of the row before the modification, regardless of whether the modifying transaction is running at the snapshot isolation or not. While the transaction that modified the data is open, another process working under snapshot isolation might request that older consistent version of the row.

Working with snapshot isolation has a performance impact in terms of transactions that modify data even when they're not working at snapshot level. Therefore, SQL Server requires you to turn on a database option to allow working with snapshot isolation in the database:

```
ALTER DATABASE testdb SET ALLOW_SNAPSHOT_ISOLATION ON;
```

If this option is turned off, snapshot isolation will not be allowed in the database and row versions will not be recorded in tempdb for snapshot isolation purposes.

To demonstrate working with snapshot isolation, run the following code from connection 1 (making sure you first set the database option just shown):

```
SET NOCOUNT ON;
USE testdb;
GO
BEGIN TRAN
  UPDATE dbo.T1 SET col2 = 'Version 2' WHERE keycol = 2;
  SELECT col2 FROM dbo.T1 WHERE keycol = 2;
```

The value of *col2* is changed from 'Version 1' to 'Version 2'. Notice that I did not request to change the session's isolation level to snapshot. Rather, the session works in the default read committed isolation level. However, because you turned on the database option that allows snapshot isolation, this transaction had to store the state of the row before the change (*col2* = 'Version 1') in tempdb.

You can examine the row versions that SQL Server currently maintains in the version store by querying the sys.dm_tran_version_store view:

```
SELECT * FROM sys.dm_tran_version_store;
```

Currently, you will find one row in the version store.

Next run the following code in connection 2, which sets the session's isolation level to snapshot, opens a transaction, and reads the contents of T1:

```
SET NOCOUNT ON;
USE testdb;
GO
SET TRANSACTION ISOLATION LEVEL SNAPSHOT;
BEGIN TRAN
  SELECT col2 FROM dbo.T1 WHERE keycol = 2;
```

You will get the output 'Version 1', which was the most recent consistent state of the data when the transaction started (that is, when the first statement in the transaction was issued). Of course, SQL Server acquired that version of the row from the version store.

Now commit the transaction in connection 1:

```
COMMIT TRAN
SELECT col2 FROM dbo.T1 WHERE keycol = 2;
```

The current committed state of the value is now 'Version 2'. However, the snapshot isolation level is still in effect for the open transaction in connection 2, and remember that when reading data you're supposed to get the latest consistent version when the transaction started. Therefore, the row cannot be removed yet from the version store.

Issue the following query in connection 2:

```
SELECT col2 FROM dbo.T1 WHERE keycol = 2;
```

You will still get the value 'Version 1'.

Note that if another process opens a transaction and modifies data, another version of the row (the one with the value 'Version 2') will be added to the linked list in tempdb in front of the existing one. When connection 1 reads the data again, it will end up traversing a longer linked list. This means that the longer transactions working under snapshot isolation remain open, the linked lists in tempdb grow longer, and readers end up traversing longer linked lists.

A cleanup process runs about every minute to remove unneeded row versions from the linked lists. However, it will only remove a contiguous section within the linked list starting at the tail of the list (that is, the oldest version). This means that long-running transactions might prevent the cleaning of intermediate versions following the oldest one even if they are no longer needed. This cleanup architecture is similar to the cleanup architecture of records in the transaction log.

Bearing the row versioning architecture in mind, you should try to minimize the length of your transaction when working with the snapshot isolation level. Also, you should understand that the snapshot isolation level is not suitable to all environments, but only to environments that mostly read and occasionally modify data.

At this point, commit the transaction in connection 2 and reread the data:

```
COMMIT TRAN
SELECT col2 FROM dbo.T1 WHERE keycol = 2;
```

You will get the latest committed value 'Version 2'.

Conflict Detection   Snapshot isolation also provides update-conflict detection capabilities. Remember that snapshot isolation allows you to work in an optimistic concurrency model. When you read data, you don't acquire any locks. You might want to access data and perform calculations based on the data you accessed for a later update in the same transaction. If in between the time you first accessed the data and the time you attempted to modify it another process modified that data, SQL Server will detect the update conflict and abort your transaction. If appropriate, you can reissue the transaction, which will rely on the new state of the data.

As an example of update-conflict detection in action, issue the following code in connection 1:

```
-- Connection 1, Step 1
SET NOCOUNT ON;
USE testdb;
GO
SET TRANSACTION ISOLATION LEVEL SNAPSHOT;
BEGIN TRAN
  SELECT col2 FROM dbo.T1 WHERE keycol = 2;
```

Under the snapshot isolation level, you opened a transaction and queried the data, getting back the value *Version 2*. Suppose that you now perform calculations based on the input and then want to modify the data. You issue the following code (still in connection 1), changing the value to *Version 3* and committing the transaction:

```
-- Connection 1, Step 2
  UPDATE dbo.T1 SET col2 = 'Version 3' WHERE keycol = 2;
COMMIT
```

The code completed successfully because there was no update conflict—no other process modified the data in between the time you read it and updated it.

Now, still in connection 1, open a new transaction and query the data:

```
-- Connection 1, Step 3
BEGIN TRAN
  SELECT col2 FROM dbo.T1 WHERE keycol = 2;
```

You will get back the value *Version 3*. In connection 2, update this value, changing it to *Version 4*:

```
-- Connection 2, Step 1
SET NOCOUNT ON;
USE testdb;
GO
UPDATE dbo.T1 SET col2 = 'Version 4' WHERE keycol = 2;
```

Back in connection 1, imagine that you have used the *col2* value in a calculation and determined that you should update the value to *Version 5*:

```
-- Connection 1, Step 4
  UPDATE dbo.T1 SET col2 = 'Version 5' WHERE keycol = 2;
```

SQL Server detects that someone modified the data in between your read and write, terminates your transaction, and produces the following error, which notifies you of the update conflict:

```
Msg 3960, Level 16, State 2, Line 1
Snapshot isolation transaction aborted due to update conflict. You cannot use snapshot
isolation to access table 'dbo.T1' directly or indirectly in database 'testdb' to update,
delete, or insert the row that has been modified or deleted by another transaction. Retry
the transaction or change the isolation level for the update/delete statement.
```

You can write exception-handling code that will reissue the transaction in the event it fails after an update conflict. In the next chapter, you can find coverage of exception handling with examples of the treatment of update conflicts.

Note that snapshot isolation is not suitable for modification-intensive environments with the potential for many update conflicts. Rather, it is recommended for environments that mainly read data, with occasional modifications and infrequent update conflicts.

For cleanup, change the value of *T1.col2* in the row where *keycol* = 2 back to *'Version 1'*:

```
UPDATE dbo.T1 SET col2 = 'Version 1' WHERE keycol = 2;
```

At this point, close all connections.

Read Committed Snapshot

"Read committed snapshot" is a new implementation of read committed isolation that can be used on a per-database basis. The database option READ_COMMITTED_SNAPSHOT controls which version of read committed is used. As soon as you set this database option to ON, all sessions working at the read committed level (default) will actually be working at the read committed snapshot level. This is a database global behavioral change that you get just by setting the database option to ON.

The read committed snapshot isolation level differs from the snapshot isolation level in two ways. The first difference is that readers get the latest consistent version of data that was available when the *statement* started, as opposed to when the transaction started. Also, this isolation level does not detect update conflicts.

This isolation level is especially useful for applications that you migrate from platforms that support obtaining earlier consistent versions of data, such as when an application migrates from Oracle to SQL Server.

The version store maintained for this isolation level is typically smaller than for snapshot isolation, and the linked lists of row versions do not grow long so easily because row versions can be removed from the linked lists sooner.

To look at the read committed snapshot isolation level, first turn on the database option in the testdb database:

```
ALTER DATABASE testdb SET READ_COMMITTED_SNAPSHOT ON;
```

Open two new connections, and issue the following code from connection 1:

```
SET NOCOUNT ON;
USE testdb;
GO
BEGIN TRAN
  UPDATE dbo.T1 SET col2 = 'Version 2' WHERE keycol = 2;
  SELECT col2 FROM dbo.T1 WHERE keycol = 2;
```

The default isolation level is read committed as always, but that level is now functioning in its new (snapshot) implementation. The code opened a new transaction, modified the value of *T1.col2* in the row where *keycol* = 2 from 'Version 1' to 'Version 2', and queried it. Before the value was modified, SQL Server stored the row with 'Version 1' in case another session later requests it.

Query the data in connection 2:

```
SET NOCOUNT ON;
USE testdb;
GO
BEGIN TRAN
  SELECT col2 FROM dbo.T1 WHERE keycol = 2;
```

You will get back the value 'Version 1'. This is the latest consistent state of the data that was available when the SELECT statement started.

Commit the transaction in connection 1:

```
COMMIT TRAN
```

At this point, the latest consistent version of the data is 'Version 2'. In connection 2, issue the following query:

```
  SELECT col2 FROM dbo.T1 WHERE keycol = 2;
COMMIT TRAN
```

You will get back the value 'Version 2'. Had you worked with the snapshot isolation level, you would have gotten back 'Version 1'.

> **Tip**   If you want to request a shared lock while working with the read committed snapshot isolation level, you can do so by specifying the READCOMMITTEDLOCK table hint. Using this hint, a reader will be blocked when requesting a shared lock on a resource that is under modification (exclusively locked). This hint allows readers to work at a similar level to read committed while at read committed snapshot level.

At this point, close all connections.

Restore the testdb database to its default settings:

```
ALTER DATABASE testdb SET ALLOW_SNAPSHOT_ISOLATION OFF;
ALTER DATABASE testdb SET READ_COMMITTED_SNAPSHOT OFF;
```

For your convenience, Table 9-6 provides a summary of all isolation levels, the problems that each allows or prevents, the supported concurrency model, and whether or not the isolation detects update conflicts for you.

Table 9-6 Summary of Isolation Levels

Isolation	Dirty Reads	Lost Updates	Nonrepeatable Reads	Phantoms	Concurrency Model	Update Conflict Detection
Read Uncommitted	Yes	Yes	Yes	Yes	Pessimistic	No
Read Committed	No	Yes	Yes	Yes	Pessimistic	No
Repeatable Read	No	No	No	Yes	Pessimistic	No
Serializable	No	No	No	No	Pessimistic	No
Snapshot	No	No	No	No	Optimistic	Yes
Read Committed Snapshot	No	Yes	Yes	Yes	Optimistic	No

Save Points

SQL Server does not support a true sense of nested transactions. When you issue a ROLLBACK TRAN command within a transaction, SQL Server rolls back all activity performed as of the outermost BEGIN TRAN. If you issue a BEGIN TRAN statement within an existing transaction, you don't really open a new transaction. Rather, SQL Server simply increments an internal counter that you can query via the @@trancount function. A COMMIT TRAN statement decrements the counter by one, and only the outermost COMMIT TRAN, which decrements the counter to zero, really commits the transaction. SQL Server will limit the number of levels you can open with BEGIN TRAN statements to 32.

SQL Server supports save points, which allow you to undo some partial activity within a transaction. To do so, you need to mark a save point by issuing a SAVE TRAN <savepoint name> statement and later issue a ROLLBACK TRAN <savepoint name> to undo the activity that was performed as of that save point.

As an example, remember that in the previous chapter I demonstrated how you can maintain your own custom sequence (autonumbering mechanism). I demonstrated a solution that maintains a synchronous sequence. That is, when a transaction modifies the sequence value to increment it, it acquires an exclusive lock and keeps it until the transaction terminates. Other transactions attempting to increment the sequence value will be blocked—in other words, the synchronous sequence queues requests for new sequence values. That's exactly what you want to establish in some cases where you want to prevent gaps in the sequence—for example, when you use the sequence to generate invoice IDs.

There might be cases, though, in which you don't care about gaps in the sequence and simply want to generate unique values—for example, to maintain keys across tables that would not overlap. In these cases, you're after an asynchronous sequence that will not block. You want the sequence value to be locked for a fraction of time so that you can increment it and prevent multiple processes from acquiring the same sequence value. But you don't want it to be locked for the duration of the whole transaction.

You can achieve such a sequence by creating a sequence table with an IDENTITY column like this:

```
USE tempdb;
GO
IF OBJECT_ID('dbo.AsyncSeq') IS NOT NULL
  DROP TABLE dbo.AsyncSeq;
GO
CREATE TABLE dbo.AsyncSeq(val INT IDENTITY);
```

Remember that an IDENTITY value increment is not considered part of an external transaction. That is, if within a transaction you insert a row to a table with an IDENTITY column, the identity increment is not rolled back if the transaction rolls back. Furthermore, the identity resource is not locked past the individual increment. To obtain a new sequence value, you simply load a row to the AsyncSeq table and return the value from the SCOPE_IDENTITY function. At that point, you have an asynchronous sequence.

However, keep in mind that the sequence table will keep on growing larger and larger. From time to time, you will probably want to clean it. If you clean it with a TRUNCATE TABLE command, the IDENTITY seed will be reset, which is not a good thing. If you clear it with a DELETE statement, the activity will be fully logged; therefore, it will take a while. During the deletion, SQL Server most likely will escalate the fine-grained exclusive locks to a full-blown exclusive table lock. This means that during the clearing activity, processes will not be able to obtain new sequence values.

You can use save points to get around this issue. Run the following code to create the stored procedure usp_AsyncSeq, which solves the problem:

```
IF OBJECT_ID('dbo.usp_AsyncSeq') IS NOT NULL
  DROP PROC dbo.usp_AsyncSeq;
GO
CREATE PROC dbo.usp_AsyncSeq
  @val AS INT OUTPUT
AS
BEGIN TRAN
  SAVE TRAN S1;
  INSERT INTO dbo.AsyncSeq DEFAULT VALUES;
  SET @val = SCOPE_IDENTITY()
  ROLLBACK TRAN S1;
COMMIT TRAN
GO
```

The stored procedure's code issues a BEGIN TRAN statement so that it can define a save point. The code defines the save point S1 and inserts a row into the AsyncSeq table, generating a new IDENTITY value. The code continues by assigning the newly generated IDENTITY value (via the SCOPE_IDENTITY function) to the output parameter @*val*. The code then issues a rollback to the save point S1. The rollback will not affect an external transaction if one was open when the procedure was invoked, because it reverts to the save point. The code finally issues a COMMIT TRAN statement that doesn't have any changes to commit, but just terminates the BEGIN TRAN statement.

Whenever you need to get a new sequence value, invoke the usp_AsyncSeq procedure, which returns the output parameter's value to a local variable like so:

```
DECLARE @key AS INT;
EXEC dbo.usp_AsyncSeq @val = @key OUTPUT;
SELECT @key;
```

As you can see, save points can really come in handy.

Deadlocks

Deadlocks occur when two or more processes block each other such that they enter a blocking chain that cannot be resolved without the system's intervention. With no intervention, processes involved in a deadlock would have to wait indefinitely for one another to relinquish their locks.

SQL Server automatically detects deadlock situations and resolves them by terminating the transaction that did less work. The transaction that was chosen as the deadlock victim will receive error 1205. You can trap such an error with exception-handling code and determine a course of action. Exception handling with deadlock examples is described in the next chapter.

SQL Server gives you a tool to control precedence between sessions in terms of which will be chosen as the deadlock victim. You can set the DEADLOCK_PRIORITY session option to one of the following values: LOW, NORMAL (default), or HIGH. Precedence in terms of choosing the deadlock victim will be based on deadlock priorities, and then by the amount of work.

Some deadlock scenarios are desirable—or more accurately, by design. For example, by using the repeatable read isolation level you prevent lost updates by creating a deadlock instead. Of course, there are other techniques to avoid lost updates—for example, having readers specify the UPDLOCK hint when reading data. But generally speaking, you might expect some deadlocks to occur to have the benefit of providing some consistency. However, I have to say that in my experience, most deadlocks I've seen are undesired ones caused by lack of sufficient indexes, unnecessarily long-running transactions, and so on. By understanding the concurrency architecture of the product you might be able to reduce undesired deadlocks, but it's very hard to avoid them altogether. So you still need to maintain exception-handling code that deals with those—for example, by retrying the transaction.

In the following sections, I'll provide deadlock examples and suggest ways to troubleshoot and avoid them.

Simple Deadlock Example

Let's start with a simple and classic deadlock example. I apologize if you've seen such examples a thousand times already. I promise to be more exciting in the following examples. Here I just want to make sure that the basics are covered, so bear with me.

Open two new connections, and call them connections 1 and 2. Issue the following code from connection 1:

```
SET NOCOUNT ON;
USE testdb;
GO
BEGIN TRAN
  UPDATE dbo.T1 SET col1 = col1 + 1 WHERE keycol = 2;
```

The code opened a new transaction and modified a row in T1. To achieve the modification, the transaction obtained an exclusive lock on the row. Because the transaction remains open, it keeps the exclusive lock on the row.

Issue the following code from connection 2, which updates a row in T2 within a transaction and keeps the transaction open, preserving the exclusive lock on the row:

```
SET NOCOUNT ON;
USE testdb;
GO
BEGIN TRAN
  UPDATE dbo.T2 SET col1 = col1 + 1 WHERE keycol = 2;
```

Issue the following code from connection 1, which attempts to read data from T2:

```
  SELECT col1 FROM dbo.T2 WHERE keycol = 2;
COMMIT TRAN
```

The SELECT query is blocked because it attempts to acquire a shared lock on the row in T2 that is locked exclusively by the other transaction. This is a normal blocking situation–it's not a deadlock yet. Connection 2 might terminate the transaction at some point, releasing the lock on the resource that connection 1 needs.

Next issue the following code from connection 2, attempting to query the data from T1:

```
  SELECT col1 FROM dbo.T1 WHERE keycol = 2;
COMMIT TRAN
```

At this point, the two processes enter a deadlock, because each is waiting for the other to release its locks. SQL Server intervenes, terminating the transaction in connection 2 and producing the following error:

```
Msg 1205, Level 13, State 51, Line 1
Transaction (Process ID 54) was deadlocked on lock resources with another process and has
been chosen as the deadlock victim. Rerun the transaction.
```

Don't you find it a bit ironic that SQL Server uses the terminology "has been chosen" to notify a process of the failure? Sort of reminds me of some spam messages notifying me that I've been chosen and won some prize. But I shouldn't digress.

Connection 1 has now obtained the lock it waited for. It reads the data and commits.

This particular deadlock can be avoided if you swap the order in which you access the tables in one of the transactions, assuming that this swap does not break the application's logic. If both transactions access the tables in the same order, such a deadlock will not happen. You can make it a practice when developing transactions to access tables in a particular order (say, by table name order), as long as this makes sense to the application and doesn't break its logic. This way you can reduce the frequency of deadlocks.

Deadlock Caused by Missing Indexes

Another example for a deadlock demonstrates the most common cause for deadlocks that I've stumbled into in production systems—lack of sufficient indexes. Processes might end up being in conflict with each other even when they need mutually exclusive resources. This can happen when you're lacking indexes on filtered columns. SQL Server has to scan all rows if there's no index on the filtered columns. Thus a conflict can occur when one process holds a lock on a row, while another scans all rows to check whether they qualify to the filter instead of seeking the desired row directly through an index.

As an example, currently there are no indexes on *T1.col1* and *T1.col2*. Run the following code in connection 1, which opens a transaction, modifies a row in T1 where *col1 = 101*, and keeps the transaction open, thus preserving an exclusive lock on the row:

```
BEGIN TRAN
  UPDATE dbo.T1 SET col2 = col2 + 'A' WHERE col1 = 101;
```

Similarly, run the following code in connection 2, which opens a transaction, modifies a row in T2 where *col1 = 203*, and keeps the transaction open, thus preserving an exclusive lock on the row:

```
BEGIN TRAN
  UPDATE dbo.T2 SET col2 = col2 + 'B' WHERE col1 = 203;
```

Now, in connection 1, try to query a row from T2 that is not locked by connection 2:

```
  SELECT col2 FROM dbo.T2 WHERE col1 = 201;
COMMIT TRAN
```

Because there's no index on *col1*, SQL Server must scan all rows and acquire shared locks to see whether they qualify to the query's filter. However, your transaction cannot obtain a shared lock on the row that is exclusively locked by connection 2; thus, it is blocked.

A similar blocking scenario will take place if, from connection 2, you now try to query a row that is not locked from T1:

```
SELECT col2 FROM dbo.T1 WHERE col1 = 103;
COMMIT TRAN
```

Of course, a deadlock occurs, and one of the processes is "chosen" as the deadlock victim (connection 2 in this case), and you receive the following error:

```
Msg 1205, Level 13, State 51, Line 1
Transaction (Process ID 54) was deadlocked on lock resources with another process and has
been chosen as the deadlock victim. Rerun the transaction.
```

SQL Server gives you several tools to troubleshoot deadlocks. You can start SQL Server's service with the trace flags 1204 and 1222, causing deadlocks to report information in SQL Server's error log (for details, please refer to *http://msdn2.microsoft.com/en-us/library/ms178104(SQL.90).aspx*). Another powerful tool for troubleshooting deadlocks is running traces while the deadlock occurs. If you can reproduce the deadlock by invoking some specific activity from the application, you can run the trace in a controlled manner. Start the trace right before you invoke the specific activity, and stop it right after the deadlock occurs. If you cannot reproduce the deadlock manually or predict when it will take place, you will have to keep the trace running in the background, which of course has a cost.

The trace should include the following events:

- **SQL:StmtStarting** This event will be recorded for each start event of a statement in a batch. If your statements are issued from stored procedures or triggers, use the *SP:Stmt-Starting* event. Make sure you trace a *Starting* event and not a *Completed* event because the statement that will be terminated will not complete. On the other hand, a *Starting* event will be traced even for statements that are terminated.

- **Lock:Timeout** This event will be produced when a session requests a lock and cannot obtain it. It will help you see which statements were blocked.

- **Lock:Deadlock Chain** This event will be produced for each process involved in the deadlock chain. It allows you to identify the process IDs of the processes involved in the deadlock and focus on their activities in the trace.

- **Lock:Deadlock** This event simply indicates when the deadlock took place.

- **Deadlock Graph** This is a new event in SQL Server 2005, and it generates an XML value with the deadlock information. If you choose this event, you can specify in the trace's Event Extraction Settings tab that you want to save deadlock XML events separately—you can direct these deadlock graphs to a single file or to distinct files.

As an example, when I traced the deadlock I described in this section I got the trace data shown in Figure 9-1.

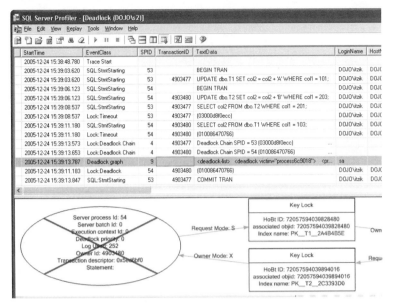

Figure 9-1   Deadlock trace

By looking at the *TextData* attribute of the *Lock:Deadlock Chain* event, you can easily identify the IDs of the processes and transactions involved in the deadlock and focus on them. Also, the *Deadlock Graph* event gives you a graphical view of the deadlock. You can follow the series of *SQL:StmtStarting* events for statements belonging to the processes involved in the deadlock. The *Lock:Timeout* events allow you to identify which statements were blocked. Analyzing this trace should lead you to the conclusion that, logically, the processes should not be in conflict and that your tables might be missing indexes on the filtered columns. If you examine the indexes on the tables, you can confirm your suspicions. To prevent such deadlocks in the future, create the following indexes:

```
CREATE INDEX idx_col1 ON dbo.T1(col1);
CREATE INDEX idx_col1 ON dbo.T2(col1);
```

Now retry the series of activities.

> **Note**   With such tiny tables as in our example, SQL Server will typically choose to scan the whole table even when indexes do exist on the filtered columns. Of course, in larger production tables SQL Server will typically use indexes for queries that are selective enough.

When you retry the activities, because our tables are so tiny, specify an index hint to make sure that SQL Server will use the index.

Start by issuing the following code from connection 1 to open a transaction and update a row in T1:

```
BEGIN TRAN
  UPDATE dbo.T1 SET col2 = col2 + 'A' WHERE col1 = 101;
```

Issue the following code from connection 2 to open a transaction, and update a row in T2:

```
BEGIN TRAN
  UPDATE dbo.T2 SET col2 = col2 + 'B' WHERE col1 = 203;
```

Go back to connection 1, and query a row that is not locked by connection 2 from T2 (and, in our case, remember to specify an index hint):

```
  SELECT col2 FROM dbo.T2 WITH (index = idx_col1) WHERE col1 = 201;
COMMIT TRAN
```

The row was obtained through the index created on *T2.col1*, and there was no conflict. The query ran successfully, and the transaction committed.

Connection 2 can now query the row from T1:

```
  SELECT col2 FROM dbo.T1 WITH (index = idx_col1) WHERE col1 = 103;
COMMIT TRAN
```

The query ran successfully, and the transaction committed.

By creating indexes on the filtered columns, you were able to avoid a deadlock. Of course, a deadlock can still happen if processes will block each other in cases where both attempt to access the same resources. In such cases, if possible, you might want to consider applying the approach I suggested in the previous section—namely, revising the order in which you access the tables in one of the transactions.

Make sure that you don't drop the index on T1, as it is used in the following section's example.

Deadlock with a Single Table

Many programmers think that deadlocks can take place only when multiple tables are involved. Keep in mind that a table can have multiple indexes, meaning that multiple resources can still be involved even when multiple processes interact with a single table.

Before I demonstrate such a scenario, let's first run the following UPDATE statement to make sure that *T1.col2* is set to 102 where *keycol = 2*:

```
UPDATE dbo.T1 SET col1 = 102, col2 = 'B' WHERE keycol = 2;
```

To generate a deadlock, first run the following code in connection 1:

```
SET NOCOUNT ON;
USE testdb;
GO
WHILE 1 = 1
  UPDATE dbo.T1 SET col1 = 203 - col1 WHERE keycol = 2;
```

An endless loop invokes, in each iteration, an UPDATE statement against T1, alternating the value of *col1* between 102 and 101 in the row where *keycol = 2*.

Next issue the following code from connection 2:

```
SET NOCOUNT ON;
USE testdb;
GO
DECLARE @i AS VARCHAR(10);
WHILE 1 = 1
  SET @i = (SELECT col2 FROM dbo.T1 WITH (index = idx_col1)
           WHERE col1 = 102);
```

Again, I used an index hint here just because the T1 table is so tiny and SQL Server might decide not to use the index in such a case. This code also invokes an endless loop, where in each iteration, it issues a SELECT statement against T1 that returns the value of *col2* where *col1 = 102*.

After a few seconds, a deadlock should occur, and the transaction in connection 2 will be terminated. And this is to show that a deadlock can in fact take place even though the processes involved interact with a single table. See if you can figure out the cause of the deadlock.

The chain of events that lead to the deadlock is illustrated in Figure 9-2.

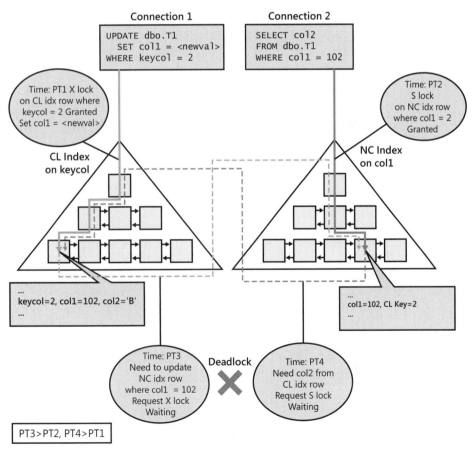

Figure 9-2   Deadlock with a single table

Currently, the table T1 has a clustered index defined on *keycol* and a nonclustered one defined on *col1*. With both endless loops running concurrently, there are bound to be occasions where both UPDATE and SELECT statements start running more or less at the same point in time ($PT1 \approx PT2$). The UPDATE transaction obtains an exclusive lock in the clustered index on the row where *keycol* = 2. It modifies the value of *col1* from 102 to 103. Then at point in time PT3 (where $PT3 > PT2$), it attempts to obtain an exclusive lock on the row in the nonclustered index where *col1* = 102 in order to modify the column value there as well.

Before the UPDATE transaction manages to obtain the lock on the row in the nonclustered index (attempt at point in time PT3), the SELECT transaction obtained a shared lock on that row (at point in time PT2). The SELECT transaction then (at point in time PT4, where $PT4 > PT1$) attempts to obtain a shared lock on the clustered index row that is currently locked by the UPDATE transaction. The SELECT transaction needs the row from the clustered index in order to return the *col2* value from that row. And you've got yourself a deadlock!

Now that you've figured out this deadlock, try to think of ways to avoid it. For example, obviously if you drop the nonclustered index from T1, such a deadlock will not occur, but such a solution can hardly be considered reasonable. You'll end up with slow queries and other types of deadlocks, such as the ones I described in the previous section. A more viable solution would be to create a covering index for the SELECT query that includes *col2*. Such an index will satisfy the SELECT query without the need to look up the full data row from the clustered index, thus avoiding the deadlock.

When you're done, run the following code for cleanup:

```
USE testdb;
GO
IF OBJECT_ID('dbo.T1') IS NOT NULL
  DROP TABLE dbo.T1;
IF OBJECT_ID('dbo.T2') IS NOT NULL
  DROP TABLE dbo.T2;
```

Conclusion

There's a lot to consider when developing applications for multiple concurrent users working with SQL Server. Most importantly, you have to understand the concurrency vision implemented in the product. SQL Server 2005 introduces new snapshot isolation levels, providing you with different concurrency models to choose from.

This chapter covered the fundamentals required when developing applications to allow multiple users to work concurrently. It covered transactions, lock resource types, lock modes, isolation levels, savepoints, and deadlocks.

Chapter 10
Exception Handling

Exception handling is one of the areas of T-SQL that was improved dramatically with the release of Microsoft SQL Server 2005. Previous versions of SQL Server had very limited exception-handling support. SQL Server 2005 introduces a new exception-handling construct and much better support for exception handling in general. In this chapter, I'll briefly go over the limitations of exception handling in SQL Server 2000 and then discuss the new functionality available in SQL Server 2005.

Exception Handling Prior to SQL Server 2005

The support for exception handling in SQL Server 2000 had several limitations. It was non-structured, it was awkward, and it wasn't capable of trapping all errors.

The main tool it provided you for exception handling was the *@@error* function, which returned an integer representing the way the last statement terminated (with 0 indicating success and a non-zero error code indicating lack of success). You had to assign the value of *@@error* to your own local variable immediately after each suspect statement. Otherwise, you'd lose that value, as it would be overridden by the statement that followed the suspect one. Then you had to switch between the possible error codes and determine a course of action. You had to either provide exception-handling code after each suspect statement or label an exception handling block and pass control to it using a GOTO command. Either way, the result was typically nonstructured code that was very hard to maintain.

Even worse, there were many errors that you simply couldn't trap, even ones that were not considered severe. Some errors simply terminated your batch and didn't give the exception-handling code a chance to run, so you had to deal with those at the caller. Examples of errors that terminated your batch include conversion errors and deadlock.

There's a simple test you can perform to check whether an error terminates the batch or not. Simply print something immediately after the statement that generates the error. Then check whether output was generated. For example, the following code does invoke the PRINT statement after a divide-by-zero error is generated:

```
SELECT 1/0;
PRINT 'Trappable error.';
```

This tells you that a divide-by-zero error is trappable. On the other hand, the following code doesn't invoke the PRINT statement after the conversion error is generated, telling you that a conversion error terminates the batch:

```
SELECT 'A' + 1;
PRINT 'Trappable error.';
```

Similarly, resolution or compilation errors terminate the batch and are not trappable—for example, referring to a nonexisting object:

```
SELECT * FROM NonExistingObject;
PRINT 'Trappable error.';
```

Another tricky part about exception handling in SQL Server 2000 was dealing with volatile functions, such as @@error and @@rowcount, that change their values after each statement that is run. The @@error function gives you an integer representing the way the last statement terminated. The @@rowcount function gives you the number of rows affected by the last statement. In many cases, you needed both for exception handling. However, if you used separate SET statements to assign the function result values to your own variables (as shown in the following code), the second SET statement would not assign the correct value to @rc.

```
<suspect_statement>
SET @err = @@error;
SET @rc = @@rowcount;
```

What you end up getting in @rc is the number of rows affected by the first assignment (namely 0), instead of the number of rows affected by the suspect statement. To trap both function result values, you could use a single assignment SELECT statement:

```
SELECT @err = @@error, @rc = @@rowcount;
```

Here's a small example of how to trap both values immediately after a suspect query:

```
SET NOCOUNT ON;
USE Northwind;
GO

DECLARE @custid AS NCHAR(5), @err AS INT, @rc AS INT;
SET @custid = N'ALFKI';

SELECT OrderID, CustomerID, EmployeeID, OrderDate
FROM dbo.Orders
WHERE CustomerID = @custid;
```

```
SELECT @err = @@error, @rc = @@rowcount;
-- exception handling code goes here
SELECT @err AS error_number, @rc AS row_count;
```

If the suspect code appeared within a stored procedure and you wanted the caller of the procedure to deal with the error, you had to pass the *@@error* and *@@rowcount* values through the return status/output parameters of the procedure. For example, the following usp_GetCustomerOrders procedure returns orders for a given customer ID and date range:

```
CREATE PROC dbo.usp_GetCustomerOrders
  @custid   AS VARCHAR(5),
  @fromdate AS DATETIME = '19000101',
  @todate   AS DATETIME = '99991231 23:59:59.997',
  @numrows  AS INT OUTPUT
AS

-- Input validation goes here

DECLARE @err AS INT;

SELECT OrderID, CustomerID, EmployeeID, OrderDate
FROM dbo.Orders
WHERE CustomerID = @custid
  AND OrderDate >= @fromdate
  AND OrderDate < @todate;

SELECT @numrows = @@rowcount, @err = @@error;

RETURN @err;
GO
```

The procedure returns the *@@error* value as the return status, and it returns the *@@rowcount* value through an output parameter called *@numrows*. Listing 10-1 has code that invokes the stored procedure and applies exception handling.

Listing 10-1   Handling errors in usp_GetCustomerOrders procedure

```
SET LOCK_TIMEOUT 5000;
DECLARE @err AS INT, @rc AS INT;

EXEC @err = dbo.usp_GetCustomerOrders
  @custid   = N'ALFKI', -- Also try with N'ABCDE'
  @fromdate = '19970101',
  @todate   = '19980101',
  @numrows  = @rc OUTPUT;

SELECT @err AS error_number, @rc AS row_count;

IF @err = 0 AND @rc > 0 BEGIN
  PRINT 'Processing Successful';
  RETURN;
END
```

```
IF @err = 0 AND @rc = 0 BEGIN
  PRINT 'No rows were selected.';
  RETURN;
END

IF @err = 1222
BEGIN
  PRINT 'Handling lock time out expired error.';
  RETURN;
END
-- other errors
-- IF @err = ...
BEGIN
  PRINT 'Unhandled error detected.';
  RETURN;
END
```

If the query completes with no errors and returns rows, the first IF statement will print the message 'Processing Successful' and exit. If the query completes with no errors and returns no rows, the second IF statement will print the message 'No rows were selected.' and exit. The PRINT statement represents the section of code where you might want to take care of a no-rows situation. If an error took place, the code switches between the possible errors using a series of IF statements. To test the code, run it for the first time. You will get back three orders for the requested customer in the requested date range, and you will identify a successful run—that is, @@error was 0 and @@rowcount was 3 (>0).

Next open a new connection and run the following code to lock the Orders table:

```
BEGIN TRAN
  SELECT * FROM dbo.Orders WITH (TABLOCKX);
```

Now go back to the original connection, and run the code in Listing 10-1 again. After about five seconds, a lock timeout expiration error will be generated, and you will get the following output:

```
Msg 1222, Level 16, State 56, Procedure usp_GetCustomerOrders, Line 13
Lock request time out period exceeded.
error_number row_count
------------ -----------
1222         0

Handling lock time out expired error.
```

When you're done, issue a rollback in the second connection to terminate the transaction:

```
ROLLBACK
```

There are other limitations to exception handling in SQL Server 2000. In addition to the error number you get from the @@error function, there's no other information available about the error—not the message, not the severity, and not the state.

> **More Info**   You can find interesting information about exception handling in SQL Server at Erland Sommarskog's Web site: *www.sommarskog.se*. Erland is a very active SQL Server MVP, and the subject of exception handling is very close to his heart.

Exception Handling in SQL Server 2005

Now that I've covered exception handling and exception-handling limitations in SQL Server 2000, I'll discuss exception handling in SQL Server 2005.

TRY/CATCH

SQL Server 2005 introduces the new TRY/CATCH construct. To use it, you place the suspect code in a BEGIN TRY/END TRY block, followed by a BEGIN CATCH/END CATCH block. When an error is encountered in the TRY block, the error is "trapped," and control is passed to the nearest CATCH block, where you have your exception-handling code. If you trap an error, no error message will be generated and sent to the caller. If you want to throw an error to the caller, you can do so using the RAISERROR command. If no error was generated in the TRY block, the CATCH block is skipped.

To demonstrate using the TRY/CATCH construct, first run the following code, which creates the database testdb and within it the Employees table:

```
IF DB_ID('testdb') IS NULL
  CREATE DATABASE testdb;
GO
USE testdb;
GO

IF OBJECT_ID('dbo.Employees') IS NOT NULL
  DROP TABLE dbo.Employees;
GO
CREATE TABLE dbo.Employees
(
  empid   INT         NOT NULL,
  empname VARCHAR(25) NOT NULL,
  mgrid   INT         NULL,
  CONSTRAINT PK_Employees PRIMARY KEY(empid),
  CONSTRAINT CHK_Employees_empid CHECK(empid > 0),
  CONSTRAINT FK_Employees_Employees
    FOREIGN KEY(mgrid) REFERENCES Employees(empid)
);
```

Run the following simple example twice:

```
BEGIN TRY
  INSERT INTO dbo.Employees(empid, empname, mgrid)
    VALUES(1, 'Emp1', NULL);
  PRINT 'INSERT succeeded.';
END TRY
```

```
BEGIN CATCH
  PRINT 'INSERT failed.';
  /* handle error here */
END CATCH
```

The first time you ran it, the INSERT statement raised no error, so the PRINT statement following it produced the output '*INSERT succeeded.*'. The CATCH block was skipped in this case. The second time you ran the code, the INSERT failed on a primary key violation and control was passed to the CATCH block. The CATCH block in this case simply printed the output '*INSERT failed.*'.

If an error is generated outside of a TRY block, control is passed to the previous level in the calling stack (the caller). For example, suppose that *proc1* invoked *proc2* within a TRY block and that *proc2* invoked code not in a TRY block and this code generated an error. The error is passed to *proc1*, and control is passed to the CATCH block corresponding to the TRY block that invoked *proc2*. If no TRY block is found up the call stack, the error is passed to the client application.

> **Note**   Resolution/compilation errors (for example, referring to an object that does not exist) are not trappable in the same level even when invoked within a TRY block. However, the previous level in the calling stack will trap such an error. So it might be a good practice to encapsulate code that might fail on such errors within a stored procedure and invoke the stored procedure in a TRY block.

The TRY/CATCH construct has many advantages over the SQL Server 2000 exception-handling tools. The code is now structured and elegant. All errors are trappable, except for errors with a severity level of 20 and up (for example, hardware failures). And now you also have a set of useful and convenient new functions available in the CATCH block, replacing the problematic @@ functions. The following section describes the new functions.

New Exception-Handling Functions

Remember that one of the most annoying limitations in SQL Server 2000 was the way @@ functions related to exception handling behaved. You had to grab them explicitly and place them into your own variables immediately after every suspect statement. If you did not, you'd lose their values. Furthermore, the information you got back about the error itself was limited only to the error number. In SQL Server 2005, you now have several functions available in the CATCH block, including:

- ERROR_NUMBER()
- ERROR_MESSAGE()
- ERROR_SEVERITY()
- ERROR_STATE()

- ERROR_LINE()

- ERROR_PROCEDURE()

Their names pretty much explain their meanings. In addition to the first four, which give you all pieces of information regarding the error that was generated, you have two other functions that allow you to even get the code line number where the error took place and the procedure name (or NULL if it did not occur in a procedure). The really great thing about these functions, beyond the fact that you get much more information, is that their values don't change throughout the CATCH block. You don't have to access them right away. Rather, you can access them anywhere you like within the CATCH block. So now you'd probably prefer to use ERROR_NUMBER, of course, instead of *@@error*.

> **Note** If you trap an error with a TRY/CATCH construct, the error is not thrown to the caller. If you want to throw it to the caller as well, you have to explicitly invoke a RAISERROR command. You can use the error message information returned by the functions, but you will not be allowed to throw the original error number. It will be a user error number (50000).

To demonstrate the use of these functions, run the code in Listing 10-2.

Listing 10-2 New exception-handling functions

```
PRINT 'Before TRY/CATCH block.';

BEGIN TRY

  PRINT '  Entering TRY block.';

  INSERT INTO dbo.Employees(empid, empname, mgrid)
    VALUES(2, 'Emp2', 1);
  -- Also try with empid = 0, 'A', NULL

  PRINT '    After INSERT.';

  PRINT '  Exiting TRY block.';

END TRY
BEGIN CATCH

  PRINT '  Entering CATCH block.';

  IF ERROR_NUMBER() = 2627
  BEGIN
    PRINT '    Handling PK violation...';
  END
  ELSE IF ERROR_NUMBER() = 547
  BEGIN
    PRINT '    Handling CHECK/FK constraint violation...';
  END
  ELSE IF ERROR_NUMBER() = 515
```

```
    BEGIN
      PRINT '    Handling NULL violation...';
    END
    ELSE IF ERROR_NUMBER() = 245
    BEGIN
      PRINT '    Handling conversion error...';
    END
    ELSE
    BEGIN
      PRINT '    Handling unknown error...';
    END

    PRINT '    Error Number  : ' + CAST(ERROR_NUMBER() AS VARCHAR(10));
    PRINT '    Error Message : ' + ERROR_MESSAGE();
    PRINT '    Error Severity: ' + CAST(ERROR_SEVERITY() AS VARCHAR(10));
    PRINT '    Error State   : ' + CAST(ERROR_STATE() AS VARCHAR(10));
    PRINT '    Error Line    : ' + CAST(ERROR_LINE() AS VARCHAR(10));
    PRINT '    Error Proc    : ' + ISNULL(ERROR_PROCEDURE(), 'Not within proc');

    PRINT '  Exiting CATCH block.';

  END CATCH

  PRINT 'After TRY/CATCH block.';
```

The code loads a valid row to the Employees table and should not generate an error. It prints messages in key locations of the code so that you will be able to easily figure out from the output which sections of the code were reached. Upon encountering an error in the TRY block, control is passed to the CATCH block. The CATCH block examines the return value of the ERROR_NUMBER() function to determine a course of action. It then just prints the values from the different functions to return information about the error. The first time you invoke the code in Listing 10-2, it should cause no error and produce the following output, which indicates that the CATCH block was not reached at all:

```
Before TRY/CATCH block.
  Entering TRY block.
    After INSERT.
  Exiting TRY block.
After TRY/CATCH block.
```

Next run the code again, and it will cause a primary key violation error, of course, producing the following output:

```
Before TRY/CATCH block.
  Entering TRY block.
  Entering CATCH block.
    Handling PK violation...
    Error Number  : 2627
    Error Message : Violation of PRIMARY KEY constraint 'PK_Employees'.
                    Cannot insert duplicate key in object 'dbo.Employees'.
    Error Severity: 14
    Error State   : 1
```

```
   Error Line   : 7
   Error Proc   : Not within proc
 Exiting CATCH block.
After TRY/CATCH block.
```

Similarly, you can try different errors by specifying *0, 'A', NULL* in the *empid* column, as suggested in the comment following the INSERT statement.

Errors in Transactions

In SQL Server 2000, your session could be in one of two possible transaction states: active and committable transaction, or no open transaction. SQL Server 2005 adds a third transaction state called "failed" or also informally referred to as "doomed." A transaction can enter this state when an error takes place in a TRY block while an explicit transaction is open and active. In this state, the transaction is open (still holding all locks) on one hand, but on the other hand it is uncommittable. That is, the transaction cannot submit any code that causes writes to the transaction log. In other words, the transaction cannot modify data; rather, it can only read data. Before you apply any modification, you have to first roll back the failed transaction.

Typically, errors with a severity level of 17 and higher would cause a transaction to enter this failed state. You can make all errors enter this state by setting the XACT_ABORT session option to ON. The nice thing about this new state is that it allows you to keep locks on resources that would have otherwise been released. You can query data to investigate the cause of the failure, and when you're ready to apply changes, you can roll back the existing transaction and immediately start a new one. Without support for this failed state, SQL Server would have had no choice but to roll back some types of errors that can now enter a failed state—for example, deadlocks.

The following section describes how you should react to errors based on the transaction state, which you can get by querying the XACT_STATE function.

Using XACT_STATE

XACT_STATE is a function that you invoke in the CATCH block to get the current transaction state. It returns 0 for *no active transaction*, 1 for *active and committable*, and −1 for *active but uncommittable*. To demonstrate the use of this function and how to determine the transaction state, I'll use the code in Listing 10-3.

Listing 10-3   Exception handling with transaction states

```
BEGIN TRY

  BEGIN TRAN
    INSERT INTO dbo.Employees(empid, empname, mgrid)
      VALUES(3, 'Emp3', 1);
    /* other activity */
  COMMIT TRAN
```

```
    PRINT 'Code completed successfully.';

  END TRY
  BEGIN CATCH

    PRINT 'Error: ' + CAST(ERROR_NUMBER() AS VARCHAR(10)) + ' found.';

    IF (XACT_STATE()) = -1
    BEGIN
      PRINT 'Transaction is open but uncommittable.';
      /* ...investigate data... */
      ROLLBACK TRAN; -- can only ROLLBACK
      /* ...handle the error... */
    END
    ELSE IF (XACT_STATE()) = 1
    BEGIN
      PRINT 'Transaction is open and committable.';
      /* ...handle error... */
      COMMIT TRAN; -- or ROLLBACK
    END
    ELSE
    BEGIN
      PRINT 'No open transaction.';
      /* ...handle error... */
    END

  END CATCH
```

This code loads a row for employee 3 into the Employees table using an explicit transaction in a TRY block. The CATCH block checks the transaction state before determining a course of action. The first time you run the code in Listing 10-3, there should be no errors, because it's a valid new employee. Run the code a second time, and you will get the following output:

```
Error: 2627 found.
Transaction is open and committable.
```

Because a primary key violation is not considered a severe error, it neither completely breaks nor fails the transaction. Rather, the transaction remains open and committable. To see an example where the transaction fails, you can simply set XACT_ABORT to ON, and rerun the code in Listing 10-3:

```
SET XACT_ABORT ON;
-- run code in listing 10-3
SET XACT_ABORT OFF;
```

This time, you get the output:

```
Error: 2627 found.
Transaction is open but uncommittable.
```

Using Save Points

When writing exception-handling code in a stored procedure, you might want to choose how to react based on whether or not the procedure was invoked from within an outer explicit transaction. For example, let's say that upon encountering an error in the stored procedure, you want to undo the procedure's activity only if the procedure opened the transaction. You don't want any side effects on an outer transaction. To achieve this, you use save points. Run the code in Listing 10-4 to create the usp_AddEmp procedure, which adds a new employee into the Employees table based on user inputs.

Listing 10-4   Creation script for usp_AddEmp stored procedure

```
IF OBJECT_ID('dbo.usp_AddEmp') IS NOT NULL
  DROP PROC dbo.usp_AddEmp;
GO

CREATE PROC dbo.usp_AddEmp
  @empid AS INT, @empname AS VARCHAR(25), @mgrid AS INT
AS

-- Save tran count aside
DECLARE @tc AS INT;
SET @tc = @@trancount;

-- If tran was already active, create a savepoint
IF @tc > 0
  SAVE TRAN S1;
-- If tran was not active, open a new one
ELSE
  BEGIN TRAN

BEGIN TRY;
  -- Modify data
  INSERT INTO dbo.Employees(empid, empname, mgrid)
    VALUES(@empid, @empname, @mgrid);
  -- If proc opened the tran, it's responsible for committing it
  IF @tc = 0
    COMMIT TRAN;

END TRY
BEGIN CATCH
    PRINT 'Error detected.';
    PRINT CASE XACT_STATE()
      WHEN 0 THEN 'No transaction is open.'
      WHEN 1 THEN 'Transaction is open and committable.'
      WHEN -1 THEN 'Transaction is open and uncommittable.'
    END;
    -- Proc opened tran
    IF @tc = 0
    BEGIN
      -- Can react differently based on tran state (XACT_STATE)
      -- In this case, say we just want to roll back
```

```
      IF XACT_STATE() <> 0
      BEGIN
        PRINT 'Rollback of tran opened by proc.';
        ROLLBACK TRAN
      END
    END
    -- Proc didn't open tran
    ELSE
    BEGIN
      IF XACT_STATE() = 1
      BEGIN
        PRINT 'Proc was invoked in an open tran. Roll back only proc''s activity.';
        ROLLBACK TRAN S1
      END
      ELSE IF XACT_STATE() = -1
        PRINT 'Proc was invoked in an open tran, but tran is uncommittable. Deferring
exception handling to caller.'
    END

    -- Raise error so that caller will determine what to do with
    -- the failure in the proc
    DECLARE
      @ErrorMessage  NVARCHAR(400),
      @ErrorSeverity INT,
      @ErrorState    INT;
    SELECT
      @ErrorMessage  = ERROR_MESSAGE(),
      @ErrorSeverity = ERROR_SEVERITY(),
      @ErrorState    = ERROR_STATE();
    RAISERROR (@ErrorMessage, @ErrorSeverity, @ErrorState);
  END CATCH
  GO
```

The procedure starts by saving the value of *@@trancount* in the local variable *@tc*. The *@tc* variable will tell you whether the procedure was invoked from an outer transaction (*@tc > 0*) or not (*@tc = 0*). If invoked from an outer transaction, the procedure will just mark a save point so that it would be able to undo only its own activity upon failure. If no transaction was open, the procedure simply opens a new one.

Then the procedure issues the INSERT statement within a TRY block and commits the transaction if the procedure opened it.

The CATCH block deals separately with a case where the procedure opened the transaction and a case where it didn't. If the former situation occurs, the code checks whether there's still a transaction open (XACT_STATE() <> 0) and simply rolls it back. Of course, you might want to react differently based on the transaction state. If the latter situation occurs, the code checks whether the transaction is open and committable, and in such a case rolls it back. If it's open and not committable, you're not allowed to roll back a transaction to a save point, so the code constructs an error message and throws it to the caller.

To test the procedure, first clear the Employees table:

```
TRUNCATE TABLE dbo.Employees;
```

Next run the following code twice, but not within an explicit transaction:

```
EXEC usp_AddEmp @empid = 1, @empname = 'Emp1', @mgrid = NULL;
```

The first run succeeds. The second run produces the following output:

```
Error detected.
Transaction is open and committable.
Rollback of tran opened by proc.
Msg 50000, Level 14, State 1, Procedure usp_AddEmp, Line 66
Violation of PRIMARY KEY constraint 'PK_Employees'. Cannot insert duplicate key in object
'dbo.Employees'.
```

Now run it again, but this time within an explicit transaction:

```
BEGIN TRAN
  EXEC usp_AddEmp @empid = 1, @empname = 'Emp1', @mgrid = NULL;
ROLLBACK
```

You get the following output:

```
Error detected.
Transaction is open and committable.
Proc was invoked in an open tran. Roll back only proc's activity.
Msg 50000, Level 14, State 1, Procedure usp_AddEmp, Line 66
Violation of PRIMARY KEY constraint 'PK_Employees'. Cannot insert duplicate key in object
'dbo.Employees'.
```

This time the procedure identified that it was invoked from an outer transaction, and upon error, rolled back only its own activity (to the savepoint). To demonstrate a failed transaction, set XACT_ABORT ON and try again:

```
SET XACT_ABORT ON;

BEGIN TRAN
  EXEC usp_AddEmp @empid = 1, @empname = 'Emp1', @mgrid = NULL;
ROLLBACK

SET XACT_ABORT OFF;
```

You get the following output:

```
Error detected.
Transaction is open and uncommittable.
Proc was invoked in an open tran, but tran is uncommittable. Deferring exception handling to
 caller.
Msg 50000, Level 14, State 1, Procedure usp_AddEmp, Line 66
Violation of PRIMARY KEY constraint 'PK_Employees'. Cannot insert duplicate key in object
'dbo.Employees'.
```

This time the procedure identified a failed transaction opened by the caller, so it deferred the exception handling to the caller.

Deadlocks and Update Conflicts

In this final section about exception handling, I'll demonstrate how you can now trap deadlock errors and apply retry logic for them. In SQL Server 2000, you couldn't trap a deadlock error with T-SQL. I'll also show examples that deal with update conflicts detected when you work with the new snapshot isolation level. Here as well, as in a deadlock case, you might want to retry several times before you deem the activity a goner.

I'll use simple T1 and T2 tables, which you create and populate by running the following code:

```
IF OBJECT_ID('dbo.T1') IS NOT NULL
  DROP TABLE dbo.T1;
IF OBJECT_ID('dbo.T2') IS NOT NULL
  DROP TABLE dbo.T2;
GO

CREATE TABLE dbo.T1(col1 INT);
INSERT INTO dbo.T1 VALUES(1);

CREATE TABLE dbo.T2(col1 INT);
INSERT INTO dbo.T2 VALUES(1);
```

We will look at two processes that access tables T1 and T2. Those processes will always succeed individually, but will cause a deadlock if run concurrently, because they access T1 and T2 in opposite orders.

First examine the code in Listing 10-5, and for now, ignore the mention of the snapshot isolation level. Focus only on the deadlock treatment here.

Listing 10-5 Exception handling retry logic, connection 1

```
SET NOCOUNT ON;
USE testdb;
GO

-- SET TRANSACTION ISOLATION LEVEL SNAPSHOT;
SET LOCK_TIMEOUT 30000;

DECLARE @retry AS INT, @i AS INT, @j AS INT, @maxretries AS INT;
SELECT @retry = 1, @i = 0, @maxretries = 3;

WHILE @retry = 1 AND @i <= @maxretries
BEGIN
  SET @retry = 0;
  BEGIN TRY
    BEGIN TRAN
      SET @j = (SELECT SUM(col1) FROM dbo.T1);
```

```
      WAITFOR DELAY '00:00:05';
      UPDATE dbo.T1 SET col1 = col1 + 1;
      WAITFOR DELAY '00:00:05';
      SET @j = (SELECT SUM(col1) FROM dbo.T2);
    COMMIT TRAN
    PRINT 'Transaction completed successfully.';
  END TRY
  BEGIN CATCH
    -- Lock timeout
    IF ERROR_NUMBER() = 1222
    BEGIN
      PRINT 'Lock timeout detected.';
      IF XACT_STATE() <> 0 ROLLBACK;
    END
    -- Deadlock / Update conflict
    ELSE IF ERROR_NUMBER() IN (1205, 3960)
    BEGIN
      PRINT CASE ERROR_NUMBER()
              WHEN 1205 THEN 'Deadlock'
              WHEN 3960 THEN 'Update conflict'
            END + ' detected.';
      IF XACT_STATE() <> 0 ROLLBACK;
      SELECT @retry = 1, @i = @i + 1;
      IF @i <= @maxretries
      BEGIN
        PRINT 'Retry #' + CAST(@i AS VARCHAR(10)) + '.'
        WAITFOR DELAY '00:00:05';
      END
    END
    ELSE
    BEGIN
      PRINT 'Unhandled error: ' + CAST(ERROR_NUMBER() AS VARCHAR(10))
        + ', ' + ERROR_MESSAGE();
      IF XACT_STATE() <> 0 ROLLBACK;
    END
  END CATCH
END

IF @i > @maxretries
  PRINT 'Failed ' + CAST(@maxretries AS VARCHAR(10)) + ' retries.';
```

The TRY block essentially runs a SELECT against T1, waits 5 seconds, runs an UPDATE against T1, waits 5 seconds, and then issues a SELECT against T2. Notice that the code runs in a loop, with a condition based on two flags: retry required (*@retry = 1*), and number of retries is smaller than or equal to a given maximum (*@i <= @maxretries*). The *@retry* flag is initialized with 1, *@i* with 0, and *@maxretries* with 3, so of course, the code runs at least once.

The TRY block then sets *@retry* to 0 so that if all goes well, there won't be another retry. If an error is generated, and it's one you want to apply retry logic to (for example, deadlock, update conflict), in the CATCH block you set the *@retry* flag to 1, increment @i, and enter a small delay. That's basically it.

Examine the CATCH block and you will see different treatment for different errors. In a case of a lock timeout error (1222), there's no point in a retry, so you simply roll back the transaction if one is open. As for deadlocks and update conflicts, you do apply retry after rolling back the existing transaction (if one is open). Run the code in Listing 10-5 (calling the connection: connection 1). The code should complete after about 10 seconds with no problem, producing the following output:

```
Transaction completed successfully.
```

The code in Listing 10-6 is similar to the one in Listing 10-5, only with a reversed access order to the tables.

Listing 10-6   Exception handling retry logic, connection 2

```
SET NOCOUNT ON;
USE testdb;
GO

SET LOCK_TIMEOUT 30000;

DECLARE @retry AS INT, @i AS INT, @j AS INT, @maxretries AS INT;
SELECT @retry = 1, @i = 0, @maxretries = 3;

WHILE @retry = 1 AND @i <= @maxretries
BEGIN
  SET @retry = 0;
  BEGIN TRY
    BEGIN TRAN
      SET @j = (SELECT SUM(col1) FROM dbo.T2);
      WAITFOR DELAY '00:00:05';
      UPDATE dbo.T2 SET col1 = col1 + 1;
      WAITFOR DELAY '00:00:05';
      SET @j = (SELECT SUM(col1) FROM dbo.T1);
    COMMIT TRAN
    PRINT 'Transaction completed successfully.';
  END TRY
  BEGIN CATCH
    -- Lock timeout
    IF ERROR_NUMBER() = 1222
    BEGIN
      PRINT 'Lock timeout detected.';
      IF XACT_STATE() <> 0 ROLLBACK;
    END
    -- Deadlock / Update conflict
    ELSE IF ERROR_NUMBER() IN (1205, 3960)
    BEGIN
      PRINT CASE ERROR_NUMBER()
              WHEN 1205 THEN 'Deadlock'
              WHEN 3960 THEN 'Update conflict'
            END + ' detected.';
      IF XACT_STATE() <> 0 ROLLBACK;
      SELECT @retry = 1, @i = @i + 1;
      IF @i <= @maxretries
```

```
        BEGIN
          PRINT 'Retry #' + CAST(@i AS VARCHAR(10)) + '.'
          WAITFOR DELAY '00:00:05';
        END
      END
      ELSE
      BEGIN
        PRINT 'Unhandled error: ' + CAST(ERROR_NUMBER() AS VARCHAR(10))
          + ', ' + ERROR_MESSAGE();
        IF XACT_STATE() <> 0 ROLLBACK;
      END
    END CATCH
  END

  IF @i > @maxretries
    PRINT 'Failed ' + CAST(@maxretries AS VARCHAR(10)) + ' retries.';
```

Open a new connection (call it connection 2), and have the code from Listing 10-6 ready to run. Run the code in both connections, and try to start the second very close to the first (within 5 seconds). One of them will finish successfully, while the other will face a deadlock and enter retry logic. In my case, it was connection 2, which generated the following output:

```
Deadlock detected.
Retry #1.
Transaction completed successfully.
```

Naturally, once connection 2 was deadlocked and released the locks, connection 1 could finish and release its own locks. Connection 2 waited a bit, tried again, and then was successful. To demonstrate exceeding the maximum number of retries you specified, open a third connection (call it connection 3) and have the following code ready in it:

```
SET NOCOUNT ON;
USE testdb;
GO

SET LOCK_TIMEOUT 30000;
DECLARE @j AS INT;

BEGIN TRAN

  UPDATE dbo.T2 SET col1 = col1 + 1;
  UPDATE dbo.T2 SET col1 = col1 + 1;
  UPDATE dbo.T2 SET col1 = col1 + 1;

  WAITFOR DELAY '00:00:05';

  WHILE 1 = 1
  BEGIN
    SET @j = (SELECT SUM(col1) FROM dbo.T1);
    WAITFOR DELAY '00:00:01';
  END
```

This code will keep an exclusive lock on T2 as soon as the first UPDATE takes place, and then in a loop, every second, it will request a shared lock on T1 to read. If you run it concurrently with the code in connection 1, you should get repeated deadlocks in connection 1. So first run the code in connection 1, and then immediately start the code in connection 3. After about a minute, you should get the following output in connection 1:

```
Deadlock detected.
Retry #1.
Deadlock detected.
Retry #2.
Deadlock detected.
Retry #3.
Deadlock detected.
Failed 3 retries.
```

Don't forget to stop the activity in connection 3 and roll back the transaction when you're done:

```
ROLLBACK
```

Update conflicts can occur when a transaction running in the snapshot isolation level reads a row at one point in time and then tries to modify the row at a later point. If SQL Server identifies that another transaction changed the row in between those two points in time, a update conflict occurs. Your transaction might be making calculations based on values it got by first reading the data, and later using the result of the calculation to update the data. If someone modifies the data between the time you first read it and the time you modify it, your modification might not be logically valid anymore.

One feature of the new snapshot isolation level is that it detects such update conflicts for you automatically. This allows you to use optimistic concurrency control. If you read and then modify a resource, and no one else modified the resource in between, the modification will work smoothly. But if someone did modify the resource in between, when you try to modify the resource SQL Server will detect the conflict and terminate your transaction. Typically, you want to retry the transaction in such a case. The logic is so similar to retrying in a case of a deadlock that there's nothing really much to add.

To work with the snapshot isolation level, you must first enable it for the current database:

```
ALTER DATABASE testdb SET ALLOW_SNAPSHOT_ISOLATION ON;
```

Go to connection 1, and remove the comment characters (the two hyphens) from the statement that sets the isolation level to snapshot.

Now open a fourth connection (call it connection 4), and have the following code ready:

```
SET NOCOUNT ON;
USE testdb;
GO
```

```
SET LOCK_TIMEOUT 30000;

WHILE 1 = 1
BEGIN
  UPDATE dbo.T1 SET col1 = col1 + 1;
  WAITFOR DELAY '00:00:01';
END
```

This code simply issues an UPDATE against T1 every second. Now run the code in connection 1, and immediately start the code in connection 4 as well. The code in connection 1 keeps reading from T1, waiting 5 seconds, and then writing to T1. Because connection 4 changes T1 every second, connection 1 will encounter plenty of update conflicts. Feel free to stop the execution in connection 4 from time to time to see that connection 1 at some point will finish successfully. If you just allow connection 4 to keep running, after three retries connection 1 will produce the following output:

```
Update conflict detected.
Retry #1.
Update conflict detected.
Retry #2.
Update conflict detected.
Retry #3.
Update conflict detected.
Failed 3 retries.
```

Don't forget to stop the activity in connection 4 when you're done. At this point, you can close all connections.

Conclusion

Exception handling has come a long way since SQL Server 2000. It's now structured, elegant, and traps all errors except for the most severe ones. It also provides a lot of useful information via the exception-related functions. You can now have three different transaction states: no transaction open, open and committable, open and uncommittable (failed). Remember that the failed state, which is new in SQL Server 2005, allows you to keep a transaction open, holding all locks, while you're investigating data. You then must roll back the transaction before making any change.

Chapter 11
Service Broker

—By Roger Wolter

Service Broker is probably the most powerful and least understood new feature in Microsoft SQL Server 2005. Service Broker makes SQL Server a platform for building reliable, distributed asynchronous applications. When combined with other new features for SQL Server 2005 such as common language runtime (CLR) integration and the XML datatype, SQL Server is a serious platform for building data-intensive services and applications.

Service Broker is not just an application platform, however. Because of its asynchronous nature, Service Broker is also an ideal tool for making many database tasks simpler, more efficient, and more robust.

In this chapter, I'll discuss the internal details of Service Broker and how it works, and I'll provide some compelling scenarios for using Service Broker in your database applications. I'll start with the key new feature of Service Broker, the dialog conversation.

Dialog Conversations

In most messaging systems, messages are the basic unit of communication. Each message is an isolated entity, and it's up to the application logic to keep track of sent and received messages. On the other hand, most real business transactions consist of a number of related steps or operations. For example, a simple purchase order will often involve a series of message exchanges between the purchaser and supplier that continue for several weeks as items are ordered, prices are negotiated, shipment dates are agreed on, order status is communicated, shipment is confirmed, billing is completed, and payment is received. Similarly, think of the number of messages exchanged during the bidding for, purchase of, and delivery of an item from an online auction site. These simple examples illustrate that many real-world business transactions take a significant amount of time and involve many related steps.

Obviously, a business transaction that takes weeks to complete can't be handled as a single database transaction. Each step of the business transaction translates to one or more database transactions. Each database transaction is related to transactions that have already occurred and transactions that will happen in the future to complete the business transaction. The application must maintain the state of the business transaction so that it knows what has happened and what remains to be done. Because this is a database application, it's logical to assume that this application state will be maintained in the database and that updates to the state will be part of the database transactions that make up the business transaction.

The Service Broker dialog conversation was designed to make managing this type of business transaction reliable and simple. As I go through the features of dialog conversations and how they are implemented, you will see how the goal of supporting this kind of business transaction influenced the design of Service Broker. Obviously, not all business transactions fit this model of a long-running exchange of data between two systems. Many business transactions have a single step and can be executed as a single database transaction. Other business transactions only flow data in one direction—for example, a point-of-sale system at a grocery store that transfers a long series of scanned items to be inserted into a database. As you'll see, dialog conversations handle these variations well also.

Conversations

Service Broker defines a conversation as a reliable, ordered, and asynchronous transfer of messages between conversation endpoints. I'll discuss conversation endpoints in more detail later, but for now think of a conversation endpoint as something that can send or receive messages. The endpoints of a conversation might be in the same database, in different databases in the same SQL Server instance, or in different databases in different SQL Server instances.

There were originally two types of conversations defined for Service Broker. A dialog conversation is a reliable, ordered, bidirectional exchange of messages between exactly two endpoints, and a monolog conversation is a reliable, ordered stream of messages from one sending endpoint to many receiving endpoints.

Monolog conversations were cut early in SQL Server 2005, but they will probably be included in a later release. Because a monolog can be implemented as a bunch of dialogs from one sending endpoint to a bunch of receiving endpoints, the dialog conversation is more important and was implemented first. Some aspects of conversations are common to both dialogs and monologs, while other aspects apply to only dialogs or only monologs, so the Service Broker T-SQL statements include both DIALOG and CONVERSATION. Because SQL Server 2005 has only one type of conversation, this amounts to two words for the same thing, but because the differentiation will be necessary when monologs are implemented, both terms are used in the language. This usage might lead to some initial confusion, but in the long run, it will be necessary to make monologs work.

The three distinguishing features of Service Broker conversations are the reliable, ordered, and asynchronous delivery of messages. Because these are key concepts, I'll explain them in some detail:

Reliable

Reliable delivery of conversation messages means that Service Broker will keep trying to deliver the message in the face of pretty much any type of failure or interruption, including the following ones:

- The sending database is stopped and started.
- The receiving database is stopped and started.
- The network goes down.
- The network is being reconfigured.
- The sending database or receiving database is being restored from backup.
- The sending database or receiving database fails over to a disaster recovery site.
- The sending or receiving database is being moved to a different server.

This kind of reliability means Service Broker applications don't have to be written to deal with delivery issues. When a message is sent, it is delivered reliably or the conversation is put into an error state and all endpoints of the conversation are informed of the error with an error message in the endpoint queue. As you can see, Service Broker goes to great lengths to avoid declaring an error on a conversation, but there are cases in which a conversation can be damaged badly enough that it can't continue. The other common source of conversation errors is the lifetime of a conversation expiring. In many cases, it doesn't make sense to keep trying to deliver messages forever. If you haven't received a response from the airline reservation system and the plane has left already, you don't really care what the answer is. To accommodate this scenario, you can set a maximum lifetime on a conversation. If the conversation is still around when the lifetime expires, an error is declared and error messages are sent to all conversation endpoints.

Reliable delivery also means the message wasn't changed or intercepted along the way, so Service Broker provides a wide range of security options to give you the assurance you need that the message was delivered securely and intact. Even if all Service Broker security is turned off, Service Broker uses checksums to ensure that the message didn't change in transit.

In Order

Service Broker provides unprecedented facilities for message ordering within a conversation. Some messaging systems will ensure messages are delivered in order provided that they are sent in a single transaction and received in a single transaction. Messages in a Service Broker conversation will be received *and processed* in the order in which they were sent, even if they were sent in multiple transactions issued by multiple applications and received in multiple transactions by multiple different applications.

To see why this is important, imagine an order entry application that receives an order header, three order lines and an order footer. In a messaging system that doesn't ensure ordering, your application might receive an order line before it receives the order header or receive the order footer before it receives all three order lines. This means the application will have to be able to recognize messages arriving out of order and store them somewhere until the missing messages arrive—greatly increasing the complexity of the application.

Even if the messages are delivered in order, if your application is multithreaded for efficiency, the messages still might be processed out of order. For example, if thread one receives the order header and starts processing it and then thread two starts processing the first order line, it's very possible that the order line will be processed before the order header is completely processed. This chain of events could occur because the order header is generally more complex than the order line, so inserting the order line into the database will fail because the order header isn't there yet. The application can try the order line again until it works, but this is inefficient and adds to the complexity of the application. If all the messages are in a Service Broker conversation, they will be delivered and processed in the order in which they were sent so that the application doesn't have to deal with the complexities of processing messages out of order.

Asynchronous

Asynchronous delivery of messages effectively decouples the endpoints of a Service Broker conversation from each other. The application at one endpoint of a conversation sends a message and then goes on to process more work without knowing when or where the message will be processed. It's entirely possible that the sending application and the receiving application never run concurrently. For example, an inventory application might send out manufacturing orders as shortages are produced during the day, and the manufacturing orders might be read by a planning application that runs at night. Even if the sender and receiver are running concurrently, asynchronous message delivery means that the sending application doesn't have to wait around for the receiving application to finish processing the message. It can continue with other work and rely on Service Broker to reliably deliver the message to the receiver for the receiver to process when it has time available.

Asynchronous messaging means you can link fast systems and slow systems into a single application without worrying about the slow systems holding back the fast systems. For example, your new order-entry system can send shipping instructions to your clunky old shipping system without the shipping system slowing down order entry. Virtually all big, scalable, high performance applications make asynchronous calls to slower parts of the system. For example, the operating system performs disk I/O asynchronously, and the Web server makes asynchronous network calls. Another example is SQL Server, which performs many asynchronous operations internally.

With Service Broker, asynchronous processing is now available to database application writers. This means, for example, that if you want to write a trigger that does a significant amount of work without slowing down updates to the table, you can have the trigger send a Service

Broker message to another application that does the work. You can also have one stored procedure call several other stored procedures in parallel by using asynchronous Service Broker messages to start the other stored procedures. You will see an example of this later.

Now that you've seen what a conversation is and what it does, I'll spend the rest of this section talking about how Service Broker implements conversations. When I'm done, you will have a thorough understanding of how Service Broker works because almost all of Service Broker revolves around conversations. I'll cover programming and security separately—not because they aren't tightly tied to conversations, but because they're big enough to justify their own headings.

Messages

So far, I've talked a lot about messages without ever saying what they are. *Messages* are the information exchanged in a conversation. Messages have two parts:

- A message header, which contains information about the message, such as its source and destination, sequence number, and security credentials
- A message body, which the application uses to transport data

The Service Broker message body is a VARBINARY(MAX) datatype that can contain up to 2 GB of any SQL Server data that can be cast to VARBINARY(MAX). A Service Broker message can exist either in the database or on the wire. In the database, it is a row of a SQL Server table whose columns that contain metadata about the message and the message contents. On the wire, it is binary data sent in TCP/IP packets. I won't go into detail about the wire format, but the disk format will be discussed in the upcoming "Queues" section.

The header of a Service Broker message must contain a message type. The message type is just a name for the message that makes it easier to write Service Broker programs to handle messages. To see why a message type is required, think about an application for a human resources department that sends information to an employee database. One message might be an XML document with information on one employee's benefits, another might be an employee's photograph as a JPEG file, and another might be a resume created in Microsoft Office Word, and so on. Without the message type to guide you, all you would know is that all the message bodies are VARBINARY(MAX). Because Service Broker ensures ordering, you might get by with knowing the first message is XML, the second is a JPEG, and so forth. However, error messages get pushed to the front of a dialog, so that is a risky strategy. Because you can rely on Service Broker to always include the message type, you can write your application to extract the message contents into the appropriate data structure depending on the message type.

Before you can use a message type in a Service Broker application, you must create it as a database object. The message type is one of several Service Broker metadata objects that are used to enforce constraints on Service Broker dialogs. Service Broker will use only message types that are defined in the metadata for the database, so you can be confident that your application won't receive a message type you don't know about. The simplest form of a message type is just a name. The following data definition language (DDL) code snippet will create simple message type objects:

```
CREATE MESSAGE TYPE [//microsoft.com/Inventory/AddItem];
CREATE MESSAGE TYPE [//microsoft.com/Inventory/ItemAdded];
```

The only parameter in this case is the name. Notice that the name has a URL-like format. This doesn't mean that the message type exists somewhere out on the Web. This format is used to make it easier to uniquely identify a message type. This message type adds an item in an inventory application distributed by microsoft.com. The message type name is just a string, so "AddItem" would have been perfectly legal, but in a large distributed application, it's difficult to ensure that there will never be two different message types named "AddItem". The URL format isn't required, but it can make your life easier when you start putting together large distributed Service Broker applications.

> **Note**   Message type names are sent in messages between databases that might have been configured with very different collations. To make this work, message type names and all other Service Broker metadata sent in the message header use a binary collation. This means that the names must match exactly, character for character, with both case and accent sensitivity. The failure to adhere to this case-sensitive matching is a common source of application errors.

While you are free to put anything you want into a Service Broker message body, you can optionally have Service Broker do some basic checking of the message body for you as messages arrive on a conversation. This checking is specified with the VALIDATION clause of the CREATE MESSAGE TYPE command:

```
CREATE MESSAGE TYPE message_type_name
    [ VALIDATION = {   NONE
                   |  EMPTY
                   |  WELL_FORMED_XML
                   |  VALID_XML WITH SCHEMA COLLECTION
                       schema_collection_name
                   } ]
```

The NONE option, as the name implies, performs no validation and is the default. The EMPTY option ensures that the message body is NULL. Messages with a type but no body are useful as flags. For example, a message that reports that an action has completed successfully might not have any data to convey, so a message with a type of "Success" with no body might be appropriate. The WELL_FORMED_XML option loads the message body into an XML parser and rejects the message if parsing fails. The VALID_XML option loads the message body into the XML parser and validates the XML with the specified SCHEMA COLLECTION. (See Books Online for a more complete explanation of what a schema collection is and how to create one.) For purposes of this chapter, it's enough to know that the message contents must be valid based on the schemas in the schema collection. Because a schema collection can contain many schemas, it is possible to use a single schema collection to validate a number of message types.

Although using one of the XML validations will ensure that your application can handle the incoming message, Service Broker loads the message body into an XML parser to validate it and then, in most cases, the application will load it into a different parser to process it. This process can be a significant resource drain if message volumes and message sizes are large, so unless you are receiving messages from an untrusted source, it might make sense to just use validation until you have your application working correctly and then turn it off when you go into production. Because validation is configured per message type, it's possible to validate only a few message types that have a higher potential to be invalid.

All Service Broker metadata can be seen in SQL Server catalog views. The view for message types is *sys.service_message_types*. If you look at that view in a user database, you will find several system-defined message types. The message types that begin with *http://schemas .microsoft.com/SQL/ServiceBroker/* are used by the Service Broker features. The other system-defined message types are used by other features such as Query Notifications and Events, which use Service Broker to deliver messages.

Contracts

Just as message types constrain the names and contents of conversation messages, a Service Broker contract constrains which message types are allowed in a conversation. A contract, as its name implies, is an agreement among the endpoints in a Service Broker conversation as to which message types can be sent and who can send them. Because the Service Broker enforces the contract, applications that process the conversation can be assured that they won't receive any message types that they aren't equipped to handle. To further ensure this agreement, once a Service Broker contract is created, the list of message types can't be changed.

A contract, like a message type, is a piece of Service Broker metadata that is used by Service Broker to enforce constraints on conversations. Each contract has a name, a list of what message types can be sent on the contract, and information that specifies which endpoint can send the approved message type. Because the endpoints of a conversation are peers once the conversation is established, the only real differentiator among endpoints is which one started the conversation. The endpoint that started the conversation is called the INITIATOR, and the opposite endpoint is the TARGET. These labels are used to specify which endpoint can send a message type. The contract must specify the allowed sender or senders of each message type in the conversation by specifying INITIATOR, TARGET, or ANY for the message type. Put this all together and you get the following CREATE CONTRACT statement:

```
CREATE CONTRACT [//microsoft.com/Inventory/AddItemContract]
  ([//microsoft.com/Inventory/AddItem] SENT BY INITIATOR,
   [//microsoft.com/Inventory/ItemAdded] SENT BY TARGET);
```

Notice that the contract also uses a URL-like name format because it too is sent as part of the message header. The contract name uses a binary collation also, so be careful of the case when typing the name.

There's no ALTER CONTRACT statement for adding or removing message types, so you have to get the CREATE CONTRACT right. The only way to change the message type list is to drop the contract and create a new one.

The catalogue view for listing contracts is *sys.service_contracts*. The view that describes how messages are related to contracts is *sys.service_contract_message_usages*. The following query will generate a list of all the message types in the database, what contracts they are used in, and which endpoints send them:

```
SELECT  C.name AS Contract, M.name AS MessageType,
  CASE
    WHEN is_sent_by_initiator = 1
      AND is_sent_by_target    = 1 THEN 'ANY'
    WHEN is_sent_by_initiator = 1 THEN 'INITIATOR'
    WHEN is_sent_by_target    = 1 THEN 'TARGET'
  END AS SentBy
FROM sys.service_message_types AS M
  JOIN sys.service_contract_message_usages AS U
    ON M.message_type_id = U.message_type_id
  JOIN sys.service_contracts AS C
    ON C.service_contract_id = U.service_contract_id
ORDER BY C.name, M.name;
```

DEFAULT

If you ran the previous query, you might have noticed a message type named DEFAULT and a contract named DEFAULT that contains the DEFAULT message type. These were created as a result of customer feedback that writing a simple Service Broker application wasn't very simple. If you want to write an application that just sends and receives simple messages and you want to handle all messages the same, you can use the DEFAULT message type and contract so that you don't have to define your own. In the Service Broker data manipulation language (DML) commands, if you don't specify a message type or contract, DEFAULT is used.

Queues

In defining conversations, I said they were reliable and asynchronous, meaning that messages survive network and database failures and can be delivered even if the sender and receiver don't ever execute at the same time. Service Broker makes this happen by storing messages persistently in the database until they are successfully delivered so that the messages won't be lost. The place messages are stored while they are in transit is called a *queue*. Queues are very common in computer systems. They are used to store work that passes between tasks that run at different rates. For example, the operating system places disk commands on a disk queue, and the disk controller executes them when it has time available and then removes them from the queue. Using a queue means the operating system doesn't have to wait for the disk controller to be available to issue a disk command. It puts the command on the queue whenever it wants and then goes on to handle other tasks while the disk controller is processing the command. This kind of queue is different from a Service Broker queue because it exists only in memory. However, the principle of loose coupling—enabling the tasks that write to the queue and the tasks that read from it to each run at their own rate—applies to both.

Many large database applications use tables in the database as queues. An order-entry system, for example, might put a list of orders that need to be billed in a table in the billing database for the billing system to handle. The order-entry system only has to wait long enough to insert the order into the billing table. It doesn't have to wait for the bill to be generated. This approach not only allows the order-entry system to process orders faster, it allows the order-entry system to keep running when the billing system is down. Although queues are common in database applications, they are usually difficult to implement and a frequent source of problems. If multiple processes are inserting and deleting messages, blocking can cause performance issues and deadlocks. Getting locking right is difficult—too little locking causes multiple processes to get the same message, and too much locking causes deadlocks and performance problems.

At its most basic level, Service Broker is database queues done right. Service Broker queues are hidden tables that are managed by Service Broker code. Service Broker uses its own locking scheme to maximize queue performance, and queue manipulation commands built into the T-SQL language give Service Broker the tight control it needs to manage queues efficiently. This level of control is one of the primary advantages of having Service Broker built into the database. An external process couldn't get the control over query execution and locking that Service Broker uses to optimize queue operations.

Service Broker queues store messages in internal tables. Internal tables are just like normal tables except they can't be used in SQL commands because the table name is hidden. To see the name of the internal table used by a Service Broker queue, you can run this query:

```
SELECT Q.name AS QueueName, I.name AS InternalName
FROM sys.service_queues AS Q
  JOIN sys.internal_tables AS I
    ON Q.object_id = I.parent_object_id;
```

You will find, however, that trying to issue a SELECT statement against the hidden table name will fail. If you want to see the contents of a queue, you can issue a SELECT statement against the queue name. This approach works because Service Broker creates a view on the internal table with the same name as the queue name. This view is not an exact view of the internal table. Some additional columns are created through joins with the metadata tables to provide names for values that are stored as internal IDs. One of the benefits of Service Broker is that you can see what messages are available in the queue with a simple SELECT statement. If you need to run a SELECT statement on an active queue, I suggest using SELECT * FROM <*queue name*> WITH (NOLOCK), because most Service Broker actions hold locks on rows in the queue.

Queues are the only Service Broker objects that actually store data. Because of this, you can create a queue in a SQL Server schema and specify a filegroup in which you want the messages stored.

The following statement will create a Service Broker queue:

```
CREATE PROCEDURE dbo.InventoryProc  AS
  RETURN 0;
GO
CREATE QUEUE dbo.InventoryQueue
  WITH ACTIVATION (
    PROCEDURE_NAME = dbo.InventoryProc  ,
    MAX_QUEUE_READERS = 2,
    EXECUTE AS SELF);
```

Please ignore the CREATE PROCEDURE statement for now. It is necessary to make the CREATE QUEUE statement work and will be explained later. The full syntax for creating a queue is shown in the following code sample:

```
CREATE QUEUE <object>
  [ WITH
    [ STATUS = { ON | OFF }  [ , ] ]
    [ RETENTION = { ON | OFF } [ , ] ]
    [ ACTIVATION (
        [ STATUS = { ON | OFF } , ]
          PROCEDURE_NAME = <procedure>,
          MAX_QUEUE_READERS = max_readers,
          EXECUTE AS { SELF | 'user_name' | OWNER }
          ) ]
  ]
    [ ON { filegroup | [ DEFAULT ] } ]
```

Queue names are not sent in message headers, so they are just SQL Server object names with the same collation rules as normal SQL Server objects. Queues are also contained in SQL schemas, unlike the Service Broker metadata objects, so they can be referenced with three-part names.

You can ignore the ACTIVATION options for now because I'll explain them later. The STATUS option allows you to specify whether the queue should start handling messages as soon as it's created. You might want to create queues with STATUS set to OFF to keep them from getting filled up before you're ready, but be sure to use ALTER QUEUE to turn on the queue when you want to process messages.

The RETENTION option controls whether all messages should be kept around until the conversation is ended. When RETENTION is ON, all messages going both directions in a conversation are kept in the queue until the conversation ends. Turning on RETENTION might be useful if you need to back out a long-running business transaction by running compensating transactions. The messages will allow you to track what you have done so far so that you know what you have to undo. RETENTION can sometimes be useful for debugging an application also. Generally, I would advise you to use RETENTION with extreme caution. With RETENTION

ON, the queue will get very big very fast and performance might degrade significantly. The ON <*filegroup*> option tells Service Broker where to create the hidden table to store messages. Queues normally don't get too big unless RETENTION is on or the application that receives messages is not running for a while.

You might want to consider not putting queues in the DEFAULT filegroup and instead put them in their own filegroup. This will keep a sudden growth in a queue from using all the free space in one of the critical filegroups. Because a queue is built on an internal table, there is no limit to how big a queue can become other than available disk space.

A key thing to remember is that all queues have the same schema. You are not allowed to add your own columns to a queue. Although defining your own message structure in a queue might seem like an attractive option, much of Service Broker's ability to rapidly transfer and manage messages in a dialog relies on the fact that Service Broker always knows the structure of a message and a queue. For example, if only one type of message could be sent in a conversation (because a queue could only hold one message structure), message ordering would be much less effective because a single order might be sent to three or four different queues. In this case, the application would have to assemble an order from different queues with messages arriving in different order on each queue, making the application logic much more complex.

Most columns in a Service Broker queue are self-explanatory and well documented in Books Online, but there are a few worth describing in a little more detail. The *status* column tracks the history of a message in the queue. When it is first inserted the status is 1, which means it is ready to be received. After it has been read, if RETENTION is turned on, the status is set to 0, meaning it has been received and processed by the application and the transaction has been committed. If RETENTION is not on, you won't see this status because the message is deleted as soon as it is processed. A status of 2 means the message has been received out of order, so it can't be processed until the missing messages arrive. A status of 3 means the message has been sent. Sent messages won't appear in the queue unless RETENTION is turned on. With RETENTION turned on, an extra copy of the sent message is inserted into the queue. This is another reason RETENTION hurts performance.

The *priority* column is a little misleading. Service Broker receives messages in priority order, but as of the SQL Server 2005 release, the priority is always 0 and there's no way to change it. Conversations enforce message ordering, so priority within a conversation would be meaningless because messages have to be processed in order no matter what the priority is. The *priority* column in the queue is intended to set the relative priority of conversations. The development group ran out of time before we could come up with a meaningful way to set the priority, so we deferred the feature to a later release. For now, the best way to implement priority processing is to point high-priority messages at a different queue than low-priority messages and then allow the application to process them appropriately. This approach generally entails not processing messages from the low-priority queue unless the high-priority queue is empty. However, be careful when you design this, because getting the behavior you want means dealing with starvation of the low-priority queues if there are enough high-priority messages to consume all your resources. You'll also have to make sure that processing a low-priority message doesn't keep you from seeing a high-priority message arriving. (Now you understand why we couldn't come up with a workable design in time.)

The last two queue columns worth commenting on are *queuing_order* and *message_sequence_number*. These columns are often cause confusion because they appear to be the same thing. The *queuing_order* column is the order that the message was placed in the queue regardless of the conversation to which it belongs. The *message_sequence_number* column is the order of the message within its conversation. This is the order that gets enforced when messages are received. You might see gaps in the *queuing_order* values because Service Broker might skip messages to return the messages in *message_sequence_number* order within a dialog.

Service Broker queues created with the CREATE QUEUE command hold messages that have reached their final destination and are ready to be received and processed. When Service Broker needs to store messages temporarily before they reach their final destination, it puts them in the *sys.transmission_queue* view. There is one *sys.transmission_queue* in every database. The structure of the *sys.transmission_queue* is a little different from the other queues because the Service Broker needs more information to send a message over the network. If possible, Service Broker will put a sent message directly on the destination queue. This will generally be possible if the destination queue is in the same SQL Server instance as the sender, but it won't be possible if the destination is in a different instance. Service Broker has an internal routine called the *classifier*, which decides what to do with messages. The classifier will put a message in the *sys.transmission_queue* in the following cases:

- The destination is in a different SQL Server instance.

- The destination queue is disabled—STATUS = OFF. The most common cause of this is a poison message on the queue. See the "Poison Messages" section later in the chapter.

- The Service Broker is disabled in the database where the destination queue is. This is generally caused by a database being attached or restored without the ENABLE_BROKER option.

- The destination is unknown. Reliable, asynchronous delivery can't fail just because the destination isn't known. The message will hang around on the *sys.transmission_queue* and be reclassified periodically until the destination is configured or the conversation lifetime expires.

Queues are the key to understanding how Service Broker works. At its lowest level, Service Broker puts messages on queues, takes messages off queues, or moves messages between queues. Most Service Broker problems turn out to be caused by messages being on the wrong queue. One of the most important sources of troubleshooting information is the *transmission_status* column of the *sys.transmission_queue* view. If the message has tried to leave the queue and failed, the *transmission_status* column will indicate what went wrong.

Services

A Service Broker conversation is a reliable, ordered exchange of messages between endpoints. Service Broker names the endpoints with service names. *Service* is a very overloaded word, but in the case of Service Broker, a service is just a name for a conversation endpoint. This is important to remember because many people assume "service" refers to an executable somewhere. In Service Broker, service is linked to a queue that is the destination for messages sent to the endpoint identified by the service name. Why not just use the queue name? The service name is a logical name used in the code, while a queue is a physical object. This level of indirection means that applications written using service names can be deployed in different physical configurations without needing code changes.

The service object also defines which contracts can be used to establish conversations that target the service. The service that identifies the target of a conversation determines whether it will accept the conversation. Because the list of conversations is enforced by the Service Broker infrastructure, the target application can be sure that it will not receive any unexpected message types.

Here's a simple example of a CREATE SERVICE statement:

```
CREATE SERVICE [//microsoft.com/InventoryService]
  ON QUEUE dbo.InventoryQueue
  ([//microsoft.com/Inventory/AddItemContract]);
```

Notice that services are also known across the network, so the URL format for service names is recommended. This example shows only one contract, but any number of contracts can be associated with a service. Also, any number of services can be associated with a queue.

The catalogue view that exposes services is *sys.services*. This query lists service names and the queue name that receives messages targeted at the service:

```
SELECT S.name, Q.name
FROM sys.services AS S
  JOIN sys.service_queues AS Q
  ON S.service_queue_id = Q.object_id;
```

Because a service can use multiple contracts and a contract can be used in multiple services, the *sys.service_contract_usages* view shows the mapping between services and contracts. The following query displays the contracts associated with each service:

```
SELECT S.name AS [Service], Q.name AS [Queue], C.name AS [Contract]
FROM sys.services AS S
  JOIN sys.service_queues AS Q
  ON S.service_queue_id = Q.object_id
  JOIN sys.service_contract_usages  AS U
  ON S.service_id = U.service_id
  JOIN sys.service_contracts AS C
  ON U.service_contract_id = C.service_contract_id;
```

The conversation endpoint that initiates the conversation does not check the contract list of the initiator service when creating a dialog. For this reason, the contract list for initiator services is generally empty. The message types and contract used by the dialog are required to begin the dialog, so requiring the contract to be in the service list is redundant. That being said, if you want to put the contracts into the initiator service's list to document the interface, it doesn't cause any harm because Service Broker will ignore them. The danger is that if the initiator service's list is wrong, you will never know it.

Begining and Ending Dialogs

You now know about all the pieces necessary for a dialog: message types to label the messages, a contract to define which message types can be sent by each endpoint, queues to hold messages at each endpoint, and services to tie all the endpoint elements together. In this section, I will discuss the T-SQL statements to begin and end Service Broker dialogs. The endpoint that begins the dialog is called the *initiator* and the opposite endpoint is the *target*. The T-SQL command that begins a dialog is BEGIN DIALOG. The following code snippet provides an example:

```
BEGIN DIALOG CONVERSATION  @Dialog
  FROM SERVICE     [//microsoft.com/ManufacturingService]
  TO SERVICE       '//microsoft.com/InventoryService'
  ON CONTRACT      [//microsoft.com/Inventory/AddItemContract]
  WITH ENCRYPTION = OFF, LIFETIME = 3600;
```

This statement begins a dialog from the *ManufacturingService* endpoint to the *InventoryService* endpoint. The *@Dialog* is an output variable that contains a *uniqueidentifier*, which is used to refer to the dialog in other Service Broker DML commands. The FROM SERVICE and TO SERVICE parameters define the endpoint of the dialog. FROM SERVICE is the initiator, and TO SERVICE is the target. The FROM SERVICE specified must exist in the database where the BEGIN DIALOG command is executed. The TO SERVICE is not validated when the command is executed because in many cases it might be in another database.

> **More Info**   One of the more frequently asked Service Broker questions is why the FROM SERVICE parameter is a SQL Server name and the TO SERVICE parameter is a string. Although in the current implementation the TO SERVICE name will always be a SQL Server name, it's assumed that at some point in the future Service Broker will be talking to services that are not necessarily SQL Server services. For this reason, the TO SERVICE parameter is a 256-character string.

The ON CONTRACT clause specifies which contract will be used by this dialog to limit which message types can be sent on the dialog and which endpoint can send each message type. If this clause is omitted, the DEFAULT contract is used. The DEFAULT contract allows only messages of the DEFAULT type to be sent by either endpoint.

The ENCRYPTION parameter might more accurately be called "encryption required." If this parameter is set to ON, the BEGIN DIALOG command will fail if dialog security is not set up—specifically, a remote service binding must be defined for the TO SERVICE name. (See the "Dialog Security" section for an explanation of dialog security.) If the ENCRYPTION parameter is set to OFF, the decision whether or not to use dialog security is a deployment decision. When the service is deployed, the administrator can decide whether to use security for the dialog based on the requirements of the installation.

> **Tip**   When dialog security is used, the BEGIN DIALOG command will create a key to be used for encrypting the dialog messages. This dialog must be encrypted when it is stored in the database, so if ENCRYPTION is set to ON, the database must have a master key. You can create one with this command:
>
> ```
> CREATE MASTER KEY ENCRYPTION BY PASSWORD = 'Pass.word1';
> ```

The LIFETIME parameter sets the maximum time in seconds that the dialog can remain active. If the dialog still exists when the LIFETIME expires, messages of type '*http://schemas.microsoft.com/SQL/ServiceBroker/Error*' are put into the queues at both endpoints of the dialog. The state of both endpoints is changed to '*Error*' so that no more messages can be sent or received on the dialog. It's important to keep in mind that the dialog still exists until both endpoints end it, so your code needs to handle error messages.

Now that you know how to begin a dialog, you'll learn how to end one. In most applications, the application at one endpoint of the dialog will know that the dialog is complete. In a purchase order application, for example, the dialog might be complete after the purchaser has received acknowledgement that the ordered item has been paid for. The endpoint that determines that the dialog is complete will end it with an END CONVERSATION statement:

```
END CONVERSATION @dialog;
```

This command will mark the endpoint as closed, delete any messages still on the queue, and send a message of type '*http://schemas.microsoft.com/SQL/ServiceBroker/EndDialog*' to the opposite endpoint of the dialog. This message is sent with a negative sequence number so that it will be received ahead of any other messages in the queue for this dialog. When the opposite endpoint receives the end dialog message, it might continue to process any messages still in the queue, but it can't send messages on the dialog because the opposite endpoint is gone. Similarly, any messages in the sys.transmission_queue that haven't been delivered to the opposite endpoint of the dialog are deleted when an EndDialog message is received. When the endpoint has processed any outstanding messages, it should do any required cleanup and then issue an END CONVERSATION command to terminate its side of the conversation. After both endpoints have ended the dialog, Service Broker will clean up the dialog state.

In some cases, one of the endpoints will decide to end the dialog because an unrecoverable error has occurred. A simple example would be a purchase order for an invalid part number. In this case, the endpoint can specify an error number and error text to let the other endpoint know what the error was. When a dialog is ended with the error option, an error message of type '*http://schemas.microsoft.com/SQL/ServiceBroker/Error*' is sent to the opposite endpoint instead of the end conversation message. Here's an example of ending a dialog with an error:

```
END CONVERSATION @dialog WITH ERROR = 31472
  DESCRIPTION = 'Invalid Purchase Order number furnished';
```

While developing a Service Broker application, you'll see that it's not unusual to end up with a number of "orphaned" dialogs. These are dialogs that are still hanging around after the application that used them is gone. Dialogs usually end up in this state either because the application didn't call END CONVERSATION on one of the endpoints or the target wasn't configured correctly and the dialog lifetime expired before the dialog was established. You can get rid of these dialogs by ending them with cleanup code—for example:

```
END CONVERSATION @dialog WITH CLEANUP;
```

This command will unconditionally terminate the dialog without sending a message to the opposite endpoint, and it will discard any unprocessed messages. Therefore, it should be used only if you're sure the dialog is no longer in use. You can use this statement in scripts to clean up large numbers of orphaned or expired conversations. For example, this script will clean up all conversations in an error state:

```
DECLARE @handle AS UNIQUEIDENTIFIER;
DECLARE conv CURSOR FOR
  SELECT conversation_handle
  FROM sys.conversation_endpoints
  WHERE state = 'ER';
OPEN conv;
FETCH NEXT FROM conv INTO @handle;
WHILE @@FETCH_STATUS = 0
BEGIN
  END Conversation @handle WITH CLEANUP;
  FETCH NEXT FROM conv INTO @handle;
END
CLOSE conv;
DEALLOCATE conv;
```

If you remove the WHERE clause from the SELECT statement, this script will get rid of all conversations in the database. This obviously requires administrator privileges to run and should be done only to clean up test data. It should never be done on a system with real dialogs running.

Conversation Endpoints

You have learned by now that Service Broker dialogs are reliable, persistent conversations. In this section, I'll discuss how reliability and persistence are implemented. The state that Service Broker maintains about a conversation is stored in the *sys.conversation_endpoints* view.

To ensure reliable exactly once delivery, Service Broker must keep track of what messages it has received. Because dialog messages must be in order, Service Broker doesn't have to keep a list of all the messages it has received. It is enough to keep track of the highest numbered message received successfully on the conversation. The *receive_sequence* column is the sequence number of the next message expected on this conversation. Large Service Broker messages might be sent as a number of smaller message fragments. Each fragment is tracked and acknowledged so that the whole message doesn't have to be resent if there's an error. The *receive_sequence_frag* column tracks the fragment number of the last fragment received. Note that if a fragment or message is received out of order, it is not thrown away. It is retained so that it doesn't have to be received again, but the *receive_sequence* and *receive_sequence_frag* values are not updated until all the missing fragments have been received. The *send_sequence* column tracks the sequence numbers of messages sent so that the dialog knows which sequence number to assign to the next message.

> **Note**   The actual sequence number stored is not the sequence number of the last message or fragment received or sent, but rather the next sequence number expected. For example, when message 4 has been received successfully, the *receive_sequence* column will contain 5 because that is the next sequence expected. Because of this, when a message is received, its sequence number is compared to the *receive_sequence* column. If the numbers match, the message is marked as received and the *receive_sequence* is incremented. Similarly, when a message is sent, the value in the *send_sequence* column is used as its sequence number and the column is incremented after the message is sent.

The *service_id* column identifies the service associated with this conversation endpoint. You can join with the *sys.services* view to find the name of the service. The *far_service* column gives the name of the service at the opposite endpoint of this conversation. This is a name instead of an identifier because the far endpoint might be in another database. If the dialog has been successfully established and a message has been received from the opposite endpoint, the *far_broker_instance* column will be filled with the GUID taken from the *service_broker_guid* column of the *sys.databases* entry for the database where the remote endpoint is located. Together, these columns determine the two endpoints of the conversation. Notice that there is no information about the network address of either endpoint. This is to allow either endpoint to move to a different network location during the lifetime of a dialog without affecting message delivery. Moving active dialog endpoints is a very powerful feature that provides flexibility and resilience in a Service Broker network.

The *state* and *state_desc* columns of the *sys.conversation_endpoints* view display the state of the conversation endpoint. The *state* column is a two-character abbreviation for the full state description given in the *state_desc* column. The full list of possible states and their meaning is given in Books Online, but I'll highlight some of the more important states here.

- **CO, or CONVERSING**   This is the normal state for a conversation in progress. Both endpoints are active and talking to each other.

- **ER, or ERROR**   This means the conversation has encountered an unrecoverable error. The most common error is that the conversation lifetime has expired. Remember that even though the conversation is in an error state, it will not go away until both endpoints have called END CONVERSATION.

- **DI, or DISCONNECTED_INBOUND**   This means that the opposite end of the conversation has called END CONVERSATION but this endpoint hasn't. If you see many conversations in this state, the code handling this endpoint is not calling END CONVERSATION when it should.

- **CD, or CLOSED**   This means the conversation is closed completely. On the target side of a conversation, Service Broker will keep the conversation around in a CLOSED state for about half an hour to prevent replay attacks where an attacker saves and then resends a message. If the conversation endpoint entry is still there when the replayed message arrives, it will be ignored. After a half hour, the message lifetime will have expired, so a replayed message will be discarded.

One of the more confusing aspects of the *sys.conversation_endpoints* view is the *conversation_handle* and *conversation_id* columns. Both of these are GUIDs that are used to identify a conversation. The *conversation_handle* is the handle used to address the dialog in T-SQL commands such as SEND or END CONVERSATION. Each endpoint has a different handle so that Service Broker knows which endpoint you are referring to in the command. For example, if both endpoints of a dialog are in the same database, the two endpoints are in the same view. In this case, they have to be different so that Service Broker knows whether you are sending a message from the initiator to the target or from the target to the initiator. The *conversation_id* is the same for both endpoints of the conversation. It is included in each message header so that Service Broker can determine which conversation a message belongs to.

There are several more columns in the *sys.conversation_endpoints* view, but I have covered the most interesting ones here. The rest of the columns are either security related or useful only to Microsoft Product Support Services (PSS) or the development team trying to isolate a problem.

Conversation Groups

One of the more difficult aspects of writing asynchronous messaging applications is dealing with multiple applications or multiple threads receiving messages from a queue simultaneously. To understand why this is an issue, think about a purchase order arriving in a message queue. The purchase order is sent as multiple messages—a header message, multiple order-line messages, and a footer message. If multiple threads receive messages from the same purchase order, one or more order lines might be processed before the purchase order header. These transactions would fail because the header isn't in the database yet. Transactional messaging handles this situation because when the order-line transactions fail, the transaction rolls back and the message is put back on the queue. However, it's possible for an order line to be processed multiple times before the header is present. This is inefficient but manageable. However, if an order footer closes out the purchase order before the last order line is processed, data might be lost. Because of these problems, many messaging applications are written with only one receiving process for each queue. This approach obviously doesn't scale well, but it is often necessary to maintain consistency in the data.

The multithreaded reader problem is a bigger issue with Service Broker conversations because Service Broker ensures in-order processing of messages in a conversation. If one thread processes message 20 and another thread processes message 21 of a conversation, it's possible for 21 to complete before 20, which violates message ordering. Service Broker solves this problem through use of conversation group locking.

Every conversation is associated with a conversation group. When an application sends or receives messages, Service Broker locks the conversation group so that no other code can receive or send messages on the locked conversation until the transaction holding the lock completes. This means that even if your application has hundreds of queue readers active, a conversation can be accessed by only one queue reader at a time. This is a very powerful feature because it means that even when thousands of messages are being processed simultaneously, the messages for a particular conversation are processed on one thread at a time. The logic for processing a conversation can assume that a given conversation is processed sequentially, so it doesn't have to deal with the issues associated with multithreaded applications. After the transaction that is processing messages for a conversation group commits, the lock is released and the queue reader goes on to process the next message on the queue, which might be from a different conversation group. Messages in a given conversation group might be processed by many different threads during the life of the conversation group, but they are processed on only one thread at a time.

By default, there is a one-to-one correspondence between conversations and conversation groups. Each conversation group is a row in the *sys.conversation_groups* view. When a conversation endpoint is created, a GUID is generated and a row is inserted into the *sys.conversation_groups* view with the GUID in the *conversation_group_id* column. The conversation endpoint is made part of the conversation group by using the *conversation_group_id* value as a foreign key in the *conversation_group_id* column of the *sys.conversation_endpoints* view. Obviously, any number of conversation endpoints can be made members of a conversation group by using the *conversation_group_id* foreign key. When the conversation group is locked, the lock applies to all conversation endpoints related to the conversation group. To understand why locking a group of conversations is useful, think about a typical order-entry application implemented in Service Broker. When an order is received, the order processing logic might create dialogs to the inventory service, shipping service, credit check service, and accounts receivable service and send messages to all these services in the initial order transaction. These services will process the messages they received from the order service and send responses. The responses will arrive back on the order queue in a random order that is based on how long it took to process the message. If these response messages are processed by different threads, the order-processing logic will have to deal with responses being processed on different threads simultaneously. On the other hand, if all the dialogs related to a particular order are put into the same conversation group, receiving a response from any of the dialogs in the group will lock the group and ensure that other messages from dialogs in the locked conversation group will only be processed by the thread that holds the lock. Thus, all the conversations in the conversation group will be single threaded. This means that the logic that runs in a highly parallel multithreaded system can be written as a single-threaded application because Service Broker manages concurrency.

There are three ways to group conversations into a conversation group in the BEGIN DIALOG command. You can specify the conversation handle of a conversation already in the group, you can specify the conversation group ID of an existing conversation group, or you can use your own GUID to create a new conversation group. The method you choose depends on what you know at the time you begin the dialog.

For example, if you want to create dialogs from the manufacturing service to the inventory and PO services in the same conversation group, the commands would look something like this:

```
BEGIN DIALOG  @ManufacturingHandle
   FROM SERVICE    [//microsoft.com/ManufacturingService]
   TO SERVICE      '//microsoft.com/InventoryService'
   ON CONTRACT     [//microsoft.com/Inventory/AddItemContract];

BEGIN DIALOG  @POHandle
   FROM SERVICE    [//microsoft.com/ManufacturingService]
   TO SERVICE      '//microsoft.com/POService'
   ON CONTRACT     [//microsoft.com/Inventory/AddPOContract]
   WITH RELATED_CONVERSATION = @ManufacturingHandle;
```

If the order service receives an order message and wants to begin a dialog to the inventory service in the same conversation group as the incoming order dialog, it would take the conversation group ID out of the incoming message and begin the inventory dialog like this:

```
BEGIN DIALOG  @POHandle
   FROM SERVICE    [//microsoft.com/OrderService]
   TO SERVICE      '//microsoft.com/InventoryService'
   ON CONTRACT     [//microsoft.com/Inventory/CheckContract]
   WITH RELATED_CONVERSATION_GROUP = @OrderGroupID;
```

This second syntax also allows you to make up your own conversation group ID. If the conversation group specified in the RELATED_CONVERSATION_GROUP parameter doesn't exist, a conversation group with that ID will be created. This approach allows you to use an existing GUID as the conversation group identifier. For example, if the order ID in your order database is a GUID, you can use it as the conversation group for dialogs related to that order. This makes relating incoming messages to the correct order simple. Be sure that the GUID you are using is unique, however. If it isn't, you might end up with unrelated dialogs in the same conversation group.

Sending and Receiving

Now that you have learned how to configure and begin a dialog, you're ready to learn how to send and receive messages on the dialog. The T-SQL command for sending a message on a conversation is SEND, and the command for receiving a message is RECEIVE. These command names can be misleading because there might or might not be a network involved in sending and receiving messages. The SEND command puts a message on a queue, and the RECEIVE command removes a message from a queue. In some cases, the message is transferred across a network to the destination queue, but if possible, the SEND command inserts the message into the destination queue directly and the RECEIVE command deletes the message from the same queue. Arguably, these commands should have been ENQUEUE and DEQUEUE, but most messaging systems use SEND and RECEIVE so these names were adopted.

The SEND command inserts a message into a queue. If the destination queue is available and is in the same database instance where the SEND command was executed, the message is inserted directly into the destination queue. Otherwise, the message is inserted into the transmission queue in the local database. The RECEIVE command dequeues a message from the destination queue. If the RETENTION option is OFF for the queue, the RECEIVE command translates to a DELETE ... OUTPUT command that deletes the chosen rows from the queue and returns the deleted rows. If the RETENTION option is ON, the *status* column of the messages received is updated from 1 to 0 and the updated rows are returned. Because the RECEIVE is done in a database transaction, if the transaction rolls back the delete or update is undone and the messages are put back on the queue as if nothing had happened.

The SEND command needs only three parameters: the handle of the dialog to send on, the message type to use for the message, and the contents of the message. The dialog handle might come from a BEGIN DIALOG command, from a received message, or from the application state. If the supplied dialog does not exist or is in the DI, DO, ER, or CD state, the SEND will fail. One of the more common Service Broker errors is the one returned from a SEND on a closed dialog. The message type supplied must exist in the local database and must be allowed in the contract for the dialog specified. If no message type is supplied, the DEFAULT message type is used and the dialog must be using the DEFAULT contract. The message can be any SQL type that can be cast to VARBINARY(MAX). The SEND command does the CAST internally, so you can supply any compatible type. The message content can be supplied as a variable or as a literal value. Putting this all together, the SEND command looks like this:

```
SEND ON CONVERSATION @Dialog
  MESSAGE TYPE [//microsoft.com/Inventory/AddItem]
  (@message_body);
```

Notice that although a message has 14 columns, the SEND command has only three parameters. The other columns are obtained from Service Broker metadata based on the *conversation_handle* parameter. The conversation endpoint information is used to route and secure the sent message. It is important to remember that at its lowest level, a SEND is just an INSERT command. The major difference is that SEND uses the Service Broker metadata to fill in the required routing and security information from the established conversation associated with the SEND by the conversation endpoint parameter before the message row is inserted into the queue. The SEND command can be executed with the same tools as the INSERT command—ADO.NET, ODBC, OLE DB, Management Studio, SQL scripts, and so on. This means you can add Service Broker commands to your application without installing any new software or learning new APIs.

The syntax of the RECEIVE command is similar to the SELECT command. You specify the message columns you want to receive, the queue you want to receive from, and optionally a limited WHERE clause. Here's a typical RECEIVE command:

```
RECEIVE TOP(1)
  @message_type = message_type_name,
  @message_body = message_body,
  @dialog       = conversation_handle
FROM dbo.InventoryQueue;
```

In this case, I chose to use the TOP(1) clause to receive only a single message. This is much less efficient than receiving multiple messages with each command, but the contents of a single message can be loaded into SQL variables for use in a stored procedure or script. A RECEIVE in a client-side program should retrieve all available messages as a record set.

The next section of the RECEIVE statement is the list of columns to be retrieved. It has the same syntax as a column list in a basic SELECT statement. In the example, only three columns are returned. These three columns are the minimum set of columns necessary to process a message. The *message_type_name* column indicates what kind of message has been received. You must always know the message type because even if the contract limits a service to a single incoming message type, error and end dialog messages might be received and must be processed appropriately. Using the *message_type_id* column instead of the name would be a little more efficient because an internal join is eliminated. However, there is no way to control the ID assigned to a message type, so using the ID isn't recommended unless you use only system message types that have stable IDs.

The FROM clause specifies which queue to receive messages from. The RECEIVE statement finds the oldest conversation group with messages available on the queue that is not already locked by another transaction. The command then locks the conversation group and uses a DELETE or UPDATE with OUTPUT command to retrieve the messages. Even if there are message on the queue from various conversation groups, only the messages from a single conversation group will be returned by a RECEIVE command. This approach ensures that a RECEIVE command will lock only one conversation group at a time, which improves parallelism. It is possible and, in many cases, desirable for a single transaction to hold multiple conversation group locks, but each RECEIVE statement locks only a single conversation group. If your program has done a lot of work to restore the state for a conversation group, receiving messages from another conversation group will require throwing that state away and retrieving the state for the new conversation group. If there are more messages on the queue for the original conversation group, it will be more efficient to retrieve them while you have the state loaded. To support this, you can specify which conversation group to receive messages from:

```
RECEIVE top(1)
  @message_type = message_type_name,
  @message_body = message_body,
  @dialog       = conversation_handle
FROM dbo.InventoryQueue
WHERE conversation_group_id = @CGID;
```

If there are no messages from the specified conversation group on the queue, this statement returns no rows.

There are also rare circumstances when it make sense to send a message and then wait for the response from that message. This is normally a bad thing to do because it negates the advantages of asynchronous messaging. However, in some cases, the application needs to know that an action is complete before continuing. In this case, you can receive messages from a particular conversation:

```
RECEIVE top(1)
    @message_type = message_type_name,
    @message_body = message_body
FROM dbo.InventoryQueue
WHERE conversation_handle = @dialog;
```

The problem with the RECEIVE statement is that if there are no messages available on the queue, it returns immediately—just like a SELECT statement that finds no records. In some cases, this is the desired behavior because if the queue is empty, the application can do other things. On the other hand, in many cases polling the queue is a waste of resources. To use resources more efficiently, Service Broker allows you to wrap the RECEIVE statement in a WAITFOR statement. The WAITFOR statement allows the RECEIVE statement to return immediately if there are messages in the queue but wait until a message arrives if the queue is empty. The RECEIVE statement now looks like this:

```
WAITFOR (
  RECEIVE top(1)
    @message_type = message_type_name,
    @message_body = message_body,
    @dialog      = conversation_handle
  FROM dbo.InventoryQueue
), TIMEOUT 2000;
```

The TIMEOUT clause defines when the WAITFOR statement should give up and return if no messages arrive. In this case, if there are no messages after 2000 milliseconds (ms), the statement will return no rows (*@@ROWCOUNT = 0*). If a message arrives before the timeout expires, the statement returns immediately. If the TIMEOUT clause is omitted, the statement will wait until a message arrives on the queue no matter how long it takes.

Important   The RECEIVE and SEND keywords must start the commands. Most SQL keywords that start commands—such as SELECT, INSERT, and UPDATE—are known to the parser as terminal keywords. This means that whenever the parser sees one of these keywords, it knows that a new command is starting. SEND and RECEIVE are not marked as terminal keywords because they are not part of ANSI SQL. To ensure that the parser knows that a new command is starting, the command before SEND or RECEIVE must end with a semicolon (;). The exception to this is a RECEIVE statement inside a WAITFOR statement.

Sample Dialog

In this section, I'll present a simple Service Broker application that demonstrates how all this fits together. I'll start with an application that runs in a single database and, in subsequent sections, show how to move this application into a distributed environment.

The application to be built is an inventory application that accepts items from a manufacturing application and adds them to inventory. To simplify the code, it will be completely implemented as T-SQL stored procedures. In reality, one or more of the services would probably be either an external application connecting to the database or a CLR stored procedure.

A stored procedure called *AddItemProc* will send a message to the *InventoryService* with an XML body that contains an item to be added to the inventory. The procedure *InventoryProc* receives the message from the *InventoryQueue*, inserts a row in the Inventory table, and sends a response back to the *ManufacturingService*. The procedure *ManufacturingProc* receives the response message from the *ManufacturingQueue* and updates the State table with the response information. Figure 11-1 shows how this works.

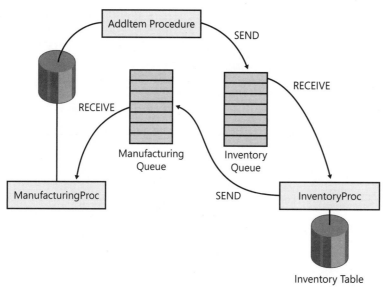

Figure 11-1   Add inventory sample

First, run the code in Listing 11-1 to create the Service Broker objects required to implement the Inventory service that receives and processes *AddItem* messages.

Listing 11-1   Inventory service metadata

```
CREATE DATABASE Inventory;
GO
USE Inventory;
GO
```

```
----------------------------------------------------------------
-- Create the message types we will need for the conversation
----------------------------------------------------------------


CREATE MESSAGE TYPE [//microsoft.com/Inventory/AddItem];
CREATE MESSAGE TYPE [//microsoft.com/Inventory/ItemAdded];

/*--------------------------------------------------------------
-- Create a contract for the AddItem conversation
----------------------------------------------------------------*/

CREATE CONTRACT [//microsoft.com/Inventory/AddItemContract]
  ([//microsoft.com/Inventory/AddItem] SENT BY INITIATOR,
   [//microsoft.com/Inventory/ItemAdded] SENT BY TARGET);
GO

/*--------------------------------------------------------------
-- Create the procedure to service the Inventory target queue
-- Make it an empty procedure for now.  We will fill it in later
----------------------------------------------------------------*/

CREATE PROCEDURE dbo.InventoryProc  AS
  RETURN 0;
GO

/*--------------------------------------------------------------
-- Create the Inventory Queue which will be the target of
-- the conversations.  This is created with activation off.
----------------------------------------------------------------*/

CREATE QUEUE dbo.InventoryQueue
  WITH ACTIVATION (
    STATUS = ON,
    PROCEDURE_NAME = dbo.InventoryProc  ,
    MAX_QUEUE_READERS = 2,
    EXECUTE AS SELF
  ) ;

/*--------------------------------------------------------------
-- Create the Inventory Service.  Because this is the Target
-- service, the contract must be specified
----------------------------------------------------------------*/

CREATE SERVICE [//microsoft.com/InventoryService] ON QUEUE dbo.InventoryQueue
  ([//microsoft.com/Inventory/AddItemContract]);

/*--------------------------------------------------------------
-- Create a table to hold the inventory we're adding
-- This isn't meant to be realistic - just a way to show that the
-- service did something
----------------------------------------------------------------*/
```

```
CREATE TABLE dbo.Inventory
(
  PartNumber    NVARCHAR(50)     Primary Key Clustered NOT NULL,
  Description   NVARCHAR (2000) NULL,
  Quantity      INT NULL,
  ReorderLevel  INT NULL,
  Location      NVARCHAR(50) NULL
);
GO
```

There's nothing too exciting here. One thing that might seem odd is that the *InventoryProc* stored procedure is empty. This is done so that the name can be used to specify the activation parameters for the queue without creating the whole procedure. The other way to do this is to create the queue without activation and then use ALTER QUEUE to add activation after the stored procedure exists. This approach works well for me because I have a tendency to forget to do activation if I don't do it when I create the queue. The Inventory table has a few columns to illustrate how to transfer data from a message to a table, but it's obviously not a realistic inventory table. Listing 11-2 has the real logic to implement the Inventory service that processes the *AddItem* messages.

Listing 11-2   Inventory service program

```
ALTER PROCEDURE dbo.InventoryProc
AS

Declare @message_body AS xml;
Declare @response      AS xml;
Declare @message_type AS sysname;
Declare @dialog        AS uniqueidentifier ;
Declare @hDoc          AS int;
--  This procedure will just sit in a loop processing event messages in
--  the queue until the queue is empty
WHILE (1 = 1)
BEGIN
  BEGIN TRANSACTION
  -- Receive the next available message
  WAITFOR (
     RECEIVE top(1) -- just handle one message at a time
       @message_type = message_type_name,
       @message_body = message_body,
       @dialog       = conversation_handle
     FROM dbo.InventoryQueue
     ), TIMEOUT 2000

  -- If we didn't get anything, bail out
  IF (@@ROWCOUNT = 0)
  BEGIN
    ROLLBACK TRANSACTION
    BREAK;
  END
```

```
/*------------------------------------------------------------------
-- Message handling logic based on the message type received
------------------------------------------------------------------*/

  -- Handle End Conversation messages by ending our conversation also
  IF (@message_type = 'http://schemas.microsoft.com/SQL/ServiceBroker/EndDialog')
  BEGIN
    PRINT 'End Dialog for dialog # ' + cast(@dialog as nvarchar(40));
    END CONVERSATION @dialog;
  END
   -- For error messages, just end the conversation.  In a real app, we
   -- would log the error and do any required cleanup.
  ELSE IF (@message_type = 'http://schemas.microsoft.com/SQL/ServiceBroker/Error')
  BEGIN
    PRINT 'Dialog ERROR dialog # ' + cast(@dialog as nvarchar(40));
    END CONVERSATION @dialog;
  END
   -- Handle an AddItem message
  ELSE IF (@message_type = '//microsoft.com/Inventory/AddItem')
  BEGIN
    SET @response  = N'Item added successfully'
    -- Parse the message body and add to the inventory
    BEGIN TRY
      INSERT INTO dbo.Inventory
(PartNumber, Description, Quantity, ReorderLevel, Location)

      select itm.itm. value ('(PartNumber/text())[1]', 'nvarchar(50)')
          as PartNumber,
        itm.itm.value('(Description/text())[1]', 'nvarchar(2000)')
          as Description,
        itm.itm.value('(Quantity/text())[1]', 'int')
          as Quantity,
        itm.itm.value('(ReorderLevel/text())[1]', 'int')
          as ReorderLevel,
        itm.itm.value('(Location/text())[1]', 'nvarchar(50)')
          as Location
        from @message_body.nodes('/Item[1]') as itm(itm);

    END TRY
    BEGIN CATCH
      ROLLBACK TRANSACTION
      -- Create a new transaction to send the response
      BEGIN TRANSACTION
        SET @response  = ERROR_MESSAGE();
        -- ToDo - log the error
        -- ToDo - poison message handling
    END CATCH;
    -- Send a response message confirming the add was done
    SEND ON CONVERSATION @dialog
      MESSAGE TYPE [//microsoft.com/Inventory/ItemAdded] (@response);
    -- We handle one message at a time so we're done with this dialog
    END CONVERSATION @dialog;
  END -- If message type
  COMMIT TRANSACTION
END -- while
GO
```

The process flow of this procedure is the basis of almost all Service Broker services. The procedure is a continuous loop that receives a message at the top, processes the message with conditional logic based on the message type received, and then goes back to the top and receives another message. The loop continues until the @@ROWCOUNT after RECEIVE is 0, which indicates the queue is empty. Each loop is a separate transaction, which means there is only one message per transaction. This is not optimal, but it makes the logic easier to follow, so I usually do this for samples. A high-performance Service Broker application would read all the messages available for a conversation group in a single RECEIVE statement and then process them all at once. If the message volume is high, you might also consider going through the loop a few times before committing the transaction. This approach makes the logic more efficient, but it also makes the processing logic much more complex.

The message processing logic is the T-SQL equivalent of a C# "switch" statement with three different sections for the three message types that might be found on the queue. It's important to remember that because a RECEIVE statement specifies a queue, any messages type allowed on the queue might be received. This means that if there are two or more services associated with the queue, the logic in the queue reader must be able to process any message allowed on any of the services.

The first two message types are error and end dialog. These two message types can be received by any service, so all service logic must have logic to handle them. At a minimum, the message-handling logic must contain an END CONVERSATION to close out this end of the dialog. If some cleanup is required before ending the conversation, handling these messages will be more complex.

The last message type is the *AddItem* message. The message body is an XML document that contains the data required to add a row to the Inventory table. The sample code processes the message with a Nodes query that inserts the XML data in the Inventory table. The error-handling logic is not robust, and it's there only to illustrate where real error-handling would go. If there is an error in the insert statement—a primary key violation, perhaps—the CATCH block will roll back the transaction and put the error message into the response message. The problem with doing that is that if the error is unrecoverable, as it would be if the message contained a duplicate key, the message would be put back in the queue. When the same message is read again, it would fail again and be rolled back again. This behavior would put the stored procedure into a tight loop. A message such as this that can never be processed correctly is called a *poison message*. Transactional messaging applications must deal with poison messages. (See the "Poison Messages" section later in the chapter for details about how to deal with them.) To avoid getting into a loop, the sample unconditionally ends the conversation whether the message was processed successfully or not. This is probably not what you would want to do in a real application.

After inserting the message contents into the Inventory table, the response message is sent back to the *ManufacturingService* and the dialog is ended. The response message contains either a message indicating success or the error text if the insert failed. The *@dialog* variable used for the SEND and END DIALOG was obtained from the received message, so the message will be routed back to the calling dialog.

Now that a service is ready to process messages, let's implement a stored procedure to send the *AddItem* message to this service. This stored procedure will begin a dialog to the *InventoryService* and send a message on the dialog. The FROM SERVICE for this dialog will be the *ManufacturingService*. Because the BEGIN DIALOG command uses the *ManufacturingService* as the FROM SERVICE, the *ManufacturingService* is the initiator of the dialog and the *InventoryService* is the target. Listing 11-3 creates the queue and service for the *ManufacturingService*, and it creates the stored procedure to send the *AddItem* message.

Listing 11-3   Dialog initiator procedure

```
/*-----------------------------------------------------------------
-- Create an empty procedure for the initiator so we can use it
-- in the activation parameters when we create the queue
-----------------------------------------------------------------*/

CREATE PROCEDURE dbo.ManufacturingProc  AS
  RETURN 0;
GO


/*-----------------------------------------------------------------
-- Create the initiator queue.  Activation is configured
-- but turned off
-----------------------------------------------------------------*/

CREATE QUEUE dbo.ManufacturingQueue
  WITH ACTIVATION (
    STATUS = ON,
    PROCEDURE_NAME = dbo.ManufacturingProc  ,
    MAX_QUEUE_READERS = 2,
    EXECUTE AS SELF
    );

/*-----------------------------------------------------------------
-- Create the Manufacturing service.  Because it is the initiator, it
-- doesn't require contracts.
-----------------------------------------------------------------*/

CREATE SERVICE [//microsoft.com/ManufacturingService]
  ON QUEUE dbo.ManufacturingQueue;


/*-----------------------------------------------------------------
-- Create a table to hold the state for our conversation
-- We use the conversation handle as a key instead of the
-- conversation group ID because we just have one conversation
-- in our group.
-----------------------------------------------------------------*/
```

```
CREATE TABLE dbo.InventoryState
  (
    PartNumber      UNIQUEIDENTIFIER  Primary Key Clustered NOT NULL,
    Dialog          UNIQUEIDENTIFIER NULL,
    State           NVARCHAR(50) NULL
  );
GO


/*-----------------------------------------------------------------
-- Create the initiator stored procedure
-------------------------------------------------------------------*/

CREATE PROCEDURE AddItemProc
AS

DECLARE @message_body       AS xml;
DECLARE @Dialog             AS uniqueidentifier;
DECLARE @partno             AS uniqueidentifier;

--Set the part number to a new GUID so we can run
--this an unlimited number of times
SET @partno = NEWID();

-- Populate the message body
SET @message_body = '<Item>
   <PartNumber>' + CAST (@partno as NVARCHAR(50)) + '</PartNumber>
   <Description>2 cm Left Threaded machine screw</Description>
   <Quantity>5883</Quantity>
   <ReorderLevel>1000</ReorderLevel>
   <Location>Aisle 32, Rack 7, Bin 29</Location>
</Item>';

BEGIN TRANSACTION
-- Begin a dialog to the Hello World Service

BEGIN DIALOG  @Dialog
  FROM SERVICE     [//microsoft.com/ManufacturingService]
  TO SERVICE       '//microsoft.com/InventoryService'
  ON CONTRACT      [//microsoft.com/Inventory/AddItemContract]
  WITH ENCRYPTION = OFF, LIFETIME = 3600;

-- Send message
SEND ON CONVERSATION @Dialog
  MESSAGE TYPE [//microsoft.com/Inventory/AddItem] (@message_body);

-- Put a row into the state table to track this conversation
INSERT INTO dbo.InventoryState
  VALUES (@partno, @Dialog, 'Add Item Sent');
COMMIT TRANSACTION
GO
```

This service uses the message types and contract created for the *InventoryService*, so they don't have to be created again. If you create this service in another database, you must first create the message types and contract.

AddItemProc is a simple procedure. It populates the message body with an XML document, begins a dialog to the *InventoryService*, and sends the message. For each message sent, a row is inserted into the InventoryState table. The InventoryState table tracks the progress of the *AddItem* messages, so a user can see the progress of the dialog.

To see whether this works, run the following:

```
EXEC AddItemProc
```

If everything is working correctly, there should be a row in the Inventory table and a row in the InventoryState table. Because you haven't written the logic to handle the response yet, there should be a response message in the *ManufacturingQueue*.

You have now sent a message on a dialog, processed the message, and sent a response message. All that's left to do is process the response message. To do this, run the code in Listing 11-4 to create another simple Service Broker service with a message processing loop. The process flow will be the same as that for the inventory procedure.

Listing 11-4   Manufacturing procedure

```
ALTER PROCEDURE dbo.ManufacturingProc
AS

DECLARE @message_body AS xml;
DECLARE @message_type AS sysname;
DECLARE @dialog       AS uniqueidentifier ;

--  This procedure will just sit in a loop processing event messages in
--  the queue until the queue is empty

WHILE (1 = 1)
BEGIN
  BEGIN TRANSACTION

  -- Receive the next available message
  WAITFOR (
    RECEIVE top(1)
        @message_type=message_type_name,
        @message_body=message_body,
        @dialog = conversation_handle
    FROM dbo.ManufacturingQueue
    ), TIMEOUT 2000;

  -- If we didn't get anything, bail out
  IF (@@ROWCOUNT = 0)
    BEGIN
      ROLLBACK TRANSACTION
      BREAK;
    END
    IF (@message_type =
      'http://schemas.microsoft.com/SQL/ServiceBroker/EndDialog')
```

```
        BEGIN
            PRINT 'End Dialog for dialog # ' + CAST(@dialog as nvarchar(40));
            END CONVERSATION @dialog;
        END
    ELSE IF (@message_type =
      'http://schemas.microsoft.com/SQL/ServiceBroker/Error')
    BEGIN
        PRINT 'Dialog ERROR dialog # ' + CAST(@dialog as nvarchar(40));
        END CONVERSATION @dialog;
    END
    ELSE IF (@message_type = '//microsoft.com/Inventory/ItemAdded')
    BEGIN
        UPDATE dbo.InventoryState  SET State = CAST(@message_body
            AS NVARCHAR(1000)) WHERE Dialog = @dialog;
    END
    COMMIT TRANSACTION
END -- while
GO
```

This procedure is almost identical to *InventoryProc*, with the exception of the *ItemAdded* message type handling. The logic just updates the state table with the status returned in the message body. Notice that the initiator side of the dialog is actually two different stored procedures—one that begins the dialog and sends the message, and another that handles the responses. This is a normal pattern for asynchronous services. The dialog initiator sends a message to a background service and then either goes on to do something else or goes away. When the response is received, it is handled in the background. In some cases, the response is just recorded in the database; in other cases, it might be communicated back to the user through an e-mail message or something similar.

You've now seen a simple Service Broker conversation in action. The logic might seem complex at first, but keep in mind that most Service Broker applications follow the same pattern. So, once you understand it, you can apply it to a number of applications. In fact, this processing pattern is so common that it has been incorporated into a sample object model that ships with SQL Server 2005. Install the SQL Server samples, and look for the ServiceBrokerInterface sample. The sample service incorporates the message loop handling, and you just have to supply the logic to handle the messages received. In the next two sections of this chapter, I'll move the ManufacturingService first to another database in the same instance to demonstrate dialog security and then to another instance to demonstrate remote communications with Service Broker.

Poison Messages

One of the advantages of transactional messaging is that if the transaction that is processing a message fails and rolls back, the message is still on the queue because the RECEIVE command is also rolled back. The application can then receive the message again, and if it processes successfully this time, the transaction will commit and the message will disappear from the queue. This is why writing transactional message processing applications is much easier than writing nontransactional message applications.

The down side of transactional messaging occurs when processing a message produces an error that retrying won't fix. For example, in the sample application that inserts an item into the inventory table, if there is already an item with the same part number and the part number column has a unique constraint, then no matter how many times the message is processed it will fail. The application will then go into a tight loop processing the message, rolling back the transaction, and then receiving the same message again. A message that can't be processed is known as a *poison message*. If left unchecked, this kind of message will cause the application to hang on the same message and have a major negative impact on the performance of the entire database. To prevent this, if Service Broker detects five rollbacks in a row on a queue, it will disable the queue to stop the poison message. This action is a last resort, however, because the application that uses the queue will stop until the administrator ends the offending dialog and re-enables the queue.

The right way to deal with poison messages is to prevent them. If the application fails to process a message, it should roll back the transaction and then decide whether processing the same message again will be likely to succeed. If the error was something like a deadlock or a lock timeout, it is worth trying again. However, if the error is a constraint violation that won't be resolved the next time the message is processed, the conversation that contains the message should be ended and an application error should be logged. If it makes sense in the application to continue the dialog without the poison message, you can commit the receive to get rid of the poison message and go on with the dialog. The approach to handling poison messages depends on the application, the dialog, and even which message failed—so there's no single right way to handle them. There is one wrong way, which is to always roll back errors and rely on Service Broker to handle them by disabling the queue.

Dialog Security

As with any feature that sends data across the network, security is a vital part of the Service Broker infrastructure. Service Broker includes a number of security options that support the level of security appropriate to the network vulnerability and data criticality. Service Broker security must solve the unique issues presented by asynchronous messaging. Because the applications communicating over a Service Broker conversation might never be running at the same time, normal connection-oriented network security won't provide the full range of security options required by Service Broker. This section describes how dialog security is implemented in the Service Broker and how to configure it.

Dialog security doesn't make sense if both dialog endpoints are in the same database. To configure dialog security, you'll need to move one of the endpoints of our sample application to a different database. To keep things simple, you'll move the initiator to another database in the same SQL Server instance. To set this up, create a database called Manufacturing. Create the message types and contract, as you did in Listing 11-1, and then run the two scripts that set up the initiator (which are provided in Listing 11-3 and Listing 11-4). If this all works correctly, execute *AddItemProc* in the Manufacturing database to begin a dialog and send a message to the *InventoryService*. You should find that the message never makes it to the *InventoryQueue* and instead ends up in the *sys.transmission_queue* in the Manufacturing database with a message in the *transmission_status* column that indicated a bad security context. This statement will display the messages in the *sys.transmission_queue* view.

```
SELECT * FROM sys.transmission_queue
```

The security context error is caused by Service Broker impersonating the owner of the Manufacturing service to send the message. Service Broker does this because a number of users can send messages on a dialog. So the send executes in the context of the service owner to ensure consistent security behavior. SQL Server 2005 considers crossing databases with an impersonated user context a security threat. To see why this is an issue, assume that Moe is the database owner (dbo) of the Inventory database and owns the *InventoryService*. If Larry is the dbo of the Manufacturing database, he can create a user in his database for Moe's login, make this user the owner of the *ManufacturingService*, and grant himself impersonation permissions for this user. Because the Moe user in the Manufacturing database is associated with the same login as the Moe user in the Inventory database, Larry has just given himself permission to execute code in the Inventory database without Moe's knowledge or permission. Although this is a bad thing if Larry isn't a trustworthy dbo, there are valid reasons for wanting to do this. To allow cross-database permissions with an impersonated security context, the system administrator can mark the impersonating database as "trustworthy." To see how this works, sign on as a system administrator and execute the following:

```
ALTER DATABASE Manufacturing SET TRUSTWORTHY ON;
```

If everything is set up correctly, the message in the *sys.transmission_queue* will be delivered and a response will be received within a minute. Check the InventoryState table in the Manufacturing database with this query to make sure it worked.

```
SELECT * FROM InventoryState
```

There is now successful communication with a service in another database, but marking the Manufacturing database as "trustworthy" gives the Manufacturing dbo a lot of power. You wanted to allow him to access the *InventoryService* in the Inventory database, but you actually gave him the ability to access any service in any database in the instance. If Larry isn't really that trustworthy, it's possible to turn off the trustworthy flag and use dialog security to give him access to only the services he really needs. Dialog security uses public key/private key certificates for authentication, so I will start with a brief explanation of asymmetric key encryption and then show how Service Broker uses it for secure message delivery.

Asymmetric Key Authentication

Asymmetric encryption involves two keys—a public key and a private key. These two keys have a special relationship. Data encrypted with the private key can be decrypted only with the public key, and data encrypted with the public key can be decrypted only with the private key. The private key is kept tightly secured on the owner's system, and the public key is given out to systems that need to communicate with the private key owner. At first glance, it looks like a great way to secure communications. If Larry and Moe need to talk, Larry gives Moe his public key and Moe gives Larry his public key. When Larry wants to send Moe something he encrypts it with Moe's public key, confident that only Moe can decrypt it. There are two issues that arise with this process. First, Larry knows that only Moe can decrypt the message, but Moe doesn't know for sure that Larry sent it to him. Larry can solve this problem by signing the message with his private key so that when Moe checks the signature with Larry's public key he will know that Larry sent it. The other, more critical problem is that asymmetric key encryption and decryption are extremely slow. The processor overhead is so great that using this technique for exchanging data is impractical.

Fortunately, symmetric key encryption is relatively efficient for exchanging large messages. Symmetric key encryption is also called "shared secret" encryption because both the sender and receiver have the same key. The issue with this process is the need to reliably exchange the secret key. This issue is especially important for Service Broker because, for optimal security, every conversation has its own symmetric key.

As you might have guessed, Service Broker combines these techniques for dialog security. The asymmetric key technique is used to securely exchange a symmetric key, and then the symmetric key is used to exchange data. Actually, Service Broker cuts down the asymmetric overhead even further by exchanging a symmetric Key Exchange Key (KEK) with the asymmetric keys and then using the KEK to exchange the session keys for each dialog. The KEK is always sent in the header of the first dialog message, but it is decrypted only if the target has lost the KEK or it has changed. Each pair of Service Broker endpoints uses a different KEK for the dialogs between them. Service Broker generates a new Key Exchange Key periodically to reduce the impact of someone using a brute-force attack to break the key.

Configuring Dialog Security

Now that you know the basics of secure data transmission and authentication with dialog security, I'll cover how to configure services to use dialog security. For mutual authentication, the initiator will need a private key and the target's public key. The target needs its private key and the initiator's public key. To provide these, Service Broker takes advantage of the support SQL Server 2005 provides for storing certificates. It's important to understand that Service Broker primarily uses a certificate as a convenient container for an asymmetric key. Service Broker never traces the issuer of the certificate. It only checks validity dates to determine a certificate's validity. For Service Broker's purposes, a self-signed certificate works just as well as a certificate from a certificate authority. To fit into the SQL Server security infrastructure, certificates need to own services and hold permissions. However, SQL Server certificates are not security principals, so they can't be assigned ownership or permissions. This means that a certificate must be associated with a user that is a security principal. The user is associated with the certificate through ownership. Certificates are not owned by schemas but are owned directly by users through the AUTHORIZATION parameter of CREATE CERTIFICATE. The other useful SQL Server 2005 feature that Service Broker takes advantage of is the user with no login. If you specify WITHOUT LOGIN in the CREATE USER statement, the user will be created without being associated with a login. This means that you can assign permissions to this user, but no external user can ever log in as this user. This arrangement helps make Service Broker applications more secure.

The BEGIN DIALOG command needs to know which certificates to use to secure the dialog. The private key comes from the owner of the *Service* object. The public key to use comes from the user specified in the REMOTE SERVICE BINDING for the service. The REMOTE SERVICE BINDING is a Service Broker object that ties a service name to a user who owns the public key associated with the remote service. The certificates corresponding to these two certificates—the public key certificate of the initiating service owner's certificate, and the private key certificate of the REMOTE SERVICE BINDING user's certificate—must be present in the target database to establish the dialog.

The private key certificate corresponding to the REMOTE SERVICE BINDING user of the initiator must have CONTROL permission on the target service, and the public key certificate corresponding to the initiator service owner's certificate must have SEND permissions on the target service. The security header sent with the first message of a dialog contains identifiers of the two certificates used to create the security header so that the target knows which certificates to use. The certificate identifier is the combination of the issuer name and the sequence number, which should be unique. The Key Exchange Key is encrypted with the public key of the REMOTE SERVICE BINDING user's certificate, and it is signed with the private key of the initiator service owner's certificate. If the target has the same certificates, it can validate the signature and decrypt the KEK. Once both endpoints have the KEK, dialogs can be established between the endpoints using the KEK to transfer the session key for the dialog without having to use the certificates until the KEK changes or is lost through a database restart. (The KEK is never persisted, so if either endpoint is restarted, a new one must be established.)

Now that you know what's needed, let's look at an example of setting up security for our sample application, as shown in Listing 11-5. This assumes you created the Manufacturing database in the cross database example.

Listing 11-5   Securing the *AddItem* dialog

```
/*---------------------------------------------------------------------
-- This script sets up dialog security between the initiator and target
-- of the AddItem dialog
---------------------------------------------------------------*/

-- First, turn off the trustworthy flag

USE master;
GO
ALTER DATABASE Manufacturing SET TRUSTWORTHY OFF;
GO
```

```
/*--------------------------------------------------------------------
-- Set up the Target Service security
-----------------------------------------------------------------*/


USE Inventory;
GO

CREATE MASTER KEY ENCRYPTION BY PASSWORD = 'Pass.word1';

-- Create a user to represent the "Inventory" Service
CREATE USER InventoryServiceUser WITHOUT  LOGIN;
ALTER AUTHORIZATION ON SERVICE::[//microsoft.com/InventoryService]
  TO InventoryServiceUser;

-- Grant control on the Inventory service to this user
GRANT CONTROL ON SERVICE::[//microsoft.com/InventoryService]
  TO InventoryServiceUser;

-- Create a Private Key Certificate associated with this user
CREATE CERTIFICATE InventoryServiceCertPriv
  AUTHORIZATION InventoryServiceUser
   WITH SUBJECT = 'ForInventoryService';

-- Dump the public key certificate to a file for use on the
-- initiating server - no private key
BACKUP CERTIFICATE InventoryServiceCertPriv
  TO FILE = 'C:\InventoryServiceCertPub';


/*-----------------------------------------------------------------
-- Set up the Initiator Service security
-----------------------------------------------------------------*/


USE Manufacturing;
GO

CREATE MASTER KEY ENCRYPTION BY PASSWORD = 'Pass.word1';

-- Create a user to own the "Manufacturing" Service
CREATE USER ManufacturingServiceUser WITHOUT LOGIN;

-- Make this user the owner of the FROM service
ALTER AUTHORIZATION ON SERVICE::[//microsoft.com/ManufacturingService]
  TO ManufacturingServiceUser;

-- Create a Private Key Certificate associated with this user
CREATE CERTIFICATE ManufacturingServiceCertPriv
  AUTHORIZATION ManufacturingServiceUser
   WITH SUBJECT = 'ForManufacturingService';

-- Dump the public key certificate to a file for use on
-- the Manufacturing server
BACKUP CERTIFICATE ManufacturingServiceCertPriv
  TO FILE = 'C:\ManufacturingServiceCertPub';
```

```
-- Create a user to represent the "Inventory" Service
CREATE USER InventoryServiceUser WITHOUT LOGIN;

-- Import the cert we got from the Inventory Service owned
-- by the user we just created
CREATE CERTIFICATE InventoryServiceCertPub
  AUTHORIZATION InventoryServiceUser
   FROM FILE = 'C:\InventoryServiceCertPub';

CREATE REMOTE SERVICE BINDING ToInventoryService
  TO SERVICE '//microsoft.com/InventoryService'
   WITH USER = InventoryServiceUser;

/*------------------------------------------------------------------
-- Finish the Target Service security setup
--------------------------------------------------------------*/

USE Inventory;
GO

-- Create a user to represent the "Manufacturing" Service
CREATE USER ManufacturingServiceUser WITHOUT LOGIN;

-- Import the cert we got from the Manufacturing Service owned
-- by the user we just created
CREATE CERTIFICATE ManufacturingServiceCertPub
  AUTHORIZATION ManufacturingServiceUser
   FROM FILE = 'C:\ManufacturingServiceCertPub';
GRANT SEND ON SERVICE::[//microsoft.com/InventoryService]
  TO ManufacturingServiceUser ;
```

This looks like a lot of code, but in reality you've just created the four certificates used for authentication and assigning permissions. Creating the public key certificates requires a certificate file exported from the private key certificate. This file is exported with the BACKUP CERTIFICATE command. If the initiator and target are located on different systems, the file must be transferred to the opposite server. However, in this case, the initiator and target are in the same instance, so it is just written out and then read back in from the same file. Also notice the trustworthy flag was set to OFF, so if this service works, it is because of dialog security.

Setting up dialog security seems like a lot of work to avoid setting the trustworthy flag. However, there is another advantage of setting up dialog security to the database—you can now detach either of these databases and attach it to a different SQL Server instance without having to change dialog security. This is what I'll do in the next section.

Routing and Distribution

In this section, I'll move the manufacturing database to another SQL Server instance to demonstrate how to configure Service Broker networking. Although communicating between two machines is more impressive, if you have only one machine, you can use two instances on the same machine to set up a remote Service Broker connection. To set up a dialog initiator in another instance to test communications, detach the Manufacturing database, move the Manufacturing.mdf and Manufacturing_log.ldf files to the second instance, and attach the database to the second instance.

In the instance you have been using for the previous samples, detach the Manufacturing database with this command:

```
sp_detach_db Manufacturing
```

Move the Manufacturing.mdf and Manufacturing_log.ldf files for the Manufacturing database to the machine where the second instance is located. If you are using a second instance on the same machine, you just need to move them to the Data directory for the second instance. Attach the Manufacturing database to the second instance with the following command:

```
CREATE DATABASE Manufacturing
    ON (FILENAME = 'C:\Program Files\Microsoft SQL Server\MSSQL.1\MSSQL\Data\Manufacturing.
mdf'),
    ON (FILENAME = 'C:\Program Files\Microsoft SQL Server\MSSQL.1\MSSQL\Data\Manufacturing_
log.ldf')
    FOR ATTACH
    WITH ENABLE_BROKER;
```

Note that the book formatting has wrapped the filename. Type these on a single line. Remember to include the ENABLE_BROKER option so that Service Broker will run after the attach. You must also encrypt the database master key with the new instance's service master key so that Service Broker can access its encrypted data:

```
USE Manufacturing;
GO
OPEN MASTER KEY DECRYPTION BY PASSWORD = 'Pass.word1';
ALTER MASTER KEY ADD ENCRYPTION BY SERVICE MASTER KEY;
```

Adjacent Broker Protocol

There are two layered protocols involved in exchanging Service Broker messages: the dialog protocol and the Adjacent Broker Protocol. The dialog protocol that's been already discussed maintains the reliable, persistent, stateful sessions between conversation endpoints. Messages are acknowledged and retried at this level, and dialog security is part of this protocol. Also, the dialog protocol is unaware of the transport protocol used to transfer messages on the network.

The "bits on the wire" protocol that Service Broker uses to send data over the network is called the adjacent broker protocol (ABP) because it communicates between SQL Server instances connected by the network. The current ABP implementation works only on TCP/IP connections, but it is designed to be extensible to other network transports in the future. The ABP is a simple protocol designed to efficiently use the available bandwidth to transfer Service

Broker messages between SQL Server instances. The ABP is so efficient that several customers have reported better performance by having the dialog initiator and target on separate machines than having them on the same machine. Of course, your results may vary.

Service Broker messages from all the *sys.transmission_queues* in all the databases on a SQL Server instance are processed by a global instance of the ABP logic. The ABP logic is called a Service Broker endpoint. This endpoint is distinctly different from a conversation endpoint. The endpoint maintains connections to all the SQL Server instances that the local instance has dialogs to. Only one TCP/IP connection is maintained between a given pair of instances.

To ensure fairness, messages waiting to be sent are referenced in a transmission list that maintains a list of all messages waiting to be sent in all the transmission queues in the instance in the order of when they were placed on the queue. Multiple messages to be sent to the same destination are placed into a single TCP/IP message for more efficient transfer. This process is called *boxcaring*. The format of an ABP message is a header that contains information about where the message is going and where it came from. It also includes the sequence number, fragment numbers, and when the message was sent. This header is used by the dialog protocol and the message body as a binary large object (LOB). The first messages from the initiator contain a security header to transfer the keys and information necessary to establish dialog security. When the first message is received back from the target, the initiator knows that the target has the security information, so subsequent messages on that dialog do not include the security header.

The Adjacent Broker Protocol also includes security features. ABP connections are only allowed between instances that have been authenticated and authorized to connect. Because this authentication is done on a connection-oriented session, Microsoft Windows authentication is supported. Certificate-based authentication is also supported to handle connections where Windows authentication won't work. Setting up ABP authentication is covered in the next section. All messages sent over an ABP connection are signed so that any message-tampering or corruption is detected. In addition, the ABP connection can be encrypted. In many cases, encryption isn't necessary because the messages are already encrypted by dialog security, but encryption at the ABP level will ensure that even messages from unsecured dialogs will be encrypted. The encryption software recognizes messages encrypted by the dialog protocol, so encrypted data is not double-encrypted.

Service Broker Endpoints

In SQL Server 2005, all network connections are handled through endpoints. The types of endpoints available are T-SQL, SOAP, Database Mirroring, and Service Broker. The CREATE/ALTER endpoint statements are used to configure the endpoints. The currently configured endpoints are listed in the *sys.endpoints* catalogue view. A Service Broker endpoint is used to configure the port that the instance will use to listen for connections and to specify what kind of security will be used on the connection. The CREATE ENDPOINT syntax includes several protocols for connections, but currently only TCP/IP is supported. The command to create a basic Service Broker endpoint looks like this:

```
CREATE ENDPOINT InventoryServer
   STATE = STARTED
   AS TCP ( LISTENER_PORT = 4030 )
   FOR SERVICE_BROKER (
      AUTHENTICATION = WINDOWS,
      ENCRYPTION = SUPPORTED);
```

The first few lines are pretty self-explanatory, the STATE = STARTED line means the endpoint will start listening for connections immediately, and the LISTENER_PORT clause means the endpoint will listen for connections on port 4030. The port you use doesn't matter as long as it is above 1024 and not already in use on your machine. If you have a tightly controlled network, your network administrator will assign port numbers for you to use. All Service Broker ABP connections must be authenticated. The WINDOWS option means a Windows authentication protocol—either NTLM or KERBEROS—will be used to authenticate the TCP/IP connections.

There are other options that let you specify which protocol to use. In situations where Windows authentication isn't possible, certificates can be used to authenticate the connection. The certificate authentication protocol used is the same SSPI protocol that Secure Sockets Layer (SSL) Internet connections use. I'll cover how to configure both kinds of authentication and how to control which servers you allow to connect to yours later in this section. The ENCRYPTION clause specifies whether encryption should be used on the ABP connection. The three options for this parameter are DISABLED, REQUIRED, and SUPPORTED. Table 11-1 explains how the settings for the two endpoints determine whether the connection will be encrypted.

Table 11-1   ENCRYPTION Settings for Two Endpoints

Endpoint 1	Endpoint 2	Encrypted
DISABLED	SUPPORTED	NO
DISABLED	DISABLED	NO
DISABLED	REQUIRED	ERROR
SUPPORTED	SUPPORTED	YES
SUPPORTED	REQUIRED	YES
REQUIRED	REQUIRED	YES
REQUIRED	DISABLED	ERROR

This clause also allows you to specify RC4 or AES as the encryption algorithm to use. AES is more secure than RC4, but RC4 is significantly faster.

Configuring Adjacent Broker Protocol Connections

The CREATE/ALTER ENDPOINT commands are used to configure the endpoint parameters for ABP. You must also configure permissions to determine which other instances are allowed to connect to the local instance. This is done by creating a SQL Server login in the local instance's master database to represent the remote instances and then granting that login CONNECT permission to the endpoint. When a remote instance connects to the Service Broker endpoint, the connection is authenticated using either a Windows protocol or the SSPI protocol, and the authenticated login is checked for CONNECT permission to the endpoint. If the authentication fails or the authenticated login fails, the connection is closed.

Windows Authentication   Windows authentication is generally easier to configure, so I'll start there. The Windows user that is authenticated is the Service Account for the instance. By default, licensed editions of SQL Server use the local system account as the service account and SQL Express uses Network Service as the service account. For this example, you'll configure a Windows server named MYPC10 for the Inventory instance and a SQL Express instance on the same server as the Manufacturing instance. Log on to the master database of the instance where the Inventory database is, and execute this script:

```
-- Create an endpoint for the inventory server
-- with Windows authentication

CREATE ENDPOINT InventoryEndpoint STATE = STARTED
  AS TCP ( LISTENER_PORT = 5523 )
    FOR SERVICE_BROKER ( AUTHENTICATION = WINDOWS );

-- Grant Network Service connect privileges

GRANT CONNECT ON ENDPOINT::InventoryEndpoint
  TO [NT AUTHORITY\Network Service];
```

That's all there is to configuring the Inventory instance. Next log on to the instance where the Manufacturing database is, and execute this script:

```
-- Create an endpoint for the manufacturing server
-- with Windows authentication

CREATE ENDPOINT ManufacturingEndpoint STATE = STARTED
  AS TCP ( LISTENER_PORT = 5524 )
    FOR SERVICE_BROKER ( AUTHENTICATION = WINDOWS );

--Create a login for remote system in this instance
-- Change to your domain and server name!

CREATE LOGIN [MYDOMAIN\MYPC10$] FROM Windows;
-- Grant Local System connect privilege

GRANT CONNECT ON ENDPOINT::ManufacturingEndpoint
  TO [MYDOMAIN\MYPC10$];
```

Notice that the local system account is seen as the machine account MYPC10$. Machine accounts work only in Kerberos environments, so if you are working on an NTLM network, you will have to either use domain account as the service accounts or use certificate authentication.

There are two shortcuts you can use if you want to do some quick development or testing without going through a lot of setup. If you use the same domain user account as the user account for both SQL Server instances and configure the endpoints for Windows authentication, the connection will work because the service account for each instance is an admin in the other instance and no additional authorization is necessary. If you are in a trusted network and don't really care who connects to the instance, you can grant CONNECT permissions to PUBLIC and any Windows user that can log on to the Windows server can connect to the Service Broker endpoint:

```
GRANT CONNECT ON ENDPOINT::InventoryServer TO Public;
```

Certificate Authentication   Certificate-based authentication for Adjacent Broker Protocol endpoints uses the same SSPI authentication protocol as SSL. SSL is the encryption used if you browse an HTTPS: site on the Internet. Although Service Broker uses the same authentication protocol as SSL, it does not use SSL because SSL encrypts everything on the wire. Because secure Service Broker dialogs are already encrypted, re-encrypting this data would be a significant waste of resources. Like mutual SSL authentication (and dialog security), certificate authentication requires each of the two endpoints to have a private key certificate. Because SQL Server might not be connected to the Internet or the private key certificate might not be issued by a certificate authority, the public key certificates required are also stored in the database. The way authentication works is similar to the dialog security process that's already been discussed, but there are some differences in the way it is configured. The following example will walk you through connecting a SQL Server instance that contains our Inventory service with another instance that contains the Manufacturing service. The setup will be the same whether the two instances are running on the same box or on different boxes. You'll start by creating the endpoint and its private key certificate in the Inventory instance. The scripts in Listing 11-6, Listing 11-7, and Listing 11-8 should all be run from the master database.

Listing 11-6   Set up inventory private key

```
/*---------------------------------------------------------------------
-- Setup Certificate authenticated Endpoint
-- on the Inventory server
----------------------------------------------------------------*/

-- Create a certificate to represent the inventory
-- server and export it to a file

CREATE CERTIFICATE InventoryCertPriv
  WITH SUBJECT = 'ForInventoryAuth';
BACKUP CERTIFICATE InventoryCertPriv
  TO FILE = 'C:\InventoryCertPub';
GO

-- Create a Service Broker Endpoint that uses this
-- certificate for authentication

CREATE ENDPOINT InventoryEndpoint STATE = STARTED
  AS TCP ( LISTENER_PORT = 4423 )
    FOR SERVICE_BROKER ( AUTHENTICATION = CERTIFICATE InventoryCertPriv );
```

Notice that the endpoint configuration specifies which certificate to use for the private key of the inventory endpoint. In this example, both instances were on the same server, so exporting the public key certificate to the C: drive makes sense. In a distributed environment, you would have to come up with another way to move the certificate to the opposite endpoint. A network-mapped directory, ftp, and e-mail are all viable alternatives.

Now that you have the private key of the inventory instance configured, you'll need to move to the manufacturing instance to create its private key and import the inventory public key by running the code in Listing 11-7.

Listing 11-7 Set up manufacturing endpoint

```
/*-------------------------------------------------------------------
-- Setup Certificate authenticated Endpoint
-- on the Manufacturing server
-------------------------------------------------------------------*/

-- Create a certificate to represent the
-- manufacturing server and export it to a file

CREATE CERTIFICATE ManufacturingCertPriv
  WITH SUBJECT = 'ForManufacturingAuth';
BACKUP CERTIFICATE ManufacturingCertPriv
  TO FILE = 'C:\ManufacturingCertPub';
GO

-- Create a Service Broker Endpoint that uses this
-- certificate for authentication

CREATE ENDPOINT ManufacturingEndpoint
    STATE = STARTED
    AS TCP ( LISTENER_PORT = 4424 )
    FOR SERVICE_BROKER (AUTHENTICATION =
    CERTIFICATE ManufacturingCertPriv);

-- Create a user and login to represent the
-- inventory server on the manufacturing server

CREATE LOGIN InventoryProxy
  WITH PASSWORD = 'dj47dkri837&?>';
CREATE USER InventoryProxy;

-- Import the certificate exported by the inventory server

CREATE CERTIFICATE InventoryCertPub
  AUTHORIZATION InventoryProxy
    FROM FILE = 'C:\InventoryCertPub';

-- Grant connect privileges to the login that
-- represents the inventory server

GRANT CONNECT ON ENDPOINT::ManufacturingEndpoint
  TO InventoryProxy;
```

Notice that you had to create both a user and login as proxies for the inventory server. The login is necessary because it must be granted the permission to connect to the endpoint to allow the Inventory instance to connect, and the user is necessary because logins can't own certificates. It should never be necessary for anyone to log into the instance with the proxy login, so the password should be long and random for maximum security.

All that's left to do is switch back to the inventory instance to import the manufacturing public key and create the required login and user by running the code in Listing 11-8.

Listing 11-8   Finish the inventory endpoint

```
/*-------------------------------------------------------------------
-- Finish the certificate-authenticated endpoint
-- on the Inventory server
-------------------------------------------------------------------*/

-- Create a user and login to represent the
-- manufacturing server on the inventory server

CREATE LOGIN ManufacturingProxy
  WITH PASSWORD = 'dj47dkri837&?>';
CREATE USER ManufacturingProxy;

-- Import the certificate exported by the Manufacturing server

CREATE CERTIFICATE InventoryCertPub AUTHORIZATION ManufacturingProxy
  FROM FILE = 'C:\ManufacturingCertPub';

-- Grant connect privileges to the login that
-- represents the Manufacturing server

GRANT CONNECT ON ENDPOINT::InventoryEndpoint
  TO ManufacturingProxy;
```

As you can see, setting up certificate authentication between instances is a little more complex than setting up Windows authentication. The advantage is that certificate authentication will work on any Windows security configuration, while Windows authentication might require Kerberos for some service accounts and might not work across domains.

Now that you have learned how to configure security for the Adjacent Broker Protocol, you will learn how Service Broker dialogs determine where messages should be delivered.

Routes

A Service Broker route is just a mapping from a service to the network address where messages to that service should be sent. Service Broker routes are simple but flexible enough to support large complex networks. Here is a basic Service Broker route:

```
CREATE ROUTE Inventory_route WITH
  SERVICE_NAME = '//microsoft.com/InventoryService',
  ADDRESS =  'TCP://mypc11:4424';
```

The routes configured in a database can be examined in the *sys.routes* view The name of the route is there so that you can ALTER or DROP it. The SERVICE_NAME is the name of the service that this route provides an address for. Remember that service names use binary collation, so the name in the route must match exactly the name of the service. (Cut-and-paste is your friend here.) A common source of routing problems is having the case of the service name wrong. The ADDRESS is the network address that messages for this service should be sent to. Service Broker supports only the TCP/IP protocol, so the address should begin with "TCP://". Next comes the network address, which can be a DNS name, a host name, or an IP address. The ":4040" in the example indicates that Service Broker should connect to port 4040 on the remote server. This port number must match the port number configured for the Service Broker endpoint in the remote instance. If two or more instances are installed on the same remote server, you target which one gets the message with the port number. Because the port number is determined when you create the remote endpoint, there is no default port number.

It's important to remember that both the initiator and target services of a dialog need endpoints. One of the more common network configuration errors is forgetting to configure the route from the target service back to the initiator. When this happens, messages are delivered successfully from the initiator to the target but no response is returned. This leads to the strange behavior that messages are received on the target queue and processed successfully, but the messages are still on the *sys.transmission_queue* of the initiator database because the acknowledgement for the messages is not delivered to the initiator. When you see the messages in the *sys.transmission_queue* of the initiator database, you think they are not being sent. In reality, they have been delivered and processed. If you use profiler to monitor Service Broker message delivery, you will see the messages being delivered to the target periodically and being rejected as duplicates. If the application sends messages only in one direction, it will appear to be working but will gradually get slower because thousands of messages a minute are being resent by the initiator and ignored by the target. With this in mind, be sure you also log in to the Inventory database and create a route back to the Manufacturing instance:

```
CREATE ROUTE Manufacturing_route WITH
  SERVICE_NAME = '//microsoft.com/ManufacturingService',
  ADDRESS =  'TCP://mypc11:4423';
```

If you have created a route from the Manufacturing database for the InventoryService and in the Inventory database for the ManufacturingService, the distributed Service Broker configuration should be complete. Log in to the Manufacturing database, and run *AddItemProc* to test your dialog. Select from the *sys.dm_broker_connections* view to see whether a network connection was established. If it was not, check *sys.transmission_queue* for an error status and monitor the broker connection traces in SQL Server Profiler.

Broker Instance

In some cases, you might need to route a dialog to a particular database in a SQL Server instance. For example, the instance might have both a production and test version of the service in two different databases. The route to the service must be able to route the dialog to the correct database in the instance. This is done by specifying the BROKER_INSTANCE parameter in the CREATE ROUTE command. The BROKER_INSTANCE is the *service_broker_guid* column of the sys.databases table for the required database. The following example shows a route with the BROKER_INSTANCE parameter specified:

```
CREATE ROUTE ManufacturingRoute WITH
  SERVICE_NAME = '//microsoft.com/ManufacturingService',
  BROKER_INSTANCE = 'A29EEDD3-27E3-4591-94D9-B97BAFBDB936',
  ADDRESS =  'TCP://mypc11:4423';
```

Incoming Routes

Service Broker uses routes in the database where the services are located to determine which remote instance messages to a service should be sent to. When the message arrives at the remote instance, Service Broker must determine what to do with the incoming message. Service Broker uses the routes stored in the msdb database to decide what to do with incoming messages. For example, if there are three or four copies of the InventoryService in an instance, a route with the BROKER_INSTANCE specified can be used to route incoming messages for the InventoryService to the correct database. This can also lead to problems if the msdb database is attached or restored without the BROKER_ENABLED flag so that Service Broker is disabled in msdb.

Wildcards and Special Addresses

Establishing a Service Broker conversation will fail if there is no route available for the TO SERVICE. This might seem unlikely to you because if you have been following along with the examples, you have created several conversations without creating a route for the services involved. The reason this works is that there is a route called *AutoCreatedLocal* that is created when a database is created. If you look at this route in the *sys.routes* view, you will see that the *remote_service_name* and *broker_instance* columns are both NULL and the address column is LOCAL. The NULL columns are what Service Broker uses as wildcards. The wildcards mean that this route will match any service name and any broker instance. A wildcard is used as the last matching criteria so that if another route matches the service name or broker instance the more specific match will always be used. You can create your own wildcard routes by not specifying one or both of the matching parameters.

The LOCAL value for the address is one of two special addresses used in Service Broker. LOCAL means that Service Broker will look for a service in the local SQL Server instance that matches the name. If the database where the route is located has a copy of the service, that copy will be used. If that database doesn't have a copy of the service, Service Broker will look in other databases in the SQL Server instance for a matching service. If more than one copy of the service is found, a random one will be chosen. Because the *AutoCreatedLocal* route is a wildcard route with an address of LOCAL, Service Broker will check for a local service if there is no matching *remote_service_name* in the *sys.routes* view.

The other special address is TRANSPORT. If no other match is found and there is a matching route with the TRANSPORT address, Service Broker will attempt to use the name of the service as a route. For example, if the service name is "TCP:\\mypc11:4040\Manufacturing", Service Broker will send the message to TCP:\\mypc11:4040. Although this might seem like a strange feature, think of an application that involves several thousand initiators connecting to a target service. Maintaining return routes for all the initiators on the target instance would be very painful. On the other hand, if each initiator names the FROM SERVICE with its network address and port, the target only needs to have a single wildcard route with the TRANSPORT address to route responses to all the initiators.

Load Balancing

If there are multiple routes for the same service name in a database, Service Broker will randomly pick one of them when sending the first message in a conversation. This provides a simple form of load balancing among a number of identical services. Notice that this balancing happens on a per-conversation, not per-message, basis. This makes sense if you realize that the first message of the conversation will insert a row in sys.conversation_endpoints at the remote database. So, if the second message goes to a different database, Service Broker will not be able to process it because there is no conversation information in sys.conversation_endpoints for the conversation the message belongs to. This is one of the few situations where having a large number of conversations is a good idea.

The issue with this type of load balancing is that it assumes all services with the same name are identical, so it doesn't matter which one you use. Depending on what the service does and how often the data used by that service changes, keeping multiple target services synchronized might be difficult. On the other hand, if the data for the service changes only rarely, replication can be used to keep the services synchronized or services can call each other with changes through a synchronization service. In other circumstances, it might make more sense for the data in the copies of the service to be partitioned. For example, one service might handle customer numbers 1 through 10000, another 10001 through 20000, and so on. In this case, the application will have to decide which copy of the service to begin the dialog with and use the broker instance in the BEGIN DIALOG command to select the appropriate one. This kind of load balancing works well if the data can be readily partitioned between services and all requests to the service know which customer number the request is for.

One possible problem to look out for is "accidental" load balancing. Whenever Service Broker finds two or more routes to a service, it will load balance dialogs among them. If you intend to have two routes, that is a good thing. However, consider a situation in which you added a route to the production version of a service and forgot to drop the route to the test version. Service Broker will send half the dialogs to test and half to production, which probably isn't what you intended. A more subtle way this happens is if you are using a LOCAL route for the service and the service exists on multiple databases in the local instance. In that case, these services will be load balanced. This generally means that about half of the dialogs will end up where you intended.

To ensure that accidental load balancing doesn't happen, you should create a route for the service and specify the broker instance instead of letting it use the default route. This way you can be sure that the dialog is going where you expect it to go. This same principle applies to messages coming into the instance from outside. If there is only the default route available in msdb, the incoming dialogs will be load balanced if there are multiple copies of the service in the instance. The fix here is the same—create a route for the service in msdb, and use the broker instance to ensure the dialog goes where you want it to.

Routes and Database Mirroring

If the SQL Server instance you are routing messages to is actually two instances that are the primary and secondary databases of a database mirroring pair, Service Broker routing can handle this very well. The CREATE ROUTE command will accept the address of the instances that contain both the primary and secondary databases:

```
CREATE ROUTE ManufacturingMirrorRoute WITH
  SERVICE_NAME = '//microsoft.com/ManufacturingService',
  BROKER_INSTANCE = 'A29EEDD3-27E3-4591-94D9-B97BAFBDB936',
  ADDRESS =  'TCP://mypc11:4040',
  MIRROR_ADDRESS =  'TCP://mypc15:5834';
```

When Service Broker opens a connection for this route, it will connect to both instances of the mirrored pair and determine which database is the primary one. If the primary fails over and the other database becomes the primary, the Service Broker running on the new primary will notify any remote Service Brokers with conversations open that it is now the primary. The remote Service Broker will then immediately start sending the messages to the new primary database. This means that not only no messages are lost when the database fails over (because all the queues are in the database), but also the remote applications will start sending to the new primary immediately. This arrangement provides an unprecedented degree of reliability for asynchronous distributed applications. In most cases, a failure will cause only a few seconds of hesitation and nothing will be lost.

Forwarding

When an incoming message arrives at the SQL Server instance, Service Broker looks in *sys.routes* in the msdb database for a route that matches the service name of the incoming message. If the address in the route is LOCAL, the message is put in the appropriate queue in a local database. If the address is a remote address, the message is put in a forwarding queue and sent to the remote instance specified in the address. Forwarding routes look exactly like other routes except they are created in the msdb database. The ADDRESS parameter in the CREATE ROUTE command was originally known as the "next hop address" because if forwarding is used, the address points to the next Service Broker in the forwarding chain, not the final destination.

Forwarding can be used to create complex network topologies, with messages forwarded from server to server until they reach their final destination. It is not necessary to persist messages to be forwarded because if they are lost, they will be re-sent from the message source if no acknowledgement is received. For this reason, the forwarding queues are memory queues. You can also configure the maximum size of the forwarding queues so that forwarded messages don't use too much memory. This command will turn on message forwarding and limit the forwarding queue to 50 MB of memory:

```
ALTER ENDPOINT InventoryEndpoint FOR SERVICE_BROKER
  (MESSAGE_FORWARDING = ENABLED,
  MESSAGE_FORWARD_SIZE = 50);
```

Scenarios

Service Broker enables a whole new class of reliable, asynchronous, database applications that could not easily be built before. With all the talk about transactional messaging, it's easy to get the impression that Service Broker is just another reliable messaging product. Although Service Broker offers unprecedented levels of reliability, availability, and performance as a transactional messaging platform, it is also extremely useful in applications that have nothing to do with networking and distribution. People often start out using Service Broker for reliable messaging and end up using it for everything from asynchronous stored procedures to batch scheduling. In this section, I'll cover a few scenarios where Service Broker provides a unique solution. This isn't meant to be en exhaustive list, but rather enough to start you thinking about how Service Broker can fit into your applications.

Reliable SOA

The latest "new thing" in software development is Service Oriented Architecture (SOA). Although there are as many definitions of SOA as there are vendors selling SOA tools, the basic idea is that your application consists of coarse-grained, loosely coupled services connected with messages. The message format defines the interface between services. Although most vendors use Web Services to handle the messaging, this is not absolutely required. Loosely coupled, autonomous services make assembling an application from reusable pieces a straightforward process. Services can be either new applications or legacy applications wrapped with a services layer to handle communication with other services.

The services that make up an application might be running on different systems located in different locations. Using traditional RPC-style synchronous communications to connect services is an issue because if any one of the services is down or unreachable, the application is down. For this reason, connecting services with reliable, asynchronous messaging is preferred in most SOA applications. This connection method is preferred because if one service is unavailable, the application might continue to run. This makes Service Broker an ideal candidate for an SOA infrastructure. Reliable, asynchronous messaging means that if a service is unavailable the application can continue to run while messages for the unavailable service are reliably queued for later processing. Because messaging is tightly integrated with the database, all of SQL Server's reliability and high-availability features, such as database mirroring, apply to messages as well as data. When a database-mirrored primary database fails over to the secondary database, the messages and the data in the database fail over to a transactionally consistent state. This means the application can be up and running again in a few seconds with no manual intervention and no loss of data.

The new development features of SQL Server 2005 enable a new class of rich data-oriented services that are hosted in a database. Using CLR stored procedures for the processing logic and Service Broker as an asynchronous execution environment, services can be contained entirely within a database. This includes all configuration and security. The advantage of this is that by detaching and attaching a database, a service can be transferred from an overloaded server to an idle server without ending active conversations or losing any messages or transactions. Moving and even duplicating services with no impact on the running application provides a great deal of flexibility in changing deployments in response to changing loads and conditions.

Asynchronous Processing

Service Broker queues and activation open up a number of possibilities for asynchronous database operations. For example, if you want to do some extensive operations in a trigger—such as creating a purchase order when an inventory update takes the on-hand quantity below the restock level—you can SEND a message to a Service Broker queue in the trigger and use an activated procedure to do the purchase order after the initiating transaction has completed. Because the majority of the work is done outside of the original transaction, the trigger has a minimal impact on performance of the main transaction. You could also write a stored procedure that uses Service Broker to start a number of asynchronous services in parallel and then waits for all of them to finish. The parallel service might be in the same database or spread out across a number of remote databases.

Because Service Broker ensures that messages on a dialog are processed in order, a dialog can be used to manage a multistep batch of SQL commands. If each message is a SQL statement or stored procedure to process, a service could be written that receives messages from the queue and executes the contents of the message by passing it to a SQL EXEC statement. A typical example of this is the night processing for a data warehouse. If the results of processing the statements are returned as response messages on the dialog, the initiator can collect the results of a number of batches. Statements that must be executed serially are placed in a dialog. Multiple dialogs can be started to enable parallel processing. Because Service Broker dialogs can be distributed, a single controlling database can start batches on a number of machines in a distributed environment. Reliable message delivery means the target machine doesn't have to be running or connected when the batch is started. When the connection is restored, the batch will be delivered and processed.

With a little imagination, a service broker user can come up with a number of uses for Service Broker's asynchronous execution capabilities. People who start using Service Broker for a specific project often end up using it for a number of other things once they discover the power of controlled asynchronous processing in a database.

Where Does Service Broker Fit?

When I talk to people about Service Broker, I inevitably get questions about how it relates to Microsoft Message Queue (MSMQ), BizTalk, or Windows Communication Foundation (WCF). This section will discuss some general guidelines for deciding whether Service Broker or one of the other messaging technologies is appropriate for your needs.

What Service Broker Is

With Service Broker, SQL Server becomes a platform for building loosely coupled, asynchronous database applications. Service Broker implements queues as first-class database objects. The queue-handling code built into the database kernel handles the locking, ordering, and multithreading issues associated with managing queues.

To support scaling out asynchronous database applications, Service Broker includes reliable, transactional messaging between SQL Server instances. Because Service Broker messaging is built into the database, it offers message integrity, performance, and reliability that most transactional messaging systems can't match. Service Broker dialogs provide ordering and delivery guarantees that no other messaging system offers.

What Service Broker Isn't

Service Broker isn't just a general-purpose messaging system. Although no other transactional messaging system offers the reliability and performance that Service Broker provides to SQL Server applications, the fact that Service Broker is built into SQL Server means that it works only for SQL Server applications.

Service Broker also supports only transactional messaging. Transactional messaging is the only way to ensure that messages are processed exactly once and in order. Because it is part of the database, Service Broker can do transactional messaging significantly better than messaging systems that aren't built into the database. If the application doesn't require transactional reliability, however, this is unnecessary overhead.

Finally, Service Broker is not just a messaging system. Although the messaging features might be very useful, a large number of Service Broker scenarios don't require messaging at all. The ability to perform asynchronous, queued database actions is very useful, even if your database application isn't distributed.

Service Broker and MSMQ

Because it is built into SQL Server, Service Broker messaging has some significant advantages over MSMQ transactional messaging:

- Service Broker can commit updates to the message queue, database data, and application state in a simple database transaction. MSMQ requires a two-phase commit to do the same thing.

- Service Broker messages can be processed by any application that can establish a database connection to the SQL Server database. Applications that process MSMQ transactional messages must run on the same physical machine as the queue.

- MSMQ message ordering is assured within a single transaction. Service Broker message ordering in a dialog is assured across transactions, sending applications, and receiving applications.

- The maximum MSMQ message size is 4 MB. The maximum Service Broker message size is 2 GB.

- Service Broker activates another queue reader process only when the current processes aren't keeping up with the load, while MSMQ triggers fire for every message that arrives.

On the other hand, MSMQ has some significant features that Service Broker doesn't have, such as:

- MSMQ offers express, reliable, and transactional message styles, while Service Broker is transactional only.

- MSMQ can communicate between virtually any pair of Windows applications. Service Broker can communicate only between applications connected to SQL Server.

- MSMQ offers both a TCP/IP binary protocol and an HTTP SOAP protocol for communications. Service Broker is binary TCP/IP only in SQL Server 2005.

Service Broker and BizTalk

Service Broker and BizTalk don't have a lot in common other than reliable message delivery and database queues. Service Broker can reliably deliver a message to another SQL Server instance with exactly-once in-order assurances. BizTalk does this also, but in addition it can manipulate the contents of messages, map message formats, manage message processing, manage workflows, manage state, send messages over multiple different transports, and so on. If your application doesn't use any of these features and just requires reliable delivery of XML documents from one SQL Server instance to another, Service Broker is probably a better alternative. However, if your application requires the more advanced BizTalk features, you will need to use BizTalk or write the logic yourself.

Service Broker and Windows Communication Foundation

Service Broker supports reliable, transactional messaging over TCP/IP using a proprietary protocol between SQL Server instances. Windows Communication Foundation (WCF) supports many messaging styles over a variety of standards-based protocols between Windows and any operating system that implements the standard protocols that WCF supports. Although WCF can't match Service Broker when it comes to connecting SQL Server applications together reliably, its total feature set and connectivity options go far beyond what Service Broker offers. You can combine the Service Broker asynchronous, reliable database platform capabilities with WCF's interoperability to build reliable, heterogeneous applications.

Conclusion

Service Broker brings the advantages of asynchronous execution and reliable messaging to SQL Server applications. Service Broker's message ordering, correlation, and activation features are unequaled by any messaging system. When combined with CLR integration, database mirroring, and the new XML features, Service Broker makes SQL Server 2005 a viable platform for building database applications and services that offer unprecedented levels of reliability and fault tolerance.

Appendix A
Companion to CLR Routines

This book has common language routine (CLR) code scattered in multiple chapters. CLR routine code for functions, stored procedures, and triggers appears in three chapters (6, 7, and 8). For your convenience and for reference purposes, I centralized all routine code from the three chapters into this appendix.

CLR User-Defined Types (UDTs) are covered in Chapter 1. The CLR code coverage there is already centralized and independent, so I didn't see any value in providing it in this appendix as well. Note that CLR User-Defined Aggregates (UDAs) are discussed in my recent book *Inside Microsoft SQL Server 2005: T-SQL Querying* (Microsoft Press, 2006) and not in this book.

You will also be provided with step-by-step instructions on how to develop and deploy the solutions in both C# and Microsoft Visual Basic.

This appendix provides the following sections, which contain the steps suggested for developing, deploying, and testing your .NET routines' code:

- Create a test database in SQL Server 2005 called CLRUtilities.
- Develop .NET code in Microsoft Visual Studio 2005.
    - Create a project.
    - Develop a class.
- Deploy the solution either automatically in Visual Studio or manually in SQL Server.
- Test the code in SQL Server.

For your reference, the step-by-step instructions will be followed by listings that contain the complete CLR-related .NET and T-SQL code that appears in the three chapters.

For a better learning experience, you might find it convenient to first follow all steps described in this appendix to create all routines that are included in the book. Then, as you read a chapter, you won't have to follow the same steps repeatedly to add each routine. Rather, you can focus on the code snippets provided inline in the chapter.

Create the CLRUtilities Database: SQL Server

All CLR routines covered in the book are created in the CLRUtilities database, which you create by running the code in Listing A-1. The code also creates the table T1, which will be used for the CLR trigger example.

Development: Visual Studio

Following are step-by-step instructions you should follow to develop the solution. All development is done in Visual Studio 2005. Follow the relevant instructions based on your language of preference (C# or Visual Basic). Note that if you're working with Visual Studio Professional edition or later, you have the option of working with the SQL Server Project template, which allows you to deploy the assembly and the routines in SQL Server automatically. In any edition of Visual Studio—including Standard—you can use the Class Library project template. This template will allow you to develop and build the assembly in Visual Studio, in which case you will have to follow with a manual process of deployment in SQL Server using T-SQL code. Both options are covered by the step by step instructions.

If this is the first time you're developing .NET code in SQL Server, I'd recommend experimenting with both options.

1. Create Project

1. Create a new project using your preferred language (C#/Visual Basic):

    (File>New>Project>Visual C# | Visual Basic)

2. Choose a project template based on the Visual Studio edition.

    For the Professional or later edition:

    Use either the Database SQL Server template (Database>SQL Server Project) or the Class Library template (Class Library).

    For the Standard edition:

    Use the Class Library template (Class Library).

3. Specify the following details in the New Project dialog box:

    Name: CLRUtilities

    Location: C:\ (or your folder of preference)

    Solution Name: CLRUtilities

    Confirm

4. Create a database reference in the Add Database Reference dialog box (relevant only if you chose the SQL Server Project template).

Create a new database reference to the CLRUtilities database, or choose an existing reference if you created one already.

Do not confirm SQL/CLR debugging on this connection.

2. Develop Code

1. Add or Rename the class.

    SQL Server Project template:

    (Project>Add Class...>Class>Name: CLRUtilities.cs | CLRUtilities.vb>Add)

    Class Library template:

    (Rename Class1.cs to CLRUtilities.cs | Class1.vb to CLRUtilities.vb)

2. Replace the code in the class with the code from Listing A-2 (C#) or Listing A-3 (Visual Basic).

Deployment and Testing: Visual Studio and SQL Server

When you're done with the code development, you need to deploy the assembly and the routines into a SQL Server database:

- Build the project into an assembly—a .DLL file on disk with the Intermediate Language (IL) code.

- Deploy the assembly into a SQL Server database. The IL code is loaded from the .DLL file into the database, and after the load, you no longer need the external file.

- Create routines (functions, stored procedures, and triggers) in the SQL Server database. This process essentially registers routines from the assembly, which already resides in the database.

All these steps can be achieved from Visual Studio with an automated process if you're working with the SQL Server Project template. If you're working with the Class Library template, from Visual Studio, you can only build the assembly. The deployment will be a manual process in SQL Server using T-SQL CREATE ASSEMBLY | FUNCTION | PROCEDURE | TRIGGER commands.

Here are the step-by-step instructions for both templates:

3. Deploy and Build Solution

1. SQL Server Project template: (Build>Deploy)

    Done

2. Class Library template: (Build>Build)

    In SQL Server, run the CREATE ASSEMBLY | FUNCTION | PROCEDURE | TRIGGER code in Listing A-4 (C#), A-5 (Visual Basic) (relevant only for the Class Library template).

When you're done with deployment, you can test and use your new routines:

4. Test Solution

Run test code in Listing A-4 (C#), A-5 (Visual Basic) without the CREATE statements.

Listing A-1   Enable CLR and create CLRUtilities database and T1 table

```
SET NOCOUNT ON;
USE master;
EXEC sp_configure 'clr enabled', 1;
RECONFIGURE;
GO
IF DB_ID('CLRUtilities') IS NOT NULL
  DROP DATABASE CLRUtilities;
GO
CREATE DATABASE CLRUtilities;
GO
USE CLRUtilities;
GO

-- Create T1 table
IF OBJECT_ID('dbo.T1') IS NOT NULL
  DROP TABLE dbo.T1;
GO
CREATE TABLE dbo.T1
(
  keycol  INT          NOT NULL PRIMARY KEY,
  datacol VARCHAR(10) NOT NULL
);
GO
```

Listing A-2   C# code

```
using System;
using System.Data;
using System.Data.SqlClient;
using System.Data.SqlTypes;
using Microsoft.SqlServer.Server;
using System.Text;
using System.Text.RegularExpressions;
using System.Collections;
using System.Collections.Generic;
using System.Diagnostics;
using System.Reflection;
```

```csharp
public partial class CLRUtilities
{
    // Validate input string against regular expression
    [SqlFunction(IsDeterministic = true, DataAccess = DataAccessKind.None)]
    public static SqlBoolean fn_RegExMatch(SqlString inpStr,
      SqlString regExStr)
    {
        if (inpStr.IsNull || regExStr.IsNull)
            return SqlBoolean.Null;
        else
            return (SqlBoolean)Regex.IsMatch(inpStr.Value, regExStr.Value ,
              RegexOptions.CultureInvariant);
    }


    // SQL Signature
    [SqlFunction(IsDeterministic = true, DataAccess = DataAccessKind.None)]
    public static SqlString fn_SQLSigCLR(SqlString inpRawString,
      SqlInt32 inpParseLength)
    {
        if (inpRawString.IsNull)
            return SqlString.Null;
        int pos = 0;
        string mode = "command";
        string RawString = inpRawString.Value;
        int maxlength = RawString.Length;
        StringBuilder p2 = new StringBuilder();
        char currchar = ' ';
        char nextchar = ' ';
        int ParseLength = RawString.Length;
        if (!inpParseLength.IsNull)
            ParseLength = inpParseLength.Value;
        if (RawString.Length > ParseLength)
        {
            maxlength = ParseLength;
        }
        while (pos < maxlength)
        {
            currchar = RawString[pos];
            if (pos < maxlength - 1)
            {
                nextchar = RawString[pos + 1];
            }
            else
            {
                nextchar = RawString[pos];
            }
            if (mode == "command")
            {
                p2.Append(currchar);
                if ((",( =<>!".IndexOf(currchar) >= 0)
                    &&
                    (nextchar >= '0' && nextchar <= '9'))
                {
                    mode = "number";
                    p2.Append('#');
                }
```

```
                if (currchar == '\'')
                {
                    mode = "literal";
                    p2.Append("#'");
                }
            }
            else if ((mode == "number")
                    &&
                    (",( =<>!".IndexOf(nextchar) >= 0))
            {
                mode = "command";
            }
            else if ((mode == "literal") && (currchar == '\''))
            {
                mode = "command";
            }
            pos++;
        }
        return p2.ToString();
    }


    // fn_RegExReplace - for generic use of RegEx-based replace
    [SqlFunction(IsDeterministic = true, DataAccess = DataAccessKind.None)]
    public static SqlString fn_RegExReplace(
        SqlString input, SqlString pattern, SqlString replacement)
    {
        if (input.IsNull || pattern.IsNull || replacement.IsNull)
            return SqlString.Null;
        else
            return (SqlString)Regex.Replace(
            input.Value, pattern.Value, replacement.Value);
    }


    // Compare implicit vs. explicit casting
    [SqlFunction(IsDeterministic = true, DataAccess = DataAccessKind.None)]
    public static string fn_ImpCast(string inpStr)
    {
        return inpStr.Substring(2, 3);
    }


    [SqlFunction(IsDeterministic = true, DataAccess = DataAccessKind.None)]
    public static SqlString fn_ExpCast(SqlString inpStr)
    {
        return (SqlString)inpStr.ToString().Substring(2, 3);
    }


    // Struct used in string split functions
    struct row_item
    {
        public string item;
        public int pos;
    }


    // Split array of strings and return a table
    // FillRowMethodName = "ArrSplitFillRow"
```

```csharp
[SqlFunction(FillRowMethodName = "ArrSplitFillRow",
 DataAccess = DataAccessKind.None,
 TableDefinition = "pos INT, element NVARCHAR(4000) ")]
public static IEnumerable fn_SplitCLR(SqlString inpStr,
    SqlString charSeparator)
{
    string locStr;
    string[] splitStr;
    char[] locSeparator = new char[1];
    locSeparator[0] = (char)charSeparator.Value[0];
    if (inpStr.IsNull)
        locStr = "";
    else
        locStr = inpStr.Value;
    splitStr = locStr.Split(locSeparator,
        StringSplitOptions.RemoveEmptyEntries);
    //locStr.Split(charSeparator.ToString()[0]);
    List<row_item> SplitString = new List<row_item>();
    int i = 1;
    foreach (string s in splitStr)
    {
        row_item r = new row_item();
        r.item = s;
        r.pos = i;
        SplitString.Add(r);
        ++i;
    }
    return SplitString;
}

public static void ArrSplitFillRow(
  Object obj, out int pos, out string item)
{
    pos = ((row_item)obj).pos;
    item = ((row_item)obj).item;
}

// Stored procedure that returns environment info in tabular format
[SqlProcedure]
public static void usp_GetEnvInfo()
{
    // Create a record - object representation of a row
    // Include the metadata for the SQL table
    SqlDataRecord record = new SqlDataRecord(
        new SqlMetaData("EnvProperty", SqlDbType.NVarChar, 20),
        new SqlMetaData("Value", SqlDbType.NVarChar, 256));
    // Marks the beginning of the result set to be sent back to the client
    // The record parameter is used to construct the metadata
    // for the result set
    SqlContext.Pipe.SendResultsStart(record);
    // Populate some records and send them through the pipe
    record.SetSqlString(0, @"Machine Name");
    record.SetSqlString(1, Environment.MachineName);
    SqlContext.Pipe.SendResultsRow(record);
    record.SetSqlString(0, @"Processors");
```

```
        record.SetSqlString(1, Environment.ProcessorCount.ToString());
        SqlContext.Pipe.SendResultsRow(record);
        record.SetSqlString(0, @"OS Version");
        record.SetSqlString(1, Environment.OSVersion.ToString());
        SqlContext.Pipe.SendResultsRow(record);
        record.SetSqlString(0, @"CLR Version");
        record.SetSqlString(1, Environment.Version.ToString());
        SqlContext.Pipe.SendResultsRow(record);
        // End of result set
        SqlContext.Pipe.SendResultsEnd();
}


// Stored procedure that returns assembly info
// uses Reflection
[SqlProcedure]
public static void usp_GetAssemblyInfo(SqlString asmName)
{
    // Retrieve the clr name of the assembly
    String clrName = null;
    // Get the context
    using (SqlConnection connection =
            new SqlConnection("Context connection = true"))
    {
        connection.Open();
        using (SqlCommand command = new SqlCommand())
        {
            // Get the assembly and load it
            command.Connection = connection;
            command.CommandText =
              "SELECT clr_name FROM sys.assemblies WHERE name = @asmName";
            command.Parameters.Add("@asmName", SqlDbType.NVarChar);
            command.Parameters[0].Value = asmName;
            clrName = (String)command.ExecuteScalar();
            if (clrName == null)
            {
                throw new ArgumentException("Invalid assembly name!");
            }
            Assembly myAsm = Assembly.Load(clrName);
            // Create a record - object representation of a row
            // Include the metadata for the SQL table
            SqlDataRecord record = new SqlDataRecord(
                new SqlMetaData("Type", SqlDbType.NVarChar, 50),
                new SqlMetaData("Name", SqlDbType.NVarChar, 256));
            // Marks the beginning of the result set to be sent back
            // to the client
            // The record parameter is used to construct the metadata
            // for the result set
            SqlContext.Pipe.SendResultsStart(record);
            // Get all types in the assembly
            Type[] typesArr = myAsm.GetTypes();
            foreach (Type t in typesArr)
            {
                // Type in a SQL database should be a class or
                // a structure
```

```csharp
                    if (t.IsClass == true)
                    {
                        record.SetSqlString(0, @"Class");
                    }
                    else
                    {
                        record.SetSqlString(0, @"Structure");
                    }
                    record.SetSqlString(1, t.FullName);
                    SqlContext.Pipe.SendResultsRow(record);
                    // Find all public static methods
                    MethodInfo[] miArr = t.GetMethods();
                    foreach (MethodInfo mi in miArr)
                    {
                        if (mi.IsPublic && mi.IsStatic)
                        {
                            record.SetSqlString(0, @"  Method");
                            record.SetSqlString(1, mi.Name);
                            SqlContext.Pipe.SendResultsRow(record);
                        }
                    }
                }
            // End of result set
            SqlContext.Pipe.SendResultsEnd();
        }
    }
}

// Generic trigger for auditing DML statements
// trigger will write first 200 characters from all columns
// in an XML format to App Event Log
[SqlTrigger(Name = @"trg_GenericDMLAudit", Target = "T1",
    Event = "FOR INSERT, UPDATE, DELETE")]
public static void trg_GenericDMLAudit()
{
    // Get the trigger context to get info about the action type
    SqlTriggerContext triggContext = SqlContext.TriggerContext;
    // Prepare the command and pipe objects
    SqlCommand command;
    SqlPipe pipe = SqlContext.Pipe;

    // Check whether the action is Insert
    switch (triggContext.TriggerAction)
    {
        case TriggerAction.Insert:
            // Retrieve the connection that the trigger is using
            using (SqlConnection connection
                = new SqlConnection(@"context connection=true"))
            {
                connection.Open();
                // Collect all columns into an XML type, cast it
                // to nvarchar and select only a substring from it
                // Info from Inserted
                command = new SqlCommand(
```

```
            @"SELECT 'New data: '
              + SUBSTRING(CAST(a.InsertedContents AS NVARCHAR(MAX))
                  ,1,200) AS InsertedContents200
                FROM (SELECT * FROM Inserted FOR XML AUTO, TYPE)
                    AS a(InsertedContents);",
              connection);
            // Store info collected to a string variable
            string msg;
            msg = (string)command.ExecuteScalar();
            // Write the audit info to the event log
            EventLogEntryType entry = new EventLogEntryType();
            entry = EventLogEntryType.SuccessAudit;
            // Note: if the following line would use
            // Environment.MachineName instead of "." to refer to
            // the local machine event log, the assembly would need
            // the UNSAFE permission set
            EventLog ev = new EventLog(@"Application",
              ".", @"GenericDMLAudit Trigger");
            ev.WriteEntry(msg, entry);
            // send the audit info to the user
            pipe.Send(msg);
        }
        break;
    case TriggerAction.Update:
        // Retrieve the connection that the trigger is using
        using (SqlConnection connection
            = new SqlConnection(@"context connection=true"))
        {
            connection.Open();
            // Collect all columns into an XML type,
            // cast it to nvarchar and select only a substring from it
            // Info from Deleted
            command = new SqlCommand(
              @"SELECT 'Old data: '
                + SUBSTRING(CAST(a.DeletedContents AS NVARCHAR(MAX))
                    ,1,200) AS DeletedContents200
                  FROM (SELECT * FROM Deleted FOR XML AUTO, TYPE)
                      AS a(DeletedContents);",
                connection);
            // Store info collected to a string variable
            string msg;
            msg = (string)command.ExecuteScalar();
            // Info from Inserted
            command.CommandText =
              @"SELECT ' // New data: '
                + SUBSTRING(CAST(a.InsertedContents AS NVARCHAR(MAX))
                    ,1,200) AS InsertedContents200
                  FROM (SELECT * FROM Inserted FOR XML AUTO, TYPE)
                      AS a(InsertedContents);";
            msg = msg + (string)command.ExecuteScalar();
            // Write the audit info to the event log
            EventLogEntryType entry = new EventLogEntryType();
            entry = EventLogEntryType.SuccessAudit;
            EventLog ev = new EventLog(@"Application",
              ".", @"GenericDMLAudit Trigger");
```

```
                    ev.WriteEntry(msg, entry);
                    // send the audit info to the user
                    pipe.Send(msg);
                }
                break;
            case TriggerAction.Delete:
                // Retrieve the connection that the trigger is using
                using (SqlConnection connection
                    = new SqlConnection(@"context connection=true"))
                {

                    connection.Open();
                    // Collect all columns into an XML type,
                    // cast it to nvarchar and select only a substring from it
                    // Info from Deleted
                    command = new SqlCommand(
                      @"SELECT 'Old data: '
                        + SUBSTRING(CAST(a. DeletedContents AS NVARCHAR(MAX))
                            ,1,200) AS DeletedContents200
                            FROM (SELECT * FROM Deleted FOR XML AUTO, TYPE)
                                AS a(DeletedContents);",
                        connection);
                    // Store info collected to a string variable
                    string msg;
                    msg = (string)command.ExecuteScalar();
                    // Write the audit info to the event log
                    EventLogEntryType entry = new EventLogEntryType();
                    entry = EventLogEntryType.SuccessAudit;
                    EventLog ev = new EventLog(@"Application",
                      ".", @"GenericDMLAudit Trigger");
                    ev.WriteEntry(msg, entry);
                    // send the audit info to the user
                    pipe.Send(msg);
                }
                break;
            default:
                // Just to be sure - this part should never fire
                pipe.Send(@"Nothing happened");
                break;
        }
    }
}

};
```

Listing A-3   Visual Basic code

```
Imports System
Imports System.Data
Imports System.Data.SqlClient
Imports System.Data.SqlTypes
Imports Microsoft.SqlServer.Server
Imports System.Text
Imports System.Text.RegularExpressions
Imports System.Collections
```

```vbnet
Imports System.Collections.Generic
Imports System.Diagnostics
Imports System.Reflection
Imports System.Runtime.InteropServices


Partial Public Class CLRUtilities

    ' Validate input string against regular expression
    <SqlFunction(IsDeterministic:=True, DataAccess:=DataAccessKind.None)> _
    Public Shared Function fn_RegExMatch(ByVal inpStr As SqlString, _
      ByVal regExStr As SqlString) As SqlBoolean
        If (inpStr.IsNull Or regExStr.IsNull) Then
            Return SqlBoolean.Null
        Else
            Return CType(Regex.IsMatch(inpStr.Value, regExStr.Value, _
              RegexOptions.CultureInvariant), SqlBoolean)
        End If
    End Function


    ' SQL Signature
    <SqlFunction(IsDeterministic:=True, DataAccess:=DataAccessKind.None)> _
    Public Shared Function fn_SQLSigCLR(ByVal inpRawString As SqlString, _
      ByVal inpParseLength As SqlInt32) As SqlString
        If inpRawString.IsNull Then
            Return SqlString.Null
        End If
        Dim pos As Integer = 0
        Dim mode As String = "command"
        Dim RawString As String = inpRawString.Value
        Dim maxlength As Integer = RawString.Length
        Dim p2 As StringBuilder = New StringBuilder()
        Dim currchar As Char = " "c
        Dim nextchar As Char = " "c
        Dim ParseLength As Integer = RawString.Length
        If (Not inpParseLength.IsNull) Then
            ParseLength = inpParseLength.Value
        End If
        If (RawString.Length > ParseLength) Then
            maxlength = ParseLength
        End If
        While (pos < maxlength)
            currchar = RawString(pos)
            If (pos < maxlength - 1) Then
                nextchar = RawString(pos + 1)
            Else
                nextchar = RawString(pos)
            End If
            If (mode = "command") Then
                p2.Append(currchar)
                If ((",( =<>!".IndexOf(currchar) >= 0) _
                    And _
                    (nextchar >= "0"c And nextchar <= "9"c)) Then
                    mode = "number"
                    p2.Append("#")
```

```vb
                End If
                If (currchar = "'"c) Then
                    mode = "literal"
                    p2.Append("#")
                End If
            ElseIf ((mode = "number") And _
                    (",( =<>!".IndexOf(nextchar) >= 0)) Then
                mode = "command"
            ElseIf ((mode = "literal") And _
                    (currchar = "'"c)) Then
                mode = "command"
            End If
            pos = pos + 1
        End While
        Return p2.ToString
End Function


' fn_RegExReplace - for generic use of RegEx-based replace
<SqlFunction(IsDeterministic:=True, DataAccess:=DataAccessKind.None)> _
Public Shared Function fn_RegExReplace( _
    ByVal input As SqlString, ByVal pattern As SqlString, _
    ByVal replacement As SqlString) As SqlString
        If (input.IsNull Or pattern.IsNull Or replacement.IsNull) Then
            Return SqlString.Null
        Else
            Return CType(Regex.Replace( _
                input.Value, pattern.Value, replacement.Value), SqlString)
        End If
End Function


' Compare implicit vs. explicit casting
<SqlFunction(IsDeterministic:=True, DataAccess:=DataAccessKind.None)> _
Public Shared Function fn_ImpCast(ByVal inpStr As String) As String
        Return inpStr.Substring(2, 3)
End Function


<SqlFunction(IsDeterministic:=True, DataAccess:=DataAccessKind.None)> _
Public Shared Function fn_ExpCast(ByVal inpStr As SqlString) As SqlString
        Return CType(inpStr.ToString().Substring(2, 3), SqlString)
End Function


'Struct used in string split functions
Structure row_item
    Dim item As String
    Dim pos As Integer
End Structure


' Split array of strings and return a table
' FillRowMethodName = "ArrSplitFillRow"
<SqlFunction(FillRowMethodName:="ArrSplitFillRow", _
    DataAccess:=DataAccessKind.None, _
    TableDefinition:="pos INT, element NVARCHAR(4000) ")> _
Public Shared Function fn_SplitCLR(ByVal inpStr As SqlString, _
    ByVal charSeparator As SqlString) As IEnumerable
    Dim locStr As String
```

```vbnet
        Dim splitStr() As String
        Dim locSeparator(0) As Char
        locSeparator(0) = CChar(charSeparator.Value(0))
        If (inpStr.IsNull) Then
            locStr = ""
        Else
            locStr = inpStr.Value
        End If
        splitStr = locStr.Split(locSeparator, _
          StringSplitOptions.RemoveEmptyEntries)
        Dim SplitString As New List(Of row_item)
        Dim i As Integer = 1
        For Each s As String In splitStr
            Dim r As New row_item
            r.item = s
            r.pos = i
            SplitString.Add(r)
            i = i + 1
        Next
        Return SplitString
    End Function

    Public Shared Sub ArrSplitFillRow( _
    ByVal obj As Object, <Out()> ByRef pos As Integer, _
      <Out()> ByRef item As String)
        pos = CType(obj, row_item).pos
        item = CType(obj, row_item).item
    End Sub

    ' Stored procedure that returns environment info in tabular format
    <SqlProcedure()> _
    Public Shared Sub usp_GetEnvInfo()
        ' Create a record - object representation of a row
        ' Include the metadata for the SQL table
        Dim record As New SqlDataRecord( _
            New SqlMetaData("EnvProperty", SqlDbType.NVarChar, 20), _
            New SqlMetaData("Value", SqlDbType.NVarChar, 256))
        ' Marks the beginning of the result set to be sent back to the client
        ' The record parameter is used to construct the metadata for
        ' the result set
        SqlContext.Pipe.SendResultsStart(record)
        '' Populate some records and send them through the pipe
        record.SetSqlString(0, "Machine Name")
        record.SetSqlString(1, Environment.MachineName)
        SqlContext.Pipe.SendResultsRow(record)
        record.SetSqlString(0, "Processors")
        record.SetSqlString(1, Environment.ProcessorCount.ToString())
        SqlContext.Pipe.SendResultsRow(record)
        record.SetSqlString(0, "OS Version")
        record.SetSqlString(1, Environment.OSVersion.ToString())
        SqlContext.Pipe.SendResultsRow(record)
        record.SetSqlString(0, "CLR Version")
        record.SetSqlString(1, Environment.Version.ToString())
        SqlContext.Pipe.SendResultsRow(record)
        ' End of result set
```

```vb
        SqlContext.Pipe.SendResultsEnd()
End Sub


' Stored procedure that returns assembly info
' uses Reflection
<SqlProcedure()> _
Public Shared Sub usp_GetAssemblyInfo(ByVal asmName As SqlString)
    ' Retrieve the clr name of the assembly
    Dim clrName As String = Nothing
    ' Get the context
    Using connection As New SqlConnection("Context connection = true")
        connection.Open()
        Using command As New SqlCommand
            ' Get the assembly and load it
            command.Connection = connection
            command.CommandText = _
              "SELECT clr_name FROM sys.assemblies WHERE name = @asmName"
            command.Parameters.Add("@asmName", SqlDbType.NVarChar)
            command.Parameters(0).Value = asmName
            clrName = CStr(command.ExecuteScalar())
            If (clrName = Nothing) Then
                Throw New ArgumentException("Invalid assembly name!")
            End If
            Dim myAsm As Assembly = Assembly.Load(clrName)
            ' Create a record - object representation of a row
            ' Include the metadata for the SQL table
            Dim record As New SqlDataRecord( _
                New SqlMetaData("Type", SqlDbType.NVarChar, 50), _
                New SqlMetaData("Name", SqlDbType.NVarChar, 256))
            ' Marks the beginning of the result set to be sent back
            ' to the client
            ' The record parameter is used to construct the metadata
            ' for the result set
            SqlContext.Pipe.SendResultsStart(record)
            ' Get all types in the assembly
            Dim typesArr() As Type = myAsm.GetTypes()
            For Each t As Type In typesArr
                ' Type in a SQL database should be a class or a structure
                If (t.IsClass = True) Then
                    record.SetSqlString(0, "Class")
                Else
                    record.SetSqlString(0, "Structure")
                End If
                record.SetSqlString(1, t.FullName)
                SqlContext.Pipe.SendResultsRow(record)
                ' Find all public static methods
                Dim miArr() As MethodInfo = t.GetMethods
                For Each mi As MethodInfo In miArr
                    If (mi.IsPublic And mi.IsStatic) Then
                        record.SetSqlString(0, "  Method")
                        record.SetSqlString(1, mi.Name)
                        SqlContext.Pipe.SendResultsRow(record)
                    End If
                Next
            Next
```

```vb
                ' End of result set
                SqlContext.Pipe.SendResultsEnd()
            End Using
        End Using
End Sub


' Generic trigger for auditing DML statements
' trigger will write first 200 characters from all columns
' in an XML format to App Event Log
<SqlTrigger(Name:="trg_GenericDMLAudit", Target:="T1", _
  Event:="FOR INSERT, UPDATE, DELETE")> _
Public Shared Sub trg_GenericDMLAudit()
    ' Get the trigger context to get info about the action type
    Dim triggContext As SqlTriggerContext = SqlContext.TriggerContext
    ' Prepare the command and pipe objects
    Dim command As SqlCommand
    Dim pipe As SqlPipe = SqlContext.Pipe

    ' Check whether the action is Insert
    Select Case triggContext.TriggerAction
        Case TriggerAction.Insert
            ' Retrieve the connection that the trigger is using
            Using connection _
              As New SqlConnection("Context connection = true")
                connection.Open()
                ' Collect all columns into an XML type,
                ' cast it to nvarchar and select only a substring from it
                ' Info from Inserted
                command = New SqlCommand( _
                    "SELECT 'New data: ' + " & _
                    "SUBSTRING(CAST(a.InsertedContents AS NVARCHAR(MAX)" & _
                    "),1,200) AS InsertedContents200 " & _
                    "FROM (SELECT * FROM Inserted FOR XML AUTO, TYPE) " & _
                    "AS a(InsertedContents);", _
                     connection)
                ' Store info collected to a string variable
                Dim msg As String
                msg = CStr(command.ExecuteScalar())
                ' Write the audit info to the event log
                Dim entry As EventLogEntryType
                entry = EventLogEntryType.SuccessAudit
                ' Note: if the following line would use
                ' Environment.MachineName instead of "." to refer to
                ' the local machine event log, the assembly would need
                ' the UNSAFE permission set
                Dim ev As New EventLog("Application", _
                    ".", "GenericDMLAudit Trigger")
                ev.WriteEntry(msg, entry)
                ' send the audit info to the user
                pipe.Send(msg)
            End Using
        Case TriggerAction.Update
            ' Retrieve the connection that the trigger is using
            Using connection _
              As New SqlConnection("Context connection = true")
```

```vb
            connection.Open()
            ' Collect all columns into an XML type,
            ' cast it to nvarchar and select only a substring from it
            ' Info from Deleted
            command = New SqlCommand( _
              "SELECT 'Old data: ' + " & _
              "SUBSTRING(CAST(a.DeletedContents AS NVARCHAR(MAX)" & _
              "),1,200) AS DeletedContents200 " & _
              "FROM (SELECT * FROM Deleted FOR XML AUTO, TYPE) " & _
              "AS a(DeletedContents);", _
                connection)
            ' Store info collected to a string variable
            Dim msg As String
            msg = CStr(command.ExecuteScalar())
            ' Info from Inserted
            command.CommandText = _
              "SELECT ' // New data: ' + " & _
              "SUBSTRING(CAST(a.InsertedContents AS NVARCHAR(MAX)" & _
              "),1,200) AS InsertedContents200 " & _
              "FROM (SELECT * FROM Inserted FOR XML AUTO, TYPE) " & _
              "AS a(InsertedContents);"
            msg = msg + CStr(command.ExecuteScalar())
            ' Write the audit info to the event log
            Dim entry As EventLogEntryType
            entry = EventLogEntryType.SuccessAudit
            Dim ev As New EventLog("Application", _
              ".", "GenericDMLAudit Trigger")
            ev.WriteEntry(msg, entry)
            ' send the audit info to the user
            pipe.Send(msg)
        End Using
    Case TriggerAction.Delete
        ' Retrieve the connection that the trigger is using
        Using connection _
          As New SqlConnection("Context connection = true")
            connection.Open()
            ' Collect all columns into an XML type,
            ' cast it to nvarchar and select only a substring from it
            ' Info from Deleted
            command = New SqlCommand( _
              "SELECT 'Old data: ' + " & _
              "SUBSTRING(CAST(a.DeletedContents AS NVARCHAR(MAX)" & _
              "),1,200) AS DeletedContents200 " & _
              "FROM (SELECT * FROM Deleted FOR XML AUTO, TYPE) " & _
              "AS a(DeletedContents);", _
                connection)
            ' Store info collected to a string variable
            Dim msg As String
            msg = CStr(command.ExecuteScalar())
            ' Write the audit info to the event log
            Dim entry As EventLogEntryType
            entry = EventLogEntryType.SuccessAudit
            Dim ev As New EventLog("Application", _
              ".", "GenericDMLAudit Trigger")
```

```
                      ev.WriteEntry(msg, entry)
                      ' send the audit info to the user
                      pipe.Send(msg)
                End Using
            Case Else
                ' Just to be sure - this part should never fire
                pipe.Send("Nothing happened")
        End Select
    End Sub

End Class
```

Listing A-4   Deployment and testing of CLR routines, C#

```
USE CLRUtilities;
GO


-- Create assembly
CREATE ASSEMBLY CLRUtilities
FROM 'C:\CLRUtilities\CLRUtilities\bin\Debug\CLRUtilities.dll'
WITH PERMISSION_SET = SAFE;
-- If no Debug folder, use instead:
-- FROM 'C:\CLRUtilities\CLRUtilities\bin\CLRUtilities.dll'
GO


---------------------------------------------------------------------
-- Scalar Function: fn_RegExMatch
---------------------------------------------------------------------


-- Create fn_RegExMatch function
CREATE FUNCTION dbo.fn_RegExMatch
  (@inpstr AS NVARCHAR(MAX), @regexstr AS NVARCHAR(MAX))
RETURNS BIT
EXTERNAL NAME CLRUtilities.CLRUtilities.fn_RegExMatch;
GO

-- Test fn_RegExMatch function
SELECT dbo.fn_RegExMatch(
  N'dejan@solidqualitylearning.com',
  N'^([\w-]+\.)*?[\w-]+@[\w-]+\.([\w-]+\.)*?[\w]+$');
GO


---------------------------------------------------------------------
-- Scalar Function: fn_SQLSigCLR
---------------------------------------------------------------------


-- Create fn_SQLSigCLR function
CREATE FUNCTION dbo.fn_SQLSigCLR
  (@rawstring AS NVARCHAR(4000), @parselength AS INT)
RETURNS NVARCHAR(4000)
EXTERNAL NAME CLRUtilities.CLRUtilities.fn_SQLSigCLR;
GO
```

```
-- Test fn_SQLSigCLR function
SELECT dbo.fn_SQLSigCLR
  (N'SELECT * FROM dbo.T1 WHERE col1 = 3 AND col2 > 78;', 4000);
GO


----------------------------------------------------------------------
-- Scalar Function: fn_RegExReplace
----------------------------------------------------------------------


-- Create fn_RegExReplace function
CREATE FUNCTION dbo.fn_RegExReplace(
  @input       AS NVARCHAR(MAX),
  @pattern     AS NVARCHAR(MAX),
  @replacement AS NVARCHAR(MAX))
RETURNS NVARCHAR(MAX)
WITH RETURNS NULL ON NULL INPUT
EXTERNAL NAME CLRUtilities.CLRUtilities.fn_RegExReplace;
GO


-- Test fn_SQLSigCLR function
SELECT dbo.fn_RegExReplace('(123)-456-789', '[^0-9]', '');
GO


----------------------------------------------------------------------
-- Scalar Functions: fn_ImpCast, fn_ExpCast
----------------------------------------------------------------------


-- Create fn_ImpCast function
CREATE FUNCTION dbo.fn_ImpCast(@inpstr AS NVARCHAR(4000))
RETURNS NVARCHAR(4000)
EXTERNAL NAME CLRUtilities.CLRUtilities.fn_ImpCast;
GO
-- Create fn_ExpCast function
CREATE FUNCTION dbo.fn_ExpCast(@inpstr AS NVARCHAR(4000))
RETURNS NVARCHAR(4000)
EXTERNAL NAME CLRUtilities.CLRUtilities.fn_ExpCast;
GO


-- Test fn_ImpCast and fn_ExpCast functions
SELECT dbo.fn_ImpCast(N'123456'), dbo.fn_ExpCast(N'123456');
GO


----------------------------------------------------------------------
-- Table Function: fn_SplitCLR
----------------------------------------------------------------------


-- Create fn_SplitCLR function
CREATE FUNCTION dbo.fn_SplitCLR
  (@string AS NVARCHAR(4000), @separator AS NCHAR(1))
RETURNS TABLE(pos INT, element NVARCHAR(4000))
EXTERNAL NAME CLRUtilities.CLRUtilities.fn_SplitCLR;
GO


-- Test fn_SplitCLR function
SELECT pos, element FROM dbo.fn_SplitCLR(N'a,b,c', N',');
GO
```

```
------------------------------------------------------------------------
-- Stored Procedure: usp_GetEnvInfo
------------------------------------------------------------------------


-- Database option TRUSTWORTHY needs to be ON for EXTERNAL_ACCESS
ALTER DATABASE CLRUtilities SET TRUSTWORTHY ON;
GO
-- Alter assembly with PERMISSION_SET = EXTERNAL_ACCESS
ALTER ASSEMBLY CLRUtilities
WITH PERMISSION_SET = EXTERNAL_ACCESS;
GO

/*
-- Safer alternative:

-- Create an asymmetric key from the signed assembly
-- Note: you have to sign the assembly using a strong name key file
USE master;
GO
CREATE ASYMMETRIC KEY CLRUtilitiesKey
  FROM EXECUTABLE FILE =
    'C:\CLRUtilities\CLRUtilities\bin\Debug\CLRUtilities.dll';
-- Create login and grant it with external access permission level
CREATE LOGIN CLRUtilitiesLogin FROM ASYMMETRIC KEY CLRUtilitiesKey;
GRANT EXTERNAL ACCESS ASSEMBLY TO CLRUtilitiesLogin;
GO
*/

-- Create usp_GetEnvInfo stored procedure
CREATE PROCEDURE dbo.usp_GetEnvInfo
AS EXTERNAL NAME CLRUtilities.CLRUtilities.usp_GetEnvInfo;
GO

-- Test usp_GetEnvInfo stored procedure
EXEC dbo.usp_GetEnvInfo;
GO


------------------------------------------------------------------------
-- Stored Procedure: usp_GetAssemblyInfo
------------------------------------------------------------------------


-- Create usp_GetAssemblyInfo stored procedure
CREATE PROCEDURE usp_GetAssemblyInfo
  @asmName AS sysname
AS EXTERNAL NAME CLRUtilities.CLRUtilities.usp_GetAssemblyInfo;
GO

-- Test usp_GetAssemblyInfo stored procedure
EXEC usp_GetAssemblyInfo N'CLRUtilities';
GO


------------------------------------------------------------------------
-- Trigger: trg_GenericDMLAudit
------------------------------------------------------------------------
```

```
-- Create T1 table
IF OBJECT_ID('dbo.T1') IS NOT NULL
  DROP TABLE dbo.T1;
GO
CREATE TABLE dbo.T1
(
  keycol  INT         NOT NULL PRIMARY KEY,
  datacol VARCHAR(10) NOT NULL
);
GO


-- Database option TRUSTWORTHY needs to be ON for EXTERNAL_ACCESS
ALTER DATABASE CLRUtilities SET TRUSTWORTHY ON;
GO
-- Alter assembly with PERMISSION_SET = EXTERNAL_ACCESS
ALTER ASSEMBLY CLRUtilities
WITH PERMISSION_SET = EXTERNAL_ACCESS;
GO


/*
-- Safer alternative:

-- Create an asymmetric key from the signed assembly
-- Note: you have to sign the assembly using a strong name key file
USE master;
GO
CREATE ASYMMETRIC KEY CLRUtilitiesKey
  FROM EXECUTABLE FILE =
    'C:\CLRUtilities\CLRUtilities\bin\Debug\CLRUtilities.dll';
-- Create login and grant it with external access permission level
CREATE LOGIN CLRUtilitiesLogin FROM ASYMMETRIC KEY CLRUtilitiesKey;
GRANT EXTERNAL ACCESS ASSEMBLY TO CLRUtilitiesLogin;
GO
*/


-- Create trg_T1_iud_GenericDMLAudit trigger
CREATE TRIGGER trg_T1_iud_GenericDMLAudit
 ON dbo.T1 FOR INSERT, UPDATE, DELETE
AS
EXTERNAL NAME CLRUtilities.CLRUtilities.trg_GenericDMLAudit;
GO


-- Test trg_GenericDMLAudit trigger
INSERT INTO dbo.T1(keycol, datacol) VALUES(1, N'A');
UPDATE dbo.T1 SET datacol = N'B' WHERE keycol = 1;
DELETE FROM dbo.T1 WHERE keycol = 1;
-- Examine Windows Application Log
GO

USE master;
GO
```

Listing A-5 Deployment and testing of CLR routines, Visual Basic

```
USE CLRUtilities;
GO

-- Create assembly
CREATE ASSEMBLY CLRUtilities
FROM 'C:\CLRUtilities\CLRUtilities\bin\Debug\CLRUtilities.dll'
WITH PERMISSION_SET = SAFE;
-- If no Debug folder, use instead:
-- FROM 'C:\CLRUtilities\CLRUtilities\bin\CLRUtilities.dll'
GO


---------------------------------------------------------------------
-- Scalar Function: fn_RegExMatch
---------------------------------------------------------------------


-- Create fn_RegExMatch function
CREATE FUNCTION dbo.fn_RegExMatch
  (@inpstr AS NVARCHAR(MAX), @regexstr AS NVARCHAR(MAX))
RETURNS BIT
EXTERNAL NAME CLRUtilities.[CLRUtilities.CLRUtilities].fn_RegExMatch;
GO

-- Test fn_RegExMatch function
SELECT dbo.fn_RegExMatch(
  N'dejan@solidqualitylearning.com',
  N'^([\w-]+\.)*?[\w-]+@[\w-]+\.([\w-]+\.)*?[\w]+$');
GO


---------------------------------------------------------------------
-- Scalar Function: fn_SQLSigCLR
---------------------------------------------------------------------


-- Create fn_SQLSigCLR function
CREATE FUNCTION dbo.fn_SQLSigCLR
  (@rawstring AS NVARCHAR(4000), @parselength AS INT)
RETURNS NVARCHAR(4000)
EXTERNAL NAME CLRUtilities.[CLRUtilities.CLRUtilities].fn_SQLSigCLR;
GO

-- Test fn_SQLSigCLR function
SELECT dbo.fn_SQLSigCLR
  (N'SELECT * FROM dbo.T1 WHERE col1 = 3 AND col2 > 78;', 4000);
GO


---------------------------------------------------------------------
-- Scalar Function: fn_RegExReplace
---------------------------------------------------------------------


-- Create fn_RegExReplace function
CREATE FUNCTION dbo.fn_RegExReplace(
  @input       AS NVARCHAR(MAX),
  @pattern     AS NVARCHAR(MAX),
  @replacement AS NVARCHAR(MAX))
```

```
RETURNS NVARCHAR(MAX)
WITH RETURNS NULL ON NULL INPUT
EXTERNAL NAME CLRUtilities.[CLRUtilities.CLRUtilities].fn_RegExReplace;
GO


-- Test fn_SQLSigCLR function
SELECT dbo.fn_RegExReplace('(123)-456-789', '[^0-9]', '');
GO


------------------------------------------------------------------------
-- Scalar Functions: fn_ImpCast, fn_ExpCast
------------------------------------------------------------------------


-- Create fn_ImpCast function
CREATE FUNCTION dbo.fn_ImpCast(@inpstr AS NVARCHAR(4000))
RETURNS NVARCHAR(4000)
EXTERNAL NAME CLRUtilities.[CLRUtilities.CLRUtilities].fn_ImpCast;
GO
-- Create fn_ExpCast function
CREATE FUNCTION dbo.fn_ExpCast(@inpstr AS NVARCHAR(4000))
RETURNS NVARCHAR(4000)
EXTERNAL NAME CLRUtilities.[CLRUtilities.CLRUtilities].fn_ExpCast;
GO


-- Test fn_ImpCast and fn_ExpCast functions
SELECT dbo.fn_ImpCast(N'123456'), dbo.fn_ExpCast(N'123456');
GO


------------------------------------------------------------------------
-- Table Function: fn_SplitCLR
------------------------------------------------------------------------


-- Create fn_SplitCLR function
CREATE FUNCTION dbo.fn_SplitCLR
  (@string AS NVARCHAR(4000), @separator AS NCHAR(1))
RETURNS TABLE(pos INT, element NVARCHAR(4000))
EXTERNAL NAME CLRUtilities.[CLRUtilities.CLRUtilities].fn_SplitCLR;
GO


-- Test fn_SplitCLR function
SELECT pos, element FROM dbo.fn_SplitCLR(N'a,b,c', N',');
GO


------------------------------------------------------------------------
-- Stored Procedure: usp_GetEnvInfo
------------------------------------------------------------------------


-- Database option TRUSTWORTHY needs to be ON for EXTERNAL_ACCESS
ALTER DATABASE CLRUtilities SET TRUSTWORTHY ON;
GO
-- Alter assembly with PERMISSION_SET = EXTERNAL_ACCESS
ALTER ASSEMBLY CLRUtilities
WITH PERMISSION_SET = EXTERNAL_ACCESS;
GO
```

```
/*
-- Safer alternative:

-- Create an asymmetric key from the signed assembly
-- Note: you have to sign the assembly using a strong name key file
USE master;
GO
CREATE ASYMMETRIC KEY CLRUtilitiesKey
  FROM EXECUTABLE FILE =
    'C:\CLRUtilities\CLRUtilities\bin\Debug\CLRUtilities.dll';
-- Create login and grant it with external access permission level
CREATE LOGIN CLRUtilitiesLogin FROM ASYMMETRIC KEY CLRUtilitiesKey;
GRANT EXTERNAL ACCESS ASSEMBLY TO CLRUtilitiesLogin;
GO
*/

-- Create usp_GetEnvInfo stored procedure
CREATE PROCEDURE dbo.usp_GetEnvInfo
AS EXTERNAL NAME
  CLRUtilities.[CLRUtilities.CLRUtilities].usp_GetEnvInfo;
GO

-- Test usp_GetEnvInfo stored procedure
EXEC dbo.usp_GetEnvInfo;
GO


---------------------------------------------------------------------
-- Stored Procedure: usp_GetAssemblyInfo
---------------------------------------------------------------------

-- Create usp_GetAssemblyInfo stored procedure
CREATE PROCEDURE usp_GetAssemblyInfo
  @asmName AS sysname
AS EXTERNAL NAME
  CLRUtilities.[CLRUtilities.CLRUtilities].usp_GetAssemblyInfo;
GO

-- Test usp_GetAssemblyInfo stored procedure
EXEC usp_GetAssemblyInfo N'CLRUtilities';
GO


---------------------------------------------------------------------
-- Trigger: trg_GenericDMLAudit
---------------------------------------------------------------------

-- Create T1 table
IF OBJECT_ID('dbo.T1') IS NOT NULL
  DROP TABLE dbo.T1;
GO
CREATE TABLE dbo.T1
(
  keycol  INT         NOT NULL PRIMARY KEY,
  datacol VARCHAR(10) NOT NULL
);
GO
```

```
-- Database option TRUSTWORTHY needs to be ON for EXTERNAL_ACCESS
ALTER DATABASE CLRUtilities SET TRUSTWORTHY ON;
GO
-- Alter assembly with PERMISSION_SET = EXTERNAL_ACCESS
ALTER ASSEMBLY CLRUtilities
WITH PERMISSION_SET = EXTERNAL_ACCESS;
GO


/*
-- Safer alternative:

-- Create an asymmetric key from the signed assembly
-- Note: you have to sign the assembly using a strong name key file
USE master;
GO
CREATE ASYMMETRIC KEY CLRUtilitiesKey
  FROM EXECUTABLE FILE =
    'C:\CLRUtilities\CLRUtilities\bin\Debug\CLRUtilities.dll';
-- Create login and grant it with external access permission level
CREATE LOGIN CLRUtilitiesLogin FROM ASYMMETRIC KEY CLRUtilitiesKey;
GRANT EXTERNAL ACCESS ASSEMBLY TO CLRUtilitiesLogin;
GO
*/


-- Create trg_T1_iud_GenericDMLAudit trigger
CREATE TRIGGER trg_T1_iud_GenericDMLAudit
 ON dbo.T1 FOR INSERT, UPDATE, DELETE
AS
EXTERNAL NAME
  CLRUtilities.[CLRUtilities.CLRUtilities].trg_GenericDMLAudit;
GO


-- Test trg_GenericDMLAudit trigger
INSERT INTO dbo.T1(keycol, datacol) VALUES(1, N'A');
UPDATE dbo.T1 SET datacol = N'B' WHERE keycol = 1;
DELETE FROM dbo.T1 WHERE keycol = 1;
-- Examine Windows Application Log
GO

USE master;
GO
```

Index

Symbol

@@error function, 391

A

ABP. *See* adjacent broker protocol (ABP)
ACID (Atomicity, Consistency, Isolation, and
  Durability), 361
adjacent broker protocol (ABP)
  certificate authentication, 453–455
  connections for endpoints, 451
  overview, 449–450
  Windows authentication, 452–453
AFTER triggers
  auditing example, 333–335
  COLUMNS_UPDATED function,
    329–332
  compared to INSTEAD OF, 336
  deleted tables, 316–318
  identifying number of rows, 318–321
  identifying type, 321–323
  inserted tables, 316–318
  nesting, 328–329
  not firing for specific statements, 324–328
  overview, 316
  recursion, 328–329
  UPDATE predicate, 329–332
arguable constructs, 111
arithmetic operations, 58–59
asymmetric key authentication in dialog
    conversations, 444–445
asynchronous delivery in dialog
    conversations, 414–415
asynchronous processing in Service Broker,
    461

Atomicity, Consistency, Isolation, and
    Durability (ACID), 361
audience for this book, xxi
auditing example in AFTER triggers,
    333–335
automatic handling of sequences, 342–344

B

BEGIN TRAN/COMMIT TRAN block, 362
beginning dialogs, 424–426
birthday problem, 8–10
BizTalk vs. Service Broker, 463
BROKER_INSTANCE parameter, 456
BULK rowset provider, 34–35
bulk-update (BU) locks, 365

C

C# .NET-based ComplexNumberCS UDA,
    60–61
career phases of T-SQL programmers,
    111–112
CASE expressions, 36
case-sensitive filters, 31
certificate authentication for endpoints,
    453–455
character-related problems
  case-sensitive filters, 31
  CHECK constraints in pattern matching,
    27–28
  IP patterns, 29–30
  LIKE predicate in pattern matching,
    26–27
  overview, 25

About the Contributors

Itzik Ben-Gan

Itzik Ben-Gan is a mentor and founder of Solid Quality Learning. A Microsoft SQL Server MVP (Most Valuable Professional) since 1999, Itzik has delivered numerous training events around the world focused on T-SQL Querying, Query Tuning, and Programming. Itzik is the author of several books on Microsoft SQL Server. He has written many articles for *SQL Server Magazine*, as well as articles and white papers for MSDN. Itzik's speaking engagements include Tech Ed, DevWeek, various SQL user groups around the world, PASS, SQL Server Magazine Connections, and Solid Quality Learning's events, to name a few.

Since 1992, Itzik has been involved in many projects covering various database and computer systems–related technologies. In addition to helping customers with their pressing needs, fixing their problems, optimizing their databases, teaching, and mentoring, Itzik has helped developers and database administrators shift to a relational/set-based mindset, improving both the performance of their code and its maintainability. Itzik's main expertise is T-SQL Querying, Query Tuning, Programming, and Internals, but he's proficient in other database areas as well. In 1999, Itzik founded the Israeli SQL Server and OLAP User Group, and he has been managing it since then.

Dejan Sarka

Dejan Sarka–MCP (Microsoft Certified Professional), MCDBA (Microsoft Certified Database Administrator), MCT (Microsoft Certified Trainer), SQL Server MVP, Solid Quality Learning Mentor–is a trainer and consultant working for many Certified Partners for Learning Solutions (CPLS) centers and development companies in Slovenia and other countries. In addition to providing professional training, he continuously works on online transaction processing (OLTP), OLAP, and Data Mining projects, especially at the design stage. He is a regular speaker at some of the most important international conferences, such as TechEd, PASS, and MCT. He is also indispensable at regional Microsoft TechNet meetings, the NT Conference, which is the largest Microsoft conference in Central and Eastern Europe, and other events. He is the founder of the Slovenian SQL Server Users Group. Dejan Sarka also developed two courses for Solid Quality Learning: *Data Modeling Essentials* and *Data Mining with SQL Server 2005*.

Roger Wolter

Roger Wolter has close to 30 years' experience in the computer industry, the last 7 years with Microsoft. He is currently a program manager on the SQL Server team specializing in SQL Server Service Broker and SQL Server Express. His projects at Microsoft have included COM+, SQLXML, the Soap Toolkit, SQL Server Service Broker, and SQL Express.

Steve Kass

Steve Kass is Associate Professor of Mathematics and Computer Science at Drew University in Madison, New Jersey. Steve graduated from Pomona College and holds a Ph.D. in Mathematics from the University of Wisconsin–Madison. He is also a Microsoft SQL Server MVP.

Lubor Kollar

Lubor Kollar is a group program manager for SQL Server at Microsoft. His team led the development of key enhancements to the relational engine, including some of the T-SQL enhancements in SQL Server 2005.

Additional SQL Server Resources for Administrators

Published and Forthcoming Titles from Microsoft Press

Microsoft® SQL Server™ 2005 Reporting Services *Step by Step*
Hitachi Consulting Services • ISBN 0-7356-2250-7

SQL Server Reporting Services (SRS) is Microsoft's customizable reporting solution for business data analysis. It is one of the key value features of SQL Server 2005: functionality more advanced and much less expensive than its competition. SRS is powerful, so an understanding of how to architect a report, as well as how to install and program SRS, is key to harnessing the full functionality of SQL Server. This procedural tutorial shows how to use the Report Project Wizard, how to think about and access data, and how to build queries. It also walks the reader through the creation of charts and visual layouts to enable maximum visual understanding of the data analysis. Interactivity (enhanced in SQL Server 2005) and security are also covered in detail.

Microsoft SQL Server 2005 Administrator's Pocket Consultant
William R. Stanek • ISBN 0-7356-2107-1

Here's the utterly practical, pocket-sized reference for IT professionals who need to administer, optimize, and maintain SQL Server 2005 in their organizations. This unique guide provides essential details for using SQL Server 2005 to help protect and manage your company's data—whether automating tasks; creating indexes and views; performing backups and recovery; replicating transactions; tuning performance; managing server activity; importing and exporting data; or performing other key tasks. Featuring quick-reference tables, lists, and step-by-step instructions, this handy, one-stop guide provides fast, accurate answers on the spot, whether you're at your desk or in the field!

Microsoft SQL Server 2005 Administrator's Companion
Marci Frohock Garcia, Edward Whalen, and Mitchell Schroeter • ISBN 0-7356-2198-5

Microsoft SQL Server 2005 Administrator's Companion is the comprehensive, in-depth guide that saves time by providing all the technical information you need to deploy, administer, optimize, and support SQL Server 2005. Using a hands-on, example-rich approach, this authoritative, one-volume reference book provides expert advice, product information, detailed solutions, procedures, and real-world troubleshooting tips from experienced SQL Server 2005 professionals. This expert guide shows you how to design high-availability database systems, prepare for installation, install and configure SQL Server 2005, administer services and features, and maintain and troubleshoot your database system. It covers how to configure your system for your I/O system and model and optimize system capacity. The expert authors provide details on how to create and use defaults, constraints, rules, indexes, views, functions, stored procedures, and triggers. This guide shows you how to administer reporting services, analysis services, notification services, and integration services. It also provides a wealth of information on replication and the specifics of snapshot, transactional, and merge replication. Finally, there is expansive coverage of how to manage and tune your SQL Server system, including automating tasks, backup and restoration of databases, and management of users and security.

Microsoft SQL Server 2005 Analysis Services *Step by Step*
Hitachi Consulting Services • ISBN 0-7356-2199-3

One of the key features of SQL Server 2005 is SQL Server Analysis Services—Microsoft's customizable analysis solution for business data modeling and interpretation. Just compare SQL Server Analysis Services to its competition to understand/grasp the great value of its enhanced features. One of the keys to harnessing the full functionality of SQL Server will be leveraging Analysis Services for the powerful tool that it is—including creating a cube, and deploying, customizing, and extending the basic calculations. This step-by-step tutorial discusses how to get started, how to build scalable analytical applications, and how to use and administer advanced features. Interactivity (which is enhanced in SQL Server 2005), data translation, and security are also covered in detail.

Microsoft SQL Server 2005 Express Edition *Step by Step*
Jackie Goldstein • ISBN 0-7356-2184-5

Inside Microsoft SQL Server 2005: The Storage Engine
Kalen Delaney • ISBN 0-7356-2105-5

Inside Microsoft SQL Server 2005: T-SQL Programming
Itzik Ben-Gan • ISBN 0-7356-2197-7

Inside Microsoft SQL Server 2005: Query Processing and Optimization
Kalen Delaney • ISBN 0-7356-2196-9

For more information about Microsoft Press® books and other learning products, visit: **www.microsoft.com/mspress** *and* **www.microsoft.com/learning**

Resources for IT Professionals
Published and Forthcoming Titles from Microsoft Press

Administrator's Pocket Consultant

- Practical, portable guide for fast answers when you need them
- Focus on core operations and support tasks
- Organized for quick, precise reference—to get the job done

Microsoft®
SQL Server™ 2005
Administrator's Pocket Consultant
William R. Stanek
0-7356-2107-1

Microsoft Windows
Server™ 2003
Administrator's Pocket Consultant
Second Edition
William R. Stanek
0-7356-2245-0

Microsoft Windows®
XP Professional
Administrator's Pocket Consultant
Second Edition
William R. Stanek
0-7356-2140-3

Microsoft Windows
Command-Line
Administrator's Pocket Consultant
William R. Stanek
0-7356-2038-5

Administrator's Companion

- Comprehensive, one-volume guide to system administration
- Real-world insights, procedures, trouble-shooting tactics, and workarounds
- Fully searchable eBook on CD

Microsoft Windows
Server 2003
Administrator's Companion
Second Edition
Charles Russel,
Sharon Crawford,
and Jason Gerend
0-7356-2047-4

Microsoft Windows
Small Business
Server 2003
Administrator's Companion
Charles Russel,
Sharon Crawford,
and Jason Gerend
0-7356-2020-2

Microsoft Exchange
Server 2003
Administrator's Companion
Walter J. Glenn
and Bill English
0-7356-1979-4

Microsoft Systems
Management
Server 2003
Administrator's Companion
Steven D.
Kaczmarek
0-7356-1888-7

Resource Kits

- In-depth technical information and tools from those who know the technology best
- Definitive reference and best practices for deployment and operations
- Essential toolkit of resources, including eBook, on CD

Microsoft
Windows Vista™
Resource Kit
Tulloch, Honeycutt,
Northrup, and Russel
with the Microsoft
Windows Vista Team
0-7356-2283-3

Microsoft Exchange
Server 2003
Resource Kit
Unkroth, Molony,
Cherny, Reid, Strachan,
English, and the
Microsoft Exchange
Server Team
0-7356-2072-5

Microsoft Windows
Server 2003
Resource Kit
Microsoft MVPs
and Partners with
Microsoft Windows
Server Team
0-7356-2232-9

Microsoft Windows
Security
Resource Kit
Second Edition
Ben Smith and
Brian Komar with
the Microsoft
Security Team
0-7356-2174-8

Self-Paced Training Kits

- Two products in one: official exam prep plus practice tests
- Features lessons, exercises, and case scenarios
- Comprehensive self-tests, trial software, and eBook on CD

Implementing and
Maintaining Microsoft
SQL Server 2005
MCTS Self-Paced Training Kit
0-7356-2271-X

Designing a Microsoft
SQL Server 2005
Database Server
Infrastructure
MCITP Self-Paced Training Kit
0-7356-2173-X

Microsoft Windows
Server 2003 Core
Requirements
Second Edition
MCSE Self-Paced Training Kit
0-7356-2290-6

Installing, Configuring,
and Administering
Microsoft XP
Professional
Second Edition
MCSA/MCSE Self-Paced Training Kit
0-7356-2152-7

Additional Windows (R2) Resources for Administrators

Published and Forthcoming Titles from Microsoft Press

Microsoft® Windows Server™ 2003 Administrator's Pocket Consultant, Second Edition

William R. Stanek • ISBN 0-7356-2245-0

Here's the practical, pocket-sized reference for IT professionals supporting Microsoft Windows Server 2003—fully updated for Service Pack 1 and Release 2. Designed for quick referencing, this portable guide covers all the essentials for performing everyday system administration tasks. Topics include managing workstations and servers, using Active Directory® directory service, creating and administering user and group accounts, managing files and directories, performing data security and auditing tasks, handling data back-up and recovery, and administering networks using TCP/IP, WINS, and DNS, and more.

MCSE Self-Paced Training Kit (Exams 70-290, 70-291, 70-293, 70-294): Microsoft Windows Server 2003 Core Requirements, Second Edition

Holme, Thomas, Mackin, McLean, Zacker, Spealman, Hudson, and Craft • ISBN 0-7356-2290-6

The Microsoft Certified Systems Engineer (MCSE) credential is the premier certification for professionals who analyze the business requirements and design and implement the infrastructure for business solutions based on the Microsoft Windows Server 2003 platform and Microsoft Windows Server System—now updated for Windows Server 2003 Service Pack 1 and R2. This all-in-one set provides in-depth preparation for the four required networking system exams. Work at your own pace through the lessons, hands-on exercises, troubleshooting labs, and review questions. You get expert exam tips plus a full review section covering all objectives and sub-objectives in each study guide. Then use the Microsoft Practice Tests on the CD to challenge yourself with more than 1500 questions for self-assessment and practice!

Microsoft Windows® Small Business Server 2003 R2 Administrator's Companion

Charlie Russel, Sharon Crawford, and Jason Gerend • ISBN 0-7356-2280-9

Get your small-business network, messaging, and collaboration systems up and running quickly with the essential guide to administering Windows Small Business Server 2003 R2. This reference details the features, capabilities, and technologies for both the standard and premium editions—including Microsoft Windows Server 2003 R2, Exchange Server 2003 with Service Pack 1, Windows SharePoint® Services, SQL Server™ 2005 Workgroup Edition, and Internet Information Services. Discover how to install, upgrade, or migrate to Windows Small Business Server 2003 R2; plan and implement your network, Internet access, and security services; customize Microsoft Exchange Server for your e-mail needs; and administer user rights, shares, permissions, and Group Policy.

Microsoft Windows Small Business Server 2003 R2 Administrator's Companion

Charlie Russel, Sharon Crawford, and Jason Gerend • ISBN 0-7356-2280-9

Here's the ideal one-volume guide for the IT professional administering Windows Server 2003. Now fully updated for Windows Server 2003 Service Pack 1 and R2, this *Administrator's Companion* offers up-to-date information on core system administration topics for Microsoft Windows, including Active Directory services, security, scripting, disaster planning and recovery, and interoperability with UNIX. It also includes all-new sections on Service Pack 1 security updates and new features for R2. Featuring easy-to-use procedures and handy work-arounds, this book provides ready answers for on-the-job results.

MCSA/MCSE Self-Paced Training Kit (Exam 70-290): Managing and Maintaining a Microsoft Windows Server 2003 Environment, Second Edition

Dan Holme and Orin Thomas • ISBN 0-7356-2289-2

MCSA/MCSE Self-Paced Training Kit (Exam 70-291): Implementing, Managing, and Maintaining a Microsoft Windows Server 2003 Network Infrastructure, Second Edition

J.C. Mackin and Ian McLean • ISBN 0-7356-2288-4

MCSE Self-Paced Training Kit (Exam 70-293): Planning and Maintaining a Microsoft Windows Server 2003 Network Infrastructure, Second Edition

Craig Zacker • ISBN 0-7356-2287-6

MCSE Self-Paced Training Kit (Exam 70-294): Planning, Implementing, and Maintaining a Microsoft Windows Server 2003 Active Directory® Infrastructure, Second Ed.

Jill Spealman, Kurt Hudson, and Melissa Craft • ISBN 0-7356-2286-8

For more information about Microsoft Press® books and other learning products, visit: **www.microsoft.com/mspress** *and* **www.microsoft.com/learning**

Resources for IT Professionals
Published and Forthcoming Titles from Microsoft Press

→ ## Microsoft Windows Server

Microsoft® Windows Server™ 2003
Resource Kit
Microsoft MVPs and Partners with
Microsoft Windows Server Team
0-7356-2232-9

Microsoft Windows Server 2003
Administrator's Companion
Second Edition
Charlie Russel, Sharon Crawford,
and Jason Gerend
0-7356-2047-4

Microsoft Windows Server 2003
Inside Out
William R. Stanek
0-7356-2048-2

Microsoft Windows Server 2003
Administrator's Pocket Consultant
Second Edition
William R. Stanek
0-7356-2245-0

**Microsoft Windows® Small
Business Server 2003 R2**
Administrator's Companion
Charlie Russel, Sharon Crawford,
and Jason Gerend
0-7356-2280-9

→ ## Microsoft Windows Client

Microsoft Windows XP Professional
Resource Kit
Third Edition
The Microsoft Windows Team with
Charlie Russel and Sharon Crawford
0-7356-2167-5

**Microsoft Windows® XP
Professional**
Administrator's Pocket Consultant
Second Edition
William R. Stanek
0-7356-2140-3

Microsoft Windows Vista™
Resource Kit
Tulloch, Honeycutt, Northrup,
and Russel with the Microsoft
Windows Vista Team
0-7356-2283-3

Microsoft Windows Vista
Administator's Pocket Consusltant
William R. Stanek
0-7356-2296-5

Microsoft Windows Command-Line
Administrator's Pocket Consultant
William R. Stanek
0-7356-2038-5

→ ## Microsoft SQL Server 2005

Microsoft SQL Server™ 2005
Administrator's Pocket Consultant
William R. Stanek
0-7356-2107-1

Microsoft SQL Server 2005
Administrator's Companion
Marci Frohock Garcia, Edward
Whalen, et al.
0-7356-2198-5

**Inside Microsoft SQL Server:
The Storage Engine**
Kalen Delaney
0-7356-2105-5

**Inside Microsoft SQL Server:
T-SQL Programming**
Itzik Ben-Gan, et al.
0-7356-2197-7

→ ## Microsoft Exchange Server 2003

Microsoft Exchange Server 2003
Resource Kit
Unkroth, Molony, Cherny,
Reid, Strachan, English, and the
Microsoft Exchange Server Team
0-7356-2072-5

Microsoft Exchange Server 2003
Administrator's Companion
Walter J. Glenn and Bill English
0-7356-1979-4

Microsoft Exchange Server 2003
Administrator's Pocket Consultant
William R. Stanek
0-7356-1978-6

→ ## Scripting

**Advanced VBScript for Microsoft
Windows Administrators**
Don Jones and Jeffery Hicks
0-7356-2244-2

Microsoft VBScript
Step by Step
Ed Wilson
0-7356-2297-3

**Microsoft Windows
Scripting with WMI:
Self-Paced Learning Guide**
Ed Wilson
0-7356-2231-0

**Microsoft SharePoint®
Products and
Technologies**
Resource Kit
Bill English with the
Microsoft SharePoint
Teams
0-7356-1881-X

**Microsoft Windows
Security**
Resource Kit
Second Edition
Ben Smith and
Brian Komar with
the Microsoft
Security Team
0-7356-2174-8

**Microsoft Systems
Management
Server 2003**
*Administrator's
Companion*
Steven D. Kaczmarek
0-7356-1888-7

**Microsoft Internet
Security and
Acceleration (ISA)
Server 2004**
*Administrator's Pocket
Consultant*
Bud Ratliff and Jason
Ballard with the Microsoft
ISA Server Team
0-7356-2188-8

See even more resources at: **microsoft.com/mspress** *and* **microsoft.com/learning**

Additional SQL Server Resources for Developers

Published and Forthcoming Titles from Microsoft Press

Microsoft® SQL Server™ 2005 Express Edition
Step by Step
Jackie Goldstein • ISBN 0-7356-2184-5

Teach yourself how to get database projects up and running
quickly with SQL Server Express
Edition—a free, easy-to-use
database product that is based
on SQL Server 2005 technology.
It's designed for building simple,
dynamic applications, with all
the rich functionality of the SQL
Server database engine and
using the same data access APIs,
such as Microsoft ADO.NET, SQL
Native Client, and T-SQL.

Whether you're new to database
programming or new to SQL Server, you'll learn how, when, and
why to use specific features of this simple but powerful database development environment. Each chapter puts you to work,
building your knowledge of core capabilities and guiding you
as you create actual components and working applications.

Microsoft SQL Server 2005 Programming
Step by Step
Fernando Guerrero • ISBN 0-7356-2207-8

SQL Server 2005 is Microsoft's
next-generation data management and analysis solution that
delivers enhanced scalability,
availability, and security features
to enterprise data and analytical
applications while making them
easier to create, deploy, and
manage. Now you can teach
yourself how to design, build, test,
deploy, and maintain SQL Server
databases—one step at a time.
Instead of merely focusing on

describing new features, this book shows new database
programmers and administrators how to use specific features
within typical business scenarios. Each chapter provides a highly
practical learning experience that demonstrates how to build
database solutions to solve common business problems.

Microsoft SQL Server 2005 Analysis Services
Step by Step
Hitachi Consulting Services • ISBN 0-7356-2199-3

One of the key features of SQL Server 2005 is SQL Server Analysis
Services—Microsoft's customizable analysis solution for business
data modeling and interpretation. Just compare SQL Server
Analysis Services to its competition to understand the great
value of its enhanced features. One of the keys to harnessing
the full functionality of SQL Server will be leveraging Analysis
Services for the powerful tool that it is—including creating a cube,
and deploying, customizing, and extending the basic calculations. This step-by-step tutorial discusses how to get started, how
to build scalable analytical applications, and how to use and administer advanced features. Interactivity (enhanced in SQL Server
2005), data translation, and security are also covered in detail.

Microsoft SQL Server 2005 Reporting Services
Step by Step
Hitachi Consulting Services • ISBN 0-7356-2250-7

SQL Server Reporting Services (SRS) is Microsoft's customizable
reporting solution for business data analysis. It is one of the key
value features of SQL Server 2005: functionality more advanced
and much less expensive than its competition. SRS is powerful,
so an understanding of how to architect a report, as well as how
to install and program SRS, is key to harnessing the full functionality of SQL Server. This procedural tutorial shows how to use the
Report Project Wizard, how to think about and access data, and
how to build queries. It also walks through the creation of charts
and visual layouts for maximum visual understanding of data
analysis. Interactivity (enhanced in SQL Server 2005) and security
are also covered in detail.

Programming Microsoft SQL Server 2005
Andrew J. Brust, Stephen Forte, and William H. Zack
ISBN 0-7356-1923-9

This thorough, hands-on reference for developers and database
administrators teaches the basics of programming custom applications with SQL Server 2005. You will learn the fundamentals
of creating database applications—including coverage of
T-SQL, Microsoft .NET Framework, and Microsoft ADO.NET. In
addition to practical guidance on database architecture and
design, application development, and reporting and data
analysis, this essential reference guide covers performance,
tuning, and availability of SQL Server 2005.

Inside Microsoft SQL Server 2005:
The Storage Engine
Kalen Delaney • ISBN 0-7356-2105-5

Inside Microsoft SQL Server 2005:
T-SQL Programming
Itzik Ben-Gan • ISBN 0-7356-2197-7

Inside Microsoft SQL Server 2005:
Query Processing and Optimization
Kalen Delaney • ISBN 0-7356-2196-9

Programming Microsoft ADO.NET 2.0 Core Reference
David Sceppa • ISBN 0-7356-2206-X

For more information about Microsoft Press® books and other learning products,
visit: **www.microsoft.com/mspress** *and* **www.microsoft.com/learning**

Additional Resources for Developers: Advanced Topics and Best Practices

Published and Forthcoming Titles from Microsoft Press

Code Complete, Second Edition
Steve McConnell • ISBN 0-7356-1967-0

For more than a decade, Steve McConnell, one of the premier authors and voices in the software community, has helped change the way developers write code—and produce better software. Now his classic book, *Code Complete*, has been fully updated and revised with best practices in the art and science of constructing software. Topics include design, applying good techniques to construction, eliminating errors, planning, managing construction activities, and relating personal character to superior software. This new edition features fully updated information on programming techniques, including the emergence of Web-style programming, and integrated coverage of object-oriented design. You'll also find new code examples—both good and bad—in C++, Microsoft® Visual Basic®, C#, and Java, although the focus is squarely on techniques and practices.

More About Software Requirements: Thorny Issues and Practical Advice
Karl E. Wiegers • ISBN 0-7356-2267-1

Have you ever delivered software that satisfied all of the project specifications, but failed to meet any of the customers expectations? Without formal, verifiable requirements—and a system for managing them—the result is often a gap between what developers think they're supposed to build and what customers think they're going to get. Too often, lessons about software requirements engineering processes are formal or academic, and not of value to real-world, professional development teams. In this follow-up guide to *Software Requirements*, Second Edition, you will discover even more practical techniques for gathering and managing software requirements that help you deliver software that meets project and customer specifications. Succinct and immediately useful, this book is a must-have for developers and architects.

Software Estimation: Demystifying the Black Art
Steve McConnell • ISBN 0-7356-0535-1

Often referred to as the "black art" because of its complexity and uncertainty, software estimation is not as hard or mysterious as people think. However, the art of how to create effective cost and schedule estimates has not been very well publicized. *Software Estimation* provides a proven set of procedures and heuristics that software developers, technical leads, and project managers can apply to their projects. Instead of arcane treatises and rigid modeling techniques, award-winning author Steve McConnell gives practical guidance to help organizations achieve basic estimation proficiency and lay the groundwork to continue improving project cost estimates. This book does not avoid the more complex mathematical estimation approaches, but the non-mathematical reader will find plenty of useful guidelines without getting bogged down in complex formulas.

Debugging, Tuning, and Testing Microsoft .NET 2.0 Applications
John Robbins • ISBN 0-7356-2202-7

Making an application the best it can be has long been a time-consuming task best accomplished with specialized and costly tools. With Microsoft Visual Studio® 2005, developers have available a new range of built-in functionality that enables them to debug their code quickly and efficiently, tune it to optimum performance, and test applications to ensure compatibility and trouble-free operation. In this accessible and hands-on book, debugging expert John Robbins shows developers how to use the tools and functions in Visual Studio to their full advantage to ensure high-quality applications.

The Security Development Lifecycle
Michael Howard and Steve Lipner • ISBN 0-7356-2214-0

Adapted from Microsoft's standard development process, the Security Development Lifecycle (SDL) is a methodology that helps reduce the number of security defects in code at every stage of the development process, from design to release. This book details each stage of the SDL methodology and discusses its implementation across a range of Microsoft software, including Microsoft Windows Server™ 2003, Microsoft SQL Server™ 2000 Service Pack 3, and Microsoft Exchange Server 2003 Service Pack 1, to help measurably improve security features. You get direct access to insights from Microsoft's security team and lessons that are applicable to software development processes worldwide, whether on a small-scale or a large-scale. This book includes a CD featuring videos of developer training classes.

Software Requirements, Second Edition
Karl E. Wiegers • ISBN 0-7356-1879-8

Writing Secure Code, Second Edition
Michael Howard and David LeBlanc • ISBN 0-7356-1722-8

CLR via C#, Second Edition
Jeffrey Richter • ISBN 0-7356-2163-2

For more information about Microsoft Press® books and other learning products,
visit: **www.microsoft.com/mspress** *and* **www.microsoft.com/learning**